POUR LA FRANCE

A GUIDE TO THE FORMATIONS & UNITS OF THE LAND FORCES OF FRANCE, 1914-1918

by

Michael Cox

& Graham Watson

With a supplementary essay by Peter Abbott

Helion & Company Ltd

Helion & Company Limited
26 Willow Road
Solihull
West Midlands
B91 1UE
England
Tel. 0121 705 3393
Fax 0121 711 4075
Email: info@helion.co.uk
Website: www.helion.co.uk

Published by Helion & Company Limited 2012

Designed and typeset by Helion & Company Limited, Solihull, West Midlands
Cover designed by Farr out Publications, Wokingham, Berkshire
Printed by Lightning Source, Milton Keynes, Buckinghamshire

Text © Michael Cox & Graham Watson, 2012

ISBN 978 1 907677 14 4

British Library Cataloguing-in-Publication Data.

A catalogue record for this book is available from the British Library.

All rights reserved. No part of this publication may be reproduced, stored in a retrieval system, or transmitted, in any form, or by any means, electronic, mechanical, photocopying, recording or otherwise, without the express written consent of Helion & Company Limited.

For details of other military history titles published by Helion & Company Limited contact the above address, or visit our website: http://www.helion.co.uk

Contents

List of Abbreviations	v
Introduction	7

Part One

The French Army in 1914	8
Corps d'Armée in 1914	14
Overseas Deployment 1914	28

Part Two

The Organisation of the Divisions	32
The Infantry Divisions	38
Active Divisions 1-43	38
War-formed Divisions 44-48	101
Reserve Divisions 51-75	109
Territorial Diviions 81-105	150
War Formed Divisions 120-170	165
Colonial Divisions 1-3, 10-11, 15-17	201
Moroccan Divisions 1-2	211
Provisional Divisions	214
The Cavalry Divisions	215
Active Divisions 1-10	215
Dismounted Divisions 1-22	224
Provisional Cavalry Divisions	226
Foreign Divisions under French Command, 1917-1918	227

Part Three

Infantry Regiments, 1914-1918	230
Active Regiments	230
Reserve Regiments	235
War Formed Regiments	240
Chasseurs à Pied	241
Regiments d'Infanterie Territoriale [RIT]	245
Regiments d'Infanterie Coloniale 1914-1918	249
Summary of French Artillery Regiments 1914-1918	265
Regiments d'Artillerie de Campagne 1914-1918	267
Heavy Artillery 1914-1918	278
Cavalry Regiments & Squadrons	281
Army of Africa Cavalry Regiments	284
Mechanised Units 1914-1918	286
Engineer Unit Organisation 1914	287
Eastern European Units of the French Army 1914-1918	291

Part Four

Army Groups & Armies	292
Allied Headquarters [GQGA]	292
Army Groups, 1914-1918	294
Introduction to Armies	297
First Army	301
Second Army	310

Third Army	326
Fourth Army	334
Fifth Army	343
Sixth Army	351
Seventh Army	361
Eighth Army [1]	365
Eighth Army [2]	368
Ninth Army [1]	372
Ninth Army [2]	374
Tenth Army	375
Formations outside France	385

Part Five

Army Corps	386
Corps d'Armee	388
'Affectation Organique' of Divisions and Corps D'Armee	430

Part Six

Introduction & List of Battles	435
1914	440
1915	453
1916	462
1917	472
1918	476
Overseas Operations	503

Part Seven

An Alphabetical Listing of French Generals	504

Part Eight

French Overseas Forces: Essay by Peter Abbott	520

LIST OF ABBREVIATIONS

AS	Artillerie d'Assaut	Assault Artillery
BA	Batallion d'Afrique	African Battalion
BC	Brigade de Cuirassiers	Cuirassiers Brigade
BCA	Batallion de Chasseurs Alpins	Alpine Brigade
BCL	Brigade de Cavalerie Légère	Light Cavalry Brigade
BCP	Batallion de Chasseurs à Pied	Light Infantry Brigade
BD	Brigade de Dragons	Dragoons Brigade
BG	Batallion du Génie	Engineer Battalion
BI	Brigade d'Infanterie	Infantry Brigade
BIC	Brigade d'Infanterie Colonial	Colonial Infantry Brigade
Bie	Batterie	Battery
BILA	Batallion d'Infanterie Légère Africaine	African Light Infantry Battalion
BM	Brigade Marocain	Moroccan Brigade
BnCL	Batallion de Chars Légère	Light Tank Battalion
CA	Corps d'Armée	Army Corps
CAC	Corps d'Armée Colonial	Colonial Army Corps
CC	Corps de Cavalerie	Cavalry Corps
CCP	Corps de Cavalerie Provisionaire	Provisional Cavalry Corps
Cie	Compagnie	Company
DAL	Detachment d'Armée Lorraine	Lorraine Army Detachment
DAV	Detachment d'Armée Vosges	Vosges Army Detachment
DC	Division de Cavalerie	Cavalry Division
DCP	Division de Cavalry à Pied	Dismounted Cavalry Division
Dd M	Division de Marche	Marching Division
DI	Division d'Infanterie	Infantry Division
DIC	Division d'Infanterie Colonial	Colonial Infantry Division
DIP	Division d'Infanterie Polonaise	Polish Infantry Division
DIT/DT	Division d'Infanterie Territoriale	Territorial Infantry Division
DM	Division Marocain	Moroccan Division DPr
DPr	Division d'Infanterie Provisionaire	Provisional Infantry Division
DPr	Division Provisionale	Temporary Division
DR	Division de Réserve	Reserve Infantry Division
ENE	Éléments non Endivisionnés	Corps Troops
Esc	Escadron	Cavalry Squadron
GAAPA	Groupe d'Artillerie à Pied d'Afrique	African Foot Artillery Group
GAC	Groupe d'Armées de Centre	Centre Army Group
GACA	Groupe d'Arillerie de Campagne d'Afrique	African Field Artillery Group
GAE	Groupe d'Armées de l'Est	Eastern Army Group
GAF	Groupe d'Armées de Flandres	Flanders Army Group
GAM	Groupe Auto-Mitrailleuse	Motorised Group
GAN	Group d'Armées du Nord	Northern Army Group
GAPA	Groupe d'Artillerie Grand Puissance	Heavy Artillery Group
GAR	Groupe d'Armées de Réserve	Reserve Army Group
GDR	Groupe de Divisions de Réserve	Group of Reserve Divisions
GMP	Gouvernement Militaire de Paris	Paris Military Government
GPE	Groupe Provisional de l'Est	Eastern Provisional Group
GPN	Groupe Provisional du Nord	Northern Provisional

GQG	Grand-Quartier-Général	General Headquarters
Gr	Groupe	Group
RAC	Régiment d'Artillerie de Campagne	Field Artillery Regiment
RACA	Régiment d'Artillerie de Campagne d'Afrique	African Field Artillery Regiment
RACC	Régiment d'Artillerie Colonial de Campagne	Colonial Field Artillery Regiment
RACH	Régiment d'Artillerie de Campagne Hippomobile	Semi-mobile Field Artillery Regiment
RACP	Régiment d'Artillerie de Campagne Portee	Lorried Artillery Regiment
RAL	Régiment d'Artillerie Lourde	Heavy Artillery Regiment
RALA	Régiment d'Artillerie Lourde d'Afrique	African Heavy Artillery Regiment
RALFV	Régiment d'Artillerie Lourde de Ferre Voie	Railway Artillery Regiment
RALGP	Régiment d'Artillerie Lourde de Grand Puissance	Very Heavy Artillery Regiment
RALH	Régiment d'Artillerie Lourde Hippomobiles	Semi-Mobile Heavy Artillery Regiment
RALT	Régiment d'Artillerie Lourde Tractuers	Tractor-drawn Heavy Artillery Regiment
RAM	Régiment d'Artillerie de Montagne	Mountain Artillery Regiment
RAP	Régiment d'Artillerie à Pied	Foot Artillery Regiment
RC	Regiment de Cuirassiers	Curassier Regiment
RCA	Regiment de Chasseurs d'Afrique	African Chasseurs Regiment
RCh	Regiment de Chasseurs à Cheval	Light Cavalry Regiment
RChars	Régiment de Chars	Tank Regiment
RD	Régiment de Dragons	Dragoons Regiment
RdMA	Régiment de Marche d'Afrique	African Marching Regiment
RdMC	Régiment de Marche Colonial	Colonial Marching Regiment
RdMIC	Régiment de Marche d'Infanterie Colonial	Colonial Infantry Marching Regiment
RdMLE/RdMRE	Régiment de Marche de la Légion Étrangere	Foreign Legion Marching Regiment
RdMMxM	Régiment de Marche Mixte Marocain	Maroccan Mixed Marching Regiment
RdMT	Régiment de Marche de Tirailleurs	Tirailleurs Marching Regiment
RdMTM	Regiment de Marche de Tirailleurs Marocain	Moroccan Tirailleurs Marching Regiment
RdMTMOcc	Regiment de Marche de Tirailleurs Marocain Occidental	Western Moroccan Marching Regiment
RdMTMOr	Regiment de Marche de Tirailleurs Marocain Oriental	Eastern Moroccan Marching Regiment
RdMTSM	Régiment de Marche de Tirailleurs Sénégalais	Senegalise Marching Regiment
RdMxIC	Régiment Mixte d'Infanterie Colonial	Mixed Colonial Infantry Regiment
RdMZ	Régiment de Marche de Zouaves	Zouave Marching Regiment
RdMZT	Regiment de Marche de Zouaves et Tirailleurs	Zouave and Tirailleurs Marching Regiment
RE	Régiment d'Étranger	Foreign Legion Regiment
RFV	Région Fortifée de Verdun	Verdun Fortified Region
RG	Régiment du Génie	Engineer Regiment
RGA	Résèrve Génèral d'Artillerie	Reserve Artillery Command
RGAL	Résèrve Groupe d'Artillerie Lourde	Reserve Artillery Group
RH	Régiment d'Hussards	Hussar Regiment
RI	Régiment d'Infanterie	Infantry Regiment
RIC	Régiment d'Infanterie Colonial	Colonial Infantry Regiment
RICM	Régiment de Marche d'Infanterie Colonial Maroc	Moroccan Colonial Infantry Regiment
RIT	Régiment d'Infanterie Territoriale	Territorial Infantry Regiment
RM	Région Militaire	Military Region
RMTA	Régiment de Tirailleurs Algériens	Algerian Rifle Regiment
RMTM	Régiment de Tirailleurs Marocain	Moroccan Rifle Regiment
RMTS	Régiment de Tirailleurs Sénégalais	Senegalise Rifle Regiment
RMTT	Régiment de Tirailleurs Tunisien	Tunisian Rifle Regiment
RS	Régiment de Spahis	Spahis Regiment
RZ	Régiment de Zouaves	Zouave Regiment

INTRODUCTION

This book is an attempt to fill a major gap in the literature of the First World War by providing English-language readers with a guide to the organisation and operations of the French Army during that conflict. The book provides detailed information on the divisions, corps and armies, which fought for France on the Western Front, and elsewhere, in the course of that war. Such information has not been available in English before, and the major French source-the Official History-is virtually unobtainable.

In his preparation of material for battlefield tours, Graham Watson became aware of this deficiency in easily accessible information on the French Army. His efforts to remedy this were accelerated by contact with Mike Cox. As co-author, with John Ellis, of the *World War One Databook*, Mike had a considerable amount of material which had to be left out of that book, for reasons of space. This book is the result of a fruitful collaboration between Graham and Mike, to which Peter Abbott has added an essay on French forces outside Europe.

The authors have focussed on the main battlefield formations: the divisions, corps and armies, for each of which, they provide details on the status, commanders, internal composition, and operational history. In addition, there are overviews of the French military effort in the form of orders of battle. The latter are supplemented by a list of the French generals who held field command during the war.

Parts One to Three concentrate on the divisions and the regiments which comprised them. Parts Four to Six will cover the higher formations: army groups, armies and corps; and, in addition, will provide detailed orders of battle, and information on French generals.

For reasons of space, our coverage of regiments and battalions is sketchier, being little more than checklists by which readers can follow the allocation of units to divisions. There are excellent French websites devoted to regimental histories which will fill the need for more detailed information at this level.

Amongst the topics which are not covered are military aviation, weapons and equipment, and uniforms and decorations. The inclusion of material on these topics would have made the book unwieldy and overlong. Again, more detailed information on these topics is available in French publications and websites.

Duncan Maclean and John Ellis made available to us their copies of the rare and invaluable texts from Tome X of the French Official History. In addition, Duncan gave invaluable help in the area of French military aviation. Peter Abbott has generously allowed us to use the relevant section of his as yet to be published opus on 'French Forces Overseas from the seventeenth century to the present day'. Peter was a sure and informed guide to us on the more arcane aspects of the Army d'Afrique and the colonial establishment. Andy Callan directed us towards the massive and very useful website www.genealogie.free.fr from which we gained much additional material on French generals. The website of the Association 1914-1918 was of great value in tracking down material on regiments, both metropolitan and colonial. .

Effectively, this book is based on the Official History: *Les Armées francaises pendant la Grande Guerre 1914-1918*. Of the 102 volumes published, the two which comprise 'Tome X' provided the bulk of the material for this book. Published in 1934, each of the two volumes is about 1,000 pages in length. Parts one to three deal with armies and corps, while parts four nine concentrates on divisions. None are accessible nor easy to consult. Hopefully our efforts will open up this material to a wider audience across the English-speaking world.

Apart from those individuals mentioned above, Ann Watson deserves a very special mention for her patience and forbearance with her husband's obsession with his computer as this book has evolved over the last four years.

As always, the authors bear full responsibility for any errors and would appreciate comments to eliminate them and improve this book.

Part One

The French Army in 1914

The French Army was made up of two major components; the Metropolitan Army and the Colonial Army. The former was built around a core of professional officers and non-commissioned officers, the Metropolitan Army was a conscript force stationed entirely in France for operations in Europe. It included the troops stationed in Algeria, which was then regarded as a province of France.

The Colonial Army was composed of volunteers from France, volunteers and conscripts from the European residents of the French empire, and non-Europeans –mainly conscripts-from those colonies. That part of the Colonial Army, which had been marines, was stationed in France to complement and reinforce the Metropolitan Army.

Control of the Army was vested in the War Minister who could be either a civilian politician or a general. He was appointed by the Prime-Minister and was responsible to him and to the National Assembly for the administration of the army. He presided over the Conseil Superieur de la Guerre which was made up of the Chief of the General Staff and ten senior generals. On mobilisation, the Chief of the General Staff would become the Commander in Chief of the forces in the field, and other members of the council would leave Paris and become the army commanders.

Conseil Superieur de la Guerre 1914 [and mobilisation appointment]

Joffre	Commander in Chief
Archinard	1 GDR
Laffon de Ladebert	Rear Services
De Langle de Cary	Fourth Army
D'Amade	Armée des Alpes
De Castelnau	Second Army
Dubail	First Army
Lanrezac	Fifth Army
Ruffey	Third Army
Sordet	Cavalry Corps

* Generals Chomer, Gallieni and Michel had retired from the council earlier in 1914

In peacetime the army was directed by the General Staff in Paris. The Chief of the General Staff was assisted by two 'Sub-chiefs'. On mobilisation the first sub Chief would take to the field with the Commander in Chief as his Chief of Staff. The other general would direct those parts of the general staff which would remain in Paris and become the principal adviser to the War Minister.

The General Staff was composed on nine directorates, each headed by a general officer. These were the Infantry, Cavalry, Artillery and Train, Engineers, Aeronautics, Military Intendance, Explosives, Army Medical Services, and Colonial Troops.

For such a large army, central control was seriously undermanned by later standards. The general staff provided posts for only five *generals de division*, nine *generals de brigade* and ten colonels. The other 110 *generals de division*, 233 *generals de brigade* and 470 colonels commanded the field and administrative units assigned to the various Corps d'Armee. In this respect the French desire to decentralise command and administration was very similar to that used by the other great armies of Europe: Germany, Italy and Austria-Hungary.

The twin pillars of French military organisation in 1914 were conscription and the army corps. Both were the result of a succession of laws designed passed after the Franco-Prussian War to remedy the defects exposed by that conflict. The latest of those laws was that of 1913 which extended the period of active military service from two years to three years.

The laws on conscription had two main functions; to provide the greater part of the manpower required to put the Metropolitan Army into the field; and to create a bond of loyalty between citizen and state. This latter was achieved by the rule that men on active service would serve with a unit in any part of France except their home area. Only after three years service in the active army would an individual serve with a locally-based regiment.

Conscription required all young men in France and throughout the empire to make themselves available for military service. In France, all men between the ages of 20 and 48 were liable for service in the army. Men became liable for conscription during the year after their 19th birthday and would be inducted into the army in October of that year. Fulfilment of military service obligations required each man to serve in differing components of the army. This required him to serve for the full twenty-eight years in the following fashion.

Active Army	3 years	Ages 20-22
Reserves-Fill out of active	2 years	Ages 23-24
Reserve Army units	9 years	Ages 25-33
Territorial Army	7 years	Ages 34-40
Territorial Reserve	7 years	Ages 41-48

Volunteers could serve between four and five years in regiments within France and between three and five years in colonial units with the option of re-engagement for a total of fifteen years service. Most volunteers were directed towards overseas service with the Colonial Army but, also, they provided the NCO's of the Metropolitan Army.

The annual requirement of the Army was met by an assessment process, which graded every potential conscript, and placed them, into various categories. In 1912, the total number of men available for military service was 314,369 of whom 220,958 were passed fit for military service. Of this age group, 23,473 were already serving as volunteers. The total was increased by the addition of 11,091 men whose service had been deferred in 1911. This meant that 232,049 were conscripted for active service in October 1913. The distribution of conscripts, amongst the various arms of the service, was 170,740 to the infantry; 1,339 to the cavalry (which had a large number of volunteers); 29,963 to the artillery; 11,138 to the engineers; 250 to aviation; 1,570 to the train; 5,593 to administrative services, and 2,491 to the African Light Infantry.

The army produced by conscription had a strength of 610,000 on 1st January 1913 and. Under the terms of the 1913 Law, which extended active military service to three years, this total strength would rise to 750,000 during 1914. The 1914 budget made provision for a total of 818,000 soldiers but his total included 27,000 gendarmerie and 80,000 in North Africa (of the latter 43,000 were not available for service in France).

In France, the army was made up of 28,701 officers and 705,863 other ranks in metropolitan regiments and a further 2,980 officers and 25,131 other ranks in those colonial regiments based in France. Added to this total of 30,785 officers and 731,631 men, were a further 2,980 officers and 78,208 men serving in North Africa.

Of the reserves, 350,000 men were allocated to the task of bringing active regiments up to war strength, and another 600,000 men were expected to man the reserve units and formations on mobilisation. The territorials totalled 920,000 (including 475,000 infantry) in units and a further 470,000 men were listed as territorial reservists. The total French manpower available on mobilisation in 1914 would be 4,186,000 which were distributed amongst the various categories and units in the following manner:*

Active	1,138,000
Reserve	1,658,000
Territorial	920,000
Territorial Reserve	470,000

Arm of service	Active	Reserves	War Strength
Infantry	453,621	482,000	734,000
Cavalry	71,108	30,000	84,000
Artillery	124,079	54,900	200,000
Engineers	22,277	18,000	40,000

*these figures include colonial troops stationed in France

The fundamental building block of French military organisation was the Military Region, whose operational component was the Corps d'Armee. France was divided into twenty military regions, which carried out most of the decentralised administration of the army. Eighteen military regions were formed in the 1870's whilst Algeria constituted a nineteenth region (with some of its units based in France). As the threat from Germany increased the 6th and 7th Military Regions-on the frontier with Germany-were split to create the 20th and 21st regions. In addition, the Colonial Corps was stationed in various parts of France under the direct command of the War Minister.

The Military Region had two personalities. The field forces within the region constituted the Corps d'Armee, which would join the operational army on mobilisation. More sedentary and localised functions such as recruiting, training, reserves, fortress troops and local defences would remain under command of the military region. The general commanding the military region would become the corps commander and his subordinate inspector of reserves would supervise the mobilisation of the reserves and territorials and command the reserve division formed in the region.

Each *corps d'armee* had a fairly standard organisation. It would have a total strength of 1,124 officers and 39,179 men who would form two infantry divisions (800 officers and 31,000 men), a cavalry regiment (30/650), an artillery brigade (four groups with a total of 12 batteries, totaling 70/1200), an engineer battalion (4/260), and. a telegraph unit (1/60). Included in the corps for peacetime administration would be either a complete cavalry brigade or a cavalry regiment. On mobilisation these would leave the corps and form ten divisions of horsemen.

It was expected that each region would form a reserve infantry division and up to four brigades of territorial infantry. Two reserve infantry regiments would join the corps but uncertainty remained on the deployment of the reserve divisions.

A major exception to the standard strength of each corps was the designation of five corps as *corps de couverture*. These corps –the II, VI, XX, XXI and VII –had a larger allocation of manpower because as frontier corps they would mobilise first and guard the frontier as the rest of the five armies assembled at their pre-designated war-stations. Each company of infantry, for example, had 200 men rather than the normal.

On mobilisation in 1914, the corps formed into five armies in a process made simpler by the allocation of geographic neighbours to the same army. The same method was used by the German Army in August 1914. As the VII Corps d'Armée was allotted to the Belfort gap far to the south of the rest of First Army, I Corps d'Armée covered the mobilisation of Fifth Army. The process of mobilisation resulted in the following deployment of forces:

5th Army
I CA   ex Lille [covering corps] III CA ex Rouen
X CA   ex Rennes
XI CA   ex Nantes

4th Army
II CA   ex Amiens [covering corps] CAC ex Paris
XII CA   ex Limoges
XVIICA   ex Toulouse

3rd Army
VI CA   ex Orléans [covering corps] V CA ex Châlons
IV CA   ex Le Mans

2nd Army

XX CA   ex Nancy [covering corps] IXCA ex Tours
XV CA   ex Marseille XVICA   ex Montpellier XVIIICA ex Bordeaux

1st Army
XXICA   ex Épinal [covering corps] VIIICA ex Bourges
XIIICA   ex Clermont-Ferrand
XIVCA   ex Lyon
VIICA   ex Besançon [covering corps for Alsace]

Strength of French Army by Arm

The Infantry

Active Army

France	North Africa	Other Territories
528 Infantry Battalions	20 Battalions Zouaves	Indo-China: 29 battalions
31 Chasseurs Battalions	40 Battalions Tirailleurs	North China: 2 battalions
4 Battalions Zouaves	9 Battalions Foreign Legion	West Africa: 13 battalions
	5 Bns African Light Infantry	Central Africa: equivalent of 8 bns
	Morocco: 47 battalions	Madagascar: 12 bns
		Antilles: equiv 1 bn
		Pacific: 2 companies

Reserves and Territorials

Reserves	Territorials
362 battalions	455 battalions
31 chasseurs battalions	7 chasseurs battalions
	12 Zouave battalions

The regular battalions were organised into regiments. There were 164 regiments with three battalions, and eight regiments with four battalions (157, 158, 159, 164, 165, 166, 170 and 173). Regiments were commanded by a colonel and had a peace strength of 1,851 or of 2,571 if part of a covering corps. Regiments had a war strength of 3,292.

Each battalion was commanded by a major and organised into four companies. Peacetime strength of a battalion was 562 men or 802 if in the covering role. Each company was divided into two *peletons*.

Chasseurs battalions comprised 1,253 men organised into six companies. War strength would be 32 officers and 1,616 men. Ten of the thirty-one chasseurs battalions provided a cyclist group for each of the cavalry divisions. Twelve of the battalions were designated Alpine.

Colonial and Armée d'Afrique Infantry comprised

16 Colonial Regiments   [52 battalions]
4 Regiments of Zouaves   [24 battalions]
9 Regiments of Tirailleurs [40 battalions]
2 Foreign Legion Regiments [12 battalions]
5 African Light Infantry battalions

The Cavalry

Cavalry Regiments were composed of 35 officers and 744 men. The regiments were:

12 regiments of Cuirassiers
32 regiments of Dragons
23 regiments of Chasseurs à Cheval

14 regiments of Hussards

The Cuirassiers and Dragoons were regarded as 'heavy cavalry' and those of Chasseurs a Cheval and Hussards were 'light cavalry'. The former would be used as 'shock troops' on the battlefield and the latter for patrol and scouting duties. The total number of cavalry squadrons in France was 324.

A further twelve regiments of cavalry were recruited in North Africa. They were six regiments of Saphis (with 28 squadrons) and six regiments of Chassuers d'Afrique (24 squadrons). One 'native' squadron served in West Africa and 22 of the above squadrons were detached to Morocco.

Out of the 81 cavalry regiments in France, sixty were allocated to ten cavalry divisions. Each cavalry division would include three cavalry brigades with a total of six regiments (or 24 squadrons) supported by a group of horse artillery with three batteries, and a 350 man cyclist group drawn from Chasseurs a Pied battalions.

One regiment of light cavalry was allocated to each corps with the four active squadrons dedicated to the corps and the two reserve squadrons of each regiment as divisional cavalry.

The one exception to this rule was the light cavalry brigade of two regiments allocated to VI *Corps d'Armee*.

In peacetime, there were three types of cavalry division, components of which were scattered across several military regions. The 1st Cavalry Division at Paris was described as a 'Heavy Cavalry Division' with one brigade of cuirassiers and two brigades of dragoons. The 3rd, 4th, 6th, 7th and 9th Cavalry Divisions were described as *'Mixte'* with one brigade of cuirassiers, one brigade of dragoons and one brigade of light cavalry. The 2nd, 5th, 8th and 10th Cavalry Divisions were described as 'Light Cavalry Divisions' with either two brigades of dragoons and one brigade of light cavalry or one brigade of dragoons and two brigades of light cavalry.

Cavalry reserves totalled 168 squadrons with a further 36 territorial squadrons in France and 3 territorial squadrons in North Africa.

Artillery

The basic unit was the battery which was usually equipped with four guns. Total number of batteries in 1914 was:

Active

France	618 field, 14 mountain, 30 horse, 58 heavy, 68 foot	788
North Africa	17 field, 8 mountain, 7 foot	32
Morocco	15 field/mountain, 7 mixed	22
Indo-China	6 field, 6 mountain, 7	19
West Africa	2 field, 1 mountain, 6 foot	9
Madagascar	1 field, 2 mountain, 3 foot	6
North China	1 mixed	1
Antilles	1 foot	1
	TOTAL	878

Reserves	240 field, 6 mountain, 55 garrison	301

Territorials   40 brigades of field artillery, 14 battalions of foot artillery, and a further six foot battalions in Algeria

The artillery regiments in France were organised as follows:

   9 regiments of foot artillery with 68 batteries for coast defence and fortress duties.
   5 regiments of heavy artillery with 24 batteries of 155mmQF and 34 batteries of other pieces: these regiments were formed in the spring of 1914 for use by the field armies.
   2 regiments of mountain artillery with 14 batteries

Each *corps d'armée* was allocated an artillery brigade of three regiments. One regiment of 4 batteries [48 guns] would remain under corps command, and the other two regiments (each of 36 guns) would supported each of the two infantry divisions within the corps. Regiments were divided into three groups, each commanded by a major; and each group contained three batteries. A battery was composed of three officers and 120 men who manned four 75mm guns. The horse artillery batteries were equipped with 3" guns.

Engineers

Active companies

France	71 field, 15 fortress, 16 railway, 14 telegraph	116
North Africa	10 field, 1 fortress, 3 railway, 3 telegraph	17
Indo China	2 companies	
Reserves	70 companies	
Territorial	126 companies allocated between 21 battalions of 4-6 each	

Aviation

Total strength   330 pilots plus another 130 under training

Organised into two types of units

Aerostation   [*dirigibles*]
Maximum of 12 companies each with one airship composed the 1st Group at Versailles

Aviation [aircraft]

Organised into squadrons [*escadrille*] of 6 aircraft and 7 pilots

Supervised by two groups, 1st Group at Dijon which covered southern France and North Africa, and

2nd Group at Reims which covered northern France. There were 27 squadrons. Of these one squadron was allotted to each corps, and the rest to the army level of command.

In addition, there were 5 fortress squadrons, 6 coast squadrons, and one section of 3 aircraft allocated to each cavalry division.

CORPS D'ARMEE IN 1914

I CORPS D'ARMÉE [LILLE]

1 Division d'Infanterie
QG – Lille

1 Brigade, Lille
43 RI, Lille
127 RI, Valenciennes

2 Brigade, Cambrai
1 RI, Cambrai
84 RI, Avesnes

1 Brigade d'Artillerie, Douai
15 RAC, Douai [1DI]
27 RAC, St Omer [2DI]
41 Rac, Douai

1BG/3RG

145 RI, Maubege
1 RAP, Dunkerque/Calais
HQ 3RG, Arras
1 Train, Lille

2 Division d'Infanterie
QG - Arras

Brigade, Arras
33 RI, Arras
73 RI, Bethune

4 Brigade, St Omer
8 RI, St Omer
110 RI, Dunkerque

Part 3 Division de Cavalerie
Sapeurs/Cylciste 3RG, Arras

4 Brigade de Cuirassiers, Arras
4 RC, Cambrai
9 RC, Douai
6 RCH, Lille [ICA]

51 Division de Reserve
QG - Lille

101 Brigade,
233 RI, Arras
243 RI, Lille
327 RI, Valenciennes

102 Brigade,
208 RI, St Omer
273 RI, Bethune
310 RI, Dunkerque

201 RI, Cambrai
284 RI, Avesnes

II CORPS D'ARMÉE [AMIENS]

3 Division d'Infanterie
QG – Amiens

5 Brigade, Amiens
72 RI, Amiens
128 RI, Abbeville

6 Brigade, St Quentin
51 RI, Beauvais
87 RI, St Quentin

2 Brigade d'Artillerie, La Fère

4 Division d'Infanterie
QG - Mézieres

7 Brigade, Mézieres
91 RI, Mézieres
147 RI, Sedan

8 Brigade, Laon
45 RI, Laon
148 RI, Rocroi

87 Brigade, Stenay
120 RI, Péronne/Stenay
9 BCP, Longwy/Stenay
18 BCP, Longuyon/Stenay

52 Division de Réserve
QG - Amiens

103 Brigade
291 RI, Mézieres
347 RI, Sedan
348 RI, Rocroi

104 Brigade
245 RI, Laon
320 RI, Stenay
49 BCP, Longwy
58 BCP, Longuyon

17 RAC, La Fère [3DI]
29 RAC, Laon
42 RAC, La Fère [4DI]

2 BG/3RG

1 RAL, La Fère
2 Train, Amiens

Part 3 Division de Cavalerie
4/42 RAC, Sissonne
19 RCh, La Fère [13BD]

Part 4 Division de Cavalerie
4/40 RAC, Mézieres

4 Brigade du Dragons, Sedan
28 RD, Sedan/Mézieres
30 RD, Sedan/Mézieres
272 RI, Amiens
328 RI, Abbeville

Part 69DR
251 RI, Beauvais
287 RI, St Quentin

Fortresses:
Longro, Les Ayvelles
Montinédy & Charlemont

III Corps d'Armée [Rouen]

5 Division d'Infanterie
QG-Rouen

9 Brigade, Rouen
39 RI, Rouen/Dieppe
74 RI, Rouen

10 Brigade, Caen
36 RI, Caen
129 RI, Le Havre

3 Brigade d'Artillerie, Versailles [GMP]
11 RAC, Rouen
22 RAC, Versaille [6DI]
43 RAC, Caen [5DI]

6 Division d'Infanterie
QG- Paris [GMP]

11 Brigade, St Denis [GMP]
24 RI, Bernay/Paris
28 RI, Evreux/Paris

12 Brigade, Paris [GMP]
5 RI, Falaise/Paris
119 RI, Liseuex/Paris

6 Brigade de Cuirassiers, St Germain [GMP]
11 RC, St Germain
12 RC, Rambouillet

11 Brigade du Dragons, Versaille [GMP]

53 Division de Réserve
QG-Rouen

105 Brigade
205 RI, Falaise/Paris
236 RI, Caen
319 RI, Liseuex/Paris

106 Brigade
224 RI, Bernay/Paris
228 RI, Evreux/Paris
329 RI, Le Havre

239 RI, Rouen/Dieppe
274 RI, Rouen

Fortress: Le Havre

3 BG/3RG

Bies 8/9, 2RAP, Le Havre
3 Train, Vernon

27 RD, Versailles
32 RD, Versailles
7 RCh, Evreux [3 CA]

IV Corps d'Armée [Le Mans]

7 Division d'Infanterie
QG - Paris [GMP]

13 Brigade, Paris
101 RI, Dreux/Paris
102 RI, Chartres/Paris

14 Brigade, Paris
103 RI, Alencon/Paris
104 RI, Argentan/Paris

4 Brigade d'Artillery, Le Mans
26 RAC, Le Mans [7DI]
31 RAC, Le Mans [8DI]
44 RAC, Le Mans

4BG/1RG
4 Train, Chartres

8 Division d'Infanterie
QG - Le Mans

15 Brigade, Laval
124 RI, Laval
130 RI, Mayenne

16 Brigade, Le Mans
115 RI, Mamers
117 RI, Le Mans

Part 7 Division de Cavalerie
[GMP] Sapeurs/cycliste, 1RG, Versaille
107 Brigade
301 RI, Dreux/Paris
302 RI, Chartres/Paris
304 RI, Argentan/Paris
108 Brigade
303 RI, Alençon/Paris
324 RI, Laval
330 RI, Mayenne
315 RI, Mamers
317 RI, Le Mans

54 Division de Réserve
QG - Le Mans

V Corps d'Armée [Orléans]

9 Division d'Infanterie
QG- Orléans

17 Brigade, Auxerre
4 RI, Auxerre/Troyes
82 RI, Montargis
18 Brigade, Blois
113 RI, Blois
131 RI, Orléans

5 Brigade d'Artillerie, Orléans
30 RAC, Orléans [9DI]
32 RAC, Orléans
45 RAC, Orléans

10 Division d'Infanterie
QG-Paris [GMP]
19 Brigade, Paris
46 RI, Fontainebleau
89 RI, Sens/Paris
20 Brigade, Paris
31 RI, Melun/Paris
76 RI, Coulommiers/Paris

7 Division de Cavalerie, Melun [GMP]
7/4 BCP, Orléans
4/30 RAC, Orléans

1 Brigade du Dragons, Fontainebleau [GMP]
7 RD, Fontainebleau

55 Division de Réserve
QG-Orléans
109 Brigade
204 RI, Auxerre/Troyes
282 RI, Montargis
289 RI, Sens/Paris
110 Brigade
231 RI, Melun/Paris
246 RI, Fontainebleau
276 RI, Coulommiers/Paris
313 RI, Blois
331 RI, Orléans

3 RAL, Orléans
5 BG/1 RG
5 Train, Fontainebleau

13 RD, Melun
8 R Ch, Orléans [5CA]

7 Brigade de Cavalerie Légère, Vendome
109 Brigade
204 RI, Auxerre/Troyes
282 RI, Montargis
289 RI, Sens/Paris

110 Brigade
231 RI, Melun/Paris
246 RI, Fontainebleau
276 RI, Coulommiers/Paris
313 RI, Blois
331 RI, Orléans

1 R Ch, Chateaudun
20 R Ch, Vendome
14 RH, Alencon [4CA]

5 Brigade du Dragons, Vincennes [GMP] [1DC]
6 RD, Vincennes
23 RD, Vincennes

3 Brigade de Cavalerie Légère, Meaux [3DC]
3 RH, Senlis
8 RH, Meaux

part 5 Division de Cavalerie
29 RD, Provins

VI Corps d'Armée [Châlons sur Marne]

12 Division d'Infanterie
QG-Reims

23 Brigade, Soissons
54 RI, Compiegne
67 RI, Soissons

24 Brigade, Reims
106 RI, Châlons
132 RI, Reims

40 Division d'Infanterie
QG- St Mihiel

79 Brigade, Commercy
154 RI, Leronville
155 RI, Commercy
26 BCP, Pont-a-Mousson

80 Brigade, St Mihiel
150 RI, St Mihiel
161 RI, St Mihiel/Reims
25 BCP, St Mihiel/Epernay

42 Division d'Infanterie
QG-Verdun

83 Brigade, Verdun
94 RI, Bar-le-Duc
8 BCP, Etain/Amiens
19 BCP, Verdun/Epernay

84 Brigade, Verdun
151 RI, Verdun
162 RI, Verdun
16 BCP, Conflans/Lille

29 BCP, St Mihiel/Epernay

6 Brigade d'Artillerie, Châlons/Marne
25 RAC, Châlons [12DI]
40 RAC, St Mihiel [40DI]
46 RAC, Châlons
61 RAC, Verdun [42DI]

6 BG/9RG
6 Train, Châlons
2 Aero Group, Reims

3 Division de Cavalerie	**4 Division de Cavalerie**	**5 Division de Cavalerie**
CG - Compiègne	CG - Sedan [2CA]	CG – Reims
	4/19 RAC, Verdun Sapeurs/Cycliste 9RG, Verdun	
3/8 BCP, Compiègne		5/29 BCP, Châlons
		4/61 RAC, Châlons Sapeurs/cycliste 9RG, Verdun
	3 Brigade de Cuirassiers, Ste Menehoulde	
13 Brigade du Dragons, Compiege	3 RC, Vouziers/Reims	3 Brigade du Dragons, Reims
5 RD, Compiègne	6 RC, Ste M/Chalons	16 RD, Reims
21 RD, Noyon		22 RD, Reims
	1 Brigade de Cavalerie Légère, St Mihiel	
	10 R Ch, Sampigny/Sézanne	7 Brigade du Dragons, Épernay
	12 R Ch, St M/Sézanne	9 RD, Épernay
		4 Brigade de Cavalerie Legere, Verdun
	5 Brigade de Cavalerie Légère, Châlons	2 RH, Verdun/Reims
	5 R Ch, Châlons	4 RH, Verdun/Reims
	15 R Ch, Châlons	

Verdun Fortress/72DR	**56 Division de Réserve**	**69 Division de Réserve**
164 RI 351 RI	111 Brigade	137 Brigade
165 RI 362 RI	294 RI, Bar le Duc	306 RI, Châlons
166 RI 364 RI	254 RI, Compiege	332 RI, Reims
5 RAP 365 RI HQ 9RG	355 RI, Commercy	138 Brigade
25 BG 56/59 BCP	112 Brigade	254 RI, Compiègne
	350 RI, St Mihiel	267 RI, Soissons
	361 RI, St Mihiel/Reims	306 RI Châlons
	65/66/69 BCP	

VII CORPS D'ARMÉE [BESANÇON]

14 Division d'Infanterie	**41 Division d'Infanterie**	**8 Division de Cavalerie**
QG- Belfort	QG-Remiremont	QG-Dole

27 Brigade, Lons-le-Saunier
44 RI, Lons-le-Saunier
60 RI, Besançon

28 Brigade, Belfort
35 RI, Belfort
42 RI, Belfort

7 Brigade d'Artillerie, Besancon
4 RAC, Remiremont [14DI]
5 RAC, Besançon
47 RAC, Hericourt [41DI]

7 BG, Besançon
7 Train, Dole

Fortress: Besançon Groupe

81 Brigade, Remiremont
152 RI, Gérardmer
5 BCP, Remiremont/Langres
15 BCP, Remiremont

82 Brigade, Bourg
23 RI, Bourg
133 RI, Belley

Belfort Fortress
171 RI
172 RI
9 RAP
28 BG
Aero Gp

8/15 BCP, Montbéliard
4/4 RAC, Besançon

8 Brigade du Dragons, Belfort
11 RD, Belfort
18 RD, Lure

8 Brigade de Cavalerie
Legere, Dole
11 R Ch, Vesoul [7CA]
14 R Ch, Dole

57 Divison de Reserve
113 Brigade
235 RI, Belfort
242 RI, Belfort
260 RI, Besançon
114 Brigade
244 RI, Lons-le-Saunier
371 RI, Belfort
372 RI, Belfort

74 Division de Reserve
223 RI, Bourg
333 RI, Belley

VIII Corps d'Armée [Bourges]

15 Division d'Infanterie
QG – Dijon

29 Brigade, Macon
56 RI, Châlons s/Soane
134 RI, Macon

30 Brigade, Dijon
10 RI, Auxonne
27 RI, Dijon

8 Brigade d'Artillerie, Bourges
1 RAC, Bourges [16DI]
37 RAC, Bourges
48 RAC, Dijon [15DI]

8 BG/4RG
8 Train, Dijon

16 Division d'Infanterie
QG – Bourges

35 Brigade, Tours
32 RI, Tours
66 RI, Tours

36 Brigade, Angers
77 RI, Cholet
135 RI, Angers

9 Division de Cavalerie, Tours
9/25 BCP, Joue-les-Tours
4/33 RAC, Tours
Sapers/Cycliste/6RG, Angers

1 Brigade de Cuirassiers, Tours
5 RC, Tours
8 RC, Tours

58 Division de Réserve
QG - Dijon

117 Brigade
232 RI, Tours
314 RI, Parthenay
325 RI, Poitiers
118 Brigade
266 RI, Tours
277 RI, Cholet
335 RI, Angers
268 RI, Le Blanc
290 RI, Chateauroux

7 RH, Niort [9CA]

IX Corps d'Armée [Tours]

17 Division d'Infanterie
QG – Chateauroux

33 Brigade, Chateauroux
68 RI, Le Blanc
90 RI, Chateauroux

34 Brigade, Poitiers
114 RI, Parthenay
125 RI, Poitiers

9 Brigade d'Artillerie, Poitiers
20 RAC, Poitiers [17DI]
33 RAC, Angers [18DI]
49 RAC, Poitiers

9 BG/6RG
9 Train, Chateauroux

18 Division d'Infanterie
QG - Angers

35 Brigade, Tours
32 RI, Tours
66 RI, Tours

36 Brigade, Angers
77 RI, Cholet
135 RI, Angers

9 Division de Cavalerie, Tours
9/25 BCP, Joue-les-Tours
4/33 RAC, Tours
Sapers/Cycliste/6RG, Angers

1 Brigade de Cuirassiers, Tours
5 RC, Tours
8 RC, Tours
7 RH, Niort [9CA]
25 RD, Angers [16BD/9DC]
Sapeurs/cycliste/6RG-10DC Angers

59 Division de Réserve
QG - Chateauroux

117 Brigade
232 RI, Tours
314 RI, Parthenay
325 RI, Poitiers
118 Brigade
266 RI, Tours
277 RI, Cholet
335 RI, Angers
268 RI, Le Blanc
290 RI, Chateauroux

X Corps d'Armée [Rennes]

19 Division d'Infanterie
QG – Rennes

37 Brigade, St Brieuc
48 RI, Guincamp
71 RI, St Brieuc

38 Brigade, Rennes
41 RI, Rennes
70 RI, Vitré

10 Brigade d'Artillerie, Rennes
7 RAC, Rennes [19DI]
10 RAC, Rennes [20DI]
50 RAC, Rennes

10BG/6RG
10 Train, Fougeres

20 Division d'Infanterie
QG - St Servan

39 Brigade, St Lô
25 RI, Cherbourg
136 RI, St Lô

40 Brigade, St Malo
2 RI, Granville
47 RI, St Malo

16 Brigade du Dragons, Rennes
24 RD, Rennes
13 RH, Dinan [10CA]

Cherbourg Fortress
2 RAP

60 Division de Réserve
QG - Rennes

119 Brigade
247 RI, St Malo
248 RI, Guincamp
271 RI, St Brieuc
120 Brigade
202 RI, Granville
225 RI, Cherbourg
336 RI, St Lô
241 RI, Rennes
270 RI, Vire

XI CORPS D'ARMÉE [NANTES]

21 Division d'Infanterie
QG – Nantes

41 Brigade, Nantes
64 RI, Acenis
65 RI, Nantes

42 Brigade, La Roche s/Yon
93 RI, La Roche s/Yon
137 RI, Fontenay

11 Brigade d'Artillerie, Vannes
28 RAC, Vannes
35 RAC, Vannes [22DI]
51 RAC, Nantes [21DI]

11BG/6RG
11 Train, Nantes

3 RAP, Brest
4 RAP, Lorient

22 Division d'Infanterie
QG - Vannes

43 Brigade, Vannes
62 RI, Lorient
116 RI, Vannes

44 Brigade, Quimper
19 RI, Brest
118 RI, Quimper

9 Brigade du Dragons, Nantes
1 RD, Lucon
3 RD, Nantes
2 R Ch, Pontivy

61 Division de Réserve
QG - Nantes

121 Brigade
264 RI, Acenis
265 RI, Nantes
316 RI, Vannes

122 Brigade
219 RI, Brest
262 RI, Lorient
318 RI, Quimper
293 RI, La Roche s/Yon
337 RI, Fontena

XII CORPS D'ARMÉE [LIMOGES]

23 Division d'Infanterie
CG – Angoulême

45 Brigade, Limoges
63 RI, Limoges
78 RI, Gueret

12BG/6RG
12 Train, Limoges

24 Division d'Infanterie
CG - Périgueux

46 Brigade, Angoulême
107 RI, Angoulême
138 RI, Magnac-Laval

47 Brigade, Bergerac
50 RI, Périgueux
108 RI, Bergerac

48 Brigade, Tulle
100 RI, Tulle
126 RI, Brive

10 Division de Cavalerie, Limoges
10/1 BCP, Limoges

10 Brigade du Dragons, Limoges
20 RD, Limoges
21 R Ch, Limoges [12CA]

62 Division de Réserve
CG - Angouleme

12 Brigade d'Artillerie, Angoulême
21 RAC, Angoulême[23]
34 RAC, Périgueux [24]
52 RAC, Angoulême

123 Brigade
263 RI, Limoges
278 RI, Gueret
338 RI, Magnac-Laval

124 Brigade
250 RI, Périgueux
307 RI, Angoulême
308 RI, Bergerac
300 RI, Tulle
326 RI, Brive

XIII Corps d'Armée [Clermont-Ferrand]

25 Division d'Infanterie
QG - St Étienne

49 Brigade, St Étienne
38 RI, St Étienne/Lyon
86 RI, Le Puy/Lyon

50 Brigade, Roanne
16 RI, Montbrison
98 RI, Roanne

13 Brigade d'Artillerie, C-F
16 RAC, Issoire [25DI]
36 RAC, C-F [26DI]
53 RAC, C-F

13 BG/4RG
13 Train, Moulins

26 Division d'Infanterie
QG - Clermont-Ferrand

51 Brigade, Riom
105 RI, Riom
121 RI, Montluçon

52 Brigade, C-Ferrand
92 RI, Clermont-Ferrand
139 RI, Aurillac

14 RD, St Étienne
[6BD/6DC]
3 R Ch, C-F [6BD/6DC]

63 Division de Réserve
QG - Clermont-Ferrand

125 Brigade
216 RI, Monbrison
238 RI, St Étienne/Lyon
298 RI, Roanne

126 Brigade
292 RI, Clermont-Ferrand
305 RI, Riom
321 RI, Montlucon

64 DR/128Brigade
286 RI, Le Puy/Lyon
339 RI, Aurillac

XIV Corps d'Armée [Lyon]

27 Division d'Infanterie
QG – Grenoble

53 Brigade, Grenoble
75 RI, Romans
140 RI, Grenoble
14 BCA, Grenoble[Maroc]
54 Brigade, Gap
52 RI, Montelimar
12 BCA, Embrun
28 BCA, Grenoble
30 BCA, Grenoble

14 Brigade d'Artillerie, Grenoble
2 RAC, Grenoble [27DI]
6 RAC, Valence/Grenoble

28 RAC, Grenoble [28DI]
1 RAM, Grenoble

5 RAL, Lyon
14BG/4RG
14 Train, Lyon

HQ 4 RG, Lyon

28 Division d'Infanterie
QG - Chambéry

55 Brigade, Lyon
22 RI, Santhony/Bourguin
99 RI, Lyon/Vienne
56 Brigade, Chambery
30 RI, Annecy
97 RI, Chambery
11 BCA, Annecy
13 BCA, Chambery
22 BCA, Albertville

6 Division de Cavalerie,
Lyon
6/13 BCP, Lyon
4/54 RAC, Lyon
Sapeurs/cycliste/4RG, Grenoble

5 Brigade de Cuirassiers, Lyon
7 RC, Lyon
10 RC, Lyon
9 RH, Chambery [14CA]

6 Brigade du Dragons, Lyon

64 Division de Réserve
QG - Grenoble

127 Brigade
275 RI, Romans
340 RI, Grenoble
52 BCA, Enbrun
68 BCA, Grenoble
128 Brigade
252 RI, Lyon
70 BCA, Grenoble

297 RI, Chambéry
357 RI, Gap

74 Division de Reserve
147 Brigade
222 RI, Santhony/Bourguin
299 RI, Lyon/Veinne
53 BCA, Chambéry
54 BCA, Grenoble
148 Brigade
230 RI, Annecy

PART ONE: 23

1 Aero Gp, Lyon

2 RD, Lyon Fortress: Lyon
Briançon Group
Grenoble Group

51 BCA, Annecy
52 BCA, Enbrun

159 RI, Briançon
11 RAP, Briançon
Parts 98RI, 38RI, 2RZ, 3RZ

5 & 11Bns/2RZ, Santhonay
5 & 11Bns/3RZ, Santhonay

XV Corps d'Armée [Marseille]

29 Division d'Infanterie
QG-Nice

57 Brigade, Antibes
111 RI, Antibes
112 RI, Toulon

58 Brigade, Marseille
3 RI, Digne/Hyere
141 RI, Marseille

Chasseurs Bns
6 BCA, Nice
7 BCA, Draguignan
24 BCA, Villefranche
27 BCA, Menton
15 Brigade d'Artillerie, Nîmes
19 RAC, Nîmes [30DI]
38 RAC, Nîmes
55 RAC, Orange [29DI]
2 RAM, Nice/Corse

15BG/7RG
15 Train, Orange
16 Train, Orange

163 RI, Nice
7 RAP, Nice [Bies 3-4]
10 RAP, Toulon
HQ7RG
23 BG
24 BG

30 Division d'Infanterie
QG-Avignon

59 Brigade, Nîmes
40 RI, Nîmes
58 RI, Avignon

60 Brigade, Aix
55 RI, St Esprit/Aix
61 RI, Privas/Aix

6 Brigade Cavalerie Légère, Tarascon [6DC]
13 R Ch, Vienne
6 RH, Marseille [15CA]
11 RH, Tarascon

Sapeurs/cycliste/7RG Avignon [8DC]

65 Division de Réserve
QG-Nice

129 Brigade
311 RI, Antibes
312 RI, Toulon
46 BCA, Nice
64 BCA, Villefranche
67 BCA, Menton
130 Brigade
203 RI, Digne/Hyere
341 RI, Marseille
47 BCA, Draguignan
63 BCA, Grasse

75 Divison de Réserve
149 Brigade
240 RI, Nîmes
258 RI, Avignon
150 Brigade
255 RI, St Esprit/Aix
261 RI, Privas/Aix

Fortress: Marseille Groupe

173 RI, Corse
Bie 1, 7RAP, Bonifacio
Bie 2, 7RAP, Ajaccio

Fortress: Corsican Groupe

XVI Corps d'Armée [Montpellier]

31 Division d'Infanterie
QG-Montpellier

61 Brigade, Béziers

32 Division d'Infanterie
QG-Perpignan

63 Brigade, Narbonne

66 Division de Réserve
QG-Montpellier

131 Brigade

81 RI, Montpellier
96 RI, Béziers

62 Brigade, Rodez
122 RI, Rodez
142 RI, Mende/Lodeve

16 Brigade d'Art, Castres
3 RAC, Castres [32DI]

9 RAC, Castres

56 RAC, Montpellier
16 BG/2RG

53 RI, Perpignan
80 RI, Narbonne

64 Brigade, Albi
15 RI, Albi
143 RI, Carcassonne

19 RD, Castres [15BD]
1 RH, Beziers [16CA] HQ 2RG, Montpellier

280 RI, Narbonne
281 RI, Montpellier
296 RI, Béziers

132 Brigade
215 RI, Albi
253 RI, Perpignan
343 RI, Carcassonne

322 RI, Rodez
342 RI, Mende/Lodeve

Fortresses: Bellegarde Mont Louis
Citadelle de Perpignan
Port Vendres-Collioure

XVII Corps d'Armée [Toulouse]

33 Division d'Infanterie
QG – Montauban

65 Brigade, Agen
7 RI, Cahors
9 RI, Agen

66 Brigade, Montauban
11 RI, Montauban
20 RI, Marmade

17 Brigade d'Artillerie, Toulouse
18 RAC, Agen [33DI]
23 RAC, Toulouse [34DI]
57 RAC, Toulouse

17BG/2RG
17 Train, Montauban

34 Division d'Infanterie
QG - Toulouse

67 Brigade, Toulouse
14 RI, Toulouse
83 RI, St Gaudens

68 Brigade, Auch
59 RI, Foix/Pamiers
88 RI, Mitrand/Auch

15 Brigade du Dragons, Montauban [10DC]
10 RD, Montauban

67 Division de Réserve
QG - Toulouse

133 Brigade
211 RI, Montauban
214 RI, Toulouse
220 RI, Marmade

134 Brigade
259 RI, Foix/Pamiers
283 RI, St Gaudens
288 RI, Mitand/Auch

207 RI, Cahors
209 RI, Agen

XVIII Corps d'Armée [Bordeaux]

35 Division d'Infanterie
QG-Bordeaux

69 Brigade, La Rochelle
6 RI, Saintes
123 RI, La Rochelle

70 Brigade, Bordeaux
57 RI, Libourne
144 RI, Bordeaux

36 Division d'Infanterie
QG-Bayonne

71 Brigade, Mont de Marsan
34 RI, Mont de Marsan
49 RI, Bayonne

72 Brigade, Pau
12 RI, Tarbes
18 RI, Pau

68 Division de Réserve
QG-Bordeaux

135 Brigade
206 RI, Saintes
234 RI, Mont de Marsan
323 RI, La Rochelle

136 Brigade
212 RI, Tarbes
257 RI, Libourne

18 Brigade d'Artillerie, Tarbes
14 RAC, Tarbes [36DI]
24 RAC, La Rochelle [35]
58 RAC, Bordeaux

3 RAP-4/5 Bies
18BG/2RG
18 Train, Bordeaux

XX Corps d'Armée [Nancy]

11 Division d'Infanterie
QG - Nancy

21 Brigade, Nancy
26 RI, Toul
69 RI, Toul
2 BCP, Lunéville/Troyes
4 BCP, St Nicholas de Port

22 Brigade, Nancy
37 RI, Troyes/Nancy
79 RI, Neufchateau

20 Brigade d'Artillerie, Nancy
8 RAC, Nancy [11DI]
39 RAC, Toul [39DI]
60 RAC, Troyes/Neufchateau

20 BG/10RG
20 Train, Versailles

part 4RI
part 82RI
HQ 10RG, Toul

Toul Fortress
167 RI
2 Brigade de Cavalerie
Légère, Lunéville
17 R Ch, Lunéville/Vitry
18 R Ch, Lunéville/Vitry

10 Division de Cavalerie
4/14 RAC, Tarbes
15 RD, Libourne

9 Brigade de Cavalerie
Légère, Tarbes [10DC]
9 R Ch, Auch [17CA]
10 RH, Tarbes [18CA]

39 Division d'Infanterie
QG – Toul

168 RI
169 RI
6 RAP
26 BG
Toul Aero Group

139 Brigade
226 RI, Toul
269 RI, Toul
42 BCP, Lunéville
44 BCP, St Nicholas
140 Brigade
237 RI, Troyes/Nancy
279 RI, Neufchateau
360 RI, Toul

73 Division de Réserve, Toul

344 RI, Bordeaux
218 RI, Pau
249 RI, Bayonne

Fortresses:
Citadelle de Bayonne
Le Portalet

70 Division de Réserve
QG - Nancy

77 Brigade, Toul
146 RI, Toul
153 RI, Toul

78 Brigade, Toul
156 RI, Toul
160 RI, Toul

2 Division de Cavalerie, Luneville
2/2 BCP, Luneville
4/8 RAC, Luneville
Sapeurs/cycliste/10RG, Toul

2 Brigade du Dragons, Luneville
8 RD, Luneville/Vtry
31 RD, Luneville/Vitry

12 Brigade du Dragons, Toul
4 RD, Commercy/Sezanne
12 RD, Troyes/Toul
5 RH, Nancy/Toul [20CA]

145 Brigade
346 RI, Toul
353 RI, Toul
356 RI, Toul
146 Brigade
367 RI, Toul
368 RI, Toul
369 RI, Toul

XXI Corps d'Armée [Épinal] (formed 1913)

13 Division d'Infanterie	**43 Division d'Infanterie**	**71 Division de Réserve**
QG - Chaumont	QG - St Dié	QG - Épinal
25 Brigade, Rembervillers	85 Brigade, Épinal	141 Brigade
17 RI, Épinal	149 RI, Épinal	349 RI, Épinal
17 BCP, Rembervillers/ Brienne	158 RI, Bruyeres/Lyon	358 RI, Bruyeres/Lyon
20 BCP, Baccarat/Brionne		370 RI, Épinal
21 BCP, Raon l'Etape/Montbelaird	86 Brigade, St Dié	142 Brigade
	1 BCP, Senones/Troyes	217 RI, Épinal
26 Brigade, Chaumont	3 BCP, St Dié/Besançon	221 RI, Langres
21 RI, Langres	10 BCP, St Dié/Langres	309 RI, Chaumont
109 RI, Chaumont	31 BCP, St Dié/Langres	

Gouvernement Militaire de Paris [all units stationed in Paris]

1 Division de Cavalerie
4/26 BCP, Vincennes
4/13 RAC, Paris
Sapeurs/cycliste/1RG

2 Brigade de Cuirassiers
1 RC
2 RC

HQ 1 RG
5 RG-
1, 2, 3 Chemin de Fer Bns
8 RG-
1, 2, 3 4 Telegraph Bns
1 Aero Station
22 BG
19 Train

5 & 11Bns, 1RZ
5 & 11Bns, 4RZ

Corps d'Armée des Troupes Coloniales

This corps was under the direct command of the Minister of War and was composed of three divisions whose units were stationed in many different Military Regions.

1 Division d'Infanterie Coloniale
QG – Paris

2 Brigade d'Infanterie Coloniale, Lyon
5 RIC, Lyon
6 RIC, Lyon

2 Division d'Infanterie Coloniale
QG - Toulon

4 Brigade d'Infanterie Coloniale, Toulon
4 RIC, Toulon
8 RIC, Toulon

5 Brigade d'Infanterie Coloniale, Paris
21 RIC, Paris
23 RIC, Paris

6 Brigade d'Infanterie Coloniale, Marseille
22 RIC, Hyéres
24 RIC, Perpignan

3 Division d'Infanterie Coloniale
QG – Brest

Corps Troops
22 BG, Versaille

1 Brigade d'Infanterie Coloniale, Brest
1 RIC, Cherbourg
2 RIC, Brest
3 Brigade d'Infanterie Coloniale, Rochfort
3 RIC, Rochfort
7 RIC, Bordeaux

Brigade d'Artillerie Coloniale, Paris
1 RACC, Lorient
2 RACC, Cherbourg
3 RACC, Vincennes-Toulon

OVERSEAS DEPLOYMENT, 1914

Summary of Overseas Garrisons

A total of 204,000 soldiers were stationed in France's overseas possessions and dependencies in 1913-1914. These were made up of 80,000 in Algeria and Tunisia, 76,303 in Morocco and 48,285 in other parts of the globe.

Algeria and Tunisia

The army in Algeria was described as the XIX Corps d'Armee and was made up of three geographical divisions. Total strength was 80,000 which was made up of 74 battalions (20 Zoauve, 40 Tirailleurs, nine Foreign Legion, and five African Light Infantry); 52 cavalry squadrons; 17 batteries of field artillery, eight of mountain artillery and eight of foot artillery; together with 17 engineer companies and nine train companies. In addition to the units listed below as being resident in Algeria and Tunisia in 1914, many battalions and squadrons were detached on temporary service in Morocco. These will be shown only in the data on the garrison in Morocco.

Division d'Alger

1 Algerian Infantry Brigade	1 Algerian Cavalry Brigade	Divisional Troops
1 RZ, Alger [4 Bn]	1 RS, Medea	1 GACA [2 batteries]
1 RTA, Blida [1, 2 Bns]	5 RCA, Alger	6 GAAPA [2 batteries]
5 RTA, Dellys [???Bn]		
9 RTA, Miliana [2, 3 Bns]		

Also in Algeria were 19Battalion du Genie,
1st and 2nd Bns of Tirailleurs Senegalais d'Afrique, Colomb-Bechar and Orléansville
Five territorial battalions of Zoauves [1, 2, 3, 10 &11], one territorial squadron of 5 RCA
One territorial battery of foot artillery.

Division d'Oran

2 Algerian Infantry Brigade	4 Algerian Infantry Brigade	2 Algerian Cavalry Brigade
2 RZ, Oran [1, 2, 3, 4 Bns]	1 REI, Sidi-bel-Abbes [2bns]	2 RS, Sidi-bel-Abbes
2 RTA, Mostaganem [1, 2, 5Bns]	2 REI, Saida [3 bns]	[5 RS formed 6.6.14]
	6 RTA, Tlcemen [1, 4 Bns]	2 RCA, Tlcemen
		6 RCA, Mascara

Divisional Troops included two GACA (two batteries), and 3rd Battery of six GAAPA. Reserves included four territorial battalions [4, 5, 6, 12] of Zouaves and a territorial squadron of six RCA

Division de Constantine

3 Algerian Infantry Brigade	3 Algerian Cavalry Brigade	Divisional Troops
3 RZ, Constantine [1, 4 Bns]	3 Spahis, Batna	3 GACA [3 btys]
3 RTA, Bone [2, 4 5 Bns]	3 Chasseurs d'Afrique, Constantine	
4 Battery, 6 GAAPA		
7 RTA, Constantine [2, 3Bns]		

Reserves included 3 territorial Battalions [7, 8, 9] of the Zoauves and one territorial squadron of the three RCA.
In addition to the forces in Algeria, the same command included the garrison in Tunisia.

Division d'Occupation de Tunisie

1 Tunisian Infantry Brigade	2 Tunisian Infantry Brigade	Tunisian Cavalry Brigade
4 RZ, Tunis [2, 3, 6 Bns]	4 RTA, Sousse [5, 6 Bns]	4 RS, Tunis
5 BILA, Le Kef	4 BILA, Gabes	4 RCA, Sfax
8 RTA, Bizerte [2, 4 Bns]		

Divisional troops were 7 GAAPA [4 batteries], five GACA 3 batteries and 29 BG.

Morocco

By 1914, the French Army had to provide an extensive force to protect its interests in Morocco. Of a total of 76,303 men, some 33,778 were Europeans, 17,062 were Algerians and Tunisians, 11,750 were Senegalese and the rest (13,892) were recruited locally. Many of the units allocated to Morocco were deployed temporarily from their home bases in France, Algeria and Tunisia. Often, they were formed into ad-hoc units entitled *'Régiments de Marche'*.

Western Morocco
14 BCP
RdM1Z [1/1Z, 2/1Z, 3/1Z]
RdM3Z [2/3Z, 4/3Z]
RdM4Z [1/4Z, 2/4Z]
RdM2RE [3, 5Bns]
2 BILA
3 BILA
RdM3T [1/3T, 3/3T]
RdM4T [1/4T, 2/4T, 3/4T]
RdM5T [1/5T, 2/5T, 3/5T]
RdM7T [1/7T, 4/7T]
RdM8T [1/8T, 5/8T, 6/8T]
2/9T
1 RMxICM, Rabat
2 RMxICM, Chauoia
3 RMxICM, Meknes
4 RMxICM, south of Fez
5 RMxICM, Fez
6 RMxICM, Marrakech
1 RCA [6 escadrons]
R de M Spahis Marocain
Esc/Spahis Senegal du Maroc
4 GACA
Artillerie Coloniale de Maroc
Bie/1RAM & Bie/2RAM
Bie/6 GAAPA
Gp Sapeurs et Mineurs
Gp Sapeurs Chemin de Fer
Gp Sapeurs Tele/Radio
2 esc d'Aviation
5 cies, 5, 16, 17 Train
Formed July 1914- 7/4 RZ newly formed –enroute to replace 1/4 and 6/4 RZ
8 GACA, Taza; 9 GACA, Meknes; 10 GACA, Fez
NB: 1RMxICM= 1BIC, 1BTS, 12BTS   4RMxICM= 8BIC, 8BTS, 11BTS
2RMxICM=7BIC, 9BTS, 10BTS   5RMxICM=4BIC, 2BTS, 3BTS
3RMxICM=9BIC, 4BTS, 13BTS   6RMxICM=6BIC, 6BTS, 7BTS

Eastern Morocco
2 RdMZ [2/2Z, 3/2Z]
1 RdM de 1REI [1, 2, 6 Bns]
1 BILA
3/1T at Fez
3/2T, 4/2T
3/6T
3/8T
4 esc/2RCA
3 esc/2RS
1 esc/1RS
4 bies/1GACA
1, 4, 5 Bies/2GACA
1 bie/3 GACA
2 bies/6 GAAPA
2 cies, Sapeurs et Mineurs
1 telegraph section, 8RG
1 det Chemin de Fer/5RG
1 cie/8 Train

Southern Morocco
2/6T
1BTM
2BTM
3BTM
4BTM
5BTM
6BTM
Esc/Spahis
Mtd Cie/1REI
1 section/RAM
Det/Genie
Det/Train

Indo China

There were 9,400 Europeans and 8,000 others, which totalled 17,400. In 1914 the garrison was divided into two geographic divisions.

1 Division Coloniale, Hanoi
1 Brigade

2 Division Coloniale, Saigon
3 Brigade

9RIC
1RT Tonkinois
4 RT Tonkinois
2 Brigade
10RIC
2 RT Tonkinois
3 RT Tonkinois
4 RACC [5 batteries]
6 Genie Coy

11RIC
RT Anamite
4 Brigade
No units allocated
5 RACC [14 batteries]
7 Genie Coy
Also 4/1REI and 5/2REI

North China

The force was made up of the 1,400 Europeans in 16RIC at Peking.

West Africa

A total of 1,200 Europeans were supported by 10,165 non-Europeans in a variety of infantry units. They were:

Battalion Infantry Coloniale de l'Afrique Occidental Francais, Dakar
1 RT Sénégalais [3 bns], St Louis
2 RT Sénégalais [3 bns], Kati
3 RT Sénégalais [3 bns], Cote d'Ivoire
4 RT Sénégalais [3 bns], Dakar
1 Bn Sénégalais du Mauritania
2 Bn Sénégalais de Timbouctu
3 Bn Sénégalais a Zinder
Escadron de Spahis Sénégalais
6 RACC [7 bies]
8 Genie Cie

Equatorial Africa

There were 5,100 locally-recruited troops in the following units:

Regiment Indigènes du Tchad Esc de Spahis du Tchad Regiment Indigènes du Gabon
Battalion Indigènes du Moyne Congo Battalion Indigènes de l'Oubangi-Chari Escadron du Cavalerie Indigènes du Congo

Djbouti

Cie de Garde Somalis

Madagascar

Some 7,700 locally recruited soldiers were supported by 4,300 European troops in the;

Battalion d'Infanterie Coloniale de l'Emyane
Battalion d'Infanterie Coloniale de Diego Suarez
1 RT Malgache [3 bns], Tananrive
2 RT Malgache [3 bns], Tamatave
3 RT Malgache [3 bns], Antsirang
BT Sénégalais en Madagascar, Majunga
Battalion Indigènes Somali
7 RACC [6 bies]
10-11 Genie Cies

West Indies

The garrison totalled 470 Europeans in Martinique who manned one artillery battery and provided one company of colonial infantry; one peleton at Guadaloupe, and one company at Guyane.

Pacific

The garrison in New Caledonia totaled 550 Europeans in a single colonial battalion, which was made up of two rifle companies and an artillery battery. There was one peleton at Tahiti.

Part Two

The Organisation of the Divisions

Divisions: An Introduction

During the First World War, the French Army raised 140 infantry divisions and 12 cavalry divisions. As with the other mass-conscript armies of Europe, and in contrast to the British and American practice, the division was not the smallest independent all-arms formation. The infantry division was a component of the main formation of manoeuvre, the Army Corps. For most of the war, a division operated as part of the same corps. Although the system began to breakdown during 1918 but even then, the French High Command deployed corps between various locations on the Western Front. As they moved, then their component divisions deployed with them, although corps had expanded from two to an average of four divisions by 1918. The relationship between division and corps is more akin to that between brigade and division in the English- speaking armies. However, as the division has become the normal method of determining the strength of an army, the authors have given more prominence to the composition and history of each division than their use by the French would warrant.

Divisions were allocated numbers in accordance with their position within the relevant army corps. For example, the 1st and 2nd Divisions held those numbers as components of the 1st Army Corps. In a similar fashion, brigades were numbered in sequence according to allocation to the divisions.

In August 1914, the French Army mobilised 93 divisions, from their respective Army Corps/Military Regions in five different categories. These were:

Active Infantry Divisions	43	numbered 1-43
Reserve Infantry Divisions	25	numbered 51-75
Territorial Infantry Divisions	12	numbered 81-92
Colonial Infantry Divisions	3	numbered 1-3
Cavalry Divisions	10	numbered 1-10

With the exception of the colonial divisions, all the infantry divisions were numbered in the same sequence.

During the course of the conflict, a further 57 infantry divisions, and two divisions of dismounted cavalry were formed and committed to battle. In addition, in 1918, the Polish Infantry Division joined the French order of battle. Those formed during the conflict were:

1914:	44-45 76-77 94-97 DM	total of 9
1915:	47-48 99-105 120-132 151-158 10DIC 15-17DIC	total of 33
1916:	46 133-134 161-170	total of 13
1917:	11DIC	total of 1
1918:	2DM 1-2DCP	total of 3

Some of the above were redesignations of older divisions, in addition, several Territorial Divisions were elevated to Active status in 1917-they were 81, 87, 88, and 97.

For reasons which are not often apparent, the following divisions were NOT formed:
49-50   78-80   93 98 106-119 135-160 159-160 4-9DIC 12-14DIC

Divisions were disbanded or used as the basis for new divisions during the course of the war. They were:

1914:	44 54 75 90 94 1DIC	total of 6
1915:	82 84 85 86 91 92 96 155	total of 8
1916:	99 101 102 103 104 105 8DC 9DC 10DC	total of 8
1917:	88 89 100 130 158 7DC	total of 6
1918:	55	total of 1

Also during 1918, the following redesignations took place:
63 to 1DIP, 65 to 2DM, 81 to 1DCP, 97 to 2DCP

SUMMARY OF DIVISIONS ON THE WESTERN FRONT

13th August 1914	66	1st January 1915	86	1st January 1916	106
5th Army	10	GPN	1	DAN	4
4th Army	9	8th Army	8	10th Army	15
3rd Army	11	10th Army	11	6th Army	20
2nd Army	13	2nd Army	14	5th Army	13
1st Army	11	6th Army	6	4th Army	7
Alsace	6	5th Army	9	2nd Army	8
GQG	6	4th Army	16	3rd Army	9
		3rd Army	9	RFV	7
		1st Army	8	1st Army	6
		DAV	4	DAL	8
				7th Army	9

1st January 1917	110	1st January 1918	98	11th November 1918	101
GAN	1	CSN	2	6th Army	9
10th Army	22	3rd Army	5	1st Army	20
3rd Army	5	6th Army	15	3rd Army	10
1st Army	9	5th Army	9	5th Army	17
6th Army	nil	4th Army	17	4th Army	17
5th Army	12	2nd Army	21	US Army	2
4th Army	14	1st Army	nil	2nd Army	nil
2nd Army	21	8th Army	15	10th Army	13
8th Army	16	7th Army	14	8th Army	5
7th Army	10			7th Army	8

The above figures are misleading in terms of the effective strength available. Divisions which were in transit from one part of the front to another often passed through the rear area of an intervening army, and are counted as part of that army on that date. Similarly, divisions in reserve or in training in the rear area of an army which is not their 'parent' are included in the strength of that army. Frontline strength, in terms of divisions in line, was much smaller than the above data would suggest. As the war progressed the proportion of divisions actually in the line declined substantially. In 1914-1916, most divisions were committed but in 1917-1918, most army corps deployed with two divisions in line, and two in reserve.

Infantry Divisions underwent one major organisational change in 1916-1917. At the outbreak of the war, infantry divisions were organised on a BINAIRE basis; with the infantry divided between two brigades of two or three regiments each. Due to severe manpower shortages, the brigade level of command was eliminated and the number of regiments reduced to three under the direction of a single infantry commander. This was the TERNAIRE division. The following table illustrates the timetable of change and should be read in conjunction with the Tables of Organisation and Equipment which follow.

Conversion from Binaire to Ternaire Divisions

Date	Division	Location	Army/CA
December 1915	58	Artois	10/XII
	152	Artois	10/IX
June 19116	48 (i)	Chemin des Dames	5/XXXVIII
	52	Verdun	2/III
	63	Verdun	2/III
	151	Verdun	2/XII
July 1916	130	Verdun	2/III
August 1916	31	Verdun	2/XI
	53	Oise	3/XIII
	158	Oise	3/-
August 1916	76	Vosges	7/-
November 1916	1	Champagne	4/I
	2	Champagne	4/I
	8	Lorraine	1/IV
	27	Chemin des Dames	5/XXXVIII
	28	Verdun	2/XIV
	42	Chemin des Dames	5/XXXII
	46	Vosges	7/-
	47	Vosges	7/XXI
	51	Champagne	4/I
	66	Vosges	7/-
	124	Chemin des Dames	5/IV
	154	Champagne	4/XVIII
	157	Vosges	7/-
	161	New-Vosges	7/-
	162	New-Champagne	4/-
	163	New-Champagne	4/V
	164	New-Vosges	7/XXXIV
December 1916	9	Verdun	2/XI
	11	Lorraine	DAL/XXXIX
	13	Vosges	7/XXI
	25	Lorraine	DAL/XIII
	26	Lorraine	DAL/XIII
	30	Chemin des Dames	5/XXXVII
	39	Lorraine	DAL/XX
	40	Chemin des Dames	5/XXXII
	43	Vosges	7/XXI
	48 (ii)	Lorraine	DAL/XXXIX
	69	Chemin des Dames	5/V or XXXVIII
	120	Lorraine	DAL/XIII
	10DIC	Oise	10/CAC
	165	New-Chemin des Dames	5/XXXII
	167	New-Lorraine	DAL/XIII
January 1917	12	Chemin des Dames	6/VI
	15	Oise	10/VIII
	16	Oise	10/VIII
	18	Chemin des Dames	6/VI
	56	Chemin des Dames	6/VI
	65	Verdun	2/XXXI
	71	Verdun	2/XXXI
	125	Reims	5/V
	127	Chemin des Dames	6/VI

	166	New-Chemin des Dames	6/VI
	168	New-Lorraine	DAL/XX
	169	New-Oise	10/VIII
	170	New-Vosges	7/XXI
Febrarury 1917	23(i)	Champagne	4/XII
	24	Champagne	4/XII
	73	Lorraine	8/XXXX
	128	Verdun	2/XXX
	134	Vosges	7/XXXIV
March 1917	7	Lorraine	8/XXXX
	55	Verdun	2/XV
	59	Verdun	2/IV
	60	Champagne	4/XII
	61	Aisne	1/XXXV
	64	Verdun	2/XXI
	67	Lorraine	8/XXXIX
	68	Lorraine	8/-
	74	Verdun	2/XV
	88	Lorraine	8/XXXIX
	123	Verdun	2/XV
	126	Verdun	2/XV
	132	Verdun	2/XVI
April 1917	20	Aisne	1/X
	62	Oise	3/XIV
	70	Oise	3/XXXIII
	81	Oise	3/XXXIII
	87	Oise	3/XIII
	97	Chemin des Dames	6/-
	121(i)	Oise	3/XXXV
May 1917	5	Aisne	1/III
	6	Aise	1/III
	14	Reims	5/VII
	19	Champagne	4/X
	29	Picardie	1/XXXVI
	32	Verdun	2/XVI
	33	Verdun	2/IV
	34	Verdun	2/I
	36	Aisne	10/XVIII
	72	Champagne	4/XVII
	131	Champagne	4/-
	2DIC	Vosges	7/ICAC
	3DIC	Vosges	7/ICAC
	15DIC	Lorraine	8/IICAC
June 1917	129	Chemin des Dames	6/III
August 1917	10	Aisne	10/V
September 1917	23(ii)	Champagne	4/XII
	41	Champagne	4/XII
	57	Macedonia	
	122	Macedonia	
	156	Macedonia	
	16DIC(I)	Macedonia	
October 1917	35	Champagne	4/XVIII
	121 (ii)	Aisne	10/XXXV
Novembver 1917	3	Verdun	2/II
	4	Verdun	2/II

	21	Chemin des Dames	6/XI
	22	Chemin des Dames	6/XI
	77	Vosges	7/XXXIII
	133	Flanders	1/XXXVI
January 1918	17	Lorraine	8/IX
	1DCP	NEW-Oise	3/ICC
	2DCP	NEW-Champagne	4/IICC
June 1917	45	Reims	5/ICAC
	48(iii)	Aisne	10/-
July 1918	37	Picardie	1/XV
	38	Aisne	10/XVIII
	153	Aisne	10/I
August 1918	17DIC	Macedonia	
	2DM	New-Lorraine	8/XXXII
October 1918	16DIC(ii)	Macedonia	

TABLES OF ORGANISATION AND EQUIPMENT

[figures 00/000 show officers/other ranks]

TYPE BINAIRE	TYPE TERNAIRE Division HQ
Division HQ [25/120]	
HQ Infantry Brigade [3/10]	HQ Infantry
Infantry Regiment [70/3250]	Infantry Regiment
3 battalions	3 battalions
Infantry Regiment [70/3250]	Infantry Regiment
3 battalions	3 battalions
• each regiment had 12 machine guns	Infantry Regiment
	3 battalions
HQ Infantry Brigade [3/10]	
Infantry Regiment [70/3250]	NB Chasseurs were organised into battalions which
3 battalions	were brigaded from 1915
Infantry Regiment [70/3250]	
3 battalions	
• each regiment had 12 machine guns	Cavalry Squadron
	-not always allocated
NB: On mobilisation, each reserve division was allocated two brigades of three regiments each, but, each regiment had two battalions only.	Divisional Artillery Regiment
	Group
	3 batteries of 4 x75mm
Cavalry Squadron [5/150] Attached from Corps cavalry regiment	Group
	3 batteries of 4 x75mm
	Group
Field Artillery Regiment [54/1600]	3 batteries of 4 x75mm
Group [16/528]	Trench Mortar Battery [4 mortars]
3 batteries of 4 x 75mm each	Heavy Artillery Battery [4 x 55mm]
Group	
3 batteries of 4 x 75mm each	Divisional Engineers
Group	3 companies
3 batteries of 4 x 75mm each total of 36 guns	
	Signals Detachment
• Territorial Divisions had 2 groups, totalling 6 batteries of 24 90/95mm guns	
Divisional Engineers [6/390]	
2 companies –3rd added 1914	
Signals Detachment	

CAVALRY DIVISION

Division HQ   [25 Officers/110 Other Ranks]

Cavalry Brigade [60/1300]   Cavalry Brigade [60/1300]   Cavalry Brigade [60/1300]
Regiment [4 sqns]   Regiment [4 sqns]   Regiment [4 sqns]
Regiment [4 sqns]   Regiment [4 sqns]   Regiment [4 sqns]

in peacetime the cavalry brigade administered a light cavalry regiment which provided corps and infantry divisional cavalry on mobilisation. During 1914 and 1915, each division formed a dismounted regiment of three battalions through the withdrawal of squadrons from the constituent regiments of cavalry

Divisional Artillery [14/370]
Horse Artillery Group   3 batteries of 75mm

Divisional Troops
Groupe Cycliste [320] permanently attached from a Battalion de Chasseurs
Engineer & Cyclist Detachment [2/34]
Signals Detachment

Infantry Divisions

Active Divisions 1 - 43

1 Division d'Infanterie

An active division in 1914 as part of I Corps d'Armée, with headquarters at Lille

Commanders
02.08.14-Alexandre Gallet
03.10.14-Joseph Bro
08.03.15-Jacques de Riols de Fonclare
06.10.16-Léon Gregoire

1 Brigade [disbanded 11.16]
43 RI, Lille	10.16 to 126DI-replaced by 233RI ex 5!DI
127 RI, Valenciennes	10.16 to 126DI

2 Brigade [disbanded 11.16]
1 RI, Cambrai	
84 RI, Avesnes	6.15 to 122DI-replaced by 201RI ex ICA

Infantry from 11.16
1 RI
201 RI
233 RI

Artillery
Groups 1-3, 15 RAC, Douai
7 Group/101 RAL [added 6.18-was 2Gp/101RL]

Cavalry
5/6 RCh, 8.14-11.15;   3/6 RCh, 11.15-7.17

Engineers & Pioneers
1914: Cie 1/1 du 3RG   1918: Cies 1/1, 1/51, 1/21 du 3RG
8.18-Pioneer Battalion 172RIT

By 13th August, the division had moved to Fifth Army's concentration area near Aubenton from which it deployed to the line of the river Meuse between Mézières and Monthermé. Two days later it moved into Belgium between Hastière and Ansermine from where it was engaged in the battle of Charleroi near St Gérard and then near Mariemburg on 25th August. During Fifth Army's long retreat to the Marne, 1DI fought near Sains-Richaumont in the battle of Guise before reaching the river Marne at Esternay. There it fought for control of the two Morin rivers in the first battle of the Marne, whence it advanced northeastwards via Dormans and Ville-en-Tardenois to enter Reims on 12th September. After actions on the outskirts of the city at Neuvillette and Cavaliers-de-Courcy, the division joined the battle of the Aisne on 16th September. It was engaged in the area around La Ferme de Cholera and Berry-au-Bac to the northwest of Reims. It remained in this area as trench warfare developed; it took part in an attack on Sapigneul between 12th and 15th October. Early in November the division moved a few kilometres westward and took part in attacks on Soupir (6th November) and Chavonne (7th-14th November) on the north bank of the Aisne.

After a relatively quiet period on the Aisne, 1DI moved eastwards to join the Fourth Army in Champagne on 20th December 1914. The division occupied a sector near Beauséjours where it took part in the French attack of 16th February 1915. The division left the line on 12th March and moved to the Longeville sector, southeast of Verdun. In the 1st Battle of Woëvre on 10th April the division attacked between Braquis and D'Hennemont and reached the Bois de Buzy. After a period of rest at Ste-Menehould in the Argonne, the division returned to the Aisne where it took up positions between

Godat and Berry-au-Bac on 26th April. It remained in the Aisne for the rest of 1915 and moved to the sector between the river Loivre and Neuville on 18th August.

The German attack on Verdun in February 1916 brought about the division's movement to that battle on 23rd February. It took up positions on the rightbank of the Meuse on 25th February. It was engaged heavily between Belleville, Bras, Côte du Poivre and d'Haudromont until 7th April. After that date the division was rotated out of the battle-part of Pétain's policy-and returned to the Aisne for a period of rest and retraining near Dormans, Fismes and Epernay. On 9th August, 1DI moved to Amiens to join Sixth Army's actions in conjunction with the BEF's attacks on the Somme. The division moved up to the line on 19th August and took part in the attacks on Maurepas on 24th August and Combles on 16th September.

After a period of recuperation near Chalons, the division returned to Fourth Army's front in Champagne on 7th October. It took up positions between Côte 193 and Ste-Marie-a-Py until 21st November. The division's time in this sector was broken by a period of training near Courtisols between 21st November and 4th January 1917.

As part of the preparations for Nivelle's spring offensive, 1DI moved, via Fismes, to join Fifth Army at Beaurieux. On 9th April the division took part in I CA's attack on the plateau and village of Craonne at the eastern end of theChemin des Dames. Although successful in comparison with the rest of the offensive, the division was moved back to a rest area on 21st April. There is no information of any unrest in the ranks of the division during this period of the Mutinies.

On 25th July, the division was moved to the North Sea coast between Dunkerque and Bergues where it became part of the often-overlooked French contribution to Haig's offensive, which began on 31st July. On that day the division 'went over the top' near Bikschote after which it occupied a sector of the line between Bikschote and Langemark until 16th October. The division trained near Calais and then attacked between St Jansbeek and Korverbeek on the 22nd and 26th of that month.

The division's stay in Flanders ended on 7th December when it moved to the sector of the river Ourcq and came under command of Sixth Army. It went into line between the Fôret de Vauclerc and the Ployon between 18th January and 9th March 1918. The division was in the rear area when the German offensive began on 21st March and was rushed up to the front near Guiscard two days later. Under German pressure, it retreated via Noyon and Mont Renaud to Ourscamp and Pontoise where it remained for several weeks. The division moved eastwards to the Aisne on 27th May and joined XICA in the ultimately successful attempt to stop the German army breaking through to the Marne. During this period it fought at Villers-Cotteréts and Chavigny. Transferred to XXXCA in Mangin's Tenth Army for the 2nd Battle of the Marne, 1DI took part in counter-attacks towards Grand- Rozoy and le Plessiers-Huleu between 18th and 28th July.

The rest of the war was spent in the relatively quiet area of Alsace. After resting near Compiegne, the division joined Seventh Army between Leimbach and Metzeral on 27th August, where it remained until 19th October. When HQ Tenth Army moved to Lorraine in anticipation of a French offensive to retake the 'lost provinces' 1DI came under Mangin's command. It was at Mirecourt in Lorraine when the Armistice was signed.

2 Division d'Infanterie

An active division in 1914 as part of I Corps d'Armée, with headquarters at Arras.

Commanders
02.08.14-Henri Deligny
08.09.14-Noel Garnier-Duplessix
21.09.14-Jean-Marie Brulard
16.07.15-Pierre Guignabaudet
17.06.17-Paul Mignot

3 Brigade [disbanded 11.16]
33 RI, Arras	11.16 to 51DI-replaced by 208RI ex 51DI
73 RI, Béthune	11.16 to 51DI

4 Brigade [disbanded 11.16]
8 RI, St Omer
110 RI, Dunkerque

Infantry from 11.16
8 RI
110 RI
208 RI

Artillery
Groups 1-3, 27 Rac, St Omer
Group 6, 101RAL [formed 6.18]

Cavalry
6/6 RCh, 8.14-11.15;   4/6 RCh, 11.15-7.17

Engineers & Pioneers
1914: Cie 1/2 du 3RG   1918: Cie 1/2, 1/92, 1/71 du 3RG
8.18-Pioneer Battalion 72RIT

As part of the Fifth Army, the division concentrated at d'Auvilliers-les-Forges in order to cover the river Meuse between Revin and Givet. On 13th August 1914 it advanced to Dinant where it defended the river between Dinant and Anhée on 15th August. By 22nd August 2DI was forced to retreat back to Charleroi, where it was engaged near St Gerard on the next day. Thereafter it conformed with the retreat of the Fifth Army to Guise. The division fought at Guê-d'Hossus on the 26th and at Sains-Richaumont. By the 30th, the retreat continued via Crécy-sur-Serre, Pontavert and Baizil to positions south of Esternay from which it began to prepare for the first battle of the Marne, which began on 6th September. In that action, as part of I Corps d'Armee, Fifth Army, it took part in the battle for the Deux Morins around Esternay, Bergères-sous- Montmirail and Fontaine-Chacun. From 10th September, 2DI advanced via Verneuil and Ville-Dommange towards Reims where it fought in the first battle of the Aisne between 13th September and 12th December 1914. After fighting around Bétheny and the Neuvillete, most of the divison's efforts were centred on the sector between Choléra and Ville-aux-Bois, to the north-west of Reims, where it took part in a French counter-attack on 12th October. On 4th November, its infantry took Sapigneul and then Côte 108 on the 11th November.

The division's first break from conflict came on 12th December 1914 when it moved to Fismes from which it joined Fourth Army's attacks during the first battle of Champagne. It attacked at Mesnil-les-Hurlus on 9th January 1915 and occupied a sector there until 2nd March, during which time it attacked at Mamelles on 16th February. After resting southeast of Verdun between 2nd March and 5th April, 2DI was allocated to Detachment Gérard for the first battle of Woëvre in which it attacked Bois de Buzy and to the east of Braquis. On 30th April and 5th May it attacked around Bois d'Ailly before withdrawal for rest at Épernay.

Between 15th May and 3rd September 1915, under command of Fifth Army, the division occupied the sector between Berry-au-Bac and Moulin Pontoy; and returned to the same area north-west of Reims, between the Miette and Sapigneul between 2nd October 1915 and 12th February 1916.

On 21st February 1916, 2DI was drawn into the battle of Verdun and was heavily engaged around Douaumont until 8th March. On 14th April, the division returnd to Fifth Army, and took up positions along the Chemin des Dames between Paissy and Soupir. The division rested from 24th July until it joined Sixth Army for the battle of the Somme. Between 3rd September and 5th October, it occupied a sector between Forest and Bois de Maurepas, during which time it seized the Ferme de Priez on the 14th and the villages of Combles and Morval on the 17th September. Withdrwan from the sector and moved back to Champagne, 2DI took over the sector between Maisons de Champagne and Butte de Mesnil from 16th to 30th November. On 6th January 1917 it moved to the sector between Maisons de Champagne and the Courtine where it withstood a German attack on 15th February.

On 8th April 1917 the division returned to the Chemin des Dames and, as part of ICA, took part in Nivelle's Offensive. It attacked between Craonne and the Ployon on the 16th but was pulled out of the line on 19th April for a long rest near Mailly and at Provins. During July, the division moved to Flanders with 1st Army. There, it occupied a sector near Bikschote, and attacked between Martje Vaert and the Broenbeek on 16th August, and into the Forêt d'Houthulst on 9th October. After these actions, the division occupied a sector north of Langemark from 21st November until 7th December.

By 17th January 1918, the division was in 6th Army behind Soissons where it remained in reserve until moved to counter the German offensive between the rivers Miette and Ployon, on the Chemin des Dames. It retreated via Fismes and Écuiry to cover the bridge over the river Oise at Choisy-au-Bac. By 2nd May it was in Fifth Army's reserve position near Beauvais. On return to the Sixth Army, it was committed to the 3rd battle of the Aisne near Montigny-Lengrain from which it re-occupied and held the front between Dammard and Troesnes until 18th July. From that date it fought for ten days on the line of the river Ourcq and took part in Sixth Army's advance during the second battle of the Marne to Rocourt St Martin. After a further period of rest, on 30th April, the division moved north of the Aisne to the Third Army's sector near Autreches. It took part in the second battle for Noyon by attacking in the sector between the river Aillette and Pont-St- Mard. It returned to the reserve on 29th August.

On 11th September 1918 the division joined the Seventh Army in the Vosges and occupied the sector between Burnhaupt-le-Haut and Leimbach until 28th October. During the last few days of the war, the division was to be found near Ceintrey preparing for Tenth Army's offensive to retake Lorraine.

3 Division d'Infanterie

An active division in 1914 as part of II Corps d'Armée, with headquarters at Amiens.

Commanders
02.08.14-Charles Regnault
02.09.14-Emilien Cordonnier
19.09.14-Ernest Caré
20.10.14-Emilien Cordonnier
03.02.15-Adrien Chrétien
22.01.16-Pierre Nayral Martin de Bourgon

5 Brigade [disbanded 11.17]
72 RI, Amiens   6.15 to 125DI replaced by 272RI ex IICA
128 RI, Abbeville   11.17 to 41DI

6 Brigade [disbanded 11.17]
51 RI, Beauvais
87 RI, St Quentin

Infantry from 11.17
51 RI
87 RI
272 RI

Artillery
Groups 1-3, 17 RAC, La Fere
Group 5, 102 RAL   [added 3.18-formerly 15Gp/102RAL]

Cavalry
5/19 RCh, 8.14-7.17;   1/19 RCh, 1.17-7.17

Engineers & Pioneers
1914: Cie 2/1 du 3RG   1918: Cies 2/1, 2/51, 2/21 du 3RG
8.18-Pioneer Battalion 13RIT

As part of the Fourth Army, the division assembled at Stenay from which it took part in the battle for the Ardennes, which began on 22nd August 1914. After fighting at Villers-la-Loue and Robelmont, the division fought at Montmédy and then at Cesse in defence of the line of the river Meuse. On 29th August 3DI began the retreat to the Marne. After moving via Ville-sur-Tourbe, St Mard-sur-le-Pont and Heiltz-le-Hutier, the division took part in Fourth Army's operations during the first battle of the Marne. Centred on Vitry, it fought at Haussignémont, Etrepy and Parguy-sur-Sauls between 6th and 12th September after which it occupied sector around Servon until 15th January 1915. During this period in the Argonne, the division engaged in mining operations, attacked and counter-attacked on 7th-11th November, 30th December and 5th January in the sector between Bois d'Hauzy and Bagatelle.

On 8th February 1915 the division moved westwards to take part in the 1st battle for Champagne and it took part in operations around Mesnil-les-Hurlus, Côte 196 and Mamelles until 12th March. As part of Detachment Gérard, the division participated in the battle for the Woëvre at Maizeray and Marcheville between 5th and 19th April: this included attacks on 6th, 12th and 13th April at the latter position. On 25th April it moved to 3rd Army's sector to the south of Verdun at Trésauvaux and Tranchée de Calonne where it assisted in the defence of the shoulder of the Verdun salient at Éparges. Apart from a brief rest period it remain here until 27th September when it moved to Perthes to take part in the attack on the Butte de Tahure, which was part of the Fourth Army's offensive during the second battle for Champagne.

On 1st December 1915, 3DI returned to the Éparges front and occupied a sector between there and Vaux-les-Palameix where it remained until 25th June 1916. After a rest period, the division joined the Sixth Army in Picardy where it took part in the battle of the Somme. It occupied the Belloy-en-Santerre sector until 16th August when it moved to the Tranchée de Souville where it remained until 18th August. From 27th August until 28th September, it was engaged in operations to the south of Belloy and to the east of Estrées-Denicourt. It was subjected to German attacks at Poivre on 10th and 15th September and then in the Tranchée de Calmon on the 17th. The division moved into reserve on 28th September and then moved to the Proyart sector, east of Bernay on 26th October. At Christmas, the division left Picardy for Lorraine, where it occupied a sector near Art-sur-Meurthe and then at Blenod-les-Toul, under command of DAL and Eighth Army until 27th March 1917.

On 27th March the division joined X Army near Epernay to prepare for Nivelle's Offensive on the Chemin des Dames. During the abortive attack of 16th April the division remained in reserve until it took over a sector north of the Godat. It attacked Mont Spin and Tranchée de Vampire on 4th, 5th and 7th May. After a rest period at Revigny from 3rd June, the division moved to the St Mihiel sector near Ligny-en-Barroy on 2nd August to prepare for the second Verdun offensive. As part of this operation, the division attacked the Germans between Côte 304 and Forges on 24th August and then took over the sector between Béthincourt and Haucourt on 31st August. It remained there until 14th January 1918. The move to the adjacent sector between Haucourt and Avocourt on 15th February was followed by a limited attack on the Bois de Malancourt on 17th March.

The division was pulled out of the Verdun area on 3rd April and by the 28th had joined First Army in Picardy where the German offensive had run out of steam. It occupied the sector between Thory, Ainval and Grivesnes. In co-operation with British forces, it took part in the attack on Sauvillers–Mongival on 27th July. After this the division moved over the river Avre to take part in the major Allied offensive in Picardy: it fought at Mailly-Raineval and Bois St Herbert between 8th and 12th August. The division left Picardy on 22nd August for a rest period near Châlons-sur-Marne.

On 5th September the division rejoined Fourth Army in Champagne. It attacked Mesnil-les-Hurlus on 26th September, reached the Galoche and freed the line of the Dormoise. Then it pursued the Germans to the Aisne and reached Condé-les-Vouziers on 13th October. On that date 3DI began another rest period at Lunéville before re-entering the line between the Domevre and Leintrey in Eighth Army's sector in Lorraine. There, it prepared for the planned liberation of Lorraine.

4 Division d'Infanterie

An active division in 1914 as part of II Corps d'Armée, with headquarters at Mézières

Commanders
02.08.14-Charles Rabier
09.12.14-Marie-Louis Guillaumat
26.02.15-Flavien Passard
03.08.15-Léonce Lebrun

21.04.16-Henri Linder
23.03.17-Horace Pentel
07.09.17-Georges Challe
11.10.17-Camille Ragueneau
12.10.17-Nicolas Remond
09.07.18-Felix Goureau

7 Brigade [disbanded 10.17]
91 RI, Mezieres   6.15 to 125DI-replaced by 328RI ex IICA 10.17-328RI to 52DI
147 RI, Sedan

8 Brigade [disbanded late 8.14-reformed 2.15-to 122DI 6.15]
45 RI, Laon   6.15 to 122DI
148 RI, Rocroi   6.15 to 122DI

87 Brigade [disbanded 11.17]
120 RI, Péronne & Stenay
9 BCP, Longwy
18 BCP, Longuyon

Infantry from 11.17
120 RI
147 RI
9 BCP
18 BCP

Artillery
Groups 1-3, 42 RAC, Stenay
Group 11, 102 RAL   [added 11.17-retitled Group 6/102 RAL 3.18]

Cavalry
6/19 RCh, 8.14-9.15;   4/19 RCh, 9.15-7.17;   3/19 RCh, 1.17-7.17

Engineers & Pioneers
1914: Cie 2/2 du 3RG   1918: Cies 2/2, 2/52, 2/71 du 3RG
8.18-Pioneer Battalion 117RIT

As part of the Fourth Army, 4DI concentrated north of Verdun between Mangiennes and Spincourt from which it took part in the battle for the Ardennes, at Gerouville and Bellefontaine, between 21st and 24th August 1914. During the retreat to the Marne, it fought at Martincourt, Luzy, Thibaudine and Yoncq on the Meuse; and at Grand Pré and Vienne-le-Chateau in the Argonne, until it halted at Chemonon-la-Ville. During Fourth Army's battles around Vitry between 6th and 15th September, it engaged the Germans at Sermaize-les-Bains, and at Pargny-sur-Saulx, and then, moved northwards through Ste-Menehould to Servon, in the Argonne. From 15th September 1914 until 18th January 1915, it took part in many actions, often involing mine warfare, between Bagatelle and Four-de-Paris, as part of the successful attempt the hold the Germans in the Argonne sector.

On 20th February 1915, the division moved to the Somme-Tourbe sector in Champagne, and attacked near Beauséjours on the 26th, and then occupied the Mesnil-lés-Hurlus sector until 23rd March. After a brief rest, the division took part in the battle of the Woevre, in Lorraine, and occupied positions in the Trésauvaux-Marchéville sector. It fought around the Eparges shoulder of the Vedun salient from 15th May until 1st October. During the second battle of Champagne, it attacked Perthes between 6th and 10th October, and then, at Tahure, on 30th and 31st October.

The division returned to Lorraine on 13th January 1916, and took over the sector between Kouer-la-Grande and Dompcervin. In response to the German assault on Verdun, the division fought around Thiaumont and the Etang-de-Vaux from 18th to 20th April.

After a period of rest, the division joined Sixth Army in Picardy on 24th June 1916. During the Somme offensive, it was involved in operations around Belloy and Berny in August and October. The division left Picardy on 23rd December 1916. After a long period of rest and re-training near Toul, it joined Tenth Army on 27th March 1917 for Nivelle's offensive on the Chemin des Dames. After a period in support, it attacked Sapigneul on 4th, 11th and 17th May. On 1st July, the division moved to the Hayette-Avocourt sector outside Verdun. On 27th August, it shuffled to the right to take over the Avocourt-Haucourt sector. After a brief rest, it moved to the Chaume-Beaumont sector on the right bank of the Meuse on 18th March 1918. It remained there until 17th May.

On 26th May 1918, the division joined Sixth Army, and took part in operations at Oulchy-le-Chateau, Neuilly-Saint-Front and Chezy-en-Orxois until 8th June in an attempt to slow down the German assault south of the Aisne. As part of 9th Army, the division took part in the second battle of the Marne at St Agnan, and Chapelle-Monthodon. On 27th July, it attacked the Foret de Riez, and advanced to the line of the Ardre.

A brief rest was followed by service with Fourth Army. It joined the line between Perthes and Beauséjours on 14th September, and, subsequently, took part in attacks at Manre, Liry and Croix from 29th September until 13th October.

On 17th October 1918, the division joined Eighth Army east of the Moselle, between Leintrey and the Sanon, where in prepared to take part in the planned offensive northwards towards Metz.

5 Division d'Infanterie

An active division in 1914 as part of III Corps d'Armée with headquarters at Rouen

Commanders
02.08.14-Elie Verrier
31.10.14-Charles Mangin
04.06.16-Henri de Roig-Bourdeville

9 Brigade [disbanded 5.17]
39 RI, Rouen/Dieppe	7.15 to 130DI replaced by 274RI ex IICA
74 RI, Rouen	

10 Brigade [to 21DI 5.17 and then to 121DI 6.17]
36 RI, Caen	5.17 to 121DI-replaced by 224RI ex 158DI
129 RI, Le Havre	5.17 to 153Bde

Infantry from 5.17
74 RI	
224 RI	
274 RI	disbanded 12.17
5 RI	added 5.17-form 6DI
114 BCP	added 6.17-from 129DI, to 70DI in 11.17
224 RI	added 11.17-from 158DI

Artillery
Groups 1-3, 43 RAC, Caen	
Group 5, 103RAL	[added 3.18-formerly Gp11/103RAL]

Cavalry
5/7 RCh, 8.14-7.17;   3/7 RCh, 1.17-7.17

Engineers & Pioneers

1914: Cie 3/1 du 3RG   1918: Cies 3/1, 3/51, 3/21 du 3RG
8.18-Pioneer Battalion 21RIT

As part of the Fifth Army, 5DI concentrated at Poix-Terron by 9th August 1914. After providing cover for the line of the Meuse between Nouvion and Mézières, the division advanced with the rest of Lanrezac's forces to the Sambre on 13th August. On the 22nd it was engaged at Châtelet during the battle for Charleroi, after which, it retreated via Renlies, Caselle and Vervins. On 29th August, it fought at Jonqueuse and Landifay in the first battle of Guise. The retreat to the Marne took the division through Laon and Pont-à-Binson to Courgivaux, from which location it fought the first battle of the Marne from 6th-10th September.

It advanced towards Reims and became engaged in heavy fighting in the northern outskirts of that city, around the Fort de Brimont. In the following months, 5DI remained in this area: in line between Courcy and the westbank of the Loivre until 11th December, and then near Berry-au-Bac until 17th May 1915. It thwarted the German attack on Bois de la Mine on 10th May.

On 26th May 1915, the division came under command of Tenth Army for the second battle of Artois. During this action it spent several periods in the line near Neuville-Saint-Vaast, beweeen Arras and Vimy Ridge. The attempt to take the ridge continued during the autumn of 1915, and 5DI attacked at Folie Ferme on 25th September. The division rested near Villers Bretonneux from 8th October and re-entered the line in Picardy, between Frise and Foucaucourt on 8th Decmeber and remained there until 18th February 1916.

After some time in support near Matz, the division moved eastwards to the Argonne, and was committed to the battle to the battle for Verdun on 2nd April 1916. It spent ten months in the Verdun sector. Initially it was in line between Thiaumont and Vaux until 21st April. It returned to the same sector on 18th May, and it took part in the abortive advance on fort Douaumont. Then it served in the Vaux-les-Palameix sector, on the Eparges shoulder of the Verdun salient from 20th June 1916 until 12th February 1917.

The division was allocated to First Army for Nivelle's Offensive. It attacked between Craonne and the Ployon on the 16th but was pulled out of the line on 19th April for a support role between Fere-en-Tardennois and Soissons until 6th June 1917. It took over the sector between Courtecon and Ferme Malval and came under German attack on Bastille Day. The division moved to the Hurtebise-Ferme de la Bovelle sector on 19th July where numerous intense actions took place. Rested and retrained from 31st August, the division moved to the Oise front and came under command of Third Army on 15th September. It occupied the line before St Quentin, between Sélency and Dallon where it remained until relieved by British troops on 14th January 1918.

After a long rest period in Picardy, the division moved into the Côte 193 sector, west of Navarin, in Champagne on 3rd March 1918. It moved eastwards to the Navarin-l'Épine de Vedegrange sector on 1st June. Two weeks later it was moved to Villers Cotterêts to join Tenth Army for the second battle of the Marne. Engaged between the Ourcq and Soissons, it attacked and took Oulchy-le-Chateau on 25th July and then advanced on Grand-Rozoy. After a brief rest there, the division participated the advance up to the Hindenburg Line. As part of XV Corp d'Armee it switched between Tenth Army and Third Army, and was engaged near Venizel on 31st August. It crossed the Aisne, and advanced through Buc-le-Long, Moncel, and Nanteuil-la-Fosse, to the Chemin des Dames at Vregny and Ferme Mennejean which it had reached by 18th September.

On 26th September, the division began the move to Flanders where it joined the 6th Army which had been newly reformed to command those French units placed under Belgian command for the liberation of Flanders. The division participated in the allied advance to Roeselare on 14th October, and fought at Thielt and along the line of the Lys. By the end of hostilities the division had reached the line of the river Schelde.

6 Division d'Infanterie

An active division in 1914 as part of III Corps d'Armée, with headquarters at Paris

Commanders
02.08.14-Georges Bloch
31.08.14-Philippe Pétain

20.10.14-Ernest Caré
05.11.15-Charles Jacquot
30.04.16-Ferdinand Pont
06.12.16-Maurice de Barescut
02.05.17-Camille Poignon

11 Brigade [disbanded 5.17]
24 RI, Bernay/Paris
28 RI, Evreux/Paris
12 Brigade   [disbanded 5.17]
5 RI, Falaise/Paris   5.17 to 5DI
119 RI, Liseux/Paris

Infantry from 5.17
24 RI
28 RI
119 RI

Artillery
Groups 1-3, 22 RAC, Veraille
Group 6, 103 RAL   [added 4.18-formerly Gp15/103RAL]

Cavalry
6/7 RCh, 8.14-7.17;   4/7 RCh, 1.17-7.17

Engineers & Pioneers
1914: Cie 3/2 du 3RG   1918: Cies 3/2, 3/52, 3/71 du 3RG
8.18-Pioneer Battalion 15RIT

As part of the Fifth Army, 6 DI concentrated at Amagne on 6th August 1914 in order to cover the line of the Meuse between Chateau de Belleville and Nouvien-sur-Meuse. From this position it advanced toward the Sambre on 13th August and was engaged with the enemy around Anderloes and Leesnes to the south of Charleroi on the 22nd and 23rd. During this action, 11 Brigade was detached to support Sordet's cavalry on the left flank of Fifth Army. Then it retreated to the south of Guise and fought back at Coujumelles between the 24th and 29th. The retreat to the Marne was resumed on the 30th, and the division moved via Barenton-Bugny and Verneuil to Montceaux-les-Provins, from which it was engaged in action to the north-east of Montmirail. During the first battle of the Marne, as part of Fifth Army's attempts to secure the lines of the two Morin rivers, 6DI fought at Champfleury and Chataigniers, and then pursued the Germans to the northwest of Reims via Jaulgonne and Muizon. During the first battle of the Aisne, the division fought in the Godat-Loivre sector and attacked Ste Marie [12-14th October], Côte 108 [1st November], Godat and Sapigneul [3-4th November] and Bois de Luxembourg [16th February 1915].

On 9th May 1915, after a brief rest, 6DI moved to Artois where it joined Tenth Army. It remained in reserve during the second battle for Artois. It entered the line at Neuville-Saint-Vaast on 3rd July and remained there, with brief periods of rest, until 8th October. The division took part in the abortive operations to seize Vimy Ridge on 25th September. Moved south to Sixth Army in Picardy, 6DI took over the sector between Frise and Foucaucourt on 21st October where its life was enlivened by mining operations. After a Christmas break at Domart-sur-la-Luce, the division re-entered the line along the river Avre, between Andechy and Maucourt, on 10th January 1916. There it sustained a German gas attack on 21st March. Three days later, it moved to Verdun.

On 8th April 1916, the division moved into the Vaux-Damloup sector above Verdun, there to contain German attacks on 11th and 13th April. Rested from 6th May, it took over the line between Thiaumont and Vaux on 26th May and was attacked there on 1st June. On 26th June, the division moved to the southern part of the salient in Lorraine where it occupied the line between Vaux-les-Palameix and Dompcevrin until 15th November, when it moved south to the adjacent sector between Dompcevrin and Keour-la-Grande. After a period of preparation and retraining, 6DI took part in the first French offensive at Verdun when it attacked and captured Bezonvaux in the Damluop sector.

The division left Verdun on 11th January 1917 and redeployed to Eighth Army's line in Lorraine where it played a support role between Forèt de Parroy and Forèt de Champenoux, near Lunéville, until it was moved to Château-Thierry, on the Marne. There it waited for the expected breakthrough by Nivelle on the Chemin des Dames. After that failure, the division took up positions on the Chemin des Dames, between l'Épine de Chevregny and the Parthenon on 29th May from which it moved to the Hurtebrise-Bovelle sector on 26th June where it remained for the rest of the summer.

Coming under command of Third Army on 15th August 1917, the division moved to Montdidier in Picardy, from where it took over the trenches facing St Quentin between Urvillers and Dallon on 2nd September. The division came out of the line on 15th January 1918 and then moved to 4th Army in Champagne. From 4th March it was located in the sector between Mamelles and Côte 193, and then between Tahure and Navarin from 1st June until 18th June.

On the latter date, the division moved westwards to Compiègne to rejoin Third Army. On 24th June it re-entered the line between Ferme Porte and St Maur and attacked from that position on 9th July.

During the third battle for Picardy, it fought at Lassigny and Canny-sur-Matz between 10th and 22nd August. After a rest at Château-Thierry, the division joined Fifth Army to the north of Reims on 17th September. The brief occupation of the line between St-Mard and a position west of Villers-en-Prayères was followed on 29th September by a period in the line between Glennes and Basilieux-lès-Fismes. Next day, the division took part in the battle for St-Thierry and moved forward to Sissonne where it remained for the rest of the conflict.

7 Division d'Infanterie

An active division in 1914 as part of IV Corps d'Armée, with headquarters at Paris

Commanders
02.08.14-Louis de Trentinian
25.09.14-Francois Desvaux
15.10.14-Francois Collas
15.05.15-Charles Weywada
22.10.17-Joseph Bulot

13 Brigade [disbanded 3.17]
101 RI, Dreux/Paris   6.15 to 124DI-replaced by 315RI ex IVCA; 315RI to 88DI 3.17
102 RI, Chârtres/Paris

14 Brigade [disbanded 3.17]
103 RI, Alençon/Paris
104 RI, Argentan/Paris

Infantry from 3.17
102 RI
103 RI
104 RI

Artillery
Groups 1-3, 26 RAC, Le Mans
Group 5, 104RAL   [added 3.18-formerly Gp4/104RAL]

Cavalry
5/14 RH, 8-10.14;   7/13 RH, 10.14-11.15; 1/14 RH, 1.17-7.17; 4/14 RH, 1.17-7.17

Engineers & Pioneers
1914: Cie 4/1 du 1RG   1918: Cies 4/1, 4/51, 4/21 du 1RG Pioneer Battalion 34 RIT 8.18-

As part of IV Corps d'Armee, in the Third Army, this division concentrated north of Verdun to cover the river Othain near Mangiennes. From there it moved north towards Latour on 21st August and took part in the battle for the Ardennes at Ethe and Ruette, and, then moved to the Meuse at Brieulles. After a fight at Marville on the 25th, the division retreated to Monfaucon in the Argonne; fought at Beauclair and Tailly [30-31st August]. After a further retreat to Ste- Menehould the division was moved westwards towards Paris.

On 7th September the division joined Sixth Army along the Ourcq and fought at Bouillancy and Silly-le- Long during the first battle of the Marne. From 10th September, the division advanced via Retheuil and Attichy to Tracy-le-Val and Carlepont during the first battle of the Aisne. After action at Puisaleine and

Bois-St-Mard, the division moved northwards to join Second Army in Picardy. Between 21st September and 27th December it was in line between Tilloloy and L'Echelle St Aurin, and fought at Andechy on 4th November.

At the beginning of 1915 the division moved to Champagne and attacked Perthes on 23rd February, after which it was in line between the Ferme de Wacques and Aubérive-sur-Suippe. It remained in this area and took part in Fourth Army's attacks on Aubérive during the second battle for Champagne on 25th September. After a rest, which began on 30th October, the division joined the eastern half of the line in Champagne, under 2nd Army, at Ville-sur-Tourbe on 7th November. It moved to the sector between the Main-de- Massiges and the river Aisne on 26th April 1916, and then that between the former location and Maisons de Champagne on 28th June.

The division moved to Verdun on 29th August and was committed to the sector between Haudromont and Thiaumont from which it attacked German positions on 3rd, 5th, 6th and 20th September. It played a support role in the first Verdun offensive during October and then settled down in the Haudromont- Douaumont sector on 28th October where it remained until 14th December 1916. It then moved south- eastwards into Lorraine to take over part of the line between the Chapelotte and Vezouve rivers.

The division returned to Verdun on 23rd June 1917 to occupy the sector along the Meuse between Louvemont, Vacherauville and Marre. During the second Verdun offensive, 7DI attacked the Côte-de-Talou and then settled down in the Damloup-Haudiomont sector, from which elements were sent to Eparges. Following a rest in the Marne Region, the division joined Fourth Army in Champagne and held the sector between Mont Cornillet and the Ferme de Marquises until 1st May 1918.

By 21st May 1918, the division had moved to Flanders where it engaged German forces around Scherpenburg and Mont Kemmel in support of the British army during the battle of the Lys. The division was recalled to the Champagne region and took part in the actions in and around the Montagne de Reims from 9th July. It fought at Leuvrigny, Festigny, Venteuil and Tincourt and took Revigny on 29th July. By 18th August, the division was back at Mont Cornillet from where its artillery was detached to support Fourth Army's attack on the Butte de Souain between 5th and 7th Octber. The division attacked St Clement-a-Arnes on 8th October and reached the Retourne, and took Givry and Ambly-Fleury in quick sucession. After a brief rest, it took part in the movement from Suippes to the Meuse on 6th November. On 11th November 1918, 7DI was at Sauville and Vendresse

8 Division d'Infanterie

An active division in 1914 as part of IV Corps d'Armee, with headquarters at Le Mans

Commanders
02.08.14-Rauol de Lartique
06.10.14-Sixte Rozée d'Infreville
02.10.17-Francois Adelbert
24.08.18-Georges Tetart

15 Brigade [disbanded 11.16]
124 RI, Laval   6.15 to 124DI-replaced by 317RI ex IV CA
130 RI, Mayenne 11.16 to 124DI

16 Brigade [disbanded 11.16]
115 RI, Mamers
117 RI, Le Mans

Infantry from 11.16
115RI
117RI
317RI   disbanded 7.18-replaced by 311RI ex 65DI
311RI   disbanded 10.18-replaced by 21RMT

Artillery
Groups 1-3, 31RAC, Le Mans
Group 6, 104 RAL   [formed and added 6.18]

Cavalry
6/14 RH, 8.14-10.14;   8/2 RCh, 10.14-11.15;   3/14 RH, 1.17-7.17

Engineers & Pioneers
1914: Cie 4/2 du 1RG   1918: Cies 4/2, 4/52, 4/71 du 1RG Pioneer Battalion 34RIT 8.18-

After mobilisation, the division concentrated near Verdun and began work on defensive positions at Ornes and Damvillers. On 21st August 1914 it took part in Third Army's actions at Virton during the battle for the Ardennes. Three days later, it retreated back to the Meuse at Cléry-Petit and Flassigny where it held the river-line before Third Army began its retreat southwards. Barely had this movement begun when IV Corps d'Armee [7DI and 8DI] was transported to the Paris region.

From 6th September the division fought along the line of the Ourcq in the first battle of the Marne, with Sixth Army. It was in action at Fublaines, advanced to Tracy-le-Mont and fought a 'fierce' action at Ferme Quennevières and Ferme Pusieux on 13th September.

On 22nd September, the division came under command of Second Army in Picardy. It fought at Rethonvillers, Etalon and Carrepuis, following which actions it occupied the line on the river Avre near Bouchier. During October, further fighting took place at Goyencourt, Villers-les-Roye [2nd October], Andechy [6th October], Quesnoy-en-Santerre [6th October] and Andechy [4th November]. From 27th December 1914 and 16th February 1915 the division was held in reserve.

Elements of the division joined 34DI in Fourth Army's attack on Perthes on 19th-20th February: these attacks were repeated on 12th-13th March. On 22nd March 1915 the division began a six-month spell in the line between Marquieses and Moscou. Then it moved to St Hilaire-le-Grand to take part in 4th Army's attacks on the Épine de Vedegrange during the second battle of Champagne. The division transferred to Second Army on 22nd October but remained in Champagne and occupied the sector between Maisons-de- Massiges and Maisons de Champagne from 21st December. It resisted German attacks on Mont Têton on 9th January 1916, and on 2nd and 22nd June 1916.

On 5th July 1916, 8DI arrived at Verdun and became committed to the sector between Haudromont and Côte de Froideterre where it attacked the Ouvrage de Thiaumont on 15th and 16th July. At the beginning of August the division returned to the Fourth Army and occupied a sector between the Butte de Mesnil and the Maisons de Champagne. This lasted until 20th October when the division was rested in the Ourcq region.

On 28th December, 8DI, now part of Tenth Army in Picardy, went into the line south of Ablaincourt- Pressoir and occupied posiitons up to the remains of the Ameins-Chaulnes railway. Its stay in this region was brief and on 7th February 1917 it was sent eastwards to Lorraine for a rest, after which, it took over the line between the river Meuse and the Etang de Vargevaux for a three week tour,

On 1st May 1917 the division rejoined Fourth Army's front before Mont Teton and carried out a series of local attacks in support of the battle of Moronvillers. This was the start of a long period of duty with Fourth Army, which included occupation of the sector Mont Haut-Mont Cornillet, the battle of the Monts [14th-15th July] and then two long periods in the front-line before Mont Cornillet [28th August-29th November 1917 and 17th January –31st May 1918].

Fifth Army took the division under command on 15th June 1918 and placed it in the Damery –Treloup sector for the second battle of the Marne. On 3rd July it seized the area around Cuisles and Vandieres-sous- Châtillon where it withstood German counter-attacks.

By 9th August, the division had rejoined Fourth Army and was back on its old stamping grounds where it was prepared and trained for the autumn offensive in Champagne and the Argonne.

On 5th October, the division began to move forward via the Monts to Suippe and Faverger. It crossed the Retourne on 13th October and reached the Canal des Ardennes at Nanteuil-sur-Aisne and Acy-Romance on the same day. From its positions on the line Rethel-Nanteuil it seized Nanteuil on the 15th and Acy on the 16th. From 5th November, it took part in Fifth Army's advance to the Meuse and reached Charleville on the 9th November 1918.

9 Division d'Infanterie

An active division in 1914, with V Corps d'Armée, with headquarters at Orléans

Commanders
02.08.14-Pierre Peslin
13.08.14-Emile Martin
22.01.15-Henri Bonfait
30.05.15-Louis Arlabosse
08.11.16-Henri Gadel
07.05.17-Maurice Gamelin

17 Brigade [disbanded 12.16]
4 RI, Auxerre/Troyes
82 RI, Montargis
18 Brigade [disbanded 12.16]
113RI, Blois   12.16 to 125DI
131RI, Orleans   7.15 to 125DI-replaced by 313RI ex V CA 66BCP
7.15 additional –from 56DI

Infantry from 12.16
41RI
82RI
313 RI   11.17   disbanded & replaced by 329RI ex 158DI
66BCP   12.17   transferred to 74DI

Artillery
Groups 1-3, 30 RAC, Orléans
Group 5, 105 RAL   [added 3.18 –formerly Gp9/105RAL]

Cavalry
5/8 RCh, 8.14-7.17;   2/8 RCh, 1.17-7.17

Engineers & Pioneers
1914: Cie 5/1 du 1RG   1918: Cies 5/4, 5/52, 5/21 du 1RG Pioneer Battalion 122 RIT 8.18-

As part of V Corps d'Armee, 9DI assembled at St Mihiel and then moved northwards up the Meuse to Vaudoncourt and Muzery. As Fifth Army advanced into the Ardennes, it attacked towards Longuyon and Tellancourt on 21st August. Over the next two days it saw action at Ville-Houdlemont, Doulcon and Brielles while trying to hold the line of the river. It was forced back through the Argonne and reached Vauquois on
2nd September. As part of Third Army's battle for Revigny, during the first battle of the Marne, it fought at Merchines, Sommaisne and Pretz-en-Argonne and succeeded in pushing the Germans back through Triaucourt and Clermont, and then engaged in heavy fighting around Varennes. When the front stabilised in the Argonne it established a line between Four-de-Paris and the river Aire where it remained for two months. On 6th November the division moved eastwards to

the sector between the Aire and Quatre Enfants where it attacked at Vauquois [8-9th December] and at Boureilles [20-24th Decmeber].

From 15th January 1915 the division was to found in the hotly-contested area around Vauquois where it was to remain until the autumn of 1916. Vauquois was the northern shoulder of the Verdun salient and was the scene of extensive mining operations by both sides. The division attacked Côte 263 on 17th February, 4th March, 4th-6th April and 13th-21st July 1915. It stopped a German attack on 21st September ands attacked Côte 385 a few days later. Most of 1916 was spent in relatively quiet as both sides held on to their positions in this small but vital area.

The division moved a few kilometres to Verdun on 11th September 1916 and was engaged in the first Verdun offensive when, with 133DI, it took part in the recovery of Fort Douaumont on 24th October, and on Vaux-devant-Damloup a week later. After a few days rest over Christmas, the division left the Argonne/Verdun area for the first time, when it joined Fifth Army at Berry-au-Bac. It trained for Nivelle's offensive in February and March 1917 and re-entered the front-line between the Miette and the Bois de Buttes on 8th April. On the first day of the offensive, 16th April, the division paticipated in V Corps' successfull attack towards Juvincourt-et-Damary.

The division remained at the eastern end of the Chemin des Dames for the rest of 1917. It undertook five tours of duty in the trenches between the Miette and the Ployon until relieved on 18th December.

After two months of labour duty with Sixth Army, the division moved to join Third Army near Noyon, on 22nd March, where it attacked north of Guiscard on the flank of the British Expeditionary Force. During this second battle for Picardy, it fought at Noyon, Mont Renaud and Thiescourt, and reached Villers-Cotterèts by the end of the month. On 13th April the division arrived at Belfort to take up positions between Leimbach and the Rhine-Rhone canal, just north of the Swiss frontier.

Two months later the division arrived in Champagne to particpate in Ninth Army's actions during the second battle of the Marne. It fought at Tincourt and Belval-sous-Chatillon during 5th Army's actions in the Montagne de Reims between 18th and 26th July. On 28th August it took up positions in the valley of the river Vesle near Breuil-sur-Vesle from which it took that town and Courlandon on 4th September, and, had closed up to the Hindenburg Line at L'Arbre de Romain by the 14th. From 29th September until 4th October

9DI was enaged in heavy fighting along the Vesle. Success at Montigny and Bouvancourt brought the division up to the line from Berry-au-Bac to Juvincourt-et-Damary, from which it advanced to Sissonne, and reached the Serre on 19th October. After ten days of rest, the division advanced to Recouverance and St Fergeux, which were reached on 3rd November. Then it took part in Fifth Army's pursuit of the Germans to the Meuse via Remaucourt, Draize, and Tournes-Houldizy. On 11th November 1918, the division reached Château-Regnault, on the river Meuse.

10 Division d'Infanterie

An active division in 1914 as part of V Corps d'Armée, with headquarters in Paris.

Commanders
02.08.14-Michel Auger
26.08.14-Charles Roques
17.09.14-Henri Gouraud
23.01.15-Henri Valdant
29.03.18-Camille Pichat

19 Brigade [disbanded 8.17]
46 RI, Fontainebleu
89 RI, Sens/Paris
20 Brigade [disbanded 8.17]
31 RI, Melun/Paris
76 RI, Coulommiers/Paris   6.15 to 125 DI –replaced by 313RI ex V CA , disbanded 8.17

Infantry from 8.17
31RI
46RI
89RI
31, 34, 51 Bns Senegalais [attached 4-11.18]

Artillery
Groups 1-3, 13 RAC, Paris
Group 8, 105RAL [added 6.18-formerly Gp2/335RAL]

Cavalry
6/8 RCh, 8.14-7.17;   4/8 RCh 1.17-7.17

Engineers & Pioneers
1914: Cie 5/2 du 1RG   1918: Cies 5/1, 5/51, 5/71 du 1RG Pioneer Battalion 29 RIT 8.18-

As part of V Corps d'Armee, 10DI concentrated at St Mihiel on 9th August 1914. It moved up to Genicourt- sur-Meuse and then on to the line of the Othain from which 5th Army commenced operations in the Ardennes on the 21st. The division advanced through Longuyon and engaged the Germans as Cosnes on the 22nd. Next day the retreat began back through Longuyon to Damvillers and then to Cuisy: it was punctuated with fighting at Ferme Haute Wal and Noers [23rd-24th], at Charpentry [27th], at Sommauthe [30th-31st] and then at Vaux-en-Dielot. By 2nd September the division had been pushed back to the line Clermont-en- Argonne, Louppy and Brabant-le-Roi. When Joffre counter-attacked on 6th September, the division took part in the battle of Revigny during which it fought in the Argonne at Nettancourt, Brabant-le-Roi, Villers- aux-Vents, and Vassincourt. By 16th September it had advanced towards Monfaucon and occupied a sector to the east of Vauquois.

Between October 1914 and August 1916, 10DI remained in the Argonne with V Corps d'Armee whose task was to secure the northern shoulder of the Verdun salient from persistent German attacks. It took part in extensive mining operations whilst in the sector between the Aire and Four-de-Paris from which it attacked German positions on 5th January 1915. After the German attack on 8th January, and a brief rest, the division moved to Vauquois where it took part in attacks on 17th February, 28th February, 1st and 3rd March, and 5th-6th April 1915. The division's line was extended southwards towards Avocourt during July 1915, and it remained there until May 1916 when it was to be found in the Quatres Enfants sector.

The division finally left the Argonne on 1st August 1916 and proceeded to Amiens for training, after which it was committed to the battle of the Somme. Under command of Sixth Army, it entered the line between Bouchavesnes and Rancourt on 14th September. It was heavily engaged on the 20th and 26th September and., after a brief respite, fought at the Bois de St-Pierre-Vaast from 14th to 29th October. Withdrawn from the line at the end of October for a period of retraining at the Camp-de-Mailly, it was allocated to 5th Army for Nivelle's planned offensive on the Chemin des Dames.

After two periods in the line between Troyon and Pontoy, and between the Miette and the Ployon, its role in the Nivelle offensive was to attack and take Ville-aux-Bois: which it did on 16th April 1917. For the rest of 1917, the division remained on the Chemin des Dames. It was in line between the Miette and Ployon [15th June-12th July]; Chevreux-Ployon [25th July-15th August]; Chevreux-Ployon [3rd- 24th September]; Chevreux-Ployon again [13th October-12th November] and Miette-Ployon [28th November-6th January 1918].

Early in 1918 the division moved to Picardy and was a component of Third Army when the German offensive began in March. From 22nd to 23rd March, it fought at Lassigny, north of Guiscard, and at Fretoy- le-Chateau, Catigny, Sermaize and Cuy during the second battle of Noyon. Its endeavours resulted in a rest in the Vosges from 6th April. As part its task in the Rhine-Rhone canal sector from 12th May 1918, it instructed newly-arrived American units.

Allocated to the Ninth Army south of the Marne on 12th July, it re-entered the front-line with the Fourth Army five days later. From initial commitments at Prunay and Mont Cornillet, it moved westwards to Fifth Army's positions on the Vesle, between Jouchery and Vandeuil on 30th July, where it remained for two months. On 30th September the division took part in the battle of St Thierry from which it advanced to the Serre between the 4th and 20th October. This advance freed several river-lines: the Vesle, the Suippe, and the Aisne. Then the division pursued the Germans to Nizy-la-Comte where it fought on 5th and 6th November, after which, the advance was resumed. During the last week of hostilities, 10DI advanced to Chaumont-Porcien, and then to Aubigny-les-Pothees and the Echelle.

11 Division d'Infanterie

An active division in 1914, as part of XX Corps d'Armée, with headquarters at Nancy

Commanders
02.08.14-Maurice Balfourier
29.08.14-Joseph Chatelain
27.09.14-Edmond Ferry
11.04.16-Eugene Vuillemot

21 Brigade [disbanded 12.16]
26 RI, Toul
69 RI, Toul
2 BCP, Lunéville 4.15 to 153DI

22 Brigade [disbanded 12.16]
37 RI, Troyes/Nancy	12.16 to 168DI-replaced by 2BCP ex 153DI
79 RI, Neufchateau	12.16 to 168DI-replaced by 4BCP ex 153DI
4 BCP, St Nicholas Port 4.15 to 153DI	

Infantry from 12.16
26 RI
69 RI
2 BCP
4 BCP

Artillery
Groups 1-3, 8 RAC, Nancy	
Group 11, 120RAL	[added 11.17-retitled Group 5, 3.18]

Cavalry
5/5 RH, 8.14-7.17;   1/5 RH, 1.17-7.17

Engineers & Pioneers
1914: Cie 20/1du 10RG   1918: Cies 20/1, 20/51, 20/21du 10RG Pioneer Battalion 142RIT 8.18-

Originally part of VI Corps d'Armee, 11DI had been transferred to the newly-created XX CA in 1913 to provide the covering force which would protect the French frontier during the period of mobilisation. On 2nd August 1914, the division assembled at the Grand Couronne de Nancy from which it moved to the Seille near Armaucourt to take part in Plan XVII: the invasion of Lorraine.

As part of Second Army, the division commenced its march towards Morhange on 14th August, fought in the battle of Morhange on the 20th, and then began to retreat back to Nancy. It fought actions at Einville, Leomont and Vitrimont at the battle for the Grand Couronne. It had begun to move from this position via Minorville towards Toul on 13th September when it was withdrawn from the line and dispatched to Picardy.

Second Army arrived in Picardy to hold the territory exposed by the gradual race to the sea in the autumn of 1914. The division took up positions south of the Somme and then moved to the Péronne-Albert road and fought a series of actions at Carnoy, Mametz, and Fricourt. From 6th October, it was fighting actions around Albert at Authuille, Bécourt and La Boiselle and, on 20th October, it was along the line of the Ancre between Gommecourt and Berles-aux-Bois, from which it attacked German positions at Monchy-aux-Bois [28-30th October].

As the race to the sea continued the division moved to Flanders on 2nd November, and arrived at Ypres on the 9th. It fought around St Eloi, Pilkem and Bikschote, and then moved north of the town to Langemark on the 16th where it remained until 30th January 1915. It was engaged at Kortecker Cabaret and the Bois Triangular during December. On 15th February, after two weeks out of the line, the division took over the trenches between Poelkapelle and the Ieper-Roeselare railway where it remained until pulled out of Flanders on 16th April.

11DI moved to Tenth Army in Artois to take part in the second battle for Artois. In line between Neuville-Saint-Vaast and Ecurie, it fought in the Labyrinthe and took part in the attack on Vimy Ridge on 16th July. The division returned to Nancy for rest and retraining after which it joined Second Army in Champagne for the planned autumn offensive. During that battle, which began on 25th September, 11DI fought between Beauséjours and Côte 196, and then moved to the Mesnil sector. The division remained in the line until 22nd December when it returned to Lorraine for more rest and retraining. On 10th February 1916, it took over the sector between Armaucourt, Bezange-la-Grande and Brin-sur-Seille.

The division was called into the Verdun salient on 20th March and committed to the Avocourt-Bethincourt sector on 27th April where it fought at Haucourt and Malancourt, and resisted the German attacks of 5th-7th April. After this, with little respite, the division was moved to the Somme where it joined Sixth Army in the Bois de Maricourt on 30th May. On 1st July 1916, it attacked Curlu and then Hem; and then at Maurepas [30th July and 7th August]. Out of the line from 10th August, it took over the Sailly-Saillisel sector on 24th November until replaced by British troops on 10th December. The division returned to Lorraine and occupied a sector north-east of Nomeny for a brief period-until 18th January 1917.

Allocated to Sixth Army for Nivelle's offensive on the Chemin des Dames [18th April], it fought on the left flank of that attack at Braye-en-Laonnais, Malval and Froidmont in order to take positions on the Oise-Aisne canal: the division managed to reach the Chemin des Dames by 5th May. After this came a further spell in Lorraine, where the division occupied the Limey-Vargevaux sector from 21st June until 4th October.

On 25th January 1918, the division returned to Verdun where it held the line between Beaumont and Bois de Chaume until 19th March. In response to the German offensive, the division was moved to Picardy and held in reserve behind the BEF near Doullens. It moved to the Oise front on 2nd June, and fought in the battle of the Matz on 9th June, and resisted German attacks on the Bois de Ressons, Méry, and Courcelles-Epayelles until the 12th. From 20th June, it held the sector between Ambleny and Fosse-en-Haut, attacking the latter on 28th June. As part of Tenth Army, the division advanced towards Soissons on 18th July, and attacked between Soissons and Pommiers on 6th August. From 17th August, it was in line between the Port and Hautebraye, and fought during the second battle for Noyon at Bieuxy and Bagneux. From 1st September, it took part in Tenth Army's movement up to the Hindeburg Line, during which it crossed the Ailette, attacked the Foret-de-Coucy and took Barisis.

Rested from 12th September, 11DI moved to Flanders on 8th October and took part in the final allied breakout from the Ypres Salient. It advanced and took Nazareth and the reached the lateral canal, and crossed the Schelde. On 10th November 1918 the division was resting at Tielt.

12 Division d'Infanterie

An active division in 1914 as part of VI Corps d'Armée, with headquarters at Reims

Commanders
02.08.14-Louis Soucher
17.09.14-Frederic Herr
15.11.14-Jean Paulinier
27.07.15-Antoine Gramat
23.05.16-Pierre Girodon
23.09.16-Georges Brissaud-Desmaillets
19.04.17-Hippolyte Penet
10.06.18-Rémy Chabord

23 Brigade [disbanded 1.17]
54 RI, Compiègne
67 RI, Soissons

24 Brigade [disbanded 1.17]

106 RI, Châlons sur Marne	1.17 to 56DI-replaced by 350RI ex 56DI
132 RI, Reims	1.17 to 56DI-not replaced
* 173 RI attached	1.15 [from 30DI] to 126DI 6.15
• 26BCP attached	1.15 [ex 40DI] to 127DI 6.15

Infantry from 1.17
54 RI
67 RI
350 RI
• 7 Indo-Chinois Bn attached 4.17-7.18

Artillery

Groups 1-3, 25 RAC, Chalons s/Marne	
Group 5, 106RAL	[added 3.18-formerly Group 8, 106RAL]

Cavalry
1/12 RCh, 1.17-7.17

Engineers & Pioneers
1914: Cie 6/1 du 9RG   1918: Cies 6/1, 6/51, 6/21 du 9RG Pioneer Battalion 142 RIT 8.18-

The division joined Third Army to the east of Verdun and, from 21st August 1914, it moved northwards from Etain through Spincourt and Beuvielle to Chiers to engage the Germans in the battle for the Ardennes. It fought at Ugny and Doncourt-le-Longuyon [22nd August], Crusnes [23rd] and Arrancy [24th] before moving the west bank of Meuse near Damville on the 25th. For several days, the division defended the crossings of the Meuse at Gercourt and Brieuilles-sur-Meuse before retreating with the rest of Third Army. It moved southwards through the Argonne, via Monfaucon and Jubecourt to Rembermont-aux-Pots where it dug in from 6th-10th September. As part of the Third Army's battle of Revigny-during 2nd battle of the Marne- 12DI fought at Sommaisne and Rembercourt, from which it advanced on 14th September towards Ville-devant-Chaumont and the Bois d'Haumont, where the front stabilised.

On 20th September, the division was moved to Éparges on the southern shoulder of the Verdun salient: it occupied the line between Loclont and Trésauvaux from which in engaged in a series of intense actions [26th December, 17th and 21st February 1915, 18th, 19th and 23rd March 1915]. From this vital point the division was involved in First Army's operations during the first battle for Woevre: it participated in a series of attacks and counter-attacks between Éparges and Calonne to secure the Verdun salient [24th and 28th April, 5th May, 3rd, 5th, 20th and 26th June].

The division rested from 2nd August and moved to Champagne on 2nd September. As part of the VI Corps d'Armee, it took part in Fourth Army's autumn offensive by fighting near Souain and then at Somme-Py. From 30th December, it occupied the line between Aubérive and Vedegrange where it attacked the Germans on 15th March 1916 and sustained a gas attack on 19th May. After a brief rest, the division was committed to Verdun on 15th June. Sent into the Bois Fumin-Damloup sector, it repulsed the Germans on 21st June and counter-attacked on 23rd June.

After this, the division retrained near Epernay and moved to the Somme. It joined Sixth Army on 5th September and attacked the German positions at Bois l'Abbaye on 15th September, and on 7th and 13th October. It remained in this sector until 18th December when it moved south to the Ourcq region for retraining.

On 5th February 1917, 12DI joined Sixth Army on the Chemin des Dames, where it took over the line on the north bank of the Aisne between Chavonne and Chivy. During Nivelle's offensive, the division was kept in support west of Craonne. On 19th April, it re-entered the line between the Canal d'Oise and the Epine de Chevregny from which it attacked the Ferme Froidmont on 5th May. The division moved to the Vosges on 13th June to take up positions between Epinal and Corcieux, and from 12th December 1917 until 25th March 1918, the division was engaged on labour duties and training between Belfort and the Swiss frontier.

In response to the German offensive, 12DI was moved to Montdidier in Picardy where it fought along the line of the Avre and resisted German attacks until the front stabilised between Montdidier and Grivesnes. This brief incursion into Picardy was followed by a return to Lorraine and the sector between Domevre and Leintrey [19th April-18th July].

The division joined Fifth Army on 29th July to participate in the final stages of the second battle of the Marne. It fought at Hartennes and Villemontoise and then occupied positions between Cirey and Vasseny. From Venizel it joined in the movement up to the Hindenburg Line, fighting near Vailly on 7th September. Pulled out of the line a week later, the division was moved to Flanders on 6th October. From 23rd October, the division took part in the allied advance to the rivers Lys and Escaut, and ended the war west of Eine.

13 Division d'Infanterie

An active division in 1914 as part of XXI Corps d'Armée with headquarters at Chaumont

Commanders
02.08.14-Frederic Bourderiat
27.08.14-Louis Baquet
13.10.14-Henri de Cadoudal
05.06.15-Albert Martin de Bouillon
22.09.18-Georges Tabouis

25 Brigade [disbanded 12.16]
17 RI, Épinal   12.16 to 170DI-not replaced
17 BCP, Rambervillers   10.15 to 77DI
20 BCP, Baccarat
21 BCP, Raon/Montbeliard

26 Brigade [disbanded 12.16]
21 RI, Langres
109 RI, Chaumont

Infantry from 12.16
21 RI
109 RI
20 BCP
21 BCP

Artillery
Groups 1-3, 62 RAC, Epinal/Bruyeres
Group 9, 121RAL   [added 11.17-retitled Group 5, 3.18]
Cavalry
5/ 4 R Ch, 8.14-7.17;   1/4 RCh, 1.17-7.17

Engineers & Pioneers
1914: Cie 21/1du 11RG   1918: Cies 21/1, 21/51, 21/21 du 11RG Pioneer Battalion 143RIT 8.18-

Detached from VII Corps d'Armee in 1913 to become part of the newly-formed XXI CA whose role was to guard the frontier with Alsace during the mobilisation and assembly of First Army. In this role, 13DI began to mobilise on 28th July and assemble at Baccarat. By 10th August it was covering the passes over the Vosges between Senones and Montigny.

On 14th August the division advanced and occupied Schirmeck from which it moved back to the Meurthe, to fight at Celles-sur-Plain and Badonvillers [22-24th August] and at Raon-l'Etape [25th]. During the battle for Mortange, the division fought for control of the Col de la Chipotte and then retreated to Epinal. During the buildup for the first battle of the Marne, the division passed rapidly westwards through Third, Fourth and Ninth Armies to fight south-east of Reims at the Camp de Mailly and Sompuis. It advanced to Souain and was engaged there for the rest of September.

The division moved to Artois and joined Tenth Army south of Lille where it took part in actions to secure the line between Loos and the canal at La Bassée. For the next year, its task was to defend the approaches to Notre Dame de Lorette, which together with Vimy Ridge, commanded the plains of northen France. In January 1915 it was in line between Noulette and Vermelles. It fought below Notre Dame de Lorette at Ablain-St-Nazaire during March; took part in the second battle for Artois during May; and in the third battle in September, by which time it had edged eastwards to Givenchy and Souchez. The division left Artois on 25th February 1916.

Two days later, the division arrived in Verdun and carried out at series of attacks in vain attempts to regain the village of Douaumont, and the Etang de Vaux during March 1916. On 20th March it moved back to Champagne and moved into the line south of Tahure, around the Butte de Souain.

Pulled out on 21st July, the division joined 10th Army in the Somme on 15th August. Initially it operated in the sector between Estrees-Deniecourt and Soyécourt where it took part in a French attack on 21st August. Then it moved southwards to the Deniecourt/Ablaincourt sector where it remained until 17th December. During this period it attacked on 17th September and took Deniecourt and then Ablaincourt by 14th October.

After a move to Lorraine, the division arrived in Belfort on 20th January 1917 to train, and to provide labourers for the defensive works around the city. After the failure of Nivelle's spring offensive in the Chemin des Dames, the division joined 6th Army there on 29th May. It manned the sector between Laffaux and Mennejean until 21st August; then between at Nanteuil-la-Fosse from 4th September; and between Mennejean and Nanteuil when it took part in the attack on Malmaison on 23rd October. As a result of success here, the division was able to take up new positions along the Oise-Aisne canal and in the Foret de Pinon. The division was pulled out of the line on 31st October for a long period of rest and retraining.

On 9th January 1918 13DI went back into the line; this time in the Vosges between Metzeral and the Ballon de Guebwiller where it remained for the next four months. Late in May it moved to the Marne region and became engaged in the third battle of the Aisne on 27th May. It resisted the German offensive around Fismes until 5th June when it moved to Champagne. It took up positions near Navarin between Côte 193 and Vedegrange. During the fourth battle for Champagne it fought at Trou-Bricot and Wacques until 15th August. During the autumn offensive in Champagne and Argonne, the division remained in support until called forward to attack between Manre and Aure on 29th September.

On 12th October the division joined Fifth Army north of Reims, and from 1st November, advanced in the Conde-les-Herpy sector to St Ferguex, from which it moved towards the Meuse via Signy l'Abbaye and Belval.

14 Division d'Infanterie

An active division in 1914 as part of VII Corps d'Armée, with headquarters at Belfort

Commanders
02.08.14-Louis Curé
14.08.14-Etienne de Villeret
17.11.14-Alexander Faës
16.01.15-Etienne Crepey
31.08.16-Edme Philipot
11.06.18-Paul Baston

27 Brigade [disbanded 5.17]
44 RI, Lons-le-Saunier
60 RI, Besançon
28 Brigade   [disbanded 5.17]
35 RI, Belfort
42 RI, Belfort   5.17 to 41DI-not replaced

Infantry from 5.17
35 RI
44 RI

60 RI

Artillery
Groups 1-3, 47 RAC, Hericourt
Group 11, 107 RAL   [added 11.17-retitled Group 5, 3.18]

Cavalry
5/11 RCh, 8.14-7.17   4/11 RCh, 1.17-7.17

Engineers & Pioneers
1914: Cie 7/1 du 7BG   1918: Cies 7/1, 7/51, 7/21 du 7BG Pioneer Battalion 8 RIT 8.18-

As part of the VII Corps d'Armee, the task of 14DI was to defend the Belfort gap between the Vosges and the Swiss frontier. The division assumed a covering role in front of Belfort on 2nd August 1914. It took part in short-lived advance into Alsace, which resulted in the capture of Mulhouse on 8th August. It retreated and advanced again towards Mulhouse which it retook on 19th August. But, five days later the division had returned to its original starting point and was entrained for Picardy.

The division joined the newly-formed Sixth Army on 28th August and became involved in the fighting along the Ourcq river next day. It was engaged at Bouiffancy and Acy-en-Multien during the first battle of the Marne. Then it advanced towards the Aisne via Vaumoise and Vic-sur-Aisne to Autreches where it fought until the front was stabilised during the first battle of the Aisne. After fighting at Autreches, Hautebraye, Chevillecourt and Viagre, the division was engaged on the plateau of Nouvron and in attacks to the north of Vingré and Ferme St Leocade until 14th December. After a brief respite, the division re-entered the battle north of Soissons. It remained in Sixth Army on the Aisne for some months: it engaged in mine warfare between Vingre and Pernant and took part in the attacks on Quennevieres on 6th and 16th June 1915. The division left the front line on 4th August.

As part of Fourth Army, in Champagne, the division took over a sector north-east of Wacques on 28th August 1915, and played a part in the second battle for Champagne during September. Again, after a period of rest, the division moved to the Epine de Vedegrange sector on 20th October and remained there for nearly two months.

Out of the line from 25th November, 14DI moved to Étain, east of Verdun on 12th February 1916. Committed to the battle for Verdun on 21st February, the division fought at Bezonvaux and at Vaux-devant- Damloup until 3rd March. It rejoined the battle on 11th April between Vaux and Damloup until 16th May when it embarked on a journey to the more 'peaceful' Vosges. A few weeks were spent east of Gerardmer, between the Lauch valley and the Col de la Schlucht before the call came to move to Picardy.

On 10th August 1916 the division entered the line between the Bois de Riez and the Bois de Hem on the front held by 6th Army. It took part in French attacks on 12th, 13th, 16th, 18th and 22nd August; and then moved to the Bouchevesnes sector where it took part in French attacks on the Bois l'Abbaye, Bois St-Pierre- Vaast and Bois Germain positions, south of Péronne. Its part in the battle of the Somme over, the division was moved to 4th Army in Champagne on 18th September.

In line between Main de Massiges, Vienne-le-Château and the Aisne from 1st October, the unit was taken out of the line on New Years Day 1917 to prepare for the spring offensive.

On 19th February, the division took up positions, to the west of Reims, between the Ferme de Luxembourg and Godat, from which it attacked Bermicourt on 16th April. After the failure of Nivelle's offensive, 14DI remain in the area and took over the line between Courcy and the Loivre on 20th May. There it stayed until called to Verdun on 22nd August. It took part in the second Verdun offensive in August 1917 when it attacked Côte 344, after which, it occupied the sector Bethincourt-Forges until 3rd January 1918.

The division was moved to Eighth Army and took over a line between Domevre and Embermesnil on 31st January where it remained until moved to Picardy in response to the German attacks on the BEF. Kept in reserve near Amiens from 12th April, it moved north into Flanders on 1st May and took over British positions near Dikkebus: it was engaged in battle on 27th May. After this action, it was held in reserve near St Omer and then near Beauvais until 14th July.

Initially allocated to the Ninth Army for the second battle of the Marne, it fought in the battle for the Montagne de Reims with Fifth Army from 16th July to 4th August. It fought at the Bois de Courton and together with the British in the valleys of the Ardre, and the Vesle. On 20th September the division joined the Fourth Army in Champagne and was engaged between Perthes and Mesnil. This was followed by an advance to Orfeuil. Retrained from 10th October, the division rejoined Fifth Army's advance on 30th October. It played a supporting role in the advance to the Meuse and was regrouping at Tourteron and Balons when the conflict ended.

15 Division d'Infanterie

An active division in 1914 as part of VIII Corps d'Armée, with headquarters at Dijon

Commanders
02.08.14-Léon Bajolle
14.10.14-Louis d'Armau de Pouydraguin
24.03.15-Ferdinand Blazer
15.06.15-Francois Collas
09.03.17-Louis Arbanère

29 Brigade [disbanded 1.17]
56 RI, Châlons sur Soane
134 RI, Mâcon

30 Brigade [disbanded 1.17]
10RI, Auxonne
27 RI, Dijon   1.17 to 16DI –not replaced

Infantry from 1.17
10 RI
56 RI
134 RI

Artillery
Groups 1-3, 48 RAC, Dijon
Group 5, 108RAL   [added 3.18-formerly Group 14/108RAL]

Cavalry
5/16 RCh, 8.14-11.15;   1/16 RCh, 1.17-7.17   2/16 RCh, 1.17-7.17

Engineers & Pioneers
1914: Cie 8/1 du 4RG   1918: Cies 8/1, 8/51, 8/21 du 4RG Pioneer Battalion 106 RIT 8.18-

After assembly at Bayon, 15DI moved forward to cover the river Meurthe: springboard for the advance of Fourth Army towards Sarrebourg in Lorraine. During the battle for Sarrebourg, the division fought at Gosselming on 20th August, and, at Gondrevarge on the 21st. Engaged in the battle for Morhange, it fought at Rozelieures, Giriviller, Magnieres, Moyen and Vallois, after which the division moved back to the Meurthe. Tranferred to the Second Army, the division moved to St Mihiel on 13th September, and to the Argonne on the 26th. It fought in the Forêt d'Apremont, north of St Mihiel, during the battle for Flirey and, when the front stabilised, occupied the line between Bois d'Ailly and the Meuse. From this position, it took part in 1st Army's operations during the battle of Woevre in the spring of 1915. It fought a series of actions around the Bois d'Ailly 5th-10th April, 22-24th April and 30th April 1915. Thereafter it remained in the same sector until 27th September 1915.

On that date it joined Second Army for the second battle of Champage. From a sector west of the Butte de Tahure it fought for control of the road between Tahure and Somme-Py from 6th October. Then it remained near Tahure until 9th December when it went for a rest in Lorraine. The division rejoined the front-line between Apremont and Koeur-la-Grande on 14th Janaury 1916 and remained there until 21st June.

On 21st July 1916 the division was committed to the Vaux Chapitre/Fleury sector on the heights above Verdun where it attacked on 27th July, resisted German attacks on 1st and 5th Ausgust, and counter-attacked at Fleury on 8th August. Three days later, the division moved back to Lorraine and took up new positions between Ancerviller and Embermesnil on 18th August.

Taken out of the line on 21st September, 15DI moved to the Santerre during December. There it joined Tenth Army east of Belloy-en-Santerre on 22nd December. Relieved by British troops on 8th January 1917, the division was moved to Champagne where it was in line from the 20th January.

The division spent eight months in the sector between the Epine de Vedegrange and Aubérive-sur-Suippe, during which time, it attacked the Bois de Mesnil on 13th February and the Maisons de Champagne 24th-30th February. On 29th August the division moved to the nearby Mesnil-Maisons sector and attacked on the line of the Galoche on 14th February 1918: where it withstood a German attack on 1st March.

In response to the German offensive, 15DI moved to the Oise and joined Third Army on 20th March. It fought at Orvillers and Berliere before retreating to secure the sector between Nampoel and Mont de Choisy. From there it moved to Sixth Army at St Mard and Quennevieres during the third battle for the Aisne. From 18th August, after a series of swift transfers back and forward between Tenth Army and Third Army, the division participated in the second battle of the Marne, the division was committed to action in Picardy. As part of the First Army, it participated in the second battle of Noyon, and moved up the right-bank of the Oise towards the Hindenburg Line. It took up positions between Servais and the Oise. On 3rd October it moved to Nesle for the attack on St Quentin and Mont-d'Origny, during which it took Fontaine-Notre-Dame, Aisonville, Bernouville and Tupigny.

From 2nd November the division was 'at rest': employed on labour duties for the Paris Military Government.

16 Division d'Infanterie

An active division in 1914 as part of VIII Corps d'Armée, with headquarters at Bourges

Commanders
02.08.14-Louis de Maud'huy
08.09.14-Jean Piarron de Mondésir
12.10.14-Charles Vandenberg
07.01.15-Jean-Joseph Roquerol
09.08.16-Alexander le Gallais

31 Brigade [disbanded 1.17]
85 RI, Cosne
95 RI, Bourges
32 Brigade [disbanded 1.17]
13 RI, Nevers   1.17 to 169DI-replaced by 27RI ex 15DI
29 RI, Autun   1.17 to 169DI-not replaced
Infantry from 1.17
27 RI
85 RI
95 RI

Artillery
Groups 1-3, 1 RAC, Bourges
Group 11, 108RAL   [added 11.17-retitled Group 6, 3.18]

Cavalry
6/16 RCh, 8.14-11.15; 3/16 RCh, 1.17-7.17   4/16 RCh, 1.17-7.17

Engineers & Pioneers
1914: Cie 8/2 du 4RG   1918: Cies 8/2, 8/52, 8/71 du 4RG Pioneer Battalion 24 RIT 8.18-

As part of the First Army, the division assembled at Châtel-sur-Moselle on 10th August 1914 and moved up to the river Meurthe four days later. On the 15th it advanced on Sarrebourg via Blamont and fought there and at Domevre on the 15th. Once Sarrebourg was occupied, the division engaged the Germans at Reding and Hoff. It re-grouped west of the Mortagne on the 21st and fought at Mattexy and Deinvillers during First Army's battle for Mortagne. In the subsequent retreat, the division moved west of the Meurthe and re- grouped at St Mihiel. With Second Army, the division fought briefly for control of the high ground above the Meuse at Woel and Doncourt-aux-Templiers on 17th September. It then moved northwards to Third Army, in the Ardennes but this movement was cancelled, and the division was diverted back towards St Mihiel where it joined in the battle for Flirey: it fought at Apremont and Bois d'Ailly from 25th September 1914. On 4th April 1915, it participated in First Army's battle for the Woevre with continued action around Bois d'Ailly. The rest of 1915 was spent in the line at Apremont. After a brief rest, 16DI resumed operations in Lorraine when it took over the sector between Paroches and Woimbey on 20th February 1916. It moved northwards to the sector between Eparges and Bonzee-en- Woevre on 18th March to protect the southern shoulder of the Verdun salient. It remained there until 3rd July. A week later it was committed to the defence of the salient and fought between Damloup and Bois Fumin for the rest of the month. The division returned to Eparges on 1st August and remained in line there until 17th September. After a long period in reserve, the division moved to the Aisne front and joined Tenth Army between Fresnes and Berny. This tour was very brief and on 21st January 1917 the division moved eastwards to Champagne and joined Fourth Army. It was allocated the sector between Four-de-Paris and the river Aisne. It moved westwards to the Marquises sector on 31st March and took part in the battle for the Monts [Moronvillers] on 16th April when it attacked German positions at the Bois de la Grille. The division returned to Verdun on 3rd May 1917, and spent six weeks in the Damloup-Haudiomont sector. It returned to 4th Army on 6th July and spent the next five months in line in the Maisons sector. After a break at Christmas, the division returned to the same sector on 2nd February 1918 and remained in line until 24th July, during which time it fought at the Maisons, Virginy and Bois d'Hauzy[15th-18th July] during the fourth battle for Champagne. On 24th July 1918, the division joined Fifth Army in the Ardre valley to the south-west of Reims and fought down river to the Vesle where it took up positions west of Muizon at Jonchery-sur- Vesle. At the battle of St Thierry on 30th September, the division crossed the Vesle and, in succession reached the Aisne-Marne canal, the Suippe, the Retourne and reached the Aisne on 13th October. Then it organised defensive positions at Thour and Nizy-le-Comte. In the final battle for the Serre, it fought at Recouvrance and went into reserve on 1st November.

17 Division d'Infanterie

An active division in 1914 as part of IX Corps d'Armée, with headquarters at Chateauroux

Commanders
02.08.14-Jean-Baptiste Dumas
06.09.14-Pierre Guignabaudet
01.07.15-Robert de Buyer
29.08.15-Paul Lancrenon
09.01.18-Joseph Gassouin

33 Brigade [disbanded 1.18]
68 RI, Le Blanc
90 RI, Chateauroux

34 Brigade [12.15 to 152DI-replaced by 304 Bde ex 152DI]
114 RI, Parthenay	12.15 to 152DI
125 RI, Poitiers	12.15 to 152DI

304 Brigade [from 152DI 12.15-disbanded 1.18]
268 RI	Disbanded 1.18-replaced by 335 RI ex 97DT
290 RI	Disbanded 1.18

Infantry from 1.18
68 RI
90 RI
335 RI
27 & 28 Bns Sénégalais   [attached from 4.18]

Artillery
Groups 1-3, 20 RAC, Poitiers
Group 6, 109 RAL   [added 3.18-formerly Group 12/106RAL]

Cavalry
5/7 RH, 8.14-7.17;   7/7 RH, 1.17-7.17
Engineers & Pioneers
1914: Cie 9/1du 6RG   1918: Cies 9/1, 9/51, 9/21 du 6RG Pioneer Battalion 54 RIT 8.18-

As part of Second Army, the division assembled at Pont-St-Vincent on 11th August 1914. It moved forward to cover the river Seille between Armaucourt and Brin. Within days IX Corps d'Armee was switched to Fourth Army in the Ardennes to cover the German advance in the north. 17DI fought at Nafraiture and Bievre in Belgium from 23rd August until IX CA moved yet again. On 29th August it joined Foch's force at St Gond, south of the Marne. During the first battle for the Marne, the division fought at Mont Toulon, Bannes, Mont Aout and Broussay-le-Grand. From 10th September it advanced towards the Aisne via Morains-le-Petit, Condé-sur-Marne, Prosnes, and took Sept Sauls and Mourmelon-le-Petit on 13th September. During the struggle for the Aisne it attacked east of Reims, with Fourth Army, to Moscou and Moronvillers and then dug in between Prosnes and Marquises.

On 19th October 1914 the IX CA was committed to another major move. It arrived in the Ypres salient on 23rd October. The division fought at Passendale, Klein Zillebeke, and occupied trenches between Wallemolen and the Ieper-Roeselare railway. On 6th December, it entered Polygon Wood and from 24th December, occupied positions at Broodseinde. On 25th March 1915 it returned to Polygon Wood.

On 5th April 1915, the division pulled out of the Ypres salient and moved southwards to join Tenth Army in Artois. Initially it occupied the sector between Ecurie and Rolincourt-to the north of Arras, and then between Grenay and Rutoire. It attacked Loos on 9th May and held off a German attack at Cinq Chemins on 16th June. On 7th August it moved south of Arras, into Picardy, to take over positions between Herleville and Maucourt but returned to Artois at the end of the month. After a period near Wailly, the division re-entered the line at Grenay and attacked towards Loos. From 6th January until 11th March 1916 it held the line at Souchez and Givenchy-below Vimy Ridge-until relieved by British troops.

After a period of indecisive marching and counter-marching, 17DI arrived at the Hayette-Bois de Canard sector, outside Verdun, on 18th April. It's stay was short as it was pulled out on 8th May and sent to Champagne. From 29th May it was to found in line between Epine de Vedegrange and Aubérive, where it remained until 9th September. This peripatetic division joined Sixth Army on the Somme on 8th October and was thrown into the battle at Sailly-Saillisel, from which it moved south of Péronne to Bois d'Abbaye in December. Relieved by British troops, the division was shuttled between Tenth, First, Fourth and Sixth Armies during the planning stages for Nivelle's attack on the Chemin des Dames. Until 20th April, it remained in reserve. Then it entered Fifth Army's front at Ville-aux-Bois, and moved to Hurtebise-Casemates on 2nd July. There, up on the Chemin des Dames, it held off German attacks on 15th -16th July and counter-attacked on 28th-29th July.

At the end of July 17DI moved to Lorraine and took over the sector between the Chapelotte and the Vezouve on 26th August. On 30th December, it moved to the Grand Couronne, outside Nancy, and was employed on labour duties until moved to Picardy on 27th March 1918. As part of First Army, it held the line of the Avre and fought the Germans near Rouvrel, but, by 23rd April, the division was on the road again. It arrived in Lorraine on 4th May and took over the sector between Maizey and Bois Loclont. Later it moved sideways to include Koeur-la-Grande at the apex of the St Mihiel salient.

On 28th July 1918 the division joined Tenth Army for the later stages of the second battle of the Marne: it fought at Chacrise and occupied Vieray and then, Venizel. A movement to the Oise sector brought it into action at Morsain, Veraponin, Mareuil and Montecouve during the second battle of Noyon. On 10th September it moved forward to the Ailette river near Vauxillon and closed up on the Hindenburg Line at Singes. As the units of Tenth Army became Third Army, the division resumed the offensive east of Laon on 21st October. It fought at the Souche during the battle for the Serre, and, from there, moved northwards towards the Meuse via Marle and Thon. This much-travelled division was at Signy l'Abbaye on 11th November 1918.

18 Division d'Infanterie

An active division in 1914 as part of IX Corps d'Armée, with headquarters at Angers

Commanders
02.08.14-Justinien Lefrevre
19.10.16-Philippe Dillemann
22.08.17-Joseph Bordeaux
12.12.17-Joseph Andlauer

35 Brigade [disbanded 1.17]
32 RI, Tours
66 RI, Tours

36 Brigade [disbanded 1.17]
77 RI, Cholet
135 RI, Angers   1.17 to 152DI-not replaced

Infantry from 1.17
32 RI
66 RI
77 RI

Artillery
Groups 1-3, 33 RAC, Angers
Group 5, 109RAL   [added 3.18-formerly Group 11, 112RAL]

Cavalry
6/7 RH, 8.14-7.17   8/7 RH, 1.17-7.17

Engineers & Pioneers
1914: Cie 9/2 du 6RG   1918: Cies 9/2, 9/52, 9/71 du 6RG Pioneer Battalion 71 RIT 8.18-

As part of the Second Army, the division assembled at Pont-St-Vincent, south of Nancy, on 11th August 1914, and then moved forward to cover the line of the river Seille between Nomeny and Clémery. The division assisted in the defence of the Grande Couronne with fighting at Champenois and Erbeviller. On 2nd September, as part of IXCA, the division moved to the Marne and joined Foch near St Gond. During the second battle of the Marne, the division fought at Euvy and Gourgançon [8th-10th September] and then moved north-eastwards towards Moronvillers where it fought between Moscou and Esperance during the first battle of the Aisne. It established positions between Esperance and Prosnes from 12th September.

On 20th October, the division moved to Flanders with IXCA, and arrived in the Zonnebeke-Broodseinde sector, outside Ieper, four days later. On 24th November, the division moved into Polygon Wood and took part in a major attack along the Menin Road 11th-17th December and withstood a German attack on 18th February 1915. After a brief rest, it occupied positions at Pilckem and endured the German gas attack of 22nd April. It left the Ypres salient on 6th May.

By 9th May, 18DI was in line facing Vimy Ridge from a line north of La Targette. From here, it took part in Tenth Army's attacks of 23rd -24th May and 16th June. After a rest in the Santerre, the division returned to Artois on 26th August. It attacked near Agny, to the south of Arras, on 25th September during the third battle of Artois. After this it occupied a sector between Loos and Grenay from 8th October until relieved by British troops on 6th January 1916. On 2nd January, the division occupied another sector of the line facing Vimy Ridge-at Angres, Calonne and the Bois de Givenchy.

Again, relieved by British forces, it left for the Argonne for rest and retraining on 3rd March. On 17th April the division entered the line between Bois Canard and Bois Avocourt on the left back of the Meuse in the Verdun salient. It repelled German attacks on 5th, 7th and 10th April before returning to the support role on 11th May. On 2nd June, it joined

Fourth Army's line between Souain and Wacques in Champagne. After three months in the trenches the division moved westwards to join Sixth Army in the battle of the Somme. It fought at Morval [12th and 18th October, and 5th November] and moved south to Bouchavesnes on 14th December. Relieved by the British on 18th January 1917 the division underwent a long period of rest and retraining in preparation for Nivelle's offensive.

18DI joined Fifth Army on the Chemin des Dames front but did not take part in the attack of 16th April. It took over the sector between Craonne and Bois de Beau Marais on 1st May; and attacked around Chevreux throughout May. After a month's rest, the division served in the Casemates/Chevreux sector until 27th July when it was pulled out and sent to Lorraine. Stationed near Toul, the division acted as a training school for newly-arrived American troops until October. On the 12th of that month it became operational in the sector between the Sanon and Bezange-la-Grande: American personnel took part in this movement. The division resumed its training role on 1st January 1918.

As a result of the German spring offensive, the division moved to Picardy on 17th May, and fought along the Avre with First Army: actions occurred at Moreuil and Senecat. During the battle for Matz in June, the division began in a support role but moved forward on 9th June to resist the German attack at Ressons and Marquelise. After a rest behind Third Army's front, the division was drawn into the second battle of the Marne. Under command of Sixth Army, it moved to Montmirail from which it attacked towards Velizy via actions at Chassins, Vincelles, Foret de Reiz and Ste Gemme. The division was pulled out of the line on 4th August and sent to Verdun where it occupied the Damloup-Beaumont sector. As part of the American-led offensive in the Argonne, from 8th October, 18DI attacked Côte 344 and Samogneux and took Bois d'Haumont and Ferme d'Ormont. Then its advanced continued towards Rosieres-aux-Salines. The division was located at Bayon on 11th November 1918.

19 Division d'Infanterie

An active division in 1914 as part of X Corps d'Armée, with headquarters at Rennes

Commanders
02.08.14-Francois Bonnier
05.09.14-Henri Bailly
16.09.16-Pierre Trouchard

37 Brigade [disbanded 5.17]
48 RI, Guincamp
71 RI, St Brieuc

38 Brigade [disbanded 5.17]
41 RI, Rennes   7.15 to 131DI-replaced by 270RI ex X CA-disbanded 5.17
70 RI, Vitré

Infantry from 5.17
48 RI
70 RI
71 RI

Artillery
Groups 1-3, 7 RAC, Rennes
Group 5, 110 RAL   [added 3.18-formerly Group 7, 110RAL]

Cavalry
5/13 RH, 8.14-7.17   3/13 RH, 1.17-7.17

Engineers & Pioneers
1914: Cie 10/1 du 6RG   1918: Cies 10/1, 10/51, 10/21 du 6RG
Pioneer Battalion 71 RIT 8.18-

As part of Fifth Army, the division assembled at Vouziers on 5th August in order to cover the crossings of the Meuse near Sedan. On the 13th it moved north via Phillipeville to the Sambre. In the subsequent battle at Charleroi, the division was engaged at Fosses-la-Ville [22nd-23rd]. From the 24th it retreated via Florennes and Hirson to Guise. After a fight at Sains-Richaumont, the division continued its retreat and reached Sézanne on the 30th. During the first battle of the Marne, in which it fought in both Fifth Army and in Ninth Army, the division contested control of the Deux Morins with combat at Sézanne, Buzy-le-Repos, and Fromentières, and then advanced towards Reims via Damery and Cormontreuil. During the first battle of the Aisne, it fought at the latter location and then advanced to the north-west of Reims. Its progress was halted when it was switched to Picardy and Artois.

The division joined Tenth Army on 5th October and was in immediate action at Neuville-Vitasse, Boisleux and Monchy-le-Preux to the east of Arras. It then occupied a sector between Agny and Berles-aux-Bois; it moved to Maison Blanch-Ecurie on 23rd February 1915; to St Laurent-Blagny-Roclincourt on 22nd April and, after the second battle of Artois, to Neuville-Saint-Vaast and the Labyrinthe on 7th July. The division left the Arras area on 25th July and was sent eastwards to Champagne.

After rest and retraining, it re-entered the line in the Argonne, under command of Third Army, between the Aire and the Haute Chevauchee from which it moved to the Ravin de la Houyette/Fontaine-aux-Charmes sector on 23rd August. There, it engaged in mining operations and resisted a German attack on 8th September. After another brief rest, the division moved closer to Verdun on 21st February 1916 when it took over the line between Dombasle-en-Argonne and Avocourt: the opening day of the German assault on the city. From 30th May, it fought on the left bank of the Meuse between Chattancourt and Marre: and attacked Mort Homme on 15th June. It moved to the right-bank at Bois d'Haudromont-Ouvrage de Thiaumont on 7th August and was heavily engaged there between 17th and 18th August.

On 2nd September 1916, the division left Verdun for Champagne. From 9th September until 8th January 1917 it held the line between Aubérive and the Epine de Vedegrange. After some retraining, it appeared on the Oise front on 12th January where it re-entered the line-between Dancourt and Popincourt on 27th February, from which it attempted to attack St Quentin on 17th March. It was pulled out on 21st March and sent back to Champagne for training, where it joined the line between Mont Cornillet and Mont Blond on 25th April. It carried out attacks on 30th April, and 4-5th May. It left the line on 15th May and arrived in Verdun on 15th June. Initially involved between Bois d'Haudromeont and Damloup, it attacked Côte 344 on 10th September. It moved to the crucial Éparges sector on 9th October and remained there throughout the winter. Its long stay was highlighted by an attack on the Calonne trenches on 4th March 1918.

After a brief period of uncertainty and rapid movement between armies as the Allies sought to respond to the German spring offensive, the division found itself in the Aisne region as part of Sixth Army. From 27th May it offered resistance to the German assaults at Hautebraye and then at Autreches, west of Vingré. On 4th June, it attacked the Plateau de St Léocade and advanced to Autreches. During the second battle of the Marne, it fought at Longpoint, and then advanced to the Vesle at Villers-Helon.

On 5th August 1918, the division moved to the Vosges and took over the sector between the upper valley of the Weiss and the valley of the river Fave. It was pulled back westwards to the Compiegne area for retraining on 17th October. On 7th November it joined Third Army's advance at Crecy-sur-Serre.

20 Division d'Infanterie

An active division in 1914 as part of X Corps d'Armée with headquarters at St Servan

Commanders
02.08.14-Elie Boe
22.08.14-Alphonse Menission
05.09.14-Martial Rogerie
08.10.14-Francois Anthoine
10.09.15-Francois Delbousquet
19.01.16-Edmond Hennocque
17.01.18-Emmanuel Putois
16.06.18-Joseph Diebold
24.06.18-Auguste Desvoyes

39 Brigade [disbanded 4.17]
25 RI, Cherbourg
136 RI, St Lo   4.17 to 87DI-not replaced

40 Brigade [disbanded 4.17]
2 RI, Granville
47 RI, St Malo

Infantry from 4.17
2 RI
25 RI
47 RI

Artillery
Group 1-3, 10 RAC, Rennes
Group 11, 110RAL   [added 11.17-retitled Group 6/110RAL 3.18]

Cavalry
6/13 RH, 8.14-7.17;   4/13 RH, 1.17-7.17

Engineers & Pioneers
1914: Cie 10/2 du 6RG   1918: Cies 10/2, 10/52, 10/71 du 6RG Pioneer Battalion 129 RIT 8.18-

By 13th August 1914, this division had assembled at Attigny and Chesne to cover the Meuse above Sedan. From here it participated in the advance of Fifth Army to the Sambre and reached Vendresse and Rocroi when it became involved in the battle for Charleroi [22-23rd]. After two days of fighting near Wagnee it was forced to retreat via Audigny towards Guise. It fought in the first battle of Guise [29-30th] and then headed south towards Sézanne. When the first battle of the Marne began on 6th September, the division fought between St Gond and the Deux Morins at Sezanne, Thoult-Trosnay, Corfelix and Bannay, after which it advanced via Bergeres-les-Vertus and Epernay to Sillery. From 13th September, the division fought at the vital Fort de la Pompelle on the eastern approaches to Reims. Further combat occurred to the north-west of the city at Cavalier de Coucy. On 25th September the division left Reims for Picardy.

During a period in which the division rotated between Second Army and Tenth Army, the division took part in the first battle of Artois. From 2nd October, it was in action at Neuville-Saint-Vaast, Mercatel and Beaurains on the outskirts of Arras. On 6th October the division established a line between Agny and Blagny from which it repelled German attacks on Arras [22-31st October] and attacked at St Laurent on 17th December. The division moved to the Ecurie-Roclincourt sector, north-east of Arras on 20th May 1915 and remained there until pulled back into reserve on 26th July.

On 10th August 1915 the division re-entered the line between the Ravin de la Houyette and the river Aisne on the western edge of the Argonne. While here, some elements of the division participated in the second battle of Champagne by supporting the offensive near Servon. The division remained in Third Army in the Argonne for nearly a year. It moved out of the area on 12th July 1916 and moved to the Somme.

As part of the Tenth Army, the division participated in the later stages of the battle of the Somme. From the sector between Maucourt and the Amiens-Chaulnes railway, it attacked Chilly on 4th-9th September. On 30th November, after a brief rest, the division moved to the adjacent sector between the railway and Ablaincourt-Pressoir. When HQ Tenth Army left the region, the division continued in the same area but under command of Third Army. On 7th February 1917, it took over the sector between Beuvraignes and Armancourt, from which, it was able to exploit the German withdrawal to the Hindenburg Line. On 17th March, the division advanced through Marngy, Dury, Tuginy and Happencourt after which it was withdrawn into reserve on 21st March.

Switched to Fourth Army in Champagne, the division participated in the battle for Moronvillers on 30th April from its positions between Cornillet and Marquises. On 15th June the division was transferred to Verdun where it took over the sector facing the Côte du Poivre and Louvement on Bastille Day. Elements of the division took part in the French offensive, which began on 8th August, and it attacked Côte 304 on the 20th August. It was moved to the Samogneux-Côte de Talou sector on 29th August, and repelled German attacks on 9th September, 2nd and 6th October.

Rested from 20th October, the division arrived in the Éparges sector on 6th November where it remained until 3rd March 1918. A further tour in the Verdun trenches began on 21st March between Bezonvaux and the Bois de Chaume. The division fought in the Bois des Caurieres on 17th April until it came out of the line on 23rd May.

Two days later, the division joined Sixth Army at Jaulgonne during the third battle of the Aisne. From 15th July, after rest at Dormans, on the Marne, the division was heavily engaged in the battles for the Marne and Champagne. It defended the front around St Agnan, Chapelle-Monthodon, Comblizy and Nesle-le-Repos until it gained conrol of the plateau de la Bourdonnerie, from which it crossed the Marne on 22nd July. By 3rd August it had cleared the valley of the Ardre at Savigny and Courville and reached the river Vesle next day: there it established a line between Breuil-sur-Vesle and Magneux.

From 26th August, the division rested in Lorraine and spent a short period in the line of the Vosges between the Fave and Chapelotte rivers. After further rest in the valley of the Meurthe, the division went back up into the on 16th October: between the Fave and Rabodeau. On 1st November it came out of the line for the last time. By 11th November 1918, the division was located between Corcieux, Arches and Thaon in preparation for Tenth Army's advance into Lorraine.

21 Division d'Infanterie

An active division in 1914 as part of XI Corps d'Armée with headquarters at Nantes

Commanders
02.08.14-René Radiquet
25.10.14-Saint-Foye Dauvin
27.08.18-Emile Giraud

41 Brigade [disbanded 11.17]
64 RI, Acenis
65 RI, Nantes   11.17 to 134DI-not replaced

42 Brigade [disbanded 11.17]
93 RI, Roche s/Yon
137 RI, Fontenay

Infantry from 11.17
64 RI
93 RI
137 RI

Artillery
Groups 1-3, 51 RAC, Nantes
Group 5, 111 RAL   [added 3.18-formerly Group 7, 111RAL]

Cavalry
5/2 RCh, 8.14-7.17   8/2 RCh, 1.17-7.17

Engineers & Pioneers
1914: Cie 11/1 du 6RG   1918: Cie 11/1, 11/51, 11/21 du 6RG Pioneer Battalion 97 RIT 8.18-

The division concentrated at Challerange on 9th August 1914, as part of Fifth Army. After XI Corps d'Armee had been transferred to Fourth Army, it moved north to cover the Meuse crossings at Sedan. On 21st August, it moved into Belgium and fought in the Ardennes at Maissin. As Fourth Army withdrew to the Marne, the division began to retreat on 23rd August when it moved back to the Meuse; by 28th August it had passed through Vendresse, Givry, and Aulny sur Marne and had reached Fère-Champenois.

During the first battle of the Marne, the division served under Foch and his Ninth Army in the battle for the Marais St Gond. The division fought at Fere-Champenois and advanced, on 10th September, via Châlons-sur-Marne to St Hilaire-le-Grand in Champagne: there, it fought the first battle of the Aisne and when the front stabilised, moved to defend Reims. On 29th September the division was transferred to Sixth Army in Picardy where it defended positions on the future Somme battlefield: Contalmaison, La Boisselle, Auchonvillers and Beaumont-Hamel. Holding a sector between Beaumont-Hamel and Hébuterne, it fought at La Boisselle on 17th December, and attacked German positions between Hebuterne and Serre on 7th June 1915.

On 27th July 1915 the division moved eastwards to Champagne and took over a sector south-west of Côte 196. Succesively under command of Group Pétain, Second Army, Fourth Army and then Second Army again, the division spent ten months in this region. During the second battle of Champagne, it attacked the Butte de Mesnil on 25th September and then took positions at Mamelles and in the Trapeze. On 2nd December it moved to the Tahure-Somme Py sector, and on, 30th April 1916, the Moscou-Baconnes sector from which it moved to Verdun on 24th May.

The division served in Verdun from May 1916 until February 1917 during which time it occupied the Bois Haudriomont-Côte Froideterre sector and attacked Douaumont on 12-16th June and 18-23rd June. On 15th June it moved to the southern sector of the salient-between Châtillon and Bonzée-en-Woëvre and later at Trésauvaux. It moved to Douaumont on 20th November and took part in the French offensive of 15th-18th December, and then moved to the Bezonvaux-Chambrette sector, where it remained until 17th February 1917.

On 12th March 1917, the division joined Sixth Army on the Aisne front, near Soissons, below the Chemin des Dames, from which it attacked positions at Laffaux.. During Nivelle's offensive, it was engaged at Vauxillon and Cerny while in line at Cerny-en-Laonnais. The division moved to Third Army's front on 10th May and re-entered the line between Urvillers and Dallon on 1st July. It was transferred back to the Sixth Army on the Chemin des Dames to occupy the sector between Panthéon and Épine de Chevregny on 24th September. It took part in the attack on the Malmaison position on 20th October and then moved to the Filain-Pargny sector. On 18th December it took over the Chavignon-Vaumaires sector and was to remain on the Chemin des Dames until the middle of 1918.

During the third battle of the Aisne, still part of Sixth Army, the division was engaged at Chassemy, Chacrise, Hartennes, Billy-sur-Ourcq and Dampleux from 27th May and 2nd June. A week later, the division arrived in the Vosges and took over Seventh Army's sector between Metzeral and the Fave. It returned to a more active front on 7th September when it was allocated to Fourth Army in Champagne. During the autumn offensive, it took part in the battle for Somme-Py and advanced north of the river Py. From 20th October, it pursued the Germans to Thugny-Trugny, south of Rethel, and reached Ambly-Fleury. Then it moved along the line Pagny-Lorquoy-Laonais and Mézières. On 8th November it went into rest at Touligny and Bancourt.

22 Division d'Infanterie

An active division in 1914 as part of XI Corps d'Armée, with headquarters at Vannes

Commanders
02.08.14-Joseph Pambet
30.09.14-Pierre Bouyssou
10.07.17-Francois Capdepont
27.03.18-Jean Renouard
28.08.18-Joseph Spire

43 Brigade [disbanded 11.17]
62 RI, Lorient
116 RI, Vannes   11.17 to 170DI- not replaced

44 Brigade [disbanded 11.17]
19 RI, Brest
118 RI, Quimper

Infantry from 11.17

19 RI
62 RI
118 RI

Artillery
Groups 1-3, 35 RAC, Vannes
Group 8, 111RAL   [added 6.18-formerly Group 2, 111RAL]

Cavalry
6/2 RCh, 8.14-11.15;   6/2 RCh, 1.17-7.17

Engineers & Pioneers
1914: Cie 11/2 du 6RG   1918: Cies 11/2, 11/52, 11/71 du 6RG Pioneer Battalion 7 RIT 8.18-

On 9th August 1914, the division assembled at Grand-Pré. It was transferred from Fifth Army to Fourth Army on 16th August and moved forward to cover bridges over the Meuse at Remilly. It advanced into Belgium on the 21st and, next day, fought at Maissin, during the battle for the Ardennes. It fell back through Sedan, fought there and at Touteron, and then retreated via Béthenville to Fère-Champenois.

During the first battle of the Marne, it fought under Foch, at the battle of Marais St Gond, with action at Lenharrée and Semoine. From 10th September, it moved forward via Nuisement-sur- Coule, Châlons-sur- Marne, and St Étienne-aux-Temple to the east of Reims at Jonchery-sur- Suippe and Ferme Wacques. During the first battle of the Aisne it was heavily engaged at Jonchery during the struggle for Reims.

On 21st September, the division moved to Picardy, where, under command of Sixth Army, it fought to control the area around Albert: the future battlefield of the Somme. It was in action at Ovillers, La Boisselle, Thiepval and Hamel and, then, took up positions between Hamel and Authuille. It moved to Fricourt and engaged in mine warfare and carried out attacks in the direction of La Boiselle on 22nd December, and on 10th-18th January 1915. It remained in the Somme sector until relieved by British units on 4th August 1915.

The division joined Pétain's force in the Champagne on 18th August and took over the Perthes-les-Hurlus sector on the 24th. It attacked and retained the Butte de Tahure position on 25th September during the second battle of Champagne. The division remained in the sector between Tahures and Mamelles until 22nd February 1916.

The division moved to Verdun and entered the line between Thiaumont and Bois d'Haudriomont on 28th March where it resisted a German attack on 17th April. It was pulled out on 22nd April and moved to the Reims area where it spent nearly three months [17th May-8th September] in the line at Berry-au-Bac. Returned to Verdun, it re-entered the line at Vaux-devant-Damloup on 29th October and remained there until 24th January 1917. It saw action at Belrupt, Vaux and Tavannes.

As part of the preparations for Nivelle's offensive, the division joined Fifth Army on 24th January 1917. On 29th March it attacked the Hindenburg Line between Laffaux and the Vesle, and was in the rear during Nivelle's abortive offensive. On 30th April it took over the line between Hurtebise and Paissy and engaged in heavy fighting on the Chemin des Dames on 5th and 7th May. Afterwards, the division joined Third Army and took over the Selency-Pontruil sector, adjacent to the BEF, on 22nd May. At rest from 20th August, it returned to the Chemin des Dames on 17th September [Colombe-Pantheon sector]. After a further rest period, it spent two tours in the sector between Ferme Rosay and Bois de Mortier [5th-25th November 1917, and 18th December 1917-11th March 1918].

As part of the Allied attempt to stem the German spring offensive, the division move to the Nesle area on 23rd March and fought along the Avre at Nesle, Roye and Rollet until 2nd April, after which it returned to the Chemin des Dames. There it remained-stationed between Vauclerc and Vaumaire until the third battle of the Aisne. It was badly cut up on the Chemin des Dames on 27th May, and had to be taken out of the line. It was reconstituted on 2nd June and sent to the Vosges where it spent in the summer in the quiet sector between Leimbach and Metzeral.

On 6th September, the division joined Fourth Army and, during the attacks on the Somme-Py positions, from 26th September, it attacked from Navarin to the Butte de Souain. It crossed the Arnes on 29th and fought between the

Retourne and the Aisne from 5th to 11th October. Withdrawn on 15th October, it moved to Baconnes where it relieved American troops. It was engaged in the battle of Chesne on 1st November and northwards towards the Meuse and was fighting at Mézières on 10th and 11th November 1918.

23 Division d'Infanterie

An active division in 1914 as part of XII Corps d'Armée, with headquarters at Angoulême

Commanders
02.08.14-Charles Leblond
22.08.14-Etienne Bapst
27.08.14-Joseph Masnou
10.01.15-Louis Arlabosse
30.05.15-Henri Bonfait

45 Brigade [disbanded 2.17]
63 RI, Limoges   2.17 to 134DI- not replaced
78 RI, Guéret

45 Brigade [reformed 6.17-disbanded again 9.17
78 RI
133RI   From 41DI 6.17 and to 164DI 9.17

46 Brigade [disbanded 2.17]
107 RI, Angoulême
138 RI, Magnac-Laval

46 Brigade [reformed 6.17-disbanded again 9.17]
107 RI
138 RI

Infantry from 9.17
78 RI
107 RI
138 RI

Artillery
Groups 1-3, 21 RAC, Angoulême
Group 5, 112RAL [added 4.18-formerly Group 11/105RAL]

Cavalry
5/21 RCh, 8.14-11.15;   5/21 RCh, 7.17-7.17;   E/21 RCh, 7.17 only

Engineers & Pioneers
1914: Cie 12/1 du 6RG   1918: Cies 12/1, 12/51, 12/21 du 6RG Pioneer Battalion 109 RIT 8.18-

On 11th August 1914, from its concentration point at Ste Menehoulde, in the Argonne, the division, as part of XII Corps d'Armee in the Fourth Army, moved north via Varennes and Stenay to Neufchateau. It fought at Menugoutte on 22nd August during the battle for the Ardennes. It began its retreat on the 23rd and had retired behind the Meuse on the 26th: it fought at Beaumont on the 27th and 28th; attacked north-eastwards at Neuville-et-Day on the 29th; and retreated from the 1st to 6th September from Tahure and Challerange to Virty-le-Francois.

From 7th September until the 18th September it took part in Fourth Army's operations during the first battle of the Marne by engaging the Germans at Sompuis and Hambauville, advancing to Minaucourt via Vèsigneul-sur-Coole, Ablancourt and Herpent; and establishing a line between Laval and Somme-Suippe. It fought at Perthes on 17th September. It moved to the defence of Reims on the 18th and, after action on the Berru Massif and at Cernay-les-Reims, it settled down to a long period of fighting in and around the Fort de la Pompelle. On 1st October it moved eastwards to Wacques and attacked St Hilaire-le-Grand on 12th and 30th October, and on 15th November and 21st December.

The division joined First Army in Lorraine on 30th March 1915. It fought in the battle of the Woevre from 2nd April. It attacked Regniéville-en-Haye, Remenauville and Fey-en-Haye and then moved to the Bois de Mort Mare-Regniéville sector on 10th May. The division rested near Toul from 10th June and then moved to Artois.

Part of Tenth Army from 19th July 1915, the division went into the line between Ecurie and Roclincourt-on the northern approaches to Arras- and remained there until 11th March 1916. During this period, it engaged in mining operations and attacked the Labyrinthe during the third battle of Artois on 25th September 1915.

On 30th March 1916 the division took over the sector between the Bois d'Haudriomont and the Meuse, north of Verdun, and took part in French attacks on 9th and 17th April, and 21st and 25th May. The division went into reserve in the Marne region on 24th June.

The division re-entered the line between Soissons and Pernant, in Fifth Army's sector of the Chemin des Dames on 10th July 1916. It moved to Troyon-Soupir on 22nd July and then left for the Somme on 23rd September. During the battle of the Somme, it occupied the sector between on the north bank of the river between Clery and the Maisonette. On 30th January 1917, the division moved to Champagne and spent the next six months in the line between the Chemin de Souain and Ste Marie a Py from which it attacked the Navarin position. It edged sideways to Côte 193 on 12th August.

In response to the Italian defeat at Caporetto, the two divisions of XII Corps d'Armee were sent to Italy on 11th November 1917. The 23DI took over at sector between Monte Tomba and the river Piave on 25th January 1918. From 27th April it fought up on the Asiago plateau at Camtelle-Penna and repelled the Austrian attack of 15th June. It rested from 23rd June to 9th August and returned to the Asiago. From 21st October it took part in the Allied offensive on the Piave and fought at Pederobra. After the armistice with Austria on 4th November, the division retired to the Asolo region.

24 Division d'Infanterie

An active division in 1914 as part of XII Corps d'Armée, with headquarters at Périgueux

Commanders
02.08.14-Charles de Garreau de la Mechenie
22.08.14-Achille Deffontaines
26.08.14-Henri Descoings
05.01.15-Louis Arlabasse
09.01.15-Antoine Meric
17.01.16-Henri Mordacq
18.11.17-Jules Priou
13.06.18-Auguste Desvoyes
15.06.18-Dominique Odry

47 Brigade [disbanded 2.17]
50 RI, Périgueux
108 RI, Bergerac

48 Brigade [disbanded 2.17]
100 RI, Tulle   6.15 to 128DI-replaced by 300 and 326RI's ex XII CA-326RI disbanded
                                       6.16 and 300RI went to 134DI 2.17

126 RI, Brive

Infantry from 2.17
50 RI
108 RI
126 RI

Artillery
Groups 1-3, 34 RAC, Périgueux
RAL Group not allocated

Cavalry
6/21 RCh, 8.14-11.15   5/21 RCh & 6/21 RCh, 7.17 only

Engineers & Pioneers
1914: Cie 12/2 du 6RG   1918: Cies 12/2, 12/52, 12/71 du 6RG Pioneer Battalion 109 RIT 8.18-

As part of the Fourth Army, the division assembled at Givry-en-Argonne on 11th August 1914. From there it moved north towards Neufchateau via Rarecourt and Malandry. During the battle for the Ardennes it fought at Pin and Izel [21st August], at Nevraumont and Rossart [22nd], and at St Medard and Deux-Villes [23rd]. By the 26th the division was back on the line of the Meuse where it fought at Mouzon [27-28th] and retreated to Ballay. After a brief counter-attack at Semuy, the retreat continued via Voncq to Somme-Py and then on to Vitry-le-Francois. Enroute, it fought at St Souplet and Ste Marie a Py [2nd September].

During the first battle of the Marne at Vitry, the division took part in heavy fighting at Courdemanges and Chatel Roual St Laurent, from which it advanced towards Laval and Wargemoulin. Dug in between Somme- Tourbe and Suippe it fought near Wacques and Aubérive from 8th September. After the front stabilised, it remained there until 20th October when it moved to the line between Marquises and Baconnes: it moved to Auberive on 28th December.

The division joined First Army in Lorraine on 25th March 1915 and fought in the battle for the Woevre at Regnieville and Remenauville. After a rest near Toul, the division arrived in Artois on 19th July. Under command of Tenth Army, it conducted mining operations between Ecurie and Neuville-Saint-Vaast, and attacked Thélus on 25th September. At the end of the month, the division moved to the eastern outskirts of Arras, between Roclincourt and the Scarpe. On 7th October it returned to Neuville-Saint-Vaast, and fought at Folie Farm on 11th October and 30-31st October. The division was withdrawn from Tenth Army on 13th April 1916 and moved to Verdun.

It joined the battle for Verdun on 4th April and sent elements in a variety of engagements between Marre, Charny and the Meuse until 27th June. On 28th June, the division joined Fifth Army west of Reims, and took over the Pontoy-Troyon sector on 17th July. Two months later the division came out of the line and division spent two tours in line between Barleux and Belloy-en-Santerre. After it was replaced by British troops it enjoyed a brief respite in the Argonne.

Between February and October 1917 the division served in the Champagne under command of Fourth Army. It served between Maisons and Courtine from 25th Febraury; between Aubérive and Suippes from 22nd March –during which period it took part in the battle of Moronvillers; between Courtine and Côte 1983 from 28th April, and between Aubérive and the Suoain-St Marie road from 12th July until 7th October.

With the other units of XII CA, the division was sent to Italy on 15th November 1917. It arrived at Verona on 28th January 1918, and moved up to the Asiago plateau on 19th March. There, around Meltar and Prunno, it resisted the Austrian attack of 15th June. During the autumn of 1918 it engaged the Austrians around Monte Sisemal. As part of the Allied offensive from the Piave, it attacked Monte Sisemol and Monte Longara [31st October-1st November]. After the armistice, the division pulled out to rest at Castelfranco.

25 Division d'Infanterie

An active division in 1914 as part of XIII Corps d'Armée, with headquarters at St Étienne

Commanders
02.08.14-Gaston Delétoille
08.09.14-Henri Chandezon
17.09.14-Georges Demange
18.05.15-Eugene Debeney
04.04.16-Camille Lévi
11.05.17-Jules Gratier

24.08.18-Joseph Joba

49 Brigade [6.15 –brigade to 120DI and replaced by 75 Brigade]
38 RI, St Étienne/Lyon   6.15 to 120DI
86 RI, Le Puy/Lyon   6.15 to 120DI
75 Brigade   [joined 6.15-replaced by 105 RI ex 26DI 12.16]
5 RdMTM
9 RdMTM   7.15 to 38DI-replaced by 1RdMZ ex 38DI

50 Brigade [disbanded 12.16]
16 RI, Montbrison
98 RI, Roanne

Infantry from 12.16
16 RI
98 RI   .18 to 48DI
105 RI

Artillery
Groups 1-3, 36 RAC, Clermont-Ferrand
Group 11, 113RAL   [added 12.17-retitled Group 5, 113RAL 2.18]

Cavalry
5/3 RCh, 8.14-11.15;   7/3 RCh, 1-7.17
Engineers & Pioneers
1914: Cie 13/1 du 4RG   1918: Cies 13/1, 13/51, 13/21 du 4RG Pioneer Battalion 106 RIT 8.18-

On 10th August 1914, the division assembled at Epinal for First Army's planned offensive. It advanced towards Sarrebourg via Rambervillers, Baccarat and Cirey and fought at Montigny and Ancerville on 14th August. During the battle for Sarrebourg [20th August] the division fought at Schneckenbusch-Oberhammer and Broudersdorf from which it retreated towards Mortange. From the 25th the division was engaged in heavy fighting at Romont, St Maurice-sur-Mortagne, Rovil- aux-Chenes until the front stabilised, briefly, at Xaffevillers on 1st September. Two weeks later the division's retreat had taken it to Epinal and on to Dreslincourt from where it entrained for Picardy.

The division joined Sixth Army on 16th September and engaged the Germans at Ribécourt, Ecouvillers, Elincourt-Ste-Marguerite, Machermont and Attiche. Then it established a line between Lassigny and Beuvraignes and fought at the Bois des Loges. It remained in this scetor until 18th January 1916, during which time it fought in the Bois Triangulaire [18th December 1914] and Massif de Thiescourt [30th September 1915].

After a two month rest, the divison entered the battle for Verdun on 7th March 1916. It resisted German attacks on the 14th and 16th March but moved back to Picardy on 19th March.

From 21st April, under command of Tenth Army-then Third Army-the division occupied the trenches between Pernant and Hautebraye until 27th September. It joined in the battle for the Somme on 15th October, when it took over the Lihons-Lihu sector, from which, it attacked Pressoire on 7th November. The division spent a further period in the line between Maucourt and the Amiens-Chaulnes railway line [25th November-13th December]. After a brief rest in Lorraine, the division moved to the river Matz front between Plessis-du-Roye and Canny-sur-Matz on 27th January 1917. It followed up the German withdrawl to the Hindenburg Line with a move forward via Lassigny to the Crozat Canal line, and took part in the attack on St Quentin on 13th April. From 7th May until 1st July 1917, the division held the sector between Urvillers and Grugies.

The division returned to operations in the Avocourt-Esnes-Malancourt sector, west of Verdun, on 25th July. From there it attacked Mort Homme and Avocourt during the second French offensive before moving to the Argonne on 23rd September. It remained between the river Aire and the Four de Paris until 8th December. Six days later it crossed to the right bank of the Meuse and took up positions between Bezonvaux and Damloup where it remained until 6th April 1918.

The division's tour of duty in Verdun continued with a three month spell in the trenches in the Ravines de Meuse sector between Forges and Côte 344. It left this sector on 18th July.

On 27th July 1918, as part of Tenth Army, the division took part in the second battle of the Marne when it became involved in action at Plessier-Huleu. Two days later it fought at Grand-Rozoy and reached the river Vesle on 4th August. Thereafter it established an new line on the left bank of the Vesle between Braine and Vasseny. During Tenth Army's move forward to the Hindenburg Line, the division crossed the Aisne canal and took Vailly on 16th September. While the division rested between 29th September and 31st October, HQ Third Army took over from HQ Tenth Army. The division rejoined the battle on 31st October and fought near Montcornet until the Armistice.

26 Division d'Infanterie

An active division in 1914 as part of XIII Corps d'Armée, with headquarters at Clermont-Ferrand

Commanders
02.08.14-Gustave Silhol
20.08.14-Ferdinand Blazer
26.08.14-Stephane Pillot
30.09.14-Louis Hallouin
07.07.15-Charles Pauffin de Saint Morel
27.10.17-Paul Toulorge
28.02.18-Jean de Belenet

51 Brigade [disbanded 12.16]
105 RI, Rion   12.16 to 25DI-not replaced
temporary attachment- 3RdeM du 1REI ex 28DI 4-7.15 –when disbanded

52 Brigade [disbanded 12.16]
92 RI, Clermont-Ferrand
139 RI, Aurillac

Infantry from 12.16
92 RI
121 RI
139 RI

Artillery
Groups 1-3, 16 RAC, Issoire
Group 8, 113RAL   [added 6.18-formerly Group 4, 311RAL]

Cavalry
6/3 RCh, 8.14-11.15

Engineers & Pioneers
1914: Cie 13/2 du 4RG   1918: Cies 13/2, 13/52, 13/71 du 4RG Pioneer Bn 170 RIT 8.18-

The division joined First Army in the Foret d'Epinal on 11th August 1914 and immediately advanced via Raon-l'Etape, Badonvillers and Cirey-sur-Vezouve towards Sarrebourg. It fought at Cirey on the 14th and at Hartzwiller on 20th-21st after which it moved to join the battle for Morhange. During this this latter conflict it was engaged in combat at Voyes and Dompstadt.

In the battle for Mortange, it fought at Domptail, Menamont and Doncierre. After its front stabilised at Angiemont on 2nd September, the division was pulled out of the line and sent with XIII CA to join the newly-formed Sixth Army in Picardy.

From 15th September, with Sixth Army, and then with Second Army [from 21st September] it fought to stem the German offensive between the Somme and the Oise. After fighting at Carlpont, Elincourt, Ste Marguerite and Lassigny, it established a front between Thiescourt and Lassingy.

On 11th November 1914 the division moved to Flanders and two days later was involved in heavy fighting in the Ypres salient at Zonnebeke after which it established a trench system in Polygon Wood. There it beat off at German attack on 27th November and counter-attacked on 29th November. Taken out of the line on

2nd December, the division moved back to Second Army in Picardy. It took over a sector between Beuvraignes and the Amiens-Roye road on 24th December 1914 and remained there until 4th October 1915. On 3rd November in moved to a new sector, closer to the Oise, between the Bois-des-Loges and Andechy and, after a brief rest, moved to the adjacent sector between the Bois-des-Loges and Belval.

In response to the German attack on Verdun, the division moved there on 22nd February 1916 and organised support defences in the Bois d'Avocourt and at Malancourt. 52 Brigade d'Infanterie was detached and fought in the Bois de Cumieres between 7th and 14th March. On 28th March, the division was pulled out of Verdun for a long rest in Picardy.

On 11th July 1916, as part of Tenth Army, the division entered the battle of the Somme at Maucourt, and attacked at Lihons and Chaulnes on 4th and 6th September, and at Pressoire on 13th November.

Rested in Lorraine from 30th November, it moved to the First Army on the Oise on 17th January 1917. From a position between Ecouvillon and Thiescourt it followed up the German retreat to the Hindenburg Line. After crossing the Crozat canal it fought at Essigny-le-Grand on 3rd and 4th April, and attacked towards St Quentin on the 13th April. It occupied new positions between Urvillers and Grugies, and then between Gruigies and between Grugies and Sélency until 15th July. The division returned to Verdun on 18th August 1917 to participate in the second French offensive, during which the division attacked Côte 304 and then occupied a line between Bethincourt and Haucourt. It moved to the Argonne on 31st August and took up a position between Avocourt and Revigny, which it held until Christmas Day. After rest and retraining, the division took over the trenches between Bezonvaux and Damloup on 2nd February 1918 and remained there until 4th May.

On 15th May, the division joined Fifth Army and was thrown into the third battle of the Aisne at Troesnes and Ferté-Milan and succeeded in securing the area, which it held until 20th June. Two days later, the division moved to Lorraine and re-entered the line between Paroches and Koeur-la-Grande, at the apex of the St Mihiel salient. From a position in the Calonne sector, it took part in the American-led attack on the St Mihiel salient on 12th September, and it advanced to Hattonchattel. Then the division moved north to Verdun and took over poisitions in the Bois de Caures. Under American command, it fought in the Bois de Caures on 18th October, in support of the advance on Monfaucon. From 3rd November, the division was in reserve at Liverdun.

27 Division d'Infanterie

An active division in 1914 as part of XIV Corps d'Armée with headquarters at Grenoble

Commanders
02.08.14-Joseph Baret
28.08.14-Ferdinand Blazer
13.01.15-Georges de Bazelaire
03.11.15-Edmond Legrand
08.06.16-Joseph Barthelemy
08.06.17-Edouard Roux

53 Brigade [disbanded 11.16]
75 RI, Romans
140 RI, Grenoble
14 BCA   11.14 to Group Serret-not replaced

54 Brigade [disbanded 11.16]

52 RI, Montélimar
157 RI, Gapseille to 44DI on mobilisation
7 BCA, Draguignan   11.14 to Group Serret,
                                      5.15 replaced by 415RI ex 155DI
                                      11.16 415RI to 163DI

Infantry from 11.16
52RI
75 RI
140 RI

Artillery
Groups 1-3, 2 RAC, Grenoble/Valence
Bie/1RAM   11.14 withdrawn without replacement Bie/2RAM   11.14 withdrawn without
                                      replacement Group 6, 114 RAL [added 3.18]

Cavalry
5/9 RH, 8.14-11.15;   3/9 RH, 1.17-7.17

Engineers & Pioneers
1914: Cie 14/1 du 4RG   1918: Cies 14/1, 14/51, 14/21 du 4RG

The division assembled at Lepanges on 9th August 1914 and immediately attacked the passes in the Vosges: the Col du Bonhomme and the Col du Sainte-Marie. After heavy fighting on the 13th and 16th, the division moved via the Saales to Schirmeck, fought at Salm and Vauquernous, and took up defensive positions on the Col de Praye and the Col de Han. The division came down from the mountains on 24th August and moved to the Meurthe, to redeploy for the battle of Mortagne. During the battle it fought at Raon- l'Etape and St Blaine-la-Roche and then moved back to the Meurthe to engage the Germans at Etival, St Remy, Nampatelize, Bourgonce, La Salle and Croix-Idoux. On 11th September it was involved in a two day attack on Senones and Raon-l'Etape after which it was withdrawn and moved to Picardy.

As part of Second Army, it became involved in heavy fighting at Maucourt [24th September], Chaulnes, Lihons and Vermandovillers in order to secure the Santerre and the approaches to Amiens. After the front stabilised it occupied a sector between Maucourt and Herleville where it counter-attacked on 17-20th December. The division remained in this area until 8th August 1915.

The division moved to Champagne and took over the line between Perthes and Bois Sabot, from which position, as part of Second Army, it took part in the second battle of Champagne. After the attack on Côte 193 [25th-29th September], the division was pulled out of the line and sent to Lorraine for retraining. It returned to the Vosges on 10th January 1916 and occupied positions at Hartmanswillerskopf, from which it was drawn to the battle at Verdun on 28th February.

In the line between Souilly and Thiaumont, the division spent three tours in the trenches around Verdun: Souilly-Thiaumont 5th March-13th May; Eparges 26th June-12th August; Vaux-devant- Damloup 12th August-28th August. It absorbed a German attack on 7th July and attacked in the Bois Chenois on 18th August.

On 6th September the division joined Fifth Army, north-west of Reims, at Berry-au-Bac where it remained until 2nd January 1917 when it moved to Picardy to take up positions between Chilly and the Amiens-Roye road. It moved to the adjacent sector between the road and the Avre on 13th March and followed up the German retreat to the Hindenburg Line. After fighting at Jossy and Hinacourt, it established a new line from the north of Vendeuil to Essigny-le-Grand. After a brief tour [25th April-8th May] at Urvillers, the division moved eastwards along the Aisne to positions between Hurtebise and the Paissy to Aillees road where it sustained a German attack on 20th May.

It came down from the Chemin des Dames on 28th June and returned to Urvillers/Moy where it remained from 24th June until 28th August. After a period of retraining, the division took part in 6th Army's attack on the Moulin de Laffaux at Malmaison [23rd September]. It advanced towards the Ailette and organised new positions at Anizy-le-Chateau and Ferme Rosal. Pulled out on 8th November, the division moved to Lorraine.

The division took over positions near the Swiss border –between Leimbach and the Rhine-Rhone canal-on

14th January 1918. The German spring offensive prompted at move to Flanders, which resulted in combat between Bailleul and Locroi from 2nd May until 7th June. It took part in the struggle for the Monts de Flandres around Kemmel.

On 2nd July 1918, the division joined Fourth Army in Champagne. After a period in support near Prosnes during which elements were involved in the 4th battle of Champagne, the division took over the sector between Moscou and the Suippe. It was not involved in any major activity and moved back to Lorraine on

27th August. There it occupied a quiet sector to the east of Lunéville, between Domevre and Leintrey until it was withdrawn for retraining on 28th October. For the rest of the war the division was located at Gerbéviller preparing for Tenth Army's attack towards Metz.

28 Division d'Infanterie

An active division in 1914 as part of XIV Corps d'Armée with headquarters at Chambéry

Commanders
02.08.14-Henri Putz
07.09.14-Emile Sorbets
19.03.16-Raoul Peillard
03.04.17-Jean Graziani
12.12.17-Jean Madelin

55 Brigade [disbanded 11.16]
22 RI, Santhony/Bourguoin
99 RI, Lyon/Vienne

56 Brigade [disbanded 11.16]
30 RI, Annecy
97 RI, Chambéry to 44DI on mobilisation
11 BCA, Annecy   1.15 to 47DI without replacement
3 RdeM du 1RE Added   12.14-to 26DI
                                     4.15-replaced by 416RI ex 154DI
                                     11.16 416RI returned to 154DI
51, 53, 62 BCA's 8.14- fom 74DI-to Gp Serret or Bordeaux 11.14

Infantry from 11.16
22 RI
30 RI
99RI

Artillery
Groups 1-3, 54 RAC, Santhony
Bie/1RAM   11.14 withdrawn without replacement
Group 5, 114RAL   [added 2.18-formerly Group 11, 114RAL]

Cavalry
6/9 RH, 8.14-11.15

Engineers & Pioneers
1914: Cie 14/2 du 4RG   1918: Cies 14/2, 14/52, 14/71 du 4RG Pioneer Bn 112 RIT 8.18-

The division's first task after assembly at Docelles on 10th August 1914 was to seize the passes across the Vosges at the Col d'Urbeis and Hingrie. This involved fierce fighting at Ste Marie-aux-Mines between 13th and 16th August, the seizure of Ville next day, and then an attack towards Schirmeck and fighting at Rothau and Bourg-Bouce. On 24th August the division moved back to the Meurthe and then on to the Dan-de-Sapt and Provencheres-sur-Faye for further action. During the First Army's battle for Morhange, the division attacked moved towards Saales and fought at Grandrupt and Menil. Then, on 27th August, it had to retreat behind the Meurthe and fight at Anozel and the Kemberg from which it moved forward on 11th September towards Laitre and Grosse-Fosse and took St Dié. On 14th September the division disengaged and moved to Picardy with the rest of Second Army.

On arrival in the Santerre the division fought the first battle of Picardy at Foucaucourt, Rainecourt and Herleville from 24th September, and then established a front line between Herleville and Frise. It remained here and fought actions on 17th October, 28th November and 1st December, before a move to a new sector near Dompierre and Carnoy on 8th April 1915.

On 1st August 1915 the division pulled of the line and left for Champagne with Second Army. After labour duties at St Remy sur Bussy, the division entered the line south-west of Perthes on 27th August. When the second battle of Champagne began on 25th September, the division attacked and took Trou Bricot and advanced on Côte 193. It renewed its assault on this position on 6th October and occupied new ground near the Butte de Souain.

The division left the front-line on 15th October and arrived in the Vosges where, after a rest, it took over positions between Altkirch and Burnhaupt-le-Bas where it remained until 29th Janaury 1916. A month later, the division moved to Verdun and went into action on 2nd March at Châtillon-sur-Côtes and Villers-sur Bonchamp. It moved to Thiaumont on 19th April and sustained heavy German attacks on 29th April and 7th May. After another period of rest, it returned to the Chatillon-Damloup sector, and elements of the division supported the offensive, which took the Damloup battery on 24th October. The division left Verdun on 29th December and arrived in Picardy on 15th January 1917.

The division occupied the area between Armancourt and the Avre and operated with British units in the move up to the Hindenburg Line, which began on 17th March. It fought at Roupy and Essigny-le-Grand and then established a new line between them. After a rest, which began on 2nd May, the division moved closer to Noyon and took up positions between Cerny-en-Laonnais and the Paissy-Ailette road on 5th May. It repulsed German attacks on 11th and 20th May before the tour ended on 22nd June. On 17th July, the division became part of Third Army between La Fere and Moy, and moved to Sixth Army's sector on the Aisne at Clavigny on 23rd August. This was followed by a move to Laffaux on 17th September, from which the division attacked between Laffaux and Bessy during the attack on the Malmaison on 25th October. It advanced to the Ailette and took up new positions between Qunicy Basse and Pont D'Anizy-le-Chateau, where it remained until 7th November.

On 8th January 1918 the division arrived in Belfort to take up positions between Fulleren and the Rhine- Rhone canal where it remained until called to Flanders in response to the German spring offensive. After its arrival on 9th April the division fought at Mont Kemmel on 15th April and then was engaged in heavy fighting around Locre and the Clytte until 27th May.

The division joined the Fifth Army during the third battle of the Aisne. From 30th May it was engaged north of the Ardre, resisted German attacks on Bligny, and organised a new sector between there and St Euphraise which was attacked on 6th June. A week later the division arrived at Lunéville for a quiet spell in the line between Embermesnil and the Sanon. From there it moved back towards the Marne region on 4th September to rejoin Fifth Army. Moved to Fourth Army, at the Epine de Vedegrange the division attacked towards Somme-Py on 20th September. It attacked Ste Marie a Py 26th September-3rd October and then, with 5th Army, attacked at Prunay and Mont Cornillet and pursued the Germans to the Selle. From 19th October, it advanced towards the Serre and fought at Conde-les-Herpy and St Germainmont, and moved on to take the position at Gomant. From 3rd November 1918, the division was resting near Epernay.

29 Division d'Infanterie

An active division in 1914 as part of XV Corps d'Armée with headquarters at Nice [8.15 Isolee 6.17 XXXVI CA]

Commanders
02.08.14-Jean-Baptiste Carbillet
18.01.16-Arthur Guyot d'Asniéres de Salins
22.04.16-Jean-Gabriel Roquerol
18.04.17-Joseph Bernard

07.04.18-Joseph Barthelemy

57 Brigade [disbanded 5.17]
111 RI, Antibes	4.16 to 133DI-replaced by 351RI ex 72DI-disbanded 5.17
112 RI, Toulon	7.15 to 126DI-replaced by 258 RI &
	4.16-258RI disbanded-replaced by 165RI ex 72DI

58 Brigade [disbanded 5.17]
3 RI, Digne/Hyeres	
141 RI, Marseille	Attached 8-11.14
6 BCP	11.14 to Group Bordeaux
23BCP	9.14 to 74DI
24BCP	11.14 to Gp Bordeaux
27BCP	9.14 to 74DI

Infantry from 5.17
3 RI
141 RI
165 RI

Artillery
Groups 1-3, 55 RAC, Orange	
Group 12, 118RAL	[added 12.17-retitled Group 5, 136RAL 3.18]

Cavalry
5/ 6RH, 8.14-11.15   7/10RD & 8/10RD, 11.15-8.16   8/10RD & 4/11RD, 8.16-7.17

Engineers & Pioneers
1914: Cie 15/1 du 7RG   1918: Cies 15/1, 15/51, 24/21 du 7RG Pioneer Battalion 63 RIT 8.18-

The division joined Second Army at St Nicholas-du-Port on 14th August 1914 and, on the same day. Advanced towards Dieuze where it fought the Germans in a three-day battle [17th-19th]. On the 20th it became involved in the battle for Morhange when it fought at Bidestorf, north-east of Dieuze and at Parroy- Damelievres.On the 25th it attacked towards Mortagne between Nermamenil and Lamath, and next day fought at Xermamenil for control of the Grand Couronne. From this point, the division was forced to retreat to the Meurthe, and then southwards towards Revigny, which it reached on 3rd September.

Tranferred to Third Army on 6th September the division fought at Vassincourt during that army's operations at Revigny, during the first battle of the Marne. By 16th September the division was enaged at Malancourt between Verdun and the Argonne. As the front stabilised it fought between Avocourt and Vauquois to establish the northern shoulder of the Verdun salient.

From then, until 26th March 1916, the division remained in line in the Verdun salient. After an attack on Forges on 28th October 1914 it established positions between Bethincourt and the Meuse, and returned to Malancourt on 6th November where it remained, with minor adjustments for the next sixteen months.

As a total contrast, the division was allocated to Nieuveport on the Belgian coast on 17th April 1916. It rested, retrained and was employed on labour duties near Beauvais from 8th October and then returned to Nieuveport on 10th January 1917, where it endured a major German gas attack on 23rd April. After a long rest outside Calais from 20th June, the division went up into the Ypres salient, as part of the French component of Haig's Third Battle of Ypres. It occupied positions near Langemark [12th September-6th October], and at Klosterschool and Drie Grachten [6-13th November] and returned to Nieuveport on 16th November. It was relieved by British troops on 4th January 1918.

After a long period in GQG reserve, the division joined First Army in Picardy on 25th March. It sought to stem the German advance towards Amiens. It fought at Hangard and along the line of the Luce, and at Bois Senecat until 14th April.

By 1st May 1918 the division was back in Verdun where it held positions between Bezonvaux and Damloup until 23rd August. Two days later it joined Third Army in the Oise front at Laffaux where it prepared for the assault on the Hindenburg Line. It attacked Vauxillon on 14th and 15th September. After a month's rest [4th October-2nd November] it joined Third Army for the final push towards the Meuse, from Vervins to Signy- la-Petit: it was regrouping between Marle and Vervins when the Armistice came into effect.

30 Division d'Infanterie

An active division in 1914 as part of XV Corps d'Armée with headquarters at Avignon [8.15 –XXXVIII CA until 12.16]

Commanders
02.08.14-Francois Colle
03.10.14-Paul Berge
15.09.15-Jean Castaing
03.11.17-Jean Sarda
01.05.18-Alphonse Monterou
22.05.18-Antoine Nérel

59 Brigade [disbanded 12.16]
40 RI, Nîmes
58 RI, Avignon
173RI, Corsica   added 8.14-1.15 to 12DI]

60 Brigade [disbanded 12.16]
55 RI, St Esprit/Aix   6.15 to 126DI-replaced by 240RI which was disbanded 12.16
61 RI, Privas/Aix

Infantry from 12.16
40 RI
58 RI
61 RI

Artillery
Groups 1-3, 19 RAC, Nîmes
Group 1, 2RAM   [added 12.16] Group 5, 136RAL[added 3.18]

Cavalry
6/6RH & 5/7RD, 8.14-11.15;   5/10RH & 6/10 RH 2.16-12.16;
7/25RD & 8/25RD 12.16-1.17;   E/5RCA 1.17-11.18

Engineers & Pioneers
1914: Cie 15/2 du 7RG   1918: Cies 15/2, 15/52, 23/21 du 7RG No pioneer battalion allocated 1918

The division concentrated at Vezelise on 8th August. As part of Second Army, it moved forward to cover the Serres between Pissot and the Sanon. It fought at Langard on the 10th and advanced eastwards to a further fight at Coincourt on the 14th. It moved back four days later and fought at Vergavillers, north-east of Dieuze, on 20th August, in the battle of Morhange. After further action near Dombasle and Rosieres, it set up a line at Hauteurs de Saffais, from which it attacked Dameleviers, Blainville-sur-Eau and Mont-sur-Meurthe. During the battle for the Grand Couronne, it engaged the Germans at Mont-sur-Meurthe and Heriménil, after which it joined the general retreat southwards towards Revigny and Bar-le-Duc.

On 3rd September, the division, as part of XV CA, transferred to Third Army and four days later fought around Bar-le-Duc. From there it advanced northwards to Malancourt and helped establish what became the northern shoulder of the Verdun salient. Based between Malancourt, Avocourt and Forges from 16th September 1914 until 8th May 1915, the division attacked the Bois des Forges on 220th-22nd December and on 17th February. It was attacked at Malancourt on 20th February.

After a brief rest, the division transferred to Champagne and occupied the line between Massiges and Ville- sur-Tourbe from 23rd May until 14th August. It moved to the eastern outskirts of Reims at St Leonards on 20th August where it remained until 22nd September. It was held in reserve at Jonchery during the second battle of Champagne. It made a brief appearance south of the Butte de Souain [9th-14th October] and resumed its operations on the eastern and northern defences of Reims on 4th November where it remained until 6th June 1916. It rotated into three sectors during this period: St Leonards-Neuvillette [4th November- 20th March]; St Leonards-Marquises [20th March-10th April]; and Bois de Zouaves [from 10th April].

On 22nd June 1916 the division arrived in the Verdun salient and took over positions between the Meuse and the Bois d'Haudromont where it remained until 20th August. It joined Fifth Army on the Aisne between Soissons and Pernant on 25th August and moved to the Troyon-Moulin Pontoy sector on the Chemin des Dames on 16th September where it remained until 16th December 1916.

After a movement via Toulouse, the division arrived in Salonika on 30th January 1917. After a period of training and acclimatisation, the division moved forward the line between Elchisu and Banista on 15th April. It moved to Jivana on 5th May and after a brief rest in Greece moved into Macedonia on 14th July. It fought at Monastir, Côte 1248 and Crete Baba Planina, during August and remained there until the Allied offensive of 15th September 1918. In that operation it pursued the enemy forces north of Lake Okrida to the Massif de Yablantia. After the Bulgarian armisticve on 30th September, the division moved through Bulgaria to Sistova. It was part of the Army of the Danube on 11th November 1918.

31 Division d'Infanterie

An active division in 1914 as part of XVI Corps d'Armée with headquarters at Montpellier

Commanders
02.08.14-Jean-Jacques Vidal
15.10.15-Henri de Cadoudal
02.01.17-Pierre Martin

61 Brigade [disbanded 8.16]
81 RI, Montpellier
96 RI, Beziers

62 Brigade [disbanded 8.16]
122 RI, Rodez
142 RI, Mende/Lodeve   6.15 to 124DI-replaced by 322RI ex XVI CA-disbanded 8.16

Infantry from 8.16
81 RI
96 RI
122 RI

Artillery
Groups 1-3, 56 RAC, Montpellier
Group 11, 116RAL   [added 12.17-retitled Group 5/116RAL 3.18]
Cavalry
5/1RH, 8.14-11.15;   1/1RH & 2/1RH 1.17-7.17

Engineers & Pioneers
1914: Cie 16/1 du 2RG   1918: Cies 16/1, 16/51, 16/21 du 2RG Pioneer Battalion 35 RIT 8.18-

After assembly at Mirecourt on 10th August, the division moved to Lunéville, from where it joined Second Army's offensive into Lorraine. It advanced via Xousse and Mazieres to Loudefring and fought at Rombach on the 17th and at Salins and Leuderfrim on the 18th. During the battle for Morhange, the division moved towards Bayon [21st] and fought at Bonviller [22nd]. As part of the move back, the division fought at Grebwiller in the battle for the Grand Couronne [25th]. On 12th September the division moved southwards to a position east of Lunéville.

Transferred to First Army, the division retreated via Nimey and arrived at Royalmeix on the 21st, and, from there was engaged in the battle of Flirey. It fought at Bernicourt, Beaumont, and at Seicheprey until the front stabilised; and then established a line between Bois Mort Mare and Flirey.

On 12th October 1914, the division began to move to Flanders. It arrived in the Ypres salient on 26th October and was thrown into action between Wallemolen and Poelkapelle. After heavy fighting it established a sector between Zwatelen and St Eloi. It moved to the adjacent sector between St Eloi and Hollebecke on 8th December and attacked the German lines on 15th-16th December. The division was pulled out of the salient on 3rd February 1915.

A month later, it entered Fourth Army's line in Champagne between Côte 196 and Beauséjour where it fought in the first battle of Champagne 12th-20th March. It was still in this sector when the second battle of Champagne began on 25th September. From Valmy it attacked towards the Butte de Tahure and Côte 173. On 14th October it moved to the Côte 193-Souain sector where it participated in a series of attacks and counter-attacks 14th-17th December. It was withdrawn for rest and retraining on 26th December.

After a two month break in Fifth Army's training area, on 20th February 1916, the division took over the sector along the Aisne between Condé-sur-Aisne and Moussy where it remained until 9th July. Transferred to Verdun, the division was committed to the line before the Ouvrage de Thiaumont on 29th July; it resisted German attacks on 8th August. After a short break, the division moved to the Argonne where it engaged in extensive mine warfare between the Haute Chevauchée and the river Aire from 4th September until 16th December. In the following months, the division edged closer to Verdun: at Avocourt 16th December-1st February 1917; before Mort Homme 27th February-2nd July; between Chattancourt and the Meuse 20th July until 1st September. It attacked towards Mort Homme during the second French offensive on 20th August and consolidated gains between Bethincourt and Forges. After this very long period of activity in Verdun, the division rested in Lorraine during September and October 1917.

On 5th November 1917, the division re-entered the line, between Burnhaupt-le-Haut and Leimbach in the Vosges and remained there until 7th February 1918. Employed on labour duties, the division moved to Flanders on 31st March as part of the response to the German spring offensive. It was thrown into the action around Locre on 29th April and helped to consolidate positions in the heights to the south of Ypres until 17th May.

It moved back to Lorraine on 30th May and was committed to the Brin/Bezange-la-Grande sector in Lorraine on 2nd June. It began the move to the Aisne on 23rd August and joined Tenth Army four days later. From 3rd September, it attacked positions on the Hindenburg Line and moved across the Ailette to take Quincy Basse and Bois Mortier. On 12th October it attacked the Massif St Gobain and moved on to the Serre. By 5th November the division was resting in the Ourcq region where it was employed on labour duties at the time of the Armistice.

32 Division d'Infanterie

An active division in 1914 as part of XVI Corps d'Armée with headquarters at Perpignan

Commanders
02.08.14-Achille Bouchez
28.02.17-Guillaume Daydrein

63 Brigade [disbanded 5.17]
53 RI, Perpignan   6.15 to 124DI-replaced by 342RI ex XVI CA-disbanded 5.17
80 RI, Narbonne

64 Brigade [disbanded 5.17]
15 RI, Albi
143 RI, Carcassonne

Infantry from 5.17
15 RI
80 RI
143 RI

Artillery
Groups 1-3, 3 RAC, Castres
Group 6, 116RAL   [added 4.18-formerly Group 14/116RAL]

Cavalry
6/ 1RH, 8.14-11.15;   3/1RH & 4/1RH, 1.17-7.17

Engineers & Pioneers
1914: Cie 16/2 du 2RG   1918: Cies 16/2, 16/52, 16/71 du 2RG Pioneer Battalion 35 RIT 8.18-

Once assembled at Mattaincourt on 11th August 1914, the division joined Second Army's offensive into Lorraine. It advanced via Veho and Auricourt to Angwiller and then participated in the battle for Morhange [20th] during which it fought at Mulhwald and then moved on to Bremoncourt. In the battle for the Grand Couronne [25th] it counter-attacked towards the Mortange and took the town after fighting at Einvaux, Rozelieures and the Bois de Bareth. It moved to Einville on 13th September and, as part of First Army, began the retreat for days later when it moved to Essey-le-Nancy, and from there, to Arainville [21st September]. During the battle for Flirey [23rd] it fought at Bois de Vorsogne, Flirey and Mort Mare. When the front stabilised it occupied a line between Flirey and Seichesprey where it remained until 6th October.

After a brief stay on the Aisne front between Moussy and Paissy the division arrived in Flanders on 29th October. It joined the battle for the Ypres salient north of Wijtschate and fought between there and St Eloi until 8th January 1915. It took part in French attacks at Wijtschate on 13th and 17th December.

After a rest in Artois, the division joined Fourth Army in Champagne on 11th February and entered the line east of Souain on 6th March. It was involved in mine warfare in the Bois de Sart between Côte 196 and Mesnil until 26th August. On 25th September, it took part in the second battle of Champagne when it attacked Mont Tetu and then Bois Marbeau and Chausson. From 6th October it consolidated new positions between the Main de Massigies and the Maisons de Champagne; it attacked the Butte de Tahure- unsuccessfully-on 31st October and moved into reserve a week later.

As part of Fifth Army, the division re-entered the line along the Aisne between Venizel and Pernant on 25th January 1916 and remained there until 9th July when it moved to the Argonne for rest and retraining. On 13th August, the division moved into the Thiaumont-Vaux Chapitre sector in the heights above Verdun and, from there, attacked on 23rd and 29th August. It moved back to the Argonne and went into line between Four de Paris and the Haute Chevauchée on 16th September where it engaged in extensive minewarfare along the river Aire until 17th January 1917.

The division remained in the Verdun sector for most of 1917. It undertook four tours in the trenches: Hayette-Bois Canard 21st January-15th March; Hayette-Avocourt 11th April-20th June; Mort Homme 30th July-30th August; and Bethincourt-Forges 30th August-6th November. It repelled a German attack on Côte 304 on 25th January, and supported the second French offensive on 20th August.

The division moved to the Vosges, and undertook labour duties until it entered the line between Leimbach and Burnhaupt-le-Haut on 3rd Febraury 1918; It attacked Aspach-le-Haut on 23rd February but was pulled out on 27th March for a move to Flanders in response to the German spring offensive.

It arrived in Flanders on 28th April and joined battle at the Clytte on 4th May and engaged in fierce fighting in the high ground on the southern flank of the Ypres salient, especially at Côte 44 and Kleine Vierstraat until 16th May. Then the division moved to Nancy and took over positions in the Lorraine front between Brin and Clémery on 31st May. It moved to the Aisne on 20th August.

The division joined Tenth Army's battles on the Hindenburg Line on 28th August when it attacked up the right bank of the Ailette towards Coucy-le-Chateau. From 6th September it organised new positions between the Fôret de St Gobain, Quincy Basse and Fresnes. When the offensive restarted on 12th October, the division entered the Fôret de St Gobain and took Couvron-et-Aumencourt and Pouilley-sur-Serre and then consolidated its gains. Now part of 3rd Army, the division advanced towards the Meuse on 3rd November and had reached Cul des Sartes by 11th November 1918.

33 Division d'Infanterie

An active division in 1914 as part of XVII Corps d'Armée with headquarters at Montauban

Commanders
02.08.14-Jean-Francois de Villemejane
31.08.14-Louis Guillaumat
09.12.14-Francois Desvaux
14.01.15-Auguste Blanc
02.06.15-Nicolas Delmotte
17.01.16-Auguste Eon
18.02.18-Edmond Buat
30.03.18-Albert Tanant

65 Brigade [disbanded 5.17]
7 RI, Cahors   7.15 to 131DI-replaced by 207RI ex XVII CA-disbanded 5.17
9 RI, Agen

66 Brigade [disbanded 5.17]
11 RI, Montauban
20 RI, Marmade

Infantry from 5.17
9 RI
11 RI
20 RI

Artillery
Groups 1-3, 18 RAC, Agen
Group 6, 117RAL   [added 4.18-formerly Group 14/117RAL]

Cavalry
5/9 RCh, 8.14-11.15;   4/9 RCh 1.17-7.17

Engineers & Pioneers
1914: Cie 17/1 du 2 RG   1918: Cies 17/1, 17/51, 17/21 du 2RG Pioneer Battalion 110 RIT 8.18-

On 11th August 1914, the division joined Fourth Army at Suippes and then moved north to Grand-Pré and Mouson to join in that army's attempts to hold off the Germans in the Ardennes. On 22nd August the division fought at Ochamps, Foret de Lucht and Bertrix, and then pulled back to Bouillon and then to Mouzon where the retreat stopped on the 26th. After fighting at Autrecourt-et-Pourron and Pourron-et- Raucourt, the division pulled back from the Meuse and reached the Aisne at Voncq on the 29th. It continued to move back through St Marie-a-Py, St Etienne-aux-Temple and Chepy to Dompierre, which it reached on the 31st.

During the first battle of the Marne, Fourth Army fought to hold positions around Vitry, which involved 33DI in fighting at Grandes Perthes and then attacking towards Beauséjour and Mesnil where the front ground to a halt. From 13th September, the division established and held positions between Beauséjour and the Hurlus from which it took part in the first battle of Champagne on 20th December. From 20th Janaury 1915 it was engaged in the Mesnil-Moulin de Perthes sector and made attacks on Perthes on 15th-16th February and 10th March. After a period of consolidation it withdrew on 3rd April and moved to Artois.

The division joined Tenth Army on 28th April and entered the line between Ecurie and Roclincourt on 1st May. During the second battle of Artois it attacked Thélus, on the eastern flank of Vimy Ridge and then moved to the Roclincourt-Agny sector outside Arras on 20th May. Here it remained until 2nd March 1916. It attacked Beauvrains on 29th September during the third battle of Artois.

Rested from 2nd March, the division entered the line between Arracourt and the Sânon in Lorraine on 9th April and remained there until 19th April when it moved back to the Champagne and took over positions between Maisons de Champagne and the Butte de Mesnil. It attacked German positions on 15th May and 22nd June. On 4th July the division disengaged and moved to Verdun.

From 13th July, the division was involved in heavy fighting at Thiaumont and Vaux Chapitre in the heights above Verdun. It attacked on 24th July and fought at Fleury 2nd -3rd August. Then it moved to the Bois d'Haudromont sector where it took part in the French offensive of 24th October. Rested from 25th November it moved to the Champagne region on 4th March 1917.

From its sector between Prosnes and Aubérive, it took part in Fourth Army's battle for Moronvilliers at Teton and Casque. Another move began on 3rd May and the division took over the Koeur-la-Grande to Etang de Vargevaux sector of the St Mihiel salient. It remained there until 15th November when the division began a move to Verdun.

In the Bezonvaux-Bois de Chaume sector from 10th December, the division moved to the Calonne- Haudiomont-Damloup sector on 28th February 1918, and then moved to the Bezonvaux-Beaumont sector on 18th May. After intense fighting on 27-28th May it was pulled out on 6th June.

The division was transferred to Sixth Army for the second battle of the Marne when it fought in the sector between Troesnes and Faverolles [29th June], and then between Neuilly-St-Front and Mont-Notre-Dame [18th July].

After a brief rest which began on 1st August, the division joined Tenth Army for the battle for Noyon [27th August]; it helped free the line of the Ailette and moved up to the Hindenburg Line via Coucy-le-Chateau and Fresnes. It was in line between Fresnes and Barisis-aux-Bois 12th-28th September, and took part in the attack on Mont-d'Origny [17th October] during which it fought at Thenelles and Oringy-Ste-Benoite. After a period in the support role, it occupied Momignes and Beauwetz during the second battle of Guise [2nd November]. On 11th November 1918 it was resting at La Capelle.

34 Division d'Infanterie

An active division in 1914 as part of XVII Corps d'Armée with headquarters at Toulouse

Commanders
02.08.14-Henri Alby
11.04.15-Paul de Lobit
14.12.17-Victor Savatier

67 Brigade [disbanded 5.17]
14 RI, Toulouse   7.15 to 131DI-replaced by 209RI ex XVII CA-disbanded 3.17
83 RI, St Gaudens

68 Brigade [disbanded 5.17]
59 RI, Foix/Pamiers
88 RI, Mitrand/Auch

Infantry from 5.17
59 RI
83 RI
88 RI

Artillery
Groups 1-3, 23 RAC, Toulouse
Group 12, 117RAL   [added 1.18-retitled Group 5/117RAL 5.18]

Cavalry
6/9 RCh,8.14-1.17;   6/9 RCh, 1.17-7.17

Engineers & Pioneers
1914: Cie 17/2 du 2RG   1918: Cies 17/2, 17/52, 17/71 du 2RG Pioneer Battalion 27 RIT 8.18-

The division, as part of XVII Corps d'Armee joined Fourth Army at Somme-Bione on 11th August 1914 and moved immediately via Apremont to Jehonville to engage the Germans. During the battle for the Ardennes [22nd August] it fought at Jehonville, Offagne and Bertrix. It retreated back to the Meuse at Villers-devant- Mouzon and fought at Remilly and Thelonne on the left bank of the river on the 26th. From there it retreated to the Aisne at Semny, and then moved southwards via Attigny, St Souplet, St Hilaire-aux-Temple and Mairy-sur-Marne.

During Fourth Army's part in the first battle of the Marne at Vitry, the division fought at Ferme Certine and at Ferme Perrier [6th –11th September] and then advanced via Cheppes and Poix to Perthes-les-Hurlus. It remained at Perthes until 2nd April 1915. During this time it fought the Germans on 13th and 26th September and mounted an attack on Le Bonnet-du-Preter on 8th December. During the first battle of Champagne it took Perthes on 8th January and carried out further attacks on 16th February and 18th March.

On 5th May the division entered Tenth Army's sector at Roclincourt, north of Arras. During the second battle of Artois it attacked Thélus on 9th, 16th and 20th May after which it moved to Blagny to continue the battle between the Scarpe and Roclincourt. It attacked St Laurent on 25th September and then moved to the Agny-Ficheux sector, and then on 3rd November, it returned to Roclincourt. The division left Arras on 4th March 1916 and travelled to Lorraine for a period of training and rest.

It arrived in Verdun on 23rd March 1916, and fought in the Bois d'Avocourt from 27th March until 24th June when in moved to the Champagne. On 29th June it took over the sector between the Butte de Mesnil and Maisons de Champagne from which it mounted an attack on 20th July, In changed sector on 8th August- to Marquises/Moscou and resisted the German attack on the Ouvrages de Marquises on 10th October. It endured a 'severe' gas attack on 31st January 1917.In the spring it took part in Fourth Army's battle for Moronvillers when it attacked Mont Blond and Mont Cornillet.

On 24th April 1917 the division moved to line between Verdun and St Mihiel and occupied trenches between Paroches and the Bois Loclont. It moved into the Verdun salient on 13th November and fought there until 31st March 1918. During the winter it fought at the Bois de Caurieres, Bois de Chaume, Bethincourt-Forges [2nd January-4th March], and between Eparges and Calonne [12th-31st March].

In response to the German spring offensive, the division arrived in Flanders on 18th April and fought near Danouter to prevent the Germans taking control of the Mont Noir heights. Successful in this task, the division returned to Lorraine on 3rd May.

From 22nd May it occupied the line between the Etang de Vargevaux and Paroches until 12th August when it moved to Picardy. There, it joined First Army near Lihons on 24th August where it replaced British troops, and advanced towards the Hindenburg Line near Chaulnes. It moved against St Quentin on 5th September and fought at Savy Dallon [13-18th September] and took up positions on the Ham-St Quentin road. On 7th October it moved to Itancourt and attacked Mont- d'Origny on 15th October when the line of the river Oise was freed as far as Longchamps and Noyal, It was engaged in the second battle of Guise on 4th November after which it went into reserve.

35 Division d'Infanterie

An active division in 1914 as part of XVIII Corps d'Armée with headquarters at Bordeaux

Commanders
02.08.14-Charles Exelmans
04.09.14-Albert Marjoulet
03.10.14-Francois Bonnier
07.05.15-Alfred Cornille
06.11.16-Paul Bonet
16.06.17-Henri Mareschal

69 Brigade [disbanded 10.17]

6 RI, Saintes   6.15 to 123DI-replaced by 249RI ex XVIII CA-disbanded 10.17
123 RI, La Rochelle

70 Brigade [disbanded 10.17]
57 RI, Libourne
144 RI, Bordeaux
Infantry from 10.17
57 RI
123 RI
144 RI

Artillery
Groups 1-3, 24 RAC, La Rochelle
Group 5, 118 RAL   [added 3.18-formerly Group 14, 118RAL]

Cavalry
5/10 RH, 8.14-11.15;   5/10 RH & 7/10 RH, 7.17 only

Engineers
1914: Cie 18/1 du 2 RG   1918: Cies 18/1, 18/51, 18/21 du 2RG Pioneer Battalion 27 RIT 8.18-

Under prewar plans, 35DI, as part of XVIIICA was to join Second Army but, after the division's concentration at Pagny-la Blanche Côte, the Corps was switched to Fifth Army on 18th August. As a result the division moved to Liesson and, from there, advanced to the Sambre via Beaumont and Fontaine Valmont on 21st August. During the battle of Charleroi the division fought at the latter location and at Lobbes. They were forced to retreat and subsequently moved back to Parpeville via Avesnes and Nouvien to fight the battle of Guise on 29th August. Thereafter, it continued to retreat towards the Marne via Chevressis-les-Dames, Alnois-sur-Laon, Dormans and Tréfols to Villers-St-Georges.

During the fight for the Deux Morins, in the first battle of the Marne, the division fought at Montceaux-les-Provins and Sancy-les-Provins from where it began to advance on 10th September to Chateau-Thierry, Mareuil-en-Dole and Breuil-sur-Vesle to the Aisne. From 14th September it was involved in heavy fighting at Corbeny, Craonne, Ville aux Bois and Choléra. After a short move to Beau Maris and Craonnelle, it occupied the line between Temple and the Pontoy. After sustaining a German attack on 26th September, it counter-attacked at Vauclerc on 12th and 14th October.

From 17th October 1914 until 16th April 1916, the division occupied the sector along the Aisne, between Moussy and Paissy, and, was engaged in many local actions. It moved to the Argonne for a rest on the latter date.

On 2nd May 1916 the division arrived in Verdun and fought between the Etang de Vaux and the Ferme de Thiaumont until 20th May when it returned to rest in the Argonne. It joined 3rd Army's line between Four de Paris and the Ravin de la Houyette on 9th June and remained there until 2nd October.

The division re-entered the line in Tenth Army's front between Berny and Belloy-en-Santerre on Christmas Day. It remained in trenches adjacent to those held by the BEF until 12th Febraury 1917. After a rest, it spent two weeks in line near the Avre, had another spell of retraining, and joined the line on the Aisne on 4th April. As part of Tenth Army-Nivelle's breakthrough force-it remained at Fismes and at the Plateau d'Ailles, until 22nd April when it took up positions between Vauclerc and Hurtebise. It fought on the Plateau du Casemates on 5th and 6th May. On 6th June, it left the Chemin des Dames for the Swiss Frontier, which it observed between 8th July and 12th September. On 5th October it joined 4th Army at Valmy and was put into the line between Côte 193 and the Souain/Ste Marie-a-Py road until 4th March 1918.

As a result of the German spring offensive, the division joined Third Army on 23rd March 1918 for the defence of positions on the Oise during the first battle of Noyon where it was involved in heavy fighting at Mont Renaud [25th-30th March] and at Missy-aux-Bois [31st March]. Pulled out of line on 9th May it moved to Sixth Army on the Aisne on 30th May. During the third battle of the Aisne, the division fought off German attacks on Missy-aux-Bois. After a brief rest in the Argonne, the division occupied the line between the Aire and Beauvrain until relieved by Italian troops on 12th August.

After the division joined First Army in Picardy on 20th August, it relieved British troops between the Chavatte and Chilly and advanced to the Hindenburg Line on the 27th. It fought at the Ingon on 29th-31st August and then crossed the Somme and advanced towards St Quentin on the 4th September. It took positions between Savy and Dallon on the 6th where it remained until the 15th. After a month-long rest at La Fère, the division attacked Mont-d'Origny on 16th October and moved to the line of the Serre two days later. Between 18th and 30th October it attacked German positions north and south of Péron and advanced towards Ferte-Chevresis. From there it went into reserve at La Fère on 2nd November 1918.

36 Division d'Infanterie

An active division in 1914 as part of XVIII Corps d'Armée with headquarters at Bayonne

Commanders
02.08.14-Théophile Joannic
19.09.14-Simon Bertin
19.08.15-Charles Lestoquoi
10.08.16-Gabriel Paquette
26.04.18-Eugene Mittelhauser

71 Brigade [disbanded 5.17]
34 RI, Mont-de-Marsan
49 RI, Bayonne

72 Brigade [disbanded 5.17]
12 RI, Tarbes   6.15 to 123DI-replaced by 218 RI ex XVIII CA-disbanded 5.17
18 RI, Pau

Infantry from 5.17
18 RI
34 RI
49 RI

Artillery
Groups 1-3, 14 RAC, Tarbes
Group 11, 118RAL   [added 12.17-retitled Group 6, 118RAL, 3.18]

Cavalry
6/10 RH, 8.14-11.15;   6/10 RH & 8/10 RH, 7.17 only

Engineers
1914: Cie 18/2 du 2RG   1918: Cie 18/2, 18/52, 18/71 du 2RG
Pioneer Battalion 117 RIT 8.18-

Originally intended to join Second Army, the division concentrated at Coussey on 9th August but was diverted with the rest of XVIII CA to Fifth Army on the 18th. Two days later, from Solre-le-Chateau, the division moved north to the Sambre and became involved in the battle for Charleroi.

It fought at Gozée and Biesme-sur-Thuin and was forced to retreat on the 24th. It moved back to Villers-le- Sec via Beaumont and St Algis, and fought at Ribemont during the battle of Guise [29th]. The retreat continued via Cerny-les-Bucy and Anizy-le-Chateau to St Martin-des-Champ.

During the first battle of the Marne, the division fought with Fifth Army for control of the Deux Morins at Rupereux and Marchais-en-Brie [6th-9th September]. Success here was followed by an advance north- eastwards via Chateau-Thierry, Villers-en-Fère and Magneux to Craonnelle. During the first battle of the Aisne [14-26th September], the division fought at the eastern end of the Chemin des Dames between Craonnelle and Hurtebise, after which, it established a line between Moulin Pontoy and Hurtebise. It remained in this sector until 24th April 1916. During this long stay, it was attacked by the Germans on 25th January 1915 and then attacked near the Feule de Caverne.

On 27th April 1916 the division joined Second Army for duty in the Verdun salient. It entered the line between Thiaumont and the Etang de Vaux on 20th May but remained only for one week before a movement to the Argonne. From 20th June until 22nd September it occupied positions between the Ravin de Huyette and the Aisne. This was followed by a long period of rest and retraining after which it joined Tenth Army in Picardy and occupied trenches between Genermont and Berny from 22nd December 1916 until 12th January 1917. After relief by the British, the divison was held in reserve for Nivelle's offensive.

On 22nd April 1917, the division took over the sector between Craonne and Vauclerc, and, under command of Tenth Army, took positions along the Chemin des Dames between Craonne and the California plateau on 4th and 5th May. It held those positions against German counter-attacks until 15th June. After a brief rest, the division was allocated to the Belfort sector at the southern end of the Vosges. There, it went into the line between Leimbach and the Rhine-Rhone canal on 8th July and remained there until 12th September.

The division joined Fourth Army in Champagne on 1st October and remained there until 7th March 1918. After a brief tour between Auberive and the Souain/Ste Marie-a-Py road, it spent most of this period between Mamelles and Côte 193. It played a part in the seizure of the Plateau de Galoches on 13th February.

The division was in reserve when the German spring offensive began and it was moved to Picardy where it joined Third Army on 24th March. It fought in the second battle of Picardy south of Ayencourt, and resisted German attacks on Ployron, Courcelles-Épayelles, and Domfront, and retook Assainvillers and Ayencourt [28-29th March]. When the front stabilised it held the line between Ayencourt and Tronquoy. From 15th April it held the Rollet/Vaux sector and fought in the battle of Matz at Ployron and Courcelles-Epayelles [9th June].

On 21st June the division moved to the Argonne for rest and retraining, after which it held the line between the river Aire and the Bois d'Avocourt until 26th August. The division joined 10th Army's advance to the Hindenburg Line on 15th September where in fought for the Plateau de Pinon and then established new positions between the Fôret de Pinon and the Ailette. When the offensive restarted on 12th October, it attacked the Massif de Laniscourt and took Verneuil sur Serre [19th October]. From 25th October until the end of hostilities, the division was in Thid Army reserve at Crèpy-en-Valois.

37 Division d'Infanterie

Formed as Constantinois Division, on mobilisation, from units stationed in Algeria [XIX Corps] [10.14-6GDR 12.14-XXXV CA 8.15-VII CA 7.16-?]

Commanders
02.08.14-Louis Comby
00.06.15-Léon Deshayes de Bonneval
00.02.16-Henri Niessel
00.11.16-Noel Garnier-Duplessix
06.06.18-Henri Simon

73 Brigade [disbanded 7.18]
RdM 2Z (3 bns) 3.15 retitled 2RMZ
RdM 2T (2 bns) & RdM 5T (1bn) 	9.14 retitled 1RdMT
	4.15 retitled 2 RdMT RdM 6T (2bns)
	9.14 amalgamated into 1 RdMT

74 Brigade [disbanded 7.18]
RdM 3Z (3 bns) 3.15 retitled 3RdMZ
RdM 3T (3 bns) & RdM 7T (1bn)	9.14 retitled 2RdMT 4.15 retitled 3RdMT
7.18 to 51DI

Infantry from 7.18
2 RdMZ
3 RdMZ

2 RdMT

Artillery
Groups 1-3, RACA
Group 12, 117RAL　　　　　　　　　　　　　[added 2.18-retitled Group 7/117RAL 3.18]

Cavalry
1-4/6 RCA 10.14 to Bde Prov de Ch'dAfrique
6/11RCh & 7/11 RCh, 8.15-10.16; 3 /1 RD & 4/1 RD, 10.16-11.18

Engineers & Pioneers
1914: Cie 8/17, 8/22 du 4RG, Cie 19/1 du 19BG
1918: Cie 19/1, 19/51 du 91BG, Cie 7/17 du 7BG Pioneer Bn 38 RIT 8.18- [reserve bn 7.17-]

After transfer form Algeria, the division joined Fifth Army at Rocroi on 15th August 1914. It advanced with X CA towards the Sambre via Mareimbourg and Philippeville and engaged the Germans at Fosse and Mettet during the battle for Charleroi [22-23rd August]. It retreated throught Florennes, Hirson, Nampcelles and Lugny and fought in the first battle of Guise on the 29th, and continued to retreat towards the Marne via Laon, Fismes and Verneuil.

In the first battle of the Marne it fought at Courgivaux on 6th September and was transferred to the newly- formed Sixth Army at Compiègne three days later. Fighting along the line of the Oise, it engaged the Germans at Cuts, Pommeraye and Lombray during the first battle of the Aisne [15th September] and repulsed the Germans at Tracy-le-Val [26th September]. As the front stabilsied the division established positions at Quennevières and remained there until 9th July 1915. It took part in local attacks on Quennevières [30-31st October], Tracy [17th November] and St Mard [21-25th December], and Ferme Quennevières [6th and 18th June 1915]. The division's last month with 6th Army was spent in the line between Quennevières and Moulin-sous-Touvent.

After a six week rest the division joined Fourth Army in Champagne of 30th August at St Hilaire-le-Grand where it fought in the second battle of Champagne. It moved to the Epine de Vedegrange on 25th September and went into reserve on 2nd October.

On 12th February 1916 the division took over positions facing Louvement, the Côte de Talou and the Côte du Poivre in the heights above Verdun, and was heavily engaged during the first days of the German attack on Verdun. Pulled out on 26th February, the division was moved to Avocourt-Bois Carré on the leftbank of the Meuse on 13th April and then to Souville, up above Verdun, on 12th July. It attacked towards Fleury on 15th-17th July and was pulled out of the salient on 29th July.

On 12th August 1916 the division joined the relatively quiet sector between Pont-a-Mousson and Armaucourt in Lorraine but moved back to Verdun on 27th September. It fought at Douaumont, in the Bois de Chaume and Bois de Caurieres from 30th October until 20th December. A further long period of rest and recuperation followed. The division arrived in the outskirts of Reims on 14th February 1917 and held positions at Chevaliers-de-Courcy and Neuville, from which it attacked Mont Spin and the Bois de Sechamps on 16th April, during the second battle of the Aisne. The division left Reims on 22nd April.

The division held positions in Lorraine between Moncel and the Sanon [22nd May-8th August] and then spent two months resting and retraining near Toul and Bar-le-Duc. It returned to Verdun on 1st October, and became heavily involved in the French offensives around the city. It fought at Damloup and in the Bois de Caurieres, and later, at Côte 344 until 6th December. It spent the winter in Lorraine along the Seille between Chenicourt and Clémery.

In response to the German spring offensive, the division moved to Picardy and joined 1st Army in its defence of the approaches to Amiens. It fought at Hangard and Villers-Bretonneux [29th April] and remained there until relieved by the Australians and Canadians on 2nd August. During the allied offensive it fought at Hailles and the Bois Senécat [8th August] and took part in the second battle for Noyon [27th August]. It pursued the Germans and established positions east of Tergnier, which it held until 27th September. On 23rd October it advanced to La Fere and then on to the river Serre [26th October] and held positions at Herle-la- Vieville. It participated in the second battle of Guise [4th November] and moved north towards the Meuse. On 11th November 1918 the division was located near Sologne and Baileux.

38 Division d'Infanterie

Formed as the Algérois Division, on mobilisation, from units in Algeria [XIX Army Corps] [10.14-XXXII CA-1.15]

Commanders
02.08.14-Paul Muteau
13.09.14-Jean-Marie Brulard
12.10.14-Georges de Bazelaire
13.01.15-Alexis Hély d'Oissel
21.05.15-Jean-Gabriel Rouquerol
22.04.16-Arthur Guyot d'Asnières de Salins
16.10.18-Julien Dufieux

75 Brigade [withdrawn 1.15 for re-organisation-to 25DI 6.15]
RdM 1Z (3 bns)	12.14 formed 1RdMZ
	1.15 to 76Brigade and replaced by 5RdMT RdM 1T (1 bn)
	12.14 amalgamated into 3RdMT
RdM 9T (2bns)	12.14 formed 3RdMT
	3.15 retitled 9RdMT
	6.15 to 25DI

76 Brigade [disbanded 7.18]
RdM 4Z (4 bns)	12.14 retitled 6RdMZ and then 4RdMZ in 1.15
RdM 4T (2bns)	10.14 to DM –not replaced
RdM 8T (2 bns)	12.14 formed 5RdMT & to 75Bde
	1.15 replaced by 1RdMZ -to 25DI
	7.15 replaced by 8RdMT

Brigade de Fusiliers Marin [replaced 75 Bde 1.15] [returned to Navy 3.16]
1 Fusiliers Marin
2 Fusiliers Marin

4 Marocain Brigade 12.15-disbanded 7.18
RdMICM
4 RdMZT
Somali Bn attached 9.16-9.17 and 4.18

Infantry from 7.18
4 RdMZ	
8 RdMT	9.18 to 56DI-replaced by 10 Gp de Chasseurs
RICM	8.18 to 2DM
4 Mixte	

Artillery
Groups 1-3, 32 RAC	
Group 12, 115RAL	[added 1.18-retitled Group 8/117RAL 2.18]

Cavalry
1-4/5 R Ch d'Afrique   10.14 3 sqns to Bde Prov de Ch d'Afrique
E/5 RCA, 10.14-10.15;   1/9 RCh & 2/9 RCh, 4.16-6.17;
E/6 RCA & E/6 RCA,   6.17-11.18; Half E/6RCA & E/5RS, 11.18-

Engineers & Pioneers
1914: Cie 19/2 du 19BG, Cie 1/29 du 3RG
1918: Cies 19/2, 19/52 du 19BG, Cie 1/25 du 3RG Pioneer Battalion 74RIT 8.18-

The division arrived from Algeria on 18th August to join Fifth Army. It moved to the Sambre via Froidchappelle and Walcourt, and fought at Châtelet and Somzée on the 22nd. After the battle of Charleroi it joined 5th Army's retreat to the Marne. It retreated through Sains-Richaumont via Chevresis and fought at the first battle of Guise [29th August]. After fighting at Ribemont it continued the retreat to Provins via Chavonne, Treloup and Montmirail. In the first battle of the Marne, it remained in the second line until the Army's began to advance on 10th September towards the Chemin des Dames. During this advance it fought at Chateau-Thierry and Fisme, and during the first battle of the Aisne, it fought between Hurtebise and Paissy for control of the Chemin des Dames. After combat at the Ferme de la Cruete [12th October] it was pulled and transferred to Flanders on the 26th.

It entered the struggle for Ypres on 29th October and was engaged in heavy fighting at Luychem, Bikschote and the Maison de Passuer from which it established a line along the Yser. During December it fought at Verbrandenmolen and Hollebecke. On 17th January 1915 the division went into the line at Nieuvepoort, and remained there until 29th April 1916.

The division joined the struggle for Verdun on 30th May 1916 and during the ensuing six months fought at Côte 304 and Avocourt, at Thiaumont from 3rd August, at Haudriomont from 21st October and at Louvement from 15th December until 20th December. It seized Fort Douaumont on 24th October.

After a period of retraining south of the Aisne, the division joined 6th Army on 3rd February 1917. It was held in reserve until 15th April when it attacked near Jumigny and took German positions south of the Ailles, from which it repulsed an attack on the 25th. The division was pulled back into reserve on 29th April and remained in that state until 20th August. It took up positions between the Pantheon and Colombe until 18th September. Another rest was followed by the attack on Malmaison on 23rd October.

From 31st October 1917 until 25th April 1918 the division was employed on labour duties in the Marne region.

On the latter date it moved to Picardy to join Third Army's fight for the Matz; there it resisted German attacks on Orvillers and Sorel. Regrouped and retrained, it moved to the Oise on 8th May.

During the third battle of the Aisne it occupied the line between Sempigny and Varesnes and then attacked Mont de Choisy. After a period in line between Tracy-le-Val and Bailly [11th June-14th July] it moved to Chavigny and attacked positions along the Aisne front at Longpont and then advanced to Hartennes [14th- 23rd July]. It returned to the Oise on 4th August and from its line between Belly and Bois St-Mard fought in the second battle of Noyon [19th August]: it attacked between Carlpont and the Oise between Noyon and Pontoise.

On 6th September, the division moved to the Vosges for rest and retraining. On 22nd September it occupied the line between Fulleren and Burnhaupt-le-Grand, which was extended to the Swiss frontier before the division move north to Lorraine on 2nd November. At the end of hostilities, it was resting and retraining between Épinal and Remiremont.

39 Division d'Infanterie

An active division in 1914 as part of XX Corps d'Armee with headquarters at Toul

Commanders
02.08.14-Georges Dantant
16.11.14-Louis Curé
13.03.15-Pierre Nourrison
25.10.16-André Massenet
02.06.18-Aramnd Pougin

77 Brigade [disbanded 12.16]
146 RI, Toul
153 RI, Toul

78 Brigade [disbanded 12.16]
156 RI, Toul

160 RI, Neufchateau 12.16 to 160DI-not replaced
Infantry from 12.16
146 RI
153 RI
156 RI

Artillery
Groups 1-3, 39RAC, Toul
Group 12, 104RAL   [added 2.18-retitled Group 6/120RAL 4.18]

Cavalry
6/5 RH, 8.14-11.15;   2/5 RH, 1.17-7.17

Engineers & Pioneers
1914: Cie 20/2 du 10RG   1918: Cies 20/2, 20/52, 20/71 du 10RG Pioneer Battalion 132 RIT 8.18-

As part of XX CA, the division concentrated near Moncel, to cover the assembly of Second Army. On 14th August it advanced towards Morhange via Chateau-Salins and fought at Morhange on the 20th, after which, it retired to the rightbank of the Moselle at Ville-en-Vermois. It fought at Crevic, the Bois d'Einville, Courbessaux and Drouville during the struggle for the Grand Couronne [24th August]. On 13th September it retreated to Manoncourt-en-Woevre and then on to Toul which it reached on 19th September. From there it moved to Picardy with Second Army.

On 25th September the division fought at Fonquescourt, south of Somme, and moved north of Albert to fight at Fricourt and Mametz. It moved north to the Ancre to engage the Germans at Fonquevillers and Hebuterne on 22nd-23rd October.

The division arrived in the Ypres salient on 3rd November and fought south of the town, between Wijtschate, St Eloi and Kruistraat until 16th November, when it moved towards Langemark, and attacked at Woolemolen on 11th December. From 3rd March 1915 it occupied positions between Polygon Wood and the Ypres/Roulers railway until 12th April.

As part of Tenth Army, the division went in line at La Targette, on the slopes of Vimy Ridge, on 18th April and took part in fighting there on 9th May. From 27th May until 7th July the division held the lines in the Neuville-Saint-Vaast/Ecurie sector where it attacked on 16th June.

After a period of rest near Lunéville, the division joined Fourth Army in the Beaséjours sector. During the second battle of Champagne it fought at Maisons de Champagne and attacked and occupied the Ouvrage de la Defaite until 26th December.

Retrained near Revigny, the division arrived in Verdun on 25th February 1916 and took up positions between the Meuse and Douaumont where it was heavily engaged until 12th March. It moved to the Côte 304 sector on 31st March and endured German attacks between 7th and 10th April. On 21st April it left Verdun for Picardy.

In line north of Maricourt, the division took part in Sixth Army's offensive on the Somme on 1st July 1916.

It attacked Hardecourt-aux-Bois, and, on 25th July, attacked north of Maurepas, and again there on 30th July and 8th August. Rested from 10th August, it took over the Sailly-Saillisel sector on 14th November and remained there until relieved by British troops on 7th December.

After a brief rest in Lorraine, the division took over the Troyon-Moussy sector of the Aisne front on 25th January 1917. It retrained at Chateau-Thierry from 15th February and re-entered the line at Moussy-Chivy on 20th March. From there it attacked Braye-en-Laonnaise on 16th April-the second battle of the Aisne and consolidated positions between Malval and Courtecon. It moved to the Epine de Chevregny/Malval sector on 16th May and to Lorraine on 5th June. From 25th June, it occupied the Pont-a-Mousson/Brin sector. It remained with Eighth Army and transferred to the Chenicourt/Clemery sector on 15th October. From 4th November 1917 until 3rd January 1918 the division retrained near Toul.

Between 10th January and 29th March 1918 the division faced Côte 344 outside Verdun and then moved to Flanders in response to the German spring offensive. It arrived at Mount Kemmel on 25th April and struggled to hold the ridge between Kemmel and the Clytte until 6th May.

By 26th May, the division was to be found near Soissons struggling to contain the German attack across the Aisne on Sixth Army. It fought between Couvrelles and Soissons until 3rd June. Then it trained American forces near Paris and rejoined Sixth Army for operations at Chateau-Thierry on 22nd June. If fought there and towards Vaux on 1st-6th July and took Chateau-Thierry on 21st July.

Withdrawn from Sixth Army on 30th July it moved to Verdun where it took over the sector between the Etang de Vargevaux and Chauvoncourt on 8th August. On 13th September, under American command, it took part in the battle of St Mihiel. It attacked between the Etang de Vargevaux and the Bois d'Ailly and established new positions between Hattonchattel and the Bois de Chaufour. From 28th October, the division rested near Toul and, on 9th November, began preparations at Nomeny for Tenth Army's planned advance on Metz.

40 Division d'Infanterie

An active division in 1914 as part of VI Corps d'Armée with headquarters at St Mihiel [1.15-XXXII CA]

Commanders
02.08.14-Emile Hache
15.08.14-Gaston Leconte
19.12.16-Louis Bernard
19.09.17-Joseph Laignelot

79 Brigade [disbanded 12.16]
154 RI, Leronville	12.16 to 165DI-replaced by 251RI ex 69DI
155 RI, Commercy	12.16 to 165DI- not replaced
26 BCP, Pont-a-Mousson	6.15 to 127DI via 12DI

80 Brigade [disbanded 12.16]
150 RI, St Mihiel
161 RI, St Mihiel/Reims
25 BCP, St Mihiel — 6.15 to 127DI
29 BCP, St Mihiel — 6.15 to 127DI

Infantry from 12.16
150 RI
161 RI
251 RI

Artillery
Groups 1-3, 40 RAC, St Mihiel
Group 5, 132RAL [added 3.18-formerly Group 14/120RAL]

Cavalry
5/10 RD & 6/10RD, 8.14-10.15; 2/20 RCh, 1.17- 7.17

Engineers & Pioneers
1914: Cie 6/2 du 9RG   1918: Cie 6/2, 6/52, 4/22 du 9RG Pioneer Battlion 145 RIT 8.18-

After assembly at Flirey on 14th August 1914, to cover the crossing of the Moselle at Pont-a-Mousson, the division moved northwards to Fresnes-en-Woëvre to join Third Army's defence of the Ardennes. It attacked towards Crusnes and Joppécourt [21st August], and fought at Fillieres, Ville-au-Montois and Mercy-le-Haut. It moved further west on the 25th to Chaumont-devant-Damvillers to cover the Meuse crossings, and arrived in the Argonne at Romagne-Monfaucon on the 31st August. Next day the division moved via Elize-la-Petite to Ivoiry and Rampont.

During the first battle of the Marne, it participated in Third Army's struggle around Revingy and fought at Deuxnouds-devant-Beauzee, Courcelle-sur-Aire and Neuville-en-Verdunois on the northern approaches to Verdun. It moved via Souilly to Ville-devant-Chaumont, on 14th September, and then on to Troyon-sur-Meuse, on the 20th, where the front stabilised. It held the sector between Maizey and Suezey until 17th December. During this period it attacked German positions on 16th and 17th November.

On 9th January 1915 the division took over the sector between Bagatelle and the Vienne/Binarville road in the Argonne. Apart from mine warfare, it repulsed German attacks on Bois Grurie [29th January], Bagatelle [7th February], Binarville [20th-21st June] and Bagatelle [30th June]. Elements took part in the French attacks north of Vienne on 14th –17th July, after which, the division moved to the nearby sector between the Four de Paris and Fontaine-aux-Charmes where it repulsed an attack on 2nd August. The division left the Argonne on 11th August, and moved westwards to join Fourth Army in Champagne.

The division took over the St Hilaire-le-Grand sector on 29th August and participated in the second battle of Champagne when it attacked on 25th September and 6th October. It remained in this sector until 30th December 1915. After a rest the division returned to the front-line on 21st Febraury 1916 when it took over the Courtine-Tahure sector. This tour was cut short and the division was pulled out a week later and retrained for operations at Verdun.

It arrived in the line between Bethincourt and Mort Homme on 15th March. Elements were engaged in the Bois de Corbeaux on 8th April and on 22nd April the division was attacked north of Cumieres. It endured German attacks from the Mort Homme position on 23rd-30th May and then left for Lorraine on 2nd June. Three weeks later it took over the quiet sector in Lorraine between St Agnant and the Meuse, only to move further east to positions between the Chapelotte and Vezouve on 7th August. The division went into reserve on 21st August, prior to a move to Picardy, where it arrived on 11th September.

The division joined Sixth Army during the battle of the Somme and fought between Frégicourt and St-Pierre-Vaast from 20th September. It advanced on Sailly [1st-4th October] and took the position [7th-15th October]and repulsed a German counter-attack on 17th October. On 5th November, it took over the line between Sailly-Saillisel and Rancourt where it engaged in hard fighting until 17th November when the division left for a rest in the Argonne. From 29th December 1916 until 28th January 1917, the division held the sector between the Aisne and the Maisons de Champagne.

In anticipation of Nivelle's offensive, it joined Fifth Army outside Reims on 5th February. During that offensive it attacked the Mont de Sapigneul and Côte 108 and then took over the line between Berry-au-Bac and the Miette. The division went into reserve on 6th June.

It was back in the Verdun on 21st July 1917 and remained there until 24th September. After a tour of the trenches between Damloup and the Bois de Caurieres it move to the Beaumont-Fosse sector on 27th August. From Verdun the division moved south to Clemery and the Bois de la Pretre where it remained until 23rd May 1918.

It was arrived back at the Montagne de Reims on 28th May and fought at Fleury-la-Riviere during the third battle of the Aisne. Further heavy fighting took place in the same area from 15th July when it was engaged at Bois du Rois, Fleury-la-Riviere, Cuchery and Basilieux-sous-Chatillon.

On 20th July it returned to Lorraine where it rested until 21st August. Between that date and 15th October, the division occupied the quiet sector between Bezange-la-Grande and Brin.

The division joined Fourth Army on 19th October, and took part in the offensive towards Vouziers and Conde-les-Vouziers which began on 30th October. It reached Chesne on 5th November and had closed up to the Meuse near Sedan, when the Armistice came into effect.

41 Division d'Infanterie

An active division in 1914 as part of VII Corps d'Armee with headquarters at Remiremont [8.14-Isolee 10.14-XXXIV CA 12.14-Isolee 7.16-VII CA]

Commanders
02.08.14-Paul Superbie

03.09.14-Desirée Bataille
13.09.14-Edouard Bolgert
22.09.14-Georges Claret de la Tour
17.09.16-Paul Mignot
17.06.17-Pierre Guignabaudet
31.05.18-Pierre Bablon

81 Brigade[12.14 to 66DI]
152 RI, Gérardmer
5 BCP, Remiremont
15 BCP, Remiremont

82 Brigade[disbanded 9.17]
23RI, Bourg
133RI, Belley   6.17 to 23DI –replaced by 42RI ex 14DI
46BCA   8.14 added from Gp de Vosges-5.15 withdrawn

152 Brigade [added 9.14 from Interior]
363 RI   9.17 to 161DI
373 RI   6.16 disbanded
37 RIC   6.15 to 16DIC, 3.16 replaced by 229RIex 66DI
                             11.17 replaced by 128RI ex 3DI
70 BCA   5.15 withdrawn
41 BCA Added   2.15-from 71DI: 3.16 to 66DI

132 Brigade [added 12.14 from 66DI] [6.16 to 76DI then 63DI –disbanded 10.16]
215 RI   11.15 to 161DI
253 RI   11.15 to 161DI
343 RI   6.16 disbanded
22 BCA   5.15 withdrawn

Infantry from 9.17
23 RI
42 RI
128 RI

Artillery
Groups 1-3, 4 RAC, Remiremont
Group 6, 107RAL [added 2.18-formerly Group 8/107RAL]

Cavalry
6/11 RCh, 8.14-8.15;   7/11 RCh, 8.14-12.14;   7/14 RD & 8/14 RD, 8.15-1.16
1/3 RCh & 2/3 RCh 1.16-6.17;   2/3 RCh, 1.16-6.17

Engineers & Pioneers
1914: Cie 7/2 du 7BG   1918: Cies 7/2, 7/52 du 7BG, Cie 13/24 du 4RG Pioneer Battalion 54RIT 8.18-

As part of VII Corps d'Armee the division mobilised on 4th August 1914 to cover the passes in southern Alsace at the Col de la Schlucht and Col de Bussang. Three days later it advanced towards Mulhouse but was forced to retire back to Rougemont-le-Château and Massevaux on the 10th. On the 14th, as part of the Armee d'Alsace, it returned to Mulhouse and fought at Dornach on the 19th. A further retreat began on the 24th and the division fell back to Gérardmer. It was involved in heavy fighting at Arnould [29th August] and attacked northeards towards the Cols Maudray and Journaux. On 13th September, it moved via St Dié to the line between Lesseux and Fontenelle and engaged in further heavy fighting for the Massif de l'Ormont between Spitzenburg, Charemont and Forain. When the front line stabilised, the division remained in the Vosges between the Chapelotte and the Fave. It fought at Chapelotte during February and March 1915; for Côte 637 on 22nd June; at Laonnais on 24th July; and at Chapelotte on 25-26th April 1916.

On 11th June 1916, the division finally left the Vosges and moved to Picardy. It joined Sixth Army's line between the Bois de Hem and the Somme on 16th July; and attacked between Hem, Monaru and the Bois de Riez on 31st July, 7th and 8th August. On 27th August it moved to the Forest/Cléry sector and attacked towards Bouchavesnes on 3rd September: it took Bouchavesnes on 12th September, and then, two days later, pulled out for a rest in the Argonne region.

The division took over the Fourth Army's sector between the Four de Paris and Vienne-le-Chateau on 29th September and remained there until 31st December. The division moved westwards to 5th Army at Reims on 19th January 1917. It occupied the Sapigneul/Cavaliers-de- Courcy sector to the north-west of the city. During the second battle of the Aisne, it attacked towards Bermericourt. On 18th June it moved eastwards to the Courtine and Côte 193 and remained with Fourth Army until 16th September. On 2nd October, the division moved to 2nd Army and joined the line around Verdun at Mormont and Côte 344 on 17th October where it remained until 21st November.

Between 29th December 1917 and 22nd April 1918, the division was in Lorraine and occupied the line between the Sanon and Bezange-la-Grande. In response to the German spring offensive, it was moved to Flanders. It was pitched into the fighting around Loker on 1st May and was involved in heavy fighting there until 8th July.

During the second battle of the Marne [with rapid movements between Fifth, Tenth, Fourth and Fifth] the division fought at Villers-Cotterèts on 17th July and at Faverolles next day. It advanced to the Vesle at Oulchy-le-Château on the 25th July, and after a brief rest, it advanced on 24th August, from Soissons to the Laffaux position on the Hindenburg Line; and fought at Vailly until 21st September.

The division arrived back in Flanders on 3rd October and fought with the Belgian Army in the Cretes de Flandres, and moved forward from Poelkapelle towards Roeselare which it attcked on 14th-15th October.

From 31st October it fought with British and American forces in the advance to the Schelde. By 10th November the division had established itself on a line west of Oudenaarde.

42 Division d'Infanterie

An active division in 1914 as part of VI Corps d'Armée with headquarters at Verdun [9.14-Humbert 10.14-XXXIV CA]

Commanders
02.08.14-Martial Verraux
30.08.14-Paul Grossetti
07.11.14-Denis Duchêne
09.03.15-Louis Deville
26.08.18-Maurice de Barescut

83 Brigade [disbanded 11.16]
94 RI, Bar-le-Duc
8 BCP, Étain
19 BCP, Verdun   6.15 to 127DI-replaced by 261RI 7.16 to 64DI

84 Brigade [disbanded 11.16]
151 RI, Verdun   11.16 to 69DI-replaced by 332RI ex 69DI
162 RI, Verdun   11.16 to 69DI-not replaced
16 BCP, Conflans   To 83 Bde 1-7.15 and again in 7.15
261RI additional 6.15-7.16   [ex 150BI –to 64DI]

Infantry from 11.16
94 RI
332 RI
8 BCP

16BCP

Artillery
Groups 1-3, 61RAC, Verdun
Group 12, 116RAL   [added 12.17-retitled Group 6/132RAL 3.18]

Cavalry
7/9 RCh,11.14-11.15;   3/20 RCh, 12.16-7.17

Engineers & Pioneers
1914: Cie 6/3 du 9RG   1918: Cie 6/3, 6/53, 6/72 du 9RG Pioneer Battalion 103 RIT 8.18-

On mobilisation the division's task was to assemble on the Woevre plain to the east of Verdun and cover the concentration of Third Army. The division organised defences between Herbeuville and Eparges and then joined the movement of 3rd Army northwards into the Ardennes. On 21st August, it fought at Crusnes, at Pierrepont and Bazailles [22nd], and at Neuillonpont [24th] and then retreated towards Cheppy in the Argonne. From 29th August, the division fell back via Verdun to Villeneuve-le-Charleville.

During the first battle of the Marne, and Third Army's operations around St Gond, it fought there and at Somey-aux-Bois, Talus-St Prix and Corfélix. It advanced to Connatre on 9th September and pursued the Germans northwards towards Aubérive, which it reached on the 14th. After fighting there it engaged the Germans at Prosnes and Marquises. The division moved to Reims on the 22nd and was involved in heavy fighting around the Fort de la Pompelle on the eastern outskirts of the city; it remained in line between the fort at the suburb of St Leonards until 17th October.

The division moved to Dunkerque on that date and became involved in the struggle to retain Ypres. It fought along the Yser, inland from Nieuvepoort and towards Diksmuide, and then along the canal d'Yser at Woumen, Korrtecker, Bikschote, and Verlandenmolen until 30th December, It struggled to for control of Hill 60 on 14th and 25th December.

By 17th January 1915 the division had taken over positions in the Argonne between Four de Paris and Bagatelle where it engaged in the mine warfare and frequent local actions which were typical of the fighting in and around Vauquois until 19th July. On 31st August, the divison joined Fourth Army's sector in Champagne between Aubérive and St Hilaire-le-Grand. During the second battle of Champagne it atacked on 6th October and resisted the Germans on 15th October. From 30th December 1915 until 3rd March 1916 the division was employed on labour duties near Mourmelon.

The division took up positions between Douaumont and Haudromont, on the heights above Verdun, on 10th March. It moved to the left bank at Hayette on 6th April and enduring German gas attacks on 9th-11th April and 12th May. Pulled out on 19th May it took up positions in the quiet sector in Lorraine between the Vezouve and Parroy on 7th June. After a rest it was moved to Picardy. The division joined Sixth Army for the battle of the Somme on 19th September. It fought around Rancourt and carried out a series of attacks on 25th-30th September, and then moved northwards to the St Pierre-Vaast sector. It fought in the Bois de Reuss on 1st and 5th November.

For the remainder of 1916, the division was employed on labour duties in the Marne region. After a very brief tour in the trenches around Aubérive [6th-23rd January 1917] the division retrained for Nivelle's offensive. As part of 5th Army, the division attacked Berry-au-Bac on 18th April. Pulled out of line a month later, the division arrived at Verdun on 27th June where it occupied three parts of the line in succession; Damloup-Louvemont [27th June-18th July]; Bois de Caurieres/Chambrettes [5th August-28th August]; and Eparges/Haudiomont [17th September-5th October]. It attacked the Bois Wavrille during the French offensive of 20th August.

After a brief rest near Toul, the division occupied the line in Lorraine between Bois-de-la-Pretre and Limey from 1st November 1917 until 5th April 1918. During this period it fought a local action at Remenauville on 12th February.

The division moved to Picardy in response to the German spring offensive. As part of First Army, it fought and held the Hangard sector from 1st May. On 8th August, as part of the allied offensive from Amiens, it fought in the Bois de Moreuil and took Villers-aux-Érables and Fresnoy and moved towards Roye until withdrawn on 13th August.

A rest in Lorraine was followed by assignment to Third Army on 26th October when it advanced from Falaise and Vouziers towards Chesne. It fought at Vouziers, Chestres, Quatre-Champs and Noirval until 6th November. From that date, the division was in reserve at Courtisols.

43 Division d'Infanterie

An active division in 1914 as part of XXI Corps d'Armée with headquarters at St Dié

Commanders
02.08.14-Pierre Lanquetot
06.02.15-Léon Lombard
03.12.15-Antoine Baucheron de Boissoudy
16.10.16-René Mollandin
23.07.17-Camille Michel

85 Brigade [disbanded 12.16]
149 RI, Épinal
158 RI, Bruyeres/Lyon   7.15 to 86 Bde

86 Brigade [disbanded 12.16]
1 BCP. Senones/Troyes
3 BCP, St Dié/Besançon   7.15 to 85 Bde; 11.16 to 170DI-not replaced
10 BCP, St Dié/Langres   7.15 to 85 Bde; 11.16 to 170DI-not replaced
31 BCP, St Dié/Langres

Infantry from 12.16
149 RI
158 RI
1 BCP
31 BCP

Artillery
Groups 1-3, 12 RAC, Bruyeres   4.15 two btys replaced by two from 14RAC which became
Group 3/12RAC
Group 6, 121 RAL   [added 7.18-formerly Group 2, 321RAL]

Cavalry
6/4 RCh, 8.14-11.15 & 1.17-7.17

Engineers & Pioneers
1914: Cie 21/2 du 11RG   1918: Cies 21/2, 21/52, 21/71 du 11RG Pioneer Battlion 143 RIT 8.18-

As part of XXI Corps d'Armee the division covered the assembly of First Army by attacking in the Vosges at Col de Ste Marie, the Col de Bonhomme and the Marches des Saales on 8th August 1914. It took Schirmeck after heavy fighting on the 14th and then moved via the Donon to support the attack on Sarrebourg. After combat at Biberkirch [18th-20th], the division crossed the Meurthe south-east of Baccarat; fought at Montigny [24th] and, in support of the battle at Mortagne, at Ste Barbe and the Col de la Chipota [26th]. It retreated via Girecourt-sur-Durbion to Montier-en-Del on 1st September.

On 7th September it joined Fourth Army for the battle of Vitry/first battle of the Marne and fought at Signal de Sompuis and then pursued the Germans towards Suippes and Souain. It fought west of Souain for the rest of September, and was pulled out of the line on 1st October for a move to Artois.

The division defended Tenth Army's positions around Notre-Dame-de-Lorette from 5th October: it fought at Carency and Ablain-St-Nazaire, and then established a front line between Carency and Aix-Noulette. The division moved up into the Ypres salient on 1st November and became engaged in fighting at Wijtschate and St Eloi and in Polygon Wood until 25th November.

On 31st December 1914 it returned to its former positions below Notre-Dame-de-Lorette and remained there for the whole of 1915. There it fought on 3-8th March, on 8-16th May, 25th-29th May and 16th June. At the end of June it moved slightly southwards to Souchez and attacked from there towards Angres during the third battle of Artois.

The division left Artois on 11th January 1916 for rest and retraining, and arrived in Verdun on 5th March to occupy positions between Eix and Vaux to cover the road from Verdun to Étain. It was attacked on 31st March and 2nd April. Pulled out on 10th April it moved to the Fourth Army in Champagne where it held the line between Tahure and the Butte de Mesnil from 1st May until 25th July. The division joined Tenth Army in Picardy and took over the line between Soyécourt and Vermandovillers on 17th August. As part of the battle of the Somme, it attacked Soyécourt on 5th-9th September; moved to Ablaincourt on 15th October and fought there on 7th and 15th November; and held the Ablaincourt-Genermont sector from 15th-26th December.

After a month in reserve, the division arrived in the Vosges on 1st February 1917 and occupied positions on the Swiss Frontier and at Belfort until 12th April.

In reserve during Nivelle's offensive, the division went up onto the Chemin des Dames between the antheon and Colombe on 28th May. From the Colombe-Nanteuil sector it attacked towards Mennejean and Ainsy-le-Chateau during the battle for Malmaison on 10th October. When its gains were consolidated it returned to the Vosges for a long rest. It took up its former positions on the Swiss frontier on 5th December, and moved to the Col du Bonhomme/Provenchères-sur-Fave sector on 22nd January 1918. It was pulled out on 5th April to go into reserve behind Fifth Army.

It joined the third battle for the Aisne on 27th May. After fighting on the south bank of the Vesle, it retreated to Veuilly and stabilised the front between there and Hautevesnes. After a period in the secondline of Fourth Army at Herpont and Dampierre-le-Château [from 3rd to 17th June] it rejoined that army at Navarin and Tahure. Moved to Côte 193 and Mamelles on 1st July, the division resisted German attacks and counterattacked towards Trou-Bricot and Mesnil on 15th July. The division moved to the Perthes-les- Hurlus/Trou Bricot sector on 24th September. Two days later, in the battle for Somme-Py it pursued the Germans to Aure and Manre where it established a support line on 29th September. When the advance resumed on 3th October, it moved into positions south of Orfeuil and then on to Banogne and Recouvrance. After fighting north of Thour it crossed the Serre 25th-27th October. Rested [30th October-6th November] it rejoined Fourth Army's advance to the Meuse and was in the support line at Chaumont Porcien on 11th November.

War-formed Divisions 44-48

44 Division d'Infanterie

Formed 11th August 1914 in 14th and 15th Military Regions.

Commanders
11.08.14-Albert Soyer
24.08.14-Jean de Vassart d'Andernay

88 Brigade
97 RI, Chambery	9.14 to 77DI
159 RI, Briancon	9.14 to 77DI

89 Brigade
157 RI, Gapseille	9.14 to 76DI
163 RI, Nice	9.14 to 76DI

Artillery
Group 12 btys/6RAC; 1bty/53RAC
Group 22 btys/6RAC; 1bty/9RAC
Group 32 btys/38RAC; 1 bty/57RAC
Group 42 btys/38RAC; 1 bty/58RAC

Cavalry
1-4/4 RCA

Engineers
Cie 14/13, 14/17, 14/22 du 4RG

The division was formed near Lyon on 11th August 1914 from a variety of spare regiments in the 14th and 15th Military Regions. By 18th August it had joined the Armée d'Alsace for the short-lived offensive against Mulhouse. It fought at Altkirch and Illfurth and held positions there until 21st August. On 22nd August, the division was moved northwards to join 1st Army north-east of Rambervillers. As part of XXICA, it fought in the battle of Mortagne at Menil, Ste Barbe and at the Col de la Chipote. The division was disbanded on 5th September and its units were used to form the Division de Vassart and the Division de Barbot [76DI & 77DI].

45 Division d'Infanterie/45 Division d'Afrique

Formed in Algeria as the Oranie Division on 24.8.14 from reserve units in North Africa

Commanders
02.08.14-Antoine Drude
02.12.14-Ferdnand Quiquandon
23.09.16-Stansilaus Naulin
10.06.18-Roger Michaud

89 Brigade –retitled 91 Brigade 31.10.14 [disbanded 6.18]
RdM1bisZ [2 bns 1Z, 1 bn 4Z]	12.14- Retitled 7RdMZ
6.15-retitled 3RdMZT	
4.18-retitled 6RdMT	6.18 to 58DI RdM3bisZ [3 bns]
	12.14- retitled 5RdMZ
	1.15- retitled RdM3bisZ

90 Brigade [disbanded 6.18]

RdM2bisZ [[3 bns]]   1.12.14-retitled 3RdMZ
                                                    10.15 to Army d'Orient- not replaced
RdM2T [1 bn 1T, 1 bn 2T, 1bn 8T]   1.12.14-retitled 6RdMT
4.15-retitled 1RdMT
1 BA   Added 10.14
3 BA   Added 11.14

Infantry from 6.18
RdM3bisZ
1RdMT
Group Bns d'Afrique [1BA, 2BA, 3BA]   2 BA added 5.18

Artillery
Group 5, RAC d'Afrique
Group 6, 52RAC 4.15 destroyed and replaced by 1bie/41RAC
& 1bie/1RAP
1.16 formed Group/15RAC [3 btys by 7.16]
Group 6, 58RAC

275RAC   Formed from the above 7.17
Group 7, 118RAL   Added 2.18-formerly Group 12, 109RAL

Cavalry
1 RdeM Ch'Afrique   Attached 10.14 only-rejoined 12.14 until 7.15
9/7 RCh, 6.15-11.15
3 Esc/6RS, 1.16-1.17
E/18 RD, 1.18-11.18

7/24 RD & 8/24 RD, 11.15-1.16
4/RS, 1.17-1.18
2/18 RD, 1.18-11.18

Engineers & Pioneers
1914=Cie 17/1M du Maroc
1918=Cie 26/4M, 17/51M du 2RG
& Cie 11/25 du 6RG
Pioneer Bn 17RIT   Added as reserve 7.17-became Pnr Bn 8.18

The division arrived in France on 24th August 1914 and joined Sixth Army to the south of Paris on 3rd September. During the first battle of the Marne, it fought along the line of the Ourcq at Penchard, Chambry, Barcy and Étrépilly. From 10th September, it fought in the first battle of the Aisne and advanced eastwards via Lizy-sur-Ourcq and Longpont to occupy a sector near Soissons. On 23rd and 30th September it took part in attacks at Perrière and Montagne Neuve.
On 5th October the division joined Tenth Army in Artois. During the first battle of Artois, it took part on actions at Bailleul, Roclincourt, Thélus and Écurie; all north of Arras. When the frontline stabilised, it took up positions between Roclincourt and la Targette where it remained until 6th April 1915. It fought at Écurie on 5th , 26th-29th November, and 7th-8th December, and 17th-18th February.

On that date, the division moved northwards into the Ypres Salient between Poelkapelle and Langemark where it sustained a German gas attack on 22nd April. It took part in attacks on Pilkem Ridge on 16th, 17th and 30th May. On 8th June, it moved to a new sector along the Yser between Boezinge and Steenstraat. The division was withdrawn on 30th September and remained in reserve between Bergues and Nieuveport until 11th March 1916.

The division joined Second Army at Verdun on 20th April and occupied the line between Hayette and the Bois d'Avocourt from 9th-23rd May. It moved to Lorraine on 30th May and occupied positions between the Vezouve and the Chapelotte until 9th August. It joined 6th Army on the Somme on 25th August and fought between L'Hopital and Forest from 4th-16th September after which it was withdrawn and returned to Flanders. After a period of rest near Dunkerque, the division re-entered the line at Nieuvepoort on 6th October and remained there until 12th January 1917.

The early part of 1917 was spent training and in labour duties with a brief spell in Third Army's sector between Beuvraignes and the Bois de Loges, 4th-15th March. It joined Fourth Army in Champagne on 1st April and, from a position near Prosnes, took part in the battle of the Monts on 17th April. On 19th May, the division joined Fifth Army north-west of Reims. During the next ten months it did five tours in the line: Neuville/Loivre [26th May-18th August]; Sapigneul/Miette [14th September-6th October]; Sapigneul/Godat [22nd October-16th November]; Courcy/Godat [16th November-11th December] and Courcy/Betheny [26th January-29th March 1918].

In response to the German spring offensive, the division moved to Picardy on 29th March 1918 and fought between Grivesnes and Montdidier with First Army during the battle of the Avre. It returned to the Reims area on 20th May. During the third battle of the Aisne, with Fifth Army, it fought along the Vesle between Rosnay and Ormes. It occupied positions to the east of Reims from 4th July until 6th August. During the fourth battle of Champagne, it resisted German attacks on 15th July. During the second battle of the Marne, it returned to the Vesle where it remained until 8th September. After a short rest, it joined Fifth Army's movement from the line of the Vesle towards the Hindenburg Line. It fought at Glennes, and at the Arbe de Romain, before taking up a new position north of the Vesle on 20th September. On 10th October, the division moved into positions near Bourgogne, on the river Suippe, from which it advanced to St Germainmont and le Thour during the battle for the Serre. It consolidated gains north of St Germainmont until 5th November. The division was resting at Condé-en-Brie on 11th November 1918.

46 (Chasseurs) Division d'Infanterie

Formed on 21st March 1916

Commanders
04.03.16-Jules Gratier
11.05.17-Camille Levi
24.08.18-Jules Gratier

1 Brigade de Chasseurs 3.16-11.16 [ex 66DI]
7 BCP
13 BCP
47 BCP
53 BCP 6.16 –to 8 Bde-replaced by 1 BCP tal

5 Brigade de Chasseurs 3.16-11.16 [ex 66DI]
22 BCP
23 BCP
62 BCP
63 BCP 6.16 to 8 Bde –replaced by 2 BCP tal

8 Brigade de Chasseurs 6.16-11.16
6 BCP   11.16 to 66DI-replaced by 15BCP ex 66DI
53 BCP Ex 1 Bde
63 BCP Ex 5 Bde
4 BCP tal

Infantry from 11.16
1 Group-7, 13, 47BCP
2 Group-22, 53, 62BCP
3 Group-15, 23, 63BCP

Artillery
Group 6, 29 RAC   Ex 81DT

Group 6, 32 RAC	Ex 103DT 11.16 to 164DI
Group 4, 2RAM	Ex Vosges 7.16 replaced by Gp/27RAC ex XXXIV CA
Group 6, 55RAC	Added 11.16 from 157DI
227 RAC	Formed from above 4.17
Group 7, 131RAL	Added 4.18-formerly Group 10/113RAL

Cavalry
7/12RH, 3.16-11.16
E/8 RCh, 7.16-6.17
4/18 RD, 6.17-11.18

Engineers & Pioneers
1916   Cie 27/2 du 11RG
        Cie 28/3 du 28BG
        Cie 12/15 du 6RG
1918   Cie 27/2 du 11RG
        Cie 12/25 du 6Rg
8.17-Pioneer Bn 5BCPtal

The division was formed in the Vosges by taking command of battalions of chasseurs, which were already in line between the Col de la Schulcht and the Col de Ste Marie where it remained until 12th July 1916.

On 30th July 1916 the division joined Sixth Army in the Somme. It entered the line between Maurepas and Hem on 18th August, and fought between Hopital and Forest on 3rd-5th September. From 13th until 21st September it occupied positions between Rancourt and the Ferme du Priez. It moved to Sailly-Saillisel on 31st October and took part in attacks towards the Bois de St-Pierre-Vaast on 1st, 5th, 9th and 11th November.

The division left the Somme on 31st November and returned to the Vosges where it took over the sector between Metzeral and Leimbach on 7th December. The division was pulled out on 27th January 1917 and sent to the Marne region to prepare for Nivelle's spring offensive.

During that offensive, the second battle of the Aisne, the division waited with the rest of Tenth Army for the breakthrough, which never happened. It transferred to Fifth Army on 21st April and did two tours in the trenches north-west of Reims: Courcy/Loivre [28th April-20th May] and Sapigneul/Neuville [20th-25th May]. On 23rd August, after a long period of rest and training, the division joined Tenth Army in positions along the Chemin des Dames between Chevreux and the Plateau des Casemates. The division was withdrawn on 31st October and prepared for transfer to Italy.

After a period in reserve near Verona, the division arrived at Monfenera on 13th February 1918 and remained in line there until 24th March when events in France forced its recall.

The division arrived in Flanders on 15th May and took over the line between Dickkebus and Kemmel on 28th May. It attacked German positions on 31st May and 13th June. On 29th June the division began the move from Flanders to Champagne where it arrived on 2nd July. Kept in reserve at St Remy-sur-Bussy during the fourth battle of Champagne, elements fought at Perthes and Souain during the second battle of the Marne.

On 8th August 1918 the division joined First Army in Picardy and fought near Piennes and Rollet. On 29th August it advanced towards the Hindenburg Line via Etelfay, Fescamps, Tilloloy, Crapeaumesnil and Frétoy-le-Chateau. During the battle for St Quentin which commenced on 28th September, the division fought to free the line of the St Quentin Canal between Marcourt and Essigny-le-Petit. On 17th October, it participated in the battle for Mont- d'Origny and the second battle of Guise, by taking over part of the Sambre-Oise Canal. From there it fought in the battle of Thiérache and then advanced towards the Meuse. It liberated Bone and Nouvion on 6th November, d'Etrerungt on 8th November and Galgeon on 9th November. It was resting at Trélon on 11th November 1918.

47 (Chasseurs) Division d'Infanterie [retitled 47 Division de Marche, 5-11.16]

Formed 16 January 1915 in the Vosges from chasseurs battalions

Commanders
16.01.15-Ferdinand Blazer
24.03.15-Louis d'Armau de Pouydraguin
22.08.17-Philippe Dillemann

Infantry 1.15-11.15
2 Bde-11, 12, 51, 54 BCA	2.15 –62 BCA and 54 BCA swopped
3 Bde-14, 30, 52, 62 BCA	
4 Bde-6, 23, 24BCA	67BCA added 2.15
Group Lancon –47, 63, 64BCA	From Brigade Mixte Klein 2.15,
-broken up 11.15	

* 151 Infantry Brigade attached from 66DI 4.15-to 129DI 6.15
• 5 Brigade de Chasseurs attached 8-11.15 then to 66 DI
• between 5.16 and 11.16 the division was entitled 47 Division de Marche

Infantry 11.15-5.16
2 Bde- 11, 12, 51, 52BCA	
3 Bde-14, 30, 54, 70 BCA	
4 Bde-115, 46, 24, 64BCA	5.16-independent in Vosges

Infantry 5-11.16
2 Bde-11, 12, 51, 52 BCA
3 Bde-14, 30, 54, 70 BCA

Infantry from 11.16
4 Group- 1, 12, 51 BCA	
5 Group- 14, 52, 54 BCA	
6 Group-30, 70, 115 BCA	115BCA ex 4 Bde in Vosges

Artillery
Group 6, 9RAC	Added 1.15
3 btys from 21, 15, 49 RAC's	Added 4.15
Group 6, 1RAM	Added 1.16- 7.16
Group 5, 2 RAM	Added 1.16- 7.16
Group 4, 56 RAC	7.16 replaced above two groups
256 RAC	Formed from above groups 7.17
Group 8, 131RAL	Added 3.18-formerly Group 9/108RAL

Cavalry
5/26 RD, 12.15-1.16
3/3 RCh, 1.16-6.17
4/3 RCh, 1.16-11.16
5/25RD, 6.17-11.18
6/25 RD, 6.17-11.18

Engineers & Pioneers
1915   Cie 27/3 du 11RG
1918   Cie 27/3, 27/53 du 11RG
        Cie 15/22 du 7RG
7.17-Pioneer Battalion 4BCP tal

Formed in the Vosges from chasseurs battalions which were in line between the Col de Bonhomme and Metzeral, the division continued to hold this line until 5th June 1916.

On 25th June moved to the Somme and joined Sixth Army. It went into the line east of Maricourt on 11th July where it remained until 27th July; it attacked towards Maurepas and the Curlu chapel on 20th July. After a brief respite near Corbie, the division moved to positions south of Maurepas on 7th August. It attacked on 11th-13th, 16th and 18th August and was withdrawn on the 20th. On 14th September, it took over the line between Cléry-sur-Somme and the Bois l'Abbé from which it attacked German positions on 25th September One month later, the division moved back to the Vosges and occupied the sector between the Cold de Ste Marie and the Chapelotte from 24th November until 26th January 1917.

There followed a long period of retraining with Tenth Army for Nivelle's spring offensive during which battle the division remained in reserve in the valley of the Ardre. On 1st June it took up positions along the Chemin des Dames between Chevreux and the road from Reims to Laon. It remained there until 4th July when it moved to Lorraine for further training. After a brief period with Fourth Army in the line between Courtine and Côte 193 in Champagne, the division left the Western Front 27th October.

As part of the allied force sent to Italy after the debacle at Caporetto, the division arrived at Verona on 12th November. It moved forward to the front-line at Monte Tomba on 4th December where it occupied trenches until 9th January 1918. It remained in reserve south of Bassano until 18th March when it returned to the front and occupied a sector at Monte Val Bella until 7th April.

Recalled to France in response to the German spring offensive, the division joined Sixth Army south of the Aisne on 1st June. It took part in actions around the Ferme de la Loges-aux- Bouefs and Chézy-en-Orxois from 7th June. During the second battle of the Marne, it fought near Dammard at Monnes, Cointicourt, Latilly, Sommelans, Grisolles, Rocourt, Coincy and Brecy between 18th and 26th July.

On the latter date, the division moved to join First Army in Picardy for the planned offensive in front of Amiens. Between 9th and 28th August, it fought near Berny-sur-Noye, and then advanced to Andechy, Roye and then Carrèpuis and Waucourt. On 31st August, it occupied the line of the Canal du Nord east of Nesle where it remained until 4th September.

After further retraining, the division rejoined First Army on 27th September for the battle of St Quentin during which it attacked le Tronquoy and advanced to the north-east of the city where it remained until 10th October. It resumed the advance on 25th October and took part in the battle of the Serre at Pleine-Selve from which it moved forward to the Guise-Marle road.

During the second battle of Guise, and the subsequent pursuit to the Meuse, it advanced to the railway between the Capelle and Hirson, 5th-9th November. On 11th November, it was resting between Englancourt and Froidestrées.

48 Division d'Infantrie

Formed on 6 February 1915 from a variety of spare metropolitan and colonial units in VII CA, 6th Army.

Commanders
08.02.15-Gabriel Delarue
21.03.15-Francois Capdepont
15.09.16-Joseph Joba
23.07.17-Léon Prax
19.07.18-Louis Schuler

Infantry 2.15-6.16

95 Brigade	170RI, 174RI
96 Brigade	2 RdMZT, RdMTM

Infantry 6-9.16
170 RI
174 RI
2RdMZT
• RdMTM not with division 6-9.16

Infantry 9-12.16
95 Brigade	170RI, 174RI-to 167DI 12.16
96 Brigade	2 RdMZT, RdMTM (to 153DI 12.16)

Infantry 12.16-9.17
1 RdMZ Ex 25DI
9 RdMT Ex 25DI
2 RdMZT

Infantry 9.17-6.18
95 Brigade	1 RdMZ, 9 RdMT
96 Brigade	2 RdMZT, 412RI [ex 153 BI-to 58DI 6.18]

Infantry from 6.18
1 RdMZ	
9 RdMT	9.18 to 25DI-replaced by 98RI
2 RdMZT	7.18 retitled 13 RdMT

Artillery
Groups 5 & 6, 15RAC	1.15-5.17 -to 2 groups new 5RAC
Group 5, 19RAC	1.15-5.17 -to 1 group new 5RAC
Groups 1-3, 5RAC	Formed 5.17
Group 12, 111RAL	Added 2.18-rettiled Group8/111RAL 3.18

Cavalry
7/7 RH, 8.15-10.15
8/7 RH, 9.15-10.15
3/11RCh, 7.16-7.17
4/11RCh, 7.16-6.17
5/1 RD, 7.17-11.18
6/1 RD, 7.17-11.18

Engineers & Pioneers
1915   Cie 15/12 du 7RG, Cie 20/22 du 10RG
1918   Cie 15/12, 15/62 du 7RG, 20/22 du 10RG
7.17- Pioneer Battalion 78RIT

After its formation at Montgobert, in Picardy, on 6th February 1915, the division joined Fourth Army in Champagne. From 10th until 24th March it occupied the line between Mesnil-les-hurlus and Côte 196 during the latter stages of the first battle of Champagne. On 28th April it moved to the Meuse front held by First Army and took part in the 1st battle of the Woëvre at Bois Haut on 29th April-13th May, and occupied positions between Tresauvaux and the Tranchée de Calonne from 1st May.

The division joined Tenth Army in Artois on 14th May. During the second battle of Artois, it fought between Ablain-St-Nazaire and Notre Dame-de-Lorette before movement to nearby positions north-east of Aix- Noulette on 28th May. On 10th June it moved south of Arras to Angres and engaged in a series of attacks and counterattacks on 16th-18th June. The division was withdrawn on 5th July and moved south to the Aisne for a long rest. It joined Sixth Army and served between Pernant and Autreches, 2nd August-19th September. On 29th September in took up Fourth Army's positions at Navarin for the second battle of Champagne where it remained in line until 22nd November.

A period of rest, in the Argonne, was followed by a transfer to Verdun on 16th February 1916. It fought for control of the village of Douaumont between 25th February and 8th March. After a rest in Lorraine, the division fought between Douaumont, Etang de Vaux and Thiaumont from 25th April until 11th May. Pulled out of the Verdun salient, the division was moved westwards to Reims and took up Fifth Army's line at the Bois de Zoauves on 4th June. The division moved to the Somme on 11th July and took part in the battle of the Somme. At first it fought between Hem, the Somme canal and

Monacu [25th July-14th August] and then towards Mont St Quentin to the north of Cléry [4th-18th September]. It left the Somme on 22nd September and moved to Lorraine where it took over positions near Pont-à-Mousson. The division remained in the Moselle front until 4th April 1917.

The division joined Fourth Army and fought between Mont Cornillet and Mont Blond, 12th-31st May, and took over the line between the river Aisne and the Maisons de Champagne, 7th June-8th July. The division transferred to Verdun and remained in reserve during the second offensive in August 1917. From 2nd September, the division occupied the line outside Verdun from Samogneux to Forges. It was withdrawn on 2nd January 1918 for a period of retraining in Lorraine.

On 4th April 1918, the division joined Fifth Army when it went into line between Champs and Pont-St- Mard. Pulled out on 9th May, it joined Mangin's Group [later 10th Army] for the battle of the Matz on 10th June. It fought between Wacquemoulin and St Maur until 13th June. As part of Tenth Army, it fought during the second battle of the Marne from Villers Cotterêts to Longpont and St Pierre-Aigle. It fought at Longpont and Villers-Helon from 18th to 21st July after which it was withdrawn, to prepare for future offensives by Tenth Army. It fought in the second battle of Noyon from 18th August to 2nd September. It engaged the Germans at Nampoel, Blerancourt and Folembray and advanced towards the Massif de St Gobain where it organised positions south of Barisis aux Bois.

The division joined Fourth Army for the battle of Somme-Py which began on 29th September. During this battle it took the Kreuz-Berg redoubt, Aure, Mont de Chery and Mont de Loisy. It had reached the Aisne between Voncq and Condé-lès-Vouziers before it was withdrawn on 16th October. It remained in a support role with Fourth Army between Vouziers and Tourteron until the end of hostilities.

49-50 Divisions d'Infanterie- not formed

Reserve Divisions 51 - 77

51 Division d'Infanterie

The reserve division of the 1st Military Region which formed at Arras on mobilisation.

Commanders
02.08.14-René Boutegourd
13.05.15-Claude Rouvier
28.01.16-Albert Boullange
28.08.18-Joseph Ecochard

101 Brigade [disbanded 11.16]
233 RI, Arras	11.16 to1DI-replaced by 33RI ex 2DI
243 RI, Lille	6.16 disbanded
327 RI, Valenciennes	11.16 to 162DI-not replaced

102 Brigade [disbanded 11.16]
208 RI, St Omer	11.16 to 2DI-replaced by 73DI ex 2DI
273 RI, Bethune	
310 RI, Dunkerque	6.16 disbanded

Infantry from 11.16
33RI
73RI
273RI — Disbanded 8.18-replaced by 3 RdMT-ex
37DI in 7.18

Artillery
4 Gp/15 RAC	4.17 became 215RAC
4 Gp/27 RAC	4.17 became 215RAC
5 Gp/41 RAC	4.17 became 215RAC
5 Gp/101RAL	3.18-added –ex 2Gp/101RAL

Cavalry
5/4 RC, 8.14–11.15d
6/4 RC, 8.14-11.15d
2 /11RH,11.15-6.16
E/11 RH, 11.15-6.16
5/16RCh, 6.16-7.17

Engineers & Pioneers
1914   Cie 1/13, 1/24 du 3RG Cie 22/17 du 1RG
1918   Cie 1/13, 1/63, 1/24 du 3RG
8.18=Pioneer Battalion 25RIT   8.18-added –from XXXIIICA

As part of the 4th GDR, the division assembled at Vervins between 9th and 19th August. It then joined Fifth Army in its advance into Belgium. The division moved northwards towards Dinant via Rocroi and fought at Onhaye on 23rd August. It retreated towards Guise and during the first battle of Guise it fought at Voulpaix on 30th August. Its retreat continued to Sézanne. During the first battle of the Marne, during which it was detached to Ninth Army [9th-12th September] and it took part in Fifth Army's operations to free the Deux Morins and fought at St Gond. After fighting at Soizy-aux-Bois it advanced to St Leonard on the eastern outskirts of Reims where it took part in the first battle of the Aisne.

The division remained with Fifth Army at Reims until 26th May 1915. At first it occupied positions between Coucy and the Neuvillette. It moved to the Fort de la Pompelle on 17th October, and, from there, to positions between the Fort and the Ferme de Marquises on 20th April 1915.

The division joined Second Army in Picardy on 27th May 1915 and attacked Serre, north of Albert, 10th- 16th June. After a rest, it took over the line between Maucourt and Herleville where it remained until 28th September. It joined Fourth Army on 1st October and took part in the latter stages of the second battle of Champagne. It fought at Navarin and attacked to the east of the Souain towards the Somme-Py road on 6th October. The division moved to Verdun on 15th October, and, after a period of retraining, took over the line south of the town between the Verdun to Étain road and Éparges on 6th December. It had just moved to the Beaumont-Bezonvaux sector when that area bore the brunt of the German attack on 21st February 1916. After ten days of severe fighting and heavy losses around Louvement, the division was withdrawn.

A long period of rest, retraining and labour duties in Lorraine preceded a return to more active duties when the division joined Sixth Army in Picardy on 9th July 1916. It re-entered the line south of Foucaucourt on 18th July and attacked the Bois Etoile on 20th July, and then, consolidated its gains between the Bois Etoile and Soyécourt. It moved to a new sector between the Ferme de Lihu and Lihons on 25th August and took part in several attacks on the Bois de Chaulnes during September and October. The division was withdrawn on 16th November and moved to Fourth Army in Champagne where it took up positions between Courtine and the Maisons de Champagne on 25th November. It remained there until 12th January 1917.

On 31st January the division joined Fifth Army to prepare for Nivelle's offensive on the Chemin des Dames. On 13th March it took over a sector between the Ployon and Hurtebise but moved back into reserve on 8th April where it remained during the abortive offensive on 16th April.

At the end of the month the division moved to Flanders to join 1st Army, the French contribution to Haig's offensive at Ypres. In the line between Reningelst and Nordschoole, it attacked at Bikschote on 31st July. It remained in this area with several minor changes of sector until 31st October 1917. The division spent the winter of 1917-1918 retraining at Calais and then near Crécy-en-Brie.

The division joined Sixth Army on the Chemin des Dames on 9th March 1918 when it took over positions between Vauclerc and the Ployon. Pulled out on 12th May, it fought at Chaudun and Vierzy during the third battle of the Aisne [31st May-6th June] and consolidated positions taken by Tenth Army north of Dommiers. On 10th June, it took over the line between Couevres-et-Valsery and Fosse-en-Basse and fought at Laversine. During the second battle of the Marne, it rested at Chelles, and then rejoined the line between Troissy and Courthiézy. On 15th July, after service with Fifth, Ninth and Sixth Armies, the division joined Fourth Army and attacked at Igny-les-Jard on 15th July.

The division was pulled out of the line on 18th July and sent to the southern Vosges. From 25th August until 14th October it occupied Seventh Army's positions between Fulleren and the Swiss frontier. By 22nd October the division had moved to Picardy where it joined First Army's attack on Nouvion and participated in the battle of Thierache on 7th November. On Armistice Day, the division was moved towards Liessies.

52 Division d'Infanterie

The reserve division of the 2nd Military Region formed at Mézières on mobilisation.

Commanders
02.08.14-Hyacinthe Coquet
02.09.14-Jules Battesti
27.09.14-Charles de Pelacot
25.10.14-Jean-Gabriel Rouquerol
21.05.15-Jean Piarron de Mondésir
30.12.15-Jean Boyer

103 Brigade [disbanded 6.16]
291 RI, Mezieres   [disbanded 6.16]

347 RI, Sedan [disbanded 6.16]
348 RI, Rocroi

104 Brigade [disbanded 6.16]
245 RI, Laon
320 RI, Peronne
49 BCP, Longwy   6.16 to Verdun Fortress
58 BCP, Longuyon   10.15 to AO

Infantry from 6.16
245RI   10.17 disbanded & replaced by 328RI ex 4DI
320RI
348RI   5.18 disbanded-replaced by 10 RMT

Artillery
4 Gp/17 RAC   4.17 to 217RAC
5 Gp/29 RAC   4.17 to 217RAC
4 Gp/42 RAC   4.17 to 217RAC
7Gp/102 RAL

Cavalry
5/21RD, 8.14-6.15
6/21RD, 8.14-6.15
7/3 RD, 6-11.15d
1/14RCh, 8.16-8.18
2/14RCh, 8.16-11.16 & 7.17-9.18
E/1RS, 8.18-11.18

Engineers & Pioneers
1914   Cie 2/13, 2/19, 2/24 du 3RG
1918   Cie 2/13, 2/63 dur 3RG Cie 6/22 du 9RG
7.17   279 RIT -became pioneer bn 8.18
5.18 added-ex 3Gp/302RAL

The division assembled at Mezieres on 13th August 1914. Its initial task was the defence of the bridges across the Meuse between Mézières and Givet. The German advance forced a retreat towards Sedan and it fought at Frenois and Donchery on 28th August. From 29th August until 6th September it retreated with Fourth Army towards Connantray. It joined Foch's Detachment on 29th August [Ninth Army from 31st August] and fought in the battle for the Marais de St Gond during the first battle of the Marne. It took part in actions at Connantre, Fere-Champenois and Linthes [7th-9th September] and then advanced northwards towards Reims.

From 14th September 1914 until 22nd May 1916 division fought in and around Reims. It was transferred from Ninth Army to Fifth Army on 7th October while fighting between Cernay and Betheny. Most of its time was spent in the northern approaches to Reims between Cavaliers and St Leonard where the most intense fighting occurred around Fort Brimont. The division moved a short distance eastwards on 5th November 1915 when it took over the line between St Leonard and the Marquises but, after a short break, returned to the outskirts of Reims on 20th March.

The division joined the battle for Verdun on 4th June and fought between Thiaumont and the Bois de Vaux Chapitre until 15th June. It was sent to the Vosges where it took over a 'quiet' sector between Leimbch and the Vallee de la Luache on 3rd July. The division remained in the southern end of the line until 1st September 1917. Mostly engaged between Leimach and Metzeral, it guarded the Swiss frontier during July and August 1917.

On 11th September 1917, the division re-entered the line north of Verdun between the Bois de Chaume and the Bois des Fosses from where it took part in the second offensive. Pulled out on 28th September, it too over positions along the St Mihiel salient between Paroches and Koeur-la-Grande on 15th October. It remained in this area until 8th May 1918, by which time it had moved northwards to the adjacent sector between Maizey and the Tranchée de Calonne on 15th January 1918. On 17th May it returned to Verdun and took up positions north of the town between Beaumont and Côte 344 where it remained until 12th July.

The division joined Sixth Army, on 21st July, along the Ourcq during the second battle of the Marne where it remained in reserve near Lizy sur Ourcq. It took over the Braine-Courcelles sector on 21st August. On 4th September it began to move up to the Hindenburg Line, and, as part of Fifth Army, freed the line of the river Vesle and established positions between Presles and St Mard which were held until 23rd September. Three days later, the division re-entered the line between Merval and a posiiton south-east of Glennes, from which it took part in Fifth Army's battle for St Thierry [1st October]. It advanced to the Aisne canal between Maizy and Oeuilly and then reached Sissonne where it occupied positions towards the Selve on 21st October.

There it engaged the Germans during the battle for the Serre and then pursued them towards the Meuse between 5th and 11th November. It had reached Revin and Laifour when hostilities ended.

53 Division d'Infanterie

The reserve division of the 3rd Military Region formed at Rouen on mobilisation.

Commanders
02.08.14-Georges Perruchon
07.09.14-Felix Journée
18.10.14-Francois Loyzeau de Grandmaison
23.01.15-Henri Berthelot
03.08.15-Joseph Micheler
26.03.16-Georges Lebouc
18.01.17-Henri Mesple
05.04.17-Amédée Guillemin

105 Brigade [disbanded 8.16]
205 RI, Falaise and Paris
236 RI, Caen
319 RI, Liseuex and Paris

106 Brigade [disbanded 8.16]
224 RI, Bernay and Paris   8.16 to 158DI
228 RI, Evreuex and Paris   8.16 to 158DI
329 RI, Le Havre   8.16 to 158DI

Infantry 8.16-8.18
205 RI
236RI   7.18-replaced by Cz Bde
319RI

1 Czechoslovak Brigade 7.18-
21 RCh Tcheco
22 RCh Tcheco

106 Brigade-reformed 8.18
205RI
319RI

Artillery
4 Gp/11 RAC   4.17-243 RAC
4 Gp/22 RAC   4.17-243 RAC

4 Gp/43 RAC
5 Gp/135 RAL

4.17-243 RAC
New formed and added 5.18

Cavalry
5/27 RD, 8.14-1.16d
6/27 RD, 8.14-1.16d
9/8 RH, 1.16-6.17d
E/10RH, 1.16-12.16d

Engineers & Pioneers
1914   Cie 3/13, 3/19, 3/24 du 3RG
1918   Cie 3/13, 3/63, 3/24 du 3RG
8.18-Pioneer Battalion 25RIT

On mobilisation the division joined 4GDR at Vervins from where it moved northwards with the rest of Fifth Army. Not engaged during the battle of Charleroi, the division began to retreat on 24th August and, during the first battle of Guise, it fought at Urvillers and Moy [29th August] and then continued its movement south via St Gobain and Villers-St-Georges. During 5th Army's battle for the Deux Morins, during the first battle of the Marne, it was held in reserve and then pursued the Germans towards Berry-au-Bac. From 14th September until 4th October, it engaged the enemy between Berry-au-Bac and Côte 108 [1st battle of the Aisne], and established a line between Berry and Sapigneul. The division was transferred to Second Army, in Picardy, on 7th October, Between 13th October 1914 and 20th April 1915, it held the line between La Boiselle, Fricourt, Mametz and Maricourt [the future British battleground of the Somme]. On 10th May, the division joined Tenth Army's front in Artois when it took up positions north-west of Arras between Neuville-Saint-Vaast and Ecurie: it fought in the Labyrinthe during the second battle of Artois. After a rest near St Pol, which began on 28th June, and at Charmes, the division was transferred to Champagne on 20th September. During the second battle of Champagne, it participated in Fourth Army's attacks on the Butte de Tahure [25th September-19th October].

After a two month rest, the division joined Sixth Army in the Oise sector on 10th December 1915 and remained there until 27th April 1916. During this period it undertook three tours in the line: between Pernant and Moulin sous Touvent [10.12.15-21.1.16]; Tracy-le-Val and Moulin-sous-Touvent [24.1.16-2.3.16] and Hautebraye/Ferme Quennevières [2.3.16-27.4.16]. After another period of retraining, the division moved northwards to the Somme and rejoined Sixth Army at Foucaucourt. During the battle of the Somme, it occupied the sector between Fay and Estrées-Denicourt and took part in several attacks on the latter position. Pulled out on 6th August, it returned to Hautebraye-Quennevières on 20th August. It was under command of Tenth Army until 29th October when positions in the Oise front were taken over by First Army. The division moved to the Ribécourt-Ecouvillon sector on 15th December and remained there until 16th March 1917.

On 22nd March 1917, now under command of Third Army, the division moved forward to occupy the area, between Quierzy, Chauny and Moy left devastated by the German withdrawal to the Hindenburg Line. It established a new line between Vendeuil and la Fere which was extended to Moy on 20th June. The division enjoyed a rest from 19th July and joined Tenth Army on the Chemin des Dames on 18th August. On 28th October Sixth Army replaced Tenth Army when the latter HQ was sent to Italy. It occupied the sector between Courtecon and Malval until 20th November, and then that between Vauclerc and Chevreux, 29th November-15th December; and between Ferme Brunin and Chevreux, 24th December 1917 until 24th March 1918.

The division was rushed to Picardy in response to the German spring offensive. From 2nd April until 13th June, it fought at Rollot, Plessis-de-Roye and Plemont. It established a line between the Plemont and Thiescourt, from which it fought at Mont Renaud. During the battle for the Matz, 9th-13th June, it fought at Chevincourt, Melicocq and Machemont.

On 13th June the division was moved to the Vosges and there took over the line between Leimbach and the Rhine-Rhone canal on 26th June. It remained there until 15th September when it returned to 5th Army. It was kept in reserve during the battle for Champagne and Argonne. Taken over by 4th Army on 9th October, it occupied a sector between Voncq and Conde-les-Vouziers where it fought the Germans until 31st October. After a rest at St Souplet, it was returning to the front, via Vittel, when the Armistice was signed.

54 Division d'Infanterie

Formed at Le Mans, 4th Military Region, on mobilisation.

Commander
02.08.14-Jules Chailley

107 Brigade [to VICA 5.9.14 and disbanded 7.10.14]
301 RI, Dreux and Paris	10.14 to VICA
302 RI, Chartres and Pari s	10.14 to VICA
304 RI, Argentan and Paris	10.14 to VICA

108 Brigade [to 72DI]
303 RI, Alencon and Paris	10.14 to 72DI
324 RI, Laval	10.14 to 72DI
330 RI, Mayenne	10.14 to 72DI

Artillery
4 Gp/26 RAC	10.14 to 65DI
4 Gp/31 RAC	10.14 to VICA
5 Gp/44 RAC	10.14 to VICA
5 & 6 Esc/1 R Ch	10.14 to 76DI

Cavalry
5/1 RCh
6/1 RCh

Engineers
Cies 4/13, 4/19 and 4/24 du 1RG

On mobilisation the division joined 3GDR in positions north of Verdun, between Damvillers and Eix, at Spincourt and Gouraincourt. On 21st August, it took part in Third Army's movement to the north-east and fought at Spincourt and Gouraincourt. From 23rd August the division fell back south of Verdun and fought
in the approaches to the developing salient. The division was broken up on 4th September when 107 Brigade came under command of VI Corps d'Armee and 108 Brigade was transferred to 72DI. Formal disbandment took place on 27.10.14.

55 Division d'Infanterie
The reserve division of the 4th Military Region formed at Orléans on mobilisation
Commanders
02.08.14-Louis Leguay
05.11.14-Eugene Buisson d'Armandy
16.01.15-Henri de Laporte d'Hulst
14.08.16-Jospeh Mangin

109 Brigade [disbanded 3.17]
204 RI, Auxerre	
282 RI, Montargis	5.16 disbanded
289 RI, Sens and Paris	

110 Brigade [disbanded 3.17]
231 RI, Melun and Paris	5.16-disbanded
246 RI, Fontainebleu	
276 RI, Colommiers	3.17 to 154Brigade

Infantry from 3.17

204RI
246RI
289RI

Artillery

5 Gp/13 RAC	4.17 to 230 RAC.
4 Gp/30 RAC	4.17 to 230 RAC.
4 Gp/45 RAC	4.17 to 230 RAC.
7Gp/105 RAL	New formed and added 6.18

Cavalry

5/32RD,	8.14-11.15d
6/32RD,	8.14-11.15d
5/6 RH,	11.15–6.16
6/6 RH,	11.15- 6.16
1/18RD,	8.16–7.17
2/18RD,	8.16-6.17
3/8 RCh,	6.17-7.17 or 1.18

Engineers & Pioneers

1914   Cie 5/13, 5/19, 5/24 du 1RG
1918   Cie 5/13, 5/63, 5/24 du 1RG
8.18-Pioneer Battalion 67RIT   From VIICA

As part of 3GDR the division assembled near St Mihiel by 17th August 1914 and, from there, it covered the Moselle at Pont-a-Mousson. As part of the Army of Lorraine, it advanced towards Metz on 25th August and fought on the Orne at Conflans-en-Jarny and Puxe. In conformation with the retreat of that army it moved back towards St Mihiel from which it began to move to Paris on 27th August.

The division joined Sixth Army in Picardy and fought at Roye, Guerbigny and Tilloloy from 29th Agust until 5th September. During the first battle of the Marne, it fought for the line of the Ourcq at Iverny, Monthyon and Barcy [5th-13th September] after which it moved north-eastwards towards the river Aisne at Soissons. After the first battle of the Aisne, it took up positions between Soissons and Pernant and remained there until 13th January 1915. A week later it returned to the Chemin des Dames and took over Sixth Army's sector between Maison Rouge and Venizel. It moved to the adjacent sector of Venizel/Condé-sur-Aisne on 22nd March 1915 where it remained until 30th April. On 9th May it joined Tenth Army in Artois, and from 11th May occupied lines between Notre Dame-de-Lorette and Vimy Ridge at Carency and Ablain-St- Nazaire. After a short break [5th-23rd June] it moved to the neighbouring sector at Souchez where it fought in the third battle of Artois in the autumn of 1915.

The division left Artois on 23rd November 1915 and re-entered the line in Fifth Army's sector, north west of Reims, between Berry-au-Bac and Moulin Pontoy on 11th February 1916. On 20th June, the division was withdrawn and prepared for combat in the Verdun salient. It took up positions on the left bank of the Meuse, between Côte 304 and Bois d'Avocourt on 12th July and it fought in this sector until 1st September. It

moved to the right bank on 21st September and spent the next month between Bois d'Haudromont and Ouvrage de Thiaumont. It returned to the left bank on 2nd November and remained in line between Bois Camard and Avocourt until 5th February 1917. The division's final tour at Verdun lasted from 14th February until 15th April when it found itself in the trenches between Louvemont and the river Meuse. On 22nd April, the division moved up the Meuse to the St Mihiel salient where it occupied the line between the Etang de Vargevaux and the river until 23rd May.

On 5th June 1917, the division moved to Fourth Army and spent a month in line between Casque and Têton, after which it moved to the Chemin des Dames. It served with Tenth Army between the Miette and Ployon until 4th October. On 29th October it moved along the Chemin des Dames to the Chevreux-Casemates sector. Pulled out of the line on 29th November 1917, it returned to the Miette-Ployon sector on 6th January

1918. From 28th January the division rested and retrained in the Ourcq region and, in response to the

German spring offensive, was sent to Picardy on 23rd March. For two months it fought along the Oise in the first battle of Noyon. On the right bank of the river, it established positions at Manicamp and Varesnes.

When the Germans attacked this position during the third battle of the Aisne, the division was engaged in prolonged defensive actions between Moulin-sous-Touvent and Autreches. During this period it fought at Ferme Quennevières as well [6th July]. In 18th August the division fought in the second battle of Noyon and advanced towards the Ailette via Pont St Mard.

The division was withdrawn from the line on 29th August and had been disbanded by 10th September 1918.

56 Division d'Infanterie

The reserve division of the 6th Military Region formed at Châlons-sur-Marne on mobilisation

Commanders
02.08.14-Frederic Micheler
16.08.14-Théodore de Dartein
26.01.16-Frederic Hellot
29.06.17-Georges Demetz

111 Brigade [disbanded 1.17]
294 RI, Bar-le-Duc	1.17 to 166DI-replaced by 132RI ex 12DI
354 RI, Leronville	6.16-disbanded
355 RI, Commercy	1.17-to 127DI

112 Brigade [disbanded 1.17]
350 RI, St Mihiel	1.17 to 12DI –replaced by 106RI ex 12DI
361 RI, St Mihiel and Reims	6.16 disbanded
65 BCP, St Mihiel	
66 BCP, Pont-a-Mousson	7.15 to 9DI
69 BCP, St Mihiel	

Infantry from 1.17
106 RI	
132 RI Ex 12DI	
10 Gp Chasseurs-49, 65, 69 BCPs	9.18 to 38DI-replaced by 8RdMT
29 Senegalais Bn	

Artillery
4 Gp/25 RAC	4.17 to 225 RAC
4 Gp/32 RAC	4.17 to 225 RAC
4 Gp/40 RAC	4.17 to 225 RAC
6Gp/106 RAL	New formed and added 4.18

Cavalry
5/3 RH, 8.14–8.16d
6/3 RH, 8.14-8.16d
E/6RCA, 9.16–12.16
E/6RCA, 9.16-12.16
2/12RCh, 1.17-7.17

Engineers & Pioneers
1914   Cie 6/11, 6/17, 6/22 du 9RG
1918   Cie 6/11, 6/61 du 9RG Cie 8/25 du 4RG
8.18=Pioneer Battalion 42RIT   From XXXICA

On 17th August 1914 the division joined 3GDR to the east of Verdun with the intention of covering the plain of the Woëvre to the east of the town. On 25th August, as part of the Armée de Lorraine, the division fought along the Orne near Olley and Buzy, after which, it joined in the general retreat. On 28th August the division began to move to Picardy where it joined 6th Army and fought at Senlis on 2nd September. During the first battle of the Marne, as part of 5GDR, it fought in the Ourcq region at Montgé, St Soupplets and Mareilly, and then pursued the Germans to Mercin and Pernant during the first battle of the Aisne.

During the 'race for the sea' the division established a series of positions in Picardy: between the Bois-des- Loges, Beuvraignes and Tilloloy [3rd-14th October]; between Fricourt and Authuille, outside Albert [21st- 30th October]; and between Hébuterne, Hannescamp, Berles- aux-Bois and Ferme Touvent [from 30th October]. Once the line of trenches had been established the division remained in the Ancre area until 5th September 1915.

The division transferred to Fourth Army on 26th September 1915 and was involved immediately in the second battle of Champagne. Until 10th October, it fought near Navarin and the Butte de Souain. After a month-long rest, it re-entered the line between L'Epine de Vedegrange and the Ferme de Wacques on 25th November and remained in this position until 14th April 1916.

On 16th May 1916, the division moved into the line above Verdun between Ferme Thiaumont and Haudromont. After two weeks it was withdrawn and sent to the outskirts of Reims where it manned positions at the Bois de Zoauves until 7th September. On 27th September it joined Sixth Army and fought at Morval, Combles and Frégicourt during the latter stages of the battle of the Somme. Withdrawn on 10th October, it re-entered the line between Cléry-sur- Somme and Bois l'Abbé on 21st October.

From 23rd September 1916 until 5th April 1917 the division was retraining for Nivelle's offensive on the Chemin des Dames. From positions between Moussy and Soupir the division took part in Sixth Army's attack on 16th April. It attacked towards Bouvettes, took Ostel and advanced towards the Oise-Aisne canal near Chevregny. During May it fought between Chevregny and the canal until moved to a new sector between Mennejean and Pantheon on 16th May.

The division was withdrawn from the line on 29th May and sent to the Vosges where it occupied a quiet sector between Leimbach and Metzeral from 29th June 1917 until 22nd January 1918. Following a two month period of training, the division was moved to Picardy in response to the German spring offensive. It took part in First Army's actions along the Avre and fought between Montdidier and Ayencourt [26th March-1st April]. It moved eastwards to Lorraine on 9th April. Between 18th April and 27th July it held the line between the Sanon and Bezange-la-Grande, and then, rejoined First Army in Picardy.

From 9th August until 8th September, the division fought between Andechy and the Avre and engaged the Germans at L'Échelle-St Aurin, and at St Mard, which resulted in an advance on the Canal du Nord and Ham. After that, the division held positions south of St Quentin [29th September-13th October] and then took part in First Army's assault of the Mont-d'Origny. It moved along the Oise and fought at Origny-St Benoite and advanced towards Guise.

The division moved to Lorraine on 31st October to join Tenth Army which was being prepared for the advance on Metz. The division was at Mirecourt when hostilities ended.

57 Division d'Infanterie

The reserve division of the 7th Military Region formed at Belfort on mobilisation.

Commanders
02.08.14-Frederic Bernard
03.02.15-Emilien Cordonnier
08.05.15-Eugene Debeney
18.06.15-Georges Demange
12.08.15-Henri de Cadoudal
23.10.15-Paul Leblois
16.01.17-Charles Jacquemot
14.12.17-Ernest Siben

05.03.18-Léon Génin

113 Brigade [disbanded 9.17]
235 RI, Belfort   10.16 disbanded
242 RI, Belfort   9.17 disbanded
260 RI, Besancon

114 Brigade [disbanded 9.17]
244 RI, Lons-le-Saunier   10.16 disbanded
371 RI, Belfort
372 RI, Belfort

Infantry from 9.17
260RI
371RI
372RI

Artillery

5 Gp/5 RAC	4.17 to 204RAC
6 Gp/5 RAC	4.17 to 204RAC
4 Gp/47 RAC	4.17 to 204RAC
---	10.15 2 btys/1RAM and 1 bty 8 Gp'Afrique added-became Gp 4 or 5/1RAM 1.18

No RAL allocated

Cavalry
5/11RD, 8.14-10.15
6/11RD, 8.14-8.14
E/18RD, 8.14-10.15
E/4RCA, 10.15-11.18

Engineers & Pioneers
1914   Cie 28/1, 28/21 du 28BG
1918   Cie 28/1, 28/6, 28/21 du 28BG
No Pioneer Battalion allocated

From mobilisation until 8th October 1915 the division was stationed at Belfort. Elements of the division joined the advance into Alsace and fought at Mulhouse on 9th and 10th August 1914. It fought in the battles for Mulhouse until 28th August and then occupied trenches to the east of Belfort for the next thirteen months. During this long period, it engaged in a series of minor actions at Carspach, Aspach, Burnhaupt-le-Haut, and Ammertswiller. In October 1915 the division left Belfort for Macedonia, where it would spend the rest of the war.

The division began to disembark at Salonika on 15th October 1915 and it was moved north to positions in the Vardar valley near the confluence of that river with the Cherna. Between 3rd and 29th December it was forced to retreat towards Salonika where it established defensive positions at Daoudli and Kiorzine.

Between 5th and 26th August 1916 it fought in the battle of Doiran and then moved to Monastir [3rd October] where it was engaged in a lengthy series of actions until 28th March 1917. Then it moved to a new sector at Côte 1248 where it remained until 14th August. After a short period of retraining, it moved west of Lake Prespa and took part in another series of battles between 29th August 1917 and 10th June 1918. During this period, it established a line near the border with Albania. From 10th June until 15th September 1918 it fought at Kamia and moved into Albania where it occupied Sinaprente and Koukri. During the allied offensive in the autumn of 1918, the division attacked along the Ockrida and advanced to Elbassan.

From 20th October the division was resting near Monastir.

58 Division d'Infanterie

The reserve division of the 8th Military Region formed at Dijon on mobilisation

Commanders
02.08.14-César Besset
31.08.14-Georges Claret de la Touche
22.09.14-Edouard Bolgert
22.08.15-Henri Niessel
26.02.16-Charles Leroux
13.06.18-Jules Priou

115 Brigade [to 66DI 10.14]
229 RI, Autun	
256 RI, Chalons-sur-Soane	10.14 to 116Bde-replaced by 213RI
334 RI, Macon	

116 Brigade [disbanded 12.15]
213 RI, Nevers	10.14 to 115Bde-replaced by 256 R!
285 RI, Cosne	12.15 disbanded
295 RI, Bourges	

131 Brigade [transferred from 66DI 10.14] [disbanded 12.15]
280 RI	12.15 disbanded
281 RI	
296 RI	12.15 to 152DI

Infantry, 12.15-6.18
256 RI	6.18 disbanded
281 RI	6.18 disbanded
295 RI	6.18 disbanded

Infantry from 6.18
412 RI	Ex 48DI
6 RMT	Ex 45DI 10.18 to 169DI-replaced by 39RI
ex 169DI	
11 RMT Ex 59DI	

Artillery
4 Gp/1 RAC	4.17 to 248 RAC
5 Gp/37 RAC	4.17 to 66DI –replaced by 4/3RAC
4.17-248 RAC	
4 Gp/48 RAC	4.17 to 248 RAC
7 Gp/108 RAL	New formed and added 8.18

Cavalry
5/6 RD, 8.14-11.15
6/26RD, 8.14-10.14
5/21RCh, 11.15-3.17
6/21RCh, 11.15-12.16d
E/6RCA, 3.17 –7.17

Engineers & Pioneers
1914   Cie 8/13, 8/19, 8/24 du 4RG
1918   Cie 8/13, 8/63, 8/24 du 4RG

8.18-Pioneer Battalion 64RIT

Initially allocated to 1GDR in the Armée d'Alsace, the division's first task was to secure the passes over the Vosges between the Col de la Schlucht and the Valley of the Thur from which it advanced towards the Fave on 18th August. This was part of First Army's advance into Alsace which brought the division into action east of Saales on 20th August. Then the division moved back to the Meurthe and took part in the battle of Mortange at Coinches. After a rest at Corcieux the division returned to the Vosges on 14th September when it took up positions between the Col du Bonhomme and Thann.

On 6th October the division began to move to Artois where it joined Second Army between La Bassée and Vermelles on 14th October. Then, as part of Tenth Army, it remained in line here until 31st May 1915 during which time it fought at Vermelles during the second battle for Artois. It was relieved by British troops and moved to Angres where it was in line from 21st June until 31st August. During the third battle of Artois it held the sector between Neuville-Saint-Vaast and Ecurie and attacked Thélus on 11th October. The division was pulled out of the line on 23rd December and went into reserve near Avesnes-le-Comte.

The division moved into the Ypres salient on 21st February 1916 and took up positions between Steenstraate and Boezinge where it remained until 19th May. It moved to Picardy and joined Sixth Army in the Santerre, for the battle of the Somme. It held the line between the Amiens-Chaulnes railway and Rouvroy 13th June-19th July, and between Armancourt and Andechy [25th July-6th December]; and from south of Maucourt to the Amiens-Chaulnes railway [10th December 1916-26th January 1917].

After a lengthy period of training at Valbonne, the division moved to Alsace and entered the line between Leimbach and the Rhine-Rhine Canal on 14th March and remained there until 16th June. It joined Fifth Army, east of Reims, on 8th August and was in line near Betheny until 30th January 1918. After a further period of training, the division joined Fourth Army and occupied trenches between the Maisons de Champagne and the Butte de Mesnil [18th March-26th April] after which it moved to Third Army in the Oise sector on 22nd May. From a line between Rollot and Orvillers-Sorel it fought in the battle of Matz, 9th June. Withdrawn next day, it joined Tenth Army on 16th July and fought at Vierzy, Villemontoire and the Bois d'Hartennes during the second battle of the Marne. Switched back to the Oise on 18th July, it participated in Third Army's operations during the second battle of Noyon. It fought between Ecouvillon and Ferme Attiche and moved forward to the Hindenburg Line: it took Cannectancourt [21st August], Evricourt [22nd August], Happlincourt [4th September] and reached Salency before a rest period which began on 6th September.

The division joined First Army back on the Oise front near Vendeuil on 25th September and took part in the assault on Mont-d'Origny on 15th October. Five days later, it fought in the battle for the Serre at Herie-la-Vievittle. In reserve from 1st November, it rejoined First Army on the 5th and advanced northwards to the Meuse via Fontaine-les-Vervins, Origny et Thierahce and Signy-le-Petit until the Armistice. Elements had reached Cul-des-Sartes on that date.

59 Division d'Infanterie

The reserve division of the 9th Military Region formed at Angers on mobilisation

Commanders
02.08.14-Julien Charley de la Masseliere
20.08.14-Jean Kopp
22.12.14-Emile Brasier de Thuy
08.09.15-Jean Laroque
11.03.16-Antoine Dessort
27.07.16-Paul Henrys
20.05.17-Henri Claudel
10.06.18-Joseph Vincendon

117 Brigade [disbanded 3.17]
232 RI, Tours
314 RI, Parthenay   4.16 disbanded
325 RI, Poitiers

118 Brigade [disbanded 3.17]
266 RI, Tours   4.16 disbanded
277 RI, Cholet
335RI, Angers   3.17 to 154 BI then 97DI

Infantry from 3.17
232 RI
277 RI   9.18 disbanded and replaced by 370 US Infantry Regiment
325 RI

Artillery
4 Gp/20 RAC   4.17 to 220 RAC
4 Gp/33 RAC   4.17 to 220 RAC
5 Gp/49 RAC   4.17 to 220 RAC
8 Gp/109 RAL   Added 8.18-ex 3/333RAL

Cavalry
5/25RD, 8.14-1.16d
6/25RD, 8.14-1.16d
1/6RH, 1.16-6.16
2/6RH, 1.16-6.16
1/1RD, 10.16-8.17
2/1RD, 10.16-8.17

Engineers & Pioneers
1914   Cie 9/13, 9/19, 9/24 du 6RG
1918   Cie 9/13, 9/63, 9/24 du 6RG
8.18-Pioneer Battalion 141RIT

As part of 2GDR in Second Army the division assembled at Laxou and advanced on 18th August to occupy Sivry and Ste Genevieve. During the battle for Morhange, it fought at Nomeny and Manoncourt-sur-Seille [20th August]. In the ensuing battle for the Grand Couronne of Nancy they engaged the Germans at Ste Genevieve and Loisy-sur-Moselle and then re-occupied Pont-à-Mousson on 12th September.

Between 14th September 1914 and 8th February 1916, the division occupied trenches along the Seille between Armaucourt and Pont-a-Mousson. During this period it engaged in small scale actions at Chenincourt, Aulnois and at Xon and Norroy [13-18th February 1915].

On 27th February 1916 the division began labour duties at Verdun from which it returned to Lorraine on 5th April and took up positions between Arracourt and the Sanon on 16th April. The division moved to the Bezange-la-Grande/Armaucourt sector on 1st June. It was withdrawn on 30th September and remained out of the line until 4th January 1917.

The division went into the line between Louvemont and Chambrettes, outside Verdun, on 4th January but moved southwards to the St Mihiel salient between the Bois Loclont and Paroches on 23rd January. After two months at this location the division was moved north-westwards to Champagne where it entered Fourth Army's line before Mont Cornillet on 16th May 1917. On 21st July the division was moved back to Lorraine, and took up positions between the Sanon and Moncel on 6th August. It moved to the Embermesnil/Domevre sector on 19th October and remained in line until 3rd February 1918.

As part of the French response to the German spring offensive, the division joined First Army in Picardy and fought near Mailly-Raineval [9th-29th April] and established a new line north of Ainval and Thory. The division returned to Verdun on 9th May and spent the next three months in trenches between Damloup and Trésauvaux. It switched back to Picardy and 1st Army where it fought in the second battle of Noyon at Chavigny and Juvigny [26th August-3rd September]. From positions in front of the Hindenburg Line it took part in Tenth Army's attack at Vauxillon [16th September-16th October]. During this action it fought at Anizy-le-Chateau and Bois de Mortier and then advanced towards Laon. After

HQ Third Army took over from HQ Tenth Army on 27th October, the division moved north towards the line of the Serre, east of Crécy- sur-Serre. In the last few days of the war it advanced to the Belgian frontier and had reached Cul-des-Sarts on 11th November.

60 Division d'Infanterie

The reserve division of the 10th Military Region formed at Rennes on mobilisation.

Commanders
02.08.14-Maurice Joppé
25.09.14-Géraud Réveillac
16.02.16-Henri Patey
24.02.18-Charles Jacquemot

119 Brigade [disbanded 3.17]
247 RI, St Malo	3.17 to 153 Bde
248 RI, Guincamp	
271 RI, St Brieuc	6.16 disbanded

120 Brigade [disbanded 3.17]
202 RI, Granville	
225 RI, Cherbourg	
336 RI, St Lo	6.16 disbanded

Infantry from 3.17
202 RI
225 RI
248 RI

Artillery
4 Gp/7 RAC	4.17 to 207 RAC
4 Gp/10 RAC	4.17 to 207 RAC
5 Gp/50 RAC	4.17 to 207 RAC
7 Gp/110 RAL	New formed and added 6.18

Cavalry
5/24RD, 8.14–11.15d
6/24RD, 8.14-11.15d
7/7 RCh. 10.15 –8.16d
8/7 RCh, 10.15-8.16d
1/11RD, 8.16-7.17
2/11RD, 8.16-5.17
1/13 RH, 7.17-8.17

Engineers & Pioneers
1914	Cie 10/13, 10/19, 10/24 du 6RG
1918	Cie 10/13, 10/63, 10/24 du 6RG
8.18=Pioneer Battalion 28RIT	Ex XCA

The division joined Fifth Army near Rethel on 11th August 1914 and moved northwards into the Ardennes on 18th August. It occupied bridges over the Semois and fought at Mogimont. Forced back to the Meuse at Donchery it fought at Hannogne-Ste-Martin and Bois de la Marfée on 28th August. The division took part in Fifth Army's long retreat to the Marne; enroute it fought at Tourteron on 30th August. During the first battle of the Marne, it took part in Ninth Army's operations for control of the Marais St Gond by fighting at Sommesous and Montepreux. It advanced to Ste Hilaire-le-Grand and fought near Souan during the first battle of the Aisne. After this, it established a frontline from Wacques to a point west of Souain which later included the Bois Sabot. During the 1st battle of Champagne it engaged in mining operations around Bois Sabot.

The division remained in Champagne until 23rd June 1916. It moved to the Moscou/Marquises sector on 17th September 1915 and then to the Aubérive/Moscou sector on 29th October. Its final move was to the Baconnes/Vaudesincourt sector on 3rd May 1916. The division took up positions between the Bois Haudromont and the Côte de Froidterre, on the heights above Verdun, on 23rd June. After three weeks of hard fighting it returned to Champagne and rejoined Fourth Army before Tahure on 23rd July. It moved to the Côte 193 position on 29th August and remained there until 28th April 1917 when it moved westwards to another sector of Fourth Army: between the Souain/Ste Marie-a-Py railway and Aubérvive. Here in engaged in the battle of the Monts until 30th June.

The division returned to Verdun on 13th October 1917 and went into the line between the Bois Caurieres and the Bois Chaume. It took part in the second offensive on 25th-29th October and on 6th-9th November. It was withdrawn on 15th November and re-appeared in the front-line on 8th December-in the Argonne between the Aire and the Four de Paris. It was rested from 23rd March 1918 and allocated to Sixth Army on the Chemin des Dames on 31st March.

It began a three month stint in the line between Ayencourt and Mesnil-St-Georges on 5th May, and was moved on 8th August to Montdidier where it took part in First Army's operations in the battle of Amiens. It remained with First Army and moved up to the Hindenburg Line on 30th August. It fought at Grivillers, Tilleloy, Popincourt and reached the Crozat canal, after which it took Ly-fontaine and Vendeuil. On 8th October, it advanced from Vendeuil via Nuevillette and Thenelles towards St Quentin after which it fought at Mont-d'Origny.

Pulled out of the line on 16th October, the division moved to the Vosges where it took up positions between the Fave and the Rabodeau. On 6th November it extended its line to the Chapelotte and was there when hostilities ended.

61 Division d'Infanterie

The reserve division of the 11th Military Region formed at Vannes on mobilisation.

Commanders
02.08.14-Paul Virvaine
31.08.14-Celeste Deprez
22.02.15-Robert Nivelle
23.12.15-Joseph Cherrier
11.06.16-Charles Vandenberg
19.03.17-Louis Modelon
15.07.18-Anatole Blondin

121 Brigade [disbanded 3.17]
264 RI, Acenis
265 RI, Nantes
316 RI, Vannes   6.16 disbanded

122 Brigade [disbanded 3.17]
219 RI, Brest
262 RI, Lorient   3.17 to 81DI-not replaced
318 RI, Quimper   6.16-disbanded
Infantry from 3.17
219 RI
264 RI
265 RI

Artillery
5 Gp/28 RAC   11.14 group dissolved
                                            5.15 2 bies/28RAC and 1 bie/32 RAC joined ex 6GDR
                                            1.16 these bies became Gp 5/28 RAC

4 Gp/35 RAC 4.17 to 251 RAC
4 Gp/51 RAC 4.17 to 251 RAC
7 Gp/111 RAL New formed and added 6.18

Cavalry
5/1RD, 8.14–11.15d
6/1RD, 8.14-11.15d
E/7RS, 12.16–7.17
E/7RS, 12.16-7.17
4/2RCh, 7.17-11.18

Engineers & Pioneers
1914   Cie 11/13, 11/19, 11/24 du 6RG
1918   Cie 11/13, 11/63, 11/24 du 6RG
8.18=Pioneer Battalion 112RIT   From VICA

After a short period of training near Paris, the division arrived at Arras on 25th August 1914, and soon it was in action, with the rest of the newly-formed Sixth Army. It fought at Ginchy and Sailly-Saillisel, and to the south of Arras on 28th August, and then retreated westwards towards Amiens. From there it moved to Nanteuil-le-Haudouin. During the first battle of the Marne, it fought along the Ourcq, 7th-10th September,at Villers-St-Genet, Bois de Montrolles and at Betz. Then it advanced to Moulin-sous-Touvent during the first battle of the Aisne. As the trench lines became established, the division dug in between Autreches and Quennevieres.

It remained here from 2nd October 1914 until 26th January 1916. It resisted German attacks on the Bois St- Mard on 21st and 25th December and attacked Touvent on 6th and 11th January 1915.

The division remained with Sixth Army for much of 1916 as that army prepared for the battle of the Somme. It was in line between Tracy-le-Val and the river Oise [24th February-25th April]; between Fontaine-lès- Cappy and Herleville [30th May-18th June], between Foucaucourt and Fontaine [25th June-4th July]; between Estrées-Deniecourt and Soyécourt [30th July-17th August] and again in that sector [26th August-8th September]. During the battle of the Somme, it attacked and took Fay on 1st July, and Bois Foster next day; and fought for Estrées on 21st and 25th July, and for Estrées-Deniecourt on 31st August and 4th-7th September. During this period the division passed to Tenth Army on 5th August.

On 25th September 1916, the division moved southwards to the Oise front where, under command of Third Army, it took over the line between Pernant and Hautebraye. Control passed to First Army on 29th October, and the moved to the Plessis-du-Roye/Ecouvillon sector on 2nd December, and by 23rd January 1917 it occupied trenches in front of the Massif de Thiescourt. As a result of the German withdrawal to the Hindenburg Line, the division moved forward to Moy and established new positions between Cerizy and Vendeuil. It remained there until 25th June. It re-entered the frontline on 14th July facing St Quentin between Selency and Dallon.

The division left Third Army and rejoined Sixth Army-now on the Chemin des Dames-on 25th October 1917 and soon found itself at the beginning of two tours there. It occupied the Pargny Filain/Chavignon sector [29th October-21st December 1917]; the Chavignon/Bois Mortier sector [7th January-27th May 1918].

The division fought at Vauxillon during the third battle of the Aisne [27th-30th May 1918] and, after transfer from Sixth Army to Tenth Army, established positions at Villers Cotterêts. The division was withdrawn from the line on 8th June and sent to the Vosges for a rest in a quiet sector. It manned positions between the Chapelotte and Domevre from 18th June, and between Domevre and Embermésnil from 18th July until 4th September.

Three days later, the division joined Fourth Army in Champagne where it took part in the battle of Somme- Py, 26th September-12th October. It fought at Somme-Py and then on the line of the Arnes from which it pursued the Germans north to Retourne which it reached on 11th October. On 18th October it moved to Rethel and took up a line between Thugny-Trugny and Ambly-Fleury-west of Attigny-from which it began to advance towards the Meuse on 5th November. On 9th November it liberated Mézières.

The reserve division of the 12th Military Region formed at Angouleme on mobilisation.

Commanders
02.08.14-Francois Ganeval
21.09.14-Henri Wirbel
10.11.14-Jean Paulinier
15.11.14-Maurice Baumgarten
10.02.15-Maurice François
14.08.17-Eugene Margot
29.03.18-Nicolas Girard

123 Brigade [disbanded 4.17]
263 RI, Limoges 6.16-disbanded
278 RI, Gueret
338 RI, Magnac

124 Brigade [disbanded 4.17]
250 RI, Perigueux	6.16 disbanded
307 RI, Angouleme	
308 RI, Bergerac 4.17 to 81DI	

Infantry from 4.17
278 RI	1.18 –disbanded & replaced by 279RI ex 81DI
307 RI	
338 RI	

Artillery
4 Gp/21 RAC	4.17 to 221RAC
4 Gp/34 RAC	4.17 to 221RAC [reduced to 2 bies 8.14]
5 Gp/52 RAC	4.17 to 221RAC reduced to 1 bie 8.14]
4 Gp/53RAC	4.17 to 221RAC [added 2.15-ex XIIICA]
7 Gp/112 RAL	8.18-added-ex 3/312RAL

Cavalry
5/20RD, 8.14–11.15d
6/20RD, 8.14-11.15d
7/14RH, 2.16 –6.17d
8/14RH, 2.16-6.17
1/14RCh, 6–7.17

Engineers & Pioneers
1914   Cie 12/13, 12.19, 12/24 du 6RG
1918   Cie 12/13, 12/63, 12/24 du 6RG
1.18=Pioneer Battalion 65RIT

After a period of duty near Paris, the division arrived at Douai on 25th August 1914. It joined the newly- formed Sixth Army. It attempted to hold the Germans north of the Arras-towards but, after fighting at Moislains and Mesnil-sur-Arruaine it was forced to retreat southwards to the line of the Ourcq. During the first battle of the Marne, it established reserve positions for Sixth Army at Plessis Belleville and Monthyon from which it advanced towards Crepy-en-Valois and Jaulzy. In the first battle of the Aisne, it fought near Moulin-sous-Touvent, after, which, it moved north to Picardy.

As part of Second Army, from 4th October 1914, it held the line between Bouchoir and Maucourt until 12th January 1916. The division was taken over by Sixth Army on 2nd August 1915 and moved to new positions on 28th February 1916. In succession it held the Avre/Maucourt sector [28th February-18th June]; Armancourt/Rouvroy sector [18th June-

26th July] and the Andechy/Maucourt sector [26th July-28th September]. On 16th October, now part of Tenth Army, it began to play a more active role in the battle of the Somme when it took up positions between Pressoire and Ablaincourt. It took Ablaincourt on 7th November and held it against a German counter-attack on 15th November. The division came out of the line on 8th December. On Christmas Day 1916, the division joined Third Army. It held the line at Andechy/Armancourt [31st December 1916-8th March 1917]. After two days in line between Andechy and the Amiens/Roye railway it advanced into the wasteland left by the German retreat to the Hindenburg Line. It took Andechy and moved to Ham where it was engaged in clearance work until 3rd April.

After a month's rest between Dunkerque and Bergues, the division joined Sixth Army on the Chemin des Dames on 10th May. It held the line between Mennejean and Bessy [12th-29th May] and between Quincy Basse and Vauxillon [17th June-20th July]. It attacked the Germans at Vauxillon on 20th June and repelled a counter-attack next day. It returned to the Oise where it held Third Army's positions between the Fere and Moy [11th August 1917-30th January 1918].

After a period of retraining and labour duties, the division moved to Picardy on 23rd March. It sought to stem the German spring offensive, and fought at Canny-sur-Matz, Conchy-les-Pots, Roye-sur-Matz and Lassigny. Then, until 15th April it established a line between Plessis-du-Roye and the Berlière. The division moved to the Vosges on 19th April and occupied the line beteween the Fave and the Chapelotte from 30th April until 15th July.

During the second battle of the Marne, the division fought with Sixth Army at Fère-en-Tardenois [27th July] and on the Vesle [4th August] and advanced to reach Bazoches on 13th August. After three days under American command, the division was transferred to 5th Army on 9th September and took up new positions between Romain and Merval. On 14th September it began to close up to the Hindenburg Line and fought near Glennes and the Arbour de Romain. It organised a new line between Glennes and Villers-en-Prayeres on 19th September, and fought from there along the line of the Aisne on 30th September. After a rest near Chateau-Thierry [6th-28th October], the division took over the line east of St Quentin-le-Petit, and from there, began to advance northwards to the Meuse on 5th November. By 11th November, it was north of Monthermé.

63 Division d'Infanterie

The reserve division of the 13th Military Region formed at Clermont-Ferrand on mobilisation.

Commanders
02.08.14-Léon Lombard
17.11.14-Georges Julien
30.12.15-Auguste Hirschauer
20.06.16-Joseph Andlauer
03.07.17-Joseph Ecochard

125 Brigade [disbanded 6.16]
216 RI, Montbrisone
238 RI, St Étienne   6.16-disbanded
298 RI, Roanne
126 Brigade [disbanded 6.16]
292 RI, Clermont-Ferrand 6.16-disbanded
305 RI, Riom
321 RI, Montluçon   6.16 to 133DI-not replaced

Infantry from 6.16
216 RI
298 RI
305 RI

Artillery
4 Gp/16 RAC   4.17 to 216 RAC
4 Gp/36 RAC   4.17 to 216 RAC
5 Gp/53 RAC   4.17 to 216 RAC

7 Gp/113 RAL   New formed and added 4.18

Cavalry
5/14RD, 8.14-11.15
6/14RD, 8.14-111.5d
1/21RCh,11.15-6.16
2/21RCh,11.15-6.16
3/14RCh, 6.16-7.16
4/14RCh, 6.16-7.16
E/2RCh, 7.16-8.16
E/2RCh, 7.16-8.16
3/14RCh, 8.16-6.17
4/14RCh, 8.16-6.17

Engineers & Pioneers
1914   Cie 13/13, 13/19, 13/24 du 4RG
1918   Cie 13/13, 13/63 du 4RG
       Cie 22/22 du 1RG
No pioneer battalion allocated

1st Division Polonaise
Commander: Joseph Ecochard 02.09.18-Jean Vidalon
Formed from 63 DI 6.8.18
Composed of-
1 RI Polonaise,
2 RI Polonaise,
3 RI Polonaise,
216 RAC,
7/113RAL,
1Gp/1RAC Polonaise, Pioneer Bn/131RIT, Esc/3RCh,
Esc Chevaux Legers Polonaise,
1Cie Genie Polonaise

After assembling at Vesoul, the division joined 1GDR in the Armée d'Alsace on 19th August 1914. It participated in the offensive towards Mulhouse and moved to Asspach, Burnhaupt and Hagenbach, and then retreated to Thann by 27th August.

The division moved westwards to join Sixth Army for the first battle of the Marne. It took up positions on the Ourcq and fought at Brégy, Fosse-Martin, Puisieux, Vincy-Manouevre and Ecouen, 6th-10th September, after which, it pursued the Germans past Villers-Cotterêts and Fontenay to the north bank of the Aisne. There it engaged the enemy at Nouvron-Vingré and Cuissy-en-Almont between 13th and 20th September. After this action, it established and remained in the trench line between Pernant and Venizel. It stayed there until 28th January 1916. Transferred to Fifth Army on 4th August 1915, the division took over the sector between Berry-au-Bac and the Loivre on 16th February 1916.

The division was pulled out on 20th May and arrived in the Verdun salient on 1st June. There, it was deployed on the heights above Verdun between the Bois Fumin and Damloup. From 3rd until 6th June it attempted, and failed, to relieve the garrison of Fort Vaux. The division was pulled out on 18th June and sent to the Vosges. There it spent two months holding positions between the Schlucht and Col de Ste Marie, and Metzeral. The division returned to the Bois Fumin on 29th September and took part in the second Verdun offensive 23rd-30th October when elements joined 74DI's attack on the Damloup battery.

The division moved to the northern side of the St Mihiel salient on 23rd November and remained there until 1st April 1917. Then it went back to the Vosges for a mont in line between the Chapelotte and the Col Ste Marie. The division returned to Verdun on 23rd June and served in the trenches downstream of the town between Marre and Hayette from 1st July until 19th August. It moved to the vital Éparges shoulder of the Verdun salient on 5th October and after a month there it moved to the left bank of the Meuse. It held posiitons before Côte 344 and Ferme Mormont from 30th November 1917 until 19th January 1918. On 22nd February it moved a short distance westwards to the Argonne sector between the Four de Paris and Bois Beaurains where it remained until 21st June 1918. It moved to the adjacent sector between Hayette and the river Aisne on 4th July but did not stay long there.

It joined Sixth Army during the second battle of the Marne and fought on the Ourcq front from 20th July until 3rd August. It fought at Coiney [23rd July], at Fere en Tardenois and Trugny [18th July] and at Saponay [29th July]. The division was pulled out of the line and sent to the Camp-de-Mailly where it commenced conversion to 1st DI Polonaise on 6th August 1918.

64 Division d'Infanterie

The reserve division of the 14th Military Region formed at Grenoble on mobilisation.

Commanders
02.08.14-Charles Hollender
07.09.14-Jules Compagnon
28.05.16-Paul Colin

127 Brigade [disbanded 3.17]
275 RI, Romans	6.16 disbanded
340 RI, Grenoble	
52 BCP, Embrun	8.14 to GAV
68 BCP, Grenoble	8.14 to GAV
35 RIC	6.15 to 16DIC-replaced by 227RI
	7.15 227RI replaced by 261RI ex 42DI

128 Brigade [disbanded 3.17]
252 RI, Montelimar	3.17 to 157DI
286 RI, Le Puy	6.16 disbanded
339 RI, Aurillac	
70 BCP, Grenoble	8.14 to GAV

Infantry from 3.17
261 RI
339 RI
340 RI

Artillery
4 Gp/2 RAC	4.17 to 202 RAC from 4/2, 6/2, 4/14 RAC
4 Gp/1 RAM	9.14 to GAV-replaced by Gp 4/14RAC ex 68DI
5 Gp/1 RAM	9.14 to GAV-not replaced until 5.15
	5.15-Gp/3RAL
	11.15 Gp/3RAL became 2 btys, 2RAC
	10.16-extra bty 2RAC from XXXICA made up to Gp 6/2RAC
202 RAC	Formed 4.17
5 Gp/131 RAL	4.18-added –ex 10/108RAL

Cavalry
5/13RCh, 8.14 –3.16
6/13RCh, 8.14-3.16
1/24RD, 6.16-7.17
2/24RD, 6.16-7.17

Engineers & Pioneers

1914 Cie 8/14 du 4Rg
1918 Cie 8/14, 8/64, 14/4T du 4RG
8.18-Pioneer Battalion 26RIT   From IIICA

When the division's original task of defending the Alpine frontier with Italy proved unnecessary, it was moved north to join Second Army in Lorraine. It arrived at Saffais and Belchamp on 24th August and, next day, advanced on Mont-sur-Meurthe and Lamath and from there northwards to take part in the battle for the Grand Couronne de Nancy, 28th Aiugust-25th September 1914. It fought in the Foret de Champenoux, 5th- 13th September and then took up positions near Sorneville.

It arrived at Toul and engaged the Germans in the battle of Flirey on 26th September. It fought at Richecourt and Lahayville, after which it established First Army's sector between Seicheprey and Richecourt where it remained until 12th March 1915. During this period it became involved in several local actions around Mort Mere. It moved to the adjacent sector between Richecourt and St Agnant on 12th March and stayed there until 1st October 1915. The division was transferred to Champagne and took over Fourth Army's sector between Navarin and Wacques on 4th October. There, it consolidated the gains acquired during the second battle of Champagne. It returned to the St Agnant sector on 7th January 1916.

After a period of retraining [20th May-26th June] after which some elements of the division were fed into the battle of Verdun, the complete formation took over the line between Chattancourt and Marre on 26th July. Rested from 13th October, the division took over a new sector at Verdun on 24th October. It remained in line between Côte 304 and the Bois Camard until 22nd January 1917: during this period it endured German attacks on 6th-10th December and 28th-29th December. Then it moved to the Avocourt sector where it remained in line for nine months until 25th September 1917.

The division was selected to be a component of the allied force, which was sent to Italy after the disaster at Caporetto. It arrived at Vicenza on 11th November and was engaged in labour duties there and at Bassano until 8th January 1918. On that date, it entered the line at Mont Tomba but returned to the reserve six weeks later. The division began to return to France on 24th March and arrived in Picardy on 6th April.

Thrown into the second battle of Picardy it was engaged in the construction of defensive lines between Rouvrel and Hailles. With the crisis over, the division moved to Lorraine on 9th May and took over positions on the Moselle between Clemery and the Bois-de-la-Pretre on 22nd May. Pulled out on 9th August, the division joined Tenth Army, on the Oise, and fought in the second battle of Noyon, from 23rd August to 11th September. After action at Crecy-sur-Mont, it moved forward to the Ailette and fought at Courson and north of Vauxillon in the approaches to the Hindenburg Line.

After a three week rest, the division joined First Army on 30th September for the battle for St Quentin, during which it pursued the Germans to the Oise-Sambre canal. On 4th-5th November it crossed the canal and fought in the second battle of Guise. It reached Tupigny but was withdrawn for a rest period on 6th November. At the armistice it was at rest near Rumigny.

65 Division d'Infanterie

The reserve division of the 15th Military District formed at Nice on mobilisation.

Commanders
02.08.14-Brice Bizot
19.09.14-Henri Le Gros
08.02.15-Horace Pentel
14.05.16-Anatole Blondin
15.07.18-Louis Modelon

129 Brigade [disbanded 1.17]
311 RI, Antibes
312 RI, Toulon   1.17-disbanded
46 BCA, Nice   8.14 to GAV
64 BCA, Villefranche   9.14 to Bde Mxt Klein

67 BCA, Menton   9.14 to Bde Mxt Klein
34 RIC   6.15 to 16DIC-replaced by 302RI ex VICA
                                             6.16-disbanded

130 Brigade [disbanded 1.17]
203 RI, Digne
341 RI, Marseille
47 BCA, Draguignan   9.14 to Bde Mxt Klein
63 BCA, Grasse   9.14 to Bde Mxt Klein
38 RIC   6.15 to 16DIC-replaced by 304 RI ex VICA
                                             6.16-disbanded

Infantry from 1.17
203 RI
311 RI
341 RI

Artillery
4 Gp/55 RAC   4.17 to 255 RAC
4 Gp/2 RAM   8.14 to GAV-replaced by Gp/26Rac ex 54DI 9.14;
4.17-to 255RAC
5 Gp/2 RAM   8.14 to GAV-replaced by Gp90/3RAL 10.14- which became Gp90/55RAC
1.16
                                             4.17 to 255 RAC

No RAL

Cavalry
5/11RH, 8.14-5.16
6/11RH, 8.14-5.16
3/24RD, 5.16-7.17
4/24RD, 5.16-7.17

Engineers & Pioneers
1914   Cie 15/11, 15/24 du 7BG
1918   Cie 15/11, 15/61 du 7BG Cie 14/54 du 4RG
No Pioneer Battalion allocated

Redundant in its planned defensive role on the Italian frontier, the division joined the Army of Lorraine on 26th August 1914. As part of 3GDR, its role was to defend the heights of the Meuse downstream from Verdun. From 7th September it took part in Third Army's defensive battle of Revigny and fought at Amblaincourt, Beauze-sur-Aire, and Seraucourt. Once the trench line solidified, it established First Army's positions along the northern edge of the St Mihiel salient between Maizey and Paroches. It moved to Koeur-la-Grande on 3rd November and played a passive role in the battle of Woëvre. On 6th June 1915 it moved to the southern part of the salient and remained in the line between Regniéville-en-Haye and Fey-en-Haye until 20th May 1916.

On 4th June 1916, the division was ordered into the Verdun battle and for six months it fought on the left bank of the Meuse at Chattancourt, Hayette and Charny. It attacked Mort Homme on 28th December 1916 and then moved to the Argonne flank of the Verdun salient on 15th January 1917. Between then and 26th September 1917, it occupied positions between the river Aire and the Four de Paris.

Selected to be part of the allied force, which was sent to Italy after the defeat at Caporetto, the division arrived at Brescia on 31st October. It was committed to frontline duty on the Paive river, between Pederobba and Rivasecca, on 2nd December 1917. The division returned to the reserve on 30th January 1918.

The division began its return journey to France on 26th March and re-appeared in the front line on 8th April when it joined First Army in Picardy. During the second battle of Picardy, it fought at Mailly-Raineval and Thory until 18th May. After a period of retraining near Toul, the division returned to the southern wing of the St Mihiel salient on 1st June. It moved to the Moselle –at Regniéville en Haye –on 29th June.

On 4th August 1918 the division began to be transformed into 2 Division de Maroc.

66 Division d'Infanterie

The reserve division of the 16th Military Region formed at Montpellier on mobilisation.

Commanders
02.08.14-Francois Voirhaye
27.08.14-Olivier Mazel
06.10.14-Arthur Guerrier
29.01.15-Marcel Serret
31.12.15-Charles Nollet
12.05.16-Gustave Lacapelle
19.04.17-Georges Brissaud-Desmaillets

131 Brigade [10.14 to 58DI –replaced by 115 Brigade]
280 RI, Narbonne
281 RI, Montpellier
296 RI, Béziers

132 Brigade [12.14 to 41DI –replaced by 81 Brigade]
215 RI, Albi
253 RI, Perpignan
343 RI, Carcassonne

115 Brigade [added 10.14-ex 58DI] [disbanded 3.16]

213 RI	Vice 256 RI to 116BI 3.16 to 157DI
229 RI	3.16 to 41DI
334 RI	3.16 to 133DI

81 Brigade [12.14 ex 41DI] [11.16 disbanded]

152 RI	11.16 to 164DI
5 BCP	3.16 to 7 BCh –replaced by 64BCA ex 4 BCh
52 BCP	8.15 to 3BCh - replaced by 15BCP ex indep
	3.16 to 7 BCh- not replaced

151 Brigade [1.15 ex 71 DI] [4.15 to 47DI]
297 RI
357 RI
359 RI

Independent Chasseurs Battalions from 14th Military Region 10.14-1.15
12 BCA 1.15 to 2 BdeCh
13 BCA 1.15 to 2 BdeCh
28 BCA 3.15 to Gp Boussat
30 BCA 1.15 to 3 BdeCh
68 BCA 3.15 to Gp Boussat
15 BCP 1.15 to GAV

1 Brigade de Chasseurs [1.15-7.16]

7 BCA
13 BCA
27 BCA   8.15 to 6 BdeCh-replaced by 47 BCA ex Gp
53 BCA

Group Boussat [formed 3.15]
26 BCA   8.15 to 6 BdeCh
68 BCA   8.15 to 6 BdeCh
5 BCA(T)   8.15 withdrawn
7 BCA(T)   8.15 withdrawn

6 Group de Chasseurs [formed 8.15 from Gp Boussat] [disbanded 11.16]
27 BCA   11.16 to 7Gp
28 BCA   11.16 to
67 BCA   11.16 to 8 Gp
68 BCA   111.6 to 8 Gp

5 Group de Chasseurs [11.15 ex 47DI] [3.16 to 46DI]
22 BCA
23 BCA
62 BCA
63 BCA

7 Group de Chasseurs [3.16 formed out of 81 Brigade] [disbanded 11.16]
5 BCP   11.16 to 9 GpCh
15 BCP   11.16 to 46DI
41 BCP   11.16 to 164DI

4 Group de Chassuers [5.16 ex 47DI] [11.16 to 47DI]
24 BCA   11.16 to 9Gp
46 BC   11.16 to 7 Gp
115 BCA   11.16 to 47DI
3 BCP(T)   11.16 to garrison duties

Infantry 11.16 –11.17
7 Gp de Chasseurs [6, 27, 46 BCA's]   6BCA ex 46DI; 46 BCA disbanded 11.17
8 Gp de Chasseurs [28, 67, 68 BCA's]   67 BCA to 11.17
9 Gp de Chasseurs [5, 24, 64 BCA's]

Infantry from 11.17
7 Gp de Chasseurs [6, 27, 67 BCA's]
8 Gp de Chasseurs [17, 28, 68 BCA's]   17BCA ex 77DI
9 Gp de Chasseurs [5, 24, 64 BCA's]
2 BCA(T)

Artillery
5 Gp/ 9 RAC   1.15 to 47DI-replaced by 1bty/1RAM and 1bty/2RAM ex Vosges 7.15 remained in Vosges-not replaced
                                    7.16 Gp/26 RAC added –ex XXXIVCA
                                    4.17 to 240 RAC
4 Gp/56 RAC   5.16 to 47DI-replaced by bty/1RAM and Gp/2RAM ex Vosges
                                    7.16 replaced by Gp/40RAC-ex XXXIVCA
                                    4.17 to 240 RAC
4 Gp/ 3 RAC   10.14 to 58DI-replaced by Gp/37 RAC ex 58DI
                                    4.17 to 240 RAC
7 Gp/116RAL   4.18 added –ex 14/110RAL

Cavalry
5/19RD, 8.14-12.14
6/19RD, 8.14-12.14
6/26RD, 10.14-12.15
7/11RCh, 12.14-8.15
4/4RCh, 12.15–6.17d
7/13RCh, 12.15-11.16
3/25RD, 6.17-11.18
4/25RD, 6.17-11.18

Engineers & Pioneers
1914   Cie 16/13, 16/19, 16/24 du 2RG
1918   Cie 16/13, 16/19, 16/24 du 2RG
7.17-Pioneer Battalion 2BCA tal

The division assembled at Montbeliard by 16th August 1914. Allocated to the Armée d'Alsace, it took part in operations to seize Mulhouse. It fought near Brunstatt and Flaxlanden and then organised defensive positions south-east of the Rhine-Rhone canal. The division was pulled out of the line on 24th August and put to work on defensive positions at Montbeliard and Delle.

On 15th September 1914 the division arrived in the Vosges and took over the line between the Fave and the Col du Bonhomme, where it remained until 4th July 1916. During this long period it was engaged in a series of local actions. These included Lesseux [24th September 1914], Tete du Violu [31st October and 3rd November 1914], Tête de Faux [2nd December 1914], Gare d'Aspach [10th December 1914], Steinbach [January 1915], Metzeral [April-June 1915], and Hartsmannswillerkopf [October 1915-January 1916].

The division joined Sixth Army in the battle of the Somme on 15th August 1916 when it took over trenches between Bois de Hem and Cléry-sur-Somme: it participated in attacks on Clery on 24th August, and 3rd-5th September. It rested from 5th September and re-entered the line at Sailly-Saillisel on 10th October. After a number of local but intense conflicts there the division was pulled out on 27th October.

It arrived back in the Vosges on 1st November and took over the line between Metzeral and the Col de Ste Marie on 29th November. It left these positions on 14th January 1917 and after a long period of retraining it joined 5th Army for the second battle of the Aisne. It fought at Craonne and the Bois de Beau Marais from 18th April until 2nd May [transferred to 10th Army on 21st April] and then held positions around Craonne, between Chevreaux and the California Position until 18th June. It moved to Sixth Army, further west along the Chemin des Dames, and held a series of positions between the Pantheon and Chevregny until 26th October. It attacked the Epine de Chevregny on 30th July and fought in the battle of Malmaison on 23rd October-when it attacked Pargny-Filain.

The division returned to positions in the Vosges on 15th December when it arrived in the line betweeb Guebwiller and Leimbach. Pulled out on 31st March 1918, it joined First Army in Picardy and fought at Bois Senecat, Rouvrel and Hailles. In the allied offensive from Amiens, it fought at Morisel and Moreuil [8th-10th August]. Transferred to Tenth Army, it supported the advance on the Hindenburg Line and organised new positions between Vauxillon and Moisy, 29th August-18th September. It rejoined First Army and took part in the attack on Mont-d'Origny, [16th October-5th November] and advanced to the Sambre canal at Hannapes and Étreux. It liberated the line of the canal in the second battle of Guise. From 5th November, the division rested at Ham.

67 Division d'Infanterie

The reserve division of the 17th Military region formed at Montauban on mobilisation.

Commanders
02.08.14-Henri Marabail
10.08.15-Ernest Aimé
08.09.16-Joseph Savy
04.05.18-Léon Bousquier

133 Brigade [disbanded 3.17]

211 RI, Montauban	4.16 disbanded
214 RI, Toulouse	3.17 to 157DI
220 RI, Marmade	

134 Brigade [disbanded 3.17]

259 RI, Foix	4.16 disbanded
283 RI, St Gaudens	
288 RI, Mirande	

Infantry from 3.17

220 RI	12.17 disbanded-replaced by 369RI ex88DI
283 RI	
288 RI	

Artillery

4 Gp/18 RAC	4.17 to 218 RAC
4 Gp/23 RAC	4.17 to 218 RAC
5 Gp/57 RAC	4.17 to 218 RAC
7 Gp/134 RAL	6.18-added –ex 3/334RAL

Cavalry

5/10RD, 8.14 only
6/10RD, 8.14 only
2/19RCh, 11.15-8.16d
6/19RCh, 11.15-8.16
E/6RCA, 9.16 –6.17
E/6RCA, 9.16-6.17
1/12RH, 7.17-11.18
2/12RH, 7.17-5.18d

Engineers & Pioneers

1914=Cie 17/13, 17/19, 17/24 du 2RG
1918=Cie 17/13, 17.63, 17/24 du 2RG
1.18=Pioneer Battalion 32RIT

By 22nd August 1914 the division had joined 3GDR east of Verdun. There it fought at Eton and Longeau before falling back on Bezonvaux. From 27th August until 2nd September it fought south of Verdun, at Paroches and Samogneux, as the line between the Verdun salient and the St Mihiel salient was created. During Third Army's battle of Revigny [first battle of the Marne], it fought at Ippecourt and then at St Remy, Dompierre and Ranzieres during October. From then until 5th April 1915, it held First Army's front between Vaux-les-Palameix and Seuzey, and then to Bois Loclont. The division fought at Lamorville during the first battle of Woevre and then established a line between Maizey and Vaux-les-Palameix which it held until 16th January 1916.

Tranferred northwards to Verdun, it fought on the left bank of the Meuse, at Bethincourt, Forges and Mort Homme until 12th March. The division was transferred to Fifth Army at Reims where it fought at Betheny and Neuvillette, 22nd April-22nd August 1916. It returned to Verdun and fought between Vaux Chapitre and the Ouvrage de Thiaumont from 2nd to 22nd September.

The division returned to the Moselle front on 6th October 1916 and remained there until 30th June 1917. It held positions near Fey-en-Haye and at Limey. On 19th August, it joined Sixth Army on the Chemin des Dames where it did three tours in the trenches: Pantheon/Epine de Chevregny [19th August-26th September and 5th-29th October] and Ferme Brunin/Ferme Malval [20th November-26th December]. It took part in Sixth Army's attack on Malmaison from 23rd-27th October when it took Filain.

After a long period of retraining at Ville-en-Tardenois, the division occupied Fifth Army's positions between Sapigneul and the Miette [2nd February 1918-18th March 1918], after which it was hurriedly moved to Picardy in response to the German spring offensive. During the second battle of Picardy it fought at Mortemer, Orvillers-Sorel and Rollot until it was withdrawn on 23rd May.

The division remained in reserve during the third battle of the Aisne and then fought with Third Army on the Matz [10th June-10th August]. It fought at Mont de Caumont and held the line between Chevincourt and Machermont. As part of the allied offensive which commenced on 8th August, the division attacked the Thiescourt plateau, liberated Ribecourt, and moved forward to new positions between the Divette and Noyon. After a short break, it continued to participate in the advance of First Army when it advanced from the Barisis-aux-Bois/Oise line towards the Serre. Between 10th and 20th October, it liberated the area between the Oise and the Serre. During the battle for the Serre, it fought at Anguilcourt, Nouvion-Catillon, Catillon-du-Temple, Mesbrecourt and Assis-sur-Serre and then organised a line in the freed areas.

The division was at rest near Sains-Richaumont from 5th November 1918.

68 Division d'Infanterie

The reserve division of the 18th Military Region formed at Bordeaux on mobilisation.

Commanders
20.08.14-Emile Brun d'Aubignosc
27.09.14-Joseph Mordrelle
13.03.15-Joseph Kaufmant
25.04.15-Léon Prax
02.03.17-Jean-Louis Menvielle

135 Brigade [disbanded 3.17]
206 RI, Saintes
234 RI, Mont de Marsan
323 RI, La Rochelle   6.16 disbanded

136 Brigade [disbanded 3.17]
212 RI, Tarbes   3.17 to 88DI
257 RI, Lilbourne   6.16 disbanded
344 RI, Bordeaux

Infantry from 3.17
206 RI
234 RI
344 RI

Artillery
4 Gp/14 RAC   9.14 to 64DI –not replaced until
10.15-Gp/62RAC ex 71DI
4.17 to 224 RAC
5 Gp/24 RAC   4.17 to 224 RAC
4 Gp/58 RAC   4.17 to 224 RAC
Gp7/130 RAL   7.18 added- ex 3/310RAL

Cavalry
5/15RD, 8.14-1.16
6/15RD, 8.14-1.16
9/10RH, 1.16-8.16
10/10RH,1.16-8.16
3/18RD, 8.16–10.17

4/18ED, 8.16-3.17
3/12RH, 11.17-11.18
4/12RH, 11.17-11.18

Engineers & Pioneers
1914=Cie 18/13, 18/19, 18/24 du 2RG
1918=Cie 18/13, 18/63, 18/24 du 2RG
7.17=Pioneer Battalion 73RIT

The division joined 2GDR, in Second Army, and occupied positions near Dombasle and Cercueil [15th August 1914] from which it advanced to Delme and took part in the battle of Morhange. During this battle it fought at Viviers, Faxe and Delme. From 21st August it fell back towards Art-sur-Meurthe and took up a new position at Amance. It fought at Champenoux, Erbéviller and the Foret de Champenoux during the

battle for the Grand Couronne de Nancy [5th-13th September]. Transferred south to First Army, it re-entered the line between Bezange-la-Grande and Armaucourt on 13th September and remained there until 14th February 1916.

It entered the contest for Verdun at Eix on 27th February and fought for Damloup until 8th June. After a brief rest, it was moved to the Bois Carre/Bois d'Avocourt sector on the left bank of the Meuse where it repulsed a German attack on 12th August. On 25th August it took over positions between the Ouvrage de Thiaumont and Bois de Vaux Chapitre and engaged in heavy fighting [3rd-12th September].

After a short rest, the division returned to Lorraine and held the line between Armaucourt and the Sanon from 29th September 1916 until 22nd May 1917.

The division joined Sixth Army [and then Tenth Army] on the Chemin des Dames when it arrived at the Courtecon/Ferme de la Bovelle sector on 6th July. It moved to the Malval/Courtecon sector on 19th September and played a minor support role in the battle for Malmaison, after which it was withdrawn for rest and retraining on 19th October.

On 8th December 1917 the division re-entered the Verdun salient and took over positions at Beaumont and the Bois de Chaume which it held until 29th January 1918. After another rest, it moved to the left bank positions at Forges and the Bois d'Avocourt on 1st March. It remained there until 17th July 1918.

During the second battle of the Marne [from 30th July], the division fought with Tenth Army from the Ourcq to Tardenois, and engaged the Germans at Cramaille and Severnay. On 4th August it reached the Vesle and established a new line Braine/Limé and later to Baroches. The division then moved to Fourth Army in Champagne. Initially located between Wacques and Auberge-de- l'Esperance, it fought in the battle of Somme-Py [26th September-14th October] and pursued the Germans across the Py to the Arne. By 12th October it had reached Retourne from which it went into reserve.

From 24th October until the armistice, the division was located in the Vosges where it occupied the line between Burnhaupt-le-Haut and Leimbach.

69 Division d'Infanterie

Formed at Reims on mobilisation with units from 2nd and 6th Military Regions.

Commanders
02.08.14-Henri Le Gros
08.09.14-Henri Neraud
05.11.14-Pierre Berdoulat
29.04.15-Emile Taufflieb
28.05.16-Louis Monroe dit Roe

137 Brigade [disbanded 12.16]
287 RI, St Quentin   12.16 to 165DI-not replaced
306 RI, Châlons sur Marne   6.16 disbanded

332 RI, Reims   11.16 to 42 DI- not replaced
138 Brigade [disbanded 12.16]
254 RI, Compiègne   6.16 disbanded
267 RI, Soissons
251 RI, Beauvais   12.16 to 40DI
48 BCP- new unit   6.15 to 121DI

Infantry from 12.16
151 RI   Ex 42DI
162 RI   Ex 42DI
267 RI   9.17 disbanded-replaced by 129RI ex 153Bde
29 Bn Tirr.Sénégalais   7.18 attached

Artillery
4 Gp/46 RAC & Bty/44RAC   6.16 to Gp/46RAC 4.17 to 268RAC
5 Gp/46 RAC & Bty/29RAC   6.16 to Gp/46RAC 4.17 to 268RAC
6 Gp/28 RAC & Bty/50 RAC   6.16 to Gp/28RAC 4.17 to 268RAC
7 Gp/132 RAL   6.18-added- ex 2/332RAL

Cavalry
5/5RD, 8.14 –11.15d
6/5RD, 8.14-11.15d
5/10RH,11.15 –2.16
6/10RH,11.15-2.16
5/25RD, 6.16–11.16
6/25RD, 6.16-11.16
4/20RCh, 12.16-11.18

Engineers & Pioneers
1914   Cie 22/13, 22/17, 22/22 du 1RG
1918   Cie 22/13, 22/63 du 1RG Cie 13/25 du 4RG
8.18=Pioneer Battalion 86RIT   From ICA

By 15th August 1914 the division had joined 4GDR, Fifth Army, at Vervins from which it advanced northwards on 21st August to Montignies-St-Christophe. It fought there during the battle of Charleroi until 24th August. During Fifth Army's retreat to the Marne, the division moved southwards via St Hilaire-sur- Helpe to Moy and fought in the first battle of Guise between Urvillers and Bay. During the initial phases of the first battle of the Marne, the division remained in reserve at Villers St Georges. From 7th September it advanced through Montmirail, Cierges and Jonchery towards Reims and established a line south of the Neuvilette and Sapigneul which it held until 4th October. A week later it moved west along the Aisne to positions at Condé and Moussy. After some fighting at Vailly and Soupir [30th October-3rd November] the division remained in this sector until 20th February 1916.

The division joined the battle for Verdun on 8th April 1916 and, after a few days near Fort Vaux, it was transferred to the left bank of the Meuse to meet the German offensive on Mort Homme. It fought for Mort Homme and for Cumieres throughout May 1916 and was withdrawn from the salient on 24th June.

It spent the next year with Fifth Army, north-west of Reims. From 16th June 1916 until 8th February 1917 it was line between Berry-au-Bac and Moulin Pontoy; between Sapigneul and the Miette, 3rd March-10th April; and north east of Berry-au-Bac, 14th April –7th May. During the second battle of the Aisne it attacked the Bois Claque-Dents on 16th April.

The division re-entered the frontline outside Verdun on 17th July and occupied lines between Damloup and Louvemont until 16th September. It took part in the second Verdun offensive on 20th August, and fought in the Bois de Chaume, 8th-14th September. Two days later it was withdrawn for a long period of rest and retraining near Vancouleurs in Lorraine.

Until 17th January 1918, the division was employed as a training unit for newly-arrived American troops. On that date it resumed an operational role, and took over the quiet sector in Lorraine between the Etang de Vargevaux and Limey. It moved to the adjacent Seicheprey/Bois-de-la-Pretre sector on 4th April where it remained for the next two months.

The division joined Third Army in its defence of the Matz line on 9th June and fought in and around Antheuil. Rested from 18th June, the division joined Tenth Army on 18th July and fought in the second battle of the Marne. Following a period in reserve at Villers Cotterêts, it advanced towards Missy-aux-Bois on 22nd July and by 2nd August had reached a line on the south bank of the Aisne between Venizel and Soissons. From 29th August it took parrt in 10th Army's assault on the Hindenburg Line. It crossed the Aisne and took Crouy on 2nd September and reached Vregny three days later.

On 6th September the division moved to Lorraine and went into reserve near Nancy. From 12th October until the armistice, it held the line on the Seille between Brin-et-Han. It was transferred to Tenth Army on 10th November as that army prepared for the advance on Metz.

70 Division d'Infanterie

The reserve division of the 20th Military Region formed at Neufchateau on mobilisation.

Commanders
02.08.14-Charles Bizard
13.08.14-Emile Fayolle
21.06.15-Alphonse Nudant
26.02.16-Henri Galon
28.11.16-Emile Tantot

139 Brigade [disbanded 4.17]
226 RI, Toul
269 RI, Toul
42 BCP, Luneville
44 BCP, St Nicholas

140 Brigade [disbanded 4.17]
237 RI, Troyes   6.16 disbanded
279 RI, Nancy   4.17 to 81DI- not replaced
360 RI, Neufchateau

Infantry from 4.17
226 RI
269 RI   1.18 disbanded –replaced by 17 Group-42,
44BCP, 114BCA
360 RI
42 BCP & 44 BCP   1.18 to 17Group
Artillery
4 Gp/8 RAC   4.17 to 208 RAC
5 Gp/60 RAC & Bty/5RAC   4.17 to 208 RAC
6 Gp/60 RAC & Bty/59RAC   4.17 to 208 RAC
5 Gp/133 RAL   2.18 –added –ex 12/103RAL
3.18-redesignated
Cavalry
5/23 RD, 8.14-11.15d
6/23 RD, 8.14-11.15d
E/4RS, 11.15-7.17
E/4RS, 11.15-7.17
Engineers & Pioneers
1914   Cie 20/11, 20/17, 20/22 du 10RG

1918   Cie 20/11, 20/61 du 10RG Cie 15/23 du 7RG
8.18-Pioneer Battalion 26RIT   From IIICA

The division assembled at Nancy on 8th August 1914 and was engaged in the preparation of defense works until the battle of Morhange in which it fought at Amance, Leyr, Jeaudecourt and Hoeville. During the battle for the Grand Couronne de Nancy, it fought at Hoeville [25th August], St Libaire [1st September], Courbessaux [5th September], and the Foret de St Paul [8th-9th September]. From 13th September, it consolidated defences around Hoeville, Serres and Bauzemont.
On 3rd October, it joined Tenth Army in Artois when it took up positions facing Vimy Ridge at La Targette and Carency. The division remained in Artois until 20th February 1916. During this long period it participated in the first, second and third battles of Artois. In the first battle it fought at Neuvireul, Oppy and Arleux-en-Gonelle and then at Souchez and la Targette. During the second battle in May 1915, it fought at Carency and Ablain-St-Nazaire. During the autumn battles it fought at Givenchy, Souchez and la Folie.

The division entered the battle for Verdun on 20th March 1916 when it moved up into the heights above the town near the Ferme de Thiaumont and the Etang de Vaux. Pulled out on 6th April, it moved to the St Mihiel salient and occupied the line between Limey and Fey-en-Haye from 15th May until 29th July 1916.

When the division took over Sixth Army's sector between Barleux and the river Somme on 19th August it began a lengthy period of activity during the battle of the Somme. It took part in attacks on Ommiecourt-les- Cléry [5th September] and on the Bois l'Abbé [12th-16th September]. From 1st October it occupied a less active sector between Feullieres and Barleux from which it moved to Sixth Army's line between Ferme

Quennevières and Hautebraye on 10th December. The German withdrawal to the Hindenburg Line caused the division to move forward into the wasteland in front of the Massif St Gobain, 17th March-4th May 1917. After a brief tour between Barisis and the Oise, the division joined Sixth Army on the Chemin des Dames. It held the line between Malval and the Epine de Chevregny from 21st June to 25th July 1917.

The summer of 1917 was spent in training near Lure and then on labour duties near Belfort. The division was stationed between the Rhine-Rhone canal and Leimbach from 11th September 1917 until 28th March 1918.

A further period of retraining near Bruyeres was interrupted by the German spring offensive. The division was moved to Picardy and fought with Third Army and then with First Army at Rollot and at le Tronquoy until 17th April. Therafter, the division resumed its rest and retraining in Lorraine-at Remiremont and Gerardmer.

After a month in line between Metzeral and the Fave, in the Vosges [11th May-16th June], the division moved to the Marne and joined Tenth Army on 18th June. It was held in reserve until 12th July when it occupied a sector between Bailly and Bois St Mard. After several transfers between Tenth Army and Third Army, the division its participation in the allied offensives on 12th August. During the third battle of Picardy it fought at Mareuil-Lamotte and from 30th August moved up to the Hindenburg Line north west of the Fere. Pulled out for a rest on 14th September, the division moved north to Flanders.

From 12th October until 3rd November, the division fought as part of the French contribution to the final allied advance out of the Ypres salient and into occupied Belgium. Initially, it fought in the Foret d'Houthulst out of which it advanced on 15th October. It fought at Tielt and liberated Nevelle on 20th October. Thereafter it moved forward to the line of the Schelde. From 3rd November 1918, it was in reserve at Deinze.

71 Division d'Infanterie

The reserve division of the 21st Military Region, which was formed as a fortress division at Epinal on mobilisation.

Commanders
02.08.14-Joseph Kaufmant
13.03.15-Jospeh Mordrelle
07.06.17-Jules Ganter
28.10.18-Paul Barbier

141 Brigade [disbanded 1.17]
349 RI, Epinal   6.16 disbanded
358 RI, Bruyeres and Lyon
370 RI, Epinal   1.17 to 170DI

142 Brigade [disbanded 1.17]
217 RI, Epinal
221 RI, Langres
309 RI, Chaumont   6.16 disbanded

151 Brigade-attached 9.14-1.15 then to 66DI [later 129DI]
297 RI
357 RI
359 RI
41BCP ex XIIICA- to 41DI 2.15

Infantry from 1.17
217 RI
221 RI
358 RI

Artillery
4 Gp/4 RAC   4.17 to 262 RAC
4 Gp/62 RAC   4.17 to 262 RAC
5 Gp/62 RAC   4.17 to 262 RAC
5 Gp/138 RAL   New formed and added 5.18

Cavalry
5/12RH, 8.14-12.14
6/12RH, 8.14-12.14
5/19RD, 12.14-1.16
6/19RD, 12.14-1.16d
5/12RH, 1.16 –4.17
6/12RH, 1.16-4.17
2/11RD, 5.17-7.17
4/10RCh, 7.17-11.18

Engineers & Pioneers
1914=Cie 27/1, 27/21 du 11RG
1918=Cie 27/1, 27/51, 27/21 du 11RG
8.18-Pioneer Battalion 131RIT   from VIIICA

On 14th August 1914 the division left Epinal and joined First Army to take and cover the passes in the Vosges between the Col du Bonhomme and the Col Ste Marie. It fought for the latter pass on 22nd-25th August and then retreated across the Meurthe and back to Épinal. It remained there until 9th September when it advanced back to the Meurthe and seized positions between the Avricourt railway and the valley of the Celles. It established new positions between that railway and the Chapelotte on 14th September. It remained in this sector until 10th June 1916, during which time it fought a series of limited actions near Badonvillers and the Ferme de Chamois.

In June 1916 the division was moved to the Verdun salient and entered the line byween Damloup and the Bois Fumin on 6th July. Two weeks later it was moved to the northern flank of the salient-the Argonne- and carried out three tours in the trenches there: Avocourt/Aire [22nd July-19th December 1916]; Hayette/Charny [6th January-27th February 1917] and Four de Paris/Aisne [28th March-4th June 1917].

The division joined Fourth Army in Champagne and served in its sector between Auberive and the Soauin/Ste Marie-a-Py road from 28th June until 15th July. After this short tour it moved further west to Fifth Army and spent a long period in the trenches around Sapigneul from 27th July 1917 until 11th May 1918.

After a brief spell in Flanders, 29th May-8th July 1918, during which time the division fought near Loker, it returned to 4th Army and fought with that army at Prosnes on 15th July. During the second battle of the Marne, it took part in operations between Moscou and Mont Cornillet.

The division took part in Fourth Army's autumn offensives. From positions between the Aisne and Vienne- le-Chateau it fought for Ville-sur-Tourbe and the Bois d'Hauzy, 29th September-21st October 1918. Four days later, it took over the line between Olizy and Falaise and fought at the latter location before participation in the battle of Chesne on 4th-5th November.

The division was resting at Chaussée-sur-Marne when hostilities ended.

72 Division d'Infanterie

A reserve division formed as a fortress division at Verdun on mobilisation.

Commanders
02.08.14-Jules Heymann
31.10.14-Etienne Bapst
03.03.16-Louis Ferradini

143 Brigade [re-organised 3.16]
351 RI, Verdun   3.16 to 29DI
362 RI, Verdun
56 BCP, Conflans
59 BCP, Longuyon   3.16 to 144 Bde

143 Brigade [3.16- 5.17]
164 RI
326 RI   1.17 disbanded
56 BCP   5.17 to Assault Artillery then to 77DI

144 Brigade [reorganised 3.16]
364 RI, Verdun   7.15 to 132DI-replaced by 164 RI ex Gp Verdun
365 RI, Verdun   7.15 to 107 Bde-replaced by 165RI ex Gp Verdun- to 29DI 3.16
366 RI, Verdun   7.15 to 132DI

144 Brigade [3.16-5.17]
324 RI
365 RI
59 BCP   3.17 to 153BI, then to 154BI and to 97DI 4.17

108 Brigade- added 9.14 –to 132DI 7.15
303 RI   7.15 to 132 DI
324 RI   7.15 to 107 Bde
330 RI   7.15 to 132 DI

107 Brigade-added 7.15-disbanded 3.16
324 RI   Ex 108 BI-to 144 BI
365 RI   Ex 144 BI-to 144 BI

Infantry from 5.17
164 RI

324 RI
365 RI 7.18 disb.replaced by 1RdMZT ex 153DI

Artillery
4 Gp/61 RAC 4.17 to 261 RAC
5 Gp/59 RAC " Bty/11RAC, Bty/41RAC, Bty/45RAC "
5 Gp/130 RAL Newly formed and added 4.18

Cavalry
5/2RH, 8.14-8.16
5/4RH, 8.14-7.15
1/3 RD, 1.17-7.17
2/3 RD, 1.17-4.17 & 6.17-7.17

Engineers & Pioneers
1914 Cie 25/1, 25/21 du 9RG
1918 Cie 25/1, 25/51, 25/21 du 9RG
8.18-Pioneer Battalion 31RIT   from XXXCA

The division remained in the Verdun area from mobilisation until 25th February 1916. During the first weeks of the war it engaged the Germans at Fresnes-en-Woevre [17th-24th August]. Étain [25th August], Béthincourt [29th August] and on the right bank of the Meuse, outside Verdun [10th-29th September] and again at Etain [4th-20th October]. From 20th October 1914 until 25th February 1916 it held the line between Vacherauville and Douaumont. It was virtually destroyed in the first days of the German assault on Verdun and remants were pulled out of the line after five days of intense fighting.

A rebuilt division joined the battle of the Somme on 6th July 1916. As part of Sixth Army, it fought at Feuilleres and Flaucourt and then at Biaches and Bois Blaize until 24th July. After a rest near Montdidier, it took over the line between Dancourt and the Bois des Loges on 11th August. From there it fought towards Armancourt and engaged in mining operations at Beuvraignes. On 4th December it moved to the Pressoire/Ablaincourt sector where it remained until 10th January 1917.

The division returned to Verdun and between 21st January and 5th May 1917, held positions on the Meuse heights between Vaux-devant-Damloup and Chatillon. It moved to Champagne on 8th May and began a long period of service with Fourth Army. It undertook five tours in the frontline between 12th May 1917 and 27th March 1918. They were Mont Haut/Casque [12th May-9th June]; Têton/Mont Haut [30th June-23rd July]; Maisons de Champagne/Butte de Mesnil [5th August-3rd September]; Têton/Mont Haut [14th September-7th November] and Auberive/Vaudesincourt/Prosnes [28th February-27th March].

On 23rd April 1918 the division joined Third Army in the Oise region where it held the line between the Oise and Cannectancourt and fought at Marchermont during the battle of the Matz [9th June-1st July]. During the second battle of the Marne, it fought with Tenth Army for the Montagne de Paris [19th-22nd July] and secured the line of the Aisne between Fontenay and Soissons. During the second battle for Noyon [20th August], it fought at Pommiers. In the autumn offensives, during which HQ Third Army took over from HQ Tenth Army, it occupied a sector between Jouey and Aizy, advanced to the Ailette [25th September], and reached Samousy [12th October]. During the battle for the Serre, the division pursued the Germans to the Souche and took Vesles-et-Caumont and Pierrepont. It advanced towards the Meuse via Chivres and Montcornet, 5th-7th November, after which it went into reserve. On 11th November 1918 the division was moving between Gizy, Pierrepont and Notre Dame de Liesse.

73 Division d'Infanterie

A reserve division formed at Toul as a fortress division on mobilisation.

Commanders
02.08.14-Joseph Chatelain
29.08.14-Charles Martin de Laporte d'Hulst

09.09.14-Henri Lebocq

145 Brigade [disbanded 2.17]
346 RI, Toul
353 RI, Toul   6.16-disbanded
356 RI, Toul

146 Brigade [disbanded 2.17]
367 RI, Toul
368 RI, Toul   6.16-disbanded
369 RI, Toul   2.17- to 88DI

Infantry from 2.17
346 RI
356 RI
367 RI

Artillery
4 Gp/12 RAC   4.17 to 239 RAC
4 Gp/39 RAC   " Bies from 37/49/52RAC
Gp/24 RAC   4.15 ex 153DI –to 129DI 10.16
7Gp/138 RAL   Added 7.18-ex 2/338RAL

Cavalry
5/4RD, 8.14–11.15d
6/12RD, 8.14-11.15d
5/16RCh, 11.15-8.16
6/16RCh, 11.15-8.16
1/12 RH, 8.16-4.17
2/12 RH, 8.16-7.17
5/11 RH, 12.16-8.17d
6/11 RH, 12.16-8.17d
1/11 RD, 7.17 –9.18
2/11 RD, 7.17-9.18
6/ 7RD, 11.18-

Engineers & Pioneers
1914   Cie 26/1, 26/3, 26/21 du 10RG
1918   26/3, 26/53, 26/21 du 10RG
7.18-Pioneer Battalion 45RIT

After a few weeks engaged in the preparation of defensive positions at Toul, the division fought at Pont-a- Mousson, 5th-10th September 1914 and then fought at Troyon from 12th –19th September. During this latter period of conflict it fought at Heudicourt and St Maurice. Between 21st and 28th September it fought in the battle of Flirey between Flirey and the Fôret de Puvenelle. After action at Lironville, the plateau de Mamey and at Fey-en-Haye, the front was stabilised. The division took up positions between the Bois-de-la-Pretre and Bois Mort Mare and held them from 28th September 1914 until 1st September 1915. On that latter date it moved to the adjacent sector between Bois and Fey where it remained until 18th July 1916.

On 28th August 1916, the division entered the struggle for Verdun and between then and 11th September fought in the Bois de Vaux Chapitre [especially 5th-6th September]. It moved back to Lorraine and took up positions between the Vezouve and Embermésnil on 20th September. Its area of responsibility was extended to the Sanon on 29th September and the division remained in line until 27th May 1917.

The division served in the Argonne, between Hayette and the Bois d'Avocourt from 25th June until 22nd July 1917 after which it moved to the Swiss frontier where it was in line between 8th August 1917 and 13th May 1918.

It joined Sixth Army near Château-Thierry on 31st May 1918 and fought in the third battle of the Aisne between Vinly and Chéry-en-Orxois [7th-8th June] and in the fourth battle of Champagne at Courtemont [15th-25th July]. As the latter battle merged into the second battle of the Marne, the division crossed the Marne between Sauvigny and Courtemont and entered the Foret de Riex [22nd July].

After a brief rest, the division returned to the Argonne and held positions between Haute Chevauchée and Avocourt from 23rd August until 20th September. During the last three days of this tour, the division came under command of the American army. It rejoined 4th Army and fought in the battle of Somme-Py during October. It fought at the Crete d'Orfeuil [4th-8th October] and pursued the enemy to Attigny where it organised a line [12th-23rd October].

The division left Champagne on 23rd October and took up positions in the Vosges, between the Chapelotte and the Vezouve on 31st October.

74 Division d'Infanterie

Reserve division of the 14th Military Region formed at Chambéry on mobilisation.

Commanders
02.08.14-Louis Bigot
29.02.16-Charles de Lardemelle

147 Brigade [disbanded 3.17]
222 RI, Santhony	
299 RI, Lyon	
36 RIC	6.15 to 16DIC-replaced by 43, 50 & 71BCP's
3.16-43BCP to 133DI	
53 BCA, Chambéry	8.14 to 28DI
54 BCA, Albertville	10.14 to GAV then to 77DI

148 Brigade [disbanded 3.17]
223 RI, Bourg	6.16 –disbanded
230 RI, Annecy	
333 RI, Belley	3.17 to 157DI
51 BCA, Annecy	8.14 to 28DI
62 BCA, Albertville	8.14 to 28DI
43, 50 & 71 BCP's	10.14 added-ex XIIICA-to 47 Bde 6.15

Infantry from 3.17
222 RI	12.17 –disbanded-66BCP ex 9DI
230 RI	
299 RI	
50 & 71 BCP's	12.17-to 16Group-50,66,71 BCPs
	6.18-Gp dissolved-replaced by 5RdMTM

Artillery
4 Gp/54 RAC	4.17 to 254 RAC
4 Gp/1 RAM [2 bies]	8.14 to GAV- 9.14 replaced by Bty/2RAC
5 Gp/1 RAM [3 bies]	8.14 to GAV- 9.14 replaced by Bty/2RAC extra bty added 2.16
4.17 to 254RAC	
5 Gp/14RAC	8.15-added –ex XXXIIICA
4.17 to 254RAC	
6 Gp /138 RAL	2.18-ex 12/115RAL

Cavalry
5/2 RD, 8.14-1.16

7/11RCh, 9.16-3.17
8/11RCh, 9.16–3.17
1/12 RH, 4.17 -7.17
E/1RS, 7.18-11.18

Engineers & Pioneers
1914   Cie 13/14 du 4RG
1918   Cie 13/14, 13/64 du 4RG Cie 10/25 du 6RG
7.18-Pioneer Battalion 101RIT   From XVCA

When the Italian threat to the Alpine frontier failed to materialise the division was sent northwards to join Second Army in Lorraine. From 23rd August 1914, it occupied a defence line along the Moselle at Charmes and Bayon, and then ,fought in the battle of the Grand Couronne during which it took Gerbéviller on 28th August. On 5th September it fought at Rehainviller and the Bois St Mansuy, and took part in attacks on Chauffontaine and Herimenil.

From 12th September 1914 until 28th December 1915 the division occupied positions near Lunéville, in the sector near the Arracourt/Avricourt railway. It fought in a series of local actions at Réchicourt-la-Petite [26th October and 22nd November] and at Embermenil [18th June]. On 10th July the division moved to the adjacent sector between the Vezouve and the Sanon and continued to fight a series of local actions, principally near Leintrey. On 30th September it front was extended to Bezange-la-Grande.

After a period of rest and retraining, and labour duties on the right bank of the Meurthe, the division took over the line between Pont-à-Mousson and Armaucourt on 3rd February 1916. It was pulled out on 18th August and retrained for operations in the Verdun salient. It took part in the first French offensive at Verdun and fought at Bois Vaux Chapitre and then at the Damloup Battery between 21st and 30th October. It moved south of the salient and took over the line between Dompcevrin and Bois Loclont on 15th November. It returned to the salient on 1st February 1917 when it arrived in the Louvemont/Chambrettes sector where it remained until 7th March.

On 31st March 1917, the division joined Fourth Army in its trenches between Maisons de Champagne and the Aisne. It left there on 11th June to join Fifth Army north-west of Reims. Between 2nd July 1917 and 14th May 1918, the division occupied positions around Sapigneul, between the Miette and Godat. During the third battle of the Aisne [25th May-5th June], as part of Sixth Army, it defended positions on the Aisne between Condé and Pont Rouge. This was followed by further action on either side of the river at Chavigny and Vertefeuille.

After a rest and retraining period near Verberie, the division joined Third Army on 6th July and occupied the sector between Antheuil and Villers-sur-Coudun until 23rd August. It fought on the right bank of the Oise at Marque, Gury and Plessis du Roye during the third battle of Picardy. Transferred to Fourth Army on 4th September, it took part in that army's autumn offensive [25th September-16th October]. From Ville-sur- Tourbe, it fought between Massiges and the Aisne. By 16th October the division had advanced to the Dormoise and the Bouconville, crossed the Aisne again and had taken Olizy and had reached Mouron. From 23rd October until 3rd November, it held the line between Falaise and Olizy. It remained in reserve at Autry and Montcheutin. Withdrawn from the line on 6th November, the division was at Possessée when the armistice was signed.

75 Division d'Infanterie

The reserve division of the 15th Military Region formed at Avignon on mobilisation.

Commanders
02.08.14-Charles Vimard
25.09.14-Eugene Buisson d'Armandy

149 Brigade [11.14 to XVCA-disbanded 6.15]
240 RI, Nîmes
258 RI, Avignon
42 RIC

150 Brigade [11.14 to VCA-disbanded 6.15]
255 RI, St Esprit
261 RI, Aix
44 RIC

Artillery
4 Gp/19 RAC	11.14 to VCA then 12.14 to XXXVCA
6 Gp/2 RAM	11.14 remained in Verdun Fortress
5 Gp/38 RAC (2 btys)	11.14 to VCA

Cavalry
7/9 RCh
8/9 RCh

Engineers
Cie 15/12 du 7RG

Withdrawn from the Alpine front when the threat from Italy did not materialise, the division joined the Armée de Lorraine at Étain on 22nd August. It fought near Étain at St Maurice and Gussainville before retreating towards Verdun on 26th August. It was moved north of the town to fight in the Bois d'Ormont and at Flabas on 1st September. It fell back through Douaumont and Fleury to positions south of Verdun. Between 7th and 9th September, as part of 3GDR, it took part in Third Army's battle of Revigny [part of the first battle of the Marne], and fought at Souilly and Ippecourt. Between 10th and 23rd September it struggled to establish a line south of Verdun and fought at Vigneulles-les-Hattonchatel and the Tranchee de Calonne [20th-21st September]. Thereafter it occupied the rightbank of the Meuse between Chauvoncourt and Dompcervin and attacked and failed to save St Mihiel on 25th September. It occupied the line between Chauvoncourt and Koeur-la-Grande-at the apex of the St Mihiel salient until 2nd November.
The division was disbanded at Pierrefitte on 6th November 1914.

76 Division d'Infanterie

Formed 05.9.14 as Division de Vassart, mainly from units of 44DI. Numbered 12.10.14

Commanders
08.09.14-Jean de Vassart d'Andernay
08.03.18-Erenest Siben
89 Brigade [disbanded 10.16]
157 RI	Ex 44DI
163 RI	Ex 44DI 6.15 to 97Bde-replaced by 210RI
ex VIIICA	

2nd Colonial Brigade [6.15 to 15DIC]
5 RIC
6 RIC

97 Brigade [formed 6.15] [disbanded 10.16]
163 RI	Ex 89 Brigade 10.16 to 161DI
227 RI	Ex VIII CA

Infantry from 10.16
157 RI
210 RI
227 RI

Artillery
2 btys/6RAC & 1 bty/53RAC	4.17 to 274RAC

2 btyd/38RAC & 1 bty/57RAC
2 btys/2RACC
Gp/53 RAC
4.17 to 274RAC
Gp/2RAM

4.17 to 274RAC
2.15 added 12.16 to XXICA –replaced by

1.17 added-remained with division after 4.17

Cavalry
5/1 RCh, 9.14-6.16
6/1 RCh, 9.14-6.16
5/11 RH, 6.16-8.16
6/11 RH, 6.16-8.16
E/5RCA, 8.16-11.18
E/5RCA, 8.16-10.16

Engineers & Pioneers
1914= Cie 27/6 du 11RG
1918=Cie 7/52T du 4RG Cie 27/6 du 11RG Cie 15/24 du 7RG
No Pioneer Battalion allocated

The division formed in the Vosges from components of 44DI and, after labour duties near Rambervillers, it attacked Col de Chipotte on 12th September and then pursued the Germans to Raon-l'Etape and Celles. The division moved north to the St Mihiel salient on 26th September and fought at Bouconville during the battle of Flirey. It occupied the sector between St Agnant and Rambucourt until 12th March 1915 when it moved to the adjacent sector between Flirey and Seicheprey. During the first battle of the Woëvre it attacked Mort Mare between 5th and 10th April. The division was withdrawn on 10th January 1916.

It arrived in the Verdun salient on 16th March and spent a month in line between Bethincourt and the Bois d'Avocourt, after which it returned to the Vosges. It occupied positions between the Col Ste Marie and the Chapelotte from 6th June until 7th September. On the latter date its front was extended to the Col du Bonhomme.

The division left the Vosges on 28th November 1916 and arrived in Salonika on 4th January 1917. During its service in Macedonia, it served in the line from 15th-23rd February 1917 [Albanian frontier between Koritsa and the Col de Tchafa Kiarits]; 2nd March-6th August 1917 [Monastir]; 14th August 1917-19th April 1918 [Monastir/Côte 1248]; 8th May-1st July 1918 [Albanian frontier near Lake Okrida]; and 5th July-14th September 1918 [Monastir]. It took part in the allied advance which began on 14th September. It took the Cols de Lopatitsa and Koukouretchani, and moved forward to Egri Palanka and Kioustendil.

After the collapse of the Central Powers the division moved north into Serbia. It became part of the Army of the Danube and remained active into 1919.

77 Division d'Infanterie

Formed 08.09.14 as Division Barbot, mainly from units of 44DI. Also known as 'B' Division 30.09.14 and numbered 12.10.14

Commanders
08.09.14-Ernest Barbot
11.05.15-Paul Stirn
14.05.15-Stephane Pillot
24.01.16-Gaspard de Cugnac
17.12.16-Marius Guillemot
09.01.18-Anthoine Peschard D'Ambly
17.04.18-Bernard de Serrigny

88 Brigade [disbanded 11.17]
97 RI	Ex 44DI
159 RI	Ex Gp Besancon 10.15 to 93 Bde
17 BCP 10.15	Ex 13DI 11.17 to 66DI
57 BCP 10.15	Ex GpCh

Group de Chasseurs [10.15 replaced by 93 Brigade]
54 BCP	12.14 to GAV
57 BCP	10.15 to 88 Bde 11.17 disbanded
60 BCP	10. 15 to 93 Bde
61 BCP	10.15 to 93 Bde

93 Brigade [formed 10.15] [disbanded 11.17]
159 RI	Ex 88 Bde
60 BCP	Ex GpCh
61 BCP	Ex GpCh

Infantry from 11.17
97 RI
159 RI
14 Gp de Chasseurs [56, 60, 61 BCP's]   56 BCP ex Assault artillery 11.17

Artillery
2 Btys/6RAC & 1 bty/9RAC	4.17 to 6 RAC
2 btys/38RAC & 1 bty/58RAC	" Gp6/6RAC "
6 Gp/133 RAL	New formed and added 3.18

Cavalry
E/4RS, 11.16-10.17
E/4RS, 11.16-10.17

Engineers & Pioneers
1914   Cie 14/13 du 4RG
1918   Cie 14/13, 14/63 du 4RG Cie 15/73 du 7RG
7.18-Pioneer Battalion 122RIT   From VCA

Formed from elements of 44DI, the division was thrown into the battle for Morhange immediately. It fought at St Remy and on the Salle, 5th-12th September. After a movement towards the Meurthe, it fought at Senones, Laitre and Launois and established a line between Senones and Badonviller between by 28th September.

The division arrived in Artois on 1st October 1914 and for the next 18 months fought a series of battles for the control of Vimy Ridge. Initially located to the north-east of Arras at St Laurent, Blagny and Roclincourt, it moved to La Targette on 14th November. From there it atacked towards Carency and Souchez during the second battle of Artois. General Barbot was killed in action on 11th May 1915. After a move to Cabaret Rouge on 2nd June, the division fought in the autumn battles around Souchez and and the Bois de Givenchy. Throughout this long period in Artois, the division engaged in numerous local battles and endured extensive mining operations on the western slopes of Vimy Ridge.

After a brief period in the Verdun salient, at Vaux-devant-Damloup/Ferme Dicourt [13th March-3rd April 1916] the division returned to Lorraine. It occupied a sector of the St Mihiel salient between Flirey and the Etang de Vargevaux from 15th May until 27th July.

On 19th August 1916, the division entered the battle of the Somme near Barleux. It fought between Barleux and Cléry-sur-Somme —the approaches to Péronne-until 1st October. After a two week rest, it fought between Biaches and Cléry until 4th November. From 29th November 1916 to 17th March 1917 it held First Army's sector between Pernant and Hautebraye from which it moved forward into the area of devastation left behind as the Germans retreated to the

Hindenburg Line. On 17th March it moved forward towards the Massif de St Gobain and established a new line from Quincy Basse to Coucy-la-Ville, which was extended to Barisis on 30th March.

The division held sectors of the Sixth Army on the Chemin des Dames between Malval/Epine de Chevregny and the Pantheon from 3rd June until 27th July 1917. After some training near Lure, the division arrived at Belfort on 3rd September. It occupied the line between Fulleren and the Rhine-Rhone canal from 10th September 1917 until 19th January 1918. A long period of retraining and labour duties at Belfort and Baccarat was interrupted by the German spring offensive.

From 23rd March until 1st May 1918, the division fought with Third Army in Picardy. It arrived at Lassigny and fought at Canny-sur-Matz, Plémont and Plessis-du-Roye, and then consolidated gains. It returned to the Vosges on 12th May and occupied positions between Leimbach and Metzeral for the next six weeks.

The division joined the second battle of the Marne on 15th July when it fought from Festigny-les-Hameaux through Leuvrigny and Montvoisin to the Marne. After a brief respite it fought at Ste Euphraise and Blighy on from 21st July until 3rd August. From 24th August until 29th September, it occupied lines in the suburbs of Reims.

It arrived in Flanders on 30th September and fought at Hooglede, crossed the Leie and took Deinze during the battle for Belgium [12th October-3rd November]. The division was resting at Ruysslede when hostilities came to an end.

78-80 Divisions d'Infanterie not formed

Territorial Divisions 81 - 92

81 Division d'Infanterie Territoriale

The territorial division of the 2nd Military Region formed at Amiens on mobilisation
08.04.17 elevated to an active service division
10.01.18 retitled 1 Division Cavalerie à Pied

Commanders
02.08.14-Lucien Marcot
06.10.14-Théophile Jouannic
08.12.14-Léon Bajolle

161 Brigade [replaced by 186 Brigade ex 87DIT 8.15]
11 RIT, Beauvais
12 RIT, Amiens

162 Brigade [disbanded 4.17]
14 RIT, Abbeville	3.17 replaced by 308RI ex 62DI
1.18 disbanded	
16 RIT, Peronne 3.17-?	

186 Brigade, 8.15-4.17
100 RIT Ex 87DIT
102 RIT Ex 87DIT

Artillery
T Gp/29 RAC	12.15 withdrawn-eventually to 46DI 3.16
T Gp/29 RAC	11.16 to 165DI T
Gp/10 RAC	12.15 ex 87DIT T
Gp/43 RAC	12.15 ex 87DIT

Cavalry
5/9 RC, 8.14–11.15d
6/9 RC, 8.14-11.15d
6/4 RCh, 11.15-2.16
7/19RD, 2.16-1.17
E/3RS, 1.17-1.18

Engineers
None

ACTIVE DIVISION 4.17-1.18
262 RI	Ex 61DI 1.18 to 161DI
279 R	Ex 70DI 1.18 to 62DI
308 RI	Ex 62DI 1.18 disbanded
270 RAC	Ex Gps 10/43/58 RAC 1.18 to 1DCP
E/3Rspahis	1.18-to parent regt-not replaced
1 Bn Malgache	Attached 7.17-1.18
Cie 4/3T, 4/53T, 4/26 du 1RG	4.18=4/59, 4/26 du 1RG, 19/3 du 19BG

Initially employed in guarding lines of communications in Flanders, the division moved back to Abbeville on
27th August and, from there, to Artois. It became involved in the first battles of Picardy and of Artois when it engaged the
Germans to the south of Arras. It fought at Vaulx-Vraucourt [26th September], Courcelles, Achiet-le-Grand and Bucquoy

[29th September-4th October], at Essarts, Hannescamp and Foncquevillers [5th-6th October] and at Monch-aux-Bois [10th October].

The division returned to Flanders on 7th November, and took up positions along the Leie and fought at Lombartsijde [7th-11th November]. It then manned the defensive line around Dunkerque until 30th August 1915. After this it moved to Arras and held defensive posiitons at Angres and Fosse Calonne during the third battle of Artois. It retired from the line on 10th February 1916 and was employed on labour duties in the Santerre until 1st July 1916.

For the rest of its existence, the division held the line in the Oise region. It did five tours in the trenches: Tracy-le-Mont/Oise [1st July –19th November 1916]; Ferme Quenneviere/Oise [5th-23rd March 1917]; Quincy Basse/Ferme le Bessay [11th May-19th June 1917]; Qunicy Basse/south of Vauxillon [12th July/15th August 1917] and Urvillers/Moy [27th August-9th January 1918].

82 Division d'Infanterie Territoriale

Territorial division of the 3rd Military Region formed at Rouen on mobilisation

Commander
02.08.14-Charles Vigy

163 Brigade
17 RIT, Bernay	6.15-independent
18 RIT, Evreux	6.15-to IICAC
164 Brigade	
21 RIT, Rouen	6.15 to XICA
22 RIT, Rouen	6.15 to XICA

Artillery
T Gp/11 RAC & T p/11RAC	8.15 to 88DIT

Cavalry
7/7 RCh

Engineers
Cie 3/1T du 3RG

The division manned defensive lines, north of Arras, between the Scarpe and the Lys. It fought the Germans at Tournai on 24th August 1914. Then it became involved in the first battle of Picardy by fighting at Flers and Longueval [26th September] and at Miraumont [28th-30th September]. When the front stabilised it formed and held the line between Pusieux and Serre until 25th October. During this period, it fought at Pusieux [4th October] and Foncquevillers [11th October].

From October 1914 until March 1915, the division was engaged in labour duties near Montdidier, in front of Amiens, and between the Somme and the Ancre. From 15th March until 23rd June it held the line between Hamel and Beaumont Hamel. It was disbanded 23-29.06.15 [ordered 24.6.15]

83 Division d'Infanterie Territoriale

Territorial division of the 4th Military Region formed at Paris on mobilisation

Commanders
02.08.14-Charles Groth
23.09.16-Alfred Galopin
20.12.17-Alexandre Gallet

165 Brigade
29 RIT,	Dreux	8.15 replaced by 237RIT

30 RIT, Chartres 8.15 replaced by 230RIT
166 Brigade
31 RIT, Alencon 8.15 replaced by 285RIT
32 RIT, Argentan 8.15 replaced by 232 RIT

Artillery
T Gp/45 RAC 11.16 to 99DIT –replaced by Gp/58RAC-ex
99DIT 4.17 to 81DI-not replaced

Cavalry
7/1 RCh, 8.14–3.16
8/1 RCh, 8.14-3.16
E/3RS, 3.16-10.16
E/1RS, 8.16-10.16
E /7RCh,10.16-11.18
E/7RCh, 10.16-11.18

Engineers
NONE

This division remained in the Paris garrison throughout the war

84 Division d'Infanterie Territoriale

Territorial division of the 4th Military Region formed at Le Mans on mobilisation

Commanders
02.08.14-Henri de Ferron
30.09.14-Joseph Chatelain

167 Brigade
25 RIT, Laval 7.15 to XXXIIICA
26 RIT, Magnac 7.15 to IIICA

168 Brigade
27 RIT, Mamers 7.15 to XVIICA
28 RIT, Le Mans 7.15 to XCA

Artillery
T Gp/44 RAC & T Gp/44RAC 11.14 one gp disbanded and replaced by gp/16RAC
 4.15 the other gp/44RAC to XXXIIICA- replaced by Gp/28RAC
 7.15 both groups to IIICA

Cavalry
7 & 8/ 14 RH   7.15 to 130DI

Engineers
Cie 4/1T du 4 RG

Initially employed on defensive works between Arras and Cambrai, during which it fought the Germans near Cambrai on 26th August, the division took part in the first battle of Picardy. On 26th September, it fought at Rocquigny, Transloy and Puisieux and then established a line between Hébuterne and Gommecourt. From 4th October it established a new line between Monchy-au-Bois and Berles-au-Bois. The division was then pulled out and employed on labour duties in Artois for the rest of its career. It was disbanded 07.07.15 [ordered 3.7.15]

85 Division d'Infanterie Territoriale

Territorial division of the 9th Military Region formed at Tours on mobilisation

Commanders
02.08.14-Tell Chapel
09.01.15-Louis Comby
169 Brigade
65 RIT, Chateauroux   6.15 to XXXVIICA
66 RIT, Le Blanc 6.15 to XXXVIICA
170 Brigade
67 RIT, Parthenay   6.15 to VIICA
68 RIT, Poitiers   6.15 to XXXVCA

Artillery
T Gp/32 RAC   6.15 to XXXVII CA
2 btys/9RAC   12.14 joined from XXXVCA
6.15-XXXVCA

Cavalry
7 & 8/7RH   6.15 to 48DI
1916-Cie 15/12 du 7RG

Engineers
Cies 4/14 & 5/2T du 1RG

Employed in the defences of Paris until December 1914, the division spent most of its time in the construction of defensive positions on the Aisne. It occupied the sector on that river, between Venizel and Condé-sur-Aisne from 16th January until 24th March 1915. It was disbanded 14.06.15 [ordered 6.6.15]

86 Division d'Infanterie Territoriale

Territorial division of the 9th Military Region formed at Tours on mobilisation.

Commanders
02.08.14-Raymond Mayniel
01.10.14-Charles Leblond
27.05.15-Amédée Nicolas

171 Brigade
69 RIT, Chateaurenault   6.15 to XXXVCA
70 RIT, Angers   6.15 to XIIICA

172 Brigade
71 RIT, Angers   6.15 to XIIICA
72 RIT, Cholet   6.15 to XIIICA

Artillery
T Gp/49 RAC   6.15 to XIIICA

Cavalry
7 & 8/25 RD   6.15 to 120DI

Engineers
No genie   1.15 Cie 9/3T du 6RG added

After four months in the Paris garrison, the division was employed on labour duties in Picardy for the rest of its existence. It was disbanded 18.06.15 [ordered 6.6.15]

87 Division d'Infanterie Territoriale

Territorial division of the 10th Military Region formed at Rennes on mobilisation

To active division status 05.04.17

Commanders
02.08.14-Francois Roy
24.05.15-Maurice Joppé
05.04.17-Louis Arlabosse
02.06.18-Francois Dhers

173 Brigade 4.17-INDEPENDENT BRIGADE
73 RIT, Guincamp
74 RIT, St Brieuc

174 Brigade [6.16 to XXXVICA]
76 RIT, Vitre
79 RIT, Granville
80 RIT, St Lo

186 Brigade 4.15-8.15 [to 81DIT]
100 RIT
102 RIT

161 Brigade 6.16 ex 81DIT 4.17-INDEPENDENT BRIGADE
11 RIT
12 RIT

Artillery
T Gp/49 RAC & T Gp/50 RAC	4.15 one Gp reduced to hvy bty
Gp/10 RAC & Gp/43RAC	4.15 ex 151DI –to 81DIT 12.15
	12.15 replaced by 2btys/3RACC ex Dakar
	4.17 all artillery to 87DI as 269 RAC

Cavalry
7/24 RD, 8.14-11.15
8/24 RD, 8.14-1.17
9/7 RCh, 11.15-4.17

Engineers
Cie 10/3T du 6RG

ACTIVE DIVISION 4.17-
72 RI	Ex Algeria –there since 12.16-ex 125DI
91 RI	Ex Algeria-there since 12.16-ex 125DI
136 RI	Ex 20DI
269 RAC	Formed from above plus Gp/59RAC ex XXXICA
	9.17 Gp/269 –which had been Gp/59RAC to XXXIVCA-replaced by Gp/30RAC
5 Gp/133 RAL	Added 6.18
4/11 RD, 4.17-9.18	
E/11RD, 1.18- 9.18	

Cie 10/3T, 10/53T du 6RG   1918-Cie 10/3T, 10/53T or 10/.55T, 10/23 du Pioneer Bn   6RG [discrepancy in Official History]
300 RIT added 7.17-pioneer bn 8.18

After initial employment on defensive works around Le Havre, the divison moved to Flanders on 7th October 1914. It fought in the Ypres salient until 5th June 1916. For most of this period the division was in line along the Ijzer canal between Boezinge and Steenstraat. It played a part in both the first battle of Ypres and the second battle in 1915. It was subjected to the first use, by the Germans, of gas when it was attacked near Langemark on 22nd April 1915.

On 15th June 1916, the division joined Third Army on the Oise front and remained there for the next twelve months. It was in line between Belval and the Oise [15th June-18th December 1916]; between the Oise and Ecouvillon-when it moved towards Noyon as the Germans retreated to the Hindenburg Line [12th-18th March 1917]; Sélency and Pontruit [20th May-9th June 1917].

In the latter part of 1917, the division served with Sixth Army on the Chemin des Dames. It was in line between the Ferme Boyelle and Courtecon [21st June-10th July]; Malval and the Epine de Chevregny [18th August-12th September and 9th October to 9th November]-elements fought during the battle for Malmaison; and between Pargny-Filain and Vaumaire [26th November-19th December].

Transferred to the Fourth Army in Champagne, the division held the line between Teton and Auberive from 17th January to 30th March 1918. It fought with 10th Army at Longpont, and then at Chavigny and St Pierre-Aigle during the third battle of the Aisne. During the second battle of the Marne, it continued with Tenth Army and fought from Buzancy and Villemontoire, and pursued the Germans to points east of Soissons.

On 15th August 1918, the division transferred to the Vosges and took up positions between the Fave and the Chapelotte. Two weeks later it moved to the Moselle and occupied positions between the Sanon and Embermésnil until 17th October. The division returned to Champagne and remained in 4th Army's reserve. It was at Bouy on 11th November 1918.

88 Division d'Infanterie Territoriale

Territorial division of the 11th Military Region formed at Nantes on mobilisation
06.03.17 became an Active Division

Commander
02.08.14-Alexandre Gallet

175 Brigade 3.17 to INDEPENDENT BRIGADE
81 RIT, Nantes   .16 replaced by 212RI ex 68DI
82 RIT, Acenis   1.17 replaced by 315RI ex 7DI

176 Brigade 3.17 to INDEPENDENT BRIGADE
83 RIT, La Roche sur Yon   .16 replaced by 369 RI ex 73DI
84 RIT, Fontenay   Disbanded 1916?
Artillery
T Gp/20 RAC   4.15 to XXXIIICA T Gp/28 RAC 4.15 to VIICA
Gps 3 & 4??/53 RAC   4.15 added from XXXIIICA-8.15 to XCA and replaced by 2 gps/11RAC ex 82DIT third gp new formed 3.17 to become 271RAC

Cavalry
5/3 RD, 8.14 –11.15d
6/3 RD, 8.14- 11.15d
E/4 RCh,11.15-2.16
7/24 RD, 2.16-11.16
8/24RD, 2.16-11.16
E/1 RS, 11.16-7.17

Engineers

Cie 11/3T du 6RG

1917-Cies11/3T, 11/53T, 11/23 du 6RG

ACTIVE DIVISION, 3-12.17

212 RI Ex 68DI	11.17 disbanded
315 RI Ex 7DI	11.17 disbanded
369 RI Ex 73DI	12.17 to 67DI
271 RAC	12.17 disbanded
Esc/1 Spahis	7.17 replaced by 3/12RH & 4/12RH ex 129DI-withdrawn 12.17

Cie 11/3T, 11/53T, du 6RG only on formation
11/3T, 11/53T, 11/23 du 6RG from 7.17

The division arrived in Flanders on 22nd August 1914 and after a brief encounter with the Germans at Tournai and Templeuve, it worked on defence lines near Lens, then at Amiens, and then at Corbie. During the first battle of Picardy it fought at Beaulencourt and Transloy [26th September]; at Beaumont Hamel, Beaulencourt and Miraumont [27th September-4th October] and then at Hébuterne [4th-8th October].

It held 10th Army's line between Berles-au-Bois and Bretencourt from 14th November 1914 until 16th February 1916. During this period, it played a defensive role in the second and third battles of Artois by making secure the southern approaches to Arras.

After several weeks of labour duty near Nancy, the division re-entered the line between Flirey and the Etang de Varegvaux, on the southern flank of the St Mihiel salient, on 25th July 1916. Pulled out on 17th November, it spent the first half of 1917 on the Moselle. It occupied positions between Nomeny and Brin [14th January-6th March] and between Nomeny/Brin and Pont-a-Mousson [17th March-28th June].

The division's final period of service was with Sixth Army on the Chemin des Dames. It held the line between Malval and Epine de Chevregny [24th July-19th August and 11th September –10th October] and between Filain and Malval [28th October-29th November 1917].

The division disbanded on 15th December 1917.

89 Division d'Infanterie Territoriale

Territorial division of the 12th Military Region formed at Limoges on mobilisation.

Commanders
02.08.14-Louis Renaud
12.09.14-Frederic Bourdériat
16.11.14-Alexandre Gallet
21.11.14-Louis de Trentinian
25.04.15-Gustave de Cornulier-Luciniere
01.07.15-Louis Baquet

177 Brigade [6.17 –independent]
89 RIT, Limoges
90 RIT, Magnac and Laval

178 Brigade [6.17-independent]
93 RIT, Perigueux
94 RIT, Angouleme

215 Brigade [created 8.16 –to independent status 3.17]
17 RIT
130 RIT

135 RIT

Artillery
T Gp/52 RAC
T Gp/37 RAC   10.14 added- from GMP

Cavalry
7/21 RCh, 8.14-11.15
8/21 RCh, 8.14-11.15
5/14 RD, 11.15-1.16
4/9 RCh, 1.16-3.17
4/18 RD, 3.17-6.17

Engineers
8/21 RCH   8.14-11.15
No engineers allocated on formation   1.15 Cie 3/2T du 1RG added
Cie 3/52 du 1RG added later

After service in the Paris garrison, the division arrived in Flanders on 8th October 1914 and served there until 20th April 1915. It organised defences between Reninghelst and the Mont de Cats, and then served alongside the Belgian Army between Zuydschute and Noordschute. From 23rd October until 9th December it held the line along the Ijzer canal between the bridge at Knocke and St Jacobs Kapelle. Then it moved to Dixmude until withdrawn on 30th December. After a long period at rest, the division resumed its front-line duties at Poelkapelle on 30th March 1915.

The division took over Sixth Army's positions along the Aisne between Venizel and Condé on 29th April 1915. It held this line, with extensions towards Soissons and Soupir, until 11th December 1916. It joined Fifth Army in the eastern outskirts of Reims on 16th Febraury 1917 and helped defend the city during the second battle of the Aisne. It pulled out of the line on 5th May and moved to Epernay where it was disbanded on 17th June 1917. [ordered 29.5.17]

90 Division d'Infanterie Territoriale

Territorial division of the 16th Military Region –began to form at Montpellier-but cancelled.

Commander
02.08.14-Georges Bunoust

179 Brigade
125 RIT, Narbonne
126 RIT, Perpignan

180 Brigade
127 RIT, Carcassonne
128 RIT, Albi

Artillery
T Gp/9 RAC

Cavalry
7 &8/1 RH

Engineers
Cie 16/?T du 2RG

12.08.14 elements of the infantry sent to North Africa-rest to Valbonne 28.9.14 to join 94DIT Cavalry and Artillery remained at depots.

Dissolved by 16.09.14

91 Division d'Infanterie Territoriale

Territorial division of the 17th Military Region formed at Toulouse on mobilisation.

Commanders
02.08.14-Paul Lacroisade
08.01.15-René Radiquet
181 Brigade
129 RIT, Agen   6.15 to IICAC
130 RIT, Marmade   6.15 to XIICA
131 RIT, Cahors 6.15 to VIIICA
182 Brigade
132 RIT, Montauban   6.15 to VIIICA
133 RIT, Toulouse   6.15 to ???
134 RIT, Foix   6.15 to I CAC
135 RIT, Mirande   6.15 to XII CA
133 RIT is not shown in the Official History, Tome X, as serving in this division.

Artillery
T Gp/57 RAC & T Gp/57 RAC   6.15 to IVCA
6.15 to 124 & 125 DI's
Cavalry
7 & 8/10 RD
Engineers
Cie 17/1T du 2RG

After employment on defensive works north of Paris, the division joined 4th Army in Champagne on 15th October. From 21st December 1914 until 15th June 1915 it held the line between Aubérive and Moscou. It was disbanded on 15th June [ordered 6.6.15]

92 Division d'Infanterie Territoriale

Territorial division of the 18th Military Region formed at Bordeaux on mobilisation

Commanders
02.08.14-Henri Calvel
01.09.14-Pierre Leré
12.02.15-Paul Muteau
16.02.15-Joseph Rualt

183 Brigade
141 RIT, Mont de Marsan	7.15 to IXCA
142 RIT, Bayonne	7.15 to XXCA

184 Brigade
143 RIT, Pau	7.15 to XXICA
144 RIT, Tarbes	7.15 to XXICA

Artillery
2 T Gps/14 RAC	7.15 –2 btys to 43DI, 2 btys to XXICA, two btys to XXXIIICA and then to 74DI
Gp5?/31 RAC	4.15 added- but soon passed to 88DT and then to XVIICA

Cavalry
7 & 8/10 RH   7.15 to 131DI
Engineers
Cie 18/1T du 2RG

Labour duties in the Paris region and then at Amiens ended when the division entered the frontline in Artois between Vermelles and Angres. During the first battle of Artois it fought at Vermelles, La Bassée and Aix- Noulette on the eastern approaches to Notre Dame de Lorette.

From 12th December 1914 it occupied the line outside Arras between Calonne and the Rutoire. It played a support role in the second battle of Artois. It was disbanded on 7th July 1915 [ordered 3.7.15]

93 Division d'Infanterie Territoriale

Not formed but 185 Brigade formed as 'isolee' in GMP

94 Division d'Infanterie Territoriale

Formation ordered 19.9.14 –began assembly at Camp Valbonne 26.9.14, under command of Général Villemnejane-but disbanded 3.10.14

Composition would have been:

187 Brigade
109 RIT, Vienne
110 RIT, Romans

188 Brigade
111 RIT, Montelimar
1, 2, 4 BCP(T)

Other units
2 groups RAC [regt not specified]
7 & 8/13 RCh
Cie du 16BG[T]

95 Division d'Infanterie

Formation ordered 22.09.14 but cancelled 3.10.14. Would have been commanded by Général Palat.

96 Division d'Infanterie Territoriale

Territorial division formed in Champagne 11.10.14

Commander
11.10.14-Barthelemy Palat

191 Brigade
108 RIT	To II CA
112 RIT	To II CA

192 Brigade
97 RIT	To VI CA
117 RIT	To VI CA

Artillery
T Gp/9 RAC & T Gp/38 RAC   To XVI CA

Cavalry
7 & 8/14 RD   To Gp Parisot

Engineers
16/1T Cie/2RG

From 16th October 1914 until 15th June 1915, the division operated in the rear of Fourth Army near Prosnes. It was disbanded on 15th June 1915 [ordered 6.6.15]

97 Division d'Infanterie Territoriale

Territorial division formed at Paris 24.10.14-To active division status 4.17

Commanders
24.10.14-Brice Bizot
10.03.16-Charles Huguet
12.06.16-Claude Lejaille

193 Brigade [4.17-independent]
91 RIT, ???	8.15 replaced by 291RIT
106 RIT, Bourguin	8.15 replaced by 301 RIT

194 Brigade [4.17 –independent]
120 RIT, Pont St Esprit	8.15 replaced by 211 RIT
122 RIT, Montpellier	8.15 replaced by 300 RIT

• original bns in both brigades dispersed to Army commands 6-8.15-replaced by units from the Territorial Reserve which took numbers 291, 301, 211 and 300 during 8.15

Artillery
Gp5/54 RAC & Gp5/56 RAC

Cavalry
7/19 RD, 10.14-11.15d
8/19 RD, 10.14-11.15d
8/2RCh, 11.15-8.16

Engineers
Cie 17/2T, 17/52T & 17/25 du2RG

ACTIVE DIVISION, 4.17-1.18 [infantry from 154BI isolee]
255 RI	10.17 –disbanded –replaced by 334RI ex
164DI	
303 RI	
335 RI	
59 BCP	10.17 to 164DI

Artillery
Gp/54RAC & Gp/56 RAC ex 97DIT	6.17 joined by Gp/59RAC ex XXXICA
	7.17 to 273RAC

Cavalry
5/3 RD 4.17-6.17
E/6RCA 6.17-1.18
E/6RCA 6.17-1.18

Engineers
Cie 17/2T, 17/52T, 17/25 du 2RG1.18-Cie 17/6, 17/56, 17/25 du 2RG

The division was employed in the Paris garrison until September 1915. It took over 5th Army's positions on the eastern outskirts of Reims on 18th September 1915. It remained in this sector until 4th December 1916. After labour duties near Fismes, the division moved to the Argonne where it took over the line at Avocourt on 1st June 1917. After several engagements in that sector it was pulled out on 26th July. Then it re-entered the trenches of Verdun at Esnes on 8th August 1917. It helped capture Côte 304 on 20th August and then pulled out ten days later. Between 20th September 1917 and 19th January 1918 it held Fourth Army's sector in Champagne between Teton and Auberive.

Division disbanded and reformed as 2 Division Cavalerie à Pied on 2nd January 1918.

98 Division d'Infanterie Territoriale

Formation ordered 28.10.14 but cancelled 7.11.14

99 Division d'Infanterie Territoriale

Formed in the Paris Garrison 16.02.15

Commander
16.02.15-Raoul de Lartigue

197 Brigade
136 RIT, St Gaudens
322 RIT, ??

198 Brigade
261 RIT, ??
282 RIT, ??

Artillery
Gp ?/58 RAC	8.16 to 83DI
Gp 5/20RAC	4.15 from 152DI, 11.15 to 115RAL/XV CA Gp5/51 RAC 4.16 added
from 102DIT	8.16 to 165DI

Cavalry
8/11 RH, 2.15-2.16
7/1 RCh 2.16-8.16

Engineers
Cie 5/1T, 5/51T du 1RG Added 1.16

The division served in the Paris garrison until it took up labour duties in Picardy on 31st August 1915. It served in the line between Herleville and Maucourt, 27th September 1915 to 1st February 1916. After further labour duties, it disbanded 13th August 1916.

100 Division d'Infanterie Territoriale

Formed in the Paris Garrison 19.02.15

Commanders
18.02.15-Georges Dantant
26.06.15-René Radiquet
23.12.15-Henri Tassin
06.10.16-Erasme de Contades-Gizeux

199 Brigade [1.17-independent until disbanded 5.17]
201 RIT	5.17 disbanded
209 RIT	9.17 disbanded

200 Brigade [1.17-independent until disbanded 5.17]
309 RIT   8.17 disbanded
315 RIT   6.17 disbanded
Artillery
Gp/35 RAC   1.17 to 158DI –to 3/219RAC 4.17
Gp/20RAC   12.15 added –passed to 165DI in 11.16

Cavalry
9?/19RD, 2–11.15d
5 /21RCh, 11.15–8.16

Engineers
Cie-none on formation   7.16 Cie 10/4T, 10/54T du 6RG added

Apart from labour duties, the division's only active service was a period in the line with 4th Army between Baconnes and Prosnes, 16th June-14th August 1916 It disbanded 05.01.17 [ordered 29.12.16]

101 Division d'Infanterie Territoriale

Formed at Bourges 25.05.15 [ordered 13.5.15]

Commanders
19.05.15-Jean-Baptiste Lasserre
19.05.16-Antoine Beaudemoulin

201 Brigade [11.16 to independent]
233 RIT
279 RIT

202 Brigade [11.16 to independent]
259 RIT
268 RIT

Artillery
Gp/23 RAC   11.16 to 134DI
Cie-none on formation   1.16-Cies 20/5T, 20/55T du 10RG added

After a period of labour duties in the Aisne and Verdun areas, the division spent two periods in the line in Lorraine. Between 21st May and 18th September 1916 it served between the Etang de Vargevaux and St Agant, and then, between Koeur-la-Grande and Dompcevrin, 18th September to 18th November 1916. It was disbanded 26th November 1916[ordered 8.11.16]

102 Division d'Infanterie Territoriale

Formed at Courtine 25.05.15

Commanders
19.05.15-Jean-Francois Villemejane
28.01.16-Claude Rouvier

203 Brigade [disbanded 5.16]
286 RIT
292 RIT

204 Brigade [disbanded 5.16]
326 RIT

342 RIT

Artillery
Gp 5/51 RAC   Ex 153DI-to 99DI 5.16

Cavalry
7?/28RD 5.15 -11.15
7/8 RCh 11.15-5.16

Engineers
Cie-none allocated

The division moved from Paris and took over 6th Army's sector between Andechy and the Bois des Loges, in Picardy, 30th September 1915. It returned to labour duties near Amiens on 3rd November 1915, and disbanded on 1st May 1916 [ordered 23.4.16]

103 Division d'Infanterie Territoriale

Formed at Courtine 02.08.15 [ordered 5.7.15]

Commander
14.07.15-Antoine Beaudemoulin

205 Brigade [disbanded]
248 RIT
260 RIT

206 Brigade [disbanded]
283 RIT
330 RIT

Artillery
Gp6/32 RAC   3.16 to 46DI

Cavalry
7/4RH -11.15
7/9 RCh 11.15 –2.16

Engineers
Cie-none on formation   1.16-11/4T du 6RG added

Until 6th October 1915 the division worked on defences around Paris. It joined 6th Army between the Oise and Tracy-le-Val and remained in line until 1st March 1916, when it was disbanded.

104 Division d'Infanterie Territoriale

Formed in the Paris Garrison 01.08.15

Commanders
15.07.15-Barthelemy Palat
30.04.16-Claude Rouvier

207 Brigade [disbanded 1.17]
240 RIT	1.17-disbanded
276 RIT	1.17-disbanded

208 Brigade [disbanded 10.16]
295 RIT	9.16-disbanded
311 RIT	1.17-disbanded

Artillery
Gp6/37 RAC   11.16 to 168DI

Cavalry
E/9RCh -11.15d
7/13 RH 11.15 –8.16d

Engineers
Cie-none on formation   7.16-Cie 12/3T du 6RG added

The division took over Sixth Army's sector between Thiescourt and the Bois des Loges on 30th September 1915. It moved to the Belval/Oise sector on 1st November. Rested from 2nd March 1916, it spent two weeks in the line near Lihons [12th-26th August] and disbanded 5th November 1916 [ordered 1.11.16]

105 Division d'Infanterie Territoriale

Formed at Belfort 14.10.14 as Groupement Sud de la Mobile Defence de Belfort and given number 105 on 09.08.15

Commanders
14.10.14-Matuzynski
12.12.14-Louis Château
17.04.15-Henri Le Gros
12.08.15-Charles Vigy
28.02.16-Fenélon Passaga

209 Brigade
49 RIT	3.16 disbanded
50 RIT 3.16 disbanded	

210 Brigade
98 RIT	3.16 to 133DI as 98 Regt de Marche
99 RIT	3.16 to 157DI

Artillery
Gp6/29 RAC & Gp8/5RAC   3.16 both to 133DI

Cavalry
5/17RD –1.16d

Engineers
Cie 28/4 du 28BGT   Added later-Cie 28/54 du 28Bg, Cie 12/25 du 6RG

Division served between Largue and the Swiss frontier, 15th October 1914 until 20th March 1916 when it was disbanded and used as basis for formation of 133DI.

106-119 Divisions d'Infanterie not formed

[although one recent work on Verdun mentions a 106DI with 211 Brigade [15RIT, 44RIT, 45RIT] and 212 Brigade [46RIT, 48RIT, 95RIT] in existence in February 1916. This division is not listed in the Offiical History but the brigades are mentioned in another work on Verdun.

War-formed Divisions 120 - 170

120 Division d'Infanterie

Formed in Picardy [Second Army] 18.06.15 [ordered 6.6.15]

Commanders
11.06.15-Amédée Nicolas
11.09.16-Lucien Mordacq

49 Brigade [ex 25DI] [disbanded 12.16]
38 RI   Ex 25DI
68 RI   Ex 25 DI

303 Brigade [ex 152DI] [disbanded 12.16]
408 RI
409 RI   12.16 to 167DI

Infantry from 12.16
38 RI
86 RI
408 RI

Artillery
5 Gp/ 53 RAC-ex XIIICA 6.15	4.17 to 53 RAC
6 Gp/ 53 RAC-ex XIIICA 6.15	4.17 to 53 RAC
6 Gp/ 49 RAC –ex XIIICA 7.16	4.17 to 53 RAC
6 Gp/113 RAL	3.18-added- ex 7/109RAL

Cavalry
7/25 RD -12.16
8/25 RD- 12.16
5/3 RCh 12.16-7.17

Engineers & Pioneers
1915   Cie 26/6M du 2RG
1918   Cie 26/3M, 26/56M du 2RG Cie 8/22 du 4RG
8.18-Pioneer Battalion 132RIT   ex VIIICA

From the date of its formation until 2nd November 1915 the division occupied trenches between Ribécourt and the Plemont. Taken over by Sixth Army on 1st July, it remained with that army during its second tour in the front-line, between the Bois des Loges and Andechy, 4th December 1915-17th February 1916. The division entered the battle for Verdun on 29th February at Vaux-devant-Damloup and fought there until 9th March. It spent the summer of 1916 with Tenth Army between Hautebraye and Quennevières [24th April- 23rd August] and then joined the battle of the Somme. It held the Vermandovillers sector, 8th September- 26th October, and attacked at Ablaincourt on 10th October.

The division returned to the Ribécourt/Ecouvillon sector of Tenth Army on 3rd January 1917. It moved to Canny-sur-Matz on 27th January, and from there, moved forward to Guiscard as the Germans withdrew to the Hindenburg Line. Two more tours on the Oise front followed: between Grugies and Rocourt [15th April- 27th May] and Pontruet and Selency [1st-27th June], before the division moved to the Argonne. It occupied the sector between Hayette and Esnes/Malancourt from 24th July to 19th August. After a period at the apex of the St Mihiel salient, [Koeur/Paroches, 28th August-18th October], the division returned to Verdun. In succession it held the line between Beaumont and the Bois de Chaume [24th October-9th Decmeber] and between Avocourt and the Aire [21st December 1917-15th May 1918].

During the third battle of the Aisne, the division fought at Olizy-et-Volaine on 29th May and established a defence line between Cuisles and Verneuil. On 8th July, it was placed under command of the Italian Corps at Nanteuil-la-Fosse and fought from there towards Marfaux during the 4th battle of Champagne/2nd battle of the Marne. During its actions at Marfaux it fought in co-operation with British forces.

The division returned to Verdun on 2nd August 1918 and operated under American command between Beaumont and Forges, downstream from the town. Still under command of the Americans, it moved to the Argonne sector between Haute Chevauchée and Vienne-le-Chateau on 10th September. Transferred westwards to Fourth Army, in Champagne, the division took part in the autumn offensives. On 29th September, it attacked the Plateau de Soudans and by 12th October, had reached Vouziers where it consolidated gains between Conde-le-Vouziers and Falaise. From 30th October, it fought from this area in the battle of Chesne and occupied the Plateau des Alleux on 3rd November. Two days later it advanced with 4th Army towards the Meuse and had reached Donchery when it was withdrawn into reserve on 8th November. The division was moving back to Suippes on armistice day.

121 Division d'Infanterie

Formed in the Somme region [Sixth Army]14.06.15 [ordered 6.6.15]

Commanders
14.06.15-Amédée Guillemin
18.06.16-Edmond Buat
31.12.16-Antoine Targe

92 Brigade [formerly the Independent Brigade Klein] [re-organised 6.17 –see below]
352 RI   7.15 replaced by 417RI

45 BCP	Added 7.15
55 BCP	Added 7.15

310 Brigade [ex XXXVCA] [re-organised 6.17-see below]

404 RI	New regt.
417 RI	New regt 7.15 replaced by 352RI-disbanded
4.17	
48 BCP	Added 7.15

Infantry 4.17- 6.17
404 RI
417 RI
11 Gp de Ch [45, 48, 55BCP]

92 Brigade 6.17-10.17 [disbanded]
36 RI   Ex 5DI
11 Gp de Ch [45.48. 55BCP]

310 Brigade	6.17-10.17 [disbanded]
404 RI	
417 RI	10.17 disbanded

Infantry from 10.17
36 RI
404 RI
11 Gp de Ch [45, 48, 55BCP]

Artillery

3 Gp/5 RAC-ex VIICA	4.17 to 205 RAC
4 Gp/5 RAC- ex VIICA	4.17 to 205 RAC
6 Gp/30 RAC-new formed 1.16	4.17 to 205 RAC

12 Gp/113 RAL-added 12.17   3.18 rettiled 6/135RAL

Cavalry
9/7RH -9.15
10/7RH -9.15
E/7RS 11.16–7.17d
E/7RS 11.16-7.17d

Engineers & Pioneers
1915   Cie 15/10T du 7RG
Pioneer Bn/69RIT 8.18 ex XXXVCA
1918   Cies 15/6, 15/56 du 7RG, 11/74 du 6RG

For the first six month's of its existence, the division occupied positions between Autreches and Moulin sous Touvent which were extended to Pernant on 1st September. A second tour of this sector took place from 19th January to 25th April 1916. For the rest of 1916, the division was involved in preparations for and action in the battle of the Somme. Initially between Herleville and Maucourt [30th May-21st June], it took part in a series of attacks during its time at Estrées-Deniecourt and Belloy [12th July-3rd August, 16th-29 August] and between Bernay and Belloy [19th September-16th October]. As the battle drew to a close, it occupied 10th Army's sector between Plessis du Roye and the Bois des Loges from 27th October 1916 to 30th January 1917.

After it returned to the frontline at Ressons du Matz on 12th March, it moved forward into the wasteland left by the German retreat to the Hindenburg Line. From 23rd March it took Remigny and Vendeuil and established new positions at Cerisy which were extended to Essigny, Urvillers and Moy by 25th June. After a brief rest, the division joined Tenth Army on the Chemin des Dames on 18th July between Bovelle and Cerny-en-Laonnaise. With a brief break from 20th September to 18th October, the division remained there until 17th November.

Taken over by Sixth Army, the division's next tour on the Chemin des Dames took place from 5th December 1917 until 19th April 1918 when it held positions facing the Ailette between Vauclerc and Brunin. By 23rd March 1918 this was extended to include Malval.

As part of the response to the German spring offensives, the division entered the struggle for Ypres on 4th May 1918. It fought along the Clytte until 2nd June when it went into reserve behind the Matz. From 15th June until 10th August, it held on to Third Army's positions between Antheuil and Ferme Porte. It held off German attacks on Ferme Porte on 9th July. From there it took part in the third battle of Picardy when it attacked between Marquelise and Ressons on 10th August. It took Lassigny on 21st August and established a new line between Lassigny and Plessis. During Third Army's advance towards the Hindenburg Line [28th August-14th September], the division moved from Plessis via Lagny to Travecy where it was taken over by First Army. From 28th September until 5th November the division participated in First Army's advance. It fought west of Ostel and advanced to the Ailette, and pursued the Germans to Marchais and Notre Dame de Liesse. During the battle of the Serre, it organised lines facing the Marais de la Souche. From 5th November, it moved towards the Meuse, from the Serre to Brune, then to the Aube, and on to Rocroi where it established new positions on 11th November 1918.

122 Division d'Infanterie

Formed in Fifth Army 09.12.14 as Division Tassin, with 9 and 185 Brigades
27.04.15 retitled Division Guerin, with 8 and 185 Brigades
15.06.15 numbered 122DI

Commanders
09.12.14-Henri Tassin
27.04.15-Etienne Guerin
14.06.15-Charles de Lardemelle
20.12.15-Charles Regnault
23.05.17-Auguste Gérôme

02.11.17-Jean Castaing
01.03.18-Paul Topart

8 Brigade [disbanded 9.17]
45 RI Ex 4DI
148 RI Ex 1DI

243 Brigade [disbanded 9.17]
84 RI Ex 4DI
284 RI Ex I CA   disbanded 9.17
58 BCP   10.15-added-ex 52DI-to ??? 10.17

Infantry from 9.17
45 RI
84 RI
148 RI

Artillery
6 Gp/41 RAC   4.17 to 241 RAC
7 Gp/41 RAC   4.17 to 241 RAC
7 Gp/6 RAC –added 11.15   4.17 to 241 RAC
1? Gp/1 RAM –added 11.15   4.17 to 241 RAC

Cavalry
5/6 RD -1.17
6/29RD 1.17-11.18

Engineers & Pioneers
1915   Cie 2/14, 2/14bis du 3RG
1918   Cie 2/14, 2/64, 2/24 du 3RG No Pioneer Battalion

The division served in the outskirts of Reims from its formation until 21st June 1915. On 31st July it moved north-west of Reims and occupied the line between Berry-au-Bac and the Loivre until 4th October 1915.

Selected for service in Macedonia, the division arrived at Salonika on 1st November and elements were engaged immediately in efforts to stem the retreat from the Cherna to Salonika.

During 1916, 1917 and for most of 1918, the division occupied positions on the Vardar river and fought numerous local actions. In the allied advance which began on 15th September 1918 it fought in the battle of Dorbopolie and moved towards the Turkish border.

123 Division d'Infanterie

Formed at Reims [Fifth Army] 15.06.15 [ordered 6.6.15]

Commanders
14.06.15-Charles Corvisart
30.04.17-Victor de Saint-Just

245 Brigade [disbanded 3.17]
6 RI   Ex 35DI
12 RI Ex 36DI

305 Brigade [disbanded 3.17]
411 RI Ex Gp Reims

412 RI   Ex Gp Reims   3.17 to 153Bde then 48DI

Infantry from 3.17
6 RI
12 RI
411 RI

Artillery
3 Gp/58 RAC-ex XVIIICA	4.17 to 58 RAC
4 Gp/58 RAC –ex XVIII CA	4.17 to 58 RAC
4 Gp/38 RAC –ex XVCA	4.17 to 58 RAC
6 Gp/24 RAC –formed 12.15	6.16-to XVCA
11 Gp/115RAL	Added 11.17-retitled 5/115RAL 3.18

Cavalry
6/7RD –11.15
5/6 RH, 4.17-11.18
6/6RH, 4.17 –11.18

Engineers & Pioneers
1915   Cie 8/7, 8/7bis du 4Rg
1918   Cie 8/7, 8/57 du 4RG,
15/21 du 7RG
8.18-Pioneer Battalion 101RIT   ex XVCA

The division's initial deployment was in the eastern fringes of Reims from St Leonards to Marquises where it served until 28th August 1915. Three days later it was moved to the line north-west of the city between the Miette and Ville-aux-Bois. After its sector was extended to include Moulin Pontoy and then Temple it left the line on 18th November 1915. A month later it joined Second Army's front between the Maisons de Champagne and Côte 196. It remained there until 29th April 1916.

The first of four tours in the Avocourt/Côte 304 sector of the Verdun salient began on 19th May and the division fought for control of the left bank of the Meuse, with brief rest periods, until 30th October. It moved to the right bank of the river and up into the heights above Verdun on 26th November 1916 and over the next eleven months it completed four tours in this sector. The main highlight was the second French offensive on 20th August 1917 when the division attacked Côtes 326 and 344.

On 30th September 1917, the division was transferred to the quieter sector in Lorraine between Bezange-la- Grande and Moncel where it remained until 4th June 1918.

Hurried to the Matz, it fought there with Third Army from 10th June and then established new positions at Chevincourt and Ville-sur Coudon. During the allied offensive in August, the division freed the line of the Matz, liberated Vandelicourt and took Thiescourt. After a break with began on 23rd August, it joined First Army's advance to the Hindenburg Line on 14th September. It advanced towards Tergnier and then to La Fère where it consolidated gains. During the battle of St Quentin [8th-19th October] it Essigny-le-Petit, Fonsomme and Boukincamp and fought in the Fermes Forte and Bernoville. From 16th October, it was engaged in the battle of Mont-d'Origny during which it fought at Grugies alongside British forces, and reached the Sambre-Oise canal between Tupigny and Hanappes. From 26th October, it advanced with First Army, reached the Sambre on 4th November, and had reached Robechies when the war ended.

124 Division d'Infanterie

Formed in the Champagne region [Fourth Army]15.06.15 [ordered 6.6.15]

Commanders
15.06.15-Georges Dantant
08.02.16-Georges Tatin

28.10.18-Jean Cot

247 Brigade [disbanded 11.16]
101 RI   Ex 7DI
124 RI   Ex 8DI

248 Brigade [disbanded 11.16]
53 RI	Ex 32DI-	11.17 to 163DI
142 RI	Ex 31DI-	11.17 to 163DI

Infantry from 11.16
101 RI
124 RI
130 RI   Ex 8DI

Artillery
5 Gp/33 RAC-ex 152DI	4.17 to 44 RAC
1 Gp/44 RAC -ex IVCA	4.17 to 44 RAC
2 Gp/44 RAC–ex IVCA	4.17 to 44 RAC
11Gp/104 RAL	12.17-added –retitled 7/104RAL 3.18

Cavalry
7/10 RD –10.15d
3/14RH, 11.15-11.16d
4/14RH, 11.15-11.16d
4/14RH 11.16-11.18 [reformed]

Engineers & Pioneers
1915   Cie 12/1T, 12/1Tbis du 2RG
1918   Cie 15/13 du 7RG, 26/4 du 10RG Cie 21/25 du 11RG
8.18-Pioneer Battalion 104RIT   Ex IVCA

The first eleven months of the division's service was spent in Champagne. It held the line from Aubérive to Moscou from its formation until 15th October. During the second battle of Champagne it attacked Mont Sans Nom. It moved eastwards to the sector between Main de Massiges and Ville-sur- Tourbe sector on 30th November and remained there until 30th April.

After a brief tour in the approaches to Fort Vaux, above Verdun, from 16th May until 8th June 1916 the division returned to the Main de Massiges sector where it remained until 5th October 1916 It joined Tenth Army in Picardy and took over the line between Pressoire and Ablaincourt on 8th January 1917. It was withdrawn on 18th February and returned to the Verdun salient. There it took up positions between Verdun and St Mihiel-between Paroches and Bois Loclont-on 28th March. The division was pulled out on 10th May and moved back to Fourth Army.

Between 24th May 1917 and 4th November 1918, the division served in the Champagne region with Fourth Army. It completed six tours at the front. They were Casque/Têton-Mont Sans Nom [24th May-14th June 1917]; Marquises/Mont Cornillet [18th July-22nd August 1917]; Mont Cornillet/Mont Haut [23rd September 1917-19th January 1918]; Mont Haut/Teton [8th March –21st July 1918]; Suippe/Moscou [5th August-18th September] and the Fourth Army advance, from 3rd October 1918.

During this long period of service, the highlights were heavy fighting north of Prosnes on 15th July 1918; the attack on Orfeuil and the advance to the Aisne on 5th October, and liberating the line of the Aisne near Terron and the capture of the heights above Voncq on 1st November. The division spent the last few days of the war at rest in the rear area of Fifth Army at Pont-Faverger.

125 Division d'Infanterie

Formed in the Argonne [Third Army] 15.06.15

Commanders
14.06.15-Ernest Caré
06.10.16-Joseph Diébold
22.06.18-Auguste Desvoyes
24.06.18-Joseph Diebold
20.08.18-Joseph Mangin

249 Brigade [disbanded 1.17]
76 RI   Ex 10DI
131 RI   Ex 9DI

250 Brigade [disbanded 1.17]
72 RI Ex 3DI	to Algeria 1.17 then to 87DI 4.17
91 RI Ex 4DI	1.17 to Algeria and then to 87DI 4.17 replaced by 113RI ex 9DI in 12.16

Infantry from 1.17
76 RI
113 RI
131 RI

Artillery
3 Gp/45 RAC –ex VCA	4.17 to 245 RAC
4 Gp/45 RAC –ex VCA	4.17 to 245 RAC
6 Gp/35 RAC-added 1.16	4.17 to 245 RAC
6 Gp/105 RAL	4.18 added-ex 14/101RAL

Cavalry
8/10 RD –11.15d
3/8 RCh 12.16-1.17
4/8 RCh 12.16-1.17
3/25RD 1.17-6.17
4/25RD 1.17-6.17
2/8RCh 6.17-11.18

Engineers & Pioneers
1915= Cie 11/1T du 6RG
1918= Cie 4/55, 5/2, 4/30 du 1RG
8.18-Pioneer Battalion 145RIT   Ex XXXIICA

The division spent the first fourteen months of its service in the line between the Haute Chevauchée and the Four de Paris, in the Argonne. It moved to the Somme on 20th August 1916. It served in the line between Bouchavesnes and Rancourt from 29th September until 14th November and carried out a series of attacks on the Bois de St Pierre-Vaast, north-west of Peronne. The division departed from Picardy on 17th November 1916.

It re-entered the line in Fifth Army's front to the north-west of Reims on 1st February 1917. Initially it served between Sapigneul and the Miette and then moved to the adjacent sector between the Miette and the Ployon. During Nivelle's offensive, it attacked towards Juvincourt-et Damary and occupied a new line until 2nd May.

From 3rd June 1917 until 22nd January 1918 the division served with Sixth Army on the Chemin des Dames. It completed three tours between the Ployon and Chevreux [3rd-26th July, 14th August-4th September and 23rd September-14th

October]. These were followed by one tour between the Miette and the Ployon [29th October-29th November] and a tour between the Ployon and the Foret de Vauclerc [17th December 1917- 22nd January 1918].

Following a long period of retraining at Chamant, the division was moved back into the line on 22nd March in response to the German spring offensive. With command moving frequently between Sixth and Third Armies, the division fought in the first battle of Noyon. From a position near Tergnier, it fought there and along the line of the Oise, and finally established new defences at Quierzy. The heavy losses incurred in this action necessitated a period of rest during which the division was reconstituted. From 13th April, it was in line between Berliere and Plessis-du-Roye. It moved to Orvillers and Sorel on 30th May and fought at Ricquebourg, Viugnemont and Antheuil during the battle of the Matz on 9th June. The division was pulled out on 10th June for further rebuilding and retraining.

It joined Sixth Army between Courthiezy and Jaulgonne on 27th June and resisted German attacks there during the fourth battle of Champagne [15th July]. After a month's rest the division was moved to the Seille sector in Lorraine. As part of Eighth Army, it held the line between Brin and Clémery from 20th August until 27th September. It joined 4th Army in Champagne on 30th September. During that army's autumn offensive, the division occupied a sector near Challerange and Monthois; occupied those towns on 10th October; and then moved to the Aisne where it established positions between Olizy and Falaise. It fought for those towns on 14th October. The division was rested from 28th October and then played a support role in Fourth Army's advance to the Meuse which began on 5th November. On 11th November 1918 the division was eight kilometres south-west of Rethel.

126 Division d'Infanterie

Formed in the Argonne [Third Army] 19.06.15

Commanders
14.06.15-Paul Muteau
19.12.16-Louis Mathieu

251 Brigade
55 RI	[disbanded 3.17]
Ex 30DI	
112 RI Ex 29DI	

252 Brigade
173 RI	[disbanded 3.17]
Ex 30DI	
255 RI Ex 150BI	-3.17 to 153BI then 154 BI then 97DI 4.17

Infantry from 3.17
55 RI
112 RI
173 RI

Artillery
1 Gp/ 38 RAC- ex XVCA	6.16 to 38RAC
2 Gp/ 38 RAC- ex XVCA	6.16 to 38RAC
5 Gp/ 18 RAC-formed 12.15	6.16 to XVCA-replaced by third group/38RAC
6 Gp/115RAL	4.18-added- ex 14/119RAL

Cavalry
3/9 RCh –8.15
3/6 RH 8.16 –11.18
4/6 RH 8.16-11.18

Engineers & Pioneers
1915   Cie 4/13, 4/13bis du 1RG

1918   Cie 4/13, 4/63 du 1RG

Cie 15/71 du 7RG
8.18-Pioneer Battalion 42RIT   Ex XXXICA

The division served between the Bois d'Hauzy and Vienne le Chateau, on the western edge of the Argonne, until 15th August 1915. Two weeks later it entered Fifth Army's positions around Reims. At first located between Pontoy and the Bois des Buttes [29th August-15th October], it then served on the eastern outskirts of the city between St Leonards and Marquises [21st October-13th November 1915]. After this the division moved eastwards into the Champagne sector and served with Second Army and then Fourth Army between Côte 196 and Mamelles from 2nd December 1915 until 4th May 1916.

A long period of duty in the Verdun salient began on 1st June 1916 when the division took over the line facing Côte 304 at Avocourt. Between that date and 3rd September 1917, it undertook six tours of duty in the trenches around Verdun. The first ended on 12th July 1916. The others were Avocourt/Bois Avocourt [13th August-1st November]; Meuse/Bois Haudromont [11th –22nd December-for the first offensive]; Chambrettes/Louvemont [16th January-4th February and 6th March-29th June 1917]; and between the Meuse and the Côte du Poivre [8th August-3rd September 1917]. During this last tour, the division attacked the Côte de Talou during the second French offensive on 20th August 1917.

During October 1917, the division moved to Lorraine and took over Eighth Army's positions between the Seille and Brin/Chernicourt on 18th October. The line was extended to Clémery on 31st March 1918. The division remained in line until 2nd June 1918 when it was rushed to the Matz region. There it fought with Third Army at Antheuil and Villers sur Coudon from 9th June until 6th July.

From 31st July 1918, the division operated with First Army and took part in the allied offensive which began on 8th August. It attacked from Roye towards Nesle and gained a line between the Ingon and the Somme. During the battle of St Quentin, it attacked German positions north of the city and reached Petit-Verly [8th-19th October]. Then the division rested and retrained. It was located near Guise on 11th November 1918.

127 Division d'Infanterie

Formed in Lorraine [First Army] 15.06.15   (ordered 6.6.15)

Commanders
15.06.15-Francois Briant
22.01.16-Philippe d'Anselme
09.07.18-Céleste Pigault
17.09.18-Paul Venel
10.11.18-Camille Rampont

253 Brigade [disbanded 1.17]
172 RI   Ex Gp Belfort
25 BCP Ex 40DI
29 BCP Ex 40DI

254 Brigade [disbanded 1.17]
171 RI   Ex Gp Belfort   1.17 to 166DI
19 BCP Ex 42D0I   1.17 to 166DI
26 BCP Ex 12DI   1.17 to 166DI

Infantry from 1.17
172 RI
355 RI   Ex 56DI
25 BCP & 29 BCP
* 27 Bn Sénégalais attached

Artillery

3 Gp/37 RAC –ex VIIICA	4.17 to 237 RAC
4 Gp/37 RAC – ex VIIICA	4.17 to 237 RAC
6 Gp/34 RAC-added 1.17	4.17 to 237 RAC
11GP/106RAL	Added 12.17-retitled 7/106RAL in 3.18

Cavalry
4/9 RCh- 1.16
3/12 RCh 1.17-7.17

Engineers & Pioneers
1915   Cie 26/5, 26/55 du 10RG
1918   Cie 26/5, 26/55 du 10RG Cie 6/17 du 9RG
8.18-Pioneer Battalion 86RIT   Ex ICA

Allocated to the sector between Seuzey and Palameix, [15th June-5th August] on the St Mihiel salient, the division moved to Champagne on 3rd September 1915. During its service in Fourth Army, it fought at Navarin during the second battle of Champagne [20th September-4th October] and held the line between Souain and Wacques [27th October 1915-3rd June 1916].

After a brief tour in Verdun when it fought at Bois Fumin and Damloup [22nd June-6th July], and an equally short tour on the Aisne between Pernant and Soissons [22th July-26th August] the division was sent to Picardy for the battle of the Somme. It fought between Bouchavesnes and the Bois l'Abbé [16th September- 3rd October, and 18th October-12th November]. As the battle died down the division held the line from Bouchavesnes to Rancourt [19th November-19th December].

The first half of 1917 was spent on the Chemin des Dames. Initially allocated to Sixth Army's sector between Chavonne and Troyon [17th Janaury-8th February and 7th-29th March], it moved forward in response to the German retreat to the Hindenburg Line and established new positions between Margival, Pont Rouge and Missy-sur-Aisne. During Nivelle's offensive, from a base between Soupir and Condé, the division attacked towards Chavonne and gained new positions between the Pantheon and the Epine de Chevregny, where it remained until 23rd May 1917.

For the rest of 1917, the division served in the Vosges and held the line between the Col de Ste Marie and Metzeral from 29th June until 23rd December. This was followed by a period on labour duties near the Swiss frontier.

As part of the response to the German spring offensive, the division was rushed to Picardy. It fought on the Avre at Mareuil, Grivesnes and Ainval with Third and First Armies from 27th March until 16th April 1918. By 9th May the division had moved to the Meuse and had taken over the line between Bois Loclont and Trésauvaux from which it moved to the Argonne on 6th July. It held the Four de Paris sector until 22nd July.

The division joined Tenth Army on 1st August and during the later stages of the second battle of the Marne, took Grand-Rozoy and advanced to the Vesle. During the second battle of Noyon, it fought at Nouvron- Vingre and then at Tartiers, Bieuzy and Bagnuex. On 17th September it took over positions at Saucy from which it advanced to the Ailette and eventually liberated Laon on 12th October. During the battle of the Serre, it freed the line of the Souche and advanced to Ferme Caumont.

Withdrawn from the line on 20th October, to Charmes, the division rejoined Tenth Army on 10th November 1918 to prepare for the offensive towards Metz.

128 Division d'Infanterie

Formed in Lorraine [First Army]16.06.15 (ordered 6.6.15)

Commanders
10.06.15-Georges Riberpray
14.09.17-Etienne Segonne

255 Brigade [disbanded 2.17]
167 RI   Ex Gp Toul
168 RI   Ex Gp Toul

256 Brigade [disbanded 2,17]
100 RI   Ex 24DI - 2.17 to 134DI
169 RI   Ex Gp Toul

Infantry from 2.17
167 RI
168 RI
169 RI

Artillery
3 Gp/ 52RAC -ex XIICA 4.17 to 252 RAC
4 Gp/ 52RAC -ex XIICA "
3 Gp/ 21RAC –formed 1.16   "
8 Gp/107 RAL   6.18 added-ex 2/307RAL

Cavalry
5/4 RD –11.15d
5/6 RCh 11.15-3.17
6/6 RCh 11.15-3.17
1/18RD 6.17- 7.17

Engineers & Pioneers
1915   Cie 26/1, 26/51 du 10RG
1918   Cie 26/1, 26/51 du 10RG Cie 14/22 du 4RG
8.18-Pioneer Battalion 67RIT   ex VIICA

Formed in First Army's sector between Bois-de-la-Prêtre and Fey-en-Haye, the division moved to the Argonne on 3rd July 1915. Initially it held the line bwteen Fontaine-aux-Charmes and Houyette but move to the Vienne/Binarville road on 14th September to fight in the second battle of Champagne at Servon.

Between October 1915 and March 1917, the division alternated between sectors between the Meuse and the Moselle, and in the Verdun salient. It served between Avricourt and Vezouve [26th December 1915-12th June 1916]; Froidterre and Souville [Verdun 11th-21st July]; St Agnant/Etang de Vargevaux [28th July –3rd December 1916]; Louvemont/Chambrettes [Verdun 12th December 1916-4th January 1917]; Chatillon/Trésauvaux/Eparges [16th January-22nd March 1917].

The division joined Fourth Army in time for the battle of Moronvillers [16th-24th April] and then remained in Champagne until 28th August. It served between Aubérive and Mont sans Nom [16th-24th April] and then Côte 193/Souain-Somme Py road [21st July-14th August]. It returned to Verdun and fought in the second offensive in the Bois des Caurieres [7th-21st September] and then in the Ravin des Caures, between the Meuse and the Côte du Talou [18th October-1st December].

The next few months were spent in Lorraine where the division occupied positions between the Chapelotte and Vezouve from 28th December 1917 until 23rd April 1918.

The division was moved up from its rest area near Amiens to join Sixth Army in the third battle of the Aisne on 31st May 1918. It fought at Corcy and Faverolles and then established a new line for Tenth Army between Faverolles, Corcy and Longpont, along which it fought many local actions. During the ensuing battle for Soissons it fought at Oulchy-le-Chateau from 18th-20th July. While occupying the line from Nouvron-Vingre to Autreches, it fought with Tenth Army in the second battle of Noyon [30th July-24th August]. When 10th Army closed up to the Hindenburg Line, it fought at Vregny during the battle for Vauxillon and took the Moulin de Laffaux, 14th-20th September.

Moved to Flanders, the division joined the allied breakout from the Ypres salient. From 28th September, it fought from Pilkem Ridge to Staden by 1st October. After a period in line between Iseghem and Ingelmunster, it moved to Oostroosebecke from where it broke out to the Leie on 28th October. There days later it attacked towards the Schelde near Oudenaarde and Eine. The division rested at Waregem from 4th November until the armistice.

129 Division d'Infanterie

Formed in the Vosges [Seventh Army] 15.06.15 (ordered 6.6.15)

Commanders
15.06.15-Charles Nollet
31.12.15-Louis Garbit
30.06.17-Alfred de Corn

5 Brigade de Chasseurs [8.15 became 257 Brigade]
106 BCP	Ex 152DI	
114 BCP	Ex 155DI	
115 BCP	Ex 153DI	8.15 to 47DI
120 BCP	Ex 151DI	
121 BCP	Ex 154DI	

151 Brigade [ex 47DI-became 258 Brigade 8.15]
297 RI
357 RI   Disbanded on transfer from 47Did
359 RI

257 Brigade [formed 8.15 –disbanded 6.17]
359 RI
106 BCP   Disbanded 6.17
120 BCP

258 Brigade [formed 8.15-disbanded 6.17]
297 RI
114 BCP   6.17 to 5DI
121 BCP

Infantry from 6.17
297 RI
359 RI   10.18 –disbanded –replaced by 14RMT
12 Gp de Ch (106, 120, 121 BCP)

Artillery
4 Gp/31 RAC –ex VICA   4.17 to 231 RAC
3 or 4 Gp/44 RAC –ex VICA   4.17 to 231 RAC
5 Gp/24 RAC-added 10.16-ex 73DI 4.17 to 231 RAC
8 Gp/114RAL   6.18-added-ex 2/306RAL

Cavalry
9?/10RH -8.15
10?/10RH-8.15
5/13RCh, 8.15-6.16
6/13RCh, 8.15-6.16
4/12RH, 8.16-7.17
1/6 RH, 616-8.16
2/6 RH, 6.16-8.16

3/12 RH, 8.16-7.17
4/12 RH, 8.16-7.17

Engineers & Pioneers
1915 Cie 21/2T du 11RG, 4/24 du 1RG
1918 Cie 26/6 du 10RG, 14/3 du 4RG, Cie 4/24 du 1RG
8.18-Pioneer Battalion 141RIT   ex IXCA

Formed at Bruyeres, the division moved to Plainfaing on 26th June and fought on the Linge, 20th July-26th August 1915. A month later it took over the Wacques sector of Fourth Army and fought in the second battle of Champagne [28th September-25th October]. It returned to the Bruyeres area where it performed labour duties; elements of the division joined 41DI on the Linge on 17th December. The division became fully operational again when it took over the sector between Brin, Nomeny and the Seille on 5th March 1916, where it remained until 28th May.

It joined the struggle for Verdun on 23rd June and fought in the Bois d'Haudromont, at Froideterre and for Fleury until 3rd July. It moved back to the Moselle and spent the period from Bastille Day until 6th October between Bois-de-la-Pretre and Fey-en-Haye. This was followed by a move to the Somme battlefield where it occupied Tenth Army's sector between Barleux and Belloy-en-Santerre [22nd December-12th January 1917]. On 27th January the division took over the line between the Col Ste Marie and the Chapelotte in the Vosges. Pulled out on 4th May, it began a long period of service on the Chemin des Dames when it arrived before the Epine de Chevregny on 14th June. It remained with Sixth Army until 31st October 1917. From 13th August it held the line between Vauxillon and Quincy Basse and fought at the latter location and at Bois Mortier during the battle of Malmaison [23rd -27th October].

From 20th-28th November 1917, as part of XXI Corps d'Armee it was held in reserve near Peronne in anticipation of a British breakthrough at Cambrai. When this did not happen, the division was involved in a lengthy period of rest and retraining in Picardy. It moved to Belfort and took on labour duties there on 30th January 1918. As a result of the German spring ofensive, the division was rushed to Flanders. From 5th May until 23rd May it fought with XVI Corps d'Armee along the Clytte and at Scherpenburg.

It joined Third Army for the battle of Matz on 9th June. Two days later it attacked at Coucelles-Épayelles and Méry, and established a new line from the former location to positions north of Belloy, where it remained until 5th September. During the second battle of Noyon [17th August] and the subsequent move to the Hindenburg Line, the division fought in the Bois des Loges and at Campagne, and then moved forward to Guiscard.

On 8th September, the division moved to Lorraine for a brief rest. It entered the line between the Sanon and Bezange-la-Grande on 12th September and remained there until the end of the war.

130 Division d'Infanterie

Formed in Artois [Tenth Army]15.07.15 (ordered 3.7.15)

Commanders
06.07.15-Paul Superbie
19.01.16-Paul Toulorge

260 Brigade [disbanded 7.16]
39 RI   Ex 5 DI
239 RI   Ex III CA

307 Brigade [disbanded 7.16]
405 RI   New regt- disbanded 7.16
407 RI   New regt

Infantry from 7.16
39 RI   11.17 to 169DI
239 RI   11.17 disbanded

407 RI   11.17 to 151DI

Artillery

3 Gp/11RAC –ex IIICA	4.17 to 211RAC –disbanded 11.17
4 Gp/11RAC –ex IIICA	4.17 to 211RAC –disbanded 11.17
3? Gp/28 RAC-ex IIICA 7.16	4.17 to 211RAC –disbanded 11.17

Cavalry
7/14 RH -2.16
8/14 RH-2.16
3/7 RCh 1.17 –11.17
4/7 RCh 1.17-6.17d

Engineers & Pioneers
1915   Cie 4/1T, 4/1Tbis du 1RG
1918   Cie 4/31 du 1RG, 25/6 du 9RG, Cie 27/5 du 11RG
No Pioneer Battalion allocated

The division served in Artois until 1st March 1916. Until October it spent three periods in the trenches at Neuville-Saint-Vaast, and elements of the division attacked Vimy Ridge on 25th September. It served between Roclincourt and the Scarpe, on the east fringes of Arras, from 8th October to 9th November. Its final tour in Artois was the sector between Souchez and the Bois de Givenchy from 17th December 1915 until 1st March 1916.

A move to Lorraine involved a period in the line between Bezange-la-Grande and Brin [11th March-4th June] and a tour in the Verdun salient. From 13th to 28th June it fought between Vaux Chapitre and the Ouvrage de Thiaumont and at Fleury [21st-23rd June]. After a two month spell in the Argonne between Four de Paris and Haute Chevauchée [29th July-16th September], the division returned to Verdun on 29th September. It fought at Vaux Chapitre and at the Ouvrage de Thiaumont until 23rd October.

This was followed by two spells in the trenches in Lorraine: between Trésauvaux and the Chatillon-sous-les- Côtes [7th November 1916-16th January 1917]; and between Flirey and the Etang de Vargevaux [20th Janaury-24th June 1917].

Until disbandment, the division served on the Chemin des Dames. At first it held Tenth Army's positions between Courtecon and Malval [18th July-18th August], and then between the Plateau des Casemates and the Creute [4th-16th September].

After a period of labour duties at Salency, the division was disbanded on 11th November 1917.

131 Division d'Infanterie

Formed in the Argonne [Third Army] 08.07.15 (ordered 8.7.15)

Commanders
01.07.15-Joseph Rualt
11.09.15-Pierre Duport
02.09.16-Amédée Guillemin
28.01.17-Jean-Marie Brulard
09.01.18-Pierre Duport
13.04.18-Paul Chauvet

261 Brigade [disbanded 5.17]
41 RI   Ex 19DI
241 RI   Ex X CA- disbanded 5.17

262 Brigade [disbanded 5.17]
7 RI   Ex 33DI

14 RI Ex 34DI
Infantry from 5.17
7 RI
14 RI
41 RI

Artillery
1 Gp/50 RAC –ex XCA   4.17 to 50 RAC
2 Gp/50 RAC –ex XCA   4.17 to 50 RAC
3 Gp/50 RAC –added 2.16 –ex XCA   4.17 to 50 RAC
8 Gp/110 RAL   7.18-added- ex 2/310RAL

Cavalry
7/10RH-11.15
8/10RH-11.15
3/13RH 11.15-7.17
4/13RH 11.15-7.17

Engineers & Pioneers
1915=Cie 18/1T, 18|Tbis du "RG
1918=Cie 18/30T du 2RG, 28/55 du 28BG, Cie 10/3 du 6RG
No Pioneer Battalion allocated

The division served in Third Army's sector between Four de Paris and Fontaine-aux-Charmes from 6th August 1915 until 13th June 1916. It entered the struggle for Verdun on 23rd June when it took over positions between Thiaumont and Vaux Chapitre. It repulsed German attacks on the Fort de Souville on 11th and 12th July. Two days later it left the front-line and moved to the Moselle where it took over 8th Army's sector between Flirey and Fey-en-Haye. It stayed there from 29th July until 15th November 1916 when it moved west to the adjacent sector between Flirey and the Etang de Vargevaux. The division pulled out on 23rd January 1917 to perform labour duties and undergo retraining near Toul.

On 22nd April, the division joined Fourth Army for its spring offensive on the Monts de Champagne. It attacked on 30th April from its line between the Casque and Mont Haut. It was withdrawn on 14th May and transferred to the southern fringes of the Verdun salient at the Tranchée de Calonne and Haudiomont, where it served from 11th June until 17th September.

From 26th September until 18th October, it faced Côte 344 and attacked it during the second Verdun offensive on 2nd October. It returned to Haudiomont on 2nd November and remained in that sector until 31st March 1918.

As a result of the German spring offensive, the division joined First Army in the Hangard area of Picardy on 14th April. It fought a series of intense local actions at Hangard during the April. After a month's rest it joined Sixth Army on 28th May as it attempted to thwart the German attack on the Aisne. From 2nd June, it fought with Tenth Army at Corcy, Longpont and Chavigny. During the second battle of the Marne, it fought as part of Fifth Army, Ninth Army and Fifth Army again between Villesaint, Chéne-la-Rene and Mesnil- Hultier. It reached the Marne on 20th July and fought from Levrigny towards Montvoisin. From 30th July until 18th August the division occupied Fifth Army's sector at Pompelle, on the eastern outskirts of Reims.

The division reached the Vosges on 26th August and took up positions between the Vallee de la Weiss and the Vallee de la Lauch. It transferred from Seventh Army to Eighth Army on 15th September when it moved to new positions between the Chapelotte and the Vezouve.

Withdrawn to prepare for the offensive on Dieuze, it was at Lunéville when the conflict ended.

132 Division d'Infanterie

Formed 23.09.14 as Division de Marche de Verdun. Numbered 132 DI on 02.07.15 (ordered 2.7.15)

Commanders
23.09.14-Francois Boucher de Morlaincourt

02.10.15-Louis Renaud
28.03.17-Eugene Huguenot
07.09.18-Jean Sicre

108 Brigade [ex 72 DI-disbanded 3.17]
303 RI   Ex 54DI 3.17 to 154Bde then 97DI
330 RI   Ex 54DI
364 RI   Ex 72DI –disbanded 8.16

264 Brigade [disbanded 3.17]
166 RI   Ex Gp Verdun
366 RI   Ex 72DI

Infantry from 3.17
166 RI
330 RI   9.18 disbanded and replaced by 298RI ex
63DI
366 RI

Artillery
1 Gp/57 RAC -ex XVIICA   4.17 to 257 RAC
2 Gp/57 RAC -ex XVIICA   " Btys 4, 22, 48 RAC's   "
12Gp/130 RAL   12.17-added-retitled 6/130RAL 3.18

Cavalry
5/4RH –8.16
5/1RH 11.15–11.16
6/1RH 11.15-11.16
5/3 RD 11.16-3.17
6/3 RD 11.16-3.17

Engineers & Pioneers
1915   Cie 25/3, 25/4, 6/23 du 9Rg
1918   Cie 25/4, 25/54, 6/23 du 9RG
8.18-Pioneer Battalion 31RIT   ex XXXCA

The division served in the Verdun area from formation until June 1916. At first, it guarded the eastern approaches to the city. Stationed in the Woëvre plain near Étain it fought there and at Marcheville during First Army's battle for the Woëvre [6th April 1915]. It left Étain on 9th December 1915 and moved to the Eparges shoulder of Verdun's salient on 8th January 1916 and remained there until 19th March. During the early stages of the battle for Verdun it fought between Eix and Eparges and engaged the Germans in action at Moulainville, Ronvaux, Manhueles, Champlon and Fresnes. After a brief rest, it moved south to the sector between Vaux-les-Palameix and Dompcevrin where it held the line from 8th April until 28th June 1916.
On 10th July 1916, the division joined Sixth Army in Picardy. For two months [13th July-10th September] it served in the Lihons/Vermandovillers sector. It attacked at Vermandovillers on 4th-7th September. From 24th September until 4th February 1917 it held the frontline between Andechy and Maucourt. When a retraining period at Bar-le-Duc ended the division returned to Verdun to fight between Côte 304 and Avocourt [12th March-12th April].

A long period of service in Champagne began on 17th April 1917 and did not end until 3rd August 1918. During this tour, the division sent elements into the line at Tahure. It served in full at Mont Cornillet and Mont Blond [29th May-26th June], at Teton/Mont Haut [21st July-17th September]; at Auberive/Epine de Vedegrange [26th October-1st June 1918] and between the Epine and Monty Sans Nom [1st –18th June].

Moved to the Oise region, the division fought with Tenth Army in the second battle of Noyon [19th August- 15th September]. It attacked at Choisy, Cuts, and Pommeraye [20th August] and reached the Oise [22nd August]. During the army's move up to the Hindenburg Line it liberated the Ailette canal line and then organised new positions between Barsisis-aux-Bois and St Gobain-à-Chauny. The division left Tenth Army on 15th September and prepared for a move to Flanders.

From Poelkapelle and Roeselare, it challenged German control of the rivers Leie and Schelde on 20th October. By 31st October it had reached the railway line between Kortrijk and Gand. After that date it was held in reserve at Dentergem and Markegem. On 11th November 1918 the division was located at Wannegem-Lede.

133 Division d'Infanterie

Formed from 105DIT in the Vosges [Seventh Army] 20.03.16 (ordered 3.3.16)

Commanders
20.03.16-Fénelon Passaga
19.12.16-Joseph Valentin

115 Brigade [ex 66DI after reorganisation] [to 134DI 8.16]
298 RIT Ex 105 DIT	8.16 to 134DI
334 RI Ex 66DI	8.16 to 134DI
43 BCP Ex 74DI	8.16 to 164DI

214 Brigade [ex independent] [disbanded 11.17]
402 RI Ex 157DI-disbanded	4.16-replaced by 111RI -disbanded 6.16 and replaced by 321DI ex 63DI
56 RIT	8.16 to 314 Bde and replaced by 102 & 116 BCP's ex 314 Bde

314 Brigade [ex 157DI] [8.16 to 134DI]
250 RIT Ex Gp Belfort	8.16 to 134DI
102 BCP	8.16 to 214 Bde
116 BCP	8.16 to 214 Bde

213 Brigade [former 313Bde] [ex 157DI 8.16] [disbanded 11.17]
401 RI
32 BCP
107 BCP   Disbanded 11.17
54 Sénégalaise Bn attached

Infantry from 11.17
321 RI
401 RI
15 Gp de Ch [32, 102, 116BCP's]

Artillery
8 Gp/5 RAC –ex 105DIT	4.17 to 265 RAC
9 Gp/5 RAC –ex GpVerdun	4.17 to 265 RAC
8? Gp/29RAC –ex 105DIT	4.17 to 265 RAC
6 Gp/136 RAL	Newly created and added 5.18

Cavalry
E/2RCA 8.16-7.17
E/2RCA 8.16-7.17

Engineers & Pioneers
1915   Cie 28/4, 28/54 du 28BG
1918   Cie 28/4, 28/54 du 28BG Cie 16/25 du 2RG
8.18-Pioneer Battalion 14RIT   Ex XXXVICA

The division remained near the Swiss frontier until 20th August 1916. From 11th September 1916 until 9th February 1917 it served at Verdun. At first it was stationed between Vaux Chapitre and Thiaumont from which it took part in the first French offensive on 24th October.

Between 11th and 20th December it fought at Douaumont and Vaux-devant-Damloup, and the at Bezonvaux and Haudromont. It returned to Vaux-devant-Damloup on 13th January 1917.

During Nivelle's offensive on the Chemin des Dame, the division served with Sixth Army between Longeuval, Cerny and Courtecon [14th April-9th May] and then moved to Flanders. It was part of the French contribution to Haig's third battle of Ypres from 13th May 1917 until 30th March 1918. It supported the Belgian and British armies between Bikschote and Drie Grachten [until 5th October], and from positions near Langemark took part in the 2nd Battle of Flanders at Merkem, Kloosteschool, Jansbeek and Corverbeek. During the winter of 1917-1918 it twice held the sector between St Georges and Nieuvepoort.

On 25th March 1918, in response to the German spring offensive, it moved southwards to Picardy and fought with First Army at Hangest-en-Santerre and Plessiers-Bouzainvillers, and then returned to Flanders to join with the British in their efforts to stem the German attack north of Bailleul.

Rested in Lorraine, it joined Third Army on 1st June to support that army's operations along the line of the Matz. From 20th June, it occupied a sector between the Ployron and Courcelles-Epayelles. From there it took part in the allied offensive in Picardy [9th-23rd August] when it fought at Tilloloy and Beuvraignes. After a rest, it took up positions between Castres and the St Quentin/Ham road on 13th September. During the battle for St Quentin, it fought in the Epine de Dallon, 15th September-10th October. After a further period in reserve near Noyon, the division rejoined First Army on 5th November and advanced from Tupigny towards the Oise/Sambre canal. It was fighting near Chimay when the war ended.

134 Division d'Infanterie

Formed in the Vosges [Seventh Army]18.08.16 (ordered 8.8.16)

Commanders
18.08.16-Albert Baratier
19.10.17-Henri Petit

115 Brigade [ex 133DI] [disbanded 2.17]
298 RIT 2.17 to 216BIT
334 RI   11.16 to 164DI

314 Brigade [ex 133 DI] [disbanded 2.17]
56 RIT   2.17 to 216BIT
250 RIT 2.17 to 216BIT

Infantry after 2.17
63 RI   Ex 23DI
100 RI   Ex 128DI
300 RI   Ex 24DI

Artillery [none on formation]
5 Gp/23 RAC -ex 101DIT	4.17 to 223 RAC
6 Gp/23 RAC -ex XXXVIIICA	4.17 to 223 RAC
7 Gp/23 RAC –formed 4.17	4.17 to 223 RAC
5 Gp/134 RAL	Newly created and added 4.18

Cavalry
E/2RCA 12.16-7.17

Engineers & Pioneers
1916 Cie 7/14 du 7BG, 8/1T du 4RG
1918 Cie 7/14 du 7BG, 28/1 du 28BG Cie 16/23 du 2RG
8.18-Pioneer Battalion 23RIT Ex XXXVIIICA

The division served between Carlspach and the Swiss frontier until 19th April 1917. It joined Fourth Army on 11th June and held the line between Teton and Aubérive [14th June-23rd September]. Next day it transferred westwards to Fifth Army and fought in and around Reims until 26th August 1918. It fought at Bétheny, Courcy and Cavaliers de Courcy during the third battle of the Aisne, fourth battle of Champagne and second battle of the Marne.

After a long rest, the division rejoined Fifth Army on 1st October 1918. During the battle of St Thiery, it fought from Romain and Ventelay towards the Aisne via Loge Fontaine and Bouflignereux. From 14th October, it fought around Vouziers and Condé-les-Vouziers and forced the line of the Aisne at Chestres. From 29th October until the armistice, the division rested and retrained at Pont-Faverger.

135-150 Divisions d'Infanterie not formed

151 Division d'Infanterie

Formed in Picardy [Second Army] 01.04.15 from new units (ordered 9.3.15)

Commanders
01.04.15-Pierre Lanquetot
20.05.17-Pierre des Vallieres
25.09.18-Camille Biesse

301 Brigade
403 RI	New regt
410 RI [disbanded 6.16]	New regt

302 Brigade
404 RI [disbanded 6.16]	New regt- 6.15 to 121DI-replaced by 293RI ex XI CA
120 BCP	New bn- 6.15 to 129DI-replaced by 337RI ex XI CA –6.16 merged into 293RI

Infantry from 6.16
293 RI	11.17 disbanded-replaced by 407RI ex 130DI
403 RI	
410 RI	

Artillery
5 Gp/ 10 RAC	4.15 to 87DI-replaced by 3 Gp/28RAC ex XICA 4.17 to 28RAC
5 Gp/ 31 RAC	4.15 to RAL-replaced by 4 Gp/28RAC ex XICA 4.17 to 28RAC
5 Gp/ 43 RAC	4.15 to 87DI-not replaced until 1.16 when 6 Gp/3RAC joined 4.17 to 28RAC
6 Gp/111 RAL	3.18-added –ex 8/111RAL

Cavalry
5/8 RD -11.15d
5/9 RD -11.15d
3/2 RCh 1.17-7.17
4/2 RCh 1.17-7.17

Engineers & Pioneers
1915 Cie 15/25 du 7RG
1918 Cie 15/7, 15/57, 15/25 du 7RG

8.18-Pioneer Battalion 7RIT   Ex XICA

From 17th April 1915 until 5th August 1915 the division served in the trenches between Fricourt and Carnoy-on the future British battlefield of the Somme. With the rest of Second Army the division moved to the eastern end of the line in Champagne for the autumn offensive. It occupied the sector at Ville-sur-Tourbe [31st August-25th October] and fought there during the second battle of Champagne. On 3rd November the division moved to the Côte 296/Mamelles sector. Pulled out on 5th December, it's next tour was between the Butte de Souain and Tahure [22nd December 1915-3rd May 1916]. On 2nd February it was attacked suddenly by the Germans at the Butte de Tahure.

The division joined the struggle for Verdun when it took up positions in the Bois Haudromont and Côte de Froideterre on 27th May 1916. On 24th June, after a ten day rest it appeared in the Marre/Charny sector, downstream from Verdun. It stayed there until 15th August.

On 21st August it moved from Verdun to another besieged city-Reims-and it would remain here until 28th June 1917. Most of the division's time was spent in the line between Betheny and Cavaliers-de-Coucy on the northern fringes of the city. It engaged in a series of local actions in November, May and June at Cavaliers- de-Coucy.

The division joined Tenth Army on the Chemin des Dames when it took over the sector between Hurtebise and the Casemates on 17th August. The line was extended to the Creute on 29th August. The division was withdrawn on 6th September for rest and retraining. On 31st October it moved westwards to join Sixth Army at Chavignon and Bois Mortier. It was to remain in this area until 27th May 1918, when Sixth Army was dislodged by the German offensive during the third battle of the Aisne. As that offensive developed the division fought at Folembray, Quincy le Basse and Bois Mortier from 6th-8th April and then withdrew to create a new defence line between Bois Mortier and Pont St Mard.

During the struggle on the Aisne, the division moved from its support position near Vic-sur- Aisne to Coeuvres-et-Valary and Fosse-en-Haut where it was involved in heavy fighting on 8th June. Four days later the division left the line and moved south-eastward to the Swiss frontier. It arrived there on 28th June. After two months in this quiet sector, the division joined Fourth Army in Champagne for the autumn offensive. From 26th September until 10th October it fought at Ste Marie-à-Py and advanced to the Charnes. From 25th October until 5th November it fought in the battle of the Serre during which it fought at Recouvrance and reached St Ferjeux. By 9th November it had advanced to the Meuse west of Charleville. It was in reserve at Signy-l'Abbaye when the conflict ended.

152 Division d'Infanterie

Formed 01.04.15 from new units at Camp d'Avord (ordered 9.3.15)

Commanders
01.04.15-Maurice Joppé
24.05.15-Joseph Cherrier
14.10.15-Simon Bertin
27.01.16-Francois Andrieu

303 Brigade [diverted to 2nd Army and then to 120DI 4.15]
408 RI
409 RI

304 Brigade [12.15 to 17DI]
417 RI   6.15 to 121DI-replaced by 268RI ex IXCA
106 BCP   6.15 to 5BdeCh-repl by 290RI ex IXCA
4 Moroccan Brigade   [added 4.15-to 38DI 12.15]
1 RdMICM
8 RdMT   7.15 retitled 4 RdMZT

Infantry from 12.15
114 RI   Ex 17DI
125 RI   Ex 17DI

296 RI   Ex 58DI   1.17 to 169DI-replaced by 135RI ex 18DI

Artillery
5 Gp/33RAC   4.15 to 124DI-replaced by 3 Gp/49RAC ex IXCA 4.17 to 249RAC
5 Gp/20RAC   4.15 to 99DIT- replaced by 4 Gp/49RAC ex IXCA 4.17 to 249RAC
5 Gp/12RAC   7.16 added 4.17 to 249RAC
7 Gp/109RAL   Newly created and added 7.18

Cavalry
5/13 RD –11.15d
5/26 RD -11.15
E /7RH 11.15 –11.18
E/17RH 11.15-6.17

Engineers & Pioneers
1915   Cie 2/7, 2/25 du 3RG
1918   Cie 2/7, 2/57, 2/25 du 3RG
8.18-Pioneer Battalion 38RIT   ex IXCA

The division arrived in the Boezinge/Wieltje sector in Flanders on 25th April 1915 and fought there during the second battle of Ypres. It began the move to Artois on 28th August and joined Tenth Army at Bretancourt, outside Arras. During the third battle of Artois it fought at Ficheux and then moved to the Fosse Calonne/Grenay sector where it was involved in attacks and counter-attacks at Loos on 8th and 11th October. The division rested at Fillievres from 30th December and rejoined Tenth Army's frontline at La Folie/Givenchy on 17th February 1916. It remained there until 10th March.

From 5th to 12th May 1916 the division fought at Hayette and Bois Camard in defence of Verdun but moved on quickly to Champagne. The division joined Fourth Army on 25th May and undertook three tours in the frontline: Epine de Vedegrange/Wacques [1st-7th June]; Auberive/Baconnes-Vaudesincourt road [13th-30th June]; and Marquises/Prosnes [7th July-28th August]. On 19th September it joined Sixth Army in Picardy and fought in the battle of the Somme in the approaches to Péronne until 3rd February 1917. At first it fought at Morval and Sailly Saillisel [20th October-4th November]; at Sailly Saillisel/Transloy [19th November-4th December] and held the line at Biaches/Maisonette [18th January-3rd February 1917].

The division took part in Nivelle's offensive when as part of Fifth Army it attacked at Mont Spin on 18th April, and between the Loivre and Miette on 28th April. It held Fifth Army's sector between the Neuville and the Aisne from 20th June until 29th July 1917.

The remainder of 1917 was spent in the quiet sector of the Foret de Parroy between the Vezouve and the Sanon in Lorraine [23rd August 1917-12th January 1918]. This was followed by labour duties in the Foret de Champenoux, south of Nancy; and a period of retraining in Picardy.

It joined First Army in Picardy on 15th April 1918 and was immediately involved in operations to thwart the German spring offensive. It fought at Grivnes and Ainval during the second battle of Picardy and then along the Matz [Third Army] between Breteuil and Mery where it counter-attacked on 11thJune. From 6th July until 24th August the division occupied a line between Grivesnes and Cantigny from which, during the third battle of Picardy, it advanced along the Avre. It fought at Pierrepont, Davesnescourt and Dancourt, 9th-11th August, and moved forward to Beuvraignes and Roye.

As First Army closed up on the Hindenburg Line, the division occupied positions between Nesle and the Canal du Nord, from which it took Ham [6th September] and reached Essigny-le-Grand where it consolidated gains. By 3rd October the division was in positions south of St Quentin. During the battle of Mont-d'Origny [15th October-4th November], the division fought at Aisonville and Grougis. Then in the second battle of Guise, it forced the Sambre canal and moved forward towards Hanappes with the rest of 1st Army. It reached Glageon but was pulled into reserve on 9th November. Two days later it was located at Nouvion.

153 Division d'Infanterie

formed 01.04.15 from new units at Courtine (ordered 9.3.15)

Commanders
29.03.15-Henri Deligny
20.03.16-Georges Magnan
19.12.16-Maurice Pellé
01.05.17-Fernand Goubeau

305 Brigade [4.15 to Groupement Reims]
411 RI	New regt
412 RI	New regt

306 Brigade [disbanded 7.18]
418 RI	New regt 7.18 to 72DI
115 BCP	4.15 to 5Bde de Ch-replaced by 2BCP ex 11DI
	12.16 to 11DI-replaced by 1RdMZT ex3BM
4 BCP	4.15 joined from 11DI
	12.16 to 11DI-not replaced

3 Moroccan Brigade from independent role 4.15 [disbanded 7.18]
1 RdMZT	12.16 to 306 Brigade –replaced by RdMTM ex 48DI which was retitled 1RdMTM 2.18
9 RdMZ	

Infantry from 7.18
9 RdMZ	
1 RdMZT	9.18 to 72DI-replaced by 418RI
1 RdMTM	

Artillery
6 Gp/ 3 RAC	4.15 to XXXVIIICA-replaced 8.15 by 3 Gp/60RAC ex XXCA 4.17 to 260RAC
5 Gp/24RAC	4.15 to 73DI-replaced 8.15 by 4 Gp/60RAC ex XXCA 4.17 to 260RAC
5 Gp/51RAC	4.15 to 102DIT –replaced 12.16 by
?Gp/5RAC ex XXXVIICA	4.17-to 260RAC
8 Gp/120RAL	Newly created and added 6.18

Cavalry
7/8 RCh -10.15
5/21 RCh-11.15
3/5 RH 12.16 –7.17
4/5 RH 12.16-1.17

Engineers & Pioneers
1915   Cie 9/25 du 6RG
1918   Cie 9/7, 9/57, 9/25 du 6RG
8.18-Pioneer Battalion 64RIT   ex XCA

The division joined the struggle to maintain the Ypres salient on 24th April 1915 when it arrived at Lizerne and Boezinge during the confusion caused by the German use of gas two days before. It remained in the salient until 8th June when it moved to the Arras area. It took over Tenth Army's line at Neuville-Saint-Vaast on 15th June. After heavy fighting it was pulled out on 5th July and moved to Lorraine for labour duties along the Meurthe.

As part of Second Army, the division took part in the autumn offensives in Champagne. From 25th September until 23rd December 1915 it fought around the Maisons de Champagne and then held the line there by alternating with 39DI.

After a further rest in Lorraine, the division was sent into the Verdun salient on 21st February 1916. It was one of the first reinforcements and it fought at Louvemont, Bezonvaux and Douaumont: it fought several hard battles for control of the Fort Douaumont until 7th March. From 10th to 24th April to it was engaged at Esnes and Avocourt in the effort to the stem the German attack on the left bank positions outside Verdun.

Transferred to Picardy on 24th April it trained at Abbeville for the planned allied offensive on the Somme. It went into line at Hardecourt-aux-Bois on 18th June, and fought there on 9th and 20th July. It fought at Maurepas from 7th to 21st August and, after a further period of retraining; it fought again at Maucourt and at Sailly Saillisel on 13th-28th November. There followed a long period of rest and retraining in Lorraine and in the Marne region,

The division joined Sixth Army on 7th April 1917 and fought at Cerny and Courtecon during the second battle of the Aisne, and then held positions between Cerny-Courtecon-Malaval until 8th June.

From 29th June until 4th November 1917 the division was located in the Moselle-Limey sector of Eighth Army's front. It moved northwards to Verdun and took over the line between Bois de la Chaume and Bezonvaux on 22nd January 1918. It came out of the line on 25th March and remained in readiness at Warluis and Quevauvillers to support the British Army. When that role became redundant, it joined Tenth Army on the Aisne on 3rd June. During the actions along the Aisne and the second battle of the Marne, the division worked on a support line at Taille-Fontaine and Haut-Fontaine. On 15th June it entered the frontline at Ambleny and was immediately involved in heavy fighting at Coeuvres-et-Valsery. After this, it established a line at Laversine and St Pierre-Aigle. In action south of Ambleny, from 18th July, it took Mont d'Arly and Saconin-et-Breuil, and Berzy-le-Sec on 22nd July.

Five days later the division joined First Army in the Santerre and during the allied offensive fought at Hangest, Arvillers and Erches and moved towards Andechy [8th-12th August]. Rested from 12th August until 30th September, the division joined Fifth Army for the battle of St Thierry [30th September-10th October]. From a startline south of Romains, it reached the line of the Vesle at Breuil sur Vesle [8th October] and moved on to the Aisne, towards Berry-au-Bac and Sapigneul, north-west of Reims.

The division rejoined First Army for the battle of the Serre [21st October-1st November] and fought from the Vendeuil/Hamegicourt line to Villers-le-Sec, Parpeville and Landifay. It was in reserve at Marle from 1st November 1918.

154 Division d'Infanterie

formed 17.03.15 with new units at Cuperly (ordered 9.3.15)

Commanders
29.03.15-Charles Rabier
04.09.16-André Breton

307 Brigade -until 4.15 [became independent –then joined 130DI 7.15]
405 RI	New regt-7.15 to 130DI
407 RI	New regt-7.15 to 130DI

308 Brigade [disbanded 11.16]
416 RI	New regt-7.15 to 28DI and replaced by
41RIC-to 2DIC and replaced	11.16 by 416RI ex 28DI
121 BCP	7.15 to 129DI-replaced by 43RIC-to 2DIC
11.16	

309 Brigade-from 4.15 [ex 155DI] [disbanded 11.16]
413 RI
414 RI

Infantry from 11.16
413 RI
414 RI
416 RI

Artillery

6 Gp/ 41 RAC	4.15 to XVCA-replaced by 3 Gp/6RAC ex XIVCA 4.17 to 266 RAC
5 Gp/30 RAC	4.15 to XXXVIIICA-replaced by 4 Gp/6RAC
	4.17 to 266RAC
? Gp/34 RAC	4.15 to XXXVIIICA –replaced 1.16 by 6
Gp/51RAC	4.17 to 266RAC
7Gp/114 RAL	Newly created and added 6.18

Cavalry
7/13 RCh -12.15
E/4 RCh -12.15
4/9 RH 1.17–7.17

Engineers & Pioneers
1915   Cie 5/7, 5/25 du 1RG
1918   Cie 5/7, 5/57, 5/25 du 1RG
8.18-Pioneer Battalion 97RIT   Ex VICA

From 18th April until 21st September 1915, the division held the line between Herleville and Dompiere in Picardy. It moved north to Artois and joined Tenth Army for the third battle of Artois. Initially, in line to the south of Arras at Warlus, Dainville and Agny, it moved to the north of the city on 29th September. There it fought at Givenchy and at Souchez, between Notre Dame-de-Lorette and Vimy Ridge until 30th November.

A period of rest and labour duties in Lorraine was followed by duty on the Swiss frontier from 16th February until 1st April 1916. The division began a tour of duty in the Verdun salient on 18th April when it joined the line on the heights above the Meuse at Châtillon. It moved to the Vaux/Damloup sector on 27th July and repulsed German attacks on Tavannes four days later. The division joined 4th Army's sector between the Aisne and the Main de Massiges on 18th August. It held the link between the Champagne and Argonne sectors until 3rd October. After another period of rest and retraining, it returned to Verdun on 20th December. It remained in line there until 18th January 1917.

As part of Third Army, the division spent a few days in the line between Chilly and Chaulnes [5th-22nd February] and then occupied the Bois des Loges sector from which it advanced into the territory left by the Germans as they retreated to the Hindenburg Line. Held in reserve with Tenth Army during Nivelle's offensive, the division joined the struggle for the Chemin des Dames on 7th May. For the next six months it held positions at Chevreux/Moulin Vauclerc [7th-30th May]; at Casemates/Chevreux [13th June-7th July] and at Mennejean/Vauxillon [20th August-7th November]. It was kept in reserve during the battle of Malmaison on 20th October.

For a brief period, 7th-28th January 1918, the division operated on the left flank of Third Army, alongside the BEF. When relieved by British units, the division was sent to the Haute-Alsace for retraining. This was brought to an end by the German spring offensive. The division was moved to Flanders and fought on the heights between Danouter and Loker from 22nd April until 1st May. Once the line had been secured the division returned to the reserve at Damery where it remained until sucked into the third battle of the Aisne on 28th May. For three days, it fought alongside British units at Ville-en-Tardenois and retreated up the valley of the Ardre. Although elements remained at the front, most of the division returned to the reserve.

From 12th June 1918 the division was used to train American troops in Lorraine and then it entered the line between Regniéville-en-Haye and the Etang de Vargevaux on 26th June. It remained there until 18th July when it moved further east to the line between the Sanon and Bezange-la-Grande. It remained there until 16th September.

Ten days later, the division was part of Fourth Army's autumn offensive. In the battle of Somme-Py, it advanced from the Epine de Vedegrange to the left bank of the Py south of St Souplet [27th-30th September]. On 6th and 7th October, it liberated the line of the Arnes at Hauvine and advanced towards Rethel via Thugny-Tupigny. On 22nd October the division left Fourth Army and moved to Alsace. From 2nd November to the end of the war, it held Seventh Army's sector between Fulleren and Burnhaupt.

155 Division d'Infanterie

Formation ordered 9.3.15-began 08.04.15 but abandoned 15.04.15

Commander
29.03.15-Edmond Gillain

309 Brigade [to 154DI]
413 RI	New regt
414 RI	New regt

310 Brigade [independent then to 121DI 6.15]
415 RI	New regt- to 27DI-replaced by 404RI
114 BCP	To 129DI replaced by 417RI

Artillery [all to 157DI]
7 Gp/15RAC
6 Gp/36 RAC
6 Gp/55 RAC

Cavalry
5/7 RD & 6/7 RD

Engineers
None allocated

156 Division d'Infanterie

Formed 17.03.15 as 156 DI but retitled 2 Division d'Infanterie du CEO 29.04.15 re- numbered as 156DI on 15.10.15

Commanders
16.03.15-Maurice Bailloud
26.08.16-Paul Baston
01.05.18-Albert Borius

Metropolitan Brigade [6.15 retitled 3 Brigade] [10.15 retitled 311 Brigade-disbanded 9.17]
176 RI
2 RdMA

Colonial Brigade [6.15 retitled 4 Brigade] [10.15 replaced by 1 Bde ex 1DI du CEO]
7 RMxIC	8.15 retitled 57RIC
8 RMxIC	8.15 retitled 58RIC

311 Brigade [ex 3 Brigade –disbanded 9.17]
175 RI
1 RdMA

312 Brigade [ex 1 Brigade-disbanded 9.17]
176 RI
2 RdMA 9.17   disbanded

Infantry from 9.17
175 RI
176 RI
1 RdMA

Artillery
5 Gp/17 RAC	4.17 to 242 RAC
5 Gp/ 25RAC	4.17 to 242 RAC
5 Gp/ 47 RAC	1.16 replaced by Gp/3RAC 4.17-242RAC
3 Gp/2RAM	10.15 –added –remained with division-no
RAL	

Cavalry
E/6 RCA –2.16
E/4 RCA 2.16 –7.18 or 11.18

Engineers & Pioneers
1915	Cie 5/15, 5/22 du 1RG
1918	Cie 5/15, 5/65, 5/22 du 1RG No Pioneer Battalion allocated

After assembly at Marseille and Bizerte, the division landed at Gallipoli on 1st May 1915. Until 1st October it fought in the battle for Krithia and took part in many actions between May and August. Transferred to Macedonia, the division took up positions on the Serbian/Bulgarian border on 14th October. For the next three years the division remained encamped at Salonika. During this time, it fought at Monastir on 31st August 1916 and again on 3rd March 1917. On 16th September 1918 it participated in the allied breakout from Monastir and reached the Tserko by the time of the Bulgarian armistice. During December 1918, the division moved to south-western Russia and joined the Army of the Danube.

157 Division d'Infanterie

Formed at the Camp de la Valbonne 28.04.15 (ordered 21.4.15)

Commanders
20.04.15-Edmond Gillain
15.09.15-Henri Tassin
23.12.15-Ferdinand Blazer
23.05.16-Jean-Marie Baulard
28.01.17-Antoine Beaudemoulin
04.05.18-Joseph de Bodin de la Galembert
30.05.18-Mariano Goybert

313 Brigade [4-10.15]
401 RI	
402 RI	10.15 replaced by 32 BCP
313 Brigade	[10.15-3.16]
401 RI	3.16 to 213 Bde-replaced by 53RIT
32 BCP	
107 BCP	

313 Brigade [3.16-8.16] [8.16 renumbered 213 Brigade and passed to 133DI]
53 RIT	8.16 replaced by 401RI
32 BCP	
107 BCP	

314 Brigade [3.16 to 133DI]
32 BCP	10.15 to 313 Bde –replaced by 402RI

102 BCP
107 BCP   10.15 to 313 Bde
116 BCP

210 Brigade [3.16 from 105DIT] [disbanded 11.16]
213 RI   From 66DI-had replaced 298RI 11.16 to 164DI
99 RIT   8.16 replaced by 53RIT

213 Brigade [ex independent role] [retitled 313 BI 8.16]
401 RI   Replaced 53RIT
8.16   replaced by 99RIT
133 RIT

313 Brigade [ex 213BI; disbanded 11.16]
99 RIT
133 RIT

Infantry 11.16-3.17 [3.17 all three RITs formed independent 217 Brigade]
53 RIT
99 RIT
133 RIT

Infantry from 3.17
214 RI   Ex 67DI   disbanded 6.18
252 RI   Ex 64DI   disbanded 6.18
333 RI   Ex 74DI

Infantry from 6.18
333 RI
371 US Infantry
372 US Infantry

Artillery
7 Gp/15 RAC –ex 155DI   4.17 to 236 RAC
6 Gp/36 RAC –ex 155DI   4.17 to 236 RAC
6 Gp/55 RAC –ex 155DI   11.16 to 46DI-replaced by Gp/36RAC
4.17 to 236RAC
6 Gp/134 RAL   3.18 added –ex12/112RAL

Cavalry
6/2 RH -2.16
7/3 RH - 2.16
5/15 RD 2.16 –6.16
6/15 RD 2.16-6.16
E/2 RCA 1.17-12.17

Engineers & Pioneers
1915   Cie 16/75 du 2RG
1918   Cie 28/5, 28/51 du 28BG Cie 16/75 du 2RG
8.18-Pioneer Battalion 70RIT   ex XIIICA

The division joined Fourth Army on 28th September 1915 when it took over the line between Wacques and Ste Hilaire-le-Grand. During the second battle of Champagne, elements of the division fought north of Wacques.
The division was withdrawn on 10th October and sent to Belfort where it carried out labour duties. On 27th

January 1916, it moved east into the line between Carlspach and Burnhaupt and moved on from there on 30th May to the adjacent sector between Leimbach and the Rhine-Rhone Canal. It remained there until 19th March 1917 when it was moved closer to the Swiss frontier. It left the frontier on 16th June.

On 9th July 1917 the division joined Fifth Army to the north-west of Reims. Between that date and 21st May 1918, it was in line between Courcy, the Loivre and Godat. During the third battle of the Aisne, it fought with Sixth Army between St Mard and Maizey, and retreated to the Marne at Chézy and Ferté-sous-Jouarre [27th May-4th June].

It moved to the Argonne on 10th June 1918. At first located between the Aire and the Bois d'Avocourt, it moved on 16th July to the sector between the Bois d'Avocourt and Forges, from which it extended its front to Quatre Enfants on 20th July. After a ten day rest near Valmy, the division joined Fourth Army's autumn offensive on Somme-Py on 26th September. Until 8th October, it advanced from the Dormoise to Monthois and Challerange.

The division arrived in the Vosges on 13th October and held the line between the upper valley of the Weiss and the Fave until the end of the war.

158 Division d'Infanterie

Formed in the Interior 15.08.15 (ordered 16.7.15)

Commanders
15.08.15-Auguste Blanc
21.03.17-Jules Priou

315 Brigade [disbanded 8.16]
406 RI	New regt-disbanded 8.16
419 RI	New regt-disbanded 8.16

316 Brigade [disbanded 11.16]
420 RI	New regt –disbanded 8.16
421 RI	New regt -disbanded 8.16

Infantry from 8.16
224 RI	Ex 53DI	11.17 to 5DI
228 RI	Ex 53DI	11.17 disbanded
329 RI	Ex 53DI	11.17 to 9DI

Artillery [11.17 to XXXVI CA]
6 Gp/ 19 RAC	4.17 to 219 RAC
5 Gp/ 35 RAC	4.17 to 219 RAC
6 Gp/ 52 RAC -added 9.15	4.17 to 219 RAC
no RAL	

Cavalry
5/5 RCh -6.17
6/18RCh -11.16d
4 /17RCh 6.17 –11.17

Engineers & Pioneers
1915   Cie 3/25 du 3RG
1918   Cie 14/14, 14/15, 4/23 du 3RG No Pioneer Battalion allocated

Employed on labour duties at Villers Cotterêts, the division was not committed to active operations until 1st September 1916 when it arrived in Reims to take over Fifth Army's sector at the Bois de Zouaves. Three weeks later it moved to the Troyon/Soupir sector on the Aisne, and then to the Chavonne/Pernant sector of the same river on 27th January 1917. After the German withdrawal to the Hindenburg Line, it moved to Soissons and fought at Braye and Margival. Apart from some elements at Laffaux, it was not involved in Nivelle's attack on the Chemin des Dames. Instead it held the line in various sectors of the Aisne until 31st July 1917: these were Mennejean/Jouy [19th April-18th May]; Mennejean/Vauxillon [28th May-6th June] and Hurtebise/Bovelle [11th-31st July]. From 20th August until 31st October, it held 3rd Army's line between Selency and Pontruet. The division disbanded at Guiscard on 5th November 1917.

159-160 Divisions d'Infanterie not formed

161 Division d'Infanterie

Formed in the Vosges [Seventh Army] 01.11.16 (ordered 16.10.16)

Commanders
18.1.0.16-Charles Brecard
31.03.17- Pierre de Laguiche
01.12.17- George Lebouc
27.06.18- Louis Modelon

Major Units
163 RI   Ex 76DI
215 RI   Ex 41DI   disbanded 9.18 replaced by 369 US Infantry
253 RI   Ex 41DI   9.17 disbanded-replaced by 363RI   ex 41DI
7 Gp/9RAC -ex XVICA   4.17- 267RAC
3 Gp/57 RAC –ex IVCA   4.17- 267RAC
4 Gp/57 RAC –ex IVCA   4.17- 267RAC
4 Gp/315 RAL   11.17 added 7.18 retitled 7/115RAL E/5RCA -12.16
5/14 RCh 12.16 –11.18
3/14 RCh   7.17 only
Cie 17/14, 17/64, 17/23 du 2RG
1 Bn/279RIT   7.17 added-became pioneer bn 8.18

Upon formation the division performed two tours in the Vosges between Metzeral and the Col Ste Mare, from 1st November 9th December 1916 and 11th January-28th June 1917. It moved to the Chemin des Dames and took over Tenth Army's sector between Bovelle and Courtecon on 1st August. It remained on this front until 12th April 1918. It left Courtecon on 22nd August and served in the line at Creute/Cerny-en- Laonnais, 25th September-20th October. Command tranferred to Sixth Army on 28th October, and the division returned to the front at Bois Mortier/Quincy Basse on 15th November. It moved to the adjacent Quincy Basse/Barisis sector on 12th January 1918. This sector was extended to the Oise/Aisne canal on 1st April.

The division left the Oise/Aisne front on 12th April and took over Fourth Army's sector at the Butte de Mesnil on the 24th. It moved to Tahure on 1st June and fought there during the fourth battle of Champagne [11th July]. From 18th July until 7th October, the division was engaged between Massiges and Mesnil-les- Hurlus. During the battle of Somme-Py, it moved north from the Dormoise to Bellevue, Séchault and Challerange.

Transferred back to the Vosges, it held the line between Leimbach and Metzeral from 15th October until the armistice.

162 Division d'Infanterie

Formed at Courtisols [4th Army] 25.11.16 (ordered 21.10.16)

Commanders
22.10.16-Emile Rauscher
09.12.17-Adolphe Messimy

Major Units
43 RI   Ex 1DI
127 RI   Ex 1DI
327 RI   Ex 51DI

4 Gp/28RAC -ex VIICA   4.17 to 263 RAC
3 Gp/53 RAC –ex XCA   4.17 to 263 RAC
4 Gp/53 RAC –ex XCA   4.17 to 263 RAC
8 Gp/101 RAL   3.18 added –ex 11/101RAL
1/6 RCh   1.18 withdrawn
Cie 1/14, 1/64, 1/23 du 3RG
Pioneer Bn/72 RIT   8.18 added –ex ICA

After serving in the Navarin sector of Champagne until 7th January 1917, the division was transferred to Fifth Army to prepare for Nivelle's spring offensive. It entered the line at Hurtebise on 20th January, fought at Chevreux on 12th February, and during the second battle of the Aisne, attacked the Plateau de Vauclerc [16th-21st April]. There followed a period of rest and retraining.

The division joined Fist Army in Flanders as part of the French contribution to Haig's summer offensive at Ypres. After a brief period in the line between Nordshote and Steenstraat, the division moved to Bikschote and attacked Jansbeek on 17th and 18th August. Rested and employed on labour duties the division resumed its frontline service on 27th October when it took over positions at Klostersschool and Langemark. On 21st November, it was pulled out for further retraining and a movement to the Aisne.

As part of Sixth Army, the division held the line between the Miette and the Ployon, 27th Janaury to 24th March 1918. In response to the German spring offensive, it was transferred westwards to Picardy where it fought at Mesnil St Georges, near Montdidier until 5th May. It returned to Sixth Army as the third battle of the Aisne developed. With Tenth Army from 2nd June, it fought at Porte, Vingré and Ambleny and then held the line between those locations. Subject to several local actions, as the battle developed into the second for Noyon and the second of the Marne, it fought at Fontenay [20th July] and north of the Aisne at Nouvion- Vingre, Tartiers, and Villers-la-Fosse until 26th August. During Tenth Army's movement up to the Hindenburg Line, 5th September-1st October, the division occupied a sector between Vailly and Aizy, fought at Vailly and Vauxelles, and made some progress on the Chemin des Dames.

On 3rd October 1918, the division joined Seventh Army in the Vosges and occupied the line between Metzeral and the Weiss valley until the end of the war.

163 Division d'Infanterie

Formed at Chaumury [5th Army] 15.11.16 (ordered 27.10.16)

Commanders
29.10.16-Joseph Bordeaux
13.06.17-Henri Mareschal
16.06.17-Edmond Boichut

Major Units
53 RI   Ex 124DI
142 RI   Ex 124DI
415 RI   Ex 27DI
4 or 6 Gp/32 RAC -ex XXXVIICA   4.17 to 244 RAC
1 Gp/44 RAC -ex IVCA   4.17 to 244 RAC
2 Gp/44 RAC -ex IVCA   4.17 to 244 RAC
8 Gp/104 RAL   6.18 added –ex 3/304RAL
5/9 RCh -4.17
5/1RD 4.17-7.17
2/14RH 7.17-11.18
Cie 4/12, 4/62, 4/23 du 1RG
Pioneer Bn/104RIT   8.18 added –ex IVCA

The division began its operational career when it joined the frontline, south of Verdun, between Eparges and Bois Loclont on 8th February 1917. Withdrawn on 14th June, it was transferred to Fourth Army where it took over the Mont Cornillet/Mont Haut sector on 20th July. Elements were involved in the battle of the Monts, 25th-27th July. Withdrawn on 4th October, the division took over the Teton/Mont Haut sector on 5th November and remained there until 10th March 1918.

Its period in reserve at Chalons was interrupted by the German spring offensive, and the division joined First Army on the Avre on 27th March. It fought at Mailly-Raineval [4th April], and establish a line between there and Moreuil where it remained until 10th April.

The division rejoined Fourth Army on 27th April and, apart from a few days in the rear of Fifth Army, remained with that army for the rest of the war. In line from 27th April until 31st May at Mont Cornillet/Marquises, then it moved to Prunay where it remained until 25th August. During the fourth battle of Champagne it fought north-west of Prunay. It rejoined the frontline on 17th September and fought between Aubérive and Moscou during 4th Army's autumn offensive. In succession it advanced to the Suippe [6th October], Pont-Faverger [11th October], the Retourne [12th October] and to the Aisne between Rethel and Thugny-Trugny. During the battle of Chesne, the division fought at Voncq and Terron and crossed the Aisne at Semuy [2nd November]. From 5th November, it advanced northwards towards the Meuse via Lametz and Omont. It crossed the river at Flize on 9th November

164 Division d'Infanterie

Formed at Giromagny [7th Army] 27.11.16 (ordered 8.11.16)

Commander
11.11.16-Léon Gaucher
Major Units
152 RI   Ex 66DI
213 RI   Ex 157DI   9.17 disbanded and replaced by
133RI ex 23DI
334 RI   Ex 134DI   9.17 to 97DI-replaced by 13 Gp de Chasseurs [41/43/59 BCP's] [59BCP ex 97DIT]
41 BCP Ex 66DI   9.17 to 13Gp
43 BCP Ex 133DI   9.17 to 13Gp
6 Gp/24 RAC -ex XVCA   4.17 to 232 RAC
5 Gp/32 RAC -ex 46DI   4.17 to 232 RAC
6? Gp/38 RAC -ex XVICA   4.17 to 232 RAC
7 Gp/107 RAL   Newly created and added 6.18
6/14 RCh -6.17
3/11RCh 6.17 –7.17
Cie 9/14, 9/64, 9/23 du 6RG
Pioneer Bn/21RIT   8.18 added –ex XICA

Initially in line between Carlspach and Ammertswiller, the division served in the Vosges until 13th March 1917. Moved to Tenth Army to support Nivelle's offensive on the Chemin des Dames, the division untertook three brief tours in that sector: Vauclerc/Hurtebise [10th-30th May]; Hurtebise/Casemates [15th June-4th July] and Craonne/Casemates [20th-27th July]. It moved eastwards and entered 5th Army's sector at Bétheny and Cavaliers, on the outskirts of Reims, on 19th August. Pulled out on 16th October, it arrived in the Verdun salient at Damloup and Bezonvaux on 1st November, where it served until 19th December.
On 11th January 1918, the division took over Eighth Army's positions in Lorraine between the Sanon and Embermésnil and served there until 30th April. Mainly attached to the Sixth Army, it fought in the series of battles of the Aisne and the Marne during the summer of 1918. In the third battle of the Aisne, it fought north and west of Château-Thierry [30th May-5th June]. It instructed American troops at Ferté-sous-Jouarre in June, and fought in the second battle of the Marne from Vinly and Chezy-en-Oxois to Clignon, d'Alland and Villeneuve-sur-Fere.

During August it fought on the Vesle, east of Fismes at Paars and Bazoches. During Tenth Army's movement up to the Hindenburg Line, it cleared the Germans from the Vesle, and moved up to the Aisne at St Mard and Villers-en-Prayeres.

On 18th September the division moved to Flanders and participated in the battle for the Cretes de Flandres when it fought at Hooglede, 30th September-5th October. During the allied breakout from the Ypres salient, it advanced from Ooostroosebeke to Waregem, 18th-30th October. During the last two days of the war it fought at Segelsgem and advanced to the line of the railway between Ronse and Gand..

165 Division d'Infanterie

Formed at Ville-en-Tardenois [5th Army] 24.12.16 (ordered 18.11.16)

Commander
19.11.16-Alphonse Caron

Major units
154 RI   Ex 40DI
155 RI   Ex 40DI
287 RI   Ex 69DI
5 Gp/20 RAC –ex 100DIT   4.17 to 235 RAC
? Gp/29 RAC –ex 81DI   4.17 to 235 RAC
5 Gp/51 RAC –ex 99DI   4.17 to 235 RAC
8 Gp/132 RAL   6.18 added –ex 3/332RAL
1/20RCh   1.17 added-withdrawn 7.17
Cie 25/14, 25/64, 25/23 du 9RG
Pioneer Bn/5RIT   8.18 added –ex XXXIVCA

On 27th December 1916 the division began its first operational tour when it took over Fourth Army's positions on the western fringes of the Argonne between the Aisne and Four de Paris. It left there on 24th January 1917 and joined Fifth Army for long period of training and preparation for Nivelle's offensive. During that abortive operation the division fought north-east of Berry-au-Bac, between Sapigneul and the Miette where it remained until 19th May. On 7th July, it took over the trenches at Louvemont, downstream of Verdun, and advanced towards Beaumont during the second Verdun offensive [20th-26th August]. After a rest from 29th August, the division moved to the southern shoulder of the Verdun salient where it was stationed between the Tranchée de Calonne and Eparges [13th September-13th October]. From 4th November 1917 until 31st January 1918, the division occupied Eighth Army's line in Lorraine between Chenincourt and Clémery.

A long period of retraining near Toul was interrupted by the German spring offensive and by 26th April, the division was in the Santerre where it fought with First Army at Hangard , Hailles and Castel until 2nd May. From 10th June until 10th August it fought along the Matz, with Third Army. It counter-attacked at Belloy and Lataule; organised new lines between Belloy and St Maur; and during the third battle of Picardy, it attacked Lataule, Conchy-les-Pots and Bois des Loges [10th-19th August]. From 26th August until 15th September, it fought at Canny-sur-Matz and Lassigny, and then, took part in Third Army's movement up to the Hindenburg Line. In this phase it fought at Potiere, Catigny, Chevilly, Bois de Chaptre et Guiscard, and pursued the Germans to the Crozat canal.

On 18th September, the division moved to Lorraine and held the line between Clémery and Arraye for the rest of the war. Re-allocated to Tenth Army on 10th November 1918 it would have participated in that army's planned offensive.

166 Division d'Infanterie

Formed at Igny-le-Jard [Fifth Army] 09.01.17 (ordered 15.12.16)

Commander
23.12.16-Paul Cabaud

Major units

171 RI Ex 56DI	
294 RI Ex 56DI	10.18 disbanded and replaced by
17 RdMT	
19 BCP Ex 127DI	
26 BCP Ex 127DI	
21 Bn Indo-Chinois	7.17 attached
8? Gp/6 RAC -ex RF Dunkerque	4.17 to 234 RAC
5? Gp/34 RAC –ex XXXVIIICA	4.17 to 234 RAC
5? Gp/46 RAC -ex 90Gp/VICA	4.17 to 234 RAC
8 Gp/106 RAL	6.18 added –ex 3/336RAL
4/12 RH	Withdrawn 7.17
Cie 6/14, 6/54, 6/24 du 9RG	
Pioneer Bn/28RIT	8.18 added-ex XCA

The division's early service was on the Chemin des Dames. It occupied Fifth Army's sector between Chavonne and Moussy from 20th March to 7th April 1917. It remained in reserve at Soupir during the second battle of the Aisne [16th April] and took over Sixth Army's positions between the Pantheon and Chevregny four days later. On 5th May it attacked the Ferme de Bouvettes. Out of the line, 9th-21st May, it returned to the trenches between the Epine de Chevregny and the Pantheon and remained there until 2nd June.

The division took over the Col de Bonhomme/Provencheres sur Fave sector of Seventh Army's front in the Vosges on 13th July and remained in line until 23rd January 1918. A long period of retraining and labour duties near Bruyeres was interrupted by the German spring offensive.

On 26th March 1918 it joined First Army in the struggle along the Avre where it fought near Grivesnes and then established a new line between Thory and Ainval. Then the division returned to Lorraine where it held Eighth Army's positions between Embermésnil and the Sanon from 28th April until 25th June.

The division returned to First Army in Picardy on 4th July 1918 and spent a month in line between Cantigny and Mesnil St Georges. During the allied offensive, which began on 8th August, the division moved up in a support role through Grivesnes and Beuvraignes to Roye. From 27th August it participated in the movement of First Army up to the Hindenburg Line. During this phase, it fought at Trois Doms, and between the Avre and the Canal du Nord. Then it organised new positions to the east of Jussy. During the battle of St Quentin [25th September-14th October], it moved from a reserve position at Nesle and Bethencourt to fight in the Foret de Savy alongside British troops. Then it took Fancilly-Sélency, passed to the north of St Quentin, crossed the St Quentin canal, and pursued the Germans to Montigny-en-Arronaise. After a brief rest at Chaulnes, the division rejoined First Army on 31st October. It freed the line of the Oise as far as Capelle during the second battle of Guise. On 7th November, the German delegation passed through its line at Haudroy/Capelle en route to Compiegne. In the advance to the Meuse, it passed through Fourmies and reached Monigies by the time the armistice was signed.

167 Division d'Infanterie

Formed at Neufchateau [DAL] 25.12.16 (ordered 28.11.16)

Commander

14.12.16-Henri Schmidt

Major units

170 RI Ex 48DI	
174 RI Ex 48DI	
409 RI Ex 120DI	
5 Gp/31 RAC -ex XIIICA	4.17 to 222 RAC
6 Gp/45 RAC -ex 99DI (8-11.16)	4.17 to 222 RAC
5 Gp/48 RAC -ex XXXCA	4.17 to 222 RAC

8 Gp/121 RAL
4/3RCh -ex XIIICA
Cie 13/12, 13/62, 13/23 du 4RG
Pioneer Bn/144RIT 8.18 added –ex XXICA

3.18 added –ex 11/121RAL
Until 7.17

From 25th December 1916 until 19th January 1917 the division held positions between Pont-a -Mousson and the Seille at Nomeny. This was followed by a period of retraining and labour duties near Lunéville. In the aftermath of Nivelle's failed offensive on the Chemin des Dames, the division joined 5th Army between Godat and the Loivre on 23rd April. Between 1st and 9th May it fought at Sechamp and then remained in line until 27th May. A month later the division moved into the suburbs of Reims and manned positions between Betheny and Cavaliers until 20th August. Transferred to 6th Army on 28th August, it moved westwards along the Chemin des Dames to the Craonne/Nanteuil-la-Fosse sector on 25th September. After remaining in support during the battle of Malmaison [23rd -31st October] the division pulled out and moved to the Vosges.

Seventh Army's sector between Metzeral and the Col du Bonhomme was the division's home from 20th December 1917 until 12th May 1918. As a response to the German offensive –the third battle of the Aisne-it joined Sixth Army between Veuilly-la-Poterie and Hautevesnes from which it fought along the river to the north of Clignon. During the second battle of the Marne, it advanced from Clignon and liberated Bussaires, Epaux-Bezu and Beauvardes. Withdrawn on 27th July it rested on the Ourcq and joined Fourth Army's sector between Trou Bricot and Wacques on 12th August. It engaged the Germans at the Butte de Souain and Crete d'Oirfeuil during the battle of Somme-Py [26th September-9th October]. After a period in reserve it joined the battle of Serre on 17th October. Taken over by Fifth Army on 19th October, it attacked towards Bagnogne and Recouvrance on the 27th and then organised a new line at those two locations. It advanced towards Signe l'Abbaye and reached a point south of the town by 10th November when it was withdrawn.

The division was moving between Conde-les-Herpy and Boult-sur-Suippe when the armistice came into effect.

168 Division d'Infanterie

Formed 04.12.16 at Bayon [DAL] (ordered 4.12.16)

Commanders
04.12.16-Maurice Gamelin
19.12.16-Georges Magnan
09.01.18-Eugene Hallier
24.08.18-Antoine Peschart d'Ambly

Major units
37RI Ex 11DI
79 RI Ex 11DI
160 RI Ex 39 DI
6 Gp/4 RAC Ex XXXXIX CA 4.17 to 233 RAC Cheval
Gp/33 RAC –ex 9DC Ex XXXXIX CA 4.17 to 233 RAC Cheval
6 Gp/37 RAC – 104DIT Ex XXXXIX CA 4.17 to 233 RAC Cheval
7 Gp/120 RAL Newly created and added 8.18
3/5 RH -ex XXCA Withdrawn 7.17
Cie 20/14, 20/64, 20/23 du 10RG
Pioneer Bn/24RIT 8.18 added –ex XIVCA

Apart from a brief period in the line between Nomeny and Pont-a-Mousson [19th January-1st February 1917], the division did not became actively employed until the spring of 1917. Held in Sixth Army's reserve during Nivelle's offensive on the Chemin des Dames, the division took over the line between Malval and Courtecon on 21st April. It was engaged in action on 5th, 6th and 14th May to the north of Verneuil. Pulled out on 17th May it moved back to Lorraine for further training, and, on 12th July entered the line along the Seille between Nomeny and Brin. The division remained in position until 22nd October when began two months of labour duties at Saffais.

On 1st January 1918, it took over the Samogneux/Forges sector in the Verdun salient. This was extended to include Côte 344 on 27th March. The division left the line on 18th April and was moved to Flanders where it fought a series of actions around Bailleul after which it remained in line at Koutkot until 29th June.

On 20th and 21st July, the division fought with Ninth Army in the second battle of the Marne when it attacked near Dormans and then crossed the Marne. Then it was transferred to the 5th Army where it fought at Vrigny and then moved up to the Vesle and established a line between Muizon and Reims [2nd August]. From its line outside Reims it joined the battle of St Thierry [30th September] and then advanced to the Suippe, north-west of Bourgogne where it remained until 10th October. After a brief break, the division was transferred to First Army for the battle of the Serre [18th October] during which it advanced from Ribemont to Vervins. During 1st Army's advance to the Meuse, it remained in reserve during the second battle of Guise and then moved forward to the Capelle by 11th November.

169 Division d'Infanterie

Formed at Aumale [10th Army] 22.01.17 (ordered 29.12.16)

Commander
29.12.16-Augustin Serot Almeras Latour

Major Units
13 RI   Ex 16DI
29 RI   Ex 16DI
296 RI   Ex 152DI   11.17 disbanded and replaced by 39RI ex 130DI-
                                                     10.18 to 58DI-replaced by 6 RdMT ex 58DI
6 Gp/17 RAC -ex XXXCA   4.17 to 210 RAC
8 Gp/32 RAC -ex XXXVIICA   4.17 to 210 RAC
7 Gp/36 RAC -ex XXXCA   4.17 to 210 RAC
8 Gp/108 RAL   5.18 added –ex 4/308RAL
6/16 RCh   Withdrawn 7.17
Cie 2/12, 2/62, 2/23 du 3RG
Pioneer Bn/69RIT   8.18 added –ex XXXVCA

The division served with Fourth Army in Champagne from 26th January 1917 until 23rd February 1918. Until 1st April it held the line between the Aisne and the Maisons de Champagne, and from 1st June, that between the Four de Paris and the Aisne. The division was retraining at Mailly when it was ordered to move westwards to the Oise region in response to the German spring offensive.

It arrived in the Vaux/Ayencourt sector on 4th April and remained there until 8th August. During this period it fought at Tricot [9th June] and Fretoy [11th June] during Third Army's fight for the Matz. From 13th June it established line between Ayencourt and the Ployron and fought at Rubescourt and at the Fretoy on 19th July. From 8th to 19th August it fought with 1st Army in the third battle of Picardy. It took German positions at Assainvilliers and Faverolles and then moved forward to Cessier and Loges by 16th August.

During First Army's movement up to the Hindenburg Line which began on 6th September, the division started at Ham and took Clastres [9th September], Essigny-le-Grand [19th September] and fought at Urvillers during the battle for St Quentin [1st October]. On 9th October it advanced from the line Urvillers/St Quentin and fought on the Oise at Hauteville until 13th October. The division remained in reserve for the rest of the war. It was at Guise, en route back to the front, when the armistice came into effect.

170 Division d'Infanterie

Formed at Vesoul [Seventh Army] 15.01.17 (ordered 23.12.16)

Commanders
23.12.16-Georges Rondeau
06.06.18-Joseph Bernard

Major units

17 RI	Ex 13DI	
370 RI	Ex 71DI	11.17 disbanded and replaced by 116RI ex 2DI
3 BCP	Ex 43DI	
10 BCP	Ex 43DI	
6 Gp/20 RAC	-ex XXXIIICA	4.17 to 259 RAC
3 Gp/59 RAC	-ex XXICA	4.17 to 259 RAC
4 Gp/59 RAC	-ex XXICA	4.17 to 259 RAC
7 Gp/121 RAL		7.18 added –ex 3/321RAL
3/4 RCh	-ex XXICA	Withdrawn 7.17
Cie 21/14, 21/64, 21/23 du 11RG		
Pioneer Bn/144RIT	8.18 added –ex XXICA	

After a period of frequent movements and training periods, the division entered the line for the first time on 27th May 1917 when it took up Sixth Army's positions on the Chemin des Dames at Colombe and Mennejean, and remained there until 29th September. It played a supporting role in the battle of Malmaison [23rd October] and was then held in reserve for the British attack on Cambrai [20th-29th November].

From 15th December 1917 until 4th May 1918, the division held Seventh Army's line in the Vosges between the Fave and the Chapelotte.

On 28th May it joined Sixth Army and fought in the third battle of the Aisne at Vic sur Aisne, and then retreated to Laversine and Port from which it was pulled out and transferred to Champagne on 5th June. From 17th June until 15th September, the division occupied the line between Mont Sans Nom and the Epine de Vedegrange. During the fourth battle of Champagne it there and established new positions between Wacques and Esperance. During Fourth Army's autumn offensive at Somme-Py, the division remained in the second line for most of the battle. Then it moved forward between the Aure and Somme-Py towards the Aisne which it reached by 2nd October.

Transferred to Fifth Army on 17th October, the division joined the battle for the Serre at Nizy-les-Comte and took St Quentin-le-Petit on 25th October. Three days later the division left the front for the last time. It was resting at Jonchery-sur-Vesle when the war ended.

Colonial Divisions 1 – 17

1 Division d'Infanterie Coloniale

An active division in 1914 as part of the Colonial Corps, with headquarters at Paris

Commander
02.08.14-Paul Leblois

2 Colonial Brigade
5 RIC, Lyon	To XIV CA
6 RIC, Lyon	To XIV CA

5 Colonial Brigade
21 RIC, Paris	To GQG reserve
23 RIC, Paris	To GQG reserve

3 RACC, Valenciennes
3 R Ch Af, Algeria
Cie 1RG

The division was broken up on mobilisation.

2 Division d'Infanterie Coloniale

An Active division in 1914 as part of the Colonial Corps, with headquarters at Toulon

Commanders
02.08.14-Charles Perreaux
06.08.14-Paul Leblois
23.01.15-Emile Maziller
19.02.17-Laumer Sardorge
22.06.17-Joseph Aymerich
10.11.17-Joseph Mordrelle

4 Colonial Brigade [to 16DIC 11.16-replaced by 7 Brigade]
4 RIC, Toulon
8 RIC, Toulon
6 Colonial Brigade [disbanded 5.17]
22 RIC, Marseille
24 RIC, Perpignan

7 Colonial Brigade [11.16 from 308 Bde/154DI] [disbanded 5.17]
41 RIC   Disbanded 5.17
43 RIC

Infantry from 5.17
22 RIC
24 RIC
43 RIC
Attached 5.17-??.18 : 28, 64 & 65 Bns Sénégalaise
Attached 7.18-11.18 : 28, 32 & 64 Bns Sénégalaise

Artillery
1 RACC, Lorient
5 Gp/141 RAL   11.17 added as 12/120RAL-retitled 3.18

Cavalry
3 RCA   8.14 detachd to CAC E/3RCA, 1.17-7.17
E/3RCA 1.17-7.17

Engineers & Pioneers
1914   Cie 22/1 du 1RG
1918   Cie 22/1, 22/51, 22/21 du 1RG
8.18-Pioneer Battalion 88RIT   from ICAC

After concentration at Vaubecourt, the division joined Fourth Army on 13th August 1914. It advanced on Neufchateau via Jubecourt, Monfaucon, Stenay and Chauvency. During in the battle of the Ardennes it fought at Termes, Frenois, Jamoigne, Valansary, Izel and Pin [22nd –24th August]. During the retreat southwards, the division fell back to the Meuse, fought at St Walfroy [25th], Foret de Jaulnay [27th], Châtillon-sur-Bar, Petites-Armoise and Brieulles-sur-Bar [30th] and came to a halt near St Remy-en- Bouzemont [1st September].

During Fourth Army's battle at Vitry during the first battle of the Marne [6th-14th September], the division fought at Matignicourt-et-Gencourt and then advanced towards Massiges [11th September] where it established a line between Ville-sur-Tourbe and Beauséjours. It fought off a German attack on 26th September and remained in line here until 1st June 1915. During the first battle of Champagne it participated in local actions at Beauséjours [20th, 28th December 1914 and 3rd, 13th and 17th February 1915]. Out of the line from 1st June to 13th August, the division returned to the Beauséjours sector and attacked at Massiges during the second battle of Champagne [25th September-6th October]. It consolidated gains and remained in the line until 13th November.

On 29th January 1916 the division joined Sixth Army in Picardy. Until 16th February, it occupied positions between Faucaucourt and Maucourt. After a period of retraining it returned to the same sector on 25th April. Moved to the Dompiêrre/Somme sector on 3rd June, it attacked and took Frise, Herbecourt and Flaucourt in the opening stages of the battle of the Somme. Later in the summer, it attacked Biaches and Bois Blaize [12th August]. The division left the Somme on 23rd August and moved southwards to join Third Army on the Oise front. It occupied a sector between the Bois des Loges and the Roye/Mondidier railway from 29th November. When the Germans retreated to the Hindenburg Line in March 1917, the division advanced from Candor, through Catigny and Jussy to the Crozat canal [16th-21st March].

The division arrived before the Laffaux position on 3rd April 1917 to prepare for its role in Sixth Army's planned attack on the Chemin des Dames. It attacked Laffaux on 16th April and established a new line between Bessy and the Soissons/Laon road. It left 6th Army on 15th May and moved to the Vosges where it spent a month in line near Leimbach. The division returned to the Chemin des Dames on 25th July and did two tours in the Chevreux/Casemates sector of Tenth Army [25th July-25th August; 20th September-20th October] and one tour in Sixth Army's lines at Vauclerc/Creute [7th November –7th December].

From 16th January until 27th May 1918, the division defended Fifth Army's positions at Reims between Pompelle and Marquises. In the third battle of the Aisne, it moved to shore up the defences at Vrigny and Ormes. It continued to fight there during the battle for the Montagne de Reims/second battle of the Marne [15th July-6th August]. From 18th September it occupied the sector between Prunay and Reims. In the battle of St Thierry [4th-20th October], the division fought between the Suippe and the Aisne and advanced to Condé-les-Herpes. In the battle for the Serre [20th October-5th November], it fought from the Herpy to Chateau-Porcien, and then advanced to the north until placed in reserve at Novion-Porcien on 9th November.

3 Division d'Infanterie Coloniale

An Active division in 1914 as part of the Colonial Corps, with headquarters at Brest

Commanders
02.08.14-Léon Raffenel
27.08.14-Charles Leblond
12.09.14-Georges Goullet
19.11.15-Henri Gadel
02.07.16-Richard Puypéroux

1 Colonial Brigade [1.15 to CAC Troops]
1 RIC, Cherbourg   2.15 to 15DIC-replaced by 21RIC
2 RIC, Brest   2.15 to 15DIC-replaced by 23RIC

3 Colonial Brigade [disbanded 5.17]
3 RIC, Rochfort   2.16 to 17DIC
7 RIC, Bordeaux

5 Colonial Brigade [1.15 from CAC –replaced 1 Colonial Brigade] [disbanded 5.17]
21 RIC
23 RIC

Infantry from 5.17
7 RIC
21 RIC
23 RIC
Attached 6-10.16: 58RIC Senegalaise [68, 69, 71 Bns] Attached 5.17- .18: 5, 61, 62 Bns Sénégalaise
Attached 7.18:   5, 61, 62 Bns Sénégalaise

Artillery
2 RACC, Cherbourg   By 9.14 replaced by Gp/50 RAL & Gp/3 RAC-ex CAC
                                           12.14 Gp/2 RACC added
                                           4.17 to 2RACC

6 Gp/141 RAL   3.18 added –ex ?/114RAL

Cavalry
E/3RCA,, 1.17-7.17
E/3RCA, 1.17-7.17

Engineers & Pioneers
1914   Cie 22/3 du 1RG
1918   Cie 22/3, 22/53, 22/71 du 1RG
8.18-Pioneer Battalion 88RIT   From ICAC

After assembly at Bar-leDuc, the division joined Fourth Army's advance northwards into the Ardennes. Moving via Neufchateau, Dun-sur-Meuse and Stenay, it fought at Bois St Vincent and then at Rossignol, during the battle of the Ardennes [22nd-24th August]. During the army's retreat southwards, it fought in the Foret de Diculet [24th –28th August] and then retreated to Thieblemont-Faremont. In the battle of Vitry/first battle of the Marne, it was in action at Ecriennes, Thieblemont-Faremont and Matigniecourt, and then advanced to Ville-sur-Tourbe.

From 14th September 1914 until 31st May 1915, the division held Fourth Army's sector at Ville-sur-Tourbe. After a long period of retraining, it rejoined Fourth Army between Ville-sur-Tourbe and the Aisne on 12th August. During the second battle of Champagne, it fought and organised new lines between Ville-sur-Tourbe and Massiges. The division left Fourth Army on 30th November 1915 and, after a period of rest and retraining, moved to the Somme.

In line from Foucaucourt to the Somme, with Sixth Army, from 10th February 1916, the division moved to the Dompiêrre/Fontaine-les-Cappy sector on 4th June. During the battle of the Somme, it attacked Becquincourt and Dompiêrre [1st July], Assevillers [2nd July], Flaucourt [3rd July] and Belloy [4th July]. In later stages of the battle it attacked Villers-Carbonnel [20th July] and Horgny [30th July]. Pulled out of the line on 4th August, the division returned to Fourth Army in Champagne where it took over the Butte de Souain/Wacques sector on 31st August.

Taken out of the line on 9th October, it moved to Third Army in the Oise front and held the sector between Andechy and the Roye/Montdidier railway from 3rd December 1916 until 7th March 1917. After the German withdrawal to the Hindenburg Line, it advanced to the Crozat canal at St Simon.

For the second battle of the Aisne, the division joined Sixth Army on 4th April. From the Vauxillon/Quincy Basse sector, it attacked the Bois Mortier on 16th April, and then attacked the Mont de Singes on 5th and 6th May. The division left the front on 13th May and moved to the quiet sector between the Rhine-Rhone canal and the Swiss frontier. It rejoined the struggle for the Chemin des Dames when it took over Tenth Army's sector between Hurtebise and the Plateau des Casemates on 20th July. The division completed two tours in this sector and reverted to the reserve on 10th November.

From 18th January 1918 until the end of the war the division occupied lines around Reims. As part of Fifth Army it occupied the Pompelle position until the third battle of the Aisne. From 15th July, during the fourth battle of Champagne/second battle of the Marne, it fought on the other side of Reims, between the city and the Vesle. Fighting continued until 18th September.

As the allied advance gained momentum, the division occupied the line between the suburbs of Reims and the Neuvillette from which it broke out northwards during the battle of St Thierry [4th-19th October]. It advanced via the Suippe to Bazancourt [7th October], Boult sur Suippe and Isles sur Suippe [11th October] and to Blanzy and the Retourne [12th October]. Then it crossed the Aisne and reached Balbam, Gomont and then Conde-les-Herpy and St Germainmont. During the battle of the Serre, it fought and organised new positions at Herpy.

The division was withdrawn from the line on 31st October and then joined Tenth Army to prepare for that army's advance on Metz. On 11th November 1918 it was at Xeuilley.

4-9 Divisions d'Infanterie Coloniale not formed

10 Division d'Infanterie Coloniale

Formed at Frejus 20.05.15 (ordered 5.2.15)

Commanders
20.05.15-Jean-Baptiste Marchand
26.09.15-Henri Gadel
22.12.15-Jean-Baptiste Marchand

19 Colonial Brigade [disbanded 12.16]
1 RMxIC	6.15 disbanded & replaced by 33RIC ex CAC
2 RMxIC	8.15 retitled 52RIC

20 Colonial Brigade [disbanded 12.16]
3 RMxIC	8.15 retitled 53RIC
5 RMxIC	6.15 disbanded & replaced by 42RIC ex

XVCA 12.16 to 11DIC

Infantry from 12.16

33 RIC
52 RIC
53 RIC
Attached 7.17- .18: 71, 68, 69 Bns Sénégalaise
Attached 7.18:   66, 67, 68 Bns Sénégalaise

Artillery
? Gp/3 RACC -ex IICAC	4.17 to 229 RAC 5.18 retitled 41RAC
6 Gp/29 RAC -ex IICA	4.17 to 229 RAC 5.18 retitled 41RAC
7 Gp/29 RAC -ex IICA	4.17 to 229 RAC
	5.18 retitled 41RAC
5 Gp/142 RAL	1.18 added –ex 12/107RAL

Cavalry
E/2RS, 1.17-1.18
E/2RS, 1.17-1.18

Engineers & Pioneers
1915   Cie 7/13, 7/63 du 7BG
1918   Cie 7/13, 7/63 du 7BG Cie 16/22 du 2RG
8.18-Pioneer Battalion 18RIT   from IICAC

The division joined Fourth Army in Champagne on 21st August 1915. From a sector between Souain and the Bois Sabot, it fought in the second battle of Champagne at Navarin. Withdrawn from the front on 29th September, the division spent a long period at resting and retraining in Picardy. It took over Sixth Army's sector between the Avre and Beuvraignes on 12th February 1916 and remained there until 14th August. It entered the battle of the Somme on 26th September at Belloy-en-Santerre and fought there until 21st November; it took part in French attacks on 14th and 16th October.

Out of the line until 7th February 1917, the division joined Sixth Army at Hurtebise and Chivy, on the Chemin des Dames, and fought there during Nivelle's offensive. During that battle it was in action between Hurtebise and the Paissy/Ailles road until 19th April. On 8th May the division moved to Lorraine and held the line between the Chapelotte and the Vesouve from 24th May until 27th August. Moved to Verdun, the division held positions between Beaumont and the Bois de Fosse, 24th September – 28th October. On 13th November, it re-rentered the line on the St Mihiel salient between the Etang de Vargevaux and Koeur-la- Grande where it remained until 27th May 1918.

In response to the German spring offensives, on 30th May 1918, the division joined Sixth Army and fought at Chateau-Thierry to stop the German advance. It organised a line between the town and the Marne until the Americans arrived. After a brief period in reserve, 27th June-15th July, the division fought in the fourth battle of Champagne/second battle of the Marne. It absorbed the German attacks at Reuil-sur-Marne and Troissy and then fought back at Troissy and Nesle-le-Repos. On 18th July, it supported the allied attack but left the line on 30th July and moved to Verdun.

From 7th August until 22nd September, the division held the Trésauvaux sector and then moved to the Damloup/Bezonvaux sector which it held until 6th November. From 22nd September, it was under command of the American army. For the last week of the war, it was held in reserve at Etain in preparation for a future offensive.

11 Division d'Infanterie Coloniale

Formed in Macedonia 01.01.17 (ordered 1.11.16)

Commanders
01.01.17-Jean Sicre
02.07.17-Paul Venel
04.10.17-Joseph Bordeaux
15.06.18-Léon Farret

21 Colonial Brigade
34 RIC   Ex 16DIC
35 RIC   Ex 16DIC

22 Colonial Brigade
42 RIC   Ex 10DIC
44 RIC   Ex 16DIC
• 2 bis2RZ-ex 45DI-nominally under 11DIC-but did not fight with division-under CAA command [Commandement des Armees Alliées en Orient]
* 1.17 attached- 26. 30 Bns Sénégalais

Artillery
5 Gp/ 7RAC -ex ICAC   4.17 to 21RAC
? Gp/57 RAC – ex XVIICA   " Gp/1 RACC –ex XXXVCA   "

Gp/2 RAM –ex AO 12.16 replaced by Gp/1RAM
4.17 remained in division

Cavalry
E/6RCA 11.16-11.18

Engineers & Pioneers
1917   Cie 7/2T du 7BG, 22/4 du 1RG
1918   Cie 7/2T du 7BG, 22/4 du 1RG Cie 16/26 du 2RG
No pioneer battalion

Formed on the Cherna from existing brigades in Macedonia, the division moved to Monastir on 16th March 1917 but returned to the Cherna sector on 25th April. It fought in the 'Boucle de la Cherna' on 17th May when elements joined 57DI in its attack on Côte 1248 and the rest of the division joined 16DIC in its attack on the Piton Rocheux.

From 21st May 1917 until 5th July 1918, the division occupied a sector to the north-east of Monastir. After a brief rest it took over the Bernik/Rapech sector on 2nd August and from there took part in the allied offensive which began on 15th September. By 6th November, the division had reached Semendria.

12-14 Divisions d'Infanterie Coloniale not formed

15 Divisions d'Infanterie Coloniale

Formed at Givry-en-Argonne [3rd Army] 16.06.15

Commanders
16.06.15-Joseph Bro
21.11.15-Etienne Guérin

1 Colonial Brigade [from ICAC] [disbanded 5.17]
1 RIC   2.16 to 17DIC -replaced by 57RIC Sénégalais-disbanded 5.17
2 RIC

2 Colonial Brigade [from 76DI] [disbanded 5.17]
5 RIC
6 RIC

Infantry from 5.17
2 RIC
5 RIC
6 RIC
Attached infantry-
5.16- 27 Bn Sénégalaise until ??
5.17- 66, 67, 70 Bns Sénégalaise - .18
7.18- 70 Bn Sénégalaise - .18
11.18-69, 70, 71 Bns Sénégalaise

Artillery
Gp/3 RACC   4.17 to 22 RACC
7 Gp/38 RAC   4.17 to 22 RACC
6 Gp/26 RAC –added 2.16   4.17 to 22 RACC
6 Gp/142RAL   4.18 added –ex 14/104RAL

Cavalry
E/2RS, 7.17 only
E/2RS, 7.17 only

5/13 RD, 7.17 –11.18
8/13 RD, 7.17-5.18

Engineers & Pioneers
1915   Cie 10/15T du 6RG
1918   Cie 26/2 du 10RG, 4/8 du 1RG,
16/72 du 2RG
8.18-Pioneer Battalion 18RIT   from IICAC

The division's first tour in the front-line began on 5th July 1915 when it took over Third Army's sector in the Argonne between Houyette and St Thomas. With some further adjustments of the line towards Binarville and Vienne-le-Chateau, it fought at the Bois de Beaurain [14th-15th July] and at Ravin de la Hayette [7th-12th August]. On 21st August it moved westwards to Fourth Army and fought in the second battle of Champagne between Souain and Wacques. It was involved in several attacks on the Navarin position. The division left Fourth Army on 30th September.

After a long period of retraining, the division took over Sixth Army's line between Beuvraignes and Belval on 12th February 1916. It remained there until 31st July. Its active role in the battle of the Somme began on 14th August when it fought to north of Belloy-en-Santerre until 2nd October. As part of Tenth Army, It was involved in heavy fighting near Barleux on 18th August, 4-6th September, and 17th September. After a month's rest, the division returned to the Belloy sector on 5th November and remained in the line until Christmas Day 1916.

Next, the division rejoined Sixth Army, on the Chemin des Dames. It occupied trenches between Troyon and Hurtebise [18th Janaury-10th February]; and then prepared for Nivelle's offensive. It returned to the Hurtebise/Chivy sector on 3rd March and attacked towards the Paissy/Ailly road on 16th April. Withdrawn three days later, the division was sent to the quiet sector between the Vezouve and the Sanon in Lorraine where it was in line from 26th May until 27th August.

On 17th September 1917 the division moved to the Verdun salient. It took over the line between the Bois de Caurieres and the Bois des Fosses on 26th September. Pulled out on 18th October, it spent the winter months along the St Mihiel salient. At first located between Paroches and the Bois Loclont [2nd November – 4th January] and then from Koeur-la-Grande and Bois Loclont [15th January-30th March], the division departed for Picardy on 25th April.

Sent to Picardy as part of the response to the German spring offensive, the division joined First Army. It took over the line between Thory and Mailly Raineval on 16th May. It engaged the Germans at Castel and at Mailly-Raineval throughout June and July. On 8th-10th August it took part in the allied offensive from Amiens and Montdidier and advanced to the river Avre.

Rested from 10th August until 5th September, the division moved back to Lorraine and came under American command for most of the rest of the war. From the line between Watronville and Mesnil-sous-les- Côtes, it participated in the elimination of the St Mihiel salient. During this American-led operation, it attacked Éparges and Combres and established new positions between Watronville and Fresnes-en-Woevre. From 20th October, it occupied the heights on the left bank of the Meuse above Verdun-the old 1916 battlefield-and advanced from there to Damvillers on 7th November 1918.

16 Divisions d'Infanterie Coloniale

Formed at Fey-en-Haye [First Army] 01.07.15 (ordered 24.6.15)

Commanders
25.06.15-Francois Bonnier
30.07.16-Antoine Dessort

31 Colonial Brigade [11.16 –replaced by 4 Colonial Brigade]
34 RIC [2 bns initially]   Ex 65DI 11.16 to 11DIC
36 RIC [2 bns initially]   Ex 74DI 11.16 disbanded
38 RIC [2 bns initially]   Ex 65DI 7.15 replaced by 35RIC
                                   8.16 withdrawn to form 21BIC

32 Colonial Brigade [11.16 –re-organised]
35 RIC [2 bns initially]   Ex 64DI 7.15 replaced by 38RIC
37 RIC [2 bns initially]   Ex 41DI
44 RIC [2 bns initially]   Ex VCA 8.16 withdrawn –to 21BIC

4 Colonial Brigade [from 2DIC 11.16-disbanded 9.17]
4 RIC
8 RIC

32 Colonial Brigade [from 11.16 -disbanded 9.17]
37 RIC
38 RIC

Infantry from 9.17 to 4.18
4 RIC
8 RIC
37 RIC
38 RIC

4 Colonial Brigade [4.18-10.18]
4 RIC
8 RIC

32 Colonial Brigade [4.18-10.18]
37 RIC
38 RIC   10.18 disbanded

Infantry 10-11.18
4 RIC
8 RIC
37 RIC
Attached infantry
5.16-10.16= 5, 20, 26, 28, 30, 61 Bns Sénégalaise
8.17= 56, 85, 97, 98 Bns Sénégalaise [controlled by 32BIC]

Artillery
3 Gp/9 RAC   -ex XVICA   4.17 to 209 RAC
4 Gp/9 RAC   -ex XVICA   4.17 to 209 RAC
5 Gp/42 RAC –added 3.16-ex ICAC 4.17 to 209 RAC
1 Bty/1RAM & 2 btys/2RAM added 11.16 1.18 formed Gp/2RAM

Cavalry
7/7 RCh, 7.15-10.16
8/7 RCh, 7.15-10.16
5/29 RD 11.16–11.18

Engineers & Pioneers
1915   Cie 3/1T, 3/5T du 3RG
1918   Cie 3/51T, 14/4, 8/75 du 2RG No Pioneer battalion allocated

Immediately put into the line between Fey-en-Haye on 1st July 1915, the division occupied the line between that point and the Bois-de-la-Pretre until 20th September. Nine days later it joined 4th Army for the second battle of Champagne during which it attacked Côte 193 from positions near Souain. It remained with Fourth Army until Boxing Day 1915 and during this period served between Ville-sur-Tourbe [24th October-8th November] and Main de Massiges and Maisons de Champagne [8th November-26th December].

After a rest period, the division joined Sixth Army in Picardy and took over positions between Faucaucourt and Maucourt on 14th February, which it held until 1st June. It was stationed in the line between Dompierre and the Somme from 22nd June but remained in reserve during the allied attack on 1st July. From 5th July until 22nd August it fought east of Faucourt and attacked the German lines between Barleux and Maisonette on 10th and 20th July, and then occupied its gains in that sector until 22nd August.

After a period of training and labour duties the division began to move to Macedonia on 5th November. It began to arrive at Salonika on 9th December, from which it moved up to the front at Monastir. On 10th April 1917, it took over from the Italians in the sector between Piton Rocheux and the Ravin d'Olre and remained there until 30th March 1918. On 11th May 1917 it took part in the action described as the 'Boucle de la Tcherna' when it attacked the Piton Rocheux and the Piton Jaune.

From 23rd June until 23rd October 1918, the division held the line at Serka di Legen from which it took part in the allied offensive on 16th August. It took the Massif de la Dzena and advanced towards Stroumitsa. From 23rd October it crossed in to Bulgaria and advanced on Sofia.

17 Division d'Infanterie Coloniale

Formed 22.02.15 as 1 Division d'Infanterie du CEO by order of 06.01.16–numbered 17 DIC

Commanders
16.03.15-Jospeh Masnou
06.08.15-Jean-Marie Brulard
29.02.16-Auguste Gerome
23.03.17-Georges Tetart
01.01.18-Joseph Bordeaux
29.05.18-Ernest Pruneau

1 Brigade (Metropolitaine) [to 10.15-to 2DI du CEO in exchange for 2BIC]
175 RI
1 RdMA

2 Brigade (Colonial)- until 1917
4 RMxIC   10.15 retitled 54RIC –to 1BIC
6 RMxIC   10.15 retitled 56RIC –to 1BIC

1 Colonial Brigade   [10.15-2.16]
54 RIC   Ex 4 R Mixte IC
56 RIC   Ex 6 R Mixte IC

2 Colonial Brigade   [ex 2DI du CEO 10.15; 2.16 broken up]
57 RIC   Ex 7 R Mxte IC- 2.16 to 15DIC
58 RIC   Ex 8 R Mxte IC- 2.16 to 3DIC

33 Colonial Brigade [from 2.16] [disbanded 8.18]
54 RIC
56 RIC   Disbanded 8.18

34 Colonial Brigade [from 2.16] [disbanded 8.18]
1 RIC   Ex 15DIC
3 RIC   Ex 3DIC

Infantry from 8.18
1 RIC
3 RIC
54 RIC

Artillery

5 Gp/1RAC	4.17 to 201 RAC 4.18 retitled 43RACC
5 Gp/8RAC	4.17 to 201 RAC 4.18 retitled 43RACC
3 Gp/2 RAM	6.15 replaced by Gp/25RAC
	1.16 replaced by Gp/47RAC
	4.17 to 201 RAC 4.18 retitled 43RACC
2 Gp/1 RAM	2.16 added 4.18 retitled Gp/13RAM

Cavalry
RdeM de ChD'aFr 3-6.15
E/4RCA, 4.16 –11.18

Engineers & Pioneers

1915	Cie 4/14, 4/25 du 1RG
1918	Cie 4/14, 4/64, 4/25 du 1RG No Pioneer Battalion allocated

Formed for the allied attack on the Dardanelles, the division landed at Krithia on 6th May 1915 and between that date and 17th August, carried out six attacks on the Turkish lines at Kereves Dere. Then it remained in line but relatively inactive until evacuated from Gallipoli on 6th January 1916.

The division spent a few weeks in garrison at Mudros, Tenedos and Mitylene and then moved to Salonika where it was reinforced by units from France and re-organised for service in Macedonia. At first it organised defences on the high ground north and sout east of Galatista and then, on 28th April, move to the right bank of the Struma. Upon relief by British troops on 9th June it moved to the Gola/Côte 576 sector from which it took part in the battle of Doiran on 9th-18th August. 34 Brigade remained in line when the rest of the division rested during September and October. From 12th October, the brigades operated in turn with the Serbian Army and fought between Kenali and the Tcherna during the battle for the Tcherna. After relief by Italian troops on 23rd December, the division moved to Rapech/Bernik sector. On 9th May it attacked the Bulgarian positions on the Tcherna and then remained in the line until 13th August 1918.

In the allied offensive in the autumn of 1918, the division fought alongside the Serbs in the battle of Dobroplie [15th-16th September] at the Krevitsa plateau and advanced to Ribartsi; and then took Tchitchevo and freed the Vardar at Oulantsa and eventually reached Egri Palanka.

From 12th October, the division advanced into Serbia and reached the Danube when the war ended on 4thNovember.

Moroccan Divisions 1 - 2

Division Marocaine

Formed in Morocco on 2nd August 1914 as Division d'Infanterie Coloniale du Maroc
15.09.14 retitled Division Marocaine
04.08.18 retitled 1 Division Marocaine

Commanders
02.08.14-Georges Humbert
14.09.14-Ernest Blondlat
26.06.16-Alexandre Codet
18.08.16-Jean-Marie Degoutte
02.09.17-Albert Daugan

1 Marocaine Brigade

R de M Colonial	11.14 to 4BM and then to 152DI replaced by 4 RdMT ex 38 DI
	8.18 to 2DM
	-replaced by-12 Bn Malgache and 27 and 43 Senegalaise Bns
R de M Zouaves	10.14 replaced by 2 RdM/1RE
	11.15-enlarged as RMLE
	7.15-2 RdM(2RE) ex XVIIICA
	11.15 merged into RMLE
	7.18 Bn Russe added-ex 2BM

2 Marocaine Brigade

1R de M du Tir du Maroc Occidental	11.14 to 7 RdMTM
2R de M du Tir du Maroc Oriental	11.14 merged into 7RdMTM
	-replaced by 8RdMZ
1 Bn Legion Russe attached to 8RMZ	12.17 and moved to 1BM 7.18

Artillery

Bty/8 Gpd'Afrique & Bty/9 Gp d'Afrique	1.16 bies administered by 58RAC
	4.17 Gp/5 Gp d'Afrique
	12.17-to 276 RAC
2 btys/Gp Colonial du Maroc	9.14 became Gp/3RACC
9.14 bty/Afr Occ Fr added	4.17-Gp/5 Gp d'Afrique
	12.17 to 276RAC
2 btys/4 Gp d'Afrique	4.17 to part of Gp/5 Gp d'Afrique
	12.17 became 276RAC
2 btys/29 RAC –created 12.14	4.17-part Gp/5 Gp d'Afrique
	12.17 to 276 RAC
8 Gp/112 RAL	7.18 added –formerly 12/110RAL

Cavalry
E/9 RCh 8.14-2.16
E/9 RCh 8.14-11.14
7/11RH, 11.14-2.16
5/10RD, 2.16-8.16
6/10RD, 2.16-8.16
E/5RCA, 8.16 –11.18
E/5RCA, 8.16-8.18
E/1RS, 8.18-11.18

Engineers & Pioneers
1914   Cie 19/2M du 2RG
1918   Cie 26/2M, 19/52M, 26/21M
9.17-Pioneer Battalion 32RIT

Soon after the division joined Fourth Army west of Mézières on 23rd August 1914, it was forced to retreat towards Fere-Champenoise. On 28th August, it fought at Dommery and the Forret-a-L'eau; at Bortoncourt on tbe 30th, and at Neuflize and Alincourt on 1st September. During the first battle of the Marne it operated with Ninth Army and fought at Mondemont during the battle of Marais de St Gond. From 10th September, it advanced north-eastwards via Tours-sur-Marne and Beaumont-sur-Vesle to Prunay and Marquises in Champagne. From 14th September 1914 until 23rd April 1915, it occupied Fifth Army's newly gained positions to the east of Reims, between Marquises, Sillery and Pompelle. During this period it was involved in several local engagements.

On 27th April 1915, it joined Tenth Army's positions at La Targette on the slopes of Vimy Ridge. During the second battle of Artois, it attacked Côte 140 [9th-12th May], and then, on 26th May took over the Carency/Cabaret Rouge sector. It attacked Givenchy on 16th and 22nd June and then retired to Lorraine for a long rest near Montbeliard. From 14th September until 18th October, it was back in the line in Champagne at Bois Sabot, and attacked Trou Bricot and Butte de Souain during the second battle of Champagne. It served in the St Marie à Py sector, 30th September-18th October. After a lengthy period of retraining, it joined Sixth Army between the Oise and Belval on 24th February 1916.

Taken out of the line on 6th June, it joined the battle of the Somme on 6th July at Flaucourt and carried out attacks on the Germans at Flaucourt and Belloy-en-Santerre on 7th and 13th July. It returned to the Oise at Belval on 29th July and remained there for the next three months. The winter of 1916-1917 was spent in Picardy: in the Belloy/Barleux sector [17th November-28th December] and at Beuvraignes/Armancourt [25th January-8th February 1917]. The division remained in support at Montdidier as the rest of Third Army moved into the wasteland left as the Germans retreated to the Hindenburg Line. During the spring offensive, it took part in Fourth Army's attack on the Monts and took Mont Sans Nom and Aubérive [17th-26th April]. From 5th June until 4th July it operated at the eastern end of the Chemin des Dames between the Aisne and the Miette.

After a spell of labour duties at Verdun, the division re-entered the trenches between Chattancourt and the Meuse, and from there, took part in the second Verdun offensive on 20th August when it captured the Bois des Corbeaux. After a month of rest, the division was moved to the St Mihiel salient and took over the Limey/Etang de Vargevaux sector on 3rd October. It engaged the Germans north of Flirey on 8th January 1918 and left this sector on the 21st.

Two month's of retraining were interrupted by the German spring offensive which brought about a move to Picardy where the division defended Villers-Bretonneux and the Bois de Hangard [24th April-7th May]. Transferred to 6th Army on 29th May it was involved immediately in the third battle of the Aisne when it fought at the Montagne de Paris, Missy-au-Bois and Chaudun. After regrouping at Villers Cotterêts on 1st June, it joined Tenth Army's struggles south of the Aisne at Ambleny and Fosse-en-Haut.

Redesignated on 5th July 1918 while in reserve, it rejoined Tenth Army that day and took over the line between Fosse-en-Haut and St Pierre-Aigle. During the second battle of the Marne, [18th –22nd July], it attacked at St Pierre-en-Haut and at Dommiers and Chaudun. From 27th August until 17th September it prepared for and then took part in Tenth Army's assault on the Hindenburg Line. It seized Sorny [5th September], then in the battle of Vuaxillon, it took Allement [13th-15th September].

The division had a month's rest and moved to Lorraine where it took over the Bezange-la-Grande/Brin position on 13th October. On 11th November it was there, preparing for a new offensive into Lorraine.

2 Division Marocaine

Formed at Limey [Eighth Army] 04.08.18 from HQ 65DI (ordered 13.7.18)

Commander
04.08.18-Louis Modelon

Major Units

RICM	Ex 38 DI
2 RdMTM	Ex isole –created 2.18
4 RdMTM	Ex 1DM
255 RAC	
6 Gp/131 RAL	Ex 4/301RAL
7/24RD E/5 Spahis	
Cie 15/11, 15/61du 7RG, 14/4T du 4RG	
9.18 replaced by 1/11 RD	
9.18 replaced by 4/11 RD	
Pioneer Bn 63RIT	Ex XXXIICA 8.18

After only four days in the line between Limey and the Bois-de-la-Prete [4th-8th August] the division moved to the Oise front. It joined 10th Army on 14th August and fought between Quennevieres and Puisaleine during the second battle of Noyon. It attacked between the Oise and Aisne near Nampoel [23rd August] and advanced towards the Ailette. From 26th August until 5th September it occupied a sector at Crécy-au-Mot, liberated the line of the Ailette, and moved up to the Hindenburg Line.

On 19th September, the division joined Fourth Army for the battle of Somme-Py. It fought between Massiges and Beauséjours, attacked the Butte de Mesnil and moved forward to Marvaux which it reached on 30th September. Between 17th and 25th October, it continued in Fourth Army's northward advance and reached Olizy and Beaurepair where it organised new positions.

Then the division moved to Belfort where it occupied the line between Fulleren and the Swiss frontier from 2nd November until the end of the war.

Provisional Infantry Divisions

'B' Division	ex Barbot Division 30.09.14	became 77DI 12.10.14
'Barbot' Division	formed 03.09.14	became 'B' 30.09.14
1 Division du CEO	formed 22.02.15	became 17DIC 06.01.16
2 Division du CEO	ex 156DI 29.04.15	became 156DI 15.10.15
'Guerin' Division	ex Tassin Division 27.04.15	became 122DI 15.06.15
'Tassin' Division	formed 09.12.14	became 'Geurin' 27.04.15
'Vassart' Division	formed 05.09.14	became 76DI 12.10.14
'Verdun' Division	formed 23.09.14	became 132DI 02.07.15

The Cavalry Divisions

Active Divisions 1 - 10

1 Division de Cavalerie

Headquarters at Paris

Commanders
02.08.14-Clément Buisson
28.09.14-Olivier Mazel
10.02.15-Félix Robillot
30.09.17-Joseph de Rascas de Chateau Redon

2 Brigade du Cuirassiers, Paris
1 RC, Paris
2 RC, Paris

5 Brigade du Dragons, Vincennes
6 RD, Vincennes
23 RD, Vincennes

11 Brigade du Dragons, Versaille
27 RD, Versaille
32 RD, Versaille
1 Gp Légère (Cavalry à pied)   101.4 formed from 1 esc from each regt in div)
                                 6.16 replaced by 4 RC a Pied
                                 1.18 to1DCP
I Groupe Cyclistes/26 BCP, Vincennes
IV Group/13RAC, Paris
Cie Sapeurs-cyclistes du 1RG
Auto Canons Mitrailleuse (ACM)   9.15-Gp 7
                                 6.16-Gp 1 added

As part of Sordet's Cavalry corps in Fifth Army, the division advanced into Belgium on 5th August 1914. It reconnoitred towards the Meuse between Dinant and Liege, then moved via Gembloux to the Sambre where it fought the Germans west of Charleroi on 21st August. From 23rd August to 6th September, it retreated south to Versaille. During the first battle of the Aisne, the division fought along the Ourcq at Betz and Nanteuil-les-Haudouin, and then, pursued the Germans north to Cambrai. In the 'race for the sea' it fought at Bapuame, Arras, Douai, Lens, Laventie and Bailleul [23rd September-23rd October]. In the first battle of Ypres, it fought at Wulverghem and Messines [2nd-12th November].

For most of the next four years, the division was either held in readiness for exploitation of allied success or committed elements to occasional frontline duty. It was placed on standby for the second and third battles of Artois in 1915; rotated through sectors in Picardy and the Oise; held in reserve during the battle of the Somme, and in reserve for Nivelle's spring offensive in 1917. It occupied Third Army's sector at Barisis on three occasions in 1917/1918.

During the second battle of Picardy it fought to defend the crossings of the Oise between Chauny and Noyon. It defended the crossing of the Marne at Dormans in May and at Venteuil and Tincourt in June and July. It remained in reserve during Fourth Army's autumn offensive in Champagne. In November 1918 it was held in reserve at Nancy for the planned advance into Lorraine.

2 Division de Cavalerie

Headquarters at Lunéville

Commanders
02.08.14-Antide Lescot
13.08.14-Jean Varin
08.02.18-Henri Lasson

2 Brigade du Dragons, Lunéville
8 RD, Lunéville
31 RD, Lunéville and Vitry

12 Brigade du Dragons, Toul
4 RD, Commercy
12 RD, Troyes and Toul
2 Brigade de Cavalerie Légère, Lunéville –to 10DC 02.08.14; returned to 2DC 00.06.16
17 R Ch, Lunéville and Vitry
18 R Ch, Lunéville and Vitry

2 Gp Légère (cavalerie à pied)	8.15 formed from esc ex division's regts
	6.16 provided nucleus of 1 Regt Légère & 10Gp Légère
	7.17 12 RC a P ex 7DC
	8.17 1RL [except 1Bn] to Tg Bn 5RCP
	1.18 12 RCP to 2DCP

2 Groupe Cycliste/2BCP, Lunéville
IV Gp/8 RAC, Lunéville
Cie Sapeurs-cycliste du 10RG

ACM	12.15-Gp 9
	6.16-Gp 10 added
	8.16 Gp 3 replaced Gp 10 (to Rumania)

Allocated to Second Army at Lunéville, the division operated in Conneau's corps during the battles of Sarrebourg and the Grand Couronne. In the autumn of 1914 it fought at St Mihiel and Troyon [7th September-4th October] and then was employed on reconnaissance duties in First Army until mid 1915. After service between the Sanon and Bezange [12th July-1st September] it was held in reserve during the second battle of Champagne. After two brief tours between Belfort and the Swiss border, some elements fought on foot at Lihons in the battle of the Somme. It served between on the Aisne in the winter of 1916- 1917 and remained in reserve during Nivelle's offensive. For the rest of 1917 it rotated elements, with 4DC and 7DC in Fifth Army's line between Reims and Marquises. From 16th April until 1st May 1918 it fought in Flanders. In the third battle of the Aisne, it held positions at Villers Côteret; was held in reserve for the second battle of the Marne; and fought near Montdidier in the allied offensive in Picardy. On 18th September, it returned to Flanders and fought at Passendale and then took part in the allied breakout from the Ypres salient. At the end of the war, the division was being held in reserve for the crossing of the Schelde.

3 Division de Cavalerie

Headquarters at Compiègne

Commanders
02.08.14-Aymard Dor de Lastours
05.04.16-Claude de Boissieu

4 Brigade du Cuirassiers, Douai –6.16 disbanded & replaced by 10BDgns ex 10DC
4 RC, Cambrai
9 RC, Douai

13 Brigade du Dragons, Compiègne
5 RD, Compiègne
21 RD, Noyon

3 Brigade de Cavalerie Légère, Meaux
3 RH, Senlis
8 RH, Meaux

10 Brigade du Dragons-from 10DC 6.16
15 RD
20 RD
3 Gp Légère (Cavalry a pied)   10.14 formed from esc from each regt
                                          6.16 absorbed by 9RCP
                                          1.18 9 RCP to 1DCP

3 Groupe Cycliste/18BCP, Compiégne
IV Gp/42 RAC, Sissonne
Cie/ Sapeurs-Cycliste du 3RG
ACM   8.15-Gp 12
                                           6.16 Gp 2 added

As part of Sordet's Cavalry corps, the advanced into Belgium on 5th August 1914 and reconnoitred towards Dinant and Liege, and then north of the Sambre. It fought west of Charleroi on 21st August and then retreated southwards to Versaille. In the battle of the Marne, it fought at Nanteuil-Hadouin and then during the 'race to the sea' fought at Chaulnes, Arras, Aix-Noilette, La Bassee, Lestrem, Laventie and Fromelles. Although elements fought at Messines, it remained at Cassel during the first battle of Ypres.

For the rest of the war the division either remained in reserve for major operations or contributed elements to line-holding duties. In support during the second and third battles of Artois, it rotated with 1DC in the provision of elements to the line in Picardy in 1916. It was in reserve during the battle of the Somme and then provided line-holders in the Oise sector. In reserve for Nivelle's offensive in the spring of 1917 elements served with Third Army at Quincy Basse for the rest of 1917.

The division fought at Mount Kemmel from 22nd April to 3rd May 1918 and then at Marizy-Ste Genevieve 1st-3rd June during the third battle of the Aisne. During the fourth battle of Champagne it fought at Montvoisin on 15th July. It was held in reserve during Fourth Army's autumn offensive in Champagne and the Argonne. When hostilites ended the division was moving from Epernay to Nancy.

4 Division de Cavalerie

Headquarters at Sedan

Commanders
02.08.14-Pierre Abonneau
13.10.14-Robert de Buyer
01.07.15-Gustave de Cornulier-Luciniere
12.10.17-Paul Lavigne-Delville

3 Brigade du Cuirassiers, Ste Menehoulde
3 RC, Vouziers and Reims
6 RC, Ste Menehoulde

4 Brigade du Dragons, Sedan
28 RD, Sedan and Mézières
30 RD, Sedan and Mézières

1 Brigade de Cavalerie Légère –to VI Corps Cavalry-to VI CA on mobilisation
10 R Ch, Sampigny
12 R Ch, St Mihiel

4 Brigade de Cavalerie Légère –replaced 1 BCL on mobilisation
2 RH, Verdun
4 RH, Verdun

4 Gp Légère (cavalerie à pied)	11.14 formed from esc ex regts in division
	6.16 absorbed by 5RCP ex 9DC
	1.18 5RCP to 2DCP

4 Groupe Cycliste/19 BCP, Verdun
IV Gp/40 RAC, Mézières
Cie Sapeurs-Cycliste du 9RG

ACM	9.15 –Gp 4
	5.16- Gp 15 added

Attached to Fourth Army, the division reconnoitred from Neufchateau to Biévre and Gédinne during the battle for the Ardennes. During its retreat to the Marne it fought in the first battle of Guise [29th August].From Provins it advanced to Amifontaine during the battle for the Marne and then remained in reserve during the battle of the Aisne. During the 'race to the sea' it engaged the Germans at Lens, Gorgue, Lestrem and Estaires and fought at d'Houthoulst and Bikschote on the Ijzer [16th October-17th November]. Thereafter it held a sector at Nieuvepoort until 5th February 1915. Throughout the rest of 1915 the division was held in readiness for the second battle of Artois and the second battle of Champagne. Some units fought on foot in the latter battle and then held small sections of Fourth Army's front from Baconnes to Moscou. After a period in reserve during the battle of the Somme, elements occupied sectors of the line in Picardy and then on the Aisne. Again in reserve for Nivelle's offensive, the division joined 1DC and 7DC in the task of manning the defences of Reims until January 1918. During the battle of the Avre [27th March-7th April], the division resisted the German offensive at Hargicourt and Moreuil. In the third battle of the Aisne [27th May- 7th June] it was forced to retreat to Dormans and then fight at Beuvardes. Kept in reserve during the second battle of the Marne, elements then fought on foot at Bus-la-Mésière, Grivillers and Tilloloy during the allied offensive in Picardy. From 28th September, it was held in reserve during the allied breakout from the Ypres salient. On 11th November some units were pursuing the enemy to the Schelde.

5 Division de Cavalerie

Headquarters at Reims

Commanders
02.08.14-Joseph Bridoux
10.09.14-Valthur Lallemand du Marais
28.09.14-Louis Allenou
31.03.17-Charles Brécard
06.01.18-Alphonse Lacombe de la Tour
10.09.18-Louis Simon

3 Brigade du Dragons, Reims
16 RD, Reims
22 RD, Reims

7 Brigade du Dragons, Epernay
9 RD, Epernay
29 RD, Provins

5 Brigade de Cavalerie Légère, Châlons sur Marne
5 R Ch, Châlons sur Marne
15 R Ch, Châlons sur Marne

5 Gp Légère (cavalerie à pied)	12.14 formed from esc ex div regts
	6.16 absorbed into 11RCP ex 7DC
	1.18 11RCP ro 1DCP

5 Groupe Cycliste/29BCP, Châlons s/Marne

IV Gp/61 RAC, Châlons s/Marne
Cie Sapeurs-Cycliste du 9RG
ACM   5.15-Gp 13
                                        5.16 Gp 11 added

As part of Sordet's corps, the division operated north of the Sambre with Fifth Army from 4th August 1914. It fought between the Sambre and Charleroi on 21st August and then retreated to the Marne. After conflict along the Ourcq and at Compiegne and Villers Cotterêts in the battle of the Marne, the division engaged the Germans at Nurlu, Peronne, Boyelles, Lens and Aix-Noulette during the 'race for the sea.' During the struggle for Ypres, it fought at from Lestrem to Steenstraate, and then at Nieuvepoort where it remained until 7th February 1915. During 1915 it remained in reserve during the second battle of Artois and the second battle of Champagne. From October 1915 until August 1916 it occupied the line near Prosnes and then moved to the Embermesnil/Sanon sector in Lorraine where it remained until January 1917. In reserve during Nivelle's spring offensive, it combined with 1DC and 3DC to provide elements to man Third Army's line on the Oise at Quincy Basse and Barisis from April 1917 until February 1918.

It fought on foot on the Avre in April, and the engaged the Germans south of the Aisne at Dravegny and Charmel and then retreated to the Marne at Mezy. In July it was in reserve near Epernay and then moved to the Argonne where it remained in support during the American offensive in September. By 11th November, the division was at Gondrecourt.

6 Division de Cavalerie

Headquarters at Lyon

Commanders
02.08.14-Georges Levillain
27.08.14-Antoine de Mitry
30.09.14-Henri Requichot
03.04.17-Henri Mesple

5 Brigade du Cuirassiers, Lyon 6.16 to GMP and replaced by 14BD from 8DC
7 RC, Lyon
10 RC, Lyon
• 5BC was reconstituted in GMP 8.17 with QG 15RD and rejoined the field army 8.17, possibly in an independent role.

6 Brigade du Dragons, Lyon
2 RD, Lyon
14 RD, St Étienne

6 Brigade de Cavalerie Légère, Tarasçon
11 RH, Tarasçon
13 R Ch, Vienne
14 Brigade du Dragons   -8.16 from 8DC vice 5BC
17 RD
26 RD
6 Gp Légère (cavalerie à pied)   11.14 formed from esc ex div regts
                                   5.16 absorbed into 8RCP ex 9DC
                                   1.18 8RCP to 2DCP
6 Groupe Cycliste/13BCP, Lyon
IV Gp/54 RAC, Lyon
Cie Sapeurs-Cycliste du 4RG
ACM   6.15-Gp 14
                                   8.16 withdrawn to Int
                                   5.16-Gp 17 added 10.17 to IICC
                                   7.16-Gp 8 added
                                   4.17 Gp 5 attached

11.17 Gp 6 added

As part of Conneau's corps, the division fought with First Army in the battles of Sarrebourg and Mortagne during August 1914. In the battle of the Marne it operated with 9th Army and advanced to the Suippe in Champagne. In October 1914 it fought Cassel, on the Lys, and north of Ypres between Roeselare and Langemark. From 25th January to 9th May 1915 it manned the defences of the Rhine-Rhone canal. In reserve during the second battle of Champagne, it occupied quiet sectors in Lorraine from November 1915 until March 1917.

Held in reserve during Nivelle's attack on the Chemin des Dames, it co-operated with 2DC and 4DC in the provision of dismounted troops for the defence of Reims until February 1918.

In the spring of 1918 the division fought in Flanders [12th April-6th May] and then defended the crossings of the Ourcq during the second battle of the Aisne [1st-6th June]. During the second battle of the Marne it took part in 10th Army's actions at Sergy and Fère-en-Tardenois [18th-31st July]. In the allied attack from Amiens, it operated near Roye [9th-12th August] and then moved to Flanders. It fought at Langemark [28th September-2nd October 1918] and elements participated in the allied advance to the Leie and the Schelde. It liberated the line of the Schelde on 10th and 11th November.

7 Division de Cavalerie

Headquarters at Melun

Commanders
02.08.14-Edmond Gillain
25.08.14-Victor d'Urbal
28.09.14-Alexis Hely d'Oissel
14.01.15-Hewnri Léorat
21.04.16-Eugene Feraud
02.03.17-Léon Prax

6 Brigade du Cuirassiers, St Germain [disbanded 6.16]
11 RC, St Germain	6.16 to 5DC
12 RC, Rambouillet	6.16 to 12RCP-see below

1 Brigade du Dragons, Fontainebleau
7 RD, Fontainebleau	7.17 to XXXVCA
13 RD, Melun	7.17 to IICAC

7 Brigade de Cavalerie Légère, Vendome
1 R Ch, Chateaudun	7.17 to XXXIVCA
20 R Ch, Vendome	11.14 reduced to 1esc and replaced by 10RCh ex XXXIICA
	3.15 20 RCh reconsituted
	2.16 20 RCh to XXXIICA
	.17 10RCh to XXXVIIICA

15 Brigade du Dragons [ex 10DC 6.16]
10 RD	7.17 to XXXVIICA
19 RD	7.17 to XXXIIICA
7 Gp Légère	111.14 formed from esc of div regts
	6.16 absorbed into 12RCP
	7.17 to 2DC

7 Groupe Cycliste/4 BCP, Orléans 7.17 disbanded
IV Gp/30 RAC, Orléans   7.17 to XXXIVCA   Cie Sapeurs-Cycliste du 1RG   7.17 to?
ACM   12.14-Gp 6
                        7.17 to IICC

11.15 Gp 16 added- 7.17 to IICC

Initially allocated to Third Army it fought north of Verdun, and then it the Argonne, before retreating to Vavincourt. During 3rd Army's battle at Revigny, it fought in the Argonne, on the Meuse near St Mihiel, at Etain and on the heights of the Meuse during the battle of Flirey. In October 1914 it fought near Lille and on the Lys, and at Neuve Chapelle and Richébourg. Its involvement in the struggle for Ypres brought it into action between Staden, Poelkapelle and then at Diksmuide. In 1915 it supported Tenth Army in Artois until 30th August when it moved to Champagne to support Fourth Army's autumn offensive. From 26th October 1915 until 8th July 1916 it held the line between Marquises and Prosnes. From 17th November 1916 until 15th January 1917 it was in line on the Aisne between Soissons and Pernant. Held in reserve for Nivelle's offensive, it provided troops to defend Reims with 2DC and 4DC until 21st June. The division disbanded at Fere-Champenoise on 23rd July 1917 (by order of 10.7.17).

8 Division de Cavalerie

Headquarters at Dole

Commanders
02.08.14-Louis Aubier
16.08.14-Olivier Mazel
27.08.14-Jean Gendron
04.09.14-Albert Baratier

8 Brigade du Dragons, Belfort
11 RD, Belfort   2 esc to 60DI & 2esc to 29DI
18 RD, Lure   2 esc to 55DI 7 2 esc to 68DI

14 Brigade du Dragons, Dijon [8.16 to 6DC vice 5Bcui]
17 RD, Auxonne   8.16 to 6DC
26 RD, Dijon   8.16 to 6DC

8 Brigade de Cavalerie Légère, Dole
14 R Ch, Dole   2 esc to 52DI & 2esc to 63DI
12 RH, Gray   2 esc to 73DI & 2esc to 129DI
8 Gp Légère (cavalerie à pied)   2.15 formed from one escadron from each brigade
                                      4.16 re-organised into 3 battalions with one escadron from each regiment in 8DC
                                      6.16 2 Regt Légère (3 bns) formed from 8Gp and 9 Gp Légère 8.16disbanded
8 Group Cycliste/15 BCP, Montbeliard 8.16 to IIICC
IV Gp/4 RAC, Besançon 8.16 to XXXIXCA Cie Sapeurs-cycliste du 9RG   8.16 to ?
ACM   11.4-Gp 3
                                      8.16-?
                                      4.16 Gp 5 added 8.16-?

After taking part in the advances from Belfort to Mulhouse, during which it fought at Altkirch [7th-9th August and14th-26th August], the division joined Conneau's corps for the battle of the Marne. It pursued the Germans from Amifontaine to the Aisne and then switched to Arras where it fought at Gommecourt and Monchy. After a period of line-holding between Berles and Hannescamp, the division remained in reserve for the second battle of Artois. In Fourth Army's autumn offensive in Champagne, it sent units into action at Tahure and Souain. From 4th November 1915 to 23rd July 1916 the division carried out two tours of duty between the Sanon and the Forest de Parroy in Lorraine. It disbanded at Charmes on 15th August 1916.

9 Division de Cavalerie

Headquarters at Tours

Commander

02.08.14-Jean-Francois de L'Espée

1 Brigade de Cuirassiers, Tours
5 RC, Tours	6.16-5RCP/4DC
8 RC, Tours	6.16-8RCP/6DC

9 Brigade du Dragons, Nantes
1 RD, Lucon	6.16 to XXXIXCA
3 RD, Nantes	6.16 to XXXCA

16 Brigade de Cavalerie Légère, Rennes
24 RD, Rennes	6.16 to XXXICA
25 RD, Angers	6.16 to XXXVIICA
9 Gp Légère (cavalerie à pied)	11.14 formed from 1esc from each regt in div 6.16 to 8DC
9 Grp Cyclistes/25BCP, Tours	6.16 1 Peleton to 6DC –2 peletons to ICC IV Gp/33 RAC, Tours 6.16 to XXXIXCA
Cie Sapeurs-Cycliste du 6RG	6.16 to?
ACM	11.14-Gp 8
	6.16-??

As part of Fourth Army, the division advanced towards Virton and fought in the battle of the Ardennes between Neufchateau and Paliseul. During the retreat southwards to Camp de Mailly it fought at Thin-le- Moutier and Chateau Porcien, and, in the struggle for the Marne, it fought at Sommesous and Mailly. It pursued the Germans towards Reims and remained there until 10th October. Transferred to Flanders, it went into action at St Eloi, Pilkem, Langemark and Boezinge [31st October-17th November] after which it went into reserve in Artois. It was not called upon to take part in the second battle of Artois and moved to Champagne on 20th September. It was not involved in Fourth Army's autumn offensive. It occupied the quiet sector in Lorraine between the Sanon and Parroy from 26th December 1915 until 2nd May 1916. It was disbanded at Tantonville on 1st June 1916.

10 Division de Cavalerie

Headquarters at Limoges

Commanders
02.08.14-Louis Conneau
15.08.14-Camille Grellet de la Deyte
13.09.14-Erasme de Contades-Gizeux

10 Brigade du Dragons, Limoges [6.16 to 3DC]
15 RD, Libourne
20 RD, Limoges

15 Brigade du Dragons, Montauban [6.16 to 7DC]
10 RD, Montauban
19 RD, Castres

9 Brigade de Cavalerie Légère, Tarbes-to Corps Troops on mobilisation-replaced by 2BCL
9 R Ch, Auch
19 RH, Tarbes

2 Brigade de Cavalerie Légère, Lunéville –from 2DC on mobilisation
17 R Ch, Lunéville and Vitry
18 R Ch, Lunéville and Vitry
9BCL and 2BCL not shown in OH as part of 10DC

Brigade Matuzinsky [added 12.14] [4.15 retitled 23 BCL] [disbanded 1.16]

R de M de Ch   4.15 to 22RCh
R de M du 12RH   4.15 to 16RH

1 Brigade de Marche de Chasseurs d'Afrique [1.16 vice 23BCL] [6.16 to XXXIVCA]
2 RCh d'Afrique
5 RCh d'Afrique
10 Gp Légère (cavalerie à pied)   11.14 formed from 1 esc per regts in div
                                          6.16 to 2DC
10 Grp Cycliste/1 BCP, Limoges   6.16 to IIICC
IV Gp/14 RAC, Tarbes   6.16 disbanded – 1bie to 6DC, 1 bie to 2DC Cie Sapeurs-Cycliste du 6RG   6.16 to?
ACM   12.15 Gp 10 formed
                                          6.16 to 2DC then to Romania

As part of Conneau's corps the division fought in the battle of Sarrebourg [17th-20th August] and then retreated to Rozelieures from where it moved westward to the Marne. It fought at Chateau-Thierry and moved forward to Sissonne [6th-14th September]. During the 'race to the sea' it engaged the Germans at Bapaume, Achiet-le-Grand, St Léger, Pont-a-Vendin, Vermelles and Merville. In the battle of Ypres it fought at Mesen until 11th November.

Transferred to the Vosges, it held the line between Leimbach and Burnhaupt [5th January-20th August and 7th-12th October 1915]. After labour duties on the Swiss frontier, the division disbanded at Montreux-Vieux on 1st June 1916 (ordered 20.5.16)

Dismounted Divisions 1 - 2

1 Division De Cavalrie à Pied

Formed at Vic-sur-Aisne [Third Army] 15.01.18 (ordered 21.12.17)

Commander
15.01.18-Charles Brécard

Major units

4 RC	Ex 1DC
9 RC	Ex 3DC
11 RC	Ex 5DC
270 RAC	Ex 81DI
7 Gp/103 RAL	2.18 –added –ex 12/101RAL
5/10RD & 6/10RD	Ex XXXVIICA Cie 4/26, 4/59, 19/3 du 1RG
Pioneer Bn/65RIT	Ex ?

On 22nd March 1918 the division took over from British forces at Selency and became involved the second battle of Picardy. In defended the line of the Crozat canal, and then retreated to defend the crossing of the Oise at Varesnes and Pontoise. Pulled out on 3rd April, the division carried out labour duties at Thiescourt before taking over Third Army's sector between Thiescourt and Plessis-de-Roye. From there, on 9th June, it fought for the crossings of the Oise and Matz during the battle of the Matz.

Transferred to Champagne on 16th June, the division entered the line between the Aisne and Ville-sur-Tourbe on 3rd July. With various alterations to its sector, it remained here until the autumn offensive by Fourth Army. On 26th September it fought between the Aisne and Vienne-le-Chateau and advanced along the western edge of the Argonne to Servon, Binarville and Lancon. From 18th October it occupied positions between Termes and Olizy and fought from there during the battle of Chesne [1st-3rd November].

The division was in reserve at Valmy from 3rd November until the armistice.

2 Division De Cavalrie à Pied

Formed at the Camp de Mailly [Fourth Army] 22.01.18 (ordered 4.1.18)

Commander
22.01.18-Edmond Hennocque

Major units

5 RC	Ex 4DC
8 RC	Ex 6DC
12 RC	Ex 2DC
273 RAC	Ex 97DI
8 Gp/103 RAL	New formed and added 3.18
E/6RCA & E/6RCA	Ex 97DI Cie 17/6, 17/56, 17/25 du 2RG
Pioneer Bn ???	

The division did not complete its formation until 18th March 1918 after which it was sent to Picardy in response to the German spring offensive. Between 1st and 12th April it fought with First Army along the line of the Avre at Moreuil and then established a new defence line between the Avre and Morisel. Moved to the Aisne, the division arrived at Sixth Army's sector between Pont St-Mard and Champs on 7th May. During the third battle of the Aisne it was forced to retreat to Soissons, from where it was moved to Tenth Army's positions at Valsery and Vertefeuille. It withstood a German attack at St Pierre-Aigle on 12th June.

From 14th June until 3rd July the division was rested and sent to Verdun where it occupied trenches to the south of the town between the Tranchee de Calonne and Trésauvaux. Relieved by the Americans on 8th September, it moved to the Bois Loclont/Suezey sector. Four days later it attacked the St Mihiel salient and moved forward to Hattonchatel and Thillot-sous-les-Côtes.

The division remained in reserve at Revigny from 18th October until 11th November. On the latter date, it had begun a movement back to the front at Mézières.

Provisional Cavalry Divisions

Division de Cavalerie Provisoire De Cornulier-Luciniere

Formed in Sixth Army on 29th August 1914 from elements of 1DC, 3DC and 5DC. It fought with Sordet's corps at Verberie and in the battle of the Ourcq. Disbanded 8th September 1914.

Division de Cavalerie Provisoire Beaudemoulin

Formed in Second Army on 15th September 1914 from Gillet's brigade and reserve units. It fought at Péronne, Bapaume and Courcelles-le-Comte until disbanded on 9th October 1914.

Division de Cavalerie Provisoire De Cornulier-Luciniere

Formed in Tenth Army on 7th November 1916 from elements of 4DC. It fought between the Amiens/Chaulnes railway and Maucourt until disbanded on 27th November 1916.

Division de Cavalerie Provisoire Brécart

Formed in Third Army on 27th April 1917 from elements of 1DC, 3DC and 5DC to occupy the sector between Bessy and Nanteuil-la-Fosse. During the second battle of the Aisne it attacked the Moulin de Laffaux [5th-6th May]. It was disbanded on 11th May 1917.

Foreign Divisions Under French Command, 1917-1918

The following divisions and corps served under the operational command of French Armées and Corps d'Armées during the last year of the war.

British Formations

Third Battle of the Aisne, 27th May-6th June 1918
SIXTH ARMY
IX Corps [British]
8th Division
21st Division
25th Division
50th [Northumbrian] Division

Second Battle of the Marne from 20th July 1918

TENTH ARMY
XX CA: 15th [Scottish] Division
XXXCA: 34th Division

FIFTH ARMY
VCA: 19th [Western] Division
XXII Corps [British]
51st [Highland] Division
62nd [West Riding] Division

Italian Formations

II Italian Corps
Served in the Argonne with Second Army, May-June 1918; with Fifth Army, 10th June-27th July during the battle of the Montagne de Reims; and then in the Ailette and Sissone area for the rest of the war

3 Italian Division:	Napoli and Salerno Brigades	75,76 89, 90 Infantry Regiments
8 Italian Division:	Brescia and Alpi Brigades	19,20 51, 52 Infantry Regiments

American Formations

Initially, US divisions were allocated to the 'quiet sectors' manned by Seventh Army in the Vosges and by Eighth Army to the east of the Moselle. The divisions involved were:

SEVENTH ARMY
32 US Infantry Division Belfort/Swiss Frontier	XXXXCA	18.05.18-21.07.18
5 US Infantry Division Anould	XXXIIICA	14.06.18-16.07.18
29 US Infantry Division Belfort/Swiss Frontier	XXXXCA	25.07.18-22.09.18
35 US Infantry Division Gerardmer	XXXIIICA	14.08.18-02.09.18
6 US Infantry Division Gerardmer	XXXIIICA	03.09.18-12.10.18
88 US Infantry Division Belfort/Swiss Frontier	XXXXCA	12.10.18-04.11.18

EIGHTH ARMY
1 US Infantry Division Sommervillers	IXCA	21.10.17-20.11.17
1 US Infantry Division Ansauville	XXXIICA	15.01.18-03.04.18
42 US Infantry Division Lunéville	VIICA	21.02.18-23.03.18
42 US Infantry Division Baccarat	VIICA	31.03.18-21.06.18

77 US Infantry Division Baccarat		VICA	21.06.18-04.08.18
5 US Infantry Division St Dié		XXXIIICA	17.07.18-23.08.18
37 US Infantry Division Baccarat		VICA	04.08.18-10.09.18
92 US Infantry Division St Dié		XXXIIICA	29.08.18-20.09.18
81 US Infantry Division St Dié		XXXIICA	20.09.18-19.10.18

3rd Battle of the Aisne 31st May-5th June 1918
| 2 US Infantry Division | Belleau Wood | VIICA 1.6-XXICA |
| 3 US Infantry Division | Chateau Thierry | XXXVIIICA |

Battle of Montdidier/Noyon 9th-13th June 1918
| 1 US Infantry Division | Cantigny | XCA |

2nd Battle of the Marne, 15th July-6th August 1918
I US Corps, SIXTH ARMY
26 US Infantry Division	15.07.18-13.08.18
2 US Infantry Division	23.07.18-30.07.18
42 US Infantry Division	25.07.18-06.08.18
4 US Infantry Division	28.07.18-23.08.28

III US Corps, , SIXTH ARMY
28 US Infantry Division	04.08.18-06.08.18
32 US Infantry Division	04.08.18-06.08.18
3 US Infantry Division	05.08.18-06.08.18 [also 4DI and 164DI]

SIXTH ARMY XXXVIII CA
3 US Infantry Division	15.07.18-05.08.18
28 US Infantry Division	15.07.18-04.08.18
32 US Infantry Division	28.07.18-04.08.18

XXI CA
| 42 US Infantry Division | 17.07.18-21.07.18 |

VII & II CA
| 4 US Infantry Division | 18.07.18-22.07.18 |

TENTH ARMY XXCA
| 1 US Infantry Division | 18.07.18-23.07.18 |
| 2 US Infantry Division | 18.07.18-19.07.18 |

Oise-Aisne operations 28th August-2nd September 1918
TENTH ARMY XXXCA
32 US Infantry Division

SIXTH ARMY III US Corps
28 US Infantry Division
77 US Infantry Division

Champagne-Argonne-Meuse 26th September -11th November 1918
FOURTH ARMY XXICA
| 2 US Infantry Division | 01.10.18-10.10.18 |
| 36 US Infantry Division | 07.10.18-28.10.18 [to IXCA on 18.10.18] |

SECOND ARMY
XVIICA 06.11.18-IICAC
33 US Infantry Division	07.10.18-21.10.18
29 US Infantry Division	08.10.18-30.10.18
26 US Infantry Division	18.10.18-11.11.18
79 US Infantry Division	29.10.18-11.11.18

Flanders/SIXTH ARMY 31st October-11th November 1918
37 US Infantry Division
91 US Infantry Division

[NB two other US divisions –27 and 30-served with II US Corps in the BEF]

Part Three

Infantry Regiments, 1914-1918

Active Regiments

Regiment	HQ	Division 8.14	Changes 14/18	Disbanded
1	Cambrai	1		
2	Granville	20		
3	Digne/Hyères	29		
4	Auxerre/Troyes	9		
5	Falaise/Paris	6	5.17-5	
6	Saintes	35	6.15-123	
7	Cahors	33	7.15-131	
8	St Omer	2		
9	Agen	33		
10	Auxonne	15		
11	Montauban	33		
12	Tarbes	36	6.15-123	
13	Nevers	16	1.17-169	
14	Toulouse	34	7.15-131	
15	Albi	32		
16	Montbrison	25		
17	Epinal	13	1.17-170	
18	Pau	36		
19	Brest	22		
20	Marmande	33		
21	Langres	13		
22	Santhonay	28		
23	Bourg	41		
24	Bernay/Paris	6		
25	Cherbourg	20		
26	Toul	11		
27	Dijon	15	1.17-16	
28	Evreux/Paris	6		
29	Autun	16	1.17-169	
30	Annecy	28		
31	Melun/Paris	10		
32	Toul	18		
33	Arras	2	11.16-51	
34	Mont de Marsan	36		
35	Belfort	14		
36	Caen	5	5.17-21	
			6.17-121	
37	Troyes	11	12.16-168	
38	St Etienne	25	6.15-120	
39	Rouen Nord	5	7.15-130	
			11.17-169	

			10.18-58
40	Nimes	30	
41	Rennes	19	7.15-131
42	Belfort	14	5.17-41
43	Lille	1	11.16-162
44	Lons le Saunier	14	
45	Laon	4	6.15-122
46	Fontainebleu	10	
47	St Malo	20	
48	Guincamp	19	
49	Bayonne	36	
50	Périgneux	24	
51	Beauvais	3	
52	Montélimar	27	
53	Perpignan	32	6.15-124
			11.16-163
54	Compiègne	12	
55	Pont St Esprit	30	6.15-126
56	Chalons s/Soâne	15	
57	Libourne	35	
58	Avignon	30	
59	Foix	34	
60	Besancon	14	
61	Privas	30	
62	Lorient	22	
63	Limoges	23	2.17-134
64	Acenis	21	
65	Nantes	21	11.17-134
66	Tours	18	
67	Soissons	12	
68	Blanc	17	
69	Toul	11	
70	Vitré	19	
71	St Brieuc	19	
72	Amiens	3	6.15-125
			12.16-Algeria
			4.17-87
73	Béthune	2	11.15-51
74	Rouen Sud	5	
75	Romans	27	
76	Coulommiers	10	6.15-125
77	Cholet	18	
78	Gueret	23	
79	Neufchâteau	11	12.16-168
80	Narbonne	32	
81	Montpellier	31	
82	Montargis	9	
83	St Gaudens	34	
84	Avesnes	1	6.15-122
85	Cosne	16	
86	Le Puy	25	6.15-120

87	St Quentin	3		
88	Mirande	34		
89	Sens	10		
90	Chateauroux	17		
91	Mézières	4	6.15-125	
			12.16-Algeria	
			4.17-87	
92	Clermont-Ferrand	26		
93	La Roche s/Yon	21		
94	Bar-le-Duc	42		
95	Bourges	16		
96	Béziers	31		
97	Chambéry	28	8.14-44	
			9.14-77	
98	Roanne	25	9.18-48	
99	Lyon	28		
100	Tulle	24	6.15-128	
			2.17-134	
101	Dreux/Paris	7	6.15-124	
102	Chârtres/Paris	7		
103	Alençon/Paris	7		
104	Argentan/Paris	7		
105	Riom	26	12.16-25	
106	Châlons s/Marne	12	1.17-56	
107	Angoulême	23		
108	Bergerac	24		
109	Chaumont	13		
110	Dunkerque	2		
111	Antibes	29	4.16-133	5.17
112	Toulon	29	6.15-126	
113	Blois	9	12.16-125	
114	Parthenay	17	12.15-152	
115	Mamers	8		
116	Vannes	22	11.17-170	
117	Le Mans	8		
118	Quimper	22		
119	Liseuex/Paris	6		
120	Péronne	4		
121	Montluçon	26		
122	Rodez	31		
123	La Rochelle	35		
124	Laval	8	6.15-124	
125	Poitiers	17	12.15-152	
126	Brive	24		
127	Valenciennes	1	10.16-162	
128	Amiens	3	11.17-41	
129	Le Havre	5	12.16-153 Bde	
			9.17-69	
130	Mayenne	8	11.16-124	

131	Orléans	9	6.15-125
132	Reims	12	1.17-56
133	Belley	41	6.17-23
			9.17-164
134	Mâcon	15	
135	Angers	18	1.17-152
136	St Lô	20	4.17-87
137	Tontenay	137	
138	Cognac	23	
139	Aurillac	26	
140	Grenoble	27	
141	Marseille	29	
142	Mende	31	6.15-124
			11.16-163
143	Carcassonne	32	
144	Bordeaux	35	
145	Maubege	Gp Maubege	0.14
146	Toul	39	
147	Sedan	4	
148	Givet	4	6.15-122
149	Épinal	43	
150	St Mihiel	40	
151	Verdun	42	12.16-69
152	Gérardmer	41	12.14-66
			11.16-164
153	Toul	39	
154	Lerouville	40	12.16-165
155	Commercy	40	12.16-165
156	Troyes	39	
157	Gapseille	??	8.14-44
			9.14-76
158	Bruyeres	43	
159	Briançon	Gp Briançon	8.14-44
			9.14-77
160	Neufchâteau	39	12.16-168
161	St Mihiel	40	
162	Verdun	42	12.16-69
163	Nice	Gp Nice	8.14-44
			9.14-76
			10.16-161
164	Verdun	Gp Verdun	8.15-72
165	Verdun	Gp Verdun	8.15-72
			3.16-29
166	Verdun	Gp Verdun	8.15-132
167	Toul	Gp Toul	6.15-128
168	Toul	Gp Toul	6.15-128
169	Toul	Gp Toul	6.15-128
170	Épinal	Gp Epinal	2.15-48
171	Belfort	Gp Belfort	6.15-127
			1.17-166
172	Belfort	Gp Belfort	6.15-127

173	Corsica	30	1.15-12
			6.15-126
174	Formed 3.15	48	12.16-167
175	Formed 3.15	156	
176	Formed 3.15	156	
177-200	Not formed		

Reserve Regiments

Regiment	HQ	DI/CA 8.14	Changes 14/18	Disbanded
201	Cambrai	I CA	6.15-1	
202	Granville	60		
203	Digne	65		
204	Auxerre	55		
205	Falaise/Paris	53		
206	Saintes	68		
207	Cahors	XVII	7.15-33	5.17
208	St Omer	51	11.16-2	
209	Agen	XVII	7.15-34	3.17
210	Auxonne	VIII	6.15-76	
211	Montauban	67		4.16
212	Tarbes	68	3.17-88	11.17
213	Nevers	58	10.14-66 3.16-157 11.16-164	9.17
214	Toulouse	67	3.17-157	9.18
215	Albi	66	12.14-41 11.16-161	7.18
216	Monbrisone	63		
217	Épinal	71		
218	Pau	XVIII	6.15-36	5.17
219	Brest	61		
220	Marmade	67		11.17
221	Langres	71		
222	Santhony	74		12.17
223	Bourg	74		6.16
224	Bernay/Paris	53	8.16-158 11.17-5	
225	Cherbourg	60		
226	Toul	70		
227	Dijon	VIII	6.15-64 7.15-? 10.16-76	
228	Évreux/Paris	53	8.16-158	11.17
229	Autun	58	10.14-66 3.16-41	
230	Annecy	74		
231	Melun/Paris	55		5.16
232	Tours	59		
233	Arras	51	11.16-1	
234	Mont de Marson	68		
235	Belfort	57		10.16
236	Caen	53	7.18-?	
237	Troyes	70		6.16
238	St Etienne	63		6.16
239	Rouen	III	7.15-130	11.17
240	Nîmes	75	11.14-XV	12.16

			6.15-30	
241	Rennes	X	7.15-131	5.17
242	Belfort	57		9.17
243	Lille	51		6.16
244	Lons le Saunier	57		10.16
245	Laon	52		10.17
246	Fontainebleu	55		
247	St Malo	60		3.17
248	Guincamp	60		
249	Bayonne	XIII	6.15-35	10.17
250	Périgueux	62		6.16
251	Beauvais	69	12.16-40	
252	Montélimar	62	2.17-157	8.18
253	Perpignan	66	10.14-4	9.17
			12.16-161	
254	Compiègne	69		6.16
255	St Esprit	75	10.14-V	10.17
			10.14-126	
			3.17-153/15Bde	
			4.17-97	
256	Châlons s/Soane	58		6.18
257	Libourne	68		6.16
258	Avignon	75	11.14-XV	4.16
			7.15 –29	
259	Foix	67		4.16
260	Besançon	57		
261	Aix	75	11.14-V	
			6.15-42	
			7.15-64	
262	Lorient	61	4.17-81	
			1.18-161	
263	Limoges	62		6.16
264	Acenis	61		
265	Nantes	61		
266	Tours	59		4.16
267	Soissons	69		9.17
268	Le Blanc	IX	6.15-152	1.18
269	Toul	70	1.18-88	
270	Vitré	X	7.15-19	5.17
271	St Brieuc	60		6.16
272	Amiens	II	6.15-3	
273	Béthune	51		8.18
274	Rouen	III	7.15-5	
275	Romans	64		6.16
276	Coulommiers	55	3.17-154Bde	
277	Cholet	59		9.18
278	Guéret	62		1.18
279	Nancy	70	4.17-81	

			1.18-62	
280	Narbonne	66	10.14-58	12.15
281	Montpellier	66	10.14-58	6.18
282	Montargis	55		5.16
283	St Gaudens	67		
284	Avesnes	I	6.15-122	9.17
285	Cosne	58		4.15
286	Le Puy	64		6.16
287	St Quentin	69	12.16-165	
288	Mirande	67		
289	Sens/Paris	55		
290	Châteauroux	IX	6.15-152	1.18
291	Mézières	52		6.16
292	Clermont-Ferrand	63		6.16
293	La Roch s/Yon	XI	6.15-151	11.17
294	Bar le Duc	56	1.17-166	9.18
295	Bourges	58		6.18
296	Béziéres	66	10.14-58	11.17
			12.15-152	
			1.17-169	
297	Chambéry	64	11.14-71	
			1.15-66	
			4.15-47	
			6.15-129	
298	Roanne	63	9.18-132	
299	Lyon	74		
300	Tulle	XII	6.16-24	
			2.17-134	
301	Dreux/Paris	54	10.14-VI?	???15
302	Chârtres/Paris	54	10.14-VI	6.16
			6.15-65	
303	Alençon/Paris	54	10.14-72	1.18?
			7.15-132	
			3.17-154Bde	
			10.17-97	
304	Argentan/Paris	54	10.14-VI?	6.16
305	Riom	63		
306	Châlons s/Marne	69		6.16
307	Angoulême	62		
308	Bergerac	62	4.17-81	1.18
309	Chaumont	71		6.16
310	Dunkerque	51		6.16
311	Antibes	65	7.18-8	10.18
312	Toulon	65		1.17
313	Blois	V	7.17-10	8.17
314	Parthenay	59		6.16
315	Mamers	IV	6.15-7	11.17

			3.17-88	
316	Vannes	61		6.16
317	Le Mans	IV	6.15-8	7.18
318	Quimper	61		6.16
319	Liseux/Paris	53		
320	Péronne	52		
321	Montluçon	63		6.16-133
322	Rodez	XVI	6.15-31	8.16
323	La Rochelle	68		6.16
324	Laval	54	10.14-72	7.18
325	Poitiers	59		
326	Brive	XII	5.15-24	
327	Valenciennes	51	11.16-162	
328	Abbeville	II	6.15-4	
			10.17-52	
329	Le Havre	53	8.16-158	
			11.17-9	
330	Mayenne	54	10.14-72	9.18
			7.15-132	
331	Orléans	V	8.15-10	9.17
332	Reims	69	12.16-42	
333	Belley	74	3.17-157	
334	Mâcon	58	10.14-66	
			3.16-133	
			8.16-134	
			11.16-164	
			10.17-97	
			1.18-?	
335	Angers	59	3.17-154Bde	
			10.17-97	
			1.18-17	
336	St Lô	60		6.16
337	Fontenay	XI	6.15-151	6.16
338	Magnac	62		
339	Aurillac	64		
340	Grenoble	64		
341	Marseille	65		
342	Mende	XVI	6.15-32	5.17
343	Carcassonne	66	10.14-41	
			11.16-161	
344	Bordeaux	68		
345	Maubege	Maubege		0.14
346	Toul	73		
347	Sedan	52		6.16
348	Rocroi	52		5.18
349	Épinal	71		6.16
350	St Mihiel	56	1.17-12	
351	Verdun	72	3.16-29	4.17
352	Gérardmer	VII	6.15-121	4.17
353	Toul	73		6.16
354	Le Ronville	56		6.16

355	Commercy	56	1.17-127	
356	Toul	73		
357	Gap/Marseille	spare	9.14-71	6.15
			1.15-66	
			4.15-47	
358	Bruyères/Lyon	71		
359	Briançon	spare	9.14-71	
			1.15-66	
			4.15-47	
			6.15-129	
360	Neufchâteau	70		
361	St Mihiel/Reims	56		6.16
362	Verdun/Reims	72	3.17-81	
363	Nice	54	10.14-?	
			9.17-161	
364	Verdun	72	7.15-132	8.16
365	Verdun	72		
366	Verdun	72	7.15-132	
367	Toul	73		
368	Toul	73		6.16
369	Toul	73	2.17-88	
			11.17-67	
370	Épinal	71	1.17-170	11.17
371	Belfort	57		
372	Belfort	57		
373	Corisca	Corsica		0.15

374-400 RI's not formed

War Formed Regiments

Regiment	HQ	Initial DI	Changes 15/18	Disbanded
402	St Quentin	4.15-157		4.16
403	Rouen	4.15-151		
404	Le Mans	4.15-151	6.15-121	
405	Orléans	4.15-154	7.15-130	7.16
406	St Quentin	4.15-152	6.15- 8.15-158	8.16
407	Besançon	4.15-154	7.15-130 11.17-151	
408	Bourges	4.15-152	4.15-120	
409	Chatelrenault	4.15-152	4.15-120	
410	Rennes	4.15-151		
411	Limoges	4.15-153	4.15-Gp Reims 6.15-123	
412	Limoges	4.15-153	4.15-Gp Reims 6.15-123 3.17-153 bde .17-48 6.18-23	
413	Clermont-Ferrand	4.15-154		
414	Meximeux	4.15-154		
415	Marseille	4.15-154		
416	Narbonne	4.15-154	7.15-28 11.16-154	
417	Toulouse	4.15-155	6.15-121	10.17
418	Bordeaux	4.15-153	7.18-72	
419	Bar le Duc	8.15-158		8.16
420	Toul ?	8.15-158		8.16
421	?	8.15-158		8.16

Chasseurs à Pied

1	1.15-66DI	7.16-46DI	−11.16	[7 13 27/47 53]
2	1.15-47DI		−11.16	[11 12 51 54]
3	1.15-47DI		-11.16	[14 30 53 62]
4	1.15-47DI	5.16-66DI	-11.16	[6/115 23/46 24 64]
5	6.15-129DI-8.15 11.15-66DI 3.16-46DI		-11.16	[22 23 62 63]
6	8.15-66DI		-11.16	[27 28 67 68]
7	3.16-66DI		-11.16	[6 27 46]
8	8.16-46DI		-11.16	[6 45 53 63]

In November 1916 the above brigades were reorganised into the groups which are listed below.

Groups De Chasseurs 1916-1918

1	11.16-46DI		[7 13 47]
2	11.16-46DI		[22 53 62]
3	11.16-46DI		[15 23 63]
4	11.16-47DI		[11 12 51]
5	11.16-47DI		[14 52 54]
6	11.16-47DI		[30 70 115]
7	11.16-66DI		[6 27 46/47]
8	11.16-66DI		[17/67 28 68]
9	11.16-66DI		[5 24 64]
10	1.17- 56DI	9.18-38DI	[44 65 69]
11	4.17-121DI		[45 48 55]
12	6.17-129DI		[106 120 121]
13	9.17-164DI		[41 43 59]
14	11.17-77DI		[56 60 61]
15	11.17-133DI		[32 102 116]
16	12.17- 74DI		[50 66 71] disbanded 6.18
17	1.18- 70DI		[42 44 114]

Battalions De Chasseurs à Pied 1914-1918 [including Alpine]

Active battalions

Regiment	HQ	Initial DI	Changes 15/18	Disbanded
1	Senones	43DI		
2	Lunéville	11DI	4.15-153DI	
			12.16-11DI	
3	St Dié	43DI	1.17-170DI	
4	St Nicholas	11DI	2.15-153DI	
			12.16-11DI	
5	Remiremont	41DI	12.14-66DI	IX Gp/Bde
6 Alpine	Nice	29DI	1.15-47DI	VII Gp/Bde
			6.16-46DI	
			11.16-66DI	
7 Alpine	Draguignan	29DI	1.15-66DI	I Gp/Bde
			3.16-46DI	
8	Étain	42DI		
9	Longwy	44DI	11.14-4DI	
10	St Dié	43DI	1.17-170DI	
11 Alpine	Annecy	28DI	1.15-47DI	IV Gp/Bde

12 Alpine	Embrun	27DI	10.14-66DI	IV Gp/Bde
			1.15-47DI	
13 Alpine	Chambéry	28DI	10.14-66DI 7.16-46DI	I Gp/Bde
14 Alpine	Grenoble	27DI	1.15-47DI	V Gp/Bde
15	Remiremont	41DI	10.14-66DI	III Gp/Bde
			11.16-46DI	
16	Conflans-Labry	42DI		
17	Rambervillers	13DI	10.15-77DI	VIII Gp/Bde
			11.16-66DI	
18	Longuyon	44DI	11.14-4DI	
19	Verdun	42DI	6.15-127DI	
			1.17-166DI	
20	Baccarat	13DI		
21	Raon L'Étape	13DI		
22 Alpine	Albertville	28DI	1.15-47DI	II Gp/Bde
			11.16-66DI	
			3.16-46DI	
23 Alpine	Grasse	29DI	1.15-47DI	III Gp/Bde
			11.15-66DI	
			3.16-46DI	
24 Alpine	Villefranche	29DI	1.15-47DI	IX Gp/Bde
			11.15-GAV	
			5.16-66DI	
25	St Mihiel	40DI	6.15-127DI	
26	Pont a Mousson	40DI	1.15-12DI	
			6.15-127DI	
			1.17-166DI	
27 Alpine	Menton	29DI	1.15-66DI	VII Gp/Bde
28 Alpine	Grenoble	54DR	10.14-66DI	VIII Gp/Bde
29	St Mihiel	40DI	6.15-127DI	
30 Alpine	Grenoble	27DI	10.14-66DI	VI Gp/Bde
			1.15-47DI	
31	St Dié	43DI		
32	Formed 1914?	-	9.15-157DI	XV Gp/Bde
			6.16-133DI	

Reserve battalions

Regiment	HQ	Initial DI	Changes 15/18	Disbanded
41	Senones	XIII CA	9.14-71DR	XIII Gp/Bde
			2.15-41DI	
			3.16-66DI	
			11.16-164DI	
42	Lunéville	70DR		XVII Gp/Bde
43	St Dié	XIII CA	10.14-74DR	XIII Gp/Bde
			3.16-133DI	
			8.16-164DI	
44	St Nicholas	70DR	1.17-56DI	X Gp/Bde
45	Remiremont	VII CA	6.15-121DI	XI Gp/Bde

46 Alpine	Nice	65DR	8.14-GAV 11.15-??	Disbanded 11.17
47 Alpine	Draguignan	65DR	8.14-GAV 11.15-47DI 5.16-GAV 5.16-66DI 11.16-46DI	I Gp/Bde
48	Étain	69DR	7.15-121DI	XI Gp/Bde
49	Longwy	52DR	6.16-RFV 11.16-164DI	Disbanded 4.18
50	St Dié	XIII CA	10.14-74DR	XVI Gp/Bde Disbanded 6.18
51 Alpine	Annecy	74DR	8.14-28DI 11.15-47DI	IV Gp/Bde
52 Alpine	Embrun	64DR	9.14-41DI 12.14-66DI 11.15-47DI	V Gp/Bde
53 Alpine	Chambéry	74DR	8.14-28DI 9.14-77DI 1.15-66DI 11.15-ind 3.16-46DI	II Gp/Bde
54 Alpine	Grenoble	74DR	9.14-77DI 12.14-GAV 1.15-47DI	V Gp/Bde
55	Remiremont	VII CA	6.15-121DI	XI Gp/Bde
56	Conflans-Labry	72DR	5.17-77DI	XIV Gp/Bde
57	Ramberviller	XXI CA	9.14-77DI	Disbanded 11.17
58	Longuyon	52DR	10.15-122DI 10.17-??	
59	Verdun	72DR	3.15-153BI 4.17-97DI 9.17-164DI	XIII Gp/Bde
60	Baccarat	XXI CA	9.14-77DI	XIV Gp/Bde
61	Raon L'Étape	XXI CA	9.14-77DI	XIV Gp/Bde
62 Alpine	Albertville	74DR	8.14-28DI 1.15-47DI 11.15-66DI 3.16-46DI	II Gp/Bde
63 Alpine	Grasse	65DR	9.14-Klein 1.15-47DI 11.15-66DI 3.16-46DI	III Gp/Bde
64 Alpine	Villefranche	65DR	9.14-Klein 1.15-47DI 11.15-GAV 11.16-66DI	IX Gp/Bde
65	St Mihiel	56DR		X Gp/Bde

66	Pont-a-Mouson	56DR	7.15-9DI	XVI Gp/Bde
			12.16-74DI	Disbanded 6.18
67 Alpine	Menton	65DR	9.14-Klein	
			2.15-47DI	
			8.15-66DI	
68 Alpine	Grenoble	64DR	8.14-GAV	VIII Gp/Bde
			10.14-66DI	
69	St Mihiel	56DR		X Gp/Bde
70 Alpine	Grenoble	64DR	8.14-GAV	VIII Gp/Bde
			11.15-47DI	
71	St Dié	XIII CA	10.14-71DR	XVI Gp/Bde
				Disbanded 6.18

Formed 4.15

Regiment	HQ	Initial DI	Changes 15/18	Disbanded
102	-	157DI	6.16-133DI	XV Gp/Bde
106	-	152DI	6.15-129DI	Disbanded 6.17
107	-	157DI	10.15-313BI	
			8.16-133DI	
			11.17-??	
114	-	155DI	6.15-129DI	XVII Gp/Bde
			6.17-5DI	
			11.17-70DI	
115	-	153DI	6.15-129DI	VI Gp/Bde
			8.15-47DI	
			11.15-GAV	
			5.16-66DI	
			11.16-47DI	
116	-	157DI	6.16-133DI	XV Gp/Bde
120	-	151DI	6.15-129DI	XII Gp/Bde
121	-	154DI	6.15-129DI	XII Gp/Bde

Territorial battalions 1914

Regiment	HQ	Initial DI	Changes 15/18
1T			
2T			11.17-66DI
3T	Vienne		5.16-66DI
			11.16-
4T			
5T	Grenoble		3.15-66DI
6T	Nice		
7T	Villefranche		3.15-66DI

REGIMENTS D'INFANTERIE TERRITORIALE [RIT]

[sometimes called Regiments Territoriaux d'Infanterie –RTI]

1st Region [region mostly occupied by the Germans]
1 RIT, Lille
2 RIT, Valenciennes
3 RIT, Cambrai
4 RIT, Avesnes
5 RIT, Arras   7.16-XXXIVCA   8.18-M/XXXIVCA, P/6DI, P/165DI
6 RIT, Béthune
7 RIT, St Omer   6.18-XICA   8.18-M/XICA, P/32DI, P/151DI
8 RIT, Dunkerque   7.15-XIVCA   8.18-M/XIVCA, P14DI, P/27DI

2nd Region
10 RIT, St Quentin
11 RIT, Beauvais   81 DIT-8.15
12 RIT, Amiens   81 DIT-8.15
14 RIT, Abbeville   81 DIT-3.17   8.18M-M/XXXICA, P/129DI, P/133DI
15 RIT, Laon   7.16-IXCA –1.18 8.18-P/6DI
16 RIT, Péronne   81 DIT-3.17
45 RIT, Mézières

3rd Region
17 RIT, Bernay   82DIT –6.15   8.16-89DT-3.17 7.17-45DI 8.18-P/45DI
18 RIT, Évreux   82 DIT 6.15-IICAC   8.18-M/IICAC, P/10DI, P/27DI, P/15DIC
19 RIT, Falaise
20 RIT, Lisieux
21 RIT, Rouen (N)   82 DIT 6.15-XICX   8.18-P/5DI, P/164DI
22 RIT, Rouen (S)   82 DIT 6.15-XICA –6.18
23 RIT, Caen   6.15-XXXVIIICA   8.18-M/XXXVIII, P/131DI, P/138DI
24 RIT, Le Havre   7.15-XIVCA   8.18-P/16DI, P/168DI

4th Region [many regiments in this region actually recruited from Paris]
25 RIT, Laval   84 DIT 7.15-XXXIIICA 8.18-M/XXXVIIICA, P/51DI, P/53DI
26 RIT, Mayenne   84 DIT 7.15-IIICA   8.18-M/IIICA, P/64DI, P/70DI
27 RIT, Mamers   84 DIT 7.15-XVIICA   8.18-M/XVIICA, P/34DI. P/35DI
28 RIT, Le Mans   84 DIT 7.15-XCA   8.18-M/XCA, P/60DI, P/166DI
29 RIT, Dreux   83 DIT 8.15-VCA   8.18-M/VCA, P/10DI, P/20DI
30 RIT, Chârtres   83 DIT 8.15-VCA-4.16d
31 RIT, Alençon   83 DIT 8.15-XXXCA   8.18-M/XXXCA, P/72DI, P/132DI
32 RIT, Argentan   83 DIT 8.15-   9.17-P/DM-1DM

5th Region [many regiments in this region actually recruited from Paris]
33 RIT, Sens
34 RIT, Fontainebleu   .14-XXXCA   3.16-XVICA 7.16-IVCA 8.18-M/IV, P/7DI, P/8DI
35 RIT, Melun   6.15-ICA   6.16-XVICA 8.18-M/XVICA, P/31DI, P/32DI
36 RIT, Coulommiers
37 RIT, Auxerre
38 RIT, Montargis   4.18-IXCA   8.18-IXCA, P/37DI, P/152DI
39 RIT, Blois
40 RIT, Orléans

6th Region

9 RIT, Soissons
13 RIT, Compiègne
44 RIT, Verdun
46 RIT, Reims
48 RIT, Châlons
no other RIT's listed in this region-usually 8 per region

7th Region
43 RIT, Épinal
49 RIT, Belfort   10.15-105DT-3.16d
50 RIT, Belfort   10.15-105DT-3.16d
51 RIT, Langres
53 RIT, Lons-le-Saumier
54 RIT, Besançon   7.15-VIICA   8.18-M/VIICA, P/17DI, P/41DI
55 RIT, Bourg
56 RIT, Belley

8th Region
57 RIT, Auxonne
58 RIT, Dijon
59 RIT, Châlon s/Soane
60 RIT, Mâcon
61 RIT, Cosne
62 RIT, Bourges
63 RIT, Autun   6.15-XXXIICA   8.18-M/XXXIICA, P/29DI, P/2DM
64 RIT, Nevers   6.16-XVIIICA   7.16-ICA 8.16-XCA
8.18-M/XCA, P/58DI, P/153DI

9th Region
65 RIT, Châteauroux   85 DIT   6.15-XXXVIICA 8.18-P/1DCP, P/62DI
66 RIT, Le Blanc   85 DIT   6.15-XXXVIICA-9.17d
67 RIT, Parthenay   85 DIT   6.15-VIICA   8.18-P/55DI, P/128DI
68 RIT, Poitiers   85 DIT   6.15-XXXVCA-6.18d
69 RIT, Chatellerault 86 DIT   6.15-XXXVCA   8.18-M/XXXVCA, P/121DI, P/169DI
70 RIT, Tours   86 DIT   6.15-XIIICA   8.18-M/XIIICA, P/157DI
71 RIT, Angers   86 DIT   6.15-XIIICA   8.18-P/18DI, P/19DI
72 RIT, Chôlet   86 DIT   6.15-XIIICA   7.17-ICA 8.18-M/ICA, P/2DI, P/162DI

10th Region
73 RIT, Guincamp   87 DIT-4.17 6.17-68DI   8.18-P/68DI
74 RIT, St Brieuc   87 DIT-4.17
75 RIT, Rennes   185BI   9.15-ICA-2.16
76 RIT, Vitré   87 DIT   6.16-XXXVICA-3.18
77 RIT, Cherbourg
78 RIT, St Malo   185BI   9.15-ICA –2.16   7.17-48DI 8.18-P/48DI
79 RIT, Granville   87 DIT   6.16-XXXVICA -?
80 RIT, St Lô   15-105 DIT   6.16-XXXVICA

11th Region
81 RIT, Nantes   88 DIT -.16
82 RIT, Açenis   88 DIT - 1.17
83 RIT, La Roche s/Yon 88 DIT - .16
84 RIT, Fontenay   88 DIT -.16d
85 RIT, Vannes

86 RIT, Quimper   6.15-XVIIICA 7.16-ICA   8.18-P/69DI, P/127DI
87 RIT, Brest
88 RIT, Lorient   7.15-ICAC   8.18-M/ICAC, P/2DIC, P/3DIC

12th Region
89 RIT, Limoges   89 DIT –6.17   8.18-M/XIICA
90 RIT, Magnac-Laval   89 DIT –6.17
92 RIT, Tulle
93 RIT, Perigueux   89 DIT- 6.17
94 RIT, Angoulême   89 DIT- 6.17
95 RIT, Brive
96 RIT, Bergerac
one RIT less than normal 8

13th Region
97 RIT, Riom   10.14-96DIT 6.15-VICA 8.18-M/VICA, P/21DI, P/154DI
98 RIT, Montluçon   10.15-105DIT 3.16-133DI
99 RIT, Clermont-Ferrand   10.15-105DT 3.16-157DI
100 RIT, Aurillac
101 RIT, Le Puy   10.14-XIVCA   8.15-XVCA   8.18-M/XVCA, P/74DI, P/123DI
102 RIT, St Étienne   4.15-87DT   8.15-81DT
103 RIT, Montbrison   .15-XXXICA-1.18   8.18-P/42DI
104 RIT, Roanne   7.15-IVCA   8.18-P/124DI. P/163DI

14th Region
105 RIT, Grenoble   1.16-XVCA –11.16
106 RIT, Bourguin   10.14-97DT   6.16-XXCA   8.18-M/XXCA, P/15DI, P/25DI
107 RIT, Annecy
108 RIT, Chambéry   10.14-96DT   6.15-IICA   2.16-RFV
109 RIT, Vienne   9.14-94DT   6.15-XVICA 6.16-XIIC 8.18-M/XIICA, P/23DI, P/24DI
110 RIT, Romans   9.14-94DT   6.15-XVICA 4.16-XVIIICA 8.18-M/XVIIICA, P/1DI, P/33DI
111 RIT, Montélimar   9.14-94DT 10.14-IVCA 7.16-XVICA-9.17
112 RIT, Gap   10.14-96DT 6.15-VICA 8.18-P/28DI, P/61DI

15th Region
113 RIT, Toulon
114 RIT, Antibes
115 RIT, Marseille

116 RIT, Ajaccio
117 RIT, Nîmes   10.14-96DT 6.15-IICA   8.18-M/IICA, P/4DI, P/36DI
118 RIT, Avignon   .15-XXXVIIICA –2.18d
119 RIT, Privas
120 RIT, Pont St Esprit   10.14-97DT 8.15-XXXCA –8.15
145 RIT, Aix   6.15-XXXIICA   8.18-P/40DI, P/125DI

15th Region
113 RIT, Toulon
114 RIT, Antibes
115 RIT, Marseille
116 RIT, Ajaccio
117 RIT, Nîmes   10.14-96DT 6.15-IICA   8.18-M/IICA, P/4DI, P/36DI
118 RIT, Avignon   .15-XXXVIIICA –2.18d
119 RIT, Privas

120 RIT, Pont St Esprit   10.14-97DT 8.15-XXXCA –8.15
145 RIT, Aix   6.15-XXXIICA 8.18-P/40DI, P/125DI

16th Region
121 RIT, Béziers
122 RIT, Montpellier   10.14-97DT   8.15-VCA   8.18-P/9DI, P/77DI
123 RIT, Mende RFB   6.15-XIVCA 7.15-IICA-2.18d
124 RIT, Rodez
125 RIT, Narbonne   90 DIT-9.14
126 RIT, Perpignan   90 DIT-9.14
127 RIT, Carcassonne 90 DIT-9.14
128 RIT, Albi   90 DIT-9.14

17th Region [3 regts per bde- possible because allocated to Alpine Front]
129 RIT, Agen   91 DIT 6.15-IICAC-8.17 8.18-P/20DI
130 RIT, Marmande   91 DIT 6.15-XIICA 8.16-89DT –3.17
131 RIT, Cahors   91 DIT 6.15-VIIICA   8.18-M/VIIICA, P/71DI
132 RIT, Montauban 91 DIT 6.15-VIIICA   8.18-P/39DI, P/120DI
133 RIT, Toulouse   91DIT 6.15-?
134 RIT, Foix   91 DIT 6.15-ICAC -10.17
135 RIT, Mirande   91DIT 6.15-XIICA 8.16-89DT-3.17
136 RIT, St Gaudens 2.15-99DT-8.16

18th Region
137 RIT, Saintes
138 RIT, La Rochelle
139 RIT, Libourne
140 RIT, Bordeaux
141 RIT, Mont de Marsan 92 DIT 7.15-IXCA   8.18-P/65DM-2DM & P/59DI
142 RIT, Bayonne   92 DIT 7.15-XXCA   8.18-P/11DI, P/12DI
143 RIT, Pau   92 DIT 7.15-XXICA   8.18-M/XXICA, P/13DI, P/43DI
144 RIT, Tarbes   92 DIT 7.15-XXICA   8.18-P/167DI, P/170DI

19th Region- North Africa

20th Region [only 4 regts] [as region recently formed –these could have been 6 Region]
41 RIT, Nancy
42 RIT, Toul   6.15-XXXICA   8.18-XXXICA, P/56DI, P/126DI
47 RIT, Troyes   .15-XXXIXCA-6.152 RIT, Neufchâteau

21st Region – no territorials

Battalions Territorial de Chasseurs à Pied [all Chasseurs Alpin]

1, Annecy
2, Chambéry
3, Vienne
4, Grenoble
5, Grasse
6, Nice
7, Villefranche

REGIMENTS D'INFANTERIE COLONIALE 1914-1918

RIC	HQ 1914	DIC	CHANGES 14/18	DISBANDED
1	Cherbourg	3	2.15-15	
			2.17-17	
2	Brest	3	2.15-15	
3	Rochfort	3	5.17-17	
4	Toulon	2	11.16-16	
5	Lyon	1	8.14-XIVCA	
			9.14-76DI	
			6.15-15	
6	Lyon	1	8.14-XIVCA	
			9.14-76DI	
			6.15-15	
7	Bordeaux	3		
8	Toulon	2	11.16-16	
9	Hanoi			
10	Haiphong			0.14
11	Saigon			
Dec-15	Not formed			
16	Tienstin			
17-20	Not formed			
21	Paris	1	8.14-indep	
			2.15-3	
22	Marseille	2		
23	Paris	1	8.14-indep	
			2.15-3	
24	Perpignan	2		
25-30	Not formed			
31	F .14	?		
32	F .14	?		
33	F .14	?		
34	F .14	65DI	7.15-16	
			1.17-11	
35	F .14	64DI	7.15-16	
			1.17-11	
36	F .14	74 DI	7.15-16	11.16
37	F .14	41DI	7.15-16	
38	F .14	65DI	7.15-16	10.18
39-40	Not formed			
41	F .14	XXCA	9.15-154DI	5.17
			11.16-16	
42	F .14	75DI	11.14-V CA	
			6.15-10	
			1.17-11	
43	F .14	XXCA	7.15-154DI	
			11.16-2	
44	F .14	75DI	11.14-V CA	
			7.15-16	
			1.17-11	

45-51	Not formed			
52	8.15- ex 2RMIC	10		
53	8.15- ex 3RMIC	10		
54	8.15- ex 4RMIC	17		
55	.15-ex5RMIC?		6.15	
56	8.15-ex 6RMIC	17	8.18	
57 [Senegalais]	8.15-ex 7RMIC	15		
58 [Senegalais]	8.15-ex 8RMIC		2.16??	
59 [Senegalais]	4.17 only			

Army of Africa Infantry Regiments

Regiment 1914 & subsequent changes	Division allocation
RdM1Z 12.14-1 RdMZ	38DI 7.15-25DI 12.16-48DI
RdM2Z 3.15- 2 RdMZ	37DI
RdM3Z 4.15- 3 RdMZ	37DI
RdM4Z 12.14-6 RdMZ 1.15-4RdMZ	38DI
RdMbis1Z 12.14-7 RdMZ 7.15-3RdMZT	45DI 4.18-58DI
RdMbis2Z 12.14-3RdMZ 1.15-2bisRdMZ	45DI 10.15-Salonika 10.18 disbanded
RdMbis3Z 12.14-5RdMZ 1.15-3bisRdMZ	45DI
RdMZ(DM) 10.14-8RdMZ	DM
RdMZ(3BM) 12.14-9RdMZ	IV 9.14-37DI 4.15-153DI
RdMx(3BM) 12.14-1RdMZT	IV 9.14-37DI 4.15-153DI 7.18-72DI
RdMMxM 12.14-2RdMZT	VII 9.14-DM? 2.15-48DI 12.16-25DI
RdMIC 8.14-1 RICM 9.14-RdMIC	DM 8.18-2DM
8.14-2 RICM-9.14	DM
RdMC 5.15-2RdMxIC 8.15-52RIC	
5.15-3 RMxIC 8.15-53RIC	
5.15-4 RMxIC 8.15-54RIC	1DI/CEO
5.15-5 RMxIC 6.15-RTSM	
5.15-6 RMxIC 8.15-56RIC	1DI/CEO
5.15-7 RMxIC 8.15-57RIC	2DI/CEO
5.15-8 RMxIC 8.15-58RIC	2DI/CEO
2.15 1 RdMA	1DI/CEO-156DI
2.15 2 RdMA	2DI/CEO/156DI
1 BILA	10.14-45DI
2 BILA	10.14-6.18-45DI
3 BILA	10.14-45DI
4 BILA	Morocco
5 BILA	Morocco
1 RdM 1RE (Maroc)	Morocco
2 RdM 2RE (Maroc)	Morocco
2 RdM 1RE (Fr) 11.15-RdMLE	11.15-DM
3 RdM 1RE (Fr) "	Disbanded 7.15
4 RdM 1RE (Fr) "	[Garibaldi] disbanded 3.15
2 RdM 2RE (Fr) "	1 bn disbanded 7.15
RdMT 6.15-4 RdMZT 11.18-16RdMT	4 BM 4.15-152DI
2 RdMT 12.14-6RdMT 3.15-1RdMT	45DI
RdM1&9T 12.14-3RdMT 3.15-9RdMT	38DI 12.16-48DI 9.18-25DI
RdM2T 12.14-1RdMT 4.15-2RdMT	37DI
RdM3T 10.14-2RdMT 4.15-3 RdMT	37DI 7.18-51DI
RdM4T 12.14-4RdMT	38DI 10.14-DM 7.18-2DM

RdM 5&6T	9.14-1RdMT	6.15-5RdMT	37DI 1.18-74DI
" "	12.14-6RdMT		45DI 6.18-58DI 10.18-169DI
1 RdMZT	9.14-RdMTMOcc 10.14-RdMT		DM
2 RdMZT	9.14RdMTMOr		10.14 merged into RdMT/DM
7.15-8 RdMT			38DI 9.18-56DI
9 RMT			See above-RdM1&9T
1.18-10 RdMT			52DI
2.18-11 RdMT			58DI
10.18-12RdMT			68DI
.18-13 RdMT			See above-RdMMxMaroc
10.18-14RdMT			129DI
11.18-15 RdMT			
11.18-16 RdMT			See above-RdMT
10.18-17RdMT			166DI
2.18-21RdMT			8DI
1RCIP/BM 10.14-RCIP 12.14-RdMTM			153DI
2.18-2 RdMTM			2DM
RICM11.14-1RICM 6.15-RICM			DM

Naval Infantry Temporarily Under Army Command

1 Fusiliers Marin and 2 Fusiliers Marin served with 38DI 1.15-3.16. Thereafter they returned to naval control.

West African Infantry Regiments & Battalions 1914 (Colonial Establishment)

1 RTS [3 bns]		St Louis, West Africa Kati, West Africa Cote d'Ivoire
2 RTS [3 bns]		Dakar
3 RTS [2 bns]		
4 RTS [3 bns]		
1 BTS d'Algerie		Colomb-Bechar
2 BTS d'Algerie		Orleansville
1 BTS	1 RMxICM	Rabat, Morocco Fez, Morocco
2 BTS	5 RMxICM	Fez, Morocco
3 BTS	5 RMxICM	Meknes, Morocco
4 BTS	3 RMxICM	Morocco
5 BTS	?	Marrakech, Morocco
6 BTS	6 RMxICM	Marrakesh. Morocco
7 BTS	6 RMxICM	south of Fez, Morocco
8 BTS	4 RMxICM	Chauoia, Morocco
9 BTS	2 RMxICM	Chauoia, Morocco
10 BTS	2 RMxICM	south of Fez, Morocco
11 BTS	4 RMxICM	Rabat, Morocco
12 BTS	1 RMxICM	Meknes, Morocco
13 BTS	3 RMxICM	

Divisions which commanded West African battalions were
10DI [31, 34, 51]   2 DIC [28.32.64.65]

17DI	[27, 28]	3 DIC	[5, 58, 61, 62]
56DI	[29]	10DIC	[66, 67, 68, 69, 71]
69DI	[29]	15 DIC	[27, 66, 67, 70, 71]
127DI	[27]	16DIC	[5, 20, 26, 28, 30, 56, 61, 85, 97, 98]

Overseas Recruited Regiments & Battalions 1914-1918

RdM1Z/38DI	12.14-1RdMZ/38DI	7.15-25DI	12.16-48DI
4/1Z	4/1Z	4/1Z	41/Z
5/1Z	5/1Z	5/1Z	51/Z
11/1Z	11/1Z	11/1Z	11/1Z

dM2Z/37DI   3.15-2RdMZ/37DI

1/2Z	1/2Z
5/2Z	5/2Z
11/2Z	11/2Z

RdM3Z/37DI   4.15-3RdMZ/37DI

1/3Z	1/3Z
5/3Z	5/3Z
11/3Z	11/3Z

RdM4Z/38DI 12.14-6RdMZ/38DI   1.15-4RdMZ/38DI

3/4Z	3/4Z	3/4Z
4/4Z	4/4Z	4/4Z
5/4Z	5/4Z	5/4Z
11/4Z	11/4Z	11/4Z-6.16d

RdMbis1Z/45DI   12.14-7RdMZ/45DI   7.15-3RdMZT/45DI   4.18-6RdMTA/45DI

6/1Z	6/1Z	6/1Z	5/6T
14/1Z	14/1Z	14/1Z	7/6T
6/4Z	6/4Z	3/4T	11/6T
		5.17-12/3Z	

Rdbis2Z/45DI 12.14-3RdMZ/45DI   1.15-2bisRdMZ/45DI 10.15-AO –10.18d

4/2Z	4/2Z	4/2Z	4/2Z
12/2Z	12/2Z	12/2Z	12/2Z
14/2Z	14/2Z	14/2Z	14/2Z

RdMbis3Z/45DDI   12.14-5RdMZ/45DI 1.15-3bisRdMZ/45DI

3/3Z	3/3Z	3/3Z
6/3Z	6/3Z	6/3Z
12/3Z	12/3Z	12/3Z-5.17

RdMZ/DM   10.14-8RdMZ/DM

1/1Z	1/1Z
2/3Z	2/3Z
4/3Z	4/3Z
9.14-3/2Z	3/2Z

RdMZ/3BM   12.14-9RdMZ/37DI   4.15-153DI

2/1Z	2/1Z	2/1Z
3/1Z	3/1Z	3/1Z
1/4Z	1/4Z	1/4Z

RdMMx/RdMZT/3BM 12.14-1RdMZT/37DI 4.15-153DI   7.18-72DI

2/2T	2/2T	2/2T	1/7T
1/3T	1/3T	1/3T	3/7T
1/7T	1/7T	7/7T	7/7T

RdMMxM/4BM   12.14-2RdMxZT/DM 2.15-48DI   12.16-25DI   7.18-13RdMT/48DI

2/4Z	2/4Z	2/4Z	2/4Z-d6.18	4/9T
3/3T	3/3T	3/3T	3/3T 1.18-	11/9T
1/9T	1/9T	2/5T 9.15-3/5T	3/5T	3/5T
		9/15-5/3T		

RMIC/DM   8.14-1RICM/DM   9.14-RICM/DM   6.15-RICM/DM   8.18-2DM

6 BICM	9 BICM	4 BICM	1 BICM	1 BICM
7 BICM	4 BTSM	9.14-8BTSM	4 BICM	4 BICM
9 BICM	7 BTSM	12 BTSM	8 BICM	8 BICM

2RMIC/DM –10.14   2.15-2RdMxIC 8.15-52RIC

6 BICM		
1 BTSM		
3 BTSM		

3 RMxIC 5.15- 8.15-53RIC

?	
?	
?	

4 RMxIC 515-1DI/CEO 8.15-54RIC

Bn ex 4RIC	
Bn ex 1BTSM	
Bn ex 3BTSM	

5 RMxIC 5.15- 8.15-RTSM

6 RMxIC 5.15-1DI/CEO   8.15-56RIC –17DIC d 8.18

Bn ex 6RIC	
Bn ex 3BTSM	
Bn ex 4BTSM	

7 RMxIC 5.15-2DI/CEO   8.15-57RIC-d 8.17

Bn ex 7RIC	
Bn ex 8BTSM	
Bn ex 12BTSM	

8 RMIC .15-2DI/CEO   8.15-58RIC

Bn ex 5RIC	66BIC
Bn ex 8RIC	67BIC
Bn ex 7BTSM	70BIC

1 Regt de M d'Afrique [1RdMA]/1DI/CEO/156DI

C/4Z	
Bn/3Z	5.15 to 2RMA
Bn/RE1	

2 RdMA/2DI/CEO/156DI   10.17 merged into 1RdMA

Bn ex 2Z	
E/4Z	5.15 to 1RMA

The following were penal battalions, stationed in North Africa.. Two 'battalions de marche' were formed in the autumn of 1914, Bn de Marche, 1BILA and Bn de Marche 3BILA [abbreviated to 1BA and 3BA], for service with 45DI. In the summer of 1918, a third battalion, 2BA, was formed by the transfer of men from the other two battalions in 45DI. 2BA was not related to 2BILA which had remained in North Africa .The three battalions constituted the 'Group de Bns d'Afrique' in 45DI.

1 BILA
2 BILA
3 BILA
4 BILA
5 BILA

FOREIGN LEGION

For details of these units see Peter Abbott's supplementary chapter on the French Army overseas.

1 RdM1RE(Maroc)/DM
2 RdM2RE(Maroc)
2 RdM1RE(France)   11.15-RdMLE/DM
3 RdM1RE (France)   11.15
4 RdM1RE (France)   11.15 [Garibaldi]
2 RdM2RE (France)   11.15

RdMT/4BM   6.15-4 RdMZT/152DI[post 11.18-16RMT]

2/4T	6/4Z 4.18-7/8T
1/8T	1/8T
6/8T	6/8T

2RdMT/45DI 12.14-6RdMT/45DI   3.15-1RdMT/45DI

2/1T	2/1T	2/1T

2/8T	2/8T	1/9T -9.15
		12.15-1/5T
		1/18-11/1T
6/2T	6/2T	1/1T
		9.15-3/1T

RdM1&9T/38DI   12.14-3RdMT/38DI   3.15-9RdMT/38DI   12.16-9RdMT/48DI   9.18-25DI

1/1T	1/1T	11/9T	11/9T	11/9T
2/9T	2/9T	2/9T	2/9T	2/9T
3/9T	3/9T	3/9T	3/9T	3/9T

RdM2T/37DI 12.14-1RdMT 4.15-2RdMT

2/2T	2/2T	2/2T
5/2T	5/2T	5/2T
		1.16-1/5T
		4.17-3/2T
	2/5T	6/2T
	2.15-6/2T	
	4/6T	4/6T-d1.16

RdM3T/37DI 4.15-3RdMT   7.18-3RdMT/51DI

2/3T	2/3T	2/3T
4/3T	4/3T	4/3T
5/3T	5/3T 8.15-1/3T	1/3T
3/7T		

RdM4T/38DI 10.14-RdM4T/DM   12.14-4RdMT/DM   7.18-4RdMT/2DM

1/4T	1/4T	1/4T	1/4T
6/4T	6/4T	6/4T	6/4T
	5/4T	5/4T	5/4T

RdM5&6T/37DI   9.14-1RdMT/37DI   6.18-5RdMT/74DI

2/5T	2/5T	2/5T
1/6T	5/2T	6/5T
4/6T	4/6T	11/5T
	2/2T	

RdMT5&6T/37DI   12.14-6RdMT 6.18-6RdMT/58DI 10.18-6RdMT/169DI

1/6T	5/6T	5/6T	5/6T
4/6T	7/6T	7/6T	7/6T
	11/6T	11/6T	11/6T

1RdMZT/DM 9.14- RdMTMOcc/DM   10.14-RdMT/DM   12.14-7RdMT/DM

5/4T	1/5T	1/5T	3/6T 1/16-1/6T
			8.18-8/7T
1/5T	4/7T	4/7T	4/7T 1.16-3/6T
4/7T	5/4T	2/2T	2/2T 1.18-1/2T
			10.18-10/7T
Two Z bns never arrived			

2 RdMZT   9.14-RdMTMOr

1/2T	1/2T
4/2T	4/2T
3/6T	3/6T
3/2Z	3/2Z

8 RdMT/38DI   10.14-8RdMT/42DI   7.15-8RdMT/38DI   9.18-8RdMT/56DI

4/8T	4/8T	4/8T 11.15-3/8T	4/8T
5/8T	5/8T	5/8T	5/8T
	4.15-2/8T	2/8T	2/8T

9RdMT- *see* RdM1&9T

10RdMT/52 DI   11RdMT/58DI   12RdMT/68DI   13RdMT   14RdMT/129DI
1.18-   2.18-   .18-??   see RMMxMaroc   10.18-

11/2T	4/7T	206RI	3/5T	16/2T
3/3T	9/7T		4/9T	15/6T
11/3T	11/7T		11/9T	16/6T

15RdMT   16RdMT[see above]   17RdMT/166DI   21RdMT/8DI
.18-   .18-   10.18-   .18-

15/7T		15/1T	12/5T	
Bn 218RI		16/1T	17/5T	
Bn 218RI		15/9T	16/9T	

1RdMCI   12.14-RdMTM/153DI   2.18-1RdMTM

III Bn	I 4.16-V 5.17-III	III
IV Bn	II 4.16-VI 5.17-VIII	VII 11.18-VI
V Bn	III 4.16-VII	VIII 11.18-IX
V Bn	.15-IV 8.16-nil 6.17-II	

2 RdMCI -12.14   2 RdMTM/2DM 2.18-

I Bn		I
II Bn		II
		III

Palestine /Syria

5.17-7/1T			
5.17-9/1T	6.18-9/2T		
5.17-5/115RIT			
5.17-esc/1RS	2.18-13/8T	6.18-RMOrient	

Battalions 'Etapes'

5/1T   Macedonia
8/8T   Danube
7/5T   ??

Zouaves 1914: Regiments And Battalions

Regiment 1914	Battalion	Regiment On Mobilisation	Location	Brigade & Division
1 RZ, Alger	1 Bn	RMZ	Western Morocco	1BM/DM
	2 Bn	RMZ	Western Morocco	3BM
	3 Bn	RMZ	Western Morocco	3BM
	4 Bn	RM1Z		75BI/38DI
	5 Bn	RM1Z	France/depot	75BI/38DI
	6 Bn	RM1Z		89BI/45DI
	11 Bn	RM1Z	France/reserve	75BI/38DI
	14 Bn	1RMZ	Formed 8.14	89BM/45DI
2 RZ, Oran	1 Bn	RM2Z		73BI/37DI
	2 Bn	RMMx	Eastern Morocco	3BM
	3 Bn	RMZ	Eastern Morocco	1BM/DM
	4 Bn	RM2Z		90BI/45DI
	5 Bn	RM2Z	France/depot	73BI/37DI
	11 Bn	RM2Z	France/reserve	73BI/37DI
	12 Bn	RM2Z	reserve	90BI/45DI
	14 Bn	RM2Z	Formed 8.14	90BI/45DI
3 RZ, Constantine	1 Bn	RM3Z		74BI/37DI
	2 Bn	RMZ	Western Morocco	1BM/DM
	3 Bn	RM3Z		89BI/45DI
	4 Bn	RMZ	Western Morocco	1BM/DM
	5 Bn	RM3Z	France/depot	74BI/37DI
	6 Bn	RM3Z		89BI/45DI
	11 Bn	RM3Z	France/reserve	74BI/37DI
	12 Bn	RM3Z	reserve	89BI/45DI
4 RZ, Tunis	1 Bn	RMZ	Western Morocco	3BM
	2 Bn	RmxMaroc Or		6 Army
	3 Bn	RM4Z		76BI/38DI
	4 Bn	RM4Z		76BI/38DI
	5 Bn	RM4Z	France/depot	76DI/38DI
	6 Bn	RM1Z	Western Morocco	89BI/45DI
	7 Bn	RmxMaroc Occ		
	11 Bn	RM4Z	France/reserve	76BI/38DI

Zouave Battalions 1914-1918

Battalion	Regt/Div 8.14	Later regiments	Later divisions	Disbanded
1/1Z	RMZ/DM	10.14-8RMZ	DM	
2/1Z	RMZ/3BM	12.14-9RMZ	9.14-37DI	
		4.15-9RMZ	4.15-153DI	
3/1Z	RMZ/3BM	12.14-9RMZ	9.14-37DI	
			4.15-153DI	
4/1Z	RM1Z/38DI	12.14-1RMZ	7.15-25DI	
			12.16-48DI	
5/1Z	RM1Z/38DI	12.14-1RMZ	7.15-25DI	

			12.16-48DI	
6/1Z	RM1BisZ/45DI	12.14-7RMZ 7.15-3RMZT		D 4.18
11/1Z	RMIZ/38DI	12.14-1RMZ	7.15-25DI 12.16-48DI	
14/1Z	RM1BisZ/45DI	12.14-7RMZ 7.15-3RMZT		D 4.18
1/2Z	RM2Z/37DI	3.15-2RMZ		
2/2Z	RMZT/RMMx/ 3BM	12.14-1RMZT	9.14-37DI 4.15-153DI	D 7.18 elements to 7/7T
3/2Z	RMZMOcc/DM	9,14-2RNZT 10.14-8RMZ		
4/2Z	RM2BisZ/45DI	12.14-3RMZ 1.15-2bisRMZ	10.15-AO	
5/2Z	RM2Z/37DI	3.15-2RMZ		
11/2Z	RM2Z/37DI	3.15-2RMZ		
12/2Z	RM2Z/45DI	12.14-3RMZ 1.15-2bisRMZ	10.15-AO	
14/2Z	RM2Z/45DI	12.14-3RMZ 1.15-2bisRMZ	10.15-AO	
1/3Z	RM3Z/37DI	4.15-3RMZ		
2/3Z	RMZ/DM	10.14-8RMZ		
3/3Z	RM3Z/45DI	12.14-5RMZ 1.15-3bisRMZ		

* lettered battalions to be added at later stage

REGIMENTS DE TIRAILLEURS ALGERIENS 1914: REGIMENTS & BATTALIONS

Regiment 1914	Battalion	Regiment On Mobilisation	Location	Brigade & Division
1 RTA, Blide	1 Bn	1 TM		75BI/38DI
	2 Bn	2 RMT		09BI/45DI
	3 Bn		Morocco-Fez	
2 RTA, Mostaganem	1 Bn	RMTMOcc or 2RMxZT		2BM/DM
	2 Bn	2 RMZT		73BI/37DI
	3 Bn		Eastern Morocco	
	4 Bn		Eastern Morocco	
	5 Bn	2 RMZT		73BI/37DI
	6 Bn	2 RMT		90BI/45DI
3 RTA, Bone	1 Bn	RMZ&T/1RMZT	Western Morocco	3BM
	2 Bn	RM3T		74BI/37DI
	3 Bn	RM Mx Maroc	Western Morocco	4BM
	4 Bn	RM3T		74BI/37DI
	5 Bn	RM3T		75BI/37DI
4 RTA, Sousse	1 Bn	RM4T		76BI/38DI
	2 Bn	RMT		4 BM
	3 Bn		Western Morocco	
	4 Bn	RMTMOrient	Western Morocco	2BM/DM
	5 Bn	RMTMOccidental	Western Morocco	2BM/DM
	6 Bn	4TM		76BI/38DI
5 RTA, Dellys	1 Bn	RMTMOcc Or 1RMxZT	Western Morocco	2BM/DM
	2 Bn	5TM		73BI/37DI
	3 Bn		Western Morocco	
6 RTA, Tclemen	1 Bn	RM6T		73BI/37DI
	2 Bn		Eastern Morocco	
	3 Bn	RMTMOrient/ 2RMZT	Eastern Morocco	2BM/DM
	4 Bn	RM6T		73BI/37DI
7 RTA, Constantine	1 Bn	RMZ&T	Western Morocco	3BM
	2 Bn	Tunisia-1914/19		
	M	1.18-10RMT	1.18-52DI	
8 RTA, Bizerte	1 Bn	RMT	Western Morcoo	4BM
	2 Bn	2RMT/RM2T		90BI/45DI
	3 Bn		Eastern Morocco	
	4 Bn	8TM		76BI/38DI
	5 Bn	8TM		76BI/38DI
	6 Bn	RMT	Western Morocco	4BM
9 RTA, Meliana	1 Bn	RMMixteMaroc 2MZT	Western Morocco	4BM
	2 Bn	1TM		75BI/38DI
	3 Bn	1TM		75BI/38DI

Tirailleurs Battalions 1914-1918

Regiment 1914	Battalion	Regiment On Mobilisation	Location	Brigade & Division
1/1T	1TM/38DI	12.14-3RMT 3.15-9RMT 4.15-1RMT	4.15-45DI	
2/1T	2RMT/45DI			
3/1T	Morocco	9.15-1RMT	9.15-45DI	
4/1T ???				
5/1T	Formed ??	9.16-	9.16-Macedonia	
6/1T	Formed ??	-		
7/1T	Formed 1917??		Palestine	
9/1T	Formed 1917		Palestine	
11/1T	Formed 1.18	1RMT	45DI	
15/1T	Formed 10.18	17RMT		
16/1T	Formed 10.18	17RMT		
1/2T	2 RMZT	9.14-RMTMOr 10.14-RMT 12.14-7RMT	DM	D 10.18
2/2T	2TM/37DI	9.14-1RMT 4.15-2RMT	4.15-153DI	
3/2T	Algeria	4.17-2RMT	4.17-48DI	
4/2T	2RMZT	9.14-RMTMOr 10.14 reorganised into 2/2T	DM	
5/2T	2TM/37DI	9.14-1RMT 3.15-2RMZT	3.15-48DI	
6/2T	2RMT/45DI	12.14-2RTM	12.14-37DI	
7/2T	Formed ??			
8/2T	Formed ??			
9/2T	formed		Palestine	
11/2T	Formed 1.18	1.18-10RMT	1.18-52DI	
16/2T	Formed 9.18	14RMT		
1/3T	RMZT/3BM	12.14-1RMZT	4.15-153DI-7.18	
2/3T	RM3T/37DI	4.15-3RMT		
3/3T	RMMMaroc/4BM	12.14-2RMZT 1.18-10RMT	2.15-48DI 1.18-52DI	
4/3T	RM3T/37DI	4.15-3RMT		
5/3T	RM3T/37DI	8.15-2RMZT	8.15-48DI	8.16 merged into 3/3T
6/3T	Formed ??			
7/3T	Formed ??			
11/3T	Formed 1.18	1.18-10RMT	1.18-52DI	
1/4T	4TM/38DI	12.14-4RMT	7.18-2DM	
2/4T	RMT/4BM		6.15-Morocco	
3/4T	Morocco	7.15-3RMZT	7.15-45DI	D 4.18
4/4T	Morocco –11.18			
5/4T	1 RMTM/DM	9.14-RMMOcc 12.14-4RMT	12.14-38DI 7.18-2DM	

6/4T	4TM/38DI	12.14-4RMT	12.14-38DI	
			7.18-2DM	
7-11/4T	Formed ????			
1/5T	1 RMTM/DM	9.14-RMMOcc	12.14- DM	
		12.14-7RMT	1.16-37DI	
		1.16-1RMT	12.16-45DI	
		1.18-5RMT	1.18-17DI	
2/5T	5TM/37DI	9.14-1RMT	2.15-48DI	
		2.15-2RMZT	9.15-Morocco	
3/5T	Morocco	9.15-2RMZT	9.15-48DI	
		6.18-13RMT		
4/5T	Formed ???			
5/5T	Formed ???			
6/5T	Formed 1.18	1.18-5RMT	1.18-17DI	
7/5T	Formed .18	.18-Etapes		
11/5T	Formed 1.18	1.18-5RMT	1.18-17DI	
12/5T	Formed 11.18	21RMT		
17/5T	Formed 11.18	21RMT		
1/6T	6TM/37DI	9.14 absorbed into 4/6T		
2/6T	Morocco-11.18	10.14-RMT		
		12.14-7RMT		
3/6T	2 RMTM/DM	9.14-RMMOr		
4/6T	6TM/37DI	9.14-1RMZ	3.15-?	
		3.15-??		
5/6T	Formed 1914	12.14-6RMT	1.18-45DI	
			6.18-58DI	
			10.18-169DI	
6/6T	Formed 1.18?	1.18-7RMT	1.18-DM	D 8.18
7/6T	Formed 12.14	6RMT	45DI	
			6.18-58DI	
			10.18-169DI	
11/6T	Formed 12.14	6RMT	45DI	
			6.18-58DI	
			10.18-169DI	
15/6T	Formed 9.18	14RMT		
16/6T	Formed 9.18	14RMT		
1/7T	RMZT/3BM	12.14-1RMZT	12.14-37DI	
			4.15-153DI	
			9.18-72DI	
2/7T	Tunisia –11.18			
3/7T	RM3T/37DI	4.15-1RMZT	4.15-153DI	
			9.18-72DI	
4/7T	1RMZT/DM	9.14-RMMOcc	1.18-58DI	
		10.14-RMT		
		12.14-7RMT		
		1.18-11RMT		
5/7T	Formed ??			
6/7T	Formed ??			
7/7T	Formed 7.18	7.18-1RMZT	7.18-153DI	

			9.18-72DI
8/7T	Formed 8.18	8.18-7RMT	8.18-DM
9/7T	Formed 1.18	1.18-11RMT	1.18-58DI
10/7T	Formed 10.18	10.18-7RMT	10.18-DM
11/7T	Formed 1.18	1.18-11RMT	1.18-58DI
12/7T	Formed 11.18	15RMT	
14/7T	Formed 11.18	15RMT	
15/7T	Formed 11.18	15RMT	
1/8T	RMT/4BM	6.15-4RMZT	4.15-152DI
2/8T	2RMT/45DI	12.14-8RMT	12.14-38DI
			9.18-56DI
3/8T	Morocco-11.18	[8RMT 11.15-2.16]	
4/8T	8TM/38DI		[det Morocco 4.15-2.16]
			9.18-156DI
5/8T	8TM/38DI		9.18-156DI
6/8T	RMT/4BM	6.15-4RMZT	4.15-152DI
7/8T	Formed 4.18	4 RMZT	152DI
8/8T	Formed ??		
9/8T	Formed .18		.18-Danube
13/8T	Formed 1918		Palestine
1/9T	RMMM/4BM	12.14-2RMZT	3.15-45DI
		3.15-1RMT	
2/9T	1TM/38DI		12.16-48DI
			9.18-25DI
3/9T	1TM/38DI		12.16-48DI
			9.18-25DI
4/9T	Formed 6.18	6.18-13RMT	6.18-48DI
11/9T	Formed .14?	2RMZT	3.15-38DI
		6.18-13RMT	1.18-48DI
15/9T	Formed 10.18	17RMT	
16/9T	Formed 10.18	17RMT	

ARTILLERY REGIMENTS

SUMMARY OF FRENCH ARTILLERY REGIMENTS, 1914-1918

2nd August 1914
62 Regiments d'Artillerie de Campagne
    1-62 RAC
2 Regiments d'Artillerie de Montagne
    1-2 RAM
3 Regiments d'Artillerie Coloniale
    1-3 RACC
10 Groups d'Artillerie à Cheval
    Gps from 4, 8, 13, 14, 30, 33, 40, 42, 54 and 61 RAC's
5 Regiments d'Artillerie Lourde de Campagne
    1-5 RAL
9 Regiments d'Artillerie à Pied
    1, 3, 5, 6, 7, 8, 9, 10, 11 RAP
2 Groupes d'Artillerie à Pied
    7, 8 GAP

11th November 1918
105 RA de Campagne Hippomobiles
33 RA de Campagne Portees
    1-62 RAC
    201-276 RAC
    1-3, 21-23, 41-43 RACC
3 RA de Montagne
    1-3 RAM
6 Groupes d'Artillerie à Cheval
    Gps from 8, 13, 40, 42, 51 and 61 RACs
64 RAL Hippomobiles
    1-5 RAL
    101-118, 120-21 RAL
    130-142 RAL
    301-338 RAL
20 RAL à Tracteurs
    81-90 RALT
    RALT   [from above?]
3 RALGP   [GP is grand Puissance]
5 RALFV   [FV is ferre voie –railway]
    71-78 RALGP/RALFV
5 RA de Tranchees
    ?175-179? RAT
13 RA a Pied
    1, 3, 5, 6. 7, 8, 10, 151, 154, 156, 158, 161, 163 RAP
6 RA Antiaeriens
    63RAC(AA) plus four others -64-67??
9 regiments et 7 groupements d'Artillerie d'Assaut [ie tanks]
plus several North African groupes.

NB uncertain as to whether totals apply to French Army as a whole or just the Western Front. All army group, army and some corps artillery were grouped into the Réserve Général d'Artillerie Lourde under Général Buat in February 1917. This GQG organisation was retitled Réserve Général d'Artillerie in 1.18. This meant that French artillery was distributed between three levels of command-RGA, CA and DI. RGAL/RGA divided into 5 divisions, for administrative and training purposes:

1st Division 2.17- RALGP/RALFV
2nd Division 2.17- RALT
3rd Division 2.17- naval batteries
4th Division 1.18- RAL Hippomobiles and RAT's
5th Division 1.18- RAC Portee-formed 6.17 -by 11.18 up from 27 to 35 regiments

REGIMENTS D'ARTILLERIE DE CAMPAGNE 1914-1918

1 RAC, Bourges

Gps 1-3	16DI	
Gp 4	58DI	4.17-248RAC
Gp 5	2.15-17DIC	4.17-201RAC
Gp 6	no information	

2 RAC, Grenoble

Gps 1-3	27DI	
Gp 4	64DI	4.17-202RAC
Gp 5	74DI	4.17-254RAC
Gp 6	11.15-64DI	4.17-202RAC

3RAC, Castres

Gps1-3	32DI	
Gp 4	66DI 10.14-58DI	4.17-248RAC
Gp 5	4.15-153DI-4.15 1.16-151DI	4.17-28RAC
Gp 6	1.16-156DI	4.17-242RAC

4RAC, Remiremont

Gps 1-3	41DI	
Gp 4	71DI	4.17-262RAC
Gp 5	9.14-Bty/132DI	4.17-257RAC
Gp 6	1.17-168DI	4.17-283RAC

5RAC, Besançon

Gps 1-4	VII CA 6.15-2gps/121DI	4.17-205RAC
	3.16-2gps/133DI	4.17-265RAC
		4.17-2 gps reformed as 5RAC in 48DI
Gp 5	57DI	4.17-204RAC
Gp 6	57DI	4.17-204RAC
Bty	70 DI	4.17-208RAC
Gp 7?	12.16-153DI	4.17-260RAC

6RAC, Vallances

Gps 1-4	XIV CA	4.17-206RAC
	4.15-2 gps/154DI	4.17-266RAC
	1.17-1gp/166DI	4.17-234RAC
	4.17- 2 gps reformed as 6RAC in 77DI	
Gp 5	44DI 9.14-76DI	4.17-274RAC
Gp 6	44DI 9.14-77DI	4.17-206RAC
Gp 7?	11.15-122DI	4.17-241RAC

7RAC, Rennes

Gps 1-3	19DI	
Gp 4	60DI	4.17-207RAC
Gp 5	1.17-11DIC	4.17-21RAC
Gp 6	no information	

8RAC, Nancy

Gps 1-3	11DI

Gp 4	70DI			4.17-208RAC
Gp 5		2.15-17DIC		4.17-201RAC
Gp 6	no information			

9 RAC, Castres

Gps 1-4	XVI CA	1.18 3rd gp reformed	
	7.15-2 gps/16DIC	4.17-209RAC	
	11.16-1gp/161DI	4.17-267RAC	
Gp 5	66DI	1.15-47DI 4.17-256RAC	
Gp 6		1.15-47DI 4.17-256RAC	
Bty	44DI	9.14-77DI 4.17-6RAC	

10RAC, Rennes

Gps 1-3	20DI			
Gp 4	60DI		4.17-207RAC	
Gp 5	4.15-151DI	4.15-87DI	12.15-81DI	4.17-270RAC
Gp 6	no information			

11RAC, Rouen

Gps 1-4	III CA	11.17 3rd gp reformed	
	7.15-2 gps/130DI	4.17-211RAC	
Gp 5	53DI	4.17-243RAC	
Bty	72DI	4.17-249RAC	
Gp 6	no information		

12RAC, Bruyères

Gps 1-3	43DI		
Gp 4	73DI		4.17-239RAC
Gp 5		7.16-152DI	4.17-249RAC
Gp 6	no information		

13RAC, Paris

Gps 1-3	10DI	
Gp 4	55DI	4.17-230RAC
Gps 5-6	no information	

14RAC, Tarbes

Gps 1-3	36DI		
Gp 4	68DI	9.14-64DI	4.17-202RAC
Gp 5		8.15-74DI	4.17-254RAC
Gp 6	no information		

15RAC, Douai

Gps 1-3	1DI		
Gp 4	51DI		4.17-215RAC
Gp 5/6		1.15-2 gps/48DI	4.17-5RAC
Gp 7		3.15-155DI 4.15-157DI	4.17-236RAC
Bty		4.15-47DI	4.17-256RAC
Gp 8		f.1.16-45DI	7.17-275RAC

16RAC, Issoire

Gps 1-3	26DI	
Gp 4	63DI	4.17-216RAC
Gps 5/6	no information	

17RAC, La Fère
Gps 1-3	3DI		
Gp 4	52DI		4.17-217RAC
Gp 5		3.15-156DI	4.17-242RAC
Gp 6		1.17-169DI	4.17-210RAC

18RAC, Agen
Gps 1-3	33DI		
Gp 4	67DI		4.17-218RAC
Gp 5		12.15-126DI-6.16	
Gp 6	no information		

19RAC, Nîmes
Gps 1-3	30DI		
Gp 4	75DI to10.14	1.15-48DI	4.17-5RAC
Gp 5		8.15-158DI	4.17-219RAC
Gp 6	no information		

20RAC, Poitiers
Gps 1-3	17DI		
Gp 4	59DI		4.17-220RAC
Gp 5		4.15-151DI 4.15-99/102?? 12.16-165DI	4.17-235RAC
Gp 6		1.17-170DI	4.17-259RAC

21RAC, Angoulême
Gps 1-3	23DI		
Gp 4	62DI		4.17-221RAC
Bty		1.15-47DI	7.17-256RAC
Gp 5		1.16-128DI	4.17-252RAC
Gp 6	no information		

22RAC, Versaille
Gps 1-3	6DI		
Gp 4	53DI		4.17-243RAC
Gp 5	9.14-132DI		4.17-257RAC
Gp 6	no information		

23RAC, Toulouse
Gps 1-3	34DI		
Gp 4	67DI		4.17-218RAC
Gp 5/6		8.16-134DI	4.17-223RAC

24RAC, La Rochelle
Gps 1-4	35DI		
Gp 5	68DI		4.17-224RAC
Gp 6		4.15-153DI 4.15-73DI 10.16-129DI	4.17-231RAC
Gp 7		f12.15-123DI -6.16 11.16-164DI	4.17-232RAC

25RAC, Châlons
Gps 1-3	12DI		
Gp 4	56DI		4.17-225RAC
Gp 5		3.15-156DI	4.17-242RAC
Gp 6?		6.15-17DIC- 1.16	

26RAC, Le Mans

Gps 1-3	7DI		
Gp 4	54DI	10.14-65DI	4.17-255RAC
Gp 5		2.16-15DIC	4.17-22RAC
Gp 6		7.16-66DI	4.17-240RAC

27RAC, St Omer

Gps 1-3	2DI		
Gp 4	51DI		4.17-215RAC
Gp 5		3.16-46DI	4.17-227RAC
Gp 6	no information		

28RAC, Vannes

Gps 1-4	XI CA		4.17-228RAC
		4.15-2 gps/151DI	4.17-218RAC
Gp 5	61DI		4.17-251RAC
Gp 6	69DI		4.17-268RAC
Gp		7.16-130DI	4.17-211RAC
Gp		11.16-162DI	4.17-263RAC

29RAC, Laon

Gps 1-4	II CA	11.17-3rd gp reformed	
5.15-2 gps/10DIC		4.17-229RAC	
Gp 5	52DI		4.17-217RAC
Bty	69DI	6.16-46DI	4.17-227RAC
2 Btys	12.14-DM		4.17-5 RACd'A
Gp		3.16-133DI	4.17-256RAC
Gp		11.16-165DI	4.17-235RAC

30RAC, Orléans

Gps 1-3	9DI		
Gp 4	55DI		4.17-230RAC
Gp 5		3.15-154DI-4.15	
Gp 6		1.16-121DI	4.17-205RAC

31RAC, Le Mans

Gps 1-3	8DI		
Gp 4	54DI to 11.14	6.15-129DI	4.17-231RAC
Gp 5		4.15-151DI-4.15 12.16-167DI	4.17-224RAC
Gp 6	no information		

32RAC, Orléans

Gps 1-3	38DI		
Gp 4	56DI		4.17-225RAC
Gp 5		3.16-46 DI 11.16-164DI	4.17-227RAC
Gp 6?		11.16-163DI	4.17-264RAC
Gp		11.16-164DI	4.17-232RAC
Gp		1.17-169DI	4.17-210RAC

33RAC, Angers

Gps 1-3	18DI		
Gp 4	59DI		4.17-220RAC

Gp 5   4.15-153DI/152DI   6.15-124DI   4.17-44RAC
Ex Gp Ch   1.17-168DI   4.17-233RAC

34RAC, Perigneux
Gps 1-3   24DI
Gp 4   62DI   4.17-221RAC
Gp 5   11.15-154DI   4.17-266RAC
Gp 6   1.17-66DI   4.17-234RAC
Gp 7   1.17-127DI   4.17-237RAC

35RAC, Vannes
Gps 1-3   22DI
Gp 4   61DI   4.17-251RAC
Gp 5   8.15-158DI   4.17-219RAC
Gp 6   1.16-125DI   4.17-245RAC

36RAC, Clermont Ferrand
Gps 1-3   25DI
Gp 4   63DI   4.17-216RAC
Gp 5   3.15-155 DI   4.17-236RAC
Gp 6?   1.17-169DI   4.17-210RAC

37RAC, Bourges
Gps 1-4   VIII CA   11.17-3rd gp reformed
6.15 2gps/127DI   4.17-237RAC
Gp 5   58DI   10.14-66DI   4.17-240RAC
Gp 6   1.17-168DI   4.17-233RAC
Bty   73DI   4.17-239RAC

38RAC, Nîmes
Gps 1-4   XV CA   4.18-238RAC
6.15-3 gps/126DI   4.17-38RAC
                                        6.15-1 gp/123DI   4.17-58RAC
Gp 5   11.14-75DI
Gp 6   44DI   9.14-77DI   4.17-6RAC
Gp   6.15-15DIC   4.17-22RAC
Gp   11.16-164DI   4.17-232RAC

39RAC, Toul
Gps 1-3   39DI
Gp 4   73DI   4.17-239RAC
Gp 5   no information
Gp 6   no information

40RAC, St Mihiel
Gps 1-3   40DI
Gp 4   56DI   4.17-225RAC
Gp 5   7.16-66DI   4.17-240RAC
Gp 6   no information

41RAC, Douai
Gps 1-4   I CA   11.17 3rd gp reformed

		6.15 2 gps/122DI	4.17-241RAC
Gp 5	51DI		4.17-215RAC
Gp 6		4.15-154DI	4.17-266RAc
Bty	72DI		4.17-241RAC

42RAC, Stenay

Gps 1-3	4DI		
Gp 4	52DI		4.17-215RAC
Gp 5		3.16-16DIC	4.17-209RAC
Gp 6	no information		

43RAC, Caen

Gps 1-3	5DI			
Gp 4	53DI			4.17-243RAC
Gp 5	4.15-151DI	4.15-87DI	12.15-81DI	4.17-270RAC
Gp 6	no information			

44RAC, Le Mans

Gps 1-4	IV CA	11.16-163DI		4.17-244RAC
6.15-2 gps/124DI		4.17-44RAC		
		6.15-1 gp/129DI		4.17-231RAC
Gp 5	54DI -10.14			
Bty	69DI	6.16-Gp/46RAC		4.17-268RAC

45RAC, Orléans

Gps 1-4	V CA	11.17-3rd gp reformed	
		6.15-2 gps/125DI	4.17-245RAC
Gp 5		12.16-167DI	4.17-222RAC
Gp 6	55DI		4.17-230RAC
Bty	72DI		4.17-261RAC

46RAC, Châlons

Gps 1-4	VI CA		4.17-246RAC	
Gp 5	69DI			4.17-268RAC
Gp 6		1.17-166DI	4.17-234RAC	

47RAC, Hericourt

Gps 1-3	14DI		
Gp 4	57DI		4.17-204RAC
Gp 5		3.15-156DI 1.17-17DIC	4.17-222RAC
Gp 6	no information		

48RAC, Dijon

Gps 1-3	15DI		
Gp 4	58DI		4.17-248RAC
Bty		9.14-132DI	4.17-257RAC
Gp 5		12.16-167DI	4.17-222RAC
Gp 6	no information		

49RAC, Poitiers

Gps 1-4	IX CA	1.18 3rd gp reformed	
4.15 2gps/152DI		4.17-249RAC	
Gp 5	59DI		4.17-220RAC

Bty	73DI		4.17-239RAC
Bty		4.15-47DI	7.17-256RAC
Gp		7.16-120DI	4.17-53RAC

50RAC, Rennes
Gps 1-4	X CA		4.17-250RAC
7.15 2 gps/131DI		4.17-50RAC	
Gp 5	60DI		4.17-207RAC
Gp 6		9.14-3DIC	4.17-2RACC
Gp		2.16-131DI	4.17-50RAC

51RAC, Nantes
Gps 1-3	21DI		
Gp 4	61DI		4.17-251RAC
Gp 5		4.15-153/102/106 11.16-165DI	4.17-235RAC
Gp 6		1.16-154DI	4.17-266RAC

52RAC, Angoulême
Gps 1-4	XII CA	9.18-ICAC	
		6.15 2gps/128DI	4.17-252RAC
Gp 5	62DI		4.17-221RAC
Gp 6		9.15-158 DI	4.17-219RAC
Gp		8.16-45DI -1.17	
Gp		8.14-45DI –4.15d	

53RAC, Clermont Ferrand
Gps 1-4	XIIICA		4.17-253RAC
	2.15 1 gp/62DI		4.17-221RAC
		6.15-2 gps/120DI	4.17-53RAC
		11.16-2gps/162DI	4.17-263RAC
Gp 5	63DI		4.17-216RAC
Bty	44DI	9.14-76DI	4.17-274RAC
Gp 6	no information		

54RAC, Santhony
Gps 1-3	28DI		
Gp 4	74DI		4.17-254RAC
Gps 5/6	no information		

55RAC, Orange
Gps 1-3	29DI			
Gp 4	65DI		4.17-255RAC	
Gp 5		3.15-155DI	4.15-157DI	11.16-46DI	4.17-227RAC
Gp 6?		1.16-65DI	4.17-255RAC	

56RAC, Montpellier
Gps 1-3	31DI		
Gp 4	66DI		4.17-47DIRAC
Gps 5/6	no information		

57RAC, Toulouse
Gps 1-4	XVII CA	1.18 3rd gp reformed	
	11.16 2 gps/161DI	4.17-267RAC	

		1.17 1 gp/17DIC	4.17-21RAC
Gp 5	67DI		4.17-218RAC
Bty	44DI	9.14-76DI	4.17-274RAC
Bty	73DI		4.17-239RAC

58RAC, Bordeaux

Gps 1-3	XVIII CA		4.17-258RAC
		6.15-2 gps/123DI	4.17-58RAC
		1.16-2 gps/DM	4.17-5Gpd'Af
Gp 4	68DI		4.17-224RAC
Bty	44DI	9.14-77DI	4.17-6RAC
Gp 5?		8.15-45DI	7.17-245RAC
Gp 6	no information		

59RAC, Chaumont

Gps 1-4	XXI CA		4.17-212RAC
		1.17-2gps/170DI	4.17-259RAC
Gp 5	72DI		4.17-261RAC
Bty	70DI		4.17-208RAC
Gp 6	no information		

60RAC, Troyes

Gps 1-4	XX CA	11.17 3rd gp reformed	
		8.15-2 gps/153DI	4.17-260RAC
Gp 5	70DI		4.17-208RAC
Gp 6	70DI		4.17-208RAC

61RAC, Verdun

Gps 1-3	42DI		
Gp 4	72DI		4.17-261RAC
Gps 5/6	no information		

62RAC, Épinal

Gps 1-3	13DI		
Gp 4	71DI		4.17-262RAC
Gp 5	71DI	10.15-68DI	4.17-224RAC
Gp 6	no information		

RAC's FORMED 4.17

NUMBER	FORMED FROM		FOLLOWING GROUPS	DIVISION/CORPS	FATE
201	5/1	5/8	G/47	17DIC	[4.18-43RACC]
202	4/2	6/2	4/14	64DI	
203	1/37	G/9	*	XXXV CA	
204	5/5	6/5	4/47	57DI	
205	3/5	4/5	6/30	121DI	
206	1/6	2/20	*	XIV CA	
207	4/7	4/10	5/50	60DI	
208	4/8	5/60	6/60	70DI	
209	3/9	4/9	5/42	16DIC	[4.18-42RACC]
210	6/17	8/32	7/36	169DI	
211	3/11	4/11	3/28?	130DI	
212	1/59	2/59	*	XXI CA	
213	N/A	N/A		was this regiment ever formed?	

214	G/3	G/30	*	XXXVIII CA	
215	4/15	4/27	5/41	51DI	
216	4/16	4/36	5/53	63DI	
217	4/17	5/29	4/42	52DI	
218	4/18	4/23	5/57	67DI	
219	6/19	5/35	6/52	158DI	
220	4/20	4/33	5/49	59DI	
221	4/21	2bies/34	1bie/52 & 4/53	62DI	
222	5/31	6/45	5/48	167DI	
223	5/23	G/38	*	134DI	
224	4/24	4/58	G/62	68DI	
225	4/25	4/32	4/40	56DI	
226	G/57	G/57	*	IV CA	
227	G/27	6/29	6/55	46DI	
228	1/28	2/28	*	XI CA	
229	6/29	7/29	G/3RACC	10DIC	[5.18-41RACC]
230	5/13	4/30	4/45	55DI	
231	5/24	4/31	3/44	129DI	
232	6/24	5/32	6/38?	164DI	
233	6/4	Ch/33	6/37	168DI	[Ch=Cheval Group]
234	8/6	5/34	5/46	166DI	
235	5/20	G/29	5/51	165DI	
236	7/15	6/36	G/36	157DI	
237	6/34	3/37	4/37	127DI	
238	G/18	G/41	*	XV CA	
239	4/12	4/39	Bies/37, 49, 52	73DI	
240	G/26	G/37	G/40	66DI	
241	7/6	6/41	7/41	122DI	
242	G/3Col	5/17	5/25	156DI	[Col=3RACC]
243	4/11	4/22	4/43	53DI	
244	4/32	1/44	2/44	163DI	
245	6/35	3/45	4/45	125DI	
246	1/46	2/46	*	VI CA	
247	G/5	1/47	*	VII CA	
248	4/1	4/3	4/48	58DI	
249	5/12	3/49	4/49	152DI	
250	1/50	2/50	*	X CA	
251	5/28	4/35	4/51	61DI	
252	3/21	3/52	4/52	128DI	
253	1/53	2/53	*	XIII CA	
254	G/2	5/14	4/54	74DI	
255	G/26	4/55	G/55	65DI [2DM]	
256	6/9	4/56	Bies/15, 21, 49	47DI	
257	1/57	2/57	Bies/4, 22,132DI		
258	1/58	2/58	*	XVIII CA	
259	6/20	3/59	4/59	170DI	
260	G/5	3/60	4/60	153DI	
261	5/59	4/61	Bies/11, 41, 45	72DI	
262	4/4	4/62	5/62	71DI	
263	4/28	3/53	4/53	162DI	
264	G/20	G/44	**	XXXIII CA	
265	8/5	9/5	G/29	133DI	
266	3/6	4/6	6/51	154DI	
267	7/9	3/57	4/57	161DI	

268	6/28	4/46	5/46	69DI	
269	G/49	G/59	G/3RACC	87DI	
270	G/10	G/43	G/58	81DI/1DCP	
271	G / 11	G / 11	*	88DI	disbanded 12.17
272	G/59	G/59	*	XXXI CA	
273	G/54	G/56	G/59	97DI/2DCP	
274	G/6	G/38	G/53	76DI	
275	G/15	G/58	G/5Gp d'Afrique	45DI	
276	three groups 5 Gp d'Afrique			DM [formed 12.17]	

* third group formed at various dates between April 1917 and April 1918
** no third group

1RAM, Grenoble

Gp 1	27DI 11.14-	11.15-122DI	4.17-241
Gp 2	28DI 11.14-	2.16-17DIC	4.17-43
Gp 3	1.15-66DI -7.15	5.16-66DI-7.16	
Gp 4	64/DI/74DI –9.14	1.15-66DI –7.15	5.16-66DI-7.16
Gp 5	64DI/74DI -9.14	10.15-57DI	
Gp 6	10.15-57DI –1.18		

2 RAM, Nice

Gp 1	27DI 11.14-		12.16-30DI	
Gp 2	28DI 111.4-			
Gp 3	2.15-17DIC	6.15-	10.15-156DI	
Gp 4	65DI 8.14-		3.16-46DI	1.17-11DIC
Gp 5	65DI 8.14-		1.16-47DI -7.16	1.17-76DI
Gp 6	75DI –11.14			

11.16 Bty/1RAM & 2 btys/2RAM to 16DIC -1.18 to Gp/2RAM

One source indicates the existence of 3RAM in 1918 bu no information has been found to confirm this.

1 RACC, Lorient
    2DIC
    & gp/11DIC 1-4.17 [to 21RACC]

2 RACC, Cherbourg
    3DIC 9.14- 2.15-76DI -12.16
    & gp/2 DIC 12.14-

3 RACC, Toulon
    6.15-CAC/1CAC
    5.15 gp/10DIC   4.17-229RAC
    6.15-15DIC   4.17-22RACC

21 RACC formed from groups 7RAC, 57RAC and 1RACC
                      4.17-11 DIC
22 RACC formed from groups 26RAC, 38RAC and 3RACC
                      4.17- 3 DIC
23 RACC formed from two groups 3RACC and a new group in 1.18
                      3.16-II CAC 1918

41 RACC	see 229 RAC
42 RACC	see 209 RAC
43 RACC	see 201 RAC

1 Group d'Artillerie du Campagne d'Afrique, Alger   to 37DI
2 GACA, Oran   to 37DI
3 GACA, Constantine
4 GACA, Bizerte   to DM
5 GACA, La Monouba   to 45DI later DM 4.17=276RAC

GROUPES D'ARTILLERIE à CHEVAL
GAC/4RAC   8DC- 8.16   to XXXIXCA
GAC/8RAC   2DC
GAC/13RAC   1DC
GAC/14RAC   10DC-6.16   bies to 2DC and 6DC
GAC/30RAC   7DC –7.17   to XXXIVCA
GAC/33RAC   9DC-6.16   to XXXIX CA and then see 233 RAC
GAC/40RAC   4DC
GAC/42RAC   3DC
GAC/54RAC   6DC
GAC/61RAC   5DC

RAC Portées formed 1.18

The following regiments have been identified. They do not constitute a single block of numbers. There might have been plans to create new regiments from several blocks of numbers. Those listed below appear to be the only regiments, which became operational by the end of the war. The list given below matches the number of such regiments listed as being in existence in November 1918, One source describes these regiments as RAL's.

301RAC	330RAC	407RAC	451RAC
303RAC	331RAC	409RAC	452RAC
304RAC	336RAC	412RAC	453RAC
305RAC	338RAC	413RAC	454RAC
306RAC	341RAC	414RAC	456RAC
308RAC	342RAC	416RAC	
309RAC	345RAC	417RAC	
310RAC		418RAC	
314RAC		420RAC	
315RAC			

HEAVY ARTILLERY 1914-1918

NB The following represents the best information, which could be obtained on heavy artillery. The French Official History [Tome X] indicated that the movements, and existence, of units of heavy artillery were too complex to be recorded. Apparently, individual armies used different methods of recording this information.

RÉGIMENTS D'ARTILLERIE LOUDRE DE CAMPAGNE

[formed in summer 1914 from batteries heavy batteries of certain RAC's]

1 RAL	Douai	[15RAC]	8.14-5th Army
2 RAL	Le Mans	[12RAC, 31RAC]	8.14-3rd Army
3 RAL	Orléans	[20RAC, 32RAC]	8.14-2nd Army
4 RAL	Paris	[???RAC]	8.14-4th Army ?
5 RAL	Valence	[2RAC]	8.14-1st Army

RÉGIMENTS D'ARTILLERIE LOURDE

[formed 1918: In each regiments, Gps 1-4 are Corps Troops; and the regiment bears the number of its Corps; eg 101RAL is part of I CA]

RAL	Gp 5	Gp 6	Gp 7	Gp 8
101	51 DI	2 DI	1 DI	162 DI
102	3 DI	4 DI	52DI	
103	5DI	6DI	1DCP	2DCP
104	7DI	8DI	124DI	163DI
105	9DI	125DI	55DI	10DI
106	12DI	56DI	127DI	166DI
107	14DI	41DI	164DI	128DI
108	15DI	16DI	58DI	169DI
109	18DI	17DI	152DI	59DI
110	19DI	20DI	60DI	131DI
111	21DI	151DI	61DI	22DI or 48DI
112	23DI	?24DI?	62DI	165DI or 1DM
113	25DI	120DI	63DI	26DI
114	28DI	27DI	154DI	129DI
115	123DI	126DI	161DI	??29/30DI's???
116	31DI	32DI	66DI	
117	34DI	33DI	37DI	38DI
118	35DI	36DI	45DI	
120	11DI	39DI	168DI	153DI
121	13DI	43DI	170DI	167DI
130	72DI	132DI	68DI	
131	64DI	2DM	46DI	47DI
132	40DI	42DI	69DI	
133	70DI or 87DI	77DI		
134	64DI	157DI	67DI	
135	53DI	121DI		
136	29DI or 30DI	133DI		
137				
138	71DI	74DI	73DI	
139				
140				
141	2DIC	3DIC		
142	10DIC	15DIC		

Régiments d'Artillerie Lourde [Tracteur]

Formed 1915-   duplicate regiments formed 10.17
81 RALT   281RALT
82 RALT   282RALT
83 RALT   283RALT
84 RALT   284RALT
85 RALT   285RALT
86 RALT   286RALT
87 RALT   287RALT
88 RALT   288RALT
89 RALT   289RALT
90 RALT   290RALT

Régiments d'Artillerie a Pied 1914

1 RAP	Maubege	7 batteries	3 batteries to 1RAL 1914
2 RAP	Querqueville	9 batteries	disbanded 1.5.14 to form 3 RAL [mainly]
3 RAP	Brest	6 batteries	4 batteries to 3RAL 1914
4 RAP	Paris	10 batteries	9 batteries to 4RAL 1914
5 RAP	Verdun	13 batteries	
6 RAP	Toul	12 batteries	
7 RAP	Nice	3 batteries plus 2 in Corsica	
8 RAP	Épinal	6 batteries	[to 1st Army]
9 RAP	Belfort	7 batteries	
10 RAP	Toulon	7 batteries	3 batteries to 4 & 5 RALs
11 RAP	Bersançon	8 batteries	

Groupes d'Artillerie a Pied 1914

6 GAAPA	Algeria	4 batteries
7 GAAPA	Tunisia	4 batteries

War Formed RAP's

68 RAP
142 RAP
151 RAP
154 RAP
156 RAP
158 RAP
161 RAP
163 RAP
182 RAP

Railway Regiments

[RALGP/RALFV] [each autonomous group had 3 batteries]

10.14-21.2.16	2.16-1.8.17	1.8.17-1.5.18	1.5-11.11.18
1 Gp de 19	1 Gp de 19	71 RALGP	71 RALGP
2 Gp de 19	2 Gp de 19	73 RALGP	73 RALGP
3 Gp de 19	4 Gp de 19	74 RALGP	74 RALGP
4 Gp de 19	7 RAP [ex 3/19]	77 RALGP	75 RALGP

1 Gp de 24	& ex 1/24	78 RALGP	76 RALGP
1 Gp de 27	3 RAP		77 RALGP
1 RAP	6 GAPA		78 RALGP
3 RAP	1 RAC		
5 RAP			
10 RAP			
6 GAPA			
7 GAPA			

REGIMENTS D'ARTILLERIE TRANCHEE

5 listed in 1918 of which four have been identified

175 RAT
176 RAT
177 RAT
178 RAT
179 RAT?

REGIMENTS D'ARTILLERIE ANTI-AERIEN

Six listed 1918 of which two have been identified. The missing numbers could be 64-67.

63 RAC [AA]
   RAC [AA]
   RAC [AA]
   RAC [AA]
   RAC [AA]
166 RAC[AA]

CAVALRY REGIMENTS & SQUADRONS 1914-1918

Regiments De Cuirassiers

1 RC	Paris	1DC –6.16		
2 RC	Paris	1DC		
3 RC	Vouziers	4DC-10.16		
4 RC	Cambrai	3DC	6.16-4RCP/1DC	1.18-1DCP

2 reserve escadron with 51DR until 11.15

5 RC	Tours	9DC	6.16-5RCP/4DC	1.18-2DCP
6 RC	Ste Menehould	4DC		
7 RC	Lyon	6DC- 6.16		
8 RC	Tours	9DC	5.16-8RCP	1.18-2DCP
9 RC	Doaui	3DC	6.16-9RCP	1.18-1DCP

2 reserve escadron with 81DT until 11.15

10 RC	Lyon	6DC- 6.16		
11RC	St Germain	7DC	6.16-11RCP/5DC	1.18-1DCP
12 RC	Rambouillet	7DC	7.17-12RCP/2DC	1.18-2DCP

Regiments Du Dragons

1 RD	Luçon	9DC	6.16-XXXIXCA, 129DI, 37DI, 59DI, 48DI

2 reserve escadron with 61DR until 11.15

2 RD	Lyon	6DC	

2 reserve escadron with 72DR and 88DT until 11.15

3 RD	Nantes	9DC	6.16-XXXCA

2 reserve escadron served with 52DR, 132DI, 97DT and 72DI until 7.17

4 RD	Commercy	2DC	

1 reserve escadron served with 73DR and 128DI until 11.15

5 RD	Compiègne	3DC	

2 reserve escadron served with 69DR until 11.15

6 RD	Vincennes	1DC	

1 reserve escadron served with 122DI 5.15-1.17

7 RD	Fontainebleu	7DC	7.17-XXXVCA

2 reserve escadron served with 155DI 3.15-and then with 123DI & 30DI to 11.15

8 RD	Lunéville	2DC	

1 reserve escadron served with 151 DI 8-11.15

9 RD	Épernay	5DC	

1 reserve escadron served with 151DI 8-11.15

10 RD	Montauban	10DC	6.16-3DC	7.17-XXXVIICA

2 reserve escadron served with 67DR, 40DI, DM and 1DCP 8.14-11.18

11 RD	Belfort	8DC	8.16-60DI & 29DI [later 71DI, 73DI, 87DI, 2DM]

2 reserve escadron served with 57DR until 10.15 then 15DIC from 7.17

12 RD	Troyes	2DC	

1 reserve escadron served with 73DR until 6.15

13 RD	Melun	7DC	7.17-IICAC & 15DIC

1 reserve escadron served with 152 DI 4-11.15

14 RD	St Étienne	6DC	

2 reserve escadron served with 63DR until 11.15

15 RD	Libourne	10DC	3.16-3DC

2 reserve escadron served with 68DR and then with 157DI 2-6.16

16 RD	Reims	5DC	

no apparent service by reserve esacdron

17 RD	Auxonne	8DC	8.16-6DC

1 reserve escadron served with 105DT 10.15-1.16

18 RD   Lure   8DC   8.16-55DI & 68DI then 128DI from 7.17
1 reserve escadron served with 87DT until 11.15 and with 45DI from 1.17
19 RD   Castres   10DC   6.16-7DC   7.17-XXXIIICA

2 reserve escadron served with 66DR then 71DR to 1.16 when disbanded
20 RD   Limoges   10DC   6.16-3DC
2 reserve escadron served with 62DR until 11.15
21 RD   Noyon   3DC
2 reserve escadron served with 52DR until 6.15
22 RD   Reims   5DC
no apparent service by reserve escadron
23 RD   Vincennes   1DC
2 reserve escadron served with 70DR until 11.15
24 RD   Rennes   9DC   6.16-XXXICA, 64DI, 65DI and later 2DM
2 reserve escadron served with 60DR until 11.15
25 RD   Angers   9DC   6.16-XXXVIICA, 22DI & 69DI
2 reserve escadron served with 59DR until 1.16; 69DI, 6-11.16;and 47DI from 6.17
26 RD   Dijon   8DC   6.16-6DC
2 reserve escadron served with 58DR and 66DR until 11.15
27 RD   Versaille   1DC
2 reserve escadron served with 53DR until 1.16 when disbanded
28 RD   Sedan   4DC
1 reserve escadron served with 102DT 5-11.15
29 RD   Provins   5DC   1.17-16DIC & 122DI
no apparent service by reserve escadron
30 RD   Sedan   4DC
no apparent service by reserve escadron
31 RD   Lunéville   2DC
no apparent service by reserve escadron
32 RD   Versaille   1DC
2 reserve escadron served with 55DR until 11.15

Regiments De Chasseurs à Cheval
1 RCh   Châteaudun   7DC -7.17
2 reserve escadron served with 54DR, then 76DR 10.14-6.16
2 RCh   Pontivy   XICA -11.15 then 151DI, 21DI and 61DI
2 reserve escadron allocated to 22DI 8.14
3 RCh   Clermont-Ferrrand   XIIICA –1.16 then 41DI and 47DI to 6.17 [also 167DI]
2 reserve escadron allocated to 25DI & 26DI 8.14; later one to 120DI
4 RCh   Épinal   XXICA –1.17 then 13DI,43DI,170DI
2 reserve escadron allocated to 13DI and 43DI 8.14-one to 81DT 11.15
5 RCh   Châlons-sur-Marne   5DC
1 reserve escadron served with 158DI 8.15-6.17
6 RCh   Lille   ICA -11.16 then 1DI and 162DI
2 reserve escadron served with 1DI and 2DI until 11.15 then 128DI
7 RCh   Évreux   IIICA –1.17 then 5DI, 6DI and 130DI [also 155DI]
2 reserve escadron served with 5DI and 6DI
8 RCh   Orléans   V CA- 2 to 125DI 11.15 and rest to 9&10DI 1.17
2 reserve escadron to 9DI & 10DI
9 RCh   Auch   XVIICA –2 to 126DI 6.15 and rest to 38DI 4.16
2 reserve escadron to 33DI and 34DI -later 89DT
10RCh   Sampigny   VICA   10.16-XXXIICA 7.17-XXXVIIICA
1 reserve escadron in 101DT 5-11.15 and 1 with 71DI from 7.17

11RCh   Vesoul   VIICA- 2 to 48DI 7.16 and 1 to 14DI 1.17
2 reserve escadron in 14DI and 41DI 8.14 –later 37DI & 74DI
12RCh   St Mihiel   VICA   to 1.17 then 12DI, 56DI and 166DI
no apparent service by reserve escadron
13RCh   Vienne   6DC
2 reserve escadrons served with 94DT and then 64DI until 3.16
14RCh   Dôle   8DC   8.16 to 52DI and 63DI [later 62DI]
reserve   escadrons   served   with   Group   Parizot   and   129DI   [later   161   &   164DI's]
15RCh   Châlons-sur-Marne   5DC
no apparent service by reserve escadrons
16RCh   Beaune   VIIICA to 1.17 then 15DI & 16DI
2 reserve escadrons with 15DI & 16DI then 73DI from 11.15 [later 51 & 169DI's]
17RCh   Lunéville   10DC   6.16-2DC
no apparent service by reserve escadrons
18RCh   Lunéville   10DC   6.16-2DC
no apparent service by reserve escadrons
19RCh   La Fère   IICA until 11.15 then 4DI, 67DI and 3DI
2 reserve escadrons served with 3DI and 4DI then 67DI from 11.15
20RCh   Vendome   7DC   2.16-XXIIICA 1.17-165DI, 40DI, 42DI and 69DI
no apparent service by reserve escadrons
21RCh   Limoges   XIICA
2 reserve escadrons served witj 23DI & 24DI to 11.15 then 58DI [later 23DI & 24DI]

Regiments d'Hussards
1 RH   Béziers   XVICA 1.17 to 31DI & 32DI
2 reserve escadrons with 31DI and 32DI until 11.15 then 132DI until 11.16
2 RH   Verdun   4DC
2 reserve escadrons with 72DR –later 157DI until 2.16
3 RH   Senlis   3DC
2 reserve escadrons with 56DR until 8.16
4 RH   Verdun   4DC
2 reserve escadrons served with 132DI 7.15-8.16 & 157DI 4.15-2.16
5 RH   Nancy   XXCA until 12.16 to 153DI, 11DI & 39DI [later 168DI]
2 reserve escadrons served with 11DI & 39DI from 8.14
6 RH   Marseille   XVCA until 8.15 when 2 esc to 122/126DI –rest to 59DI 1.16, then 129DI 6.16 and
                                            123DI 4.17
2 reserve escadrons served with 29DI & 30DI until 11.15 when to 55DI until 6.16
7 RH   Niort   IXCA
2 reserve escadrons served with 17DI and 18DI from 8.14
8 RH   Meaux   3DC
2 reserve escadrons served with 121DI 6.15- and 53DI 1.16-6.17
9 RH   Chambéry   XIVCA until 1.17 then 27, 154 & 163DI's
2 reserve escadrons served with 27DI & 28DI from 8.14
10RH   Tarbes   XVIIICA
2 reserve escadrons served with 35DI and 36DI: the 11.15-69DI, 2.16-30DI and then 35DI & 36DI from 7.17
11RH   Tarasçon   6DC
2 reserve escadrons served with 65DR, 5.16-76DI 12.16-73DI
12RH   Gray   8DC to 8.16 then 73DI & 129DI [later 67DI & 68DI]
2 reserve escadrons served with 71DR then 12.14-RMH and 1.16-71DI to 7.17
13RH   Dinan   XCA   11.15-2 esc to 131DI; others to 19 & 20DI's 1.17
2 reserve escadrons served with 19DI and 20DI from 8.14
14RH   Alençon   IVCA 11.15-2 esc to 124DI; others to 7 & 8DI 1.17 [also 163DI & 164DI]
2 reserve escadrons served with 7 DI 7 8DI until 10.14

ARMY OF AFRICA CAVALRY REGIMENTS

REGIMENTS DE CHASSEURS D'AFRIQUE [RCA]

1RCA, Morocco
8.14 merged into 1RMCA and served in France with XXXIIICA
2.15-retitled 1RCA
1.16 to BCA, Salonika
10.18-one escadron detached to 17DIC

2RCA, Morocco
8.14 merged into 1RMCA and served in France with XXXIIICA
2.15-transferred to 2RMCA
7.15-retitled 2RCA
1.16 allocated to 10DC and PC disbanded 31.1.16
8.16 two escadron allocated to 133DI until 12.17 and then to 29DI
12.16 two escadron allocated to 134DI
1.17 one escadron allocated to 157DI until 12.17
8.17 PC reformed with XXXVICA

3RCA, Constantine
8.14 to France where allocated to 2DIC
8.14-CAC
1.17-became divisional cavalry with two escadron to 2DIC and two others to 3DIC
8.17-restored as ICAC cavalry

4RCA, Tunis
8.14 to France where allocated to 44DI
10.14 to XXXIIICA
10.15 to BCA, Salonika where three escadrons allocated to divisional cavalry
–57DI, 156DI and 17DIC

5RCA, Alger
8.14 to France with 3BM, 38DI
10.14-5DC
11.14-XXXIICA
8.16- two escadron to DM & 76DI; latter to 161DI in 161DI 10.16, and then 30DI, 12.16
9.16- two escadron to Salonika
1.17- remaining escadron to 17DIC in Salonika

6RCA, Mascara
8.14 to France with 37DI
10.14-one escadron to 3RMCA, and rest to IIICA
12.14-to Fifth Army troops [later XXXVIIICA]
1.15-one escadron to 156DI, to 37DI 1.16 and 56DI 9.16 where joined by another escadron-both to Algeria 12.16-4.17; remaining two escadron to 67DI
4.17-regiment restored to full strength in France, but became divisional cavalry in
6.17 with two escadron to 38DI and the other two to 97DI

7RCA
Formed in France in 1DC 10.14 as RM de Colonel de Sazilly. Became 3RMCA 6.15 [1/6, 5/1, 5/5 Esc] in 37DI
8.15 retitled 7RCA and sent to Salonika 10.15 where disbanded 5.1.16

8RCA
2.15 formed from depot units in Algeria as RMCA and arrived in Egypt 3.15

8.15 retitled 8RMCA in 8.15 and sent to Salonika 10.15 where disbanded 10.12.17
One escadron to RMCS 1917

Regiments De Spahis [RS]

1 RS, Medea
10.14 merged with 2RS on arrival in France to form RMS
served in Artois 1914-15 and on the Aisne 1915 [higher formation not known]
11.15 demerged to form 1RS and 6RS
11.15 one escadron detached to 88DT until 7.16
.17 one escadron detached to Palestine
7.18 two escadron detached to 74DI and DM

2 RS, Sidi-bel-Abbes
10.14 merged with 1RS as RMS
11.15 demerged to form 2RS and 7RS –served as IICAC cavalry in Champagne and
Somme 1915-1916
1.17 broken up to form divisional cavalry for 10DIC and 15DIC

3 RS, Batna
8.14 to France where served in Artois 1914-1915 [higher formation not known]
8.16 one escadron detached to 83DT and then to 81DT
.16 rest of regiment to Salonika for the remainder of the war

4 RS, Sfax
8.14 to France where served with ICC in Artois 1914-1915
11.15 two escadron detached to 70DI and then, in 11.16, to 77DI –returned 10.17
1.16 became XXXIICA cavalry until 7.17

5RS, Morocco
formed 5.14 and sent to France 9.14 where fought in Picardy.
.15 returned to Morocco
.18 to France –served in battle of Noyon: two escadron detached to 2DM and 38DI

6 RS
1.16 formed from 1RMS and became divisional cavalry of 45DI [3 escadrons] until 1.18

7 RS
9.15 formed from 2RMS and became divisional cavalry of 121DI and 61DI until 7.17
1.16 PC served with XXXVCA until 7.17

Mixed Regiments

RdeM Chasseurs Indigenie à Cheval
Formed 1914 and then retitled- RdeM Spahis Marocain à Cheval
Composed on two escadron RCA [one from 4RCA and 8RCA] and two escadron RS. Served in the battle of the Marne.
Transferred to Salonika –date?

R Mx Cav [Chasseurs et Spahis]
Formed in Near East 1916 with one escadron/4RCA and one escadron/8RCA. Served with the 5th
Australian Cavalry Brigade in Palestine 1918

MECHANISED UNITS 1914-1918

Two types of armoured car were ordered in August 1914:
62 Peugeot Automitrailleus [AM]
74 Peugeot Auto-Canon   [AC]

First two sections formed 9.14 –by 2.14 Sections 1-5 each of 2AM/1AC u/c Cavalry Corps by 12.15-
I Cavalry Corps - Groups 1-3 –total of 9 sections each of 2AM/1AC = 18AM/9AC II Cavalry Corps- Groups 4-6 –same strength

Also-Motorcycle section added to Cyclist Group of each Cavalry Division in 11.14

1-17 Groups Auto-Mitrailleuse [GAM] formed 1917 and distributed as follows-
1DC- 1 7
2DC- 3 5 9 10
3DC- 2 12
4DC- 4 15
5DC- 11 13
6DC- 6 8 14 17 unlisted-16

MECHANISED ASSAULT ARTILLERY

Tank orders-   12.15-400 Schneider
                4.16-400 St Chamons
                12.16-150 Light Tanks

Organised into Artillerie Special, Artillerie d'Assaut [AS]
AS 1-20   Schneider – each of 4 batteries of 4 vehicles = 16 per AS AS 31-39
                St Chamon
AS 40-42   to AS 18-20 when re-equipped

I –IV Groupements formed April 1917 with V-VIII Groupements in May 1917

I Groupement   = 2 4 5 AS II   = 3
8 12 AS III   = 1 6 15 AS
IV   = 14 16 17 AS
V   = ???   [from 7 9 10 11 13 18 19 20 AS]
VI   = ???   [from 7 9 10 11 13 18 19 20 AS]
VII   = ???   [from 7 9 10 11 13 18 19 20 AS]
VIII   = ???   [from 7 9 10 11 13 18 19 20 AS]
IX   not formed
X   = 31 33 36 AS
XI   = 32 34 35 AS
XII   = 37 38 39 AS
XIII   = 40 41 42 AS

TANK REGIMENTS & BATTALIONS 1918

Formed	Regt de Chars	Bns de Chars Legere	Artillerie Special
2.18	501	1 2 3 BCL	301-309 AS
5.18	502	4 5 6	310-318
6.18	503	7 8 9	319-327
6.18	504	10 11 12	328-336

7.18	505	13 14 15	337-345
7.18	506	16 17 18	346-354
8.18	507	19 20 21	355-363
9.18	508	22 23 24	364-372
10.18	509	25 26 27	373-381
10.18	-	28	382-384
10.18	-	29	385-387
11.18	-	30	388-390
11.18	-	31	391-393

501 502 503 R Chars and 11 12 BCL in 6Army/10Army-2nd Marne

15 tanks per AS
45 tanks per Bn with a rear echelon of 9 spare tanks and 1 signal tank
165 tanks per regt

Total in service 11.18-2,756

ENGINEER UNIT ORGANISATION 1914

Engineer Regiments

There were eleven engineer regiments in 1914. Under the Law of 15th April 1914, the number of regiments had been increased from eight to eleven-probably to reflect the introduction of signal units, and the creation of XX and XXI Corps d'Armee on the eastern frontier.

These regiments were purely administrative –possibly to give colonels of the engineer branch a range of posts similar to colonels of infantry, cavalry and artillery.

Engineer Regiments were either functional or geographic. 5RG commanded the railway troops and 8RG commanded the signals units. The other regiments were responsible for units in particular parts of France.

Each regiment supervised a number of battalions, which were, in turn, divided into companies of various functional types. Battalions and companies were the principal *tactical* units.

Some engineer regiments provide the detachment of cyclist sappers allocated to each cavalry division.

Engineer Battalions

An engineer battalion was allocated to each Corps d'Armee/Military Region and bore the number of that CA/MR.

The Colonial Corps was serviced by a metropolitan battalion (22Bn).

Normally, engineer battalions commanded nine companies. These companies were-

1st Compagnie	divisional field company for first infantry division
2nd Compagnie	divisional field company for second infantry division
3rd Compagnie	corps field company
4th Compagnie	reserve corps field company which joined on mobilisation
13th Compagnie	divisional field company for the reserve infantry division
16th Compagnie	bridging company under corps command
19th Compagnie	reserve bridging company –under command of reserve division?
21st Compagnie	park company under corps command
24th Compagnie	reserve park company- under command of reserve division

Other companies were formed during the war and allocated some of the vacant numbers

In 1914, 64 field, 7 bridging, 15 fortress, 16 railway, 12 telegraph and 2 wireless companies were stationed in France. Another 10 field, 1 fortress, 3 railway, 2 telegraph and 1 wireless companies were in North Africa.

Each Military Region commanded a Territorial Engineer Battalion, which took the number of the MR, and, from which one company-either 1st or 3rd-was allocated to the relevant DIT.

Regiments du Genie 1914

1 Regiment, Versailles
4 Bn	VI CA	LeMans
5 Bn	V CA	Orleans
22 Bn	Col CA	Paris

2 Regiment, Montpellier
16 Bn	XVI CA	Montpellier
17 Bn	XVII CA	Toulouse
18 Bn	XVIII CA	Bordeaux

3 Regiment, Arras
1 Bn	I CA	Lille	[& 1 fortress coy at Maubege]
2 Bn	II CA	Amiens	
3 Bn	III CA	Rouen	

4 Regiment, Grenoble
8 Bn	VIII CA	Bourges
13 Bn	XIII CA	Clermont-Ferrand
14 Bn	XIV CA	Lyon [& 1 fortress coy at Briancon]

5 Regiment, Versailles
1 Rlwy Bn	4 coys
2 Rlwy Bn	4 coys
3 Rlwy Bn	4 coys
4 Rlwy Bn	4 coys

6 Regiment, Angers
9 Bn	IX CA	Tours
10 Bn	X CA	Rennes
11 Bn	XI CA	Nantes
12 Bn	XII CA	Limoges

7 Regiment, Avignon
15 Bn	XV CA	Marseille	[& 1 fortress coy at Nice]
23 Bn	4 bridging coys Alpine Defences		
24 Bn	3 bridging coys Alpine Defences		

8 Regiment, Mont Valerion et Rueil
1 Telegraph Bn- 4 coys
2 Telegraph Bn- 4 coys
3 Telegraph Bn- 4 coys
4 Telegraph Bn- 2 wireless coys

9 Regiment, Verdun

| 6 Bn | VI CA | Chalons |
| 25 Bn | | Verdun |

10 Regiment, Toul
| 20 Bn | XX CA | Nancy |
| 26 Bn | Toul | |

11 Regiment, Epinal
21 Bn	XXI CA	Epinal
27 Bn	3 coys, Epinal	
7 Indep Bn,	VIICA	Besancon
19 Indep Bn	3 field, 1 tel, 1 rlwy coy Algerie	
28 Indep Bn	1 fd & 3 fortress coys	Belfort
29 Indep Bn	1 coy Bizerte	

Engineer Battalions 1914-1918

Battalion	Corps d'Armée	Divisions
1 BG, Lille	I XXXVI	1 2 38 51 162
2 BG, Amiens	II XXXVI XXXVIII	3 4 52 122 152 169
3 BG, Rouen	III XXXIX IIICC	5 6 53 82 89 158 16DIC
4 BG, Le Mans	IV XXXII XXXV XXXVII	7 8 40 41 54 81 84 85 125
		126 129 130 158 163 15DIC
		17DIC 1DCP
5 BG, Orléans	V ICC	9 10 55 85 99 125 154 156
6 BG, Châlons	VI IICC	12 40 42 52 56 127 132 166
7 BG, Besançon	VII XXXIII XXXVII XXXVIII	14 37 41 134 10DIC 11DIC
8 BG, Bourges	VIII XXX XXXVIII	15 16 37 56 58 64 120 123
		134 16DIC
9 BG, Tours	IX XXXIII XXXIX	17 18 59 86 153 164
10 BG, Rennes	X	19 20 60 76 87 100 131 15DIC
11 BG, Nantes	XI XXXV IICC	21 22 45 61 88 103 121 125
12 BG, Limoges	XII IICAC	23 24 46 62 104 105 124
13 BG, Clermont Ferrrand	XIII XXXVII	25 26 41 63 69 74 167
14 BG, Lyon	XIV XXXI ICC	27 28 44 64 65 77 128 129
		158 16DIC 2DM
15 BG, Marseille	XV XXXI XXXII XXXVI	29 30 47 48 65 70 75 76 77
		85 121 123 124 126 151 2DM
16 BG, Montpellier	XVI XXXIV IICAC	31 32 66 90 94 96 133 134
		157 10DIC 11DIC 15DIC

17 BG, Toulouse	XVII	33 34 45 67 91 97 161 2DCP
18 BG, Bordeaux	XVIII	35 36 68 92 131
19 BG, Alger	XXXV XXXVII	37 38 1DM 1DCP
20 BG, Nancy	XX XXXIII	11 39 48 70 101 168
21 BG, Épinal	XXI IICAC	13 43 124 129 170
22 BG, Paris	ICAC	51 63 69 2DIC 3DIC 11DIC
23 BG, Alpine		30
24 BG, Alpine		29
25 BG, Verdun	XXX	72 130 132 165
26 BG, Toul		45 73 120 124 127 128 129
		1DM 15DIC
27 BG, Épinal		46 47 71 76 130
28 BG, Belfort	XXXIV	46 57 105 131 134 157
29 BG, Bizerte	XXXII	

Eastern European Units of the French Army 1914-1918

Governments on both sides attempted to employ soldiers from the 'minority' ethnic groups of the Austro-Hungarian Empire. Formed units from three nationalities served in the French Army. In addition many individuals from the nations of Eastern Europe served in the Legion Etranger.

Czecho-Slovak

In 1914, the Compagnie Nazdar was formed in France and allotted to the RMLE. This remained the only Czech unit in France until the spring of 1918 when a combination of volunteers from the USA and Russia, and prisoners of war [former German soldiers], formed the 21st Rifle Regiment. The high number allocated to this regiment reflected the hope that twenty regiments could be created in Russia, where they would combine into five divisions. [In practice only twelve were formed]. A second rifle regiment-the 22nd- became operational in the autumn of 1918, and two more - 23rd and 24th were in the process of formation when the war ended. The 21st and 22nd Rifle Regiments formed the 1st Czechoslovak Brigade which joined the 53rd Infantry Division in July 1918. They fought in the autumn battles in Champagne with this division.

Poland

The French controlled component of the Polish Army emerged in 1918 as the most substantial Eastern European element on the Western Front. Using a numbering system which-like the Czechs-applied to all units no matter where they served, the Poles planned to form two corps for operations under French command. Of these, only the 1st Rifle Division was ready for frontline service by the end of the war.

The major French-controlled formations and units were: I Corps d'Armee [Odry]
1st DI [Bernard]
1, 2, 3 Rifle Regiments	1 Field Artillery Regiment EscadronI/Chevaux Legers
2nd DI [Modelon]	
4, 5, 6 Rifle Regiments	2 Field Artillery Regiment EscadronII/Chevaux Legers

II Corps d'Armee [Mondesir]
3rd DI [Petidemange]
7, 8, 9 Rifle Regiments	7 Field Artillery Regiment EscadronI/3 Chevaux Legers
6th DI [Champeaux]	
10, 11, 12 Rifle Regiments	6 Field Artillery Regiment EscadronII/3 Chevaux Legers

The other divisions were 4th DI near Odessa and the 5thDI in the Ukraine. A 7th DI was planned for service under French command. The 7th DI would have commanded the 19, 20, and 21 Rifle Regiments.

Serbian

In May 1916 some 1,100 Bosnians and Serbs were formed into the 'Battalion Bosnique' but the unit was forced to disband in September 1916 as a result of internal feuding and indiscipline. A company was retained and attached to 260RI but the unit was disbanded in January 1917 for the same reasons. Thereafter individual Serbs fought either in the Legion or under Russian command in the 'Division de Volontaires Serbs' which joined other Russian forces in France in 1917.

PART FOUR

ARMY GROUPS & ARMIES

On mobilisation, General Headquarters [GQG] was established at Vitry-le-François with General Joffre as commander-in-chief. Until March 1918, GQG was the supreme authority for the conduct of the war on the Western Front. An allied headquarters [GQGA] was formed under General Foch on 26th March 1918 to co-ordinate the operations of the Belgian, British, French and American armies. GQGA rapidly became the supreme directing authority for allied strategy to win the war. In the summer and autumn of 1918, GQGA commanded the Belgian army group, the BEF, GAC, AEF and GAE: each of which had several armies under command.

ALLIED HEADQUARTERS [GQGA]

Commander in Chief: Ferdinand Foch

Chief of Staff: Maxime Weygand

Location: Beauvais
            7th April   Sarcus
            1st June   Mouchy-le-Châtel
            5th June   Bombon
            18th October   Senlis

GENERAL HEADQUARTERS, FRENCH ARMY [GQG]

Commander in Chief: Joseph Joffre
                      17th December 1916   Robert Nivelle
                      17th May 1917   Phillipe Pétain

Chief of Staff: Emile Belin
                      22nd March 1915   Maurice Pellé
                      20th December 1916   Ferdinand Pont
                      2nd May 1917   Eugene Debeney
                      23rd December 1917   Francois Anthoine
                      5th July 1918   Edmond Buat

Chief of Rear Services: Lafond de Ladébat - until 30th November 1914

Additional senior officers:

Deputy CinC: 4th October 1914-13th June 1915 [also army group commander]: Ferdinand Foch

Chief of the General Staff: 11th December 1915-17th December 1916: Noel Curieres de Castelnau
                            29th April -15th May 1917: Philippe Pétain
                            15th May 1917: Ferdinand Foch

General Reserve Artillery: from January 1917 Edmond Buat

Locations:
5th August 1914   Vitry-le-François

31st August 1914	Bar-le-Duc
6th September 1914	Châtillon-sur-Seine
28th September 1914	Romilly-sur-Seine
29th November 1914	Chantilly
10th January 1917	Beauvais
4th April 1917	Compiègne

Army Groups, 1914-1918

As the "Race to the Sea" developed at the conclusion of the First Battle of the Aisne, the number of armies, and the increasing length of the front-line, forced Joffre to devolve control to a provisional army group under General Foch. In the spring of 1915, this arrangement was made permanent with the creation of three Army Groups for the Northern, Central and Eastern sections of the Western Front. Each Army Group controlled between two and four armies, and this number varied during the course of the conflict.

Groupe d'Armees du Nord [GAN]

Formed 4.10.14 as Groupe Provisoire du Nord   [GPN]   QG at Breteuil
13.06.15 retitled Groupe d'Armées du Nord   [GAN]   QG at Cassel
06.07.18 retitled Groupe d'Armées du Centre   [GAC]   QG at Sezanne

Commanders
04.10.14 -Ferdinand Foch
27.12.16- Louis Franchet d'Esperey
10.06.18- Paul Maistre

Component Armies
04.10.14-04.11.14	2nd Army
05.10.14-14.03.16	10th Army
22.10.14-22.05.15	DAB/8th Army/DAB
13.06.15-02.08.15	2nd Army
02.08.15-12.12.16	6th Army
12.04.16-05.02.17	10th Army
26.06.16-29.11.16	3rd Army
26.10.16-22.02.17	1st Army
15.11.16-01.12.17	3rd Army
24.04.17-28.10.17	6th Army
08.05.17-28.10.17	10th Army
10.05.17-12.06.17	1st Army
01.12.17-21.07.18	6th Army
01.12.17-11.11.18	4th Army [to GAC 06.07.18]
01.12.17-29.03.18	5th Army
29.05.18-11.11.18	5th Army [to GAC 06.07.18]
17.07.18-25.07.18	9th Army
30.08.18-22.09.18	2nd Army
08.09.18-09.09.18	6th Army
23.10.18-27.10.18	3rd Army

Groupe d'Armees du Centre [GAC]

22.06.15 formed at Château Thierry
01.12.17 transferred to Italy as QG Forces Françaises d'Italie
06.07.18 reformed by retitling of GAN [see above]

Commanders
22.06.15- Noel de Curières de Castelnau
12.12.15- Fernand de Langle de Cary
02.05.16- Philippe Pétain
04.05.17- Emile Fayolle

Component Armies

23.06.15-30.03.16	4th Army	
23.05.15-30.03.16	5th Army	
23.06.15-02.08.15	6th Army	
20.07.15-28.02.16	3rd Army	[Groupe Pétain 28.02.16-02.05.16]11
02.08.15-10.08.15	2nd Army	
10.08.15-20.09.15	Gp Pétain	
20.09.15-05.01.16	2nd Army	
01.02.16-26.02.16	RFV	
26.02.16-28.02.16	2nd Army	[Groupe Petain 28.02.16-02.05.16]
02.05.16-01.12.17	2nd Army	
02.05.16-26.06.16	3rd Army	
02.05.16-01.12.17	4th Army	
02.05.16-01.01.17	5th Army	
08.05.17-01.12.17	5th Arm	

GROUPE D'ARMEES DE L'EST [GAE]

15.01.15 formed as Groupement Provisoire de l'Est [GPE]   QG at Gondrecourt
13.06.15 retitled Groupe d'Armées de l'Est [GAE] [temporarily titled Groupe Foch 21.01.17-31.03.17]

Commanders

15.01.15-	Auguston Dubail
31.03.16-	Louis Franchet D'Esperey
27.12.16-	Noel de Curiéres de Castelnau
21.01.17-	Ferdinand Foch
31.03.17-	Noel de Curiéres de Castelnau

Component Armies

08.01.15-26.10.16	1st Army
08.01.15-20.07.15	3rd Army
08.01.15-11.11.18	DAV/7th Army
11.03.15-11.11.18	DAL/8th Army
04.04.15-15.04.15	Detachment Gérard
10.08.15-01.02.16	RFV
01.12.17-30.08.18	2nd Army
16.12.17-26.03.18	1st Army
06.11.18-11.11.18	10th Army

GROUPE D'ARMEES DE RESERVE [GAR]

01.01.17 formed at Dormans to command the armies allocated to Nivelle's offensive on the Chemin de Dames –disbanded 08.05.17
23.02.18- reformed at Beauvais

Commanders
01.01.17-08.05.17-	Joseph Micheler
23.02.18-	Emile Fayolle

Component Armies
01.01.17-08.05.17	5th Army
01.01.17-08.05.17	6th Army

10.02.17-24.04.17	10th Army
23.03.18-14.09.18	3rd Army
26.03.18-28.07.18	1st Army
01.06.18-27.10.18	10th Army
21.07.18-08.09.18	6th Army
16.08.18-11.11.18	1st Army
27.10.18-11.11.18	3rd Army

The Groupe d'Armées des Flandres was formed on 15.10.18 under the command of the King of the Belgians. It was composed of the Belgian Army, the French 6th Army, and the British 2nd Army. Between this group and the rest of the French Army, the BEF constituted a further army group of the 1st, 3rd, 4th and 5th British Armies under General Haig.

Introduction to Armies and Army Groups

First Army
GAE   08.01.15-26.10.16
GAN   26.10.16-22.02.17
GAN   10.05.17-12.06.17
GAE   16.12.17-26.03.18
GAR   26.03.18-28.07.18
GAR   16.08.18-11.11.18

Second Army
GAN   04.10.14-04.11.14
GAN   14.06.15-02.08.15
GAC   02.08.15-10.08.15
GAC   20.09.15-05.01.16
GAC   26.02.16-28.02.16
GAC   02.05.16-01.12.17
GAE   01.12.17-30.08.18
GAC   30.08.18-22.09.18

Third Army
GAE   08.01.15-20.07.15
GAC   20.07.15-28.02.16
GAC   02.05.16-26.06.16
GAN   26.06.16-29.11.16
GAN   15.11.16-01.12.17
GAR   23.03.18-14.09.18
GAC   23.10.18-27.10.18
GAR   27.10.18-11.11.18

Fourth Army
GAC   23.06.15-30.03.16
GAC   02.05.16-01.12.17
GAN   01.12.17-06.07.18
GAC   06.07.18-11.11.18

Fifth Army
GAC   23.05.15-30.03.16
GAC   02.05.16-01.01.17
GAR   01.01.17-08.05.17
GAC   08.05.17-01.12.17
GAN   01.12.17-29.03.18
GAN   29.05.18-06.07.18
GAC   06.07.18-11.11.18

Sixth Army
GAC   23.06.15-06.08.15
GAN   06.08.15-12.12.16
GAR   01.01.17-08.05.17
GAN   08.05.17-28.10.17
GAN   01.12.17-21.07.18
GAR   21.07.18-08.09.18
GAC   08.09.18-09.09.18

GAF   15.10.18-11.11.18

Seventh Army [including DAV]
GAE   08.01.15-11.11.15

Eighth Army [including DAL]
GAN   22.10.14-22.05.15
GAE   11.03.15-11.11.18

Ninth Army
GAC   17.07.18-25.07.18

Tenth Army
GAN   05.10.14-14.03.16
GAN   12.04.16-05.02.17
GAR   10.02.17-24.04.17
GAN   08.05.17-28.10.17
GAR   01.06.18-27.10.18
GAE   10.11.18-11.11.18

GENERAL ARTILLERY RESERVE

Until January 1917, control of heavy and medium artillery was shared between armies and corps and control was then centralised under the Réserve Général d'Artillerie Lourde, commanded by General Buat. This was retitled the Réserve Général d'Artillerie in January 1918. For administrative purposes, the RGA was divided into five divisions on the latter date. They were:

1st Division	RALGP/RALFV
2nd Division	RALT
3rd Division	naval batteries
4th Division	RAL Hippomobiles/RAT
5th Division	RAC Portée

Although this was intended to maximise flexibility in the deployment of these weapons, it remains uncertain as to whether this was accomplished in terms of the movement of groups and batteries between armies. Was the RGA just a headquarters for planning and control of artillery, French and American sources are imprecise on this matter. The authors have been unable to find a complete listing of French artillery units. The Official History regarded the compilation and listing of heavy artillery units as too complex and too time-consuming for inclusion in that work. It cites the different methods used by each army and corps in filling out returns of artillery strength at different dates.

All that can be done here is to present a summary of artillery regiments in 1918 together with a table indicating strength in terms of equipment held in October 1918. Both tables include artillery held at divisional and corps level.

Summary of artillery regiments, 11th November 1918

RAC Hippomobile	105 regiments
RAC Portée	33 regiments
RA Montagne	3 regiments
Groupes à Cheval	6 groups
RAL Hippomobile	64 regiments
RAL à Tracteurs	20 regiments
RAL Grand Puissance	3 regiments
RAL Ferre Voie	5 regiments
RA Tranchées	5 regiments
RA à Pied	13 regiments

RA Antiaeriens	6 regiments
Tank regiments	9 regiments and 7 groups
And several North African groups	

Regiments tended to serve as complete units within divisions and corps but seem to have been deployed as semi-independent groups and batteries at higher levels.

Aviation

Many units of the 'Aviation Militaire' were organic components of the army groups, armies and army corps. These are covered in the following chapters. Due to considerations of space and the availability of other books on French aviation in World War One, all other components and aircraft, are not included in this book.

In 1918, army groups came to have control of those units, which had a wider strategic role. This resulted in the larger-scale employment of fighters and bombers. By 3rd November 1918, for example, GAC commanded 7 bomber groups, and GAE commanded 2 bomber groups, with additonal British and Italian units. These were components of the Division Aérienne, under General Duval, which was formed on 1st May 1918 with 6 fighter groups and 5 bomber groups.

From the initial allocation of recconnaissance aircraft to each of the armies, this level of command came to control a variable number of escadrilles by 1918. These would include an extensive fighter element to cover the work of the recconnaissance and artillery-spotting aircraft operated by the subordinate corps. The variations in the allocation of escadrilles between the various armies suggest a lack of a uniform table of organisation for this level of command.

Each corps was allocated one escadrille for tactical recconnaissance and artillery-spotting in 1915. This was increased to two, and then, three during 1918.

An outline of the allocation of escadrilles to armies and corps is provided within the organisational details of each formation.

- *French Aircraft of the First World War*, J J Davilla & A M Soltan, Stanton, Conn, 1997
- *Historie de l'Aviation Militaire-L'Armée de l'Air*, C Christienne & P Lissarrague, Paris 1981
- *Pictorial History of the French Air Force*, vol 1: 1909-1940, A van Haute, London 1974
- *French Military Aviation* [2nd edition], P Jackson, Leicester 1979

Armies

Armies did not exist before mobilisation in 1914 except as planning concepts. At this stage plans had been drawn up for five armies to be formed along the border with Germany. From right to left, they were designated L'Armée de Paris with QG at Rethel; L'Armée de Fontainebleau with QG at St Dizier; L'Armée de Chalons with QG at Verdun; l'Armée de Dijon with QG at Neufchäteau; and L'Armée de Dole with QG at Épinal. Upon mobilisation these five armies were numbered according to French custom, from left to right, and so became Fifth, Fourth, Third, Second and First Armies respectively. Each of the five armies was placed under the command of a member of the Conseil Supérieur de la Guerre, whose vice president was Chief of the General Staff and Commander in Chief designate [Joffre].

During the course of the conflict, another five numbered armies were formed on the Western Front. They were the Sixth, Seventh, Eighth, Ninth and Tenth Armies. In addition, a number of other formations appeared, and, occupied a position between armies and corps. Mostly, they were described as Army Detachments. Those with some degree of permanence were allocated geographic titles such as DAV [Vosges] and DAL [Lorraine], and others bore the name of their commander: Groupe Pétain or DA Gérard.

As wartime creations, each army was allocated a minimal number of 'Army Troops' in 1914. Of these the largest were a cavalry squadron, and the equivalent of a regiment of heavy artillery. Information on the growth and development of such troops is scarce. The French official history, for example, admits an inability to compile lists of troops under direct command. In particular, it indicates that, because the data on heavy artillery was compiled in different ways by different armies at different dates, the task of unravelling this information was too complicated to include in the official history.

Unfortunately, this means that a compilation of units assigned to direct army command has had to be omitted from this book.

The following histories of each individual army include dates of formation and disbandment, where appropriate; names of commanders; a summary of main battles; and then a narrative history. The latter is interspersed between extensive data on the corps and divisions, which were under the command of each army throughout its existence.

In this section, corps and divisions are included only when they were operational and thus part of the effective fighting strength of the relevant army. It was French custom to include corps and divisions, in transit from one part of the Western Front to another, under the command of the army as they passed through that armies rear area.. This gives an inflated view of army strength and such formations have been left out.

By the same token, corps and divisions which were on non-operational tasks such as resting, rebuilding, training, and labour duties have been left out.

Equally important, is that many of the apparent movements of corps between armies was the result of changes in army boundaries, rather than the physical movement of corps and divisions.

The British practice of formation designation has been followed: First Army, I Corps, and 1st Division; rather than the French practice of I Army, 1st Corps and 1st Division.

Summary of Armies and Army-Level Formations

First Army	02.08.14-11.11.18	
Second Army	02.08.14-11.11.18	
Third Army	02.08.14-11.11.18	
Fourth Army	02.08.14-11.11.18	
Fifth Army	02.08.14-11.11.18	
Sixth Army	26.08.14-11.11.18	
Seventh Army	04.04.15-11.11.18	
Eighth Army	16.11.14-04.04.15;	02.01.17-11.11.18
Ninth Army	05.09.14-05.10.14;	05.07.18-07.08.14
Tenth Army	05.10.14-11.11.18	
Armee des Alpes	02.08.14-17.08.14	
Armee d'Alsace	10.08.14-28.08.14	
Armee de Lorraine	22.08.14-27.08.14	
Armee d'Orient	03.10.15-11.08.16	
Armee Francaise d'Orient	11.08.16-11.11.18	
Armee du Danube	28.10.18-11.11.18	
CSN	23.12.17-19.04.18	
DA Belgique	22.10.14-16.11.14; 04.04.15-22.05.15	
DA Foch	29.08.14-05.09.14	
DA Gerard	04.04.15-23.04.15	
DA Lorraine	16.03.15-02.01.17	
DA Nord	17.04.18-06.07.18	
DA Maud'huy	01.10.14-05.10.14	
DA Putz/DA Vosges	08.12.14-04.04.15	
Group Mangin	06.06.18-10.06.18	
Group Petain	10.08.15-20.09.15	
RF Verdun	02.08.15-26.02.16	

First Army

[Armée de Dole at Épinal]

Commanders

02.08.14-Augustin Dubail
05.01.15-Pierre Roques
23.03.16-Olivier Mazel
31.03.16-Augustin Gérard
31.12.16-Emile Fayolle
06.05.17-Joseph Micheler
01.06.17-Henri Gouraud
15.06.17-Francois Anthoine
21.12.17-Marie Debeney

Army Troops, August 1914

Peletons/44RI
Cyclist Cie/55BCP
Escadron/14RH
Groups 1-4, 5RAL
1 Telegraph Cie
23/1 Pont Cie/7RG

Aviation

1914-MF5, Bl9, Bl10, Br17, Bl18, Bl3
1918-Spa102, Br201, Sal203, Sal204, Br234, Vr293

Main Battles

1914	1915	1916	1917	1918
Sarrebourg	Woëvre	-	2nd Aisne	2nd Picardie
Mortange			3rd Ypres	3rd Picardie
Woevre				2nd Noyon St
Flirey				Quentin Mont
				d'Origny
				2nd Guise
				Thierrache

Alsace-Lorraine 1914

Covered by XXI Corps d'Armée, First Army took over the right-hand position of the five French armies which faced the frontier with Germany. Under the command of General Dubail, a member of the Supreme War Council, the bulk of the army was concentrated east of Épinal, in the Moselle valley and upper part of the Meurthe valley. The principal line of concentration was Xures-Blamont-Badonviller-Senones.

The army consisted of VIII CA, XIII CA, XXI CA, XIV CA and VII CA. First Army had initial responsibility for the passes through the Vosges Mountains, and for the defences of Haut Alsace to the Swiss frontier. On 10th August, after the failure to take Mulhouse, the Army d'Alsace took over responsibility for this southern sector, with VIICA under command. With a total strength of 256,000 men, First Army could concentrate on the advance on Strasbourg.

First Army's deployment for the advance from the Meurthe to Strasbourg was:
VIII CA
XIII CA
XXI CA
The units of XIV CA undertook the seizure of the passes over the Vosges, centered on the Col du Bonhomme.

First Army advanced into Germany on 15th August. Its ultimate objective was Strassbourg. More immediately it advanced towards Sarrebourg, which it took on 18th August. Plans to advance on Saverne were halted by the German counterattack on 20th August. First Army was forced to retreat towards the Moselle.

It fought on the line of the Mortange, 25th August, and then established defensive positions along the Moselle between Nancy and Épinal. This action involved the deployment of VIII CA between Vallois and Matexey, XIII CA to the north of Rambervillers, and XXI CA between Raon-l'Étape and XXI CA between Ste Barbe and the Col de la Chipotte. From these positions, First Army moved north to cover Nancy and Lunéville.

During the first battle of the Marne, it held this position but gradually lost divisions to more threatened parts of the French line. On 5th September, for example, it included VIII CA [15DI, 16DI], XIII CA [25DI, 26DI], XIV CA [27DI, 28DI] and a provisional corps of Barbot and Vassin's divisions. Ten days later, as the battle of the Marne concluded, it had been reduced to XIV CA and the provisional corps.

VIII CA

From Frambois and Glonville, the corps advanced from the Meurthe towards Sarrebourg, which it took on
18th August. It fought at Réding and Gosselaing on 20th August and then retreated behind the Mortange to Hallainville and Essey-la-Cote. From 25th August, it advanced from Vallois and Matexey to reach the Meurthe on 12th-13th September.

15DI	02.08.14-14.09.14
16DI	02.08.14-14.09.14

XIII CA

Advanced from Darnieulles, via Cirey, towards Saarebourg. It fought at Hartzwiller, Schneckenbusch and Brouderoff. It retreated to the Mortagne on 21st August, and from positions to the north of Rambervillers, it attacked towards the Meurthe on 25th August, and reached Xaffévillers and the Bois d'Angelmont by 10th September.

25DI	02.08.14-13.09.14
26DI	02.08.14-13.09.14
44DI	22.08.14-27.08.14

XXI CA

Covering Corps. It advanced via the Col du Donon and Schirmeck towards Saarebourg on 18th August but was forced to retire towards Baccarat. During the battle for the Mortagne, it fought at the Col de la Chipotte and Ste-Barbe. It left the army on 2nd September.

13DI	02.08.14-02.09.14
43DI	02.08.14-02.09.14
44DI	27.08.14-02.09.14

XIV CA

Fought for the passages over the Vosges, -the Col de Bonhomme and Saales 9th-24th August14 and then moved to defend the Meurthe at Raon-l'Etape: it held the line between Baccarat and St Clémont 14th-17th September during the struggle for the Mortagne. It left Army 21st September.

27DI	02.08.14-20.09.14
28DI	02.08.14-20.09.14

Group Deletoile

Fought for the line of the Mortagne 5th-12th September and then the Meurthe until 28th September. Became
XXXI CA on 3rd October.

Vassart DI	05.09.14-28.09.14
Barbot DI	05.09.14-28.09.14

[In addition to the above corps, Conneau's Cavalry Corps was transferred temporarily from Second Army during the advance on Sarrebourg, 19-21.08.14]

LORRAINE 1914-1916

After the stabilisation of the front-line, with QG at Toul, First Army assumed responsibility for operations in Lorraine. For most of this period, its line extended from the heights of the Meuse, south of Verdun, around the St Mihiel Salient, to Toul and Nancy, and across the Moselle at Pont-à-Mousson to Lunéville. First Army remained there until October 1916.

During this period, it committed forces to action at Flirey on 21st September 1914, and east of the Verdun salient on the plains of the Woëvre in the spring of 1915. Apart from these major actions, the line was relatively quiet and stable for most of the period. The battle of Flirey sought to secure the line between the Meuse and the Moselle, and to contain the Germans within the St Mihiel Salient. In the battles on the Woëvre, First Army successfully employed VIII CA [15DI, 16DI], XVI CA [31DI, 32DI], 7DC, 64DR, 73DR and 76DR to defend the southern shoulder of the Verdun Salient at at Éparges. Together with DA Gérard –ICA [1DI, 2DI] and II CA [3DI. 4DI], First Army was able to thwart German assaults on the vital Éparges position and on the Tranchée de Calonne further south.

VI CA

Taken over from Second Army 16th September, it held the sector between Bois Mort Mare and Flirey from 22nd September until 7th October.

31DI   22.09.14-06.10.14
32DI   23.09.14-06.10.14

2 GDR

Taken over from Second Army 16th September. It held the sector from Flirey to Pont-a-Mousson and Armaucourt from 13th September 1914 until 11th March 1915. It came under direct command of GPE on
08th January 1915.

64DI   16.09.14-12.10.14
59DI   16.09.14-08.01.15
68DI   16.09.14-08.01.15
74DI   24.09.14-08.01.15

VIII CA

From 29 September 1914 it held Flirey until 4th April 1915 when it moved to the Woëvre-Apremont-Koeur sector on the northern flank of the St Mihiel Salient, it remained there until 29th September 1916 when it was taken over by DAL.

16DI   24.09.14-22.01.16
15DI   27.09.14-27.08.15
40DI   20.06.16-03.08.16

XXXI CA

Held the northern flank between Lahayville and Bois Mort Mare until 21st May 1916. Fought in the battle for Woëvre 5th April 1915.

76DI   12.10.14-10.01.16
64DI   12.10.14-29.05.16
101DT   11.01.16-21.05.16

VI CA

Transferred from Third Army 8th January 1915 to the Eparges sector where it held the Eparges/Seuzey/Maizey sector on the northern flank of the St Mihiel salient until 5th August 1915. It fought at Eparges and at Tranchée de Calonne during 1st Woëvre

12DI   08.01.15-04.08.15
65DI   08.01.15-05.08.15
67DI   08.01.15-05.08.15
127DI   15.06.15-03.08.15

Group Verdun
Transferred from Third Army 8th January 1915 –covered the Verdun sector; to RFV 10th August 1915.
72DI   08.01.15-10.08.15
131DI   08.01.15-04.04.15

Detachment d'Armée Gérard
Between 4th and 23rd April 1915, this temporary formation fought to the left of First Army as an independent formation. With QG at Verdun it secured the sector from Eix to Trésauvaux with 1CA and IICA.

I CA
1DI   04.04.15-23.04.15
2DI   04.04.15-23.04.15

II CA
Remained with First Army between Trésauvaux and Riaville until transferred to RFV on 10th August-it remained in line until 30th September 1915
3DI   04.04.15-27.09.15
4DI   04.04.15-01.10.15
48DI   29.04.15-13.05.15

XII CA
Fought in 1st Woëvre between Fey-en-Haye and Regnieville 2nd May-10th June 1915.
23DI   02.04.15-10.06.15
24DI   06.04.15-30.05.15

XXXIII CA
Inserted into the line on 31st May 1916 and served between St Agnant and Fey-en-Haye until 29th July 1916.
70DI   15.05.16-29.07.16
77DI   15.05.16-27.02.16

Army command
73DI served 28th September 1914 until 18th July 1916 in the Bois de la Prêtre sector

Oise 1916-1917

On 29th October 1916, First Army moved from Lorraine westwards to the Oise region and established a new QG at Verberie. This move was part of a general reshuffling of armies as a gap emerged when Sixth Army and Tenth Army moved further north to concentrate on the later stages of the battle of the Somme. First Army assumed responsibility for a front which stretched the boundary with Tenth Army at Bois des Loges, and then eastwards across the Oise to the Aisne at Pernant where Fifth Army took over on the Chemin des Dames.

XXXV CA
Between the Bois des Loges and Ribécourt, 25th November 1916-16th March 1917
121DI   25.11.16-25.01.17
61DI   25.11.16-17.03.17
53DI   25.11.16-05.01.17
87DI   25.11.16-18.12.16
120DI   05.01.17-22.03.17
25DI   25.01.17-23.03.17

XIII CA
Inserted into the line between Massif de Thiescourt and Ribécourt on 25th January 1917
26DI   25.01.17-19.03.17

53DI   25.01.17-16.03.17
87DI   25.01.17-17.03.17

ICC

Between Oise and Tracy-le-Val, 11th November 1916-13th March 1917.
1DC and 3DC alternate in the line

XXXIII CA

Between Quennevières and Pernant, 28th November 1916-17th March 1917.
77DI   29.11.16-17.03.17
70DI   10.12.16-17.03.17
53DI   23.01.17-16.03.17

AISNE 1917

As the new CinC, Robert Nivelle, made plans for his spring offensive in 1917, First Army was squeezed out by the insertion of Third Army to its left, and Sixth Army on the right. With its corps taken over by Third Army, it left the frontline on 22nd March and established itself between the Marne and the Seine, east of Paris. With QG at Château-Thierry it became the follow-through formation for Nivelle's breakout out along the Chemin des Dames. The CinC intended to employ four armies in what he felt was the final path to victory. Adjacent to each other, along the Chemin des Dames, Sixth and Fifth Armies would crumble the German defences, and then Tenth Army would attack at the junction of these two armies and create a corridor towards Laon. When this was achieved, First Army would move through this corridor, and exploit northwards towards the Belgian frontier. Nivelle' offensive failed on its first day-16th April 1917.

Under command were- X CA [19DI, 20DI] , XXI CA [13DI, 43DI, 167 DI], I CA [1DI, 2DI, 51DI, 162DI], II CAC [10DIC, 15DIC] and XXXIICA [42DI, 47DI, 69DI and 165DI]. All these formations remained in reserve except for XXI CA, which entered the line between Mennejean and the Panthéon on 25th May and was transferred to Sixth Army on 11th June.

FLANDERS

As a result of the French determination to play a part in the planned British offensive in Flanders in the summer of 1917, First Army moved its QG to Rexpoëde on 16th June. It took command of XXXVI CA, which had been the major component of the Dunkerque Fortified Region. It was joined by I CA and played a significant role in Haig's offensive which began on 31st July. First Army operated between the British and Belgian forces to the north of Ypres. When that offensive petered out, First Army departed from Flanders on 15th December.

I CA

In line between Boezinge, Steenstraat and Nordschoote, 7th July-15th September 1917 and then at Kloosterschool, 29th October-5th December 1917.
1DI   07.07.17-30.10.17
2DI   04.08.17-07.12.17
162DI   04.08.17-21.11.17

XXXVI CA

In line between Drei Grachten and Bikschote, 15th September –13th November 1917
133DI   03.09.17-08.11.17
29DI   12.09.17-13.11.17
The divisions allocated to both corps interchanged frequently.

LORRAINE 1918

The First Army returned to Lorraine where it set up QG at Toul from which it controlled operations along the quiet southern flank of the St Mihiel Salient between the rivers Meuse and Moselle. Among the divisions in training behind this front was the 69 Division d'Infanterie at Vaucouleurs; which helped introduce American soldiers to the operational reality of the trench life.

II CAC

Taken over from Second Army and held Maizey-Koeur-Vargevaux sector, 5th January-24th March 1918. Divisions temporarily with XXXII CA, 24th-26th March

15DIC   05.01.18-24.03.18
52DI   05.01.18-24.03.18
10DIC   05.10.18-25.03.18

XXXII CA

From Eighth Army and held the Chenincourt/Limey sector 5th January-26th March 1918.

42DI   05.01.18-26.03.18
40DI   05.01.18-26.03.18

Picardy 1918

As a direct result of the German spring offensive, which began on 21st March 1918, First Army was sent to Picardy to help fill the gap left by the virtual disintegration of the British Fifth Army. QG was established at Maignelay on 26th March, moved to Breteuil two days later, and then to Conty on 13th April. The army fought along the line of the river Avre to stem the left flank of the German advance towards Montdidier and Amiens. Although the former location was lost, the Army secured, held and consolidated a line between Hangard, on the river Luce, to Ayencourt where it met up with Third Army, which covered the Oise.

IX CA

Transferred from Eighth Army. Fought along the Avre between Grivesnes and Thory from 26th March, and then, held the line between Grivesnes and Ayencourt until 10th August

166DI   26.03.18-11.04.18
127DI   26.03.18-16.04.18
59DI   04.04.18-29.04.18
152DI   16.04.18-29.05.18
3DI   29.04.18-08.08.18
15DIC   29.05.18-02.08.18
66DI   30.05.18-02.08.18

VI CA

Transferred from Seventh Army. Fought along the Avre between Erches and Dancourt on 26th March, and then, held a line between Grivesnes and Ayencourt until 5th May.

12DI   26.03.18-05.04.18
56DI   26.03.18-09.04.18
162DI   30.03.18-05.05.18
45DI   05.04.18-28.04.18

XXXVI CA

Transferred from Dunkerque to line south-east of Moreuil, 30th March-established a line between Morisel and Mailly-Raineval by 14th April. Returned to DAN 18th April to assist the BEF on the Lys.

29DI   30.03.18-04.04.18
163DI   30.03.18-18.04.18
2DCP   04.04.18-05.04.18
17DI   04.04.18-18.04.18

II CC

In Hangard/Morisel area, 5th-8th April

29DI   05.04.18-08.04.18

2DCP   05.04.18-08.04.18

XXXI CA

Succeeded XXXVI CA and IICC on the Army's left wing on 6th April. Held the line between Hangard and Morisel. Remained in First Army for the summer/autumn offensives [see below]

64DI   06.04.18-29.04.18
2DCP   08.04.18-12.04.18
29DI   08.04.18-14.04.18
DM   12.04.18-07.05.18
131DI   14.04.18-29.04.18
18DI   17.04.18-24.05.18
165DI   29.04.18-31.05.18
37DI   29.04.18-02.08.18
42DI   07.05.18-08.08.18

V CA

From Third Army 14th April-held Morisel/MaillyRaineval positions until 26th May when succeeded by VII CA which held same positions until succeeded by X CA.

17DI   14.04.18-23.04.18
18DI   17.04.18-24.05.18
64DI   29.04.18-06.05.18
66DI   06.05.18-30.05.18
15DIC   17.05.18-30.05.18

X CA

Took over the Grivesnes-Ayencourt line on 5th May and remained there until summer offensives [see below]

60DI   05.05.18-
152DI   06.07.18-
166DI   07.07.18-

THE ADVANCE TO VICTORY 1918

First Army played a major role in the British-led offensive, which began to the east of Amiens on 8th August. With XXXI CA, IX CA, XCA and XXXV CA, it attacked alongside the Canadian Corps and achieved significant gains, freed Montdidier, and advanced to the line Lihons/Ayencourt.

This line provided the base for First Army's participation in the Allied advance to victory in the autumn of 1918. With the British Fourth Army on its left flank, it advanced further than any other French army in a series of rolling attacks, planned and co-ordinated by Foch.

By 27th August, it had advanced to St Quentin, which it freed on 3rd September with XXXI, X, XV and VIII Corps. This was followed by the battle for Mont d'Origny and the crossing of the Oise-Sambre canal on 15th October. It protected the flank of Tenth/Third Army on the Serre on 26th October. Then it advanced north-eastward and took Guise on 4th November.

The First Army advanced into Belgium and reached Chimay on 11th November, when its line was that between Bois-de-Chimay, Robechies, Baileux and Rièzes. With QG at Homblieres, it held this front with XV, XXXVI and VIII Corps; with XXXI and XX Corps in reserve.

XXXI CA

As the most northerly corps, it fought alongside the Canadians on 8th August and progressed eastwards from Moreuil. From 27th August it advanced from Ercheu, near Nesle, towards the Hindenburg Line. By 9th September it fought at Essigny-le-Grand and Contescourt to reach Grand-Seraucourt and Hinacourt. During the battle for St Quentin, it advanced from Urvillers/Neuville St Amand to reach Montigny-en-Arrouaise on 11th October. It crossed the Oise-

Sambre canal during the battle of Mont d'Origny to reach the Laon-Guise road by 27th October. It liberated Guise and moved towards La Capelle and and Haudroy on 10th November. It was in reserve near Guise on Armistice Day.

42DI 00.00.00-08.08.18
66DI 02.08.18-10.08.18
126DI 06.08.18-03.09.18
153DI 08.08.18-12.08.18
47DI 10.08.18-04.09.18
152DI 03.09.18-03.10.18
169DI 04.09.18-13.10.18
64DI 30.09.18-07.10.18
34DI 07.10.18-16.10.18
60DI 08.10.18-16.10.18
56DI 13.10.18-31.10.18
33DI 16.10.18-28.10.18
166DI 16.10.18-10.11.18

X CA

During the battle of Amiens it advanced to Beuvraignes and Roye, and then moved towards the Hindenburg Line between Vendeuil and Hinacourt. Withdrawn on 15th September.

60DI 00.00.18-15.09.18
166DI 00.00.18-10.09.18
152DI 00.00.18-24.08.18
46DI 00.00.18-05.09.18

XXXV CA

Transferred from Third Army, it held the Ayencourt/Wacquemoulin sector from 13th June until 9th August. During the allied offensive, it moved past Montdidier to the Avre and Beuvraignes to take part in the second battle for Noyon on 17th August. Withdrawn on 28th August.

169DI 09.08.18-28.08.18
46DI 09.08.18-28.08.18

XXXVI CA

Rejoined First army on 17th August and took up positions between the Chavette and Lihons on 25th August. Two days later it advanced towards the Hindenburg Line, crossed the Somme-Nesle canal and reached Grand Seraucourt and Savy. It fought at Savy Dallon 13th-18th September, and then at St Quentin. 25th September-15th October, from where it advanced to Montigny en Arrouaise and Bernoville. During the struggle for Mont d'Origny, the corps crossed the Oise-Sambre canal and advanced to Tupigny, where it fought during the second battle of Guise, 4th-5th November. By the time of the armistice, it had moved into Belgium and held positions between Chimay and the Foret de Nouvion.

153DI 17.08.18-19.08.18
35DI 24.08.18-15.09.18
34DI 29.08.18-22.09.18
133DI 15.09.18-10.10.18
166DI 22.09.18-14.10.18
64DI 07.10.18-07.11.18
15DI 10.10.18-11.11.18
152DI 14.10.18-09.11.18
33DI 17.10.18-28.10.18
133DI 28.10.18-11.11.18
166DI 09.11.18-11.11.18

XV CA

This corps was transferred from Third Army on 15th September. It had been involved in the advance of that army from Tergnier and Liez to Vendueil. Between 29th September and 16th August it took part in operations around St Quentin and achieved the line between Bernoville and Seboncourt. During the battle for Mont d'Origny it reached the Oise-

Sambre canal between Tupigny and Etruex and then crossed the canal during the second battle for Guise. By 11th November it had advanced to reach positions between Nouvion and Trélon.

37DI	15.09.18-27.09.18
123DI	15.09.18-28.09.18
60DI	15.09.18-26.09.18
47DI	26.09.18-10.10.18
46DI	28.09.18-10.10.18
123DI	07.10.18-19.10.18
66DI	16.10.18-07.11.18
46DI	17.10.18-11.11.18
126DI	18.10.18-19.10.18
123DI	26.10.18-11.11.18
51DI	07.11.18-11.11.18

VIII CA

Transferred from Tenth Army on 24th September, the corps established itself between Barisis-aux-Bois and Tergnier. During the battle for St Quentin, which began on 27th September, it advanced via Fere, Vendeuil and Urvillers to the Oise between Moy and Bernot. It participated in the actions for Mont d'Origny and the Serre between 15th October and 5th November to reach the Guise/Laon road at Chevresis-Monceau. After an advance via Hirson, it had reached Chimay/Baileux by 11th November.

67DI	24.09.18-06.11.18
123DI	24.09.18-07.10.18
58DI	25.09.18-11.11.18
60DI	26.09.18-08.10.18
35DI	16.10.18-02.11.18
37DI	23.10.18-09.11.18
168DI	09.11.18-11.11.18

XX CA

Transferred from Fifth Army to form the right wing of First Army on 13th October, it fought between Vendeuil and Ribemont during the struggle for the Serre, and reached Landifay on the Guise/Laon road by 27th October. During the second battle of Guise, it fought at Audigny and then advanced towards Froidestrées where it went into reserve on 9th November.

168DI	13.10.18-11.11.18
153DI	21.10.18-11.11.18
47DI	25.10.18-11.11.18

SECOND ARMY

[Armée de Dijon at Neufchâteau]

COMMANDERS

02.08.14-Eduoard de Curieres de Castelnau
21.06.15-Philippe Pétain
01.05.16-Robert Nivelle
10.12.16-Louis Guillamat
11.12.17-Auguste-Edouard Hirschauer

ARMY TROOPS AUGUST 1914

Peleton/27RI
Cyclist Cie/42BCP
Escadron/26RD Groups 1-4, ??? RAL Group, 3 or 4 RAL
2 Telegraph Cie
D Radio Detachment
23/2 Pont Cie., 7RG

AVIATION

1914-HF1, MF8, HF19, MF20
1918-Spa23, Vr209, Br243

MAIN BATTLES

1914	1915	1916	1917	1918
Morhange	2nd Champagne	Verdun	Verdun Offensive	St Mihiel
Grand Couronne				Argonne
1st Picardie				
1st Artois				

LORRAINE 1914

With its headquarters at Neufchâteau, Second Army concentrated along the frontier with Lorraine. Its assembly was covered by XX CA from positions to the east of Nancy. The army's initial line covered the frontier from Pont-à-Mousson, Nomeny, the Seille and to Brin, on the eastern bank of the Moselle. Under the terms of Plan XVII, its task was to advance north-eastwards into Lorraine and take up positions east of Metz, along the line Nancy-Morhange-Saarburg. Metz would be isolated and threatened from the north by Third Army.

From north to south, Second Army deployed IX CA [17DI, 18DI], XX CA [11DI, 39DI], XV CA [29DI, 30DI] and XVI CA [31DI, 32DI]. Its strength was reduced by the diversion of XVIII CA and 2DC and 10DC to Fifth Army on 18th August. The army's was supported by 2GDR [59DR, 68DR and 70DR]. Its total strength was 200,000 men.

The advance of Second Army was halted at Morhange on 20th August by the advance of the German Sixth Army. The French fell back towards Nancy and the Moselle where they fought and held the line between Pont-a-Mousson and Lunéville in the battle for the Grand Couronne which began on 24th August. Once established, this line in Lorraine was to be maintained until November 1918. Second Army continued operations in this area during the first battle of the Marne with XX CA, XVI CA and 2GDR. With a major gap between it and its neighbour, Third Army, and its comparative weakness allowed the Germans to take and hold the St Mihiel Salient on the northern flank of Second Army on 20th September. The results of battles further west on the Marne and the Aisne led to the consolidation of the remaining forces in Lorraine into First Army.

XX CA

Covering Corps, which deployed to the east of Nancy, between the Seille and the Forêt de Champenoux. It advanced towards Morhange on 14th August but was forced to retire back to the Grand Couronne at St Nicholas du Port on 21st August. In the battle for the Grand Couronne, it fought between Crevic, Courbesaux and Léomont until 13th September.

11DI	02.08.14-18.09.14
39DI	02.08.14-18.09.14
68DI	22.08.14-24.08.14
70DI	22.08.14-24.08.14

IX CA

To Fourth Army 20th August with 17DI, 18DI and 76DR.

XV CA

In the advance on Morhange, it moved forward via Moncourt and Coincourt, to Vergaville and Bidestorf. It fought at Dieuze in the battle of Morhange. It retired to Dombasle, Blainville and Saffair, and then fought between Xermaménsil and Hèrimnénil during the struggle for the Grand Couronne

29DI	02.08.14-06.09.14
30DI	02.08.14-06.09.14
64DI	23.08.14-01.09.14
72DI	01.09.14-02.09.14

XVI CA

Attacked from Lunéville towards Loudrefine, and fought at Bissing 20th August during the battle for Morhange. From 25th August it was engaged between Einvaux, Gerbéviller and Xermaménsil during the battle for the Grand Couronne. Transferred to First Army 16th September.

31DI	02.08.14-16.09.14
32DI	02.08.14-16.09.14
74DI	23.08.14-24.08.14
29DI	25.08.14-27.08.14

XVIII CA

Diverted to Fifth Army 18th August with 35DI and 36DI

2 GDR

Operated between Nomeny and Manoncourt during the Morhange operation, and after a move to Hoèville, fought at Érbéviller on 5th September and at Pont-a-Mousson on 12th September during the battle for the Grand Couronne. Transferred to First Army 16th September.

59DI	02.08.14-16.09.14
68DI	02.08.14-20.08.14
74DI	19.08.14-24.08.14
70DI	20.08.14-26.08.14
64DI	01.09.14-16.09.14

3 GDR

Temporarily transferred from Third Army for operations between Eix and the Hauts de Meuse-to the immediate southeast of Verdun, 16th-19th September

65DI	16.09.14-19.09.14
67DI	16.09.14-19.09.14
75DI	16.09.14-19.09.14

PICARDY 1914-1915

Second Army moved to Picardy and set up its QG at Creuil on 20th September 1914. With the 'Race to the

Sea' well underway after the frustrations of the battle of the Aisne, Joffre sought to extend his line northwards from the flank of Sixth Army to match the German advances in the area. When the BEF pulled out of the Aisne and moved to Flanders, and was replaced by Sixth Army, Joffre needed Second Army to establish and hold a line between the river Oise and Arras. By 26th September Second Army had six corps under command with which to thwart German attacks between Maucourt and Arras. They were:

GDT   Arras/Bapaume
XXCA   Ancre
XICA   Albert/Peronne
XIVCA   Frise/Maucourt
IVCA   Maucourt/Tilloloy
XIIICA Lassigny

Much of the fighting in this first battle of Picardy took place in territory which was to become so familiar to the British in 1916: names such as Albert, Fricourt, Mametz, Beaumont Hamel, Serre and Hébuterne featured in the battles conducted by Second Army. The Army's burden was reduced on 2nd October by the creation of Tenth Army to control operations from Arras northwards to Flanders. Second Army held the line in Picardy until 2nd August 1915 when its area was taken over by the BEF.

Groupement de Divisions Territoriale
Held the area from south of Arras to Bapaume, 6th-22nd October
81DT   06.10.14-22.10.14
84DT   06.10.14-22.10.14
88DT   06.10.14-22.10.14

XX CA
In line between Gommecourt, Hébuterne and Touvent from 25th September to 2nd November.
11DI   25.09.14-02.11.14
39DI   25.09.14-02.11.14
84DT   29.09.14-23.10.14
82DT   01.10.14-02.11.14
56DI   30.10.14-02.11.14

XI CA
Held the Somme sector, from Beaumont Hamel to Fricourt, 23rd September-11th August 1915. Transferred to Sixth Army, 2nd August
21DI   23.09.14-02.08.15
22DI   23.09.14-02.08.15
56DI   09.01.15-02.08.15
82DT   08.03.15-23.06.15
151DI   17.04.15-02.08.15
51DI   10.06.15-02.08.15

XIV CA
In the Frise-Herleville-Maucourt sector, south of the Somme, from 24th September 1914 until transferred to Sixth Army on 2nd August 1915.
27DI   24.09.14-02.08.15
28DI   24.09.14-02.08.15
62DI   04.10.14-02.08.15
154DI   14.04.15-02.08.15

IV CA
Fought at Lassigny, and then held the Maucourt-Tilloloy sector 19th-27th December 1914
7DI   21.09.14-27.12.14
8DI   22.09.14-27.12.14

53DI   13.10.14-27.12.14[Army Cmd 3-20.4.15]

XIII CA

Transferred from Sixth Army and moved from the Aisne front 21st September to operate between the Oise and the Matz near Lassigny. Held Ribécourt/Beuvraignes sector from 25th September 1914 until 15th February 1916. Returned to Sixth Army 1st July 1915

25DI   21.09.14-01.07.15
26DI   21.09.14-11.11.14
56DI   03.10.14-14.11.14
86DT   26.04.15-08.06.15

CHAMPAGNE- ARGONNE 1915-1916

On 10th August 1915, a temporary army detachment commanded by Pétain began to form at the eastern end of Fourth Army's front in Champagne. It took control of operations on the chalk plain, which was flanked by the Argonne forests on its right. Inserted between Fourth Army and Third Army, Pétain's command became Second Army on 20th September. With QG at Châlons-sur-Marne, the Army was to co-operate with its neighbour to the left, the mount a massive offensive northwards over the open, largely featureless, bare slopes of the chalk plain which extended from Reims to the Argonne. This second battle of Champagne, which began on 25th September was part of a two-fold strategy devised by Joffre to break the German hold on the Western Front. Simultaneous British and French attacks would take place in Artois and Flanders to divide German resources. Second Army attacked with XIVCA, XICA, XXCA, and ICAC against German positions between Mesnil-lès-Hurlus and Ville-sur-Tourbe. The offensive achieved little in terms of territory. Second Army was pulled out the line on 5th January 1916.

XIV CA

Held the sector from Moulin des Perthes to Bois Sabot, 10th August –15th October 1915
Fought at Tahure and Trou Bricot during Second Champagne.
27DI   10.08.15-29.09.15
28DI   10.08.15-15.10.15
16DIC   29.09.15-07.10.15

XI CA

Held the Cote 196/Perthes sector, 26th August –12th December 1915
Fought at Tahure during Second Champagne.
21DI   26.08.15-09.10.15
22DI   26.08.15-05.11.15
53DI   25.09.15-19.10.15
4DI   09.10.15-18.11.15
151DI   31.10.15-05.12.15
22DI   02.12.15-12.12.15
126DI   05.12.15-12.12.15

XVI CA

Held the Cote 193/Tahure sector, 30th September –27th December 1915
Fought at the Butte de Tahure during Second Champagne
3DI   30.09.15-26.10.15
31DI   30.09.15-27.12.15
15DI   03.10.15-27.12.15
32DI   26.10.15-05.11.15
151DI   22.12.15-27.12.15

XX CA

In line between Cote 196 and Massiges, 3rd September to 16th November 1915
Fought at Maisons de Champagne during Second Champagne

11DI   03.09.15-16.11.15
39DI   03.09.15-16.11.15
153DI   03.09.15-16.11.15

I CAC

In the sector between Massiges and the Aisne 14th August until 20th December 1915. Fought at Ville-sur-Tourbe during Second Champagne
2DIC   14.08.15-13.11.15
3DIC   14.08.15-30.11.15
151DI   31.08.15-25.10.15
32DI   24.09.15-18.10.15
16DIC   25.10.15-20.12.15
7DI   13.11.15-20.12.15
124DI   30.11.15-20.12.15

XV CA

Took over the Cote193/Mamelles sector on 12th December 1915. Transferred to Fourth Army on 5th January 1916
123DI   12.12.15-05.01.16
126DI   12.11.15-05.01.16

IV CA

Took over the Maisons de Champagne sector, 20th December 1915. Transferred to Fourth Army 5th January 1916
7DI   20.12.15-05.01.16
8DI   20.12.15-05.01.16
124DI   20.12.15-05.01.16

XV CA

Took over the Argonne sector 9th December 1915. Transferred to Fourth Army, 15th January 1916.
29DI   09.12.15-15.01.16
30DI   09.12.15-15.01.16

To the east of Third Army in the Argonne, was the fortress of Verdun which had a relatively small garrison in the town and on the heights above the Meuse. These were organised into the **Verdun Fortified Region [RFV]** on 2nd August 1915 with II CA and a few independent units which formed Secteur Nord.

Secteur Nord, formed 2nd August 1915 –became **XXX CA** 21st January 1916
Held the area to the north of Verdun, mainly on the left bank of the Meuse
72DI   02.08.15-
51DI   02.08.15-10.01.16
132DI   10.01.16-16.02.16
67DI   10.02.16-
51DI   14.02.16-
14DI   16.02.16-
37DI   20.02.16-

IICA

Held the southern flank of the salient from Éparges to Palameix from 10th August 1915
4DI   10.08.15-28.11.15
67DI   10.08.15-10.01.16
3DI   28.11.15-
4DI   10.01.16-
132DI   06.02.16-
16DI   20.02.16-

68DI   28.02.16-

VERDUN 1916-1918

When the German attack on Verdun began on 21st February 1916, RFV had only XXX CA for the immediate defence of the town. It held the heights on the right bank of the Meuse to the north-east of the town. Five days after the battle began, and when the initial scale of French losses had become apparent, Pétain was sent to the area and QG of Second Army was established at Bar-le-Duc on 26th February. The army controlled operations in the Verdun sector for the rest of the war.

A major feature of Pétain's conduct of the defence was the introduction of a roulement system by which corps and divisions were rotated into the fight for relatively short-tours. Pétain's intention was to allow formations and units to recover from the intensity of the fighting, and to confront the German's –who did not adopt a similar system-to be confronted with relatively fresh troops in each sector. As a result a major part of the French army underwent the 'Verdun experience' and that commitment is reflected in the tabular information below. A total of 76 divisions carried out a least one tour at Verdun. The intensity of the fighting in a relatively confined area meant that only a small number of divisions were involved in any major attack. For example, only three divisions took part in the attack on Douaumont on 24th October, and only five in the offensive which began on 15th December: the ground was too limited for anything larger. Initially corps were moved into the Verdun sector with their component divisions, but, as the roulement policy was developed, corps became sector commands with the temporary assignment of divisions. These sectors can be grouped into four broad geographic areas which will be indicated in the tables below. From left to right, they were:

Argonne   which was a Fourth Army area until 26th June 1916
Left Bank   which included key areas such as Mort Homme and Cote 304
Right Bank   the heights above the town which were dominated by Douaumont
Southern flank   the line from Eparges to the apex of the St Mihiel Salient, which was shared with
                    neighbouring forces such as First Army and DAL.

The allocation of corps to each sector during 1916 was:

Argonne
XV CA 26.6.16-VCA   6.8.16-XVICA

Left Bank-
27.2.16- XIIICA   14.4.16-IXCA –22.5.16
25.2.16-VIICA-8.3.16
26.3.16- I CA –8.4.16
26.3.16- XXXIICA   10.6.16-XXXICA
29.3.16- VIICA –24.4.16

Right Bank
XXXCA   25.2.16-XXCA 24.4.16
25.2.16-XXCA- 24.4.16
27.2.16-ICA –26.3.16
08.03.16-XXICA
20.3.16-XXXIICA   5.4.16-IIICA   15.6.16-VICA- 15.7.16
29.3.16-VIICA –24.4.16
08.4.16- XIICA 22.6.16-XICA
01.09.16-XIVCA –22.09.16

Southern sector
IICA   20.6.16-IIICA
07.03.16-XIVCA –01.09.16 & 22.09.16-XIVCA 25.12.16- XVCA

Corps engaged in the battle for Verdun during 1916 will be listed in accordance with date of arrival in sector.

Argonne

XVCA
15th January- Avocourt/Malancourt 16th May-Bois d'Avocourt/Cote 304 -2nd November 1916
29DI   15.01.16-26.03.16
126DI   15.01.16-02.11.16
123DI   19.05.16-30.10.16
45DI   19.05.16-23.05.16
38DI   22.06.16-27.07.16
68DI   05.07.16-08.08.16
55DI   12.07.16-01.09.16
64DI   24.10.16-02.11.16

VCA
26th June-Aire/Haute Chevauchée/Four de Paris-6th August 1916
9DI   26.06.16-06.08.16
10DI   26.06.16-01.08.16
71DI   22.07.16-06.08.16
124DI   24.07.16-06.08.16

XVICA
6th August-Four de Paris/Haute Chevauchée –to 24th January 1917
130DI   06.08.16-16.09.16
31DI   04.09.16-24.01.17
32DI   16.09.16-24.01.17

Left Bank

VII CA
Bethincourt, Forges 25th February-8th March
67DI   25.02.16-08.03.16
25DI   07.03.16-08.03.16

XIIICA
Bois d'Avocourt, Malancourt, Bethincourt 27th February-14th April 1916
25DI   27.02.16-07.03.16
26DI   28.02.16-28.03.16
76DI   23.03.16-16.04.16
11DI   24.03.16-30.03.16

ICA
Chattancourt, Marre sector 26th March-8th April
22DI   30.03.16-08.04.16
24DI   04.04.16-08.04.16
23DI   06.04.16-08.04.16

XXXIICA
Hayette, Mort Homme, Chattancourt 26th March-10th June 1916
40DI   26.03.16-02.06.16
42DI   06.04.16-19.05.16
69DI   10.04.16-24.05.16
19DI   02.06.16-10.06.16
65DI   04.06.16-10.06.16

VIICA
Bois d'Avocourt, Bois Carré 29th March-24th April 1916
- 34DI 29.03.16-24.04.16
- 37DI 13.04.16-24.04.16

IXCA
Bois d'Avocourt, Camard 13th April-19th May 1916
- 18DI 13.04.16-08.05.16
- 45DI 20.04.16-19.05.16
- 17DI 23.04.16-08.05.16
- 152DI 05.05.16-12.05.16

XXXICA
Chattancourt, Marre 10th June 1916- 24th January 1917
- 19DI 10.06.16-29.07.16
- 65DI 10.06.16-29.09.16
- 64DI 26.07.16-13.10.16
- 64DI 02.11.16-24.01.17
- 55DI 09.11.16-24.01.17
- 71DI 06.01.17-24.01.17

Right Bank

XXXCA
Northern sector of RFV 10th August 1915-25th February 1916
- 67DI to VIICA
- 37DI to XXCA
- 72DI largely destroyed by 25th February
- 51DI to XXCA
- 14DI to XXCA
- 132DI to IICA

XXCA
Louvemont, Douaumont, 25th February-24th April
- 39DI 25.02.16-27.02.16
- 153DI 25.02.16-24.04.16
- 48DI 25.02.16-08.03.16
- 37DI 25.02.16-26.02.16
- 51DI 25.02.16-26.02.16
- 14DI 25.02.16-03.03.16
- 120DI 29.02.16-09.03.16
- 13DI 03.03.16-30.03.16
- 39DI 12.03.16-21.04.16
- 11DI 30.03.16-12.04.16
- 18DI 17.04.16-24.04.16
- 17DI 18.04.16-24.04.16

ICA
Poivre, Haudromont, Douaumont 27th February-26th March
- 1DI 27.02.16-26.03.16
- 2DI 27.02.16-08.03.16
- 39DI 27.02.16-12.03.16
- 42DI 10.03.16-31.03.16

XXICA
Etang de Vaux, Damloup, Eix 8th-20th March
13DI   08.03.16-20.03.16
27DI   08.03.16-20.03.16
43DI   09.03.16-20.03.16
77DI   16.03.16-20.03.16

XXXIIICA
Douaumont, Etang de Vaux, Eix 20th March-5th April
70DI   20.03.16-05.04.16
77DI   20.03.16-05.04.16
27DI   20.03.16-05.04.16
43DI   20.03.16-05.04.16
5DI   02.04.16-05.04.16

IIICA
Thiaumont, Etang de Vaux, Vieux Chapitre 5th April-15th June
5DI   05.04.16-15.06.16
43DI   05.04.16-11.04.16
6DI   08.04.16-15.06.16
69DI   08.04.16-10.04.16
4DI   10.04.16-27.04.16
14DI   11.04.16-16.05.16
48DI   25.04.16-11.05.16
35DI   02.05.16-20.05.16
27DI   05.05.16-13.05.16
124DI   16.05.16-08.06.16
36DI   20.05.16-28.05.16
63DI   01.06.16-15.06.16
52DI   04.06.16-15.06.16

XIICA
Haudromont, Thiaumont 8th April-22nd June
22DI   08.04.16-22.04.16
23DI   08.04.16-22.06.16
24DI   08.04.16-22.06.16
28DI   22.04.16-22.06.16
56DI   16.05.16-31.05.16
151DI   27.05.16-14.06.16

VICA
Bois Fumin, Damloup 15th June-15th July
12DI   15.06.16-28.06.16
63DI   15.06.16-18.06.16
130DI   15.06.16-28.06.16
127DI   24.06.17-06.07.16
131DI   28.06.16-15.07.16
71DI   06.07.16-15.07.16
16DI   11.07.16-15.07.16
154DI   27.07.16-01.08.16

XICA
Haudromont, Froidterre 22nd June 1916-27th January 1917
21DI   22.06.16-23.06.16

23DI   22.06.16-24.06.16
24DI   22.06.16-27.06.16
30DI   22.06.17-20.08.16
129DI   23.06.16-03.07.16
151DI   24.06.16-15.08.16
60DI   27.06.16-13.07.16
8DI   03.07.16-05.08.16
37DI   12.07.16-29.07.16
128DI   13.07.16-20.07.16
33DI   20.07.16-25.11.16
15DI   25.07.17-11.08.16
38DI   03.08.16-20.12.16
31DI   05.08.16-15.08.16
19DI   07.08.16-02.09.16
32DI   11.08.16-30.08.16
68DI   25.08.16-13.09.16
7DI   29.08.16-14.12.16
73DI   05.09.16-11.09.16
67DI   05.09.16-22.09.16
154DI   05.09.16-22.09.16
74DI   07.09.16-30.10.16
133DI   17.09.16-20.12.16
55DI   22.09.16-22.10.16
130DI   25.09.16-25.10.16
63DI   01.10.16-30.10.16
38DI   21.10.16-12.12.16
9DI   23.10.16-14.12.16
37DI   02.11.16-07.01.17
22DI   11.11.16-22.12.16
123DI   25.11.16-15.01.17
126DI   11.12.16-22.12.16
6DI   15.12.16-30.01.17
128DI   18.12.16-05.01.17
154DI   20.12.16-18.01.17
59DI   04.01.17-23.01.17
133DI   10.01.17-27.01.17

XIVCA

Damloup, Eix 12th August 1916-5th September 1916
154DI   12.08.16-05.09.16
73DI   28.08.16-05.09.16
67DI   02.09.16-05.09.16

XVCA

Vaux devant Damloup/Vaux 25th December 1916-24th January 1917
5DI   25.12.16-24.01.17
22DI   25.12.16-24.01.17
130DI   25.12.16-24.01.17

Southern Flank

IICA

Éparges, Trésavaux, Vaux-lès-Palameix until 22nd June 1916
3DI   00.00.16-22.06.16

4DI   00.00.16-22.06.16
16DI   00.00.16-18.03.16
132DI   00.00.16-19.03.16
68DI   28.02.16-07.03.16

XIVCA

Eix, Châtillon, Trésauvaux, 7th March 1916-12th August 1916

28DI   02.03.16-15.04.16
68DI   07.03.16-08.06.16
154DI   09.04.16-22.07.16
28DI   05.06.16-12.08.16
27DI   26.06.16-12.08.16

IIICA

Éparges, Dompcervin, Etang de Vargevaux 20th June 1916-30th January 1917

5DI   20.06.16-01.12.16
6DI   20.06.16-30.11.16
16DI   05.08.16-17.09.16
128DI   01.11.16-30.01.17
74DI   15.11.16-30.01.17
63DI   23.11.16-30.01.17
59DI   30.11.16-30.01.17
33DI   01.12.16-30.01.17

XIVCA

Eix, Châtillon, Trésauvaux, 7th November-25th December 1916

28DI   07.11.16-25.12.16
130DI   07.11.16-25.12.16
22DI   22.12.16-25.12.16

During 1917, the pattern of deployment in the Verdun Salient continued, but at a reduced level. A total of 46 divisions were rotated through the area. Of these, sixteen were employed in the major offensive, which took place on both banks of the Meuse between 20th and 24th August, with little overall success.
Second Army deployed the following corps during 1917:

Argonne

XVI CA 27th July-XIIICA

Left Bank

XXXICA   24th January –XVICA   10th September-IICA

Right Bank

XVCA   24th January-XXXCA   24th June-XCA
XICA   27th January-XVCA   15th September- VII
Added 7th July - XXXIICA until 28th August
Added 2nd October - IICAC until 18th November

Southern Flank

IIICA   30th January-IVCA   24th June-XVIICA   18th November-IICAC

Corps are listed according to date of arrival in sector:

Argonne

XVI CA shared between Argonne and Left Bank [see below]

XIIICA

Four de Paris, Avocourt 27th July 1917-21st August 1918

4DI	27.07.17-21.08.17
97DI	27.07.17-20.08.17
25DI	27.07.17-08.12.17
3DI	18.08.17-10.09.17
26DI	20.08.17-25.12.18
60DI	08.12.17-23.03.18
120DI	07.01.18-05.05.18
169DI	03.02.18-23.02.18
63DI	23.02.18-21.06.18
25DI	21.03.18-06.04.18
3DI	23.03.18-03.04.18
68DI	03.04.18-07.07.18
157DI	10.06.18-21.08.18
35DI	21.06.18-21.08.18
127DI	07.07.18-22.07.18
36DI	11.07.18-21.08.18

Left Bank

XVICA

Four de Paris, Avocourt, Charny 24th January-7th October 1917

32DI	24.01.17-15.03.17
55DI	24.01.17-05.02.17
31DI	27.02.17-01.09.17
132DI	15.03.17-12.04.17
32DI	12.04.17-26.06.17
97DI	26.05.17-26.07.17
73DI	26.06.17-22.07.17
63DI	01.07.17-19.08.17
DM	18.08.17-03.09.17
48DI	19.08.17-07.10.17
14DI	03.10.17-03.01.18

IICA

Avocourt, Haucourt, Bethincourt, 10th September 1917-25th March 1918

3DI	10.09.17-24.01.18
4DI	10.09.17-20.02.18
34DI	02.01.18-04.03.18

Right Bank

XVCA

Louvemont, Chambrette 24th January and Cote 304, Mormont, Louvemont 27th January-15th September 1917

21DI	24.01.17-17.02.17
22DI	24.01.17 24.01.17
133DI	24.01.17-09.02.17
123DI	09.02.17-01.07.17
126DI	01.03.17-29.06.17

42DI   29.06.17-18.07.17
20DI   14.07.17-20.10.17
123DI   07.08.17-26.08.17
14DI   22.08.17-15.09.17
19DI   10.09.17-15.09.17

XXXCA

Vaux, Damloup, Tranchée de Calonne 24th January-24th June 1917
5DI   24.01.17-12.02.17
128DI   24.01.17-22.03.17
72DI   24.01.17-05.05.17
163DI   08.02.17-14.06.17
16DI   05.05.17-19.06.17
131DI   14.06.17-24.06.17
19DI   19.06.17-24.06.17

XCA

Damloup, Haudiomont, Éparges, Tranchée de Calonne 24th June 1917-17th April 1918
19DI   24.06.17-28.08.17
131DI   24.06.17-17.09.17
7DI   20.08.17-05.11.17
165DI   13.09.17-13.10.17
42DI   17.09.17-05.10.17
163DI   05.10.17-09.11.17
19DI   09.10.17-14.03.18
131DI   05.11.17-31.03.18
20DI   06.11.17-03.03.18
52DI   15.01.18-17.04.18
33DI   28.02.18-17.04.18
34DI   12.03.18-17.04.18

XXXIICA

Louvemont, Bois de Caurieres, Damloup 7th July –20th August 1917
42DI   07.07.17-20.08.17
69DI   17.07.17-20.08.17
40DI   21.07.17-20.08.17

VIICA

Cote 344/Mormont 15th September 1917-3rd January 1918
19DI   15.09.18-03.10.17
20DI   15.09.18-20.10.17
131DI   26.09.17-18.10.17
14DI   03.10.17-03.01.18
48DI   07.10.17-02.01.18
41DI   18.10.17-21.11.17
128DI   20.10.17-01.12.17
37DI   21.11.17-06.12.17

IICAC

Chaume, Caurieres 2nd October –18th November 1917
15DIC   02.10.17-18.11.17
37DI   02.10.17-18.11.17
60DI   20.10.17-18.11.17
120DI   24.10.17-18.11.17

164DI   01.11.17-18.11.17
34DI   15.11.17-14.12.17

XVIICA
Chaume, Bezonvaux, Damloup 18th November 1917-20th March 1918
33DI   18.11.17-14.12.17
120DI   18.11.17-09.12.17
164DI   18.11.17-19.12.17
68DI   09.12.17-29.01.18
25DI   14.12.17-07.02.18
153DI   22.01.18-20.03.18
11DI   25.01.18-20.03.18
131DI   29.01.18-20.03.18
26DI   02.02.18-20.03.18

SOUTHERN FLANK

IVCA
Loclont, Paroches, Keour, Vargevaux 30th January-24th June 1917
63DI   30.01.17-01.04.17
33DI   30.01.17-04.03.17
59DI   30.01.17-28.03.17
8DI   04.03.17-24.04.17
124DI   01.04.17-10.05.17
55DI   24.04.17-23.05.17
33DI   23.05.17-24.06.17

XVIICA
Bois Loclont, St Mihiel, Vargevaux 24th June-18th November 1917
33DI   24.06.17-15.11.17
34DI   24.06.17-05.11.17
52DI   15.10.17-18.11.17
15DIC   05.11.17-18.11.17
10DIC   13.11.17-18.11.17

IICAC
Bois Loclont, Vargevaux 18th November 1917-24th March 1918
10DIC   18.11.17-24.03.18
15DIC   18.11.17-24.03.18
52DI   18.11.17-24.03.18

From a total of eighteen divisions in March 1918, the role and size of Second Army was reduced drastically during the course of 1918. In part this was because the destruction of the previous two years had rendered the Verdun as an area incapable of mounting any serious attacks. In addition, the requirement for divisions further west in Picardy, the Marne and Aisne, and in Champagne virtually eliminated the forces required for any further large-scale action in Verdun. Equally important, the arrival of the American forces during the course of 1918 brought about the allocation of most of the line between the Argonne and the Moselle to the US Army. By the autumn of 1918, the US First Army was fully established in the Argonne. After the elimination of the St Mihiel Salient, the US Second Army was established between the Meuse and the Moselle. After 30th September, all remaining French formations in the area were under American operational command. The last division assigned to Second Army-26DI- left on 9th November. On Armistice Day, QG Second Army was in the process of leaving Verdun for Nancy.

Second Army deployed the following corps during 1918:

ARGONNE

XIII CA until 21st August

Left Bank

II CA   until 25th March
XVIICA 29th March-24th June

Right Bank

X CA   17th April-XVIICA until 6th November
VIICA   31st January –29th March
XVIICA until 20th March

Southern flank

IICAC   until 6th November
Corps will be detailed in order of arrival in designated sectors

XVII CA
Forges, Cote 304, Beaumont, Bezoncourt, Damloup 29th March-24th June
20DI   29.03.18-23.05.18
4DI   29.03.18-17.05.18
168DI   29.03.18-18.04.18
25DI   18.04.18-24.06.18
29DI   01.05.18-24.06.18

XXCA
Forges, Samogneux, Cote 344, Mormont 15th January-29th March
39DI   15.01.18-29.03.18
168DI   15.01.18-29.03.18
11DI   15.01.18-29.03.18
68DI   01.03.18-29.03.18
4DI   18.03.18-29.03.18

IICAC
Damloup, Calonne, Maizey, Trésauvaux 17th April-12th September 1918
33DI   17.04.18-14.05.18
52DI   17.04.18-08.05.18
17DI   04.05.18-24.07.18
59DI   09.05.18-11.08.18
34DI   28.06.18-12.08.18
26DI   03.07.18-15.09.18
39DI   08.08.18-12.09.18
2DCP   08.09.18-12.09.18

XVIICA
Damloup, Trésauvaux, Bois Loclont, Vargevaux 24th June-6th November 1918
29DI   18.07.18-23.08.18
120DI   02.08.18-10.09.18
10DIC   08.08.18-06.11.18
157DI   21.08.18-14.09.18
18DI   23.08.18-18.10.18
15DIC   22.09.18-06.11.18
Under Command US Army from 30th September in St Mihiel sector

IICAC
39DI   30.09.18-28.10.18
2DCP   30.09.18-18.10.18
10DIC 06.11.18-11.11.18
15DIC 06.11.18-11.11.18

Third Army

[Armée de Châlons at Verdun]

Commanders

02.08.14-Pierre Ruffey
30.08.14-Maurice Sarrail
22.07.15-George Humbert

Army Troops, August 1914

Peleton/106RI
Cyclist Cie/69BCP
Escadron/5 RCh
2 groups, 2RAL
3 groups, 4RAL
3 Telegraph Cie
E Radio Detachment
23/3 Pont Cie, 7RG

Aviation

914-MF2, HF7, HF13, MF16
1918-Spa79, Br209, Br217, Br226

MAIN BATTLES

1914	1915	1916	1917	1918
Ardennes	Argonne	-	St Quentin	1st Noyon
1st Marne-	RevignyVauquois		Essigny/Moy	3rd Aisne Matz
Argonne				3rd Picardie
				2nd Noyon Serre

Ardennes-Marne 1914

Covered by VI CA [12DI, 40DI, 42DI], Third Army assembled east of the Meuse where it faced the German fortress of Metz. With its headquarters at Verdun, it held the line from Mangiennes/Conflans-en- Jarisy/Chambley/Pont a Mousson with 168,000 men. Its component corps were deployed in anticipation of an advance to the Moselle between Metz and Thionville. They were IVCA [7DI, 8DI], V CA [9DI, 10DI], and VI CA [12DI, 40DI, 42DI], with further support from 7DC and 3GDR [54DR, 55DR, 56DR and 72DR].

As the German intentions became clearer, Third Army, in accordance with Joffre's prewar plans, switched to face north, and began to move into the Belgian Ardennes. From the line Virton-Arlon, its task, on 21st August was to strike the left or southern flank of those German forces in conjunction with Fourth Army on
its left flank. Both armies encountered unexpectedly stiff German opposition in the battle of the Ardennes [which some describe as the battle of Virton]. The reserve divisions of both armies had to be formed into the Army of Lorraine*, between Virton, Longwy and Étain, to protect the northern approaches to Verdun. From
25th August, all three armies were forced back by the weight of the German advance. By the beginning of September, Third Army had anchored its right wing on Verdun but its centre and left had been forced further south and with their backs to the Meuse, now faced north-west! Third Army's contribution to the first battle of the Marne was to fight at Revigny with XVCA, XXICA, 3GDR, VICA and VCA. It was able to push the Germans back to an west-east line through the Argonne between Ste Menehoulde and Monfaucon.

*__The Army of Lorraine__ was formed on 17th August 1914 under the command of Paul Durand, who was succeeded by Paul Manoury on 21st August. It disbanded on 27th August. It consisted of 3GDR [54DR, 67DR, 72DR] and 3bisGDR [56DR, 65DR, 75DR].

VI CA

Covering corps, which fought from Crusnes/Doncon to the Othain in the battle of Virton. From 6th-14th September, during the battle of Revigny/1st Marne, it fought at Ivoiry, Cuisy and Chaumont-sur-Aire. After this it established and held the line Éparges/Souzey/Maizey to the south of Verdun where it was transferred to First Army on 8th January 1915.

12DI   02.08.14-15.01.15
40DI   02.08.14-15.01.15
42DI   02.08.14-12.09.14
72DR   01.09.14-02.09.14

IV CA

Fought between Eithe and Virton during the Ardennes campaign and then retreated to Ste- Menehoulde before transfer eastwards to Sixth Army on 2nd September.

7DI   02.08.14-02.09.14
8DI   02.08.14-02.09.14
10DI   31.08.14-01.09.14

V CA

Fought at Cosnes, Gorcy, and Ville-Haudlemont during the battle of Virton. Retreated to Cierges and then, fought along the line Brabant-sur-Roi/Louppy-le-Château/Vassincourt, during the battle of Revigny. From this position the corps moved forward to the Four-de-Paris/Vauqouis line in the Argonne. It remained in the Argonne until transferred to Second Army on 26th June 1916.

9DI   02.08.14-26.06.16
10DI   02.08.14-01.08.16
125DI   15.06.15-26.06.16
19DI   04.08.15-26.05.16

3 GDR

During the battle of Virton, fought to the north-east of Verdun at Jeandelize/Etain/Eton

54DR   10.08.14-17.08.14
55DR   10.08.14-17.08.14
56DR   10.08.14-17.08.14

Argonne 1914-1916

From September 1914 until June 1916, with QG at Verdun, then Ste-Menehould [8th January 1915] and Nettancourt [11th August 1915], Third Army held the line in the Argonne, the heavily wooded area which stretched northwards towards Montmédy and the Meuse near Sedan. With relatively small forces, rarely more than two corps, it fought a series of small scale but intense actions to prevent German penetration of the northern flank of the Verdun salient. Characteristic of this warfare was the extensive mining operations around the Butte de Vauquois, which commanded the north-south route from Varennes to Clermont. During the battles of the autumn of 1915, when Fourth and Second Armies sought to break-through on the open plains to the west, Third Army continued to hold this relatively small but vital sector. In June 1916 the Argonne sector was handed over to Second Army in order to place all those forces engaged in the struggle for Verdun under a single command: Second Army.

XV CA

During 1st Marne/Revigny, it fought at Vassincourt and then moved into the Argonne on 16th September to establish a line between Bois des Forges and Malancourt.

On 31st May 1915, it was moved westwards of the Argonne to the Aisne/Massiges sector where it served until 14th August [four days after leaving Third Army].

29DI   06.09.14-26.06.16
30DI   06.09.14-08.05.15

72DR   29.09.14-04.10.15
126DI   09.06.15-15.08.15

II CA
Transferred from Fourth Army and in line Vienne/Four-de-Paris/Bois d'Hauzy until 15th January 1915
3DI   03.01.15-15.01.15
4DI   03.01.15-18.01.15

XXXII CA
Replaced II CA 12th January and served Four-de-Paris/Bagatelle until 6th August 1915
40DI   12.01.15-08.08.15
42DI   17.01.15-19.07.15
128DI   03.07.15-08.08.15
15DIC   05.07.15-08.08.15

X CA
Operated between Houyette and Four-de-Paris 4th August 1915 until 24th June 1916
40DI   06.08.15-11.08.15
128DI   06.08.15-28.08.15
131DI   06.08.15-13.06.16
15DIC   06.08.15-14.08.15
19DI   09.08.15-28.01.16
20DI   10.08.15-23.06.16

XVIII CA
Entered line Houyette/Four-de-Paris 9th June 1916 -to Fourth Army 10th June and remained in line until 2nd October 1916
35DI   09.06.16-02.10.16
36DI   20.06.16-22.09.16

OISE 1916-1917

On 26th June 1916 QG Third Army was established at Verberie, to the north of Compiègne. Third Army was inserted into the front between Tenth Army and Fifth Army. It took over the positions previously held by Sixth Army, which had moved north to the Somme. It held the line between the Bois des Loges and Pernant. Its main task was to cover the Oise valley: which was a key route towards Compiègne and Paris. The area, facing Noyon and then St Quentin would be Third Army's principal area of operations for the rest of the war. It would hold the line while major operations were conducted on either side.

II CAC
Ex Tenth Army, 26th June, and returned to that army 3rd August. Held Avre/Armancourt/Beuvraignes/BelvalBois des Loges sector
10DIC   03.06.16-31.07.16
15DIC   03.06.16-31.07.16
87DT   30.06.16-31.07.16
DM   16.07.16-31.07.16

XIII CA
Ex Tenth Army 26th June –transferred to First Army 29th October 1916
Held Tracy/Quennevières/Pernant sector 27th April-2nd December 1916
25DI   30.06.16-27.09.16
26DI   30.06.16-01.07.16
81DT   30.06.16-19.10.16
120DI   30.06.16-23.08.16

53DI   15.08.16-29.10.16
61DI   12.09.16-29.10.16

XXX CA
Ex Tenth Army. 26th June - held Maucourt/Faucaucourt/Andechy sector until 6th December
58DI   15.11.16-06.12.16
72DI   15.11.16-01.12.16
132DI   15.11.16-17.01.17

I CAC
Held Andechy/Beuvraignes/Bois des Loges sector 1st December 1916-21st March 1917
3DIC   03.12.16-07.03.17
62DI   31.12.16-23.01.17
DM   25.01.17-08.02.17
28DI   22.01.17-29.01.17
45DI   04.03.17-15.03.17
154DI   12.03.17-21.03.17

XIV CA
Took over Maucourt/Andechy sector 17th January 1917. From 21st March until 2nd April followed German retreat to Vendeuil/Roupy/Essigny-le-Grand
124DI   17.01.17-18.02.17
132DI   17.01.17-04.02.17
8DI   25.01.17-07.02.17
62DI   27.01.17-03.04.17
27DI   02.02.17-02.04.17
154DI   05.02.17-22.02.17
28DI   21.03.17-04.04.17

In March 1917, Third Army faced the complex task of slowly advancing into the area of total devastation left behind as the Germans retreated to the Hindenburg Line. As part of the overall allied strategy for the spring of 1917, Third Army attacked towards St Quentin on 13th April. Its six divisions were intended to distract German attention from Nivelle's attack on the Chemin des Dames three days later. Compared with the disaster of that offensive, Third Army's activities were limited but relatively successful. During the course of 1917, the army's area of operations shrank to the east bank of the Oise, as it gave up territory on the left to the BEF. By the summer of 1917 it held the line Moy/Fere/Servais/Barisis aux Bois.

XIII CA
Transferred from First Army and held Essigny/Roupy sector-fought in St Quentin attack
26DI   22.03.17-26.04.17
120DI   22.03.17-27.05.17
25DI   01.04.17-01.07.17
27DI   02.04.17-08.05.17
87DI   20.05.17-09.06.17

XXXV CA
From 16th March pursued the Germans from Chauny/Tergnier/Vendeuil/Servais line-fought during St Quentin offensive and reached Moy/d'Urvillers line on 4th May. Withdrawn 7th August.
61DI   22.03.17-05.08.17
121DI   22.03.17-19.07.17
53DI   23.03.17-19.07.17

XXXIII CA
Ex First Army 22nd March in the Quincy Basse/Coucy-le-Ville/Barisis sector.

70DI 22.03.17-02.06.17
77DI 22.03.17-20.05.17

XI CA
In the St Quentin/Pontruet sector from 20th May until 26th June
In line between Urvillers and Pontruet, 29th June-24th August 1917
26DI 20.05.17-15.07.17
21DI 11.05.17-24.08.17
22DI 20.05.17-20.08.17
25DI 29.06.17-01.07.17
61DI 14.07.17-24.08.17

XIV CA
27DI 29.07.17-14.08.17
28DI 29.07.17-14.08.17
62DI 11.08.17-14.08.17

XXXVII CA
In line Moy-Vauxillon-Fère from 14th August 1917 until disbanded 18th January 1918
62DI 14.08.17-30.01.18
81DI 14.08.17-09.01.18
154DI 07.01.18-28.01.18

III CA
In line Dallon/Urvillers/Selency/Pontruet from 24th August 1917 to 14th January 1918
21DI 24.08.17-05.09.17
61DI 24.08.17-18.09.17
6DI 09.09.17-15.01.18
5DI 15.09.18-14.01.18

Third Army's line was reduced to that between Urvillers and Pontruet on 10th January 1918 and it was pulled out of the line completely on 12th February. Its area of operations was added to that of Sixth Army. With QG at Maignelay, it was to be a reserve force to support the BEF on the Somme. On 23rd March, the Army moved back to the line, Ollezy/Dury/Tugny-et-Pont/Barsisis as a direct result of the German spring offensive. With the BEF, and then First Army on its left, it sought to stem the German advance down the Oise, and to hold the line between that river and the Somme, between Nesle and Barisis.

V CA
Fought in the battles for Noyon and Picardy from 22nd March until 7th April 1918 by which time the corps had reached the line from Plémont to the Berliere. Transferred to First Army on 4th April.
55DI 22.03.18-26.03.18
9DI 22.03.18-31.03.18
10DI 22.03.18-28.03.18
35DI 23.03.18-04.04.18
53DI 25.03.18-04.04.18
77DI 27.03.18-04.04.18
62DI 03.04.18-07.04.18

II CC
In action from 23rd March until 1st April between Montdidier, Roye and Nesle; and then on the line Ressons/Lassigny/Guiscard
22DI 23.03.18-01.04.18
62DI 23.03.18-01.04.18
38DI 26.03.18-01.04.18

67DI   30.03.18-01.04.18

XXXV CA

Joined Third Army at Ribécourt on 27th March and fought between Montdidier, Assainvillers and Rollot, and then established the line Ayencourt/Rollet. Moved to Orvillers on 30th May and fought between Belloy and Ressons during the battle for the Matz, 9th June. Temporarily attached to Group Mangin 10th-13th June. Was in line between Wacqmoulin/Courcelles/the Ployon/Ayencourt from 13th June until 9th August. Transferred to First Army, 2nd August.

36DI   27.03.18-21.06.18
70DI   27.03.18-17.04.18
169DI   01.04.18-09.08.18
58DI   04.05.18-10.06.18
133DI   08.06.18-09.08.18

The line remained stable until the start of the third battle of the Aisne on 27th May 1918. Although the full force of the German attack was borne by Sixth army to the right, Third Army fought to retain its positions on the Oise. In particular, it successfully held the line of the river Matz between 9th and 12th June.

XVIII CA

Served between Rollot, la Berlière, and Cuvilly from 1st April until the start of the 3rd Battle of the Aisne where it was in action between Nampcel and the Oise from 30th May until 11th June.

38DI   01.04.18-11.06.18
62DI   01.04.18-03.04.18
67DI   01.04.18-23.05.18
58DI   22.05.18-10.06.18
15DI   01.06.18-18.08.18

XXXIII CA

In line between Plémont and the Oise from 2nd April. Fought at Mont Renaud until 7th May.

35DI   02.04.18-07.05.18
53DI   02.04.18-07.05.18
1DI   05.05.18-07.05.18

As the balance of power swung in favour of the allies, Third Army played its part in the offensive, which began on 8th August. It fought in the second battle of Noyon and then moved forward towards the Hindenburg Line. It reached the line Remingy/Tergnier/Barisis by 30th August. On 14th September, Army QG at Clermont was withdrawn and divisions handed over to First Army on the left. With the advance of First Army and of Tenth Army, on the right, there was no space left for Third Army.

XXXIV CA

Served between the Plémont and the Berlière from 7th April and then moved to Orvillers-Sorel on 30th May. During the battle for the Matz, it fought from 9th June at Ressons, Marquelize, and Elincourt-Ste Marguerite. By 2nd August a line was established at Courcelles-Épayelles. From 28th August advanced forward to the Hindenburg Line to Lagny and the Crozat canal which was reached on 14th September.

62DI   04.04.18-15.04.18
77DI   28.04.18-01.05.18
125DI   28.04.18-10.06.18
1DCP   28.04.18-10.06.18
18DI   09.06.18-25.06.18
69DI   09.06.18-18.06.18
165DI   10.06.18-19.08.18
121DI   13.06.18-28.08.18
6DI   24.06.18-28.08.18
74DI   17.07.18-23.08.18

129DI   02.08.18-05.09.18

II CA
Transferred from Sixth Army on the line between the Oise and Varennes/Plémont on 7th May. Engaged in the 3rd battle of the Aisne. Fought between Orval and Écouvillon during the battle for the Matz on 9th June. Then held the line of the Matz between Chevincourt and Béthancourt until 19th June.

53DI   07.05.18-13.06.18
72DI   07.05.18-13.06.18
67DI   07.05.18-13.06.18

XV CA
On 10th June joined the battle for the Matz between Chevincourt and Antheuil, to the south of the river. On 10th August, during the allied advance, in took part in the battle for Montdidier [3rd Picardie] between Marquelize, the Plessier, and Ribécourt. Assaulted the Massif de Thiescourt on 17th August, during the second battle for Noyon. Advanced to the Hindenburg Line between Liez and Tergnier. Handed over to First Army on 14th September.

123DI   05.06.18-23.0818
1DCP   10.06.18-14.0618
67DI   10.06.18-28.08.18
11DI   10.06.18-12.06.18
72DI   13.06.18-01.07.18
74DI   06.07.18-17.07.18
70DI   12.08.18-14.09.18
58DI   17.08.18-06.09.18
37DI   27.08.18-27.09.18

Group Mangin was attached to Third Army from 10th to 13th June when it evolved into Tenth Army.

XVIII CA
Joined the second battle for Noyon, between Carlepont and Pontoise, on 11th August. Detached Tenth Army 11th-30th August and then fought towards the Hindenburg Line via Barisis and then Tegnier until 24th September. Transferred to First Army 14th September.

15DI   02.08.18-15.09.18
38DI   02.08.18-06.09.18
132DI   05.09.18-14.09.18
67DI   11.09.18-14.09.18

On 27th October 1918, with QG at Chevreux, Third Army returned to active operations. It took over XVICA, XVIIICA and XXXVCA from Tenth Army, north of Laon. Tenth Army, with its aggressive commander [Mangin], was moved to Lorraine to prepare for a major offensive on Metz. In the latter days of the war, Third Army moved up between First and Fifth Armies, to the line Crecy-sur-Serre/ Pierrepont/ Sissonne. By 11th November, its two leading corps-XVI and XXXVI had reached the Belgian border on the line Rièzes/Rocroi/Revin.

XVI CA
From 30th October on line Crecy –sur-Serre/Mortiers/Chalandry and then advanced to Cul de Saarts from 5th November.

31DI   27.10.18-04.11.18
32DI   27.10.18-11.11.18
29DI   02.11.18-11.11.18
17DI   09.11.18-11.11.18
59DI   10.11.18-11.11.18

XVIII CA
At Caumont and Tonlis during the battle for the Serre. Advanced from St Pierremont to Aubentin between 5th and 10th November.

29DI   27.10.18-02.11.18

127DI 27.10.18-31.10.18
17DI 27.10.18-09.11.18
59DI 27.10.18-10.11.18

XXXV CA
Moved from the Serre to the Souche and then from Montcornet to Rumigny and then Rocroi.
25DI 27.10.18-11.11.18
72DI 27.10.18-11.11.18

Fourth Army

[Armée de Fontainebleau at St Dizier]

Commanders

02.08.14-Fernand de Langle de Cary
11.12.15-Henri Gouraud
19.12.16-Emile Fayolle
31.12.16-Pierre Rocques
23.03.17-Francois Anthoine
15.06.17-Henri Gouraud

Army Troops, August 1914

Peletons/46RI
Cyclist Cie/44BCP
Escadron/7RD   Br237, Spa212, Vr291
1 Group/2RAL   u/c-GC 12, GC21 & GC22 [15 sqns]
4 Telegraph Cie
F Radio Detachment
21/1 Pont Cie/7RG

Aviation

1914-V14, V21
1918-Br207, Br210, Br212, B223, Br232

Main Battles

1914	1915	1916	1917	1918
Ardennes	2nd Champagne	-	Moronvillers	4th Champagne
1st Marne-Vitry				Champagne et
1st Champagne				d'Argonne Somme-Py

With QG at St Dizier, Fourth Army was formed in the Argonne, between Mouzon and Mangiennes, as a reserve force, which would reinforce the expected advance of Third Army into Lorraine and help secure the capture of Metz. For this purpose, it was allocated XIICA, XVIICA and the Colonial Corps. As the evidence of the German advance into Belgium mounted, the Fourth Army was brought forward towards the Meuse. II CA and XI CA were transferred from Fifth Army: IX CA joined from Second Army. Together with Third Army on its right, Fourth Army, with 193,000 men, advanced north into the Ardennes in an effort to reach Bertrix/Neufchâteau and attack the German left flank. During the ensuing battle of Virton it was deployed with IX CA on the left, then XI CA, XVII CA, XII CA, CAC and then II CA. Forced back to the Meuse it fought a delaying action there until 28th August on which date the army virtually disintegrated and began the long retreat southwards, which ended at Vitry.

Fourth Army fought at Vitry during the first battle of the Marne with II CA [3DI, 4DI], CAC [2DIC, 3DIC], XVIICA [33DI, 34DI] and XII CA [23DI, 24DI]. French success allowed the army to advance northwards and establish a more permanent line in the chalk uplands between Reims and the Argonne forest. By 7th October 1914, with QG at Châlons-sur-Marne, Fourth Army held the line between Bois Sabot, Ville-sur- Tourbe, and Four de Paris.

With occasional changes of army boundaries, Fourth Army would remain in this position for the next four years and fight a series of major actions in what had been the main pre-war training area of the French Army. The open country provided little opportunity for major advances. From left to right, the main locations would be St Leonards, Pompelle, Prunay, Marquises, Prosnes, Moronvillers, Mont Cornillet, Mont Haut, Mont Sans Nom, Wacques, Moscou, Aubérive, Ste Hilaire-le-Grand, Navarin, Butte de Souain, Perthes-lès- Hurlus, Butte de Tahure, Butte de Mesnil, Mesnil-lès-Hurlus, Mamelles, Main de Massige, Ville-sur-Tourbe, Bois d'Hauzy, Vienne-le-Château and Haute Chevauchée.

XII CA

Advanced from Varennes and Stenay towards Neufchâteau in Belgium on 21st August. Fought at Menugoutte and Névramont, and then retreated back to the Meuse at Mouzon and Beaumont on 27th August. During the first battle of the Marne, it fought at Courdemange and Chatel-Rouald from 6th to 13th September. After temporary detachment to Ninth Army, 18th September-7th October, the corps established positions between Aubérive and Souain. On 21st December it fought between Souain and Ste Hilaire during the first battle of Champagne.

23DI 02.08.14-30.03.15
24DI 02.08.14-30.03.15
60DI 07.10.14-21.08.15   Under Army command from 28.12.14
96DT 16.12.14-25.03.15
91DT 21.12.14-23.03.15

XVII CA

Advanced from St Médard and Sart on 23rd August and fought at Jeanville, Luchy and Bertix and then fell back on the Meuse at Romilly, During 1st Marne, its role in the battle of Vitry was to engage the Germans between Grand Perthes, Certine, and Perriere. From 13th September 1914 until 3rd April 1915, it held positions between Bois Sabot, Perthes and Beausejours. It fought at Perthes during the first battle of Champagne.

33DI 02.08.14-03.04.15
34DI 02.08.14-02.04.15

Elements of 2DI, 7DI and 8DI served with the corps between December 1914 and March 1915

CAC

After a major action at Rossignol during the battle for the Ardennes, the Colonial Corps retreated southwards to St Remy and Farémont. It fought at Matignycourt and Thieblemont during the battle of the Marne, and then, advanced back north to Ville-sur-Tourbe. It held positions between the latter location and Massiges until 1st June 1915. Engaged between Ville-sur-Tourbe and Massiges during the first battle of Champagne.

2DIC 02.08.14-01.06.15
3DIC 02.08.14-31.05.15

II CA

Covering Corps, which was transferred from Fifth Army on 8th August 1914. Fought at Virton on 22nd August, and then, retreated across the Meuse at Cesse and Luzy to Cheminon-la-Ville and Heiltz-le-Hutier. It fought there during the battle of the Marne and advanced northwards to a line between Servon and Binarville. From 17th September 1914 until 15th January 1915, it held positions of the Argonne flank between Four de Paris and Bois d'Hauzy.

3DI   09.08.14-15.01.15
4DI   09.08.14-18.01.15
10DI 06.11.14-21.01.15

XI CA

Joined Fourth Army on 16th August for the advance into the Ardennes but transferred to Foch's Detachment on 29th August.

21DI 16.08.14-29.08.14
22DI 16.08.14-29.08.14
52DI 26.08.14-29.08.14

IX CA

Joined Fourth Army on 20th August for the advance into the Ardennes but transferred to Foch on 29th August.

17DI 20.08.14-29.08.14
18DI 20.08.14-29.08.14
DM   21.08.14-29.08.14

XXI CA

Transferred from Third Army 7th Sepember, fought at Sommepuis and Mailly and moved to Ninth Army on

14th September as Fourth Army began its advance northwards.
13DI   07.09.14-14.09.14

During the winter 1914-1915, Fourth Army sought to establish its line in a series of actions, which began with the first battle of Champagne in December 1914. The initial phase involved XVII CA and the Colonial Corps. In the spring of 1915, the major participants were XXI, I, II, XVI, and IV Corps in the area between Perthes and Mesnil.

I CA
Served in Beauséjours sector 28th December 1914-12th March 1915
1DI   28.12.14-12.03.15
2DI   20.01.15-02.03.15

IV CA
Served between Marquises and Wacques, 25th March to 28th October 1915: 2nd Champagne
7DI   22.03.15-30.10.15
8DI   22.03.15-23.09.15
91DT   25.03.15-15.06.15
96DT   25.03.15-15.06.15
124DI 01.06.15-15.10.15
60DI   17.09.15-28.10.15

XVI CA
Beauséjours/Mesnil-lès-Hurlus sector, 12th March-3rd September 1915. Transferred to Group Pétain on 10th August.
48DI   16.02.15-24.03.15
31DI   05.03.15-02.09.15
32DI   06.03.15-26.08.15
4DI   12.03.15-22.03.15

IICC
In the Marquises/Aubérive sector 11th September 1915 to 7th July 1916
2DC   11.09.15-07.07.16
4DC   11.09.15-07.07.16
7DC   11.09.15-07.07.16
60DI   28.10.15-03.03.16
152DI 11.0.616-30.06.16

II CAC
Souain/Perthes sector 20th June to 14th October 1915: 2nd Champagne
10DIC 12.06.15-29.09.15
15DIC 21.08.15-30.09.15
DM   14.09.15-18.10.15
48DI   29.09.15-09.10.15
64DI   08.10.15-14.10.15

By August 1915, Fourth Army had handed over responsibility for its right flank to Second Army, and with its companion, mounted the second battle of Champagne on 25th September 1915. It employed IV, XXXII, VII, IICAC, and VI Corps in its attacks, which produced very little in terms of territory gained. A further attempt was made at Navarin on 6th October.

XXXII CA
Ste-Hilaire/Aubérive sector, 29th August-30th December 1915: 2nd Champagne
40DI   29.08.15-30.12.15
42DI   03.09.15-30.12.15

VII CA

Wacques/Aubérive sector, 18th August-25th November 1915: 2nd Champagne
14DI   28.08.15-25.11.15
157DI   27.09.15-10.10.15
129DI   28.09.15-25.10.15
48DI   14.10.15-22.11.15

VI CA

Butte de Souain/Navarin sector 20th September 1915-3rd June 1916
Fought at Navarin 25th September 1915
56DI   26.09.15-11.05.16
12DI   28.09.15-14.04.16
51DI   02.10.15-15.10.15
30DI   09.10.15-14.10.15
64DI   14.10.15-29.10.15

During the course of 1916, Fourth Army held its line while attention and resources were diverted to the battles of Verdun and the Somme.

IV CA

Transferred from Second Army 20th December 1915 in the sector between the Maisons de Champagne and the river Aisne. Served there until 20th October 1916.
7DI   20.12.15-20.10.16
8DI   20.12.15-28.06.16
124DI   20.12.15-25.07.16
34DI   29.06.16-10.08.16
60DI   23.07.16-20.10.16
8DI   10.08.16-20.10.16
124DI   19.08.16-10.10.16
3DIC   30.08.16-09.10.16

XI CA

Transferred from Second Army 27th December 1915 and served between Moscou and Aubérive until 25th May 1916.
21DI   27.12.16-23.04.16
22DI   27.12.16-22.02.16
151DI   27.12.16-03.05.16
60DI   03.03.16-25.03.16

XV CA

Transferred from Second Army 5th January 1916 in the Mamelles, Côte 196 sector and served there until 16th May 1916
123DI   05.01.16-29.04.16
126DI   05.01.16-03.05.16
33DI   26.04.16-05.05.16

XXI CA

Butte de Souain/Côte 196 sector 2nd May-25th July 1916
13DI   23.04.16-21.07.16
43DI   01.05.16-25.07.16
152DI   18.07.16-25.07.16
13DI   02.05.16-18.06.16

IX CA

Aubérive/Épine de Vedegrange/Butte de Souain sector 3rd June-4th September 1916
152DI   26.05.16-07.06.16

17DI 29.05.16-09.09.16
18DI 02.06.16-02.09.16
3DIC 31.08.16-04.09.16

XVII CA
Marquises/Aubérive sector 7th July 1916 to 24th June 1917. Monts de Champagne 17th April 1917
33DI   29.04.16-04.07.16
152DI 07.07.16-18.07.16
34DI   10.08.16-24.04.17
19DI   09.09.16-08.01.17
15DI   20.01.17-24.06.17
33DI   19.03.17-03.05.17
DM   03.04.17-26.04.17
45DI   05.04.17-22.04.17
128DI 16.04.17-16.06.17
131DI 22.04.17-14.05.17
8DI   01.05.17-26.05.17
72DI   12.05.17-09.06.17
124DI 24.05.17-14.06.17
55DI   05.06.17-24.06.17
134DI 11.06.17-24.06.17

XVIII CA
Transferred from Third Army 9th June 1916 to hold Argonne sector between Four de Paris/Aisne/Main de Massiges until 21st October 1916.
35DI   09.06.16-02.10.16
36DI   26.06.16-22.09.16
124DI 25.07.16-19.08.16

I CA
Served west of Navarin in the Maisons de Champagne sector from 25th October 1916 until 20th January 1917.
2DI   16.10.16-20.01.17
60DI 20.10.16-20.01.17
1DI   02.11.16-20.01.17
51DI 25.11.16-12.01.17

VII CA
In the Argonne sector between Main de Massiges and Four de Paris, 2nd October 1916 until 3rd January 1917.
14DI   01.10.16-01.01.17
41DI   02.10.16-31.12.16
165DI 27.12.16-19.01.17
40DI   26.12.16-03.01.17

XXXII CA
In the Maisons de Champagne/Four de Paris sector, 3rd-28th January 1917
40DI   05.01.17-28.01.17
165DI 05.01.17-25.01.17

XII CA
Served from the Maisons to west of Navarin, 20th January-11th October 1917.
1DI 20.01.17-31.07.17
2DI 20.01.17-27.02.17

60DI	20.01.17-30.06.17
23DI	30.01.17-09.10.17
24DI	25.02.17-07.10.17
15DI	22.03.17-09.08.17
169DI	22.03.17-01.04.17
74DI	31.03.17-11.06.17
41DI	18.06.17-16.09.17
71DI	28.06.17-15.07.17
128DI	21.07.17-14.08.17
47DI	14.09.17-27.10.17

VIII CA

Served in the Argonne sector between the Maisons de Champagne and Four de Paris 28th January -22nd March 1917. In the Marquises/Prosnes sector 4th-24th April for the Monts offensive; and returned to the Argonne and served between the Courtine and Four de Paris from 10th May 1917 until 15th July 1918.

16DI	28.01.17-25.04.17
169DI	28.01.17-22.03.17
15DI	01.04.17-09.08.17
74DI	10.05.17-11.06.17
71DI	10.05.17-04.06.17
48DI	07.06.17-08.07.17
169DI	01.06.17-23.02.18
16DI	06.07.17-24.07.18
72DI	05.08.17-03.09.17
15DI	25.08.17-20.03.18
72DI	02.12.17-02.03.18
161DI	24.04.18-15.07.18
1DCP	03.07.18-15.07.18
63DI	04.07.18-16.07.18

As a preliminary to Nivelle's spring offensive on the Chemin des Dames, Fourth Army mounted a major offensive on 14th April 1917. Known either as the Monts de Champagne, or Moronvillers, Fourth Army initially deployed VIII, XVII and XII Corps. On 26th April X CA was added but hopes were dashed by the failures of the major offensive further west.

X CA

In line between Marquises and the Monts, 26th April-24th June 1917: fought at Cornillet 30th April.

131DI	22.04.17-14.05.17
20DI	24.04.17-25.05.17
19DI	25.04.17-15.05.17
59DI	16.05.17-19.07.17
132DI	29.05.17-25.06.17

IV CA

In the Marquises/Monts sector 24th June 1917 to3rd October 1917. Fought at the Monts 14th July and at Tahure 9th November. Served in the Somme-Py offensive and transferred to Fifth Army 17th October 1918.

8DI	21.06.17-29.11.17
59DI	24.06.17-19.07.17
132DI	24.06.17-25.0617
124DI	18.07.17-19.01.18
60DI	03.08.17-25.09.17
163DI	05.11.17-10.03.18
7DI	20.11.17-06.03.18
87DI	17.01.18-30.03.18

8DI 17.01.18-20.07.18
163DI 27.04.18-20.10.18
132DI 28.06.18-23.07.18
27DI 07.07.18-07.08.18
71DI 15.07.18-13.08.18
10DI 17.07.18-29.07.18
8DI 23.08.18-17.10.18
7DI 23.08.18-26.09.18

XXX CA

In the Monts/Aubérive sector 24th June 1917- 27th March 1918
55DI 24.06.17-15.07.17
134DI 24.06.17-23.09.17
72DI 01.07.17-23.07.17
132DI 21.07.17-17.09.17
72DI 14.09.17-07.11.17
97DI 20.09.17-19.01.18
132DI 05.11.17-27.03.18
87DI 17.01.18-27.03.18
72DI 28.02.18-27.03.18

XVIII CA

In the Mamelles/Aubérive sector 11th October 1917-8th March 1918
35DI 08.10.17-04.03.18
132DI 18.10.17-05.11.17
36DI 27.10.17-07.03.18

III CA

In the Epine de Vedegrange/Courtine sector 8th March-20th June 1918-later enlarged to take in Aubérive/Tahure/Mont San Nom
5DI 03.03.18-15.06.18
6DI 04.03.18-18.06.18
58DI 18.03.18-26.04.18
132DI 27.03.18-01.06.18

Fourth Army took over responsibility for the Reims sector on 29th March 1918. On 15th July, Reims came under attack as the Germans sought to eliminate the left-hand shoulder of their salient, which went southwards to the Marne. The army played a supporting role in the second battle of the Marne.

I CAC

Transferred from Fifth Army 29th March 1918 and returned to Fifth Army 27th May 1918. Served in the Bétheny/Marquises on the eastern outskirts of Reims.
2DIC 29.03.18-29.05.18
3DIC 29.03.18-29.05.18
134DI 29.03.18-29.05.18

XXI CA

Served in the Tahure/Mont Sans Nom sector 23rd June-15th July 1918. Fought at Tahure during the fourth battle of Champagne 15th July and again during the second battle of the Marne on 18th July. Remained in Fourth Army for the autumn offensive during which the corps fought in the Bois Sabot/Perthes sector from 25th September until 18th October. Transferred to Fifth Army on the latter date.
13DI 23.06.18-15.08.18
43DI 23.06.18-07.09.18
170DI 17.07.18-15.09.18

46DI   18.07.18-02.08.18
167DI   12.08.18-09.10.18
13DI   05.09.18-12.10.18
4DI   13.09.18-25.09.18
68DI   14.09.18-14.10.18
170DI   23.09.18-02.10.18
43DI   24.09.18-05.10.18
61DI   02.10.18-12.10.18
73DI   03.10.18-18.10.18

XXXVIII CA

Joined the line in the Mesnil/Vienne-le-Château sector on 29th August. During the Somme-Py battle, which began on 26th September, it advanced to the line Vaux-lès-Mourin/Autry/Binarville by 1st October. It crossed the Aisne on 9th October and advanced to Olizy/Termes, and then Falaise by 13th October. It took part in the battle of the Chesne on 1st November and reached Brieulle-sur-Bar/Boult-aux-Bois by 6th November.

71DI   29.08.18-21.10.18
161DI   29.08.18-07.10.18
1DCP   29.08.18-10.10.18
74DI   25.09.18-16.10.18
1DCP   16.10.18-03.11.18
2DM   17.10.18-25.10.18
125DI   19.10.18-25.10.18
71DI   25.10.18-05.11.18
74DI   28.10.18-03.11.18
87DI   30.10.18-11.11.18

As the allied offensive began on 26th September 1918, Fourth Army began a series of attacks, which led it northwards out of its accustomed positions. On that date Fourth Army deployed seven corps between Prunay and Vienne-le-Château. They were IV, II, XXI, IX, XI, XIV and XXXVIII CA. The Army's contribution to the battle of Champagne and the Argonne in which it fought in conjunction with First American Army on its right, was the battle of Somme-Py which until 14th October. After an advance northwards, it fought the battle for the Chesne between 1st and 6th November. From there it pushed northwards towards the Meuse, and, on 11th November, had reached the line, Mèziéres, Sedan, Pont Maugis with XXXVIII, XI, IX and XIV Corps.

II CA

Fought Mesnil and Perthes during the Somme-Py battle, 25th September-13th October 1918. By the latter date had advanced to a line from the west of Voncq to Conde-lès-Vouziers.

3DI   05.09.18-13.10.18
4DI   25.09.18-13.10.18
48DI   26.09.18-16.10.18
14DI   26.09.18-10.10.18   To XIV

XI CA

Joined the line at Souain on 25th September, and advanced to the line St Etienne/St Clementen Arnes by 5th October. Reached Givry/Thugny-Trugny by 11th October. Advanced to the Meuse on 5th November towards Mèziéres/Amagne-Lucquoy.

21DI   20.09.18-08.10.18
22DI   18.09.18-15.10.18
151DI   26.09.18-10.10.18
7DI   07.10.18-20.10.18
154DI   12.10.18-25.10.18
163DI   17.10.18-20.10.18
61DI   18.10.18-11.11.18
21DI   20.10.18-08.11.18

22DI   25.10.18-11.11.18
7DI   06.11.18-11.11.18
2DCP   07.11.18-11.11.18

IX CA

Joined the line between Mesnil-lès-Hurlus and Main de Masiges on 23rd September. During the Somme-Py battle it advanced to Marvaux-Mieux/Challerange. In the battle of the Chesne, it advanced to the Plateau des Ileux/Vouziers line from 1st November. Five days later, it advanced to the river Meuse via Quatre-Champs to Sedan.

157DI   16.09.18-08.10.18
2DM   26.09.18-30.09.18
120DI   26.09.18-15.10.18
125DI   06.10.18-13.10.18
73DI   18.10.18-23.10.18
48DI   13.10.18-16.10.18
134DI   14.10.18-29.10.18
53DI   16.10.18-31.10.18
40DI   26.10.18-11.11.18
48DI   28.10.18-11.11.18
120DI   30.10.18-08.11.18

XIV CA

On 26th September joined Fourth Army between Souain and Aubérive, and took part in the Somme-Py battle. By 4th October it had reached the line St Clement à Arnes/Béthenville, Reached the Retourne 10th-11th October and, after period of rest, advanced to Terrin/Voncq and Attigny from 28th October. From 5th November it moved to the Meuse at Dom-le-Mesnil.

28DI   26.09.18-07.10.18
154DI   26.09.18-12.10.18
68DI   24.09.18-14.10.18
22DI   25.10.18-11.11.18
124DI   28.10.18-04.11.18
14DI   30.10.18-10.11.18
163DI   31.10.18-11.11.18

Fifth Army

[Armée de Paris at Rethel]

Commanders

02.08.14-Charles Lanrezac
03.09.14-Louis Franchet d'Esperey
31.03.16-Olivier Mazel
22.05.17-Joseph Micheler
10.06.18-Edmond Buat
05.07.18-Henri Berthelot
07.10.18-Louis Guillaumat

Army Troops, August 1914

Cyclist Cie/66 BCP [no peletons ex RI]
Escadron/6RD
1 group/4RAL
9 Telegraph Cie
G Radio Detachment
24/2 Pont Cie/7RG

Aviation

1914-D4, D6, C11, N12, REP15
1918-Spa76, Br216, Br 222, Br223, Group 4/1RAL
        Br231, Sal230
& u/c-GC16 [4 sqns]

Main Battles

1914	1915	1916	1917	1918
Charleroi	-	-	2nd Aisne	3rd Aisne
1st Guise				2nd Marne
1st Marne-Deux				St Thierry Serre
Morins				
1st Aisne				

With its headquarters as Rethel, Fifth Army was intended to guard the frontier with Belgium in case the Germans invaded that country. As the initial threat appeared to be further east, and not to the north in Belgium, the army lost its covering corps [IICA], another corps [XI CA] and two reserve divisions [52DR and 60DR] to Fourth Army before it began operations. [Sordet's cavalry had ridden towards Liege and found little evidence of a German presence]. As Lanrezac's concern about the German advance through Belgium grew, he moved QG to Signy-le-Petit, and gained XVIII CA and then, with 254,000 men, Fifth Army moved north between the Sambre and the Meuse to hold the line Charleroi/Namur. It fought the battle of Charleroi, 21st-23rd August, with IIICA and X CA but had to withdraw as Fourth Army had failed to secure the line of the Meuse at Givet.

During its long retreat to the Marne and beyond, Fifth Army fought an important rear-guard action, south of Guise, between the Oise and the Serre. Its retreat came to halt between Montmirail and Esternay from which position it fought for control of the Morin rivers during the first battle of the Marne. It fought with XVIIICA, 4GDR, XCA, IIICA and ICA during that battle. After its initial struggle, Fifth Army advanced northwest towards the Marne between Château-Thierry and Dormans. As the Germans retreated from the line of the river Aisne, Fifth Army crossed the Vesle and liberated Reims on 12th September.

As the front line developed into a line of trenches, Fifth Army controlled a line from the Chemin des Dames, north of Maizey to the eastern outskirts of Reims.

I CA

After cooncentration at Aubenton, the corps crossed the Meuse between Mézièrs and Givet, and advanced towards Dinant. It fought at St Gérard during the battle for Charleroi, 23rd August; and at Sains-Richaumont 29th August; during the battle of Guise. As the left wing of the Army, the corps fought at Esternay and Montmirail, and advanced to the Marne at Dormans. From 13th September, it advanced towards Reims and established positions between Cavaliers de Coucy and Bétheny. A sector between Ville-aux-Bois and Berry- au-Bac was held from 18th September until 3rd November. Then the corps moved westwards to the Chemin des Dames and took over positions between Chevreux, Soupir and Condé-sur-Aisne which were held until 8th December 1914.

1DI	02.08.14-10.12.14
2DI	02.08.14-12.12.14
51DR	20.08.14-31.08.14
69DR	29.09.14-04.10.14

II CA

Covering corps; In Mangiennes, Stenay, Spincourt area until transferred to Fourth Army, 14th August

3DI	02.08.14-14.08.14
4DI	02.08.14-14.08.14

III CA

Advanced into Belgium when it crossed the Meuse between Mézières and Sedan, and fought to the south of Charleroi 23rd-24th August, and then, between Landifay and Courjoumelles, in the battle of Guise 29th August. During the battle of the Marne, it advanced from Courgivaux and Montceaux-lès-Provins to the outskirts of Reims. There it fought on the north-western approaches to the city, between the Godat and Brimont during the battle of the Aisne. From 17th September 1914 until 27th April 1915, the corps held positions between Godat and Courcy.

5DI	02.08.14-27.04.15
6DI	02.08.14-27.04.15
38DI	16.08.14-24.08.14
37DI	28.08.14-09.09.14
Tassin	09.12.14-27.04.15

X CA

During the battle of Charleroi, the corps fought at Fosse and Mettet, followed by action near Sains- Richaumont during the battle of Guise. During the battle of the Marne, the corps advanced from Sezanne and Villeneux-lès-Charleville and was detached to the Ninth Army [10th-12th September] but reached Reims on the 13th September. After a week of fighting for the Fort de la Pompelle, the corps established a line to the north-west of the city between the Neuvillete and Cavaliers de Coucy.

19DI	02.08.14-29.09.14
20DI	02.08.14-29.09.14
37DI	16.08.14-24.08.14
51DR	31.08.14-25.09.14

XI CA

Assembled between Sedan and Romilly but transferred to Fourth Army, 16th August

21DI	02.08.14-16.08.14
22DI	02.08.14-16.08.14
69DR	15.08.14-16.08.14

4 GDR

After fighting on the Sambre, 21st-25th August, 4GDR fought between Urvillers and Moy during the battle for Guise. During the battle of the Marne, it advanced from Villers St George to Cierges and then Berry-au- Bac, and then fought between the Neuvillette and Cavaliers from 18th to 25th September.

51DR	15.08.14-20.08.14
53DR	15.08.14-26.09.14
69DR	15.08.14-29.09.14

XVIII CA

Engaged between Gozée, Thuin and Fontaine-Valmont during the battle of Charleroi, and then at Ribemont and Villers-sur-Sec during the battle of Guise. During 1st Marne, it advanced from positions north of Provins to Château-Thierry and then to the Chemin des Dames where it dug in between Craonne and Hurtebise during 1st Aisne. From 14th September 1914 until 24th April 1916, the corps held the Chemin des Dames sector from the Ailles/ Paissy road to Bois de Beau Marais

35DI	18.08.14-16.04.16	36DI	18.08.14-24.04.16
38DI	24.08.14-26.10.14	ExIII to III	
69DI	14.09.14-17.09.14		

Apart from one short break, with QG at Jonchery-sur-Vesle, Fifth Army spent the next four years defending Reims and the eastern end of the Chemin des Dames. Throughout this period, its prime responsibility was to hold the city. During this period, although there was little movement, a series of sharp engagements took place around Reims, from Fort de la Pompelle, in the east, to Bétheny and Cavaliers in the north. In addition, Fifth Army had to defend the line of the Vesle, and of the Aisne at the eastern end of the Chemin des Dames. There the high ground, which overlooked the rivers and the plain towards Reims was the scene of many encounters. The length of Fifth Army's sector on the Aisne would vary depending on requirements for other armies elsewhere.

Secteur Reims

Formed 25th October 1914 at Reims, between the Neuvillete and Marquises. Retitled **Groupement de Reims** on 26th April 1915 and then **XXXVIII Corps d'Armée** on 17th August 1915. Served on the outskirts of Reims until 9th June 1917. During the second battle of the Aisne, it fought at the Cavaliers de Courcy. Occupied the sector between the Miette and the Neuvillette from 12th June 1917 until 10th May 1918.

51DI	12.10.14-26.05.15
52DI	12.10.14-27.02.16
DM	12.10.14-23.04.15
123DI	15.06.15-23.08.15
30DI	17.08.15-22.09.15
97DT	18.09.15-04.12.16
30DI	04.11.15-07.06.16
67DI	29.04.16-22.08.16
48DI	04.06.16-27.06.16
56DI	23.06.16-07.09.16
151DI	21.08.16-28.06.17
27DI	04.09.16-02.01.17
41DI	29.01.17-12.05.17
37DI	15.02.17-01.04.17
89DT	16.02.17-05.05 17
46DI	12.06.17-25.06.17
152DI	20.06.17-29.07.17
74DI	02.07.17-14.05.18
71DI	25.07.17-23.02.18
67DI	01.02.18-18.03.18
157DI	28.03.18-21.05.18

I CA

In sector from Bois de Beau Marais to the Neuvillette, 27th April 1915-19th February 1916

1DI	22.04.15-20.02.16
2DI	22.04.15-12.02.16
122DI	27.04.15-04.10.15

XXXVII CA

Occupied the left bank of the Aisne from Pernant to Condé-sur-Aisne, 10th June 1915 to 6th February 1916, and then between the Bois de Beau Marais and the Neuvillette, 16th February 1916 to 19th January 1917. Transferred to Sixth Army 6th January 1917

63DI   10.06.15-20.05.16
89DT   10.06.15-11.12.16
55DI   08.02.16-20.06.16
22DI   17.05.16-08.09.16
69DI   06.06.16-08.02.17
30DI   23.09.16-16.12.16
158DI   23.09.16-19.01.17
10DI   13.12.16-21.01.17

XV CA

Ex Sixth Army, served between the Miette and Beau Marais, 2nd September 1915-12th November 1915
126DI   29.08.15-15.10.15
123DI   31.08.15-18.11.15

XVI CA

Served between Pernant and Condé on the Chemin des Dames, 6th February-9th July 1916
31DI   06.02.16-09.07.16
32DI   06.02.16-09.07.16
89DT   06.02.16-09.07.16

I CA

In sector Soupir/Beau Marais, 20th April-24th July 1916
2DI   14.04.16-24.07.16
1DI   21.04.16-20.07.16

XII CA

Served between Pernant and Soupir, 9th-22nd July 1916 and then between Soupir and Beau Marais, 24th July-23rd September 1916
24DI   17.07.16-17.09.16
89DT   09.07.16-30.03.17
23DI   22.07.16-23.09.16
30DI   25.08.16-23.09.16

GROUPEMENT BAQUET

Served between Soissons and Pernant, 22nd July-11th December 1916
89DI   22.07.16-11.12.16
127DI   22.07.16-26.08.16
30DI   26.08.16-16.09.16
2DC   02.12.16-11.12.16
7DC   02.12.16-11.12.16

In preparation for Nivelle's spring offensive, Fifth Army took a large section of the Chemin des Dames and became the eastern wing of the planned assault force. The army employed an substantial force of tanks to support the assault. When the attacks began on 16th April 1917, Fifth Army achieved some limited successes between Craonne and Berry-au-Bac: sufficient to lift some of the gloom of failure.

V CA

From 23rd December 1916 until 27th January 1918, operated between Moulin Pontoy and Berry au Bac. Attacked near Juvincourt on 16th April 1917 during 2nd Aisne
10DI   23.12.16-06.01.18
69DI   23.12.16-10.04.17
9DI   31.12.16-18.12.17
162DI   20.10.17-13.03.17
125DI   01.02.17-22.01.18

47DI   01.06.17-04.07.17
55DI   04.08.17-04.10.17
55DI   06.01.18-28.01.18

I CA

In line between the Ployon and Hurtebise 26th-29th January 1917, and between Vauclerc and Beau Marais, 13th March- 21st April 1917. It fought between the plateau de Vauclerc and Craonne on 16th April 1917.

1DI   17.01.17-21.04.17
162DI   26.01.17-21.04.17
51DI   31.01.17-08.04.17
2DI   08.03.17-19.04.17

VII CA

In line between Sapigneul and the Cavaliers, 13th February-12th July 1917. Attacked Mont Spin on 16th April.

41DI   29.01.17-12.05.17
14DI   19.02.17-04.07.17
37DI   08.04.17-22.04.17
40DI   14.04.17-22.04.17
152DI   19.04.17-23.05.17
46DI   28.04.17-19.05.17
45DI   19.05.17-18.08.17
157DI   09.07.17-12.07.17

XXXII CA

In the Sapigneul sector from 13th March for the second battle of the Aisne. Tranferred to Tenth Army 21st April

69DI   13.03.17-07.05.17
165DI   04.04.17-19.05.17
42DI   14.04.17-18.05.17
40DI   14.04.17-17.04.17

II CA

Held in reserve for 2nd Aisne from 4th April. In line between Mont Spin and Sapigneul, 22nd April-12th June 1917.

3DI   17.04.17-03.06.17
4DI   22.04.17-21.05.17
167DI   23.04.17-27.05.17
46DI   19.05.17-12.06.17

II CC

Held the Reims sector between Cavaliers and Marquises, 9th June 1917-21st January 1918

7DC   09.06.17-23.07.17
2DC   09.06.17-23.07.17
4DC   09.06.17-21.01.18
151DI   09.06.17-28.06.17
167DI   25.06.17-20.08.17
58DI   08.08.17-21.01.18
6DC   04.08.17-21.01.18
2DIC   16.01.18-21.01.18
3DIC   18.01.18-21.01.18

XXXIV CA

In sector Mont Spin-Cavaliers, 12th July 1917-28th March 1918

45DI   12.07.17-22.08.18
157DI   12.07.17-28.03.18
58DI   15.08.17-18.03.18

164DI 19.08.17-16.10.17
134DI 12.10.17-28.03.18

I CAC
In line between Bétheny and Marquises from 14th January 1918. Transferred to Fourth Army 29th March.
2DIC   16.01.18-29.03.18
3DIC   18.01.18-29.03.18

When 'Operation Blucher' began on 27th May 1918, Fifth Army was forced back from its long-held positions of the Chemin des Dames, as Sixth Army, on its left, collapsed. It was forced back across the Vesle but held on to its crucial position at Reims. It established a platform for future success by retaining control of the Montagne de Reims and the Ardre valley. In these crucial actions Fifth Army was assisted greatly by the attached II Italian and IX British Army Corps. From this base-line Fifth Army held the left shoulder of the German salient which extended towards the Marne, and it provided a starting position for allied success in the second battle of the Marne.

I CC
From 29th May until 20th July, this corps between the Vesle and the Marne with several transfers between armies. From 1st June it fought at Champlat and Courthièzy, and then south of the Marne between Oeuilly and Festigny-les-Hameaux. In 4th Champagne, it fought at Oeuilly and Montvoison from 15th July.
1DC   29.05.18-07.06.18
13DI   29.05.18-08.06.18
40DI   29.05.18-12.06.18
120DI 30.05.18-12.06.18
1DC   15.07.18-20.07.18
3DC   15.07.18-20.07.18
5DC   15.07.18-20.07.18
77DI   15.07.18-20.07.18
131DI 15.07.18-20.07.18

I CAC
From 27th May fought in the third battle of the Aisne between Courcy and Pompelle. Fought in the Montagne de Reims, 15th-18th July, and in and around Reims during second Marne, 18th July-30th September. It fought in the battle of St Thierry, 30th September-16th October by which time it had advanced towards Herpy. From there, it took part in the battle of the Serre, between 16th October and 6th November. It reached the line Château Porcien/Herpy by 30th October. It left the frontline for transfer to Tenth Army and the proposed Lorraine offensive on 6th November.
2DIC   29.05.18-09.11.18
3DIC   29.05.18-31.10.18
134DI 29.05.18-01.10.18
45DI   29.05.18-06.08.18
7DI   09.07.18-31.07.18
77DI   20.07.18-03.08.18
15DI   30.07.18-18.08.18
168DI 23.07.18-06.08.18
131DI 30.07.18-18.08.18
77DI   24.08.18-29.09.18

V CA
Joined Fifth Army on 30th May 1918 and fought at Ville-en-Tardenois and Vrigny during the third battle of the Aisne. Operated in sector Champlat/Vrigny from 3rd June. During 4th Champagne it was engaged between Vandieres-sous-Châtillon and Bois du Roi, 15th-18th July. In 2nd Marne, fought near Belval-sous-Chatillon and advanced to the Vesle at Breuil. Held the sector on the Vesle between Unchair and Jonchery, 7th August-14th September. Attacked north from the Vesle to Glennes and Romain, 14th-30th September. Reached the Aisne-Marne canal and progressed north towards the Suippe during the battle of St Thierry, 30th September-20th October. Then, in sector between Neufchâtel-sur-Aisne

and Berry-au-Bac, until a further attack towards the Malmaison and the Selve on 20th October. Advanced on the line Selve/Liart to Renwez and reached the Meuse on 11th November.

28DI	30.05.18-12.06.18
154DI	30.05.18-31.05.18
40DI	12.06.18-20.07.18
120DI	12.06.18-09.07.18
8DI	17.06.18-18.07.18
51DI	30.06.18-08.07.18
10DIC	15.07.18-30.07.18
7DI	15.07.18-08.08.18
1DC	16.07.18-19.07.18
9DI	18.07.18-21.10.18
168DI	21.07.18-23.07.18
14DI	24.07.18-01.08.18
10DI	31.07.18-11.11.18
20DI	31.07.18-26.08.18
45DI	08.09.18-08.10.18
62DI	19.09.18-23.09.18
52DI	23.09.18-11.11.18
53DI	24.09.18-09.10.18
10DI	30.09.18-11.11.18

XIV CA

Joined from Ninth Army at Troissy, 15th July 1918. Fought in the Ardre/Vesle area from Jonchery to the north-east of Reims, 6th August-11th September.

20DI	20.07.18-31.07.18
131DI	20.07.18-22.07.18
14DI	01.08.18-04.08.18
77DI	01.08.18-03.08.18
16DI	03.08.18-30.09.18
168DI	06.08.18-11.09.18

As the allied autumn offensive began, Fifth Army began its forward advance on 30th September in the battle for St Thierry [XXCA, IIICA, XIIICA, VCA, ICAC]. It joined the allied advance northwards towards the Serre, where it played a major role in the struggle for that line [XXICA, IVCA, XIVCA, IIICA, XIIICA, VCA, ICAC] . By 11th November, with its forward headquarters at Château Porcien, Fifth Army had advanced just beyond its original 1914 positions at Rethel. With XXI CA [9DI, 43, 62DI], V CA [10DI, 52DI], and XIII CA [13DI, 151DI], it had reached a line along the Meuse between Charleville, Château Regnault and Revin.

III CA

Transferred from Sixth Army and advanced from the Vesle to the Aisne between Villers-en- Prayère to Presles by 9th September. In sector between Basilieux-lès-Fismes and Villers-en- Prayère from 23rd September. In the battle of St Thierry, advanced from there, via Merval and Craonne to Sissonne. Retired from frontline 1st November.

6DI	09.09.18-06.11.18
52DI	09.09.18-21.10.18
164DI	09.09.18-18.09.18
62DI	23.09.18-06.10.18

XX CA

Joined from Tenth Army in positions between Braine and Beuil-sur-Vesle on 24th September. Advanced towards Berry-au-Bac and Romain during the battle of St Thierry, 30th September-10th October. During the battle of the Serre, it advanced from Vendeuil and Ribemont towards the Guise/Laon road and Landifay, 18th October-1st November. Fought near Audigny during the second battle of Guise and moved from there towards Froidestrées where it went into reserve on 9th November.

45DI	24.09.18-09.10.18

153DI 25.09.18-10.10.18
134DI 01.10.18-05.10.18

XIII CA

Occupied the sector between Reims and Jonchery on 11th September. Advanced northwards from the Vesle to Muizon and liberated the Aisne-Marne canal by 5th October. Fought from St Etienne-sur-Suippe to Asfeld-la-Ville by 13th October. Fought between Recouvrance, St Germaincourt and the Thour during the battle of the Serre, 20th-30th October. Then held the line between Recouvrance and Herpy before advancing towards the Meuse on 5th November. It had reached Bel-Air and Varidon by 11th November.

16DI   11.09.18-01.11.18
168DI 11.09.18-10.10.18
45DI   09.10.18-05.11.18
151DI 20.10.18-09.11.18
28DI   25.10.18-04.11.18
9DI   30.10.18-05.11.18
13DI   01.11.18-11.11.18
2DIC   05.11.18-09.11.18

XXI CA

Transferred from Fourth Army and fought between Recouvrance and Nizy-le-Comte during the battle of the Serre. Advanced via Signy-l'Abbaye to the Meuse near Monthermé by 11th November

170DI 15.10.18-28.10.18
43DI   20.10.18-11.11.18
167DI 22.10.18-10.11.18
62DI   28.10.18-11.11.18
9DI   05.11.18-11.11.18

IV CA

Transferred from Fourth Army 17th October between Nanteuil-sur-Aisne and Thugny-Tugny. After the battle for the Serre, it advanced to the Meuse via Laonais to Charleville.

SIXTH ARMY

COMMANDERS

26.08.14-Michel Maunoury
13.03.15-Pierre Dubois
26.02.16-Emile Fayolle
19.12.16-Charles Mangin
04.05.17-Paul Maistre
11.12.17-Denis Duchene
10.06.18-Jean Degoutte -11.09.18
15.10.18-Antoine Baucheron de Boissoudy

AVIATION

1915-Bl3, C10, MF16, C30
1918-Spa62, Sal225, Br239 & u/c GC23 [6 sqns]

MAIN BATTLES

1914	1915	1916	1917	1918
Ardennes	-	Somme	2nd Aisne	3rd Aisne
1st Marne- Ourcq				2nd Marne
1st Aisne				Flanders
1st Picardie				

MARNE 1914

On 26th August 1914 the commander and QG of the Army of Lorraine were ordered to move from Verdun to Montdidier to form QG Sixth Army. This new forces was to command those divisions being assembled north-east of Paris to protect the capital from the advancing German First Army. With its formation covered by Sordet's cavalry and VII CA, by 3rd September it commanded VII CA [14DI, 63DR], 5 GDR [55DR, 56DR], 6GDR [61Dr, 62DR] and Bridoux's cavalry corps [1DC, 3DC and 5DC] on the left flank of the BEF. IV CA joined on the 7th and XIII CA on the 11th as the army fought in the battle of the Marne. During this operation it advanced eastwards to the line of the river Ourcq and successfully threatened the German right flank. It pursued the Germans beyond the Ourcq and gained control of the area between the rivers Oise and Aisne at Poussy sur Aisne.

6 GDR

Formed 28th August and joined Sixth Army on 9th September. It fought north-east of Paris from 6th September to reach Crépy-en-Valois and Jaulzy on the 11th, and then held the line between Moulin-sous-Touvent, Tracy-le-Val, and Bailly during the battle of the Aisne, 14th September-1st October., and remained there until 15th December.

61DR   28.08.15-15.12.14
62DR   28.08.14-02.10.14
45DI   15.09.14-03.10.14
37DI   15.09.14-15.12.14

VII CA

In action between Péronne and Proyart, 29th-30th August. Fought along the Ourcq from Brécy, Manouerve to Bouillancy, 6th-13th September, and then to Fonyenay and Vic-sur-Aisne. From 13th September 1914 until 4th August 1915 it consolidated and held the sector on the Aisne between Autreches and Nouvion-Vingré. It was handed over to Fifth Army on the latter date.

14DI   28.08.14-04.08.15
63DR   28.08.14-02.02.15

121DI   14.06.15-04.08.15

5 GDR

Fought along the Ourcq from 5th September, and then north of Soissons from 13th September to 24th September. It remained in line between Soissons and Pernant until 13th Janaury 1915 when it moved eastwards to the junction of the Aisne and Vesle. On 10th June 1915 it became XXXVII CA. On 6th August it was transferred to Fifth Army.

55DR   05.09.14-30.04.15
56DR   05.09.14-30.09.14
45DI   15.09.14-03.10.14
85DT   17.01.15-24.03.15
63DI   26.02.15-06.08.15
89DT   23.04.15-06.08.15

IV CA

Fought in 1st Marne and moved from the Ourcq to Tracy/Carlpont 7th-13th September. To Second Army.

7DI   07.09.14-21.09.14
8DI   07.09.14-21.09.14

XIII CA

Fought in 1st Marne on the Ourcq from 16th September and then to Second Army.

25DI   14.09.14-21.09.14
26DI   1409.14-21.09.14

OISE-PICARDY 1914-1916

On 1st October Sixth Army relinquished responsibility for part of the Aisne front to Fifth Army. With QG established at Villers Cotterèts, its initial frontline extended from the Oise via Tracy-le-Mont, Hautebraye, Fontenay, and Soissons to Missy-sur-Aisne. Gradually, Sixth Army's area was extended northwards into Picardy. When Second Army departed for Champagne on 2nd August 1915, Sixth Army took over the front the Somme to the Oise, and gave up the Aisne front to Fifth Army. With GQ now at Verberie, its front settled down into the line between Vermandovillers and Pernant: the BEF took over its area to the north of the Somme during September 1915.

XVI CA

In line between Condé and Moussy 14th-17th October 1914.

32DI   08.10.14-28.10.14
69DI   15.10.14-17.10.14

XXXV CA

In line between the Oise and the Aisne at Autrechies/Bailly 15th December 1914-27th April 1916. Handed over to Tenth Army 12th April 1916.

37DI   15.12.14-07.09.15
61DI   15.12.14-14.04.16
48DI   31.07.15-26.09.15
121DI   04.08.15-13.12.15
103DT   01.10.15-01.03.16
53DI   02.03.16-12.04.16

XIII CA

Taken over from Second Army 1st July 1915 when in line between Beuvraignes and Ribécourt where it remained until transferred to Tenth Army on 15th February 1916.

25DI   01.07.15-08.01.16
26DI   01.07.15-15.02.16
120DI   01.07.15-17.02.16
102DT   01.10.15-03.11.15

104DT   01.10.15-15.02.16

III CA
In line Andechy, Maucourt, Lihons, Frise, 23rd October 1915-18th February 1916
6DI   24.10.15-12.12.15
62DI   25.10.15-12.01.16
5DI   08.12.15-18.02.16

IICAC
Joined the line between Armancourt, Dancourt and Bois ds Loges on 15th February 1916 and served there until 12th April 1916 when transferred to Tenth Army.
104DT   15.02.16-02.03.16
10DIC   12.02.16-12.04.16
15DIC   12.02.16-12.04.16
DM   24.02.16-12.04.16

SOMME 1916

As allied plans for an offensive in Picardy were developed, Sixth Army relinquished is southern wing. The Oise front was handed over to Third Army and Tenth Army was inserted between the two armies on 12th April 1916 to command forces in the Santerre. These changes permitted Sixth Army to concentrate on preparations for the Somme offensive in the area immediately to the right of the BEF.

During the battle of the Somme, Sixth Army initially operated astride the Somme in front of Péronne. As the battle developed its focus extended northwards towards Morval, Combles, and Sailly-Saillisel. In addition, attacks were continued in the approaches to Péronne at Belloy, Bois l'Abbé and Biaches. Although Sixth Army was unable to take Péronne, its activities took much pressure of the British Fourth Army in its series of attacks towards the ridges and woods around Bazentin, Longeuval and Flers. On 12th December 1916 QG Sixth Army handed over to an extended Tenth Army and left the front-line.

I CAC
In line, between the Avre and the Somme, from 18th February –23rd August 1916. Fought at Biaches and Belloy
2DIC   29.01.16-23.08.16
3DIC   10.02.16-04.08.16
6DI   15.02.16-28.02.16
16DIC   16.02.16-22.08.16
62DI   24.02.16-18.06.16
61DI   30.05.16-18.06.16
DM   20.06.16-15.07.16
72DI   04.07.16-24.07.16

XX CA
Served in the Maricourt sector, 3rd June-21st August, and then, between Rancourt and Sailly-Saillisel, 15th November-10th December 1916.
11DI   30.05.16-10.12.16
39DI   30.05.16-07.12.16
153DI   09.07.16-28.11.16
47DI   11.07.16-20.08.16
46DI   18.08.16-21.08.16

XXXV CA
In line between Fay, Fontaine-lès-Cappy/Maucourt, 30th May-5th August when transferred to Tenth Army.
61DI   30.05.16-17.08.16
121DI   30.05.16-12.07.16

53DI   17.06.16-20.07.16
51DI   18.06.16-05.08.16
132DI   13.07.16-05.08.16

XXX CA

In line between Foucaucourt and Armancourt from 12th June-28th June 1916 then Tenth Army

58DI   13.06.16-28.06.16
62DI   18.06.16-28.06.16

II CA

Served near Belloy and Estrées-Deniecourt 23rd July-28th December 1916. To Tenth Army on 5th August 1916.

3DI   23.07.16-05.08.16
121DI   23.07.16-03.08.16
4DI   01.08.16-05.08.16

VII CA

Fought in the Bois de Hem sector, 26th July-18th September 1916.

48DI   16.07.16-18.09.16
41DI   16.07.16-14.09.16
14DI   10.08.16-18.09.16
66DI   15.08.16-18.09.16

I CA

Fought at Combles and Morval, 20th August-10th October 1916.

1DI   19.08.16-30.09.16
45DI   20.08.16-29.09.16
46DI   21.08.16-10.10.16
2DI   03.09.16-05.10.16
56DI   27.09.16-10.10.16
18DI   09.10.16-10.10.16

XXXIII CA

Fought between Cléry, Feuillères, Biaches and Barleux, 23rd August-13th November 1916. To Tenth Army

70DI   23.08.16-19.11.16
77DI   23.08.16-11.11.16
47DI   14.09.16-25.10.16
23DI   02.11.16-11.11.16

V CA

In line between Rancourt and Bouchavesnes, 15th September-14th November 1916.

10DI   14.09.16-29.10.16
125DI   29.09.16-14.11.16

VI CA

Fought at Bois l'Abbé and Bouchavesnes, 18th September-23rd December 1916.

12DI   18.09.16-18.12.16
127DI   18.09.16-19.12.16
47DI   03.10.16-26.12.16
56DI   21.10.16-23.12.16

XXXII CA

In line between Rancourt and Ferme du Priez, 20th September-17th November 1916.

42DI   20.09.16-03.11.16
40DI   30.09.16-17.11.16

66DI   10.10.16-27.10.16
46DI   24.10.16-13.11.16
17DI   27.10.16-07.11.16

IX CA
Joined line at Morval/Sailly-Saillisel 8th October and taken over by Tenth Army on 12th December 1916
18DI   08.10.16-21.10.16
152DI 20.10.16-04.12.16
17DI   07.11.16-21.11.16

AISNE 1917-1918

On 6th January 1917 QG Sixth Army re-opened at Fismes and took over responsibility for the western half of the Aisne front from Pernant to Troyon. This move was in anticipation of the army's central role as an assault force in Nivelle's spring offensive. After the initial plans were disrupted by the German withdrawal to the Hindenburg Line, Sixth Army's front covered the line from Quicy Basse to Troyon. Sixth Army was given the task of breaking through the German positions between Laffaux and Hurtebise. It achieved little but heavy manpower losses on 16th April 1917. It remained in line and staged a limited recovery at Malmaison, 23rd-27th October.

XXXVII CA
In line from Pernant to Chavonne, 29th January-5th April 1917 and then between Nanteuil-la-Fosse and Jouy, 21st April-10th August 1917
158DI 27.01.17-18.05.17
127DI 07.03.17-29.03.17
62DI   12.05.17-20.07.17
81DI   11.05.17-15.08.17

II CAC
Entered line between Troyon and Hurtebise 16th January 1917 and withdrawn on 19th April after conflict at Ailles on the 16th during 2nd Aisne.
15DIC 18.01.17-19.04.17
10DIC 07.02.17-19.04.17
38DI   15.04.17-19.04.17

XX CA
Briefly in line between Moussy and Troyon, 25th-30th January 1917, and in same sector, 7th April-5th June when it fought at Braye-en-Laonnaise in 2nd Aisne.
39DI   14.01.17-05.06.17
153DI 16.01.17-08.06.17
133DI 16.04.17-09.05.17
11DI   18.04.17-17.05.17
168DI 21.04.17-17.05.17

VI CA
In line between Troyon and Chavonne, 19th January-4th June 1917: fought at Ostel during 2nd Aisne
12DI   15.01.17-09.05.17
56DI   15.01.17-29.05.17

XI CA
In second line, at Fere-en-Taardenois, during the assault of 16th April. Entered the line between Cerny-en- Laonnais and Hurtebise, 19th April-19th May 1917
21DI   18.04.17-09.05.17
22DI   30.04.17-18.05.17
28DI   05.05.17-16.05.17

I CAC
Fought at Laffaux, Bois Mortier and Vauxillon, 5th April-15th May 1917
3DIC 04.04.17-13.05.17
2DIC 06.04.17-15.05.17

XIV CA
In line Hurtebise/Courtecon, 18th May-24th June 1917
27DI 16.05.17-28.06.17
28DI 16.05.17-22.06.17
87DT 15.06.17-22.06.17

XXI CA
In line between Mennejean and the Panthéon, 25th May-31st October 1917. Fought at Malmaison
43DI   23.05.17-31.10.17
170DI 27.05.17-29.05.17
13DI   29.05.17-31.10.17
167DI 25.09.17-31.10.17

XXXIII CA
In line Epine de Chevregny/Courtecon, 5th June-3rd August 1917.
77DI 03.06.17-27.07.17
70DI 21.06.17-25.07.17
88DI 24.07.17-03.08.17

III CA
In line Braye-en-Laonnais/Courtecon, 25th May-7th July 1917 when transferred to Tenth Army
6DI   31.05.17-12.07.17
5DI   06.06.17-19.07.17
129DI 14.06.17-09.07.17

XXXIX CA
In line Panthéon/Braye-en-Laonnais, 3rd August-1st December 1917. Fought at Malmaison, 23rd-27th October.
66DI 27.07.17-20.09.17
87DT 03.08.17-01.12.17
88DT 03.08.17-29.11.17
67DI 19.08.17-29.10.17

XIV CA
In line Quincy Basse/Vauxillon, 17th August-19th November 1917. Fought at Malmaison 23rd October.
129DI 13.08.17-31.10.17
154DI 20.08.17-19.11.17
27DI   23.10.17-08.11.17
28DI   25.10.17-07.11.17
161DI 15.11.17-19.11.17

XI CA
In line, Panthéon/Jouy 27th August 1917-8th April 1918. Fought at Malmaison 23rd October 1917. In Coucy-le-Château/Bois Mortier sector from 8th April. Fought at Vauclerc during 3rd Aisne, 27th May 1918 and then retreated to Chauvigny/Faverolles where transferred to Tenth Army on 2nd June 1918.
38DI 20.08.17-31.10.17
22DI 17.09.17-21.03.18
66DI 17.09.17-26.10.17
21DI 20.10.17-02.06.18
61DI 29.10.17-08.06.18

151DI   31.10.17-27.05.18
87DI   26.11.17-01.12.17
22DI   20.04.18-13.06.18
43DI   27.05.18-06.06.18
74DI   27.05.18-05.06.18
157DI   27.05.18-28.05.18
1DI   28.05.18-02.06.18
39DI   28.05.18-02.06.18
170DI   28.05.18-30.05.18
131DI   29.05.18-02.06.18
DM   29.05.18-30.05.18
128DI   31.05.18-02.06.18

V CA

From Tenth Army 28th October 1917 when in line between Vauclerc and the Miette. Served there until 27th January 1918.
10DI   28.10.17-06.01.18
125DI   29.10.17-22.01.18
9DI   12.11.17-18.02.18
55DI   06.01.18-28.01.18

XXXV CA

From Tenth Army 28th October 1917 whilst in Vauclerc/Chevreux sector where it remained until 26th March 1918.
53DI   28.10.17-24.03.18
68DI   28.10.17-17.11.17
121DI   28.10.17-19.04.18
67DI   17.11.17-26.12.17

I CAC

From Tenth Army 28th October 1917 in the Chevreux/Casemates sector which it left on 28th November 1917.
3DIC   28.10.17-10.11.17
46DI   28.10.17-31.10.17
55DI   29.10.17-29.11.17
2DIC   07.11.17-28.11.17

I CA

In line, Forêt de Vauclerc/Miette sector 27th January-27th April 1918.
162DI   27.01.18-24.03.18
1DI   27.01.18-09.03.18
51DI   07.03.18-27.0418
2DI   20.03.18-31.03.18
121DI   11.04.18-19.04.18

I CC

Transferred from Third Army in the Quincy Basse/Crozat canal sector 18th January 1918. Served until 5th February.
161DI   18.01.18-05.02.18
Elements of 1DCP, 1DC and 5DC also in line.

Sixth Army bore the brunt of the German offensive on the Aisne, which began on 27th May 1918. It was forced to concede much territory and to fall back some twenty miles towards the Marne at Château-Thierry. As the second battle of the Marne developed, with Tenth Army on its left, Sixth Army kept German troops busy and allowed Tenth Army to attack deeply into the German right flank between the Ourcq and the Aisne. By the summer of 1918 Sixth Army was back on the Aisne but was withdrawn on 7th September.

XXX CA
In line Manicamp/Bois Mortier, 8th April-12th June and involved in 3rd Aisne from 27th May. To Tenth Army 2nd June
19DI   06.04.18-02.06.18
48DI   16.04.18-09.05.18
55DI   05.05.18-03.06.18
2DCP   07.05.18-31.05.18
151DI   27.05.18-01.06.18

II CA
In line Carlpont/Queirzy/Manicamp 5th April-5th May 1918.
55DI   05.04.18-05.05.18
1DI   05.04.18-05.05.18

XXI CA
From Fifth Army 27th May 1918 and fought on the Vesle from that date, and between Vaux and Hautebraye, 2nd June-23rd June when transferred to Fourth army.
DM   27.05.18-02.06.18
22DI   27.05.18-17.06.18
164DI   30.05.18-23.06.18
167DI   31.05.18-21.06.18
Also temporarily under command 29th May-2nd June-13DI 73DI 20DI 10DIC 4DC & 5DC

I CA
Fought during 3rd Aisne between Vaurezis and Soissons, 29th May-2nd June 1918 when transferred to Tenth Army.
2 DI   29.05.18-01.06.18
162DI   29.05.18-02.06.18
51 DI   29.05.18-02.06.18
170DI   29.05.18-02.06.18
35 DI   30.05.18-02.06.18
DM   30.05.18-02.06.18
2 DCP   31.05.18-02.06.18

XXXVIIICA
Transferred from Fifth Army and joined the 3rd battle of the Aisne on 30th May. Fought at Vaux, Mozy and Jaulgonne, and then, at Chateau-Thierry.
20 DI   01.06.18-27.06.18
10DIC   01.06.18-28.06.18
4DC   01.06.18-07.06.18
5DC   01.06.18-06.06.18
39DI   22.06.18-08.07.18
125DI   24.06.18-08.07.18

II CC
From Tenth Army 1st June 1918-fought north of Neuilly and St Front, and then between Troesnes and Damard until 20th June.
26DI   01.06.18-20.06.18
2DC   01.06.18-06.06.18
3DC   01.06.18-06.06.18
5DC   01.06.18-06.06.18
2DI   02.06.18-20.06.18

VII CA

Fought between Hautevesnes and Damard, and at Chézy-en-Orxois 31st May-18th July, and advanced to Bonnes and Brécy during 2nd Marne. To Tenth Army 31st July.

4DI	31.05.18-08.06.18
73DI	03.06.18-31.07.18
47DI	04.06.18-21.07.18
5DC	04.06.18-06.06.18
164DI	01.07.18-27.07.18
52DI	20.07.18-27.07.18

II CA

Entered the line between Faverolles and Damard, 20th June 1918, and fought from the Ourcq via Fere-en-Tardenois to the Vesle, 18th July-5th August

2DI	20.06.18-27.07.18
33DI	20.06.18-01.08.18
63DI	20.07.18-03.08.18
47DI	17.07.18-18.07.18
62DI	27.07.18-05.08.18
52DI	27.07.18-08.08.18

III CA

Entered the line near Hautevsesnes and Vaux and advanced to Jaulgonne, Dormans and Troissy on 8th July. Detached to Ninth Army 17th July-23rd August. Held sector from west of Baroches to Braine, 23rd August- 4th September 1918.

167DI	21.06.18-04.07.18	U/c I US Corps 4.07.18-27.07.18
51DI	08.07.18-17.07.18	
125DI	08.07.18-17.07.18	
20DI	08.07.18-17.07.18	
51DI	08.07.18-23.07.18	
77DI	15.07.18-16.07.18	
4DI	30.07.18-06.08.18	
18DI	30.07.18-04.08.18	
52DI	23.08.18-09.09.18	
164DI	23.08.18-04.09.18	

IICC

Attached to Sixth Army 12th July and transferred to Tenth Army 16th July with 2DC, 4DC and 6DC.

XI CA

Transferred from Tenth Army 29th July and fought between Braine and Limé during the battle of Tardenois, until 23rd August.

68DI	09.08.18-23.08.18
62DI	13.08.18-23.08.18

Flanders 1918

As part of the preparations for a general advance by the allied forces, QG Sixth Army was moved to Flanders to take control of the French element assigned to the Belgian-led army group which would clear Flanders of the occupying Germans. With QG at Hondschoote. it became operational on 20th September. With the Belgians on the left, and the British on the right, it took part in the final breakout from the Ypres Salient. After crossing the Leie at Tielt on 19th October, by 11th November 1918, with QG at Roulers, it had advanced to the line Elst/Paulatem.

VII CA

In line at Staden, from 27th September until 20th October. Advanced to Roeselare, 14th-15th October and to the Schelde from 20th October-11th November.

128DI   28.09.18-14.10.18
164DI   30.09.18-11.11.18
41DI   03.10.18-10.11.18

XXXIV CA

In second line during the Crêtes des Flandres, 2nd-16th October, then at Roeselare, 14th-15th October. Advanced from the Leie to the Schelde from 20th October to 11th November.

11DI   08.10.18-10.11.18
70DI   12.10.18-03.11.18
77DI   12.10.18-03.11.18
128DI   14.10.18-04.11.18
5DI   09.11.18-11.11.18

XXX CA

Moved from the Leie to the Schelde, 19th October-11th November

132DI   06.10.18-11.11.18
5DI   14.10.18-09.11.18
12DI   23.10.18-11.11.18

SEVENTH ARMY

COMMANDERS

10.08.14-Paul Pau
28.08.14-Georges Toutée
07.09.14-Henri Putz
02.04.15-Louis Maud'Huy
03.11.15-Etienne de Villeret
19.12.16-Eugene Debeney
04.05.17-Antoine Baucheron de Boissoudy
15.10.18-Georges Humbert
23.10.18-Antoine de Mitry

AVIATION

1915-MF14
1918-Sal49, Br221, R242, Br245

MAIN BATTLES

1914	1915	1916	1917	1918
	Hartmanswillerkopf			
	Linge			

Initial responsibility for the Vosges front was apportioned to First Army, but the pre-occupation of that army with events further north, and the foray towards Mulhouse by VII CA, led to the creation of a separate command on 10th August 1914.

The **Armée d'Alsace** was created to exploit the possible advance into Alsace from Belfort via Mulhouse to Colmar. General Pau was allocated VII CA [14DI, 41DI, 8DC] and 1GDR [58DR, 63DR, 68DR] together with 44DI and 57 DR. When this endeavour collapsed, his army was reduced to the **Groupement du Vosges** on 28th August. The group commanded 41DI, 58DI, 66DI, 71DI and, briefly, 10DC in holding the line between in the Vosges to the east and north of Belfort. This command was retitled XXXIV CA on 20th November 1914.

Detachment d'Armée du Vosges [DAV] took over from XXXIV CA on 8th December 1914 with QG at Remiremont, and the task of holding the sector between Avricourt and the Swiss frontier. Initially, it commanded only 66, 41,71 and 47 Divisions. This small force was supplemented, by a provisional group, on its southern wing, which began as Group Cordonnier, then Group Contades, then Group Demange, and
finally RF Belfort on 15th August 1915. RFB commanded 57DI, 105DT and 10DC. It was to evolve into the reformed XXXIV CA on 20th June 1916.

DAV was upgraded to Seventh Army on 2nd April 1915. It remained responsible for the line north from the Swiss frontier to and including the passes across the Vosges until the end of the war. Apart from some local actions in 1914 and 1915 this was a quiet sector which came to be used by the Americans in 1917-1918 as an introductory arena for newly-arrived divisions.

DAV and Seventh Army divisions 1914-1916 [independent of corps]
57 DI	02.08.14-08.10.15	Belfort
71 DI	12.08.14-11.03.15	Meurthe –to DAL
105 DT	08.10.14-20.03.16	Swiss frontier
66DI	12.09.14-04.07.16	Fave/Bonhomme

41DI	22.09.14-11.06.16	Chapelotte/Fave
47DI	16.01.15-05.06.16	Bonhomme/Metzeral
129DI	15.06.15-26.08.15	Linge
157DI	11.10.15-18.06.17	Belfort
27DI	15.10.15-28.02.16	Hartsmannswillerkopf
28DI	19.10.15-28.02.16	Altkirch/Burnhaup
129DI	26.10.15-21.12.16	Linge
154DI	03.12.15-04.04.16	Swiss frontier
46DI	23.03.16-16.07.16	Schulcht –to DAL
14DI	21.05.16-20.07.16	Schulcht
76DI	24.05.16-29.11.16	Chapelotte
52DI	03.07.16-01.09.17	Leimbach
63DI	25.07.16-29.09.16	Schulcht
47DI	26.10.16-30.03.17	Chapelotte
66DI	01.11.16-20.03.17	Metzeral
46DI	21.11.16-27.03.17	Metzeral
129DI	13.01.17-31.05.17	Chapelotte
63DI	10.04.17-23.06.17	Chapelotte

XXXIV CA

Formed from RFB 20th June 1916 to cover Belfort Gap/Swiss Frontier which it did so until 16th June 1917.

133DI	31.03.16-20.08.16
157DI	30.05.16-06.07.17
134DI	18.08.16-11.06.17
164DI	27.11.16-22.04.17
58DI	14.03.17-16.06.17

XXI CA

Corps was at rest except for one division in line between Metzeral and Leimbach.

| 47DI | 13.02.17-02.03.17 |

ICAC

In line between Leimbach and the Swiss frontier 16th June-15th July 1917.

| 2DIC | 16.06.17-16.07.17 |
| 3DIC | 16.06.17-16.07.17 |

VI CA

In line between the Chapelotte and Leimbach 29th June 1917 to 20th January 1918.

127DI	29.06.17-23.12.17
56DI	29.06.17-22.01.18
12DI	14.06.17-17.12.17
170DI	15.12.17-20.01.18
13DI	18.01.18-20.01.18

XVIII CA

In line between Leimbach and the Swiss frontier 8th July-13th September 1917

35DI	08.07.17-12.09.17
36DI	13.07.17-12.09.17
52DI	17.07.17-20.07.17

XXXX CA

In line between Fulleren and the Swiss frontier, 20th July 1917-11th November 1918

| 52DI | 20.07.17-12.08.17 |
| 73DI | 08.08.17-12.05.18 |

27DI   14.01.18-29.01.18
9DI   12.04.18-25.06.18
10DI   12.05.18-01.07.18
53DI   24.06.18-15.09.18
151DI   28.06.18-24.08.18
51DI   25.08.18-14.10.18
2DI   15.09.18-28.10.18
38DI   22.09.18-11.11.18
68DI   24.10.18-11.11.18
2DM   02.11.18-11.11.18
154DI   02.11.18-11.11.18

XXXIII CA

In line between Leimbach and Fulleren 13th September 1917-29th January 1918

77DI   03.09.17-28.01.18
70DI   10.09.17-19.01.18

XVI CA

In line between Guebwiller and Leimbach 7th November 1917 and 26th March 1918.

31DI   05.11.17-07.01.18
66DI   15.12.17-31.03.18
32DI   05.02.18-27.03.18

XIV CA

In line between Burnhaupt and Fulleren 29th January-1st April 1918.

27DI   29.01.18-01.04.18
28DI   29.01.18-11.04.18

XXI CA

In line between the Chapelotte and Guebwiller, 20th January- 17th May 1918.

167DI   20.12.17-12.05.18
13DI   18.01.18-20.05.18
170DI   20.01.18-04.05.18
43DI   22.01.18-05.04.18
62DI   30.04.18-17.05.18
70DI   11.05.18-17.05.18
77DI   12.05.18-17.05.18

XXXIII CA

In line between the Chapelotte and Leimbach 17th May-4th October 1918.

13DI   17.05.18-24.05.18
62DI   17.05.18-20.07.18
70DI   17.05.18-18.06.18
77DI   17.05.18-26.06.18
21DI   13.06.18-31.08.18
22DI   20.06.18-02.09.18
87DI   20.08.18-31.08.18
19DI   26.08.18-04.10.18
131DI   27.08.18-04.10.18
1DI   31.08.18-04.10.18
20DI   17.09.18-04.10.18

X CA

In line between the Chapelotte and the Linge, 1st October-11th November 1918.

19DI   01.10.18-24.10.18
20DI   01.10.18-10.11.18
157DI   13.10.18-11.11.18
60DI   30.10.18-11.11.18

I CA

In line from the Linge to Leimbach 4th October-11th November 1918.

1DI   04.10.18-20.10.18
162DI   09.10.18-11.11.18
161DI   15.10.18-11.11.18

EIGHTH ARMY [1]

COMMANDERS

20.10.14-Victor d'Urbal
09.03.15-Georges Humbert
05.04.15-Henri Putz

MAIN BATTLES

1914	1915	1916	1917	1918
1st Ypres	2nd Ypres			
Yser				

As the last area of fluidity on the Western Front, the area around Ypres became the scene of intense fighting in late 1914 and in the spring of 1915. French forces which were committed to the defence of the northern flank of the Ypres Salient became **Detachment d'Armée de Belgique** [DAB] on 20th October and then Eighth Army 16th November. With QG at Rousbrugge-Harlinge, it controlled French forces in both the first and second battles of Ypres. As the French presence diminished Eighth Army became DAB again on 2nd April 1915.

XXXII CA
Fought at Langemark, Diksmuide and Hollebeke, 12th October-31st December 1914.
42DI   12.10.14-31.12.14
38DI   29.10.14-17.01.15   Group Nieuport 17.01.5-10.5.16

Group Bidon
Operated between Diksmuide and Nieuvepoort from 13th October until 2nd November 1914. It was part of Group Nieuport from 2nd November.
87DT   13.10.14-02.11.14
89DT   13.10.14-02.11.14

IICC
Fought in the Ypres Salient, 16th October 1914-5th February 1915.
4DC   16.10.14-05.02.15
5DC   16.10.14-05.02.15
6DC   16.10.14-05.02.15

IX CA
Fought between Zonnebeke and Poelkapelle 22nd October 1914-9th April 1915.
17DI   22.10.14-09.04.15
18DI   22.10.14-09.04.15
43DI   01.11.14-06.12.14

XVI CA
Fought between Zillebeke and Wijtschate, 29th October 1914-3rd February 1915.
31DI   29.10.14-03.02.15
32DI   29.10.14-08.01.15

XX CA
Fought between Poelkapelle and Wijtschate, 13th November 1914-16th April 1915.
11DI   13.11.14-16.04.15
39DI   13.11.14-16.04.15
87DT   30.12.14-16.04.15

89DT   30.12.14-16.04.15

Group Hély d'Oissel
Manned the line of the Ijzer canal south of Diksmuide from 5th December until disbanded on 30th December 1914
87DT   05.12.14-30.12.14
89DT   05.12.14-30.12.14
7DC   05.12.14-29.12.14

Group Nieuport
Formed on the Flemish Coast 17th January 1915 and served there until 10th May 1916.
38DI   17.01.15-10.05.16

On 26th May 1915, DAB was retitled XXXVI CA and this remained the principal French formation in Flanders until 1917. The corps was often combined with the RFD [Dunkerque] and then taken under command of First Army on 16th June 1917. When that QG left Flanders, the remained forces were commanded by **Command Superiuer Nord** [CSN] under General Putz. With QG at Amiens he retained command of XXXVI CA and the various coastal garrisons at Boulogne, Calais and Dunkerque.

With the German offensive on the Lys, CSN was upgraded to **Detachment d'Armée Nord** h [DAN] under command of General de Mitry. At first DAN commanded XXXVI CA and 39DI but the need to hold the line with the BEF led to a massive reinforcement. Four army corps were thrown into the battle for Flanders.

XXXVI CA   17th April-2nd June 1918
II CC   19th April-5th May 1918
XVI CA   27th April-8th July 1918
XIV CA   3rd May-6th July 1918

The following divisions fought in Flanders. As they were rotated between the corps on an almost daily basis, they are listed with overall dates.

17 DI   17th April-21st April
65DI   17th April-21st April
2DC   19th April-30th April
3DC   19th April-30th April
6DC   19th April-1st May
28DI   19th April-28th April
133DI   19th April-1st May
34DC   19th April-4th May
154DI   19th April-30th April
2DC   21st April-27th April
39DI   21st April-5th May
32DI   27th April-6th July
27DI   1st May-5th June
39DI   1st May-5th May
31DI   1st May-6th July
14DI   3rd May-30th May
129DI   3rd May-23rd May
168DI   3rd May-26th June
39DI   5th May-6th May
121DI   12th May-2nd June
41DI   15th May-1st June
7DI   20th May-6th July
46DI   25th May-29th June
71DI   29th May-8th July
27DI   31st May-7th June

41DI   26th June-4th July

DAN became QG Ninth Army on 6th July and moved away from Flanders. It was succeeded by a new CSN [J-B Dumas], which commanded the garrisons of Boulogne, Calais and Dunkerque until the end of the war. Responsibility for operations in Flanders was taken over by Sixth Army on 20th September.

EIGHTH ARMY [2]

COMMANDERS

09.03.15- Georges Humbert
24.07.15- Augustin Gérard
05.11.15- Celeste Deprez
31.12.16- Augustin Gérard

AVIATION

12.1916-C42, N68, N75, N77
1918-Spa90, Br206, Br224, R241, Vr292
& u/c GC11 [5 sqns]

Detachment d'Armée de Lorraine [DAL] was formed on 11th March 1915. With QG at St Nicholas-du- Port, it was entrusted with the defence of the line from the east bank of the Moselle to the Vosges, between Pont-a-Musson and the Chapelotte. When First Army pulled out of the line in December 1916, DAL took over its positions around the St Mihiel Salient. As a result of this change, DAL became Eighth Army on 2nd January 1917 and its QG moved to Tatonville on the same date. The army remained in this 'quiet' sector for the rest of the war. It mounted no major offensives and very few local actions. In 1917 and 1918, several American divisions were attached for familiarisation with trench warfare. Gradually the army lost command of the line west of the Moselle, to First Army and then to the American Army. By November 1918, it had shrunk to a mere five divisions with QG at Falvigny-sur-Moselle. Behind it, Tenth Army was assembling for the planned offensive northwards towards Metz.

For the most part DAL commanded individual divisions until the spring of 1916. These were:
59 DI	11.03.15-08.02.16	Pont-à-Mousson to Armaucourt
68 DI	11.03.15-14.02.16	Armaucourt to Bezange-la-Grande
74 DI	11.03.15-28.12.15	Bezange-la-Grande to Avricourt
71 DI	11.03.15-10.06.16	Avricourt to Chapelotte
128DI	26.12.15-12.06.16	Avricourt to Vezouve
11DI	10.02.16-12.03.16	Armaucourt to Bezange-la-Grande

III CC was under command from 26th October 1915 until disbandment on 28th December 1916 but apart from two periods in the line, it remained in reserve throughout. Between 4th November 1915 and 23 July 1916 it occupied the sector from Parroy to Bezange-la-Grande with 6DC, 8DC and 9DC. 33DI was under command from 8th-10th April 1916. From 24th August to 28th December 1916 it occupied positions between the Sanon and the Chapelotte with 5DC, 6DC, 15DI, 73DI and then 7DI.

XVII CA
In line from the Sânon to Brin and Bezange-la-Grande, 8th March 1916-22nd April 1916.
130DI   11.03.16-23.04.16
59DI   16.04.16-22.04.16

XXXIX CA
In line between Pont-à-Mousson and Lanfroicourt, 1st April-24th October 1916 and then between the Etang de Vargevaux and the right-bank of the Moselle from 26th October 1916 to 2nd July 1918.
74DI   01.04.16-09.09.16
129DI   01.04.16-28.05.16
130DI   04.05.16-10.06.16
37DI   12.08.16-27.09.16
73DI   20.09.16-27.05.17
48DI   27.09.16-11.05.17
68DI   29.09.16-22.05.17

131DI   15.111.6-23.01.17
67DI   06.10.16-30.06.17
88DI   20.10.16-17.11.17
11DI   17.12.16-18.01.17
167DI   25.12.16-19.01.17
168DI   19.01.17-01.02.17
39DI   25.06.17-02.07.17
153DI   28.06.17-02.07.17

XXXII CA

In line between Parroy and the Chapelotte, 16th June-24th August 1916.
45DI   16.06.16-09.08.16
42DI   16.06.16-24.08.16
40DI   07.08.16-21.08.16

XXXX CA

In line between the Sânon and the Chapelotte, 28th December 1916-27th May 1917.
7DI   28.12.16-28.05.17
73DI   28.12.16-19.06.17
4DI   29.01.17-10.03.17
11DI   09.02.17-15.03.17
5DI   13.03.17-24.03.17

II CAC

In line between the Sânon and the Chapelotte, 27th May 1917-29th August 1917.
10DIC   24.05.17-27.08.17
15DIC   24.05.17-27.08.17

XX CA

In line between the Etang de Vargevaux, Limey, and Brin, 2nd July-5th November 1917.
153DI   08.06.17-04.10.17
11DI   24.06.17-04.10.17
39DI   02.07.17-04.11.17
168DI   12.07.17-05.11.17
40DI   15.10.17-05.11.17

IX CA

In line between the Sânon and the Chapelotte, 29th August 1917-21st January 1918.
17DI   06.08.17-27.03.18
59DI   06.08.17-03.02.18
152DI   26.08.17-30.12.17
18DI   15.10.17-01.01.18
128DI   28.12.17-01.04.18
41DI   29.12.17-21.01.18
164DI   11.01.18-21.01.18

XXXII CA

In line between Limey and Chenincourt, 5th November 1917-5th January 1918 when transferred to First Army.
40DI   05.11.17-05.01.18
42DI   05.11.17-05.01.18
165DI   05.11.17-05.01.18

XV CA

In line between Chenincourt and Bezange-la-Grande 23rd October 1917-5th June 1918.

123DI   23.10.17-05.06.18
126DI   23.10.17-02.06.18
165DI   05.01.18-31.01.18
37DI   28.01.18-02.04.18
32DI   31.05.18-05.06.18
31DI   02.06.18-05.06.18

VII CA

In line between Bezange-la-Grande and the Chapelotte, 21st January-12th May 1918.
14DI   21.01.18-02.04.18
41DI   21.01.18-22.04.18
59DI   21.01.18-03.02.18
164DI   21.01.18-30.04.18
128DI   01.04.18-12.05.18
56DI   18.04.18-12.05.18
12DI   19.04.18-12.05.18

XXXII CA

Returned from First Army in the Limey-Chenincourt sector on 26th March 1918 and remained until transferred to the Port-sur-Seille/Bezange-la Grande sector where it remained until 11th November 1918.
69DI   26.03.18-04.06.18
40DI   26.03.18-23.05.18
10DIC   26.03.18-27.05.18
15DIC   26.03.18-30.03.18
42DI   26.03.18-09.04.18
34DI   22.05.18-12.08.18
64DI   22.05.18-09.08.18
65DI   01.06.18-04.08.18   Became 2DM
154DI   25.06.18-18.07.18
166DI   25.06.18-19.07.18
2DM   04.08.18-08.08.18   Ex 65DI
42DI   23.08.18-16.10.18
40DI   25.08.18-15.10.18
125DI   25.08.18-27.09.18
165DI   25.09.18-10.11.18
69DI   12.10.18-10.11.18
1DM   13.10.18-10.11.18

VI CA

In line between Bezange-la-Grande and the Chapelotte, 12th May-20th October 1918.
12DI   12.05.18-18.07.18
56DI   12.05.18-25.07.18
61DI   18.06.18-04.09.18
28DI   13.06.18-04.09.18
154DI   23.07.18-16.09.18
87DI   31.08.18-17.10.18
27DI   02.09.18-28.10.18
129DI   12.09.18-20.10.18
131DI   14.09.18-20.10.18
4DI   17.10.18-20.10.18

XXXVI CA

In line between Clémery and Bezange-la-Grande 5th June-31st July 1918.
31DI   05.06.18-31.07.18

32DI   05.06.18-31.07.18

XVI CA
In line between Clémery and Bezange-la-Grande, 31st July-24th August 1918.
31DI   31.07.18-23.08.18
32DI   31.07.18-20.08.18
125DI   13.08.18-24.08.18

II CA
In line between Bezange-la-Grande and the Chapelotte, 20th October-11th November 1918.
3DI   20.10.18-10.11.18
4DI   20.10.18-11.11.18
27DI   20.10.18-08.11.18
129DI   20.10.18-11.11.18
131DI   20.10.18-11.11.18
73DI   31.10.18-02.11.18

Ninth Army [1]

Commander

29.08.14-Ferdinand Foch

Main Battles

1914
1st Marne-Marais de St Gond
1st Aisne

Foch's Army Detachment was formed on 29th August 1914, mostly out of components of Fourth Army as that army rapidly retreated southwards from the Meuse to Vitry. Foch's force was asked to fill the emerging gap between Fourth and Fifth Armies. Retitled Ninth Army on 5th September, it was to hold the line between them at the Marais de St Gond. There it fought during the first battle of the Marne. It advanced via Epernay to positions east of Reims, where most of its units were re-absorbed into Fourth Army on 7th October 1914.

IX CA
Ex Fourth Army. Was at Dommery and Fosse à L'Eau on 28th August, it moved to Bertincourt two days later. During the battle of the Marne, it fought between the Marais de St Gond to Fère-Champenois and Mondement, and advanced to Prunay/Prosnes/St Hilaire-le-Grand by 10th September. During the battle of the Aisne, it consolidated positions at St Leonards, to the east of Reims, and was absorbed into Fourth Army on 7th October.

17DI	29.08.14-07.10.14
DM	29.08.14-21.09.14
52DR	31.08.14-18.09.14
18DI	14.09.14-07.10.14
42DI	17.09.14-23.09.14

XI CA
Ex Fourth Army. It had retreated from Remilly-sur-Meuse to positions east of Fère-Champenois. In the battle for the Marais de St Gond it advanced back to Fère-Champenois and then on to Montepreux. Then fought between Jonchery-sur-Vesle and St Hilaire-le-Grand from 10th to 18th September. Transferred to Second Army.

21DI	29.08.14-21.09.14
22DI	29.08.14-21.09.14
60DR	29.08.14-18.09.14
18DI	08.09.14-14.09.14
52DI	18.09.14-21.09.14

X CA
Ex Fifth Army 9th September and advanced from Sézanne towards Reims and returned to Fifth Army on 12th September.

20DI	09.09.14-12.09.14
51DI	09.09.14-12.09.14
19DI	10.09.14-12.09.14

XXI CA
Ex Fourth Army 14th September and fought in the Souain sector until 1st October.

13DI	14.09.14-01.10.14
43DI	14.09.14-01.10.14

XII CA
Ex Fourth Army 18th September. Fought between Souain and Aubérive until 1st October.

24DI	18.09.14-01.10.14

60DI   19.09.14-10.10.14

Gp Humbert

Formed on 21st September to defend the northern approaches to Reims between the Neuvillette and Marquises. To Fifth Army, 7th October.

23DI   21.09.14-01.10.14
52DI   21.09.14-07.10.14
42DI   23.09.14-07.10.14
DM   23.09.14-07.10.14

NINTH ARMY [2]

COMMANDER

05.07.18-Antoine de Mitry

Formed along the Marne to fill a gap between Sixth and Fifth Armies which had emerged during the 3rd battle of the Aisne. It held the line of the river, facing Dormans, while adjacent armies prepared for Foch's counterstroke in the second battle of the Marne. Disbanded once victory had been achieved.

XIV CA
Ex Fifth Army 6th July: kept in reserve until transferred to Fourth Army on 14th July.
7DI   06.07.18-08.07.18
10DIC   06.07.18-08.07.18
71DI   08.07.18-14.07.18
9DI   12.07.18-15.07.18

III CA
Ex Sixth Army 17th July and returned to Sixth Army on 25th July. Served between Courthiezy, Igny- Comblizy and Troissy.
18DI   17.07.18-25.07.18
51DI   17.07.18-19.07.18
73DI   17.07.18-25.07.18
168DI   17.07.18-21.07.18
4DI, 20DI and 125DI under command but kept in reserve

ICC
Attached to Ninth Army for two days-19th & 20th July with 77DI, 131DI, 1DC & 5DC. In addition, several divisions served on a detached basis from their parent corps. They were 10DI [from XVICA], 14DI [from IICAC], and 39DI [from XXXVIII CA]. Of the above, only 77DI was employed on active operations at Fetigny-lès-Hameaux and Montvoisin.

Tenth Army

Commanders

03.10.14-Louis Maud'Huy
02.04.15-Victor d'Urbal
04.04.16-Joseph Micheler
27.12.16-Denis Duchêne
11.12.17-Paul Maistre
10.06.18-Charles Mangin

Aviation

1915- REP15
1918-Sal69, Br224, Br294

Main Battles

1914	1915	1916	1917	1918
1st Artois	2nd Artois	Somme	2nd Aisne	3rd Aisne
	3rd Artois		Malmaison	2nd Marne
			Italy	Vauxillon
				Laon/Croanne Serre

Artois 1914-1916

As the 'Race to the Sea' got underway, a gap appeared in Artois, between Second Army in Picardy and the BEF in Flanders, and Tenth Army was formed on 3rd October 1914 to fill this gap. With QG at St Pol, Tenth Army's task was to defend the city of Arras and the important high ground to the north of the city. The most important heights were Vimy ridge and the Lorette spur, possession of these would give the allies a commanding view over the coalfields and industrial areas of the Doaui plain. This plain was the heartland of prewar industrial France and it not only provided resources for the Germans but permitted them to use the strategic lateral railways of northern France.

The Tenth Army fought a series of engagements to contain and frustrate German control of the area. It succeeded in retaining control of Arras which like Reims and Verdun became a city in the frontline for the next four years. It was less successful in obtaining control of the high ground. In the second battle of Artois, 16th May-20th June 1915, it seized the Lorette spur and the village of Souchez but failed to take Vimy ridge. The third battle of Artois was part of an allied offensive, which included British attacks on Loos on the left of Tenth Army, and in Champagne. Tenth Army failed to take Vimy ridge which remained in German hands until April 1917. The army was withdrawn from Artois on 16th February 1916 when its line was taken over by the British First Army.

X CA

Established the line from Blagny to Berles-au-Bois, 6th October 1914 and moved to the Écurie/Roclincourt sector on 22nd May 1915. Left sector 26th July 1915.

19DI	02.10.14-23.02.15
45DI	05.10.14-25.02.15
20DI	06.10.14-26.07.15
88DT	14.11.14-26.07.15
17DI	18.04.15-03.05.15

XXXIII CA

D'Urbal's Corps until retitled on 12th October. Held the line along Vimy Ridge from Blagny through Roclincourt and Carency to Notre Dame de Lorette, 13th October 1914-25th February 1916. Fought at Vimy Ridge and Souchez.

45DI   05.10.14-15.10.14
70DI   05.10.14-20.02.16
77DI   05.10.14-24.02.16
45DI   30.12.14-06.04.15
DM   20.04.15-24.06.15
18DI   09.05.15-04.07.15
55DI   23.06.15-23.11.15
130DI   23.12.15-15.02.16

XXI CA

In line between La Bassée and Carency from 5th October 1914 until 19th January 1916. Engaged at La Bassée and Vermelles during 1st Artois; at Notre Dame de Lorette and Souchez in 2nd Artois; and at Givenchy in 3rd Artois.

43DI   05.10.14-01.11.14
13DI   06.10.14-25.12.15
92DT   09.10.14-07.07.15
58DI   14.10.14-31.05.15
43DI   31.12.14-11.01.16
17DI   04.05.15-08.05.15
58DI   15.05.15-31.08.15
48DI   17.05.15-05.07.15
92DT   29.05.15-07.07.15
81DT   01.09.15-11.01.16
154DI   24.09.15-30.11.15
152DI   26.09.15-01.10.15
130DI   17.12.15-23.12.15

XX CA

Held line along Vimy Ridge to Neuville-Saint-Vaast 16th April-14th July 1915. Fought at La Targette and Écurie during 2nd Artois.

39DI   18.04.15-07.07.15
11DI   20.04.15-07.07.15
53DI   10.05.15-28.06.15
5DI   25.05.15-11.06.15
153DI   15.06.15-05.07.15

XVII CA

Held line between Écurie and Roclincourt from 28th April 1915 until 5th March 1916. Fought at Écurie, Roclincourt and Thélus during 2nd Artois: and at Beaurains, St Laurent and Blagny during 3rd Artois.

33DI   28.04.15-01.03.16
34DI   28.04.15-04.03.16
17DI   01.05.15-04.05.15
88DT   23.05.15-10.11.15
130DI   08.10.15-09.11.15

IX CA

Inititially engaged between La Bassée, Vermelles and Loos 8th-19th May 1915 and then at Neuville St Vaast from 19th May until 5th July. After a rest and a brief period with Sixth Army in Picardy, it held the line between Agny and Berles from 25th-30th September. It moved to the Loos sector on the latter date and remained there until 7th January 1916.

17DI   07.05.15-05.07.15
58DI   08.05.15-31.05.15
92DT   16.05.15-07.07.15
18DI   30.05.15-04.07.15
18DI   26.08.15-03.03.16
17DI   30.08.15-17.02.16

152DI   31.08.15-22.12.15
81DT   11.01.16-10.02.16
130DI   15.02.16-01.03.16
152DI   17.02.16-10.03.16

III CA

In the Agny/Berles sector from 25th May and then at Neuville-Saint-Vaast from 5th July. It held the Roclincourt/river Scarpe sector 8th-23rd October 1915.
6DI   09.05.15-08.10.15
5DI   03.07.15-08.10.15
130DI   15.07.15-23.09.15

XII CA

In line between Neuville-Saint-Vaast and Roclincourt, 21st July 1915-14th March 1916.
23DI   21.07.15-11.03.16
24DI   22.07.15-13.03.16
58DI   25.09.15-23.10.15

Franco-British plans for 1916 envisaged a major assault in the Somme region. Although the French contribution was reduced by the requirements of Verdun, Sixth Army was allocated to the attack. In order to reduce that army's line, Tenth Army rejoined to struggle on 12th April 1916 when it took over the line between the Oise and the Aisne; from Armancourt to Pernant. QG was established at Clermont.

OISE-AISNE 1916

XIII CA

Ex Sixth Army. Quennevières/Hautebraye sector, 27th April-20th June 1916 [to Third Army]
120DI   27.04.16-20.06.16
25DI   27.04.16-20.06.16
26DI   27.04.16-20.06.16

XXXV CA

Ex Sixth Army. Tracy/Quennèvieres sector [to Third Army]
53DI   12.04.16-27.04.16
61DI   12.04.16-25.04.16

II CAC

Ex Sixth Army. Beuvraignes/Oise sector   [to Third Army]
10DIC   12.04.16-20.06.16
15DIC   12.04.16-20.06.16
DM   12.04.16-19.06.16
87DT   15.06.16-20.06.16

PICARDY 1916-1917

On 20th June, Tenth Army handed over this sector to Third Army and edged leftwards into Picardy. With QG at Breteuil, and then at Moreuil, its task was to takeover the southern part of the line there in order to permit Sixth Army to concentrate on the battle of the Somme.

Gradually, it extended its line northwards towards the Somme and became actively involved in that battle. It conducted attacks in the Santerre, and south of Péronne at Vermandovillers, Ablaincourt and Berny. On 12th December, Sixth Army was withdrawn and Tenth Army shared the Picardy front with the British until it too, was relieved by the BEF on 5th Febraury 1917.

XXX CA

Ex Sixth Army. Foucaucourt/Armancourt sector, 9th June 1916-17th January 1917. To Third Army on 15th November
- 58DI 16.06.16-06.12.16
- 62DI 28.06.16-28.09.16
- 72DI 14.08.16-01.12.16
- 132DI 24.09.16-17.01.17

X CA
Vermandoviller/Chaulnes/ Maucourt/Lihons sector 12th July 1916-2nd January 1917
- 20DI 16.07.16-02.01.17
- 26DI 16.07.16-30.11.16
- 51DI 25.08.16-16.10.16
- 25DI 15.10.16-13.12.16
- 58DI 06.12.16-25.01.17
- 8DI 28.12.16-02.10.17

II CAC
Ex Third Army. Belloy/Barleux/Bernay sector 3rd August 1916-5th January 1917
- 10DIC 03.08.16-21.11.16
- DM 17.11.16-28.12.16
- 15DIC 05.11.16-25.12.16

XXXV CA
Ex Sixth Army. Vermandovillers/Soyécourt sector 5th August- 19th September 1916
- 61DI 05.08.16-08.09.16
- 132DI 05.08.16-10.09.16
- 43DI 17.08.16-19.09.16
- 120DI 08.09.16-19.09.16

II CA
Ex Sixth Army. Estrées-Deniecourt/Belloy sector 5th August-28th December 1916.
- 3DI 05.08.16-23.12.16
- 4DI 05.08.16-23.12.16
- 121DI 05.08.16-28.12.16
- 15DIC 14.08.16-02.10.16
- 16DI 23.12.16-28.12.16

XXI CA
Vermandovillers/Ablaincourt/Estrées-Deniecourt sector, 3rd September-29th December 1916.
- 13DI 03.09.16-16.10.16
- 132DI 10.09.16-23.09.16
- 43DI 19.09.16-22.09.16
- 120DI 19.09.16-26.10.16
- 43DI 15.10.16-18.11.16
- 62DI 16.10.16-08.12.16
- 13DI 15.11.16-17.12.16
- 43DI 15.12.16-26.12.16
- 36DI 22.12.16-29.12.16

XII CA
In Cléry-sur-Somme/Biaches/Barleux sector 13th November- 16th January 1917.
- 23DI 06.11.16-20.01.17
- 70DI 13.11.16-21.11.16
- 24DI 17.11.16-16.01.17
- 129DI 22.12.16-12.01.17

VIII CA

In the Berny/Belloy sector 25th December 1916- 9th January 1917.

15DI   25.12.16-08.01.17
16DI   25.12.16-28.12.16

VI CA

Ex Sixth Army. In Bouchavesnes/Bois l'Abbé sector 12th-23rd December 1916

18DI   15.12.16-23.12.16
17DI   15.12.16-23.12.16

IX CA

In Cléry/Bois l'Abbé/Bouchavesnes sector 23rd December 1916-22nd January 1917

17DI   23.12.16-22.01.17
18DI   23.12.16-18.01.17

XVIII CA

In the Belloy/Genermont sector 22nd December 1916-13th February 1917. To Third Army on 5th February

36DI   22.12.16-12.02.17
35DI   26.12.16-12.02.17
24DI   16.01.17-05.02.17
152DI   16.01.17-05.02.17

IV CA

In the Chilly/Ablaincourt sector 2nd-25th January 1917

8DI   02.01.17-25.01.17
72DI   02.01.17-10.01.17

AISNE 1917

From February 1917, with QG at Nogent-sur-Seine, Tenth Army prepared for its intended role in Nivelle's spring offensive. He planned a major breakthrough along the Chemin des Dames by Sixth and Fifth Armies. As they crumbled the German defence lines, Tenth Army, with its corps deployed in line ahead would attack at the junction of those two armies to create a corridor northwards to Laon. Once this had been achieved, First Army would traverse that corridor, through Tenth Army and exploit northwards towards Belgium. This plan foundered on the first day, 16th April 1917. As a result, Tenth Army was deployed along the Aisne, in a sector which centered on Craonne, in order to hold the line while the rest of the army recovered from that disaster. With QG at Crugny, it maintained its line until the end of October 1917.

II CA with 3DI, 4DI, and 46DI was held in reserve for the spring offensive from 27th March until 19th April but not committed while under command of Tenth Army.

III CA with 5DI, 6DI and 47DI was held in reserve for the spring offensive from 27th March to 27th May but not committed while under command of Tenth Army.

XVIII CA

In reserve for the spring offensive and then committed to the Hurtebise/Croanne sector from 21st April. It fought at Casemates and Californie until 16th June 1917.

35DI   29.03.17-16.06.17
36DI   29.03.17-15.06.17
154DI   29.03.17-30.05.17
164DI   10.05.17-15.06.17

IX CA
From Fifth Army. In the Casemates/Chevreux sector from 18th April until 31st July 1917.
66DI   18.04.17-18.06.17
17DI   21.04.17-20.07.17
18DI   01.05.17-27.07.17
154DI   13.06.17-07.07.17
2DIC   25.07.17-31.07.17

V CA
From Fifth Army in the Moulin Pontoy/Berry-au-Bac sector 21st April until transfer to Sixth Army on 28th October 1917. Fought at Juvincourt during 2nd Aisne.
125DI   19.04.17-14.10.17
9DI   01.05.17-30.10.17
47DI   01.06.17-04.07.17
10DI   15.06.17-28.10.17
55DI   04.08.17-04.10.17

XXXII CA
From Fifth Army in the Miette/Sapigneul sector 21st April-21st May 1917.
42DI   21.04.17-18.05.17
69DI   21.04.17-07.05.17
165DI   21.04.17-19.05.17

III CA
From Sixth Army in the Chevregny/Panthéon sector 16th July-19th August 1917.
6DI   16.07.17-15.08.17
68DI   16.07.17-21.08.17
158DI   16.07.17-31.07.17
161DI   01.08.17-19.08.17
5DI   12.08.17-19.08.17

I CAC
In the Courtecon/Chevreux/Hurtebise/Casemates sector 28th July 1917 until transferred to Sixth Army 28th October 1917.
130DI   28.07.17-16.09.17
2DIC   28.07.17-28.10.17
3DIC   30.07.17-28.10.17
151DI   17.08.17-06.09.17
46DI   23.08.17-31.10.17

XXXV CA
In the Malval/Cerny/Bovelle/Hurtebise sector from 15th August 1917. Transferred to Sixth Army 28th October 1917.
161DI   15.08.17-28.10.17
5DI   15.08.17-31.08.17
121DI   18.08.17-25.09.17
53DI   18.08.17-28.10.17
68DI   17.09.17-28.10.17

Italy 1917-1918

After the Italian defeat at Caporetto, British and French forces were rushed to Italy. The French component consisted of six divisions commanded by QG Tenth Army. after preparations and acclimatisation near Verona, the army moved forward to the Piave on 14th January 1918. It did not have time to become involved in major operations. The German spring offensive in France brought about the recall of Tenth Army, and most of its forces, on 26th March 1918.

XII CA

Arrived in Italy on 11th November 1917. On Piave front at Asolo, 5th February-14th March 1918. Remained in Italy and served on the Asiago front, 24th March-25th October.

23DI   25.1.18-Tomba-15.03.18 27.04.18-Asiago –04.11.18
24DI   19.03.18-Asiago-04.11.18

XXXI CA

Arrived in Italy, 2nd December 1917. On Piave front at Monte Tomba, 5th December 1917-9th February 1918. Recalled to France 26th March 1918.

64DI   08.1.18-Tomba-15.2.18
65DI   2.12.17-Piave-30.1.18

In addition, 46DI and 47DI went out to Italy under Army Command. 46DI served at the front at Monfenera, from 13th February-24th March; and 47DI was in the line at Tomba, 4th December-9th January and at Val Bella 18th March-7th April. Both were recalled to France.

PICARDY 1918

From 16th April until 1st June 1918, Tenth Army, with QG at Beauval, and XIV CA and XXXVIII CA under command, remained in reserve in Picardy.

AISNE-MARNE 1918

In response to the severe defeat incurred by Sixth Army in the opening phase of the 3rd battle of the Aisne, Tenth Army returned to operations on 2nd June. From its new QG at Lamorlaye, it took up positions, which extended southwards from the Aisne, west of Soissons, towards the Marne. It held the western flank of the German salient, which extended to the Marne. As Foch began his counter-stroke, he gave Mangin's Tenth Army the key role. Tenth Army would attack eastwards towards Villers Cotterêts and so threaten the rear of the German forces on the Marne. This was accomplished from 18th July onwards, and Tenth Army retook Soissons on 2nd August.

In the planned autumn offensive, the task allocated to Tenth Army was to penetrate the Hindenburg Line on the St Gobain massif and advance across the high ground towards Laon.

Between 14th September and 27th October, Tenth Army accomplished this task. It moved forward from its start line, Barsis-is-Vailly, and moved up the Oise and reached positions north-west of Sissonne and the Souche by the latter date. On 27th October, QG Tenth Army, at Château de Chevreux, handed over this sector to Third Army.

This period was characterised by the frequent and often brief changes of army boundaries which resulted in the apparently frequent movements of corps to and from Tenth Army.

I CA

From Sixth Army, 2nd June. Fought between Couevres- et-Valsery, Ambleny and Vingré between that date and 17th July. Fought at Venizel, Fontenoy and Hautebraye during the second battle of the Marne. From 17th August operated from Soissons towards Chavigny and reached Laffaux on 14th September and Allemant/Jouy by 20th September.

35DI   02.06.18-04.06.18
51DI   02.06.18-01.07.18
151DI   02.06.18-12.06.18
162DI   02.06.18-06.09.18
170DI   02.06.18-05.06.18
1DM   02.06.18-30.06.18
11DI   14.06.18-01.09.18
72DI   14.07.18-29.08.18

153DI   15.07.18-22.07.18
69DI   02.08.18-06.09.18
59DI   26.08.18-02.09.18
5DI   25.08.18-08.09.18
29DI   02.09.18-20.09.18

XI CA

From Sixth Army 2nd June while retreating from the Aisne to Villers Cotterêts. Operated between Faverolles and Chavigny and moved to Longpont by 8th July. During the second battle of the Marne advanced from Longpont to Oulchy and from there to the Vesle on 29th July. Returned to Sixth Army 9th August.

1DI   02.06.18-28.07.18
61DI   02.06.18-08.06.18
74DI   02.06.18-05.06.18
128DI   02.06.18-18.07.18
131DI   02.06.18-11.06.18
87DI   06.06.18-12.07.18
48DI   08.07.18-21.07.18
5DI   14.07.18-27.07.18
41DI   15.07.18-08.08.18
68DI   26.07.18-08.08.18
127DI   01.08.18-11.08.18

XXX CA

From Sixth Army 2nd June while retreating from Nampcel/Nouvrion/Fontenoy to Nouvrion/Autreches/ Quennevières line. Advanced eastwards from line Villers Cotterêts/St Pierre- Aigle/Fontenoy; and Grand Rozoy to the Vesle, 15th-18th July. During 7th-8th August moved along the Vesle to Braine. Rested until 6th October.

19DI   02.06.18-05.08.18
55DI   02.06.18-18.08.18
1DI   13.07.18-28.07.18
48DI   15.07.18-21.07.18
25DI   26.07.18-11.08.18
127DI   08.08.18-28.08.18
128DI   11.08.18-20.09.18
2DI   13.08.18-25.08.18
17DI   21.08.18-22.10.18
64DI   23.08.18-11.09.18
66DI   24.08.18-18.09.18
2DM   26.08.18-05.09.18
31DI   03.09.18-23.09.18
36DI   14.09.18-06.10.18
59DI   15.09.18-06.10.18
121DI   27.09.18-20.10.18

XX CA

In line Villers Cotterêts-Ambleny from 6th June. Advanced to Ambleny and Chevigny 15th-17th July. Fought at Tardenois 20th July and advanced to the Vesle. Moved to Presles/Jouy sector, north of Soissons 30th August.

153DI   03.06.18-08.07.18
87DI   06.06.18-04.08.18
2DCP   06.06.18-22.07.18
1DM   05.07.18-22.07.18
69DI   16.07.18-21.07.18
58DI   20.07.18-25.07.18
17DI   02.08.18-12.08.18
25DI   11.08.18-29.09.18

162DI   06.09.18-21.09.18

IICC
Attached to Tenth Army 16th-20th July with 2DC, 4DC and 6DC

XVIII CA
From Third Army 11th June in the Aisne-Compiegne sector after the battle of the Matz. Held line Bailly/Tracy/Quennevières until second Noyon when the corps moved to Pontoise-lès-Noyon and Carlpont. Advanced to the Hindenburg Line at Barisis/Tergnier on 30th August. [detached to Third Army 2nd-11th August]
15DI   11.06.18-30.08.18
38DI   11.06.18-30.08.18
55DI   15.07.18-18.08.18
70DI   17.07.18-04.08.18
128DI   29.07.18-24.08.18
132DI   14.08.18-15.09.18
2DM   14.08.18-26.08.18

VII CA
In line between Moulin-sous-Touvent and Fontenoy from 1st August. Moved to Blerancourt during 2nd Noyon 17th August, and then advanced on the Hindenburg Line between Barisis and Quincy Basse. To Third Army 27th October.
55DI   01.08.18-18.08.18
128DI   01.08.18-24.08.18
162DI   01.08.18-11.08.18
2DM   24.08.18-05.09.18
2DI   25.08.18-31.08.18
11DI   01.09.18-08.10.18
132DI   29.08.18-05.09.18
32DI   02.08.18-17.09.18
33DI   05.09.18-17.09.18

XVI CA
In the Barisis/Bois Mortier sector from 23rd September. Advanced to St Gobain on 4th October and to the Serre at Crécy-sur-Serre/Mortiers/Chalandry on 20th October. To Third Army 27th October.
33DI   23.09.18-28.09.18
31DI   23.09.18-27.10.18
32DI   23.09.18-27.10.18
59DI   06.10.18-27.10.18

XXXV CA
In line between Presles and Jouy from 21st September. Move to the Ailette 28th September and then north of St Quentin via Ostel/Athies and Monceau-le-Wast. Reached the Serre on 16th October. Transferred to Third Army 27th October.
25DI   21.09.18-27.10.18
72DI   21.09.18-27.10.18
162DI   21.09.18-01.10.18
121DI   28.09.18-27.10.18

XVIII CA
On the Serre at Verneuil-sur-Serre, from 6th October until transferred to Third Army on 27th October.
29DI   28.09.18-04.10.18
36DI   06.10.18-12.10.18
17DI   21.10.18-27.10.18

LORRAINE 1918

QG Tenth Army arrived at Tatonville on 6th November 1918 to prepare for a major offensive northwards along the east bank of the Moselle to Metz. The collection of corps and divisions was incomplete when hostilities ended. By 11th November, elements of the following formations had arrived:

6th November	II CAC	39DI, 10DIC, 15DIC
10th November	XVII CA	18DI, 26DI
11th November	X CA	19DI, 20DI
11th November	VI CA	27DI
11th November	XXXII CA	69DI, 165DI, 1DM
11th November	I CAC	2DIC, 3DIC
11th November	III CA	6DI

OTHER ARMY LEVEL FORMATIONS IN FRANCE

The **Armée des Alpes [or Arméee de Lyon]** which formed at Lyon on 2nd August 1914, under General d'Amade with 64DR, 65DR, 74DR, 75DR and 91DT, to meet a possible threat from Italy. It disbanded on 17th August when that threat failed to materialise.

All the other temporary army level formations are dealt with in the appropriate army history. They are:

Armée d'Alsace	see Seventh Army
Armée de Lorraine	see Third Army
Détachment d'Armée Gérard	see First Army
Détachment d'Armée de Belgique	see Eighth Army [1]
Détachment d'Armée de Lorraine	see Eighth Army [2]
Détachment d'Armée des Vosges	see Seventh Army
Région Fortifiée de Verdun	see Second Army
Commandment Supérieur du Nord	see Eighth Army [1]
Détachment d'Armée du Nord	see Eighth Army [1]

Formations outside France

Gallipoli

The forces committed to the Gallipoli campaign never rose above corps level.
The Corps Expéditionnaire d'Orient [CEO] commanded two specially-formed divisions. It was retitled Corps d'Expéditionnaire des Dardanelles [CED] on 1st January 1916 and disbanded five days later.

CEO/CED
22.02.15-d'Amade   15.05.15-Gouraud   1.07.15-Bailloud   4.10.15-Brulard
1 DI du CEO   to Salonika 15th February 1916
2 DI du CEO   to Salonika 4th October 1915 [became 17DIC]

Macedonia

French Forces allocated to the Salonika from in October 1915 were described, initially, as the **Armée d'Orient [AO]**. Under command of General Sarrail, and with QG at Salonika, the AO was responsible for all French units until 11th August 1916. On that date, an allied high command was established-the **Commandment des Armées Alliés en Orient [CAA]**- with most French units allocated to the **Armée Française d'Orient [AFO]**. This command structure remained in place until October 1918, frequent movements of divisions between CAA and AFO.

During 1917, three subordinate group headquarters were established: **Groups des Divisions d'Infanterie [GDI]**.

They were the 1GDI [generals Lebouc, Gerome, and d'Anselm];
    2GDI [Generals Regnault and Patoy] and
    3GDI [General de Lobit].
Again there were frequent movements of divisions between the GDI.

The divisions allocated to the campaign in Macedonia were:
04.10.15   Division Bailloud –to 15.10.15
15.10.15   57DI
15.10.15   156DI [formerly Division de Serbie]
01.11.15   122DI
09.12.16   16DIC
08.02.16   17DIC
01.01.17   11DIC
04.01.17   76DI
09.06.17   30DI

At the conclusion of the campaign part of the French force was organised as the **Armée du Danube** with 30DI, 16DIC and elements of 76DI. Under command of General Berthelot it remained in existence until 5th May 1919.

Italy

From 31st October 1917 until 26th March 1918, the French forces, in Italy, were commanded by **QG Tenth Army**. After that date, the only French force, which remained, was **XII CA**.

Details are to found under the respective histories.

PART FIVE

ARMY CORPS

CORPS D'ARMEE

Before August 1914, the army corps was the highest level of command in the French Army. The army was divided into twenty-one military regions each of which contained an administrative organisation concerned with recruiting, training, mobilisation and local defence; and a field formation-the army corps-which commanded the active divisions and units within the region. Initially there were eighteen army corps in France with a nineteenth situated in Algeria. By 1913, the border military regions-the 6th and 7th-were divided to provide two more army corps along France's eastern frontier-the 20th and 21st.

On mobilisation, each of the twenty army corps in metropolitan France left its military region and took to the field as the principal battlefield organisation of the French Army. In accordance with pre-war planning with one army corps, of greater strength and on the frontier, covering their assembly, these twenty army corps were formed into five armies. In general, geographic proximity determined the allocation of corps to their respective armies. Fifth Army, for example, was made up of ICA [Lille], IICA [Mèziéres], IIICA [Rouen] and X CA [Rennes] from a swath of territory across northern France.

Each corps was composed of two infantry divisions based in its military region, and numbered in a sequence determined by the numerical title of the parent corps. For example, the 1st Military Region produced I Corps d'Armée with 1st and 2nd Divisions d'Infanterie [DI].

In addition, most of the reserve infantry regiments of the region were formed into a single reserve division. The remaining field units within the region became 'Corps Troops'.

The reserve divisions were grouped into ad hoc organisations called 'Groupe de Divisions de Reserve' on the basis of one per field army. These GDR would become Corps d'Armée by 1915 when new army corps, numbered from 30 to 34, were formed.

In addition to the twenty peacetime corps, and those formed from reserve units in 1915, the colonial divisions were grouped into a single corps: the Corps d'Armée Colonial [CAC]; a second colonial corps was formed in 1915. At first, there were no plans to form corps to control the ten cavalry divisions but this was soon rectified. During the mobile warfare of 1914, cavalry were grouped into two provisional corps, named after their commander, which eventually expanded into three numbered Corps de Cavalerie [CC].

The relationship between the corps and its constituent divisions remained relatively fixed throughout the war. For most of the war, the organic divisions of each corps, moved and fought with their parent corps. The relationship between corps and division was akin to that between division and brigade in the British Army: a semi-permanent relationship. Although some divisions remained independent [isolée], many reserve and war-formed divisions did become organic to a particular corps. The system began to breakdown in 1918 as the more fluid operational situation demanded greater flexibility but many corps still commanded their original divisions at the end of the conflict.

A major stimulus to change came in 1917. Most army corps had a basic two-division organisation before then but some had acquired a third or even fourth division. In 1917, there were six corps with four divisions: during the year this figure rose to fifteen. Of the fourteen corps with three divisions at the beginning of the year, none survived. The twelve corps with two divisions were increased to seventeen. The overall strength of thirty-two corps and one hundred and eight divisions remained the same. This change was designed to ensure greater operational flexibility; large corps were more suitable for lengthy line-holding duties, and the smaller for offensives.

The importance of the army-corps is underlined further by the patterns of movement between sectors of the front-line, and between that line and the rear area. More often than not, such movements were by corps rather than by individual division. By 1917, this system began to erode as more corps headquarters became controllers of static sectors for lengthy periods of time. But, movement by corps, even when that formation was larger, still remained the norm for planned movements up until November 1918.

One word of caution on corps movements: often, what appeared as a movement of a corps between armies was merely the result of the adjustment of army boundaries with the corps remaining in the same sector. This trend was particularly noticeable in major battles such as the second battle of the Marne. A similar pattern can be detected in the allocation of divisions to corps: especially when it was for a relatively short period.

Each corps had a standard allocation of 'Corps Troops' with major variations in terms of changes throughout the army.

Each army-corps had two reserve infantry regiments, each of two battalions. These were left over from the formation of the reserve divisions. In November 1915, the two regiments were withdrawn and allocated to operational divisions. They were replaced by one, or two, territorial infantry regiments. In the summer of 1918 one RIT left the corps and the other was re-organised into three battalions: a machine gun battalion and two pioneer battalions. The machine gun battalion remained with the corps but the pioneer battalions were allocated to the constituent divisions.

Divisional cavalry, was provided by one regiment of light cavalry-either a regiment of hussars or of chasseurs à cheval. Each regiment had four active escadron which remained with the corps, and two reserve escadron which were allocated to each of the infantry divisions. Major changes of organisation took place from November 1915 as divisional escadron were re-allocated. Most were returned to their parent regiment in the summer of 1916 and then returned to the division in January 1917. From July 1917 all escadron were concentrated within the regiment at corps-level.

Corps artillery consisted of both field and heavy regiments. Throughout the war, each corps had one field regiment [RAC] with 4 groups. This was reduced to two groups in June 1915 in order to provide artillery for new-formed divisions. A third group would be newly-formed and added in November 1917. The ad-hoc allocation of groups and batteries to reserve and war-formed divisions was rationalised by the creation of

new regiments in April 1917. The new RAC's were numbered in a new series starting with 201 RAC, Heavy artillery grew from a single battery or group to a complete regiment [RAL] of two groups in November 1915, and then three groups in 1918. The RAL would provide each constituent division with a group as well. In addition many corps had a single battery of 58's drawn from 175 RAC until the summer of 1918.

There is some evidence to suggest the control of corps artillery was taken over by the Réserve Général d'Artillerie in June 1918. Other evidence suggests that the artillery continued to operate with the corps until the end of the war.

The engineers of the corps were formed from the battalion, which was stationed in the home military district. Until 1917 corps engineers comprised the 3rd, 4th, 16th and 21st Companies of the relevant battalion but the 21st company was withdrawn and not replaced in January 1917.

In 1915, each army corps was allocated one squadron of aircraft for artillery spotting and reconnaissance. This was increased to two in January 1918 and to three in July 1918. A balloon company was added in 1916.

The information of each corps in the following pages includes details of formation, changes of title, commanders, corps troops, and operational history.

NB: Army Corps are described in the British fashion-by roman numerals. This was not the French custom of the time, but is adopted to provide greater clarity in the histories of armies, corps and divisions.

In the following corps histories, the term 'M' battalions refer to the Corps Machine Gun Battalion which was drawn from the Corps' territorial infantry regiment. E.g. M/72RIT indicates the Machine Gun Battalion of the 72RIT employed in I Corps d'Armée.

I CORPS D'ARMÉE

QG: Lille

Commanders
02.08.14-Louis Franchet D'Esperey
04.09.14-Henri Deligny
22.02.15-Louis Guillaumat
17.12.16-Jacques Riols de Fonclare
25.01.17-Paul Muteau
19.04.17-Gustave Lacapelle

Organic Divisions
Active 1914   51 DI, Lille 11.15-   122 DI 4-10.15
1 DI, Lille   162 DI 10.16-
2 DI, Arras

Corps Troops
201 RI, Cambrai   6.15 to 1DI
284 RI, Avesnes   6.15 to 122DI
7.16-64 RIT –8.16
7.16-86 RIT –8.16
6.17-72 RIT   8.18-M Bn/72 RIT
6 R Ch, Lille [4 escadrons]
41 RAC, Douai [4 groups]   6.15 –two groups to 122DI
                                           11.17-third group reformed
12.14-4 RAL [1 bie/120mm]   4.15 to XXX CA
4.15- gr/3RAL joins as gp/27RAC   11.15 consolidated into 101 RAL and enlarged to three groups 4.18
4.15- gr/1 RAL
1 BG
Aviation
1915-C53
1918-Sal17, Spa53, Spa255

As part of Fifth Army, I CA advanced to Dinant, retreated to the Meuse at Hastiere and Anhel, and fought in the battle of Charleroi at St Gerard [23rd August] with 1DI, 2DI and 51DI. During the retreat to the Marne it engaged the Germans at Sains Richaumont during the battle of Guise [1DI, 2DI.] During Fifth Army's fight for the two Morin Rivers, ICA [1DI, 2DI] fought at Esternay and then crossed the Marne at Dormans and advanced to the outskirts of Reims between Bétheny and the Cavaliers-de-Coucy. During the first battle of the Aisne, the corps fought at Berry-au-Bac, to the north-west of Reims between 18th September and 3rd November. On the latter date it moved leftwards along the Aisne to take up positions on the river between Braine and Condé, and then between Soupir and Chavonne where it remained until 8th December.

Transferred to Fourth army the corps [1DI , 2DI] fought in the Beauséjours area of Champagne from 28th December 1914 until 28th March 1915. It fought in the first battle of the Woëvre, under command of DA Gérard, to the south-east of Verdun between Braquis, Pareid, Buzy and Maizey from 5th-12th April. On 27th April it rejoined the Fifth Army's front near Reims and held the line to the north-west of that city, between the Neuvillette and Beau Marais until 19th February 1916 [1DI, 5DI, DPr Guerin initially].

The corps [1DI, 39DI, 59DI] arrived in the Verdun salient on 27th February 1916. Under command of Second Army, it fought between the left-bank of the Meuse and Douaumont until 8th April. It returned to Fifth Army's positions on the Chemin des Dames on 20th April. There, with 1DI and 2DI, took over the line between Soupir and Beau Marais which it held until 27th July.

After movement to Picardy, the corps made its contribution to Sixth Army's part in the battle of the Somme when it took over the Bois de Hem sector on 20th August 1916 [1DI, 2DI, 46DI and 47DI] in which it fought towards Ginchy, Combles and Sailly-Saillisel until 10th October.

From 20th October 1916 until 20th January 1917, the corps occupied Fourth Army's sector between the Maisons de Champagne and Navarin [56DI, 18DI] after which it returned to the Chemin des Dames. After a brief spell in the line between the Ployon and Hurtebise [26th-29th January 1917], the corps prepared for its part in Nivelle's offensive. It returned to the line on 13th March and, as part of Fifth Army it attacked Craonne on 16th April [1D, 2DI, 51DI, 162DI]. Withdrawn for a rest on 24th April it did not see action again until 7th July. On that date it took up positions to the north of Ypres. On 31st July, as part of First Army, [it attacked the Foret d'Houthulst [1DI, 2DI, 51DI, 162DI] and remained as a major part of the French contribution to Haig's offensive until December 1917.

Now under command of Sixth Army, the corps resumed its vigil on the Chemin des Dames on 23rd January 1918. With 1DI, 2DI and 162DI, it was in position between Vauclerc and the Miette until 27th April. When the German offensive began on 29th May it returned to the line between Coeuvres-et-Valsery, Soissons and Ambleny in a largely successful attempt to thwart the enemy [2DI, 51DI, 162]. As part of Tenth Army, it held the line between Coeuvres, Ambleny and Vingré, and was able to advance and retake Soissons during the second battle of the Marne. It fought to the north-east of Soissons, between Venizel, Fontenoy and Hautebraye during the second battle of Noyon. During Tenth Army's advance on the Hindenburg Line, it attacked at Laffaux [14th September], and reached the Allemant/Jouy line by 29th September. During this complex period, for most of the time the corps commanded 11DI, 69DI, 72DI and 162DI.

Withdrawn to the Vosges on 28th September 1918, the corps ended its war in the line between the Linge and Leimbach, which it entered on 4th October. [161DI, 162DI].

II CORPS D'ARMÉE

QG: Mézières

Commanders
02.08.14-Augustin Gérard
24.07.15-Frederic Herr
10.08.15-Denis Duchene
29.12.16-Edmond Buat
21.01.17-Henri de Cadoudal
11.06.18-Edme Philipot

Organic Divisions
3 DI, Amiens	52 DR, Amiens part 69DR
4 DI, Mèziéres	

Corps Troops
272 RI, Amiens	6.15 to 3DI
328 RI, Abbeville	6.15 to 4DI
6.15-108 RIT –2.16	
6.15-117 RIT	8.17-M Bn/117RIT
9.16-123 RIT- 2.18	
19 R Ch, La Fère [4 escadron]	
29 RAC, Laon [4 groups]	6.15- two groups to 10DIC
	11.17-third group reformed
12.14-4 RAL [1 bie/120mm]	11.15-consolidated into 102 RAL with third group added 4.18
4.15-1 gp/26 RAC added-9.15 to VI CA	
4.15-101 bie/29 RAC added	
2 BG	
Aviation	

1915-C11
1918-Br11, Br269

Originally intended to cover the assembly of Fifth Army, II CA was transferred to Fourth Army on 8th August 1914. Between 21st and 24th August it took part in operations to the north-west of Virton during the battle for the Ardennes [3DI, 4DI]. It retreated to the Meuse at Beaufort and Stenay, 27th August, and then southwards to Cheminon-la-Ville and Heiltz-le-Hutier. During Fourth Army's operations around Vitry, the corps advanced northwards from Sermaize via Ste-Menehould to Servon, 6th-17th September. Then it established positions on the western edge of the Argonne forest between Four de Paris and the Bois d'Hauzy: there it stayed until 15th January 1915.

After a brief spell in the Beauséjours sector [20th February-12th March] the corps moved into positions to the south of Verdun. Under command, successively of DA Gérard and RFV, it fought the 1st battle of the Woëvre at Marchéval. It manned the Riaville/Trésauvaux sector until 30th September 1915. It fought the vital Éparges sector from 1st December 1915 until 22nd February 1916 to maintain the integrity of the southern flank of the Verdun salient. Then it fought for four months inside the salient between Éparges and Eix [3DI, 4DI, 16DI, 132 DI].

On 23rd July 1916, the corps joined Tenth army's sector at Estrées-Deniecourt [3DI, 4DI and 121DI] where it supported the battle of the Somme. On 19th September it moved north into the more active sector between Belloy and Bernay where it remained until 28th December 1916.

After a period of rest and retraining in Lorraine, the corps was kept in readiness for Tenth Army's planned breakthrough on the Chemin des Dames in April 1917. When this did not materialise, it joined Fifth Army's sector between the Loivre and the Aisne until 12th June [3DI, 4DI and 167 DI]. It returned to the Verdun salient on 7th September when it entered the line between Béthincourt and Avocourt. Its front included Cote 304. It left this sector on 25th March 1918.

It began its period of service between the Oise and the Aisne, in the sector between Carlpont and Manicamp on 5th April. After takeover from Sixth Army to Third Army on 5th May, it moved to the Plémont/Varesnes sector where it became embroiled in the third battle of the Aisne on 29th May [1DI, 33DI, 38DI, 53DI and 72DI]. By 9th June it had become involved in Third Army's defence of the line of the river Matz [53DI, 72DI]. From positions at Orval and Ecouvillon it resisted the Germans and then moved forward via Bethincourt and Chevincourt [11th June] towards the Aisne. From 19th June it joined Sixth Army between Faverolles and Dammard and fought at Troesnes [2DI, 33DI]. In the second battle of the Marne, it advanced eastwards from the Ourcq towards the Vesle from Neuilly St Front [2DI, 33DI, 47DI, 63DI]. It left the area on 5th August.

After a period of rest in Lorraine, the corps joined Fourth Army at les Hurlus [3DI, 4DI, 14DI, 48DI] on 25th September. It fought northwards towards Orfeuil [1st October]and reached the Aisne between Condé and Voncq on 10th October. It was withdrawn from the line three days later.

On 20th October, the corps' final period of service began in the Vosges when it manned Seventh Army's defences between Bezange-la-Grande and the Chapelotte.

III CORPS D'ARMÉE

QG: Rouen

Commanders
02.08.14-Henri Sauret
28.08.14-Emile Hache
23.12.15-Robert Nivelle
21.04.16-Léonce Lebrun

Organic divisions
5 DI, Rouen	53 DR, Rouen	130 DI 7.15-11.17
6 DI, Paris		158 DI 6.17-11.17

Corps Troops

239 RI, Rouen	7.15 to 130DI
274 RI, Rouen	7.15 to 5DI
7.15-26 RIT	8.18-M Bn/26RIT
7 R Ch, Évreux [4 escadron]	
11 RAC, Rouen [4 groups]	7.15- two groups to 130DI
	7.15- two groups ex 84DT, of which one from 16RAC –1.17 [to XXICA] one from 28RAC –7.16 [to 130DI
	11.17 third group reformed
12.14-4 RAL [1 bie/120mm]	11.15 consolidated into 103 RAL with third group added 4.18
4.15-1 bie 120mm ex ICA	
4.15-101 bie/11 RAC	

3 BG
Aviation
1915-C4
1918-Sal4, Sal280

The corps advanced into Belgium as part of Fifth Army, and fought to the south of Charleroi on 24th August [5DI, 6DI, 38DI], and then retreated southwards. In the first battle of Guise on 29th August it fought at Landifay and Courjumelles [5DI, 6DI and 37DI], after which the retreat continued. In the first battle of the Marne, it fought across the Deux Morins from Montceaux-les-Provins, northeastwards to the outskirts of Reims, which it reached on 9th September. There it fought from Brimont to Godat to secure the northern approaches to the city [5DI, 6DI, 38DI]. Then it remained in the established line between Courcy and Godat until 27th April 1915.

After a transfer to Tenth Army in Artois, the corps took up positions to the east of Arras, between Agny and Berles-aux-Bois on 25th May where it remained until the conclusion of the second battle of Artois on 17th June. On 5th July it moved to new positions to the north of Arras, at Neuville-Saint-Vaast, and from there took part in the third battle of Artois [5DI, 6DI and 130DI]. It moved to adjacent sector on its right, between Roclincourt and the Scarpe on 8th October but was pulled out on 23rd October in order to move to Sixth Army in Picardy.

With 6DI, 62DI and 99DT it held the line between Frise, Lihons and Andechy until 18th February 1916.
The corps arrived in the Verdun sector on 5th April 1916 when it took over trenches on the right bank of the Meuse between Douaumont and Eix [5DI, 6DI, 27DI, 43DI]. Relieved on 15th June, it took over the Éparges sector on 20th June and remained in that line until 30th January 1917.

Much of 1917 was spent in the Aisne sector. Initially held in reserve for Tenth Army's breakthrough role in the Chemin des Dames, it took over Sixth Army's positions between Chevregny and the Panthéon on 4th June and then moved to the Courtecon/Braye sector on 16th June [5DI, 6DI, 166DI]. After Tenth Army took over the sector from Sixth Army on 16th July the corps pulled out on 19th August. It joined Third Army on the Oise front and served between Pontruet and Urvillers from 24th August 1917 until 14th January 1918. [21DI, 61DI, 158DI] After a long period of rest and retraining, the corps joined Fourth Army at Tahure on 18th March 1918 [5DI, 6DI, 132DI, 2DCP]. It was moved westwards towards the Marne on 26th June. At first it fought near Château-Thierry with Sixth Army [20DI, 51DI, 125DI] and advanced towards Jaulgonne and Troisy which it reached on 8th July. From 17th July, under command of Ninth Army, it fought south of the Marne [4DI, 18DI, 20DI, 73DI and 125DI] until it reached Arcis-le-Ponsart on 3rd August. Returned to Sixth Army, it held the line on the Vesle between Braine and Bazoches from 24th August until 4th September [52DI, 164DI].

As part of Fifth Army, the corps began to advance towards Villers-en-Prayères and Presles on 4th September [52DI and 164DI] and reached the Merval/Craonne/Sissonne line after the battle of St Thierry [6DI, 52DI and 62DI]. It remained here until 1st November when it was pulled out in preparation for Tenth Army's planned offensive towards Metz.

IV CORPS D'ARMÉE

QG: Paris

Commanders
02.08.14-Victor Boelle
17.06.15-Henri Putz
19.12.17-Ferdinand Pont

Organic Divisions
7 DI, Paris	54 DR, Le Mans	124 DI 6.15-
8DI, Le Mans		163 DI 11.16-

Corps Troops
315 RI, Mamers   6.15 to 7DI
317 RI, Le Mans   6.15 to 8DI
6.15-104 RIT –8.18
6.15-111 RIT -.7.16
7.16- 34 RIT   7.18-M Bn/34 RIT
14 RH, Alençon [4 escadron]
44 RAC, LeMans [4 groups]
                                  6.15- two groups to 124DI
                                  6.15- two groups of 57 RAC ex 91DT
                                  11.16-remaining gps 44RAC to 163DI
                                  4.17- 226 RAC formed from 2 gps/57RAC
                                  11.17 –third group/226 RAC formed
1.15-gp/21 RAC added   11.15 consolidated into 104 RAL with third group formed 4.18
1.15-bie/46 RAC added
1.15-bie/44 RAC added
4 BG
Aviation
1915-F40
1918-Sal40, Sal140, Br267

Assigned to Third Army, the corps fought in the Ardennes between Ethe and Virton, on 22nd August and then retreated to the Meuse at Marville and Flassigny from 24th August to 2nd September. After further retreats via Dun-sur-Meuse and Vienne-le-Château to Ste- Menehoulde, the corps was pulled out of the line and moved towards Paris.

It joined Sixth Army on the Ourcq, with 7DI and 8DI, and fought in the first battle of the Marne, 8th September, towards Nanteuil-le-Haudoin from which it advanced towards Noyon on the left wing of the first battle of the Aisne, 13th September. It joined Second Army's attempt to plug the gap in Picardy as the 'Race to the Sea'developed. It fought at Lassigny and Roye and successfully established a line between Maucourt and Tilloloy where it remained until 27th December 1914.

After movement eastwards to Champagne, it took over Fourth Army's sector between Marquises and Wacques-to the east of Reims-on 25th March 1915. It remained there until 28th October 1915 and fought during the second battle of Champagne with 7DI, 124DI and 60DI.

After a two-month period of rest and retraining, the corps joined Second Army on the borders between the chalk downs of Champagne and the Argonne forest when it took over the line between the Maisons de Champagne and the river Aisne. It remained in line from 20th December 1915 until 20th October 1916 [7DI, 8DI, 124DI]. Command of the area was taken over by Fourth Army on 5th January 1916.

On 2nd January 1917, the corps arrived in the Oise sector of Tenth Army and served in the Ablaincourt area for only three weeks. It travelled eastwards towards Lorraine, and took over the sector around the apex of the St Mihiel Salient, between Bois Loclont and Vargevaux on 30th January. It remained there until 24th June 1917 when it returned to Champagne.

The corps served between Prunay and Marquises, to the east of Reims, from 24th June 1917 until 15th July 1918. During this time, it fought in the battle of the Monts, 14th-15th July 1917 [8DI, 59DI, 163DI] and became involved in the fourth battle of Champagne on 15th July 1918.

It remained with Fourth Army for the autumn offensive when it advanced from Aubérive [7DI. 8DI, 124DI and 163DI] to Nanteuil-sur-Aisne on 15th October. Under command of Fifth Army from 17th October, the advance continued to the Thugny-Trugny/Nanteuil line where it took part in the battle for the Serre [8DI, 124DI]. In the last phase of the advance, it reached Charleville by armistice day.

V CORPS D'ARMÉE

QG: Orléans

Commanders
02.08.14-Charles Brochin
23.08.14-Frederic Micheler
07.07.15-Louis Hallouin
16.10.16-Antoine Boucheron de Boissoudy
01.09.17-Maurice Pellé

Organic Divisions
9 DI, Orléans   55 DR, Orleans 6.17-9.18   125 DI 1.15-
10 DI, Paris

Corps Troops
313 RI, Blois   6.15 to 9DI
331 RI, Orléans   6.15 to 10DI
6.15-29 RIT   8.18-M Bn/29RIT
6.15-30 RIT -4.16
6.15-91 RIT -8.16
6.15-122 RIT-8.18
8 R Ch, Orléans [4 escadrons]   6.15 two groups to 125 DI
45 RAC, Orléans [4 groups]   6.15 bies/38RAC to 15DI
additional 11.14-6.15: 2 bies/38 RAC   11.17 third group reformed
4.15-gr/2 RAL added   11.15 enlarged into 105 RAL with third group added 4.18
5 BG
Aviation
1915-F2
1918-Spa2, Sal105, Br250

As a component of Third Army, the corps fought in the battle for the Ardennes between Cosnes, Gorcy and Ville-Houdlemot, and then, retreated via Longuyon, Varennes and Cierges to Brabant-le-Roi. It in the battle for Revigny there, and at Louppy-le-Château and Vassincourt, and then, advanced to Clermont, Monfaucon and Baulny, in the Ardennes. Still with Third Army, from 16th September 1914 until 6th August 1916, the corps fought in the difficult country of the Argonne, centred on Vauquois, with 9DI, 10DI and 125DI.

On 15th September 1916, the corps joined Sixth Army in the battle of the Somme. The corps took part in engagements between Rancourt and Bouchavesnes until 14th November [10DI, 125DI]. After this, it joined Fifth Army at Berry-au-Bac, to the north-west of Reims, where it remained in line until 27th January 1918. During the second battle of the Aisne in April 1917, it attacked towards Juvincourt-et-Damary with some degree of success [9DI, 10DI, 125DI].

Rushed to Picardy, the corps joined Third Army, and then First Army, in the attempt to stem the German breakthrough towards Amiens. It fought between Mont Renaud and Plessis-du-Roye [9DI, 10DI], and then on the line between the Berliere and the Plémont, and finally, from 14th April, between Sauvillers and Morisel. It remained there and at Bois Sénécat until 26th May.

The German offensive on the Aisne brought about the swift return of the corps to Fifth Army on 30th May. With 28DI and 154DI it fought at Vrigny and Champlat-et-Boujacourt to stem the German advance, and establish the line Marfaux/Tréloup. On 15th July-during fourth Champagne it fought at Vandières-sous- Châtillon and Basilieux [7DI.8DI, 40DI and 10DIC], and then between Ouilly and Tincourt during the second battle of the Marne [7DI. 9DI, 40DI, 10DIC and 7DC]. It advanced Romigny/Breuil-sur-Vesle to the Vesle at Jonchery and Uchair. Progress to Romain and Glennes followed during August [9DI, 10DI, 45DI, 62DI]. In the final push for victory, the corps advanced to the Aisne-Marne canal and then to the Suippe. It fought in the battle of St Thierry on 4th October [9DI, 10DI, 53DI] and reached the Berry-au-Bac and then Neufchâtel-sur-Aisne. From there it advanced towards the Serre at Nizy-le-Comte on 20th October [9DI, 10DI and 52DI]. Its final movement was across the Selve to the Meuse, which it reached on 11th November [10DI, 52DI].

VI CORPS D'ARMÉE

QG: Châlons sur Marne

Commanders
02.08.14-Maurice Sarrail
30.08.14-Martial Verraux
15.11.14-Frederic Herr
24.07.15-Jean Paulinier
17.12.16-Antoine de Mitry
17.04.18-Pierre Duport

Organic divisions
12 DI, Reims	56 DR 9.15-	56 DI	9.15-
40 DI, St Mihiel –1.15		65 DI	12.14-
42 DI, Verdun –9.14		67 DI	1-9.15
		127 DI	6.15-
		166 DI	1.17-

Corps Troops
164 RI, Verdun		8.15 to 72DI
165 RI, Verdun		8.15 to 72DI
168 RI, Verdun		8.15 to 128DI
6.15- 97 RIT	8.18-M Bn/97 RIT	
6.15-112 RIT- 7.18		
1 Lt Cavalry Bde-		To 10.14
10 R Ch, Sampigny [4 escadrons]		10.14 to XXXII CA
12 R Ch, St Mihiel [4 escadrons]		retained as corps cavalry
46 RAC, Châlons-sur-Marne [4 groups]		11.14- two groups to XXXII CA
		11.14- gp/31RAC and gp/44 RAC added but to 129 DI 6.15
		11.15- bie/57RAC and bie/3RACC added and became bies/46 RAC
	on transfer to 166DI 1.17	
		4.17- remaining two gps/46 RAC became 246 RAC
		11.17- third group added to 246RAC
4.15- gr/4 RAL added		11.15 enlarged into 106 RAL with third group added 4.18
6 BG		
Aviation		
1915-F7		

1918-Sal5, Br7, Br141

As part of the Third Army, the corps took part in the fighting in the Ardennes, from 21st August, when it engaged the Germans to the north of Longuyon [12DI, 40DI, 42DI]. It fought at Crusnes, on the Othain, and at Arrancy [12DI, 40DI]. It was forced to retreat southwards along the western side of the Meuse, and eventually, reached Remembercourt-aux-Pots and Erise-le-Petit by 6th September. During the battle of Revigny, during the wider battle of the Marne, it fought at Chaumont-sur-Aire and Deuxnouds, and then, advanced northwards to secure positions downstream from Verdun, at Brabant-le-Roi and Bois d'Haumont [12DI, 40DI].

From 20th September 1914 until 5th August 1915, the corps held the line around Éparges on the southern shoulder of the Verdun Salient. It came under command of First Army on 8th January 1915 and took part in the battle of the Woëvre on 5th April when it engaged the Germans between Éparges and Lamerville [12DI, 65DI, 67DI].

The corps entered Fourth Army's line between Souain and Navarin on 20th September 1915. With 12DI, 56DI, 127DI and 10DIC it attacked on the 25th September, and then remained in this position until 3rd June 1916.

Twelve days later, the corps took over the trenches between Fleury and Damloup in the heights above Verdun [12DI, 52DI, 63DI, 124DI and 130DI]. It was pulled out on 1st August and sent westwards to join Sixth Army in Picardy. Its part in the battle of the Somme began on 18th September when it conducted operations between Bois l'Abbaye and Bouchavesnes, on the approaches to Péronne [12DI, 127DI, 56DI]. It remained in line until 23rd December 1916.

The corps was moved to the Aisne front, where it joined Sixth Army and occupied positions between Chavonne and Troyon [12DI, 56DI, 166DI]. In the second battle of the Aisne, it attacked between Soupir and Ostel on 16th April [12DI, 56DI, 127DI] and remained there until 4th June. After the losses suffered on the Chemin des Dames, the corps was transferred to the Vosges. Under command of Seventh Army, it held the line between the Chapelotte and Leimbach from 29th June 1917 until 20th January 1918.

The German spring offensive brought VI CA back to more active service when it joined First Army in Picardy on 26th March 1918 [12DI, 56DI, 5DC]. After initial fighting around Erches and Dancourt, it established a line to the west of Montdidier, between Ayencourt and Grivesnes. The corps left Picardy for Lorraine on 5th May.

It spent the rest of the war in the quiet sector of Lorraine between Bezange-la-Grande and the Chapelotte. It served in this part of Eighth Army's front from 12th May to 20th October 1918 [12DI, 56DI, 166]. It was returning to the same sector when hostilities ended on 11th November.

VII CORPS D'ARMÉE

GQ: Besançon

Commanders
02.08.14-Louis Bonneau
12.08.14-Frederic Vautier
17.11.14-Etienne de Villeret
02.11.15-Georges de Bazelaire
04.06.18-André Massenet

Organic divisions

14 DI, Belfort	57 DR, Besançon	37 DI	8.15-7.16
41 DI, Remiremont-8.14 &		48 DI	2.15-5.17
from 7.16		63 DI	8.14-2.15
		121 DI	6-8.15
		128 DI	2.17-
		164 DI	5.17-

Corps Troops

352 RI, Gérardmer   9.14- Bde Klein –6.15
45 BCP, Remiremont   9.14- Bde Klein –6.15
55 BCP, Remiremont   9.14- Bde Klein –6.15
7.15- 67 RIT- 8.18   no M Bn?
11 R Ch, Vesoul [4 escadrons]
5 RAC, Besançon [4 groups]   2.15 two groups to 48DI
                                          6.15 two groups to 121DI
                                          10.14 gp/47 RAC added
                                          4.15 gp/28RAC added but to 162DI 10.16
                                          12.15 gp/5 RAC added
                                          4.1917 remaining 2 gps became 247 RAC
                                          11.17 third gp added to 247RAC
                                          6.18 247 RAC transfers to RGA
    4.15-gr/4 RAL added   11.15 enlarged into 107 RAL with third group added 4.18
7 BG
Aviation
1915-C46
1918-Sal34, Sal72, Sal259

Intended to cover the line of the Vosges from the Col de la Schucht to the Swiss frontier under command of First Army, the corps [14DI, 41DI] became the nucleus of the Armée d'Alasce on 11th August. It had taken part in the first offensive of the War-towards Mulhouse on 7th August and it continued to be involved in operations in this area until 25th August. On 6th September it arrived in Sixth Army's line to the east of Paris and there it fought in the battle of the Ourcq between Bouillancy and Brégy with 14DI, 61 and 63DI's. From there it advanced to Autreches, Cuisy and Novron-Vingré, during the battle of the Aisne. Having established positions there, it remained in line until 4th August 1915 [14DI, 63DI].

Transferred to Fourth Army in Champagne the corps manned the line between Wacques and Auberive from 18th August until 25th November 1915. With 14DI, 37DI and 7DI [later 8DI] it took part in the second battle of Champagne which began on 25th September.

After a rest at Ancerville, the corps took up positions on the left bank of the Meuse, in the Verdun sector, between Avocourt and the river on 12th February 1916. It held the left bank of the river during the first phase of the battle of Verdun [29DI, 67DI]. Withdrawn on 26th March, it re-entered the battle at Avocourt on 10th April and fought there until 5th July [14DI, 48DI].

Swiftly transferred to Picardy, the corps took up Sixth Army's positions in front of Péronne on 26th July. It fought at between Cléry, Bois de Hem and Bois l'Abbaye until 18th September [14DI, 41DI, 48DI]. Moved to Champagne, it took over the line between the Main de Massiges and Four de Paris, on the western edge of the Argonne, on 2nd October 1916 and remained there until 3rd January 1917 [14DI, 41DI].

From 13th February until 12th July 1917, the corps, now part of Fifth Army, occupied the line between Sapigneul and Cavaliers. From there it attacked towards Mont Spin on 16th April with 14DI and 41DI. After a two-month rest, the corps returned to Verdun on 15th September. From its positions between Mormont and the Meuse, it took part in the offensive, which was mounted on 2nd October [19DI, 20DI]. It left the salient on 13th January 1918.

From 21st January until 12th May 1918, it occupied the quiet sector, in Lorraine, between Bezange-la- Grande and the Chapelotte with 63DI and 168DI. The German attack on the Aisne brought about a return to more active operations on 22nd May when it arrived in Picardy. It fought as part of First Army in the Bois Sénécat until 30th May [26DI, 73DI]. Transferred to Sixth Army between the Aisne and the Marne, it fought from Villers Cotterêts to Montémafroy, Veuilly-sur-Poteau, and Chézy-en-Orxois [4DI, 73DI] and established a line between Hautevesnes and Dammard. During the second battle of the Marne, it fought from Bonnes and Brécy to the Forêt de la Fère [52, 144DI].

On 1st August the corps transferred to Tenth Army in the Aisne/Oise region, and took over the line between Moulin and Fontenoy which it held until 29th August [48DI, 55DI]. In the second battle of Noyon, it attacked between Blerancourt and Audignecourt and then advanced towards the Hindeburg Line to reach the Forêt de Coucy by 17th September [2DI, 33DI, 48DI and 132DI].

The corps was transferred to Flanders and arrived at its new positions at Straden, between Ypres and Dixmuide on 27th September [41DI, 168DI]. It fought from the Leie to the Schelde with 128 and 164 DI's via Oostroosebrook and Oudenaarde, and had reached Elst by 11th November.

VIII CORPS D'ARMÉE

QG: Bourges

Commanders
02.08.14-Joseph de Castelli
12.10.14-Jean Piarron de Mondesir
08.05.15-Emilien Cordonnier
03.08.16-Alexis Hely d'Oissel

Organic divisions
15 DI, Dijon	58 DR, Dijon 6.17-	169 DI 12.16-
16 DI, Bourges		

Corps Troops
210 RI, Auxonne	6.15 to 76 DI
227 RI, Dijon	6.15 to 76 DI
6.15-131 RIT 7.18-M Bn/131 RIT	
6.15-132 RIT –8.18	
16 R Ch, Beaune [4 escadrons]	
37 RAC, Bourges [4 groups]	6.15 two groups to 127 DI and replaced by two bies/37RAC
	1.18 third group reformed
4.15-gp/38 RAC added	11.15 enlarged into 108 RAL with third group added 4.18
8 BG	

Aviation
1915-none until 1916-F71
1918-Sal54, Sal71, Sal262?

Allocated to First Army, the corps took part in the advance towards Saarebourg on 19th August 1914. It fought at Rédine and Gosselming, after which it retreated across the Mortagne at Hallainville and Essy-la- Côte, on 25th August. Returning to the offensive it fought between Mattexey and Vallois from 25th August until 13th September when it reached the Meurthe.

From 29th September 1914 until 18th September 1916 the corps held the same positions along the southern wing of the St Mihiel sector, centred on Apremont. From there it took part in the battles for Flirey and the Woëvre with 15DI and 16DI.

The corps did not leave Lorraine until the end of 1916, when it joined Tenth Army in Picardy. From 25th December 1916 until 9th January 1917 it held the line in the Santerre between Belloy and Berny [15DI, 16DI]. By 28th January the corps had moved east to the Fourth Army and entered the line between the Maisons de Champagne and Four de Paris on the fringes of the Argonne [16DI, 16DI]. It left this area on 22nd March and moved to the left wing of Fourth Army, between Marquises and Prosnes for the attack towards the Monts [16DI, 34DI and 169DI]. Pulled out from there on 26th April the corps returned to the Argonne and took up positions between Four de Paris and the Courtine on 10th May. It was to remain here until 15th July 1918. [15DI, 16DI, 174 DI, 161DI and 1DCP]. At the end of this long period it fought in the fourth battle of Champagne in the Bois de Beaurain, and in the second battle of the Marne at Mesnil-lès-Hurlus until 28th August.

On 17th September 1918, the corps joined Tenth Army on the Oise front. It held positions between Barsisis and Quincy Basse [32DI, 33DI]. Taken over by First Army on 23rd September, it took up positions between Barsisis and Tergnier, which it held until 15th October in support of the army's advance up the Oise to St Quentin. When that was achieved the corps was to found on the Oise between Moy and Bernot. It took part in the attack on Mont-d'Origny, 15th October-5th November [35DI, 37DI, 58DI, 67DI]. In the last phase of the war, it fought from Mont-d'Origny to the Serre via Vendueil to Sains Richaumont, Hirson and the Bois de Thiérache. On 11th November, the corps had reached the road between Baileux and Chimay.

IX CORPS D'ARMÉE

QG: Tours

Commanders
02.08.14-Pierre Dubois
13.03.15-Louis Curé
14.05.16-Horace Pentel
29.10.16-Henri Niessel
22.08.17-Auguste Hirschauer
17.12.17-Charles Mangin
06.06.18-Noel Garnier-Duplessis

Organic divisions
17 DI, Châteauroux   59 DR, Châteauroux 6.17-   152 DI 4.15-
18 DI, Angers

Corps Troops
268 RI, Le Blanc   4.15 to 152 DI
290 RI, Châteauroux   4.15 to 152 DI
7.15- 141 RIT –8.18
7.15- 308 RIT –8.16
7.16- 15 RIT – 1.18d
4.18- 38 RIT   7.18-M Bn/37 RIT
7 RH, Niort [4 escadrons]
 49 RAC, Poiters [4 groups]   4.15 two groups to152DI
                              1.18 third group reformed
12.14-gr/39 RAC added   11.15 enlarged to form 109 RAL with third group added 4.18
4.15 replaced by gr/49 RAC
9 BG
Aviation
1915-F33
1918-Sal33, Ar256, Ar257

After transfer from Second Army to Fourth Army, the corps advanced northwards into the Ardennes on 22nd August to reach Houdremont and Bièvres where 17DI and 18DI were joined by the Moroccan Division. During the consequent retreat to the Meuse, it fought at Dammory and Juniville. Forced to retreat to the Marne, the corps became part of Foch's Group on 29th August. During the battle for the Marais de St Gond, it fought between Fère Champenoise and the Château de Mondemont [17DI, DM]. It advanced via Jâlons to a line east of Reims between Ste Hilaire-le-Grand, Prosnes and Prunay [17DI, 18DI, 52DI, DM] where it fought until 20th October.

On 23rd October 1914, the corps arrived in the newly-created Ypres Salient and played a substantial part in the fighting around Poelkapelle and Zonnebeke during the first and second battles of Ypres. [17DI, 18DI, 6DC and 7DC]. On 8th May 1915 it moved into French Flanders and took over the line around La Bassée and Grenay for Tenth Army's second battle for Artois. It left this area on 5th July 1915, and moved further south to join Sixth Army between Maucourt and Frise. It left Picardy on 20th August and returned to Artois for Tenth Army's third major battle. Between 25th August and

30th September, it fought to the east and south of Arras at Berles and Agny[17DI, 18DI]. On 1st October, it moved to the other side of Arras to hold the Grenay/Loos sector until 7th January 1916. Four days later, it shuffled to the right to the sector, below Notre Dame de Lorette, between Calonne and Aix-Noulette.

The corps left Artois on 11th March 1916 and, by 24th April, had arrived in the Verdun Salient, where it took up positions between the Hayette and Avocourt on the left bank of the Meuse [17DI, 18DI]. There it remained until 19th May when it left for the Aubérive/Suippe sector in Champagne [17DI, 18DI]: it took over on 3rd June and departed on 4th September. By 6th October, the corps had joined the battle of the Somme in Sixth Army's vital sector between Combles and Sailly-Saillisel [17DI, 18DI, 152DI]. It shuffled sideways to the Bouchavesnes/Cléry/Bois l'Abbé sector on 23rd December. A month later it left the Somme for the Aisne.

Held in reserve by Tenth Army during the preparations for Nivelle's offensive with 17DI, 18DI and 152DI, it attacked Craonne from 18th April until 31st July 1917. The corps earned a rest when it moved to Lorraine and took over the line between the Sanon and the Chapelotte on 29th August: it remained there until 21st January 1918.

Recalled to more active service after the German spring offensive began, it reached the Avre and helped stabilise First Army's front between Thory and Grivesnes from 31st March. It remained in this area throughout the spring and summer of 1918 [127DI, 166DI]. During the Amiens offensive it fought from the Avre, west of Montdidier, 8th-10th August [3DI, 15DIC].

In mid-September, the corps joined Fourth Army in Champagne. From positions between the Main de Massiges and Mesnil-lès-Hurlus it advanced towards Somme-Py on 23rd September [2DM, 157DI, 161DI]. By 1st October it had advanced to Challerange and then to Brécy and Conde-le-Vouzier by 10th October [40DI, 42DI, 74DI and 120DI]. By the end of hostilities it had reached the Meuse between Quatre Champs and Sedan.

X CORPS D'ARMÉE

QG: Rennes

Commanders
02.08.14-Gilbert Desforges
10.11.14-Henri Wirbel
10.09.15-Francois Anthoine
24.03.17-Charles Vandenberg

Organic divisions
19 DI, Rennes   60 DR, Rennes 6.17-   131 DI 7.15-
20 DI, St Servan

Corps Troops
241 RI, Rennes	7.15 to 131 DI
270 RI, Vitré	7.15 to 19 DI
7.15- 28 RIT 7.18-M Bn/28 RIT	
6.17-64 RIT –8.18	
13 RH, Dinan [4 escadrons]	
50 RAC, Rennes [4 groups]	7.15 two groups to 131DI
	8.15 two groups/53 RAC ex 88DT and both transferred to 162DI 10.16
	4.1917-remaining two groups became 250 RAC and third group added 1.18
12.14 gr formed from bie/1RAP and bie/10 RAC 7.15 replaced by gr/7 RAC	11.15 enlarged to form 110 RAL with third group added 4.18
10 BG	
Aviation	
1915-F32	

1918-Sal32, Esc59, Spa261

As part of Fifth Army, the corps advanced into Belgium and fought at Metett and Fosse during the battle of Charleroi [19DI, 20DI]. Then it retreated via Chimay and Hirson, and fought at Sains-Richaumont, during the battle of Guise on 29th August. After it reached Sezanne, it fought in Fifth Army's struggle for the Deux Morins [19DI, 20DI, 51DI] and then advanced north-westwards to Boissy, Bannes and Epernay, to arrive at the Fort de la Pompelle, outside Reims by 9th September. On that date, the corps was taken over by Ninth Army in the struggle to retain control of Reims. It departed for Artois on 20th September.

As a component of Second Army it sought to retain French control of Artois from 2nd October in fighting around Mercatel and Neuville-Saint-Vaast [19DI, 20DI]. This achieved, and as part of Tenth Army, it setteled down to a long stay in the Arras area. It occupied the line between Berles and Blagny from 6th October 1914 until 29th July 1915 [19DI, 20DI].

The corps arrived in the Argonne to take up Third Army's positions between the Aisne and Four de Paris on 4th August. During its stay there it took part in the second battle of Champagne on 25th September 1915 [19DI, 20DI, 128DI, 131DI]. It did not leave the Argonne until 24th June 1916.

Next the corps joined Tenth Army in Picardy. From 12th July 1916 until 2nd January 1917 it operated between Maucourt and Chaulnes, and then between Chilly and Presles [20DI, 26DI, 51DI, 104DT].

Moved to the Oise region and Third Army, the corps occupied a line between Echelle and Thierry from 29th January 1917. It followed the German retreat to the Hindeburg Line along the axis Ham/Tugny/Happincourt which it reached by 31st March [28DI, DM]. As a part of Fourth Army it occupied positions near Marquises 24th April-20th June 1917 during the battle for the Monts [19DI, 20DI, 48DI, 169DI].

From 24th June 1917 until 17th April 1918, the corps sustained the French presence on the northern flank of the St Mihiel salient between Damloup and Loclont.

In response to the German spring offensive, the corps moved to First Army in Picardy where it fought on the Avre, near Montdidier, at Ayencourt and Grivesnes from 5th May [33DI, 52DI].

During the battle of Amiens, on 8th August, it advanced towards Beuvraignes [60DI, 152Di and 166DI], then took part in First Army's movement towards the Hindenburg Line. From Catigny, on 27th August, it crossed the Canal du Nord, and proceeded eastwards to Vendeuil and Hinacourt which it reached on 4th September [60DI, 166DI]. It left the Oise area on 15th September.

From 24th September until 11th November 1918, the corps manned the line between the Linge and the Chapelotte, along the crest of the Vosges. [19DI, 20DI]

XI CORPS D'ARMÉE

QG: Nantes

Commanders
02.08.14-Joseph Eydoux
10.02.15-Maurice Baumgarten
04.06.16-Charles Mangin
19.12.16-Paul Muteau
25.01.17-Louis de Maud'Huy
03.06.18-Henri Niessel
19.07.18-Léon Prax
Organic divisions
21 DI, Nantes   61 DR, Nantes 6.17-   151 DI 4.15-
22 DI, Vannes

Corps Troops

293 RI, La Roche	4.15 to 151 DI
337 RI, Fontenay	4.15 to 151 DI
4.15- 21 RIT –8.18	
4.15- 22 RIT –6.18	
6.18- 7 RIT 7.18-M Bn/7 RIT	
2 R Ch, Pontivy [4 escadrons]	
28 RAC, Vannes [4 groups]	4.15 two groups to 151DI
	4.1917 remaining two groups became 228 RAC and third group reformed 1.18
	6.18- 228 RAC transferred to RGA
12.14 gr/4 RAL added	11.15 enlarged to form 111 RAL with third group added 4.18
11 BG	

Aviation
1915-F8
1918-Sal8, Sal55, Sal251

Intended to become part of Fifth Army, the corps was re-assigned to Fourth Army on 16th August. It advanced northwards into the Ardennes and reached Maissin before being forced to retreat via Bouillon back to the Meuse between Nouvion and Remilly. At the end of Fifth Army's long retreat southwards, the corps reached Fère-Champenoise where it was taken under Foch's wing. As part of the Ninth Army it fought at Fère-Champenoise and then advanced through Châlons-sur-Marne to Jonchery-sur-Suippe and Ste Hilaire-le-Grand [21DI, 22DI, 60DI]. During the first battle of the Aisne, it engaged the enemy at Jonchery and Ste Hilaire-le-Grand.

Re-allocated to Second Army, the corps arrived in Picardy on 27th September 1914 and fought on the future British battlefield of the Somme, at Thiepval and Beaumont Hamel. It was to hold the line in front of Albert until 11th August 1915 [21DI, 22DI].

On 25th September 1915, the corps joined Group Pétain on the Champagne front where it took over positions between Cote 196 and Perthes from which it took part in the second battle of Champagne, which began on 25th September [21DI, 22DI, 53DI]. It held this sector until 12th December and two weeks later returned to the line: this time, between Souain and Mamelles [21DI, 22DI, 155DI]. It left the front-line on 2nd May 1916 and entered the struggle for Verdun on 19th June, It fought at Marre and Fleury until 27th January 1917, during which time, it took part in the offensive of 24th October 1917.

The corps was held in reserve with Sixth Army during the Nivelle's offensive in April 1917, after which, it fought at Cerny and Hurtebise, 19th April-18th May. Then it moved to the Oise front of Third Army where it undertook two tours in the trenches around Pontruet and Orvillers [21DI, 22DI, 133DI, 38DI and 38DI]: 20th May-26th June and 29th June-24th August.

It served with Sixth Army between the Panthéon and Jouy from 27th August 1917 until 8th April 1918. During this long period, it took part in the attack on Malmaison on 23rd October when it advanced towards the Oise-Aisne canal.

The corps continued to hold this position during the initial stages of the German spring offensive but was forced out of the area by the strength of the attack on Sixth Army which began on 27th May 1918 [21DI, 61DI, 74DI, 157DI]. The corps was forced to retreat from the line between the Ailette and Coucy-le-Château to Condé and Margival, and then to Villers Cotterêts. By 5th June it held on the line between Chavigny and Faverolles. From this base it fought in Tenth Army's drive eastwards from the Ourcq towards the Vesle,

from Longpont to Savieres and Cugny to reach Oulchy-la-Ville and Oulchy-le-Château by 29th July. During the battle of Tardenois, it drove forward to the Vesle via Beugneux to Limé and Braine. After it reached Baroches, it was pulled out of the line on 23rd August [41DI, 68DI].

By 2nd September 1918, the corps was in line between Damloup and Watronville, to the south-east of Verdun [52DI, 62DI, 68DI and 164DI]. After a week in this quiet sector, amidst the American forces, the corps was moved to Fourth

Army. From 25th September it fought in the battle of Somme-Py [21DI, 22dI, 61DI, 155DI] and advanced to the Arnes by 5th October. Then it crossed the Aisne between Givry and Thugny, reached Attichy on 28th October, and reached forward to the Meuse near Mézières by the end of hostilities.

XII CORPS D'ARMÉE

QG: Limoges

Commanders
02.08.14-Pierre Roques
05.01.15-Henri Descoings
12.05.16-Charles Nollet
25.10.16-Pierre Nourisson
29.03.18-Jean Graziani

Organic divisions
23 DI, Angoulême   62 DR, Angoulême
24 DI, Perigueux

Corps Troops
300 RI, Tulle   6.15 to 24DI
326 RI, Brive   6.15 to 24DI
6.15-130 RIT- 8.16
6.15-135 RIT- 8.16
8.16-109 RIT   7.18-M Bn/109 RIT
21 R Ch, Limoges [4 escadrons]
52 RAC, Angoulême [4 groups]   6.15 two groups to 128DI
                                     9.18 52 RAC transferred to ICC and not replaced
1.15- gr/7 RAC added   11.15 enlarged to form 112 RAL with third group added 4.18
12 BG
Aviation
1915-F22
1918-Sal22, Sal254

As part of Fourth Army, the corps advanced to Neufchâteau and fought at Oin and Izel. In the battle for the Ardennes, it fught at Ménugoutte and Névarumont before retirement back to the Meuse at Mouzion. After a brief struggle along the Meuse between Mouzion and Beaumont, the corps followed the rest of the army southwards deep into Champagne. It reached Vitry and from there took part in the first battle of the Marne on 6th September, when it fought at Courdemanges and Château Rouald [23DI, 24DI] From this point it advanced north to reach to Somme-Tourbe, and took up positions between Aubérive and Souain. It remained in the line there from 18th September 1914 until 25th March 1915 [23DI, 24DI, 60DI, 91DT, 93DT].

Allocated to First Army, it took part in an extensive series of actions along the southern flank of the St Mihiel Salient between Remenauville to Regniéville and Fey from 2nd April until 10th June 1915 [23DI, 24DI].
Next, the corps joined Tenth Army in Artois, when it occupied the line to the north of Arras from Roclincourt to Neuville-Saint-Vaast, from where it fought in the third battle of Artois [23DI, 24DI]. It left Artois on 14th March 1916 and took up positions to the north of Verdun on 8th April. It served between Marre, Charny, Cote du Poivre and Douaumont until 22nd June [23DI, 24DI].

On 22nd July 1916, the corps began a two-month tour of Fifth Army's line from Pernant to Soupir on the Chemin des Dames [23DI, 89DI]. It left this position on 23rd September and moved westwards to Picardy where it took over Tenth Army's front between Belloy and Cléry as the battle of the Somme subsided [23DI. 70DI]. It left this area on 16th January 1917 and returned to Champagne where it embarked on a very lengthy tour near Navarin, 20th January-11th October

1917. During this period, it fought at Souain and Auberive during the attack on the Monts on 24th April [23DI, 24DI, 60DI, 15DI, 74DI, 132DI].

As part of Tenth Army's redeployment to Italy, XII Corps left France in November and December 1917. [23DI, 24DI]. It was to remain in Italy for the rest of the war. After the withdrawal of Tenth Army at the end of March 1918, it became the major French contribution to allied victory against Austria-Hungary. It served in the Asolo sector, 5th February-14th March; in the Asiago plateau, 24th March-25th October, and on the Piave 25th October-4th November 1918.

XIII CORPS D'ARMÉE

GQ: Clermont Ferrand

Commanders
02.08.14-César Alix
11.04.15-Henri Alby
06.10.16-Georges Demange
19.03.17-Charles Vandenberg
24.03.17-Henri Linder

Organic divisions
25 DI, St Etiènne
26 DI, Clermont Ferrand
63 DR, Clermont Ferrand 6.17-
120 DI 6.15-
167 DI 12.16-6.17

Corps Troops
41 BCP, Senones   9.14 to 71DI
43 BCP, St Dié   10.14 to 74 DI
50 BCP, St Dié   10.14 to 74 DI
71 BCP, St Dié   10.14 to 74 DI
6.15- 70 RIT   7.18-M Bn/70 RIT
6.15- 71 RIT –8.18
6.15- 72 RIT –6.17
also 185 Bde [75RIT, 78RIT] 9.15-2.16
3 R Ch, Clermont Ferrand [4 escadrons]
53 RAC, Clermont Ferrand [4 groups]

2.15 one group to 62DI
6.15 one group to 120DI
10.14 gp-90/53RAC added but to 120DI 4.15
3.15 gp/31RAC added –to 167DI 11.16
8.15 gp/49RAC added –to 120DI 6.16
12.16 one gp/53RAC toAO
4.1917 253 RAC formed with remaining gp and one
    gp/53RAC ex IICAC-third gp added 4.18
6.18 253 RAC to RGA

6.15-gr/16 RAC added

11.15 enlarged to form 113 RAL with third group added 4.18

13 BG Aviation
1915-F19
1918-Sal19, Sal54, Sal264

During First Army's advance on Sarrebourg, which began on 20th August 1914, the corps reached Hartzwiller, Schneckenbusch and Brouderdorff [25DI, 26DI]. Then it retired to the far bank of the Mortagne at Ramberviller and Voymecourt. As the front stabilised on 2nd September, it established positions between the Bois d'Anglemont and Xaffévillers [25DI, 26DI, 44DI].

By 16th September, the corps had moved westwards to Picardy where it joined Second Army in its fight for Noyon, The corps fought between the Oise and Lassigny before establishing a firm line from Ribécourt to Beuvraignes which it held from 2nd October 1914 until 14th April 1916. It was transferred from Second Army to Sixth Army on 1st July 1915.
A move to the Oise front of Tenth Army, and then Third Army resulted in a long spell in the line between the Oise and Pernant which lasted from 27th April 1916 until 2nd December 1916 [25DI.26DI. 120DI].

After a brief period of retraining in Lorraine, the corps took over First Army's sector between Thiescourt and Ribémont on 25th January 1917. In response to the German withdrawal to the Hindenburg Line, it advanced towards Noyon. Withdrawn on 19th March, it came under command of Third Army two days later. From 2nd April until 29th June it held the sector from Roupy to Essigny-le-Grand [25DI, 26DI].

On 22nd July 1917, the corps arrived in the Verdun Salient and took over the left-bank sector between Béthincourt and Avocourt. It took part in the offensive of 20th August when it attacked Côte 304. It left the line on 10th September and shuffled westwards into the Argonne. It held the sector between Avocourt and Four de Paris from 27th September 1917 until 21st August 1918. [25DI, 26DI, 60DI, 120DI]. It was relieved by the Second Italian Corps on that date [which moved to the Damloup/Calonne sector 22nd August and served there until 2nd September].

It resumed a more mobile role when it was transferred to Fifth Army on 7th September in preparation for the autumn offensives. It fought between Reims and Jouvincourt, during the battle of St Thierry, which began on 30th September [16DI, 168DI], and then, advanced to the Serre via Muizon [1st October], to the Aisne- Marne canal [16DI, 45DI. 161DI]. It reached the the Suippe by 5th November, where it established a line between Thours St Germainville and the Recouvrance. In the last push towards the Meuse, with 13DI and 151DI, it advanced to Varidon and Bel-Air.

XIV CORPS D'ARMÉE

QG: Lyon

Commanders
02.08.14-Paul Pouradier-Duteil
24.08.14-Joseph Baret
03.08.16-Pierre Duport
02.09.16-Albert Marjoulet

Organic divisions
27 DI, Grenoble   64 DR, Grenoble   129 DI 6.17-
28 DI, Chambéry   154 DI 4.15-

Corps Troops
2 BI, Lyon-9.14
5 RIC
6 RIC
10.14-101 RIT-7.15
7.15-8 RIT   7.18-M Bn/8RIT
6.15-123 RIT-7.15
7.15-24RIT-8.18
9 RH, Chambéry [4 escadrons]
6 RAC, Valence [4 groups]
                              9.14 one group to 77DI
                              5.15 two groups to 154DI
                              1.15 one bie/1RAM and 2 bies/2RAM added and became gp/6RAC 6.15-to
                                   122DI 12.15
                              1.16 gp/20RAC added
                              4.16 gp/6Rac and gp/20RAC to 206 RAC
                              2.18 third gp added 206RAC
                              6.18 206 RAC to RGA

12.14 –gr/1 RAC added   11.15 enlarged to form 114 RAL with third group added 4.18
14 BG
Aviation
1915-F20
1918-Spa20, sop50, Spa263

With its divisions made up of alpine troops, the corps was assigned the task of holding the passes over the Vosges on the southern flank of the main body of First Army. It fought for control of the passes between the Col du Bonhomme and Saales. It advanced on Schirmeck on 19th August, and moved via the Salm to the Col Ste Marie in the offensive towards Saarebourg. When that failed, it retreated to the Mortange via Raon-l'Étape and then it reformed to cross over the Meurthe to Raon-l'Étape, and advance and re-capture St Dié on 13th September [27DI, 28DI, also 58DI and 71DI].

Nine days later, the corps arrived in Picardy with Second Army and successfully attempted to stall the German advance south of the Somme. Once this was achieved, the corps remained in the line between the Somme and Maucourt until 8th August 1915 [27DI, 28DI, 62DI and later, 154DI].

Transferred to the Champagne region in preparation for the planned autumn offensive, the corps came under command of Pétain's group [later Second Army] in the sector between Perthes and Bois Sabot, on 17th August 1915. From there it attacked towards Tahure and Trou Bricot on 25th September [27DI, 28DI, 31DI and later 16DIC]. It remained in line until 15th October when it was withdrawn for a period of retraining in the Vosges.

The corps returned to front-line duties on 7th March 1916, when it joined the battle for Verdun. Initially, it occupied the sector from the Woëvre to Eix but moved to the more intense sector around Tavannes on 1st August. It fought there until Christmas Day 1916. [27DI, 28DI, 68DI, 154DI].

On 17th January 1917, the corps took over Third Army's positions on the Oise front between Maucourt and Andechy [132DI, 62DI]. As a result of the German withdrawal to the Hindenburg Line, it moved eastwards from Andechy and Essigny to reached Vendeuil and Roupy by 21st March [27DI, 28DI, 62DI]. New positions were established before the corps left the front-line on 2nd April. It was withdrawn to take part in Sixth Army's limited attempts to maintain the front along the Chemin des Dames after the failure of Nivelle's offensive. It held the line between Courtecon and Hurtebis from 18th May until 24th June [27DI, 28DI, 38DI]. Then, it returned to Third Army for a brief period in the line between Urvillers, Moy and Fère, 29th July-14th August 1917, after which it prepared to take part in Sixth Army's planned attacked on Malmaison. In line between Vendeuil and Quincy Basse from 17th August, it took part in the attack on Malmaison on 23rd October when it advanced towards the Ailette river [27DI, 28DI, 129DI, 154DI, 151DI]. After this success, the corps was held in reserve in case it was required to support the British attack on Cambrai [129DI, 154DI].

On 29th January 1918, the corps took over Seventh Army's line to the north of Belfort, between Burnhaupt and Fulleren where it remained until 1st April. Recalled to more active duty by the German offensives, it was moved to Flanders. From 12th May until 30th June, it fought around Mount Kemmel in the struggle for the Ypres Salient [14DI, 32DI, 121DI].
As the main battle between the Aisne and the Marne developed in the summer of 1918, the corps joined Fifth Army at Troissy on 20th July. In the second battle of the Marne, it fought from there to Dormans, on the Marne, and then to Jonchery on the Vesle. It reached Reims on 11th September [20DI, 121DI].

For the final allied offensives, the corps operated with Fourth Army. On 25th September it arrived in the Soupir/Auberive sector and advanced northwards in the battle of Somme-Py. It reached Vaudessincourt, Ste Marie-à-Py and the Retourne between Alincourt and Juniville by 12th October [28DI, 68DI, 154DI]. In the battle for the Chesne, it attacked from the Voncq/Attigny line towards the Meuse at Dom-le-Mesnil [22DI, 163DI, 14DI].

XV CORPS D'ARMÉE

QG: Marseille

Commanders
02.08.14-Louis Espinasse
31.10.14-Jules Heymann

02.04.16-Louis de Maud'Huy
25.01.17-Jacques de Riols de Fonclare

Organic divisions
29 DI, Nice	65 DR, Nice	123 DI 8.15-
30 DI, Avignon		126 DI 6.15-

Corps Troops
6 BCA, Nice   11.14 –149 Bde-6.15
23 BCA, Grasse   240 RI
24 BCA, Villefranche   258 RI
27 BCA, Menton   42 RIC
6.16-101 RIT   7.18-M Bn/101RIT
6.16-105 RIT-11.16
6 RH, Marseille [4 escadrons]
38 RAC, Nîmes [4 groups]   6.15 two groups to 126DI
                                                    6.16 remaining two groups to 123 & 126DI and replaced by
                                                         gp/24RAC and gp/18RAC from 123 and 126DI's
                                                  -gp/24RAC to 164DI 11.16
                                                  4.15 gp/41RAC ex 154DI which became gp/41RAC in 5.16
                                                  4.1917-gp/41RAC and gp/18RAC became
                                                  238 RAC-third group added 12.17
                                                  6.18-238 RAC to RGA
4.15-gr/2 RAL added   11.15 enlarged to form 115 RAL with third group added 4.18
15 BG
Aviation
1915-C13
1918-Sal13, Sal270

The corps advanced, with the rest of Second Army towards Morhange on 14th August 1914, It advanced towards Dieuze, via Moncourt and Coincourt, and reached Vergaville and Bidestorff by 19th August. Forced to retreat, it fell back towards Lunéville, and fought around Xermaménil and Heriménil during the battle for the Grand Couronne: this saved Lunéville and Nancy from German occupation [29DI, 30DI, 64DI]. It moved to Bar-le-Duc and joined Third Army.

From 7th September 1914, the corps took part in the batle of Revigny. It fought at Vassincourt [29DI, 30DI] and took part in the army's advance northwards back into the Argonne at Malancourt. The corps would spend most of the next year in this sector. From 16th September 1914 until 20th May 1915 it fought around Vauquois, between the Bois des Forges and Malancourt; and then, between Massiges and the river Aire, until 14th August 1915 [30DI, 126DI].

Moved from Group Pétain, it left the Argonne for Fifth Army. It took over the latter's positions below the eastern end of the Chemin des Dames, between Beau Marais and the Miette on 31st August and held that line until 12th November [30DI, 123DI, 126DI].It returned to the Champagne/Argonne border, between Cote 196, Mamelles and the Courtine on 12th December 1915 and stayed there until 5th June 1916 [123DI, 126DI]. Drawn into the struggle for Verdun, it fought on the other side of the Argonne, between the Hayette and Avocourt, 16th June-2nd November 1916 [123DI, 126DI]. After a period of recuperation, the corps returned to the Salient. After a brief period along the southern flank between Damloup and Vaux-lès- Palameix, it spent most of its long stay on the right bank of the Meuse. It fought at Charrny, Bois de Caurières and Marre until 15th September 1917. As part of the offensive mounted on 20th August, the corps attacked along the Cote de Talu.

A lengthy spell in Eighth Army's quiet sector, between Chenincourt, Bezange-la-Grande and Clémery occurred between 23rd October 1917 and 5th June 1918 [123DI, 126DI].

Recalled to a more active front in response to the German spring offensives, the corps joined Third Army on 10th June. It fought along the Matz between Antheuil and Chenincourt with 123DI, 126DI and 1DCP. During the allied offensive in Picardy, which began on 8th August, the corps fought at Marquélise, on the Plessier, and at Ribécourt and then advanced to the Thiescourt Massif to take Noyon on 29th August [123DI, 67DI, 74DI, 70DI and 58DI]. From the line, Liez/Tergnier it moved up to the Hindenburg Line at Hinacourt and Vendeuil.

Transferred to First Army on 14th September, the corps attacked towards the north of St Quentin from 29th September until 16th October [126DI, 46DI, 47DI]. In the subsequent battle for Mont d'Origny on 16th October, it reached Tupigny and Pont Velli [126DI, 123DI, 66DI, 46DI]. In the battle of Guise, 4th November, it crossed the Oise-Sambre canal at Etreux and reached the line of the Nouvion [123DI, 46DI. 51DI]. From 6th November it advanced northwards to the Thiérache and end the war in the Forêt de Trélon.

XVI CORPS D'ARMÉE

QG: Montpellier

Commanders
02.08.14-Louis Taverna
07.11.14-Paul Grossetti
13.01.17-Frederic Herr
30.04.17-Pierre Corvisart
26.08.18-Louis Deville

Organic divisions
31 DI, Montpellier	66 DR, Montpellier
32 DI, Perpignan	

Corps Troops

322 RI, Rodez	Disbanded 9.14 reformed 3.15 6.15-31DI
342 RI, Mende	6.15 to 32DI
6.15-109 RIT-8.16	
6.15-110 RIT-4.16	
6.16-35 RIT	7.18-M Bn/35 RIT
6.16-34 RIT –7.16	
7.16-111 RIT-9.17	
1 RH, Béziers [4 escadrons]	
9 RAC, Castres [4 groups]	6.15 two groups to 16DIC replaced by gp/9RAC and gp/38RAC ex 93DT
	10.16-two groups to 161DI
	1.18 third group reformed
	6.18 9RAC to RGA
12.14-gr/14 RAC added	11.15 enlarged to form 116 RAL with third group added 4.18
16 BG	

Aviation
1915-F50
1918-Sal50, Br274

From its assembly point at Lunéville, the corps joined Second Army's advance towards Morhange on 20th August 1914. It fought at Loudrefins and advanced as far as Bisping before being forced to retire towards Bayon. From there it fought the battle of Grand Couronne between Einvaux, Gerbévillers and Xermaménil. Consequently, it retired to Nancy and then to Toul. [31DI, 32DI, 74DI and 29DI].

From Toul the corps joined First Army on 22nd September in the Flirey sector, where it consolidated positions between Mort Mare and Seicheprey until 7th October [31DI, 32DI]. Moved westwards to the Aisne, it served briefly with Sixth Army between Condé-sur-Aisne and Soupir: those positions had been evacuated by the BEF as it raced northwards to the Ypres area. The XVI Corps followed the BEF to Flanders. From 31st October 1914 until 3rd February 1915 it fought along Mesen Ridge, from Wijschate to Klein Zillebeke [31DI, 32DI-later 11DI, 39DI, 43DI and 9DC].

On 12th March 1915 the corps arrived in the Champagne sector and, then, served in Fourth Army's sector between Beauséjours and Mesnil-lès-Hurlus until 3rd September. It stayed in the region but transferred to Group Pétain/Second Army and fought in the Tahure/Cote 193 sector until 27th December 1915. [31DI, 32DI and 3DI, 48DI and 4DI].

The corps rejoined the line on the Aisne between Pernant and Condé on 6th February 1916 and served there, with Fifth Army, until 9th July. For the following fifteen months the corps served in various parts of the Verdun Salient. At first, it occupied the Argonne sector, between Four de Paris and Avocourt from 6th August 1916 until 29th January 1917 [31DI, 32DI, 71DI, 130DI]; then on the left bank of the Meuse from Avocourt to Charny, 24th January to 7th October 1917. During this latter tour, the corps attacked Mort Homme on 20th August: part of the major offensive which began that day.

From 7th November 1917 until 26th March 1918 the corps 'rested' in the quiet sector in the Vosges between Guebwiller, Burnhaupt and Leimbach.

The German spring offensive brought about a rapid move to Flanders in April 1918. From 5th May until 8th July, the corps fought at Danoutre, Kemmel and Locre along the southern fringes of the Ypres Salient [31DI, 32DI, 29DI, 129DI]. The corps arrived in the 'quiet' sector in Lorraine, between Clémery and Bezange-le-Grand on 24th July and remained there until 25th August.

The corps spent a week with Fifth Army on the Aisne front between Romain, Vieil and Arcy, 9th-18th September and then moved further west to join Tenth Army on the Oise. From a line between Barisis-au-Bois and Bois Mortier, it joined that army's advance on 23rd September [31DI, 32DI, 33DI]. As Tenth Army became Third Army on 27th October, the corps continued its advance to the Serre via the Forêt de St Gobain. It reached Builly-sur-Serre, Crecy-sur-Serre and Chalandry by 5th November. In the last few days of the war, the corps moved north to Cul de Saarts.

XVII CORPS D'ARMÉE

QG: Toulouse

Commanders
02.08.14-Arthur Poline
21.09.14-Jean-Baptiste Dumas
20.05.17-Paul Henrys
12.12.17-Jean Graziani
29.03.18-Edmond Buat
10.06.18-Henri Claudet
27.10.18-Frederic Hellot

Organic divisions
33 DI, Montauban	67 DR, Toulouse
34 DI, Toulouse	

Corps Troops
207 RI, Cahors	7.15 to 33DI
209 RI, Agen	7.15 to 34DI
7.15-27 RIT 7.18-M Bn/27 RIT	
9 R Ch, Auch [4 escadrons]	
57 RAC, Toulouse [4 groups]	7.15 two groups to 132DI replaced by gp/31RAC ex 88DT which became gp/57
	RAC in 7.17
	11.16 one gp/57 RAC to 16DIC
	1.18 third group reformed

6.15-gr/57 RAC added
17 BG
Aviation
1915-C56
1918-Sal56, Br281

6.18 57 RAC to RGA
11.15 enlarged to become 117 RAL with third group added 4.18

The corps served with Fourth Army until the spring of 1915. It took part in the advance northwards into the Ardennes, where it reached Jehonville, Forêt de Luchy and Bertrix. Forced to retreat back to the Meuse at Mouzon, and fought for the river line between Remilly and Autrecourt-et-Pourron. Then it joined the general southward movement of Fourth Army via Voncq to Vitry. There it fought in the first battle of the Marne between Grand Perthes and Certine [33DI, 34DI]. With victory, the corps advanced back north to the Massiges- Beauséjours area, and established a position around Perthes and Bois Sabot where it remained until 3rd April 1915.

By 1st May, the corps had moved westwards and on that same day it entered Tenth Army's line between Écurie and Roclincourt on the northern approaches to Arras. It fought in Artois until 4th March 1916. During the second battle of Artois, it fought in its lines, and then, shuffled to the right to Roclincourt on 22nd May. Consequently, it fought the third battle of Artois between St Laurent and Blagny [33DI, 34DI].

After a brief period in the 'quiet sector' between Bezange-la-Grande and Brin, in Lorraine from 8th March 1916 until 22nd April, XVII Corps returned to Fourth Army. It served between the Marquises and Monts Haut from 7th July 1916 until 17th April 1917. It left the line immediately after the spring attacks on the Monts position. [33DI, 34DI and many others]. The last eighteen months of the conflict was spent in the Verdun area.. It manned the trenches around the apex of the St Mihiel Salient, between Loclont and Vargévaux from 24th June 1917 until 18th November 1917 [33DI, 34DI, 52DI, 120DI]. On the latter date, the corps moved northwards to the heights of the right bank of the Meuse. There it occupied the trenches from Chaume to Mormont and Damloup [34DI, 120DI, 164DI].

On 22nd September 1918, the corps was transferred from Second Army-which had become a shadow of its former self-to the new resident of the region: the American First Army. Under command of the Americans, the corps operated on the right wing of the American attack on Monfaucon. From 6th October, it recovered positions downstream from Verdun, such as Somogneux, which had been in German hands since February 1916. By 6th November, it continued to secure the right flank of the American Army by an advance on Thillot and Chaufour.

XVIII CORPS D'ARMÉE

QG: Bordeaux

Commanders
02.08.14-Jacques de Mas-Latre
04.09.14-Louis de Maud'Huy
30.09.14-Albert Marjoullet
20.06.16-Auguste Hirshauer
22.08.17-Louis d'Armau de Pouydraguin

Organic divisions
35 DI, Bordeaux   68 DR, Bordeaux
36 DI, Biarritz

Corps Troops
218 RI, Pau   6.15 to 36DI
249 RI, Bayonne   6.15 to 35DI
6.15- 64 RIT –4.16
6.15- 86 RIT –4.16
4.16-110 RIT   7.18-M Bn/110 RIT

10 RH, Tarbes [4 escadrons]
58 RAC, Bordeaux [4 groups]
    6.15 two groups to 123DI
    4.17 other two groups become 258 RAC
    1.18 third group reformed
    6.18 258 RAC to RGA
12.14-gp/3RAL and gr/1RAL added
    11.15 became 118 RAL with third group from 4.18
18 BG
Aviation
1915-C6
1918-Sal6, Spa268

Originally intended for Second Army, the corps was switched to Fifth Army on 18th August 1914. It advanced north into Belgium and fought at Gozée, Biesme-sur-Thuin and Fontaine-Valmons, during the battle of Charleroi. Forced to retreat, it marched south and fought at Ribémont and Villers-le-Sec during Fifth Army's fight at Guise. Then it continued the retreat to Provins. During the first battle of the Marne, when 35DI and 36DI were joined by 38DI, it fought across the two Morins at Rupéreux, Montceaux and Sancy to advance to the Marne at Chateau Thierry. From 14th September it advanced to the Aisne and held new positions at Cerny, Hurtebise and Craonne, on the Chemin des Dames. As the front stabilised, the corps established a firm line in this area. It remained in position until 24th April 1916 [35DI, 36DI].

From 24th June until 2nd November 1916, the corps served in the Argonne, in the line between the river Aisne and Four de Paris [35DI, 36DI]. It moved to Picardy where it served between Belloy-en-Santerre, Génermont and Cléry from 22nd December 1916 until 13th February 1917 [35DI, 36DI].

Held in reserve along the Vesle, under command of Tenth Army, during Nivelle's offensive, it held positions along the Chemin des Dames between Hurtebise and Craonne from 21st April until 16th June [35DI, 36DI, 154DI]. Sent to the Vosges for a 'rest' it held positions on Seventh Army's front between Leimbach, Belfort and Fulleren, from 8th July to 13th September 1917. On 11th October, it joined the more active Fourth Army and settled into the line between Aubérive and Mamelles, where it remained until 8th March 1918 [35DI, 36DI, 47DI, 132DI].

The German spring offensive brought about the transfer of the corps to Picardy. From 25th March 1918, as part of Third Army, it fought at Cuvilly, and then retreated to Rollot and Berliere [15DI, 38DI, 62DI, 67DI]. There it remained until the second battle of the Aisne when it sought to secure positions on the Oise between Nampcel and Chauny. On 11th June it was taken over by Tenth Army and fought between Bailly, Tracy and Quennevières during the battle of the Matz [15DI, 38DI, 70DI]. It remained on the Matz sector until 30th August. During the last twelve days of this tour, it participated in the battle for Noyon when it fought between Pontoise and Carlpont. Frequently transferred between Third, Tenth and First Amies, it fought up the Oise to Tergnier and Barisis, from 30th August until 24th September [15DI, 38DI, 132DI, 70DI and 2DM]. Between 28th September and 13th October, it advanced along the right bank of the Oise, with Tenth Army; fought to the north-east of Laffaux, and took Laon [29DI, 127DI]. From 16th October until 5th November, its forward movment continued when it marched via Verneuil to the Souche, during the battle of the Serre [17DI, 36DI, 127DI]. After crossing the Serre at Aubenton, the corps went into Third Army reserve on 11th November 1918 [17DI, 59DI]

XIX CORPS D'ARMÉE

Based in Algeria and not mobilised in August 1914. Its constituent divisions were re-organised into three divisions; 37th, 38th and 45th. They were sent to France on an individual basis. The corps continued to train and administer the remaining garrisons in Algeria.

XX CORPS D'ARMÉE

QG: Nancy

Commanders
02.08.14-Ferdinand Foch

29.08.14-Maurice Balfourier
17.09.16-Georges Claret de la Touche
19.02.17-Emile Mazillier
19.07.17-Pierre Berdoulat

Organic divisions
11 DI, Nancy	70 DR, Nancy	153 DI 4.15-
39 DI, Toul		168 DI 12.16-

Corps Troops
41 RIC	4.15 to 154DI
43 RIC	4.15 to 154DI
7.15-142 RIT –8.18	
12.16-106 RIT 7.18-M Bn/106 RIT	
5 RH, Nancy [4 escadrons]	
60 RAC, Troyes [4 groups]	8.15 two groups to 153DI
	11.17 third group reformed
	6.18 60 RAC to RGA
3.15-gr/60 RAC added	11.15 enlarged to become 120 RAL with third group added 4.18
20 BG	

Aviation
1915-F35
1918-Br35, Sal70, Sal253

As the covering corps for Second Army, the corps took part in the advance towards Morhange and fought there on 20th August 1914. Forced to retire it moved back to the Grand Couronne de Nancy at St Nicholas- du-Port, it fought at Crévic, Courbesiaux and Léomont until 13th September [11DI, 39DI, 68DI, 70DI].

Two weeks later, along with the rest of Second Army, the corps arrived in Picardy. As part of the 'Race to the Sea' it fought to secure a line along the Ancre and Somme. Initially engaged at Fouquescourt, it then fought at Fricourt and Hébuterne until 2nd November [11DI, 39DI]. From 13th November 1914 until 16th April 1915 it was engaged in the Ypres Salient, where it fought at Wijtschate and Poelkapelle [11DI, 39DI, 87DT, 89DT].

On 24th April 1915, the corps joined Tenth Army in Artois. For two months it fought in and around the village of La Targette, which faced Vimy Ridge, during the second battle of Artois [11DI, 39DI, 53DI]. From 3rd September until 26th December 1915, it occupied Fourth Army's line between Côte 196 and Massiges, and took part in the second battle of Champagne, when it fought for the Maisons position [11DI, 39DI, 153DI].

The corps arrived in the Verdun Salient on 25th February 1916 where it took up positions on the endangered right bank at Louvement and Bezonvaux. It was released from this sector on 8th March and re-entered the fight on 29th March. This time it fought on the newly-threatened left bank, between Bethincourt and Malancourt until 24th April [11DI, 39DI].

After a long rest, the corps joined Sixth Army, on 3rd June 1916, for the battle of the Somme. It participated in the battle during two tours at the front. From 3rd June until 21st August, it was engaged between Maricourt, Bois de Hem, and Maurepas [adjacent to the BEF], and then from 15th November until 10th December at Rancourt and Sailly-Saillisel [11DI, 39DI, 72DI, 153DI].

When Sixth Army withdrew from the region and re-established itself along the Aisne, the corps followed and took over positions between Moussy and Troyon on 25th January 1917. After a few days, the corps went into reserve in preparation for Nivelle's offensive. From 7th April until 5th June it fought towards Braye-en- Laonnaise [11DI, 39DI, 153DI, 168DI]. From 7th July until 5th November 1917 the corps recovered in the 'quiet' sector in Lorraine between Limey, Brin, and Vargévaux. This was followed by several months in reserve.

The corps moved to Picardy in April 1918 where it was kept in reserve at Beauvais and then Picquigny until the third battle of the Aisne began. On 2nd June, it moved forward to join Tenth Army between Villers Cotterêts, Coeuvres and

Ambleny, to contain the right flank of the German salient thrust to the Marne [87DI, 153DI, 2DCP]. In the second battle of the Marne, it attacked from Vierzy to Chaudun, Sermoise, Villemontoise, Buzancy and Tigny to the Vesle and reached Vasseny and Venizel, and then Braine by 11th August. [1DM, 58DI, 87DI, 69DI, 12DI]. When Tenth Army began its advance on the Hindenburg Line, on 30th August, the corps advanced to the north of Soissons, and then to the Forêt de Condé and finally to Jouy and Presles [12DI, 25DI, 29DI].

Taken over by Fifth Army on 21st September, the corps moved eastwards to Glennes/Brieul sur Vesle, and advanced via Romains to Berry-au-Bac during the battle of St Thierry [45DI, 153DI]. From 18th October until 1st November, it advanced from Vendeuil and Ribemont, to Landifay [47DI, 153DI, 168DI]. It crossed the Serre and reached Audigny during the second battle of Guise, after which it moved on to reach Froidestrées by 9th November.

XXI CORPS D'ARMÉE

QG: Épinal

Commanders
02.08.14-Edmond Legrand
21.09.14-Paul Maistre
01.05.17-Ferdinand Pont
01.09.17-Jean-Marie Degoutte
10.06.18-Stanislaus Naulin

Organic divisions
13 DI, Chaumont
43 DI, St Dié
71 DR, Épinal
167 DI 6.17-
170 DI 1.17-

Corps Troops
57 BCP, Ramberviller — 9.14 to Barbot DI
60 BCP, Baccarat — 9.14 to Barbot DI
61 BCP, Raon L'Étape — 9.14 to Barbot DI
7.15- 143 RIT   7.18-M Bn/143 RIT
7.15- 144 RIT –8.18
4 R Ch, Épinal [4 escadrons]
 59 RAC, Chaumont [4 groups]
  8.15 two groups to XXXI CA
  4.15 gp/14RAC added from 92DT-8.15
  8.15 two groups/59RAC added and transferred to 170DI 12.16 and
     gp/2RACC added until 4.17.
  4.1917 two gps/59RAC become 212 RAC
  4.18-third group reformed
  6.18-59 RAC to RGA
1.15-gr/59 RAC added   11.15 enlarged to become 121 RAL with third group added 4.18
21 BG
Aviation
1915-C27
1918-Sal27, Sop106, Sop252

The corps covered the southern flank of First Army's main thrust towards Sarrebourg when it moved from the Col du Donon towards Saarebourg on 20th August 1914. When that advance failed, the corps retreated back to the Meurthe at Baccarat and then held the line of the Mortagne between Ste Barbe and the Col de la Chipotte from 26th August [13DI, 43DI, 44DI].

It was transferred westwards from Girecourt-sur-Durbin to Fourth Army on 7th September, to reinforce that armys' fight for Vitry during the battle of the Marne. It fought at the Camp de Mailly and then advanced northwards to Sommepuis, and the to Souain which it reached on 1st October [13DI, 23DI, 43DI].

The corps joined Tenth Army in Artois on 5th October 1914 and served with that army until 11th January 1916. At first it occupied the sector between La Bassée and Carency [13DI, 43DI, 92DT and 7DC]. On 14th October it switched to the neighbouring sector, from Vermelles to Ablain-St-Nazaire, below Notre Dame de Lorette [13DI, 43DI, 92DT]. On 9th May 1915, it shuffled to the right and took over the Souchez position from which it attacked during the second battle of Artois. On 25th September, it attacked around Givenchy and Ablain-St-Nazaire, in the third battle of Artois [13DI, 43DI, 81DT, 154DI].

The corps served at Verdun from 8th –20th March 1916 in the vital Douamont/Vaux sector, after which it moved to Champagne [13DI, 43DI, 48DI, 120DI]. It served with Fourth Army, in line between Cote 196 and Souain from 2nd May until 25th July [13DI, 43DI]. It moved to Tenth Army in Picardy and served between Vermandovillers and Estrées-Deniecourt from 3rd September until 29th December 1916 [13DI, 43DI, 120DI].

It rested in the Vosges region until April 1917 when it moved to Château-Thierry as part of First Army which was held in reserve in anticipation of success on the Aisne. When that did not materialise, the corps joined Sixth Army between Mennejean and Panthéon. From there it participated in the battle of Malmaison on 23rd –31st October 1917 [13DI, 43DI, 167DI, 170DI]. It left the line on the latter date and returned to the Vosges, where it served between the Ballon de Guebwiller and the Chapelotte from 20th January to 17th May 1918.

When the Germans attacked Sixth Army on the Aisne, the corps moved to the threatened area and fought on the Vesle at Bazoches. Forced to retreat, it moved back to the Marne and by 2nd June, established a line at Hautevesnes and Vaux- which included Bois Belleau [13DI, 43DI, 39DI, 22DI]. Three weeks later, the corps moved eastwards to the Tahure sector in Champagne where it fought in the fourth battle of Champagne and the second battle of the Marne to secure positions between Mesnil and Mamelles [13DI, 43DI, 52DI, 170DI]. From there it advanced on 25th September via Bois Sabot and Perthes to Somme-Py [13DI, 43DI, 167DI, 170DI]. Thereafter it continued to advance northwards with Fourth Army, and then with Fifth Army from 18th October. It reached the Arnes on 3rd October; the Aisne at Givry on 11th October; to Viel-St Remy, and then to Signy l'Abbaye and Monthermé by 11th November [43DI, 167DI, 62DI and 9DI].

XXXII-XXIX CORPS D'ARMÉES

Not formed

XXX CORPS D'ARMÉE

Formed as Northern Section of RFV 10.08.15 –retitled XXX CA on 21.01.16

Commanders
12.08.15-Michel Coutançeau
19.01.16-Adrien Chrétien
10.06.18-Hippolyte Penet

Organic divisions

72 DI   1.16-
131 DI 1.16-

Corps Troops
34 RIT -7.15
120 RIT –7.15
7.15-31 RIT   7.18-M Bn/31 RIT
7.15-134 RIT –10.17

6.16- 3 RD
1.16-one group/17RAC [new] — 1.17 to 169DI
2.16-one group/36 RAC — 1.17 to 169DI
2.16-one group/48 RAC — 11.16 to 167 DI
no RAC 1.-17-1.18
1.18-313 RALT attached temporarily
5.16-gr/102 RAL added — 7.18 replaced by 130 RAL Genie-25/3 25/5 8/17 Cies
Aviation
1916-C18
1918-Sal18, Sal278

Served on the right bank of the Meuse from 10th August 1915. It was destroyed in the initial German attack of 21st February 1916 and withdrawn four days later [72DI, 51DI, 14DI].

The corps was rebuilt sufficiently take over line between Fouquescourt and Armancourt in Picardy. There it served succesively under command of Sixth Army, Tenth Army and Third Army until 17th January 1917 [51DI, 58DI, 132DI]. It returned to Verdun and took over the southern sector between Vaux-devant- Damloup and the Tranchée de Calonne on 24th Janaury 1917 and remained there until 24th June when it moved to Champagne [5DI, 72DI, 128DI, 163DI]. There, it held the line between the Monts and Aubérive until 27th March 1918.

In response to the German spring offensives, the corps took over Sixth Army's positions between Varesnes, Manicamp and Bois Mortier on 8th April 1918 [19DI, 151DI, 161DI]. When the second battle of the Aisne began, it fought at Fontenoy and Nampcel, and then to Nouvrion, Autreches and Quennevières [19DI, 55DI, 151DI, 2DCP]. From Longpont, as part of Tenth Army, it advanced to Volaine, Chavigny, Villers-Helu and Grand Rozoy on 15th July. It took over the Vasseny/Braine sector on 7th August. During Tenth Army's battle of second Noyon, and the subsequent advance to the Hindenburg Line, the corps moved to Crecy, Vauxillon and Quincy Basse, on the east bank of the Oise [2DI, 17DI, 128DI and then 64DI, 2DM, 66DI and 1DM]. It fought for Vauxillon on 14th October and advanced to Allemant. Between 23rd September and 13th October, the corps advanced to Anizy-le-Château.

Pulled out of the Oise front, the corps was transferred to Flanders for the final offensive there, during which it advanced from the Leie to the Schelde, from Tielt to Gottem and Eine by 11th November 1918.

XXXI CORPS D'ARMÉE

Formed as CAP Delatoille 05.09.14 and became XXXI CA 12.10.14

Commanders
08.09.14-Gaston Delétoile
02.01.17-Sixte Rozée d'Infreville
25.02.18-Paul Toulorge

Organic divisions
64 DI 10.14-
65 DI 5.16-8.18 to 2DM
70 DI 10.14-12.16

Corps Troops
6.15-42 RIT   7.18-M Bn/42 RIT
6.16-24 RD
1.15-group/37 RAC — 4.15 to VIII CA
4.15-two groups/2RAC [new] — 12.16-one to 64DI and other split
8.15-two groups/59 RAC ex XXI CA which — 33CA/170DI
became 272 RAC in 4.17
2.18 third gp/272 RAC formed

6.18 272 RAC to RGA
4.15-gr/56 RAC added
1.16-gr/108 RAL added   7.18 merged as 131 RAL
Genie-14/4T 14/17 15/5T 15/16 Cies
Aviation
1916-F44
1918-Br44. Br275

As a provisional grouping, with Barbot and Vassart divisions, the corps fought in the battle of Mortagne, 5th- 12th September 1914. From north-east of Rambervillers, it fought between Raon-l'Étape and Senones, and then, advanced to Badonviller where it engaged the Germans from 22nd to 28th September. Transferred to the Woëvre with First Army on 3rd October, it operated between Apremont and Laheyville until 21st May 1916. It fought at Mort Mare during the first battle for the Woëvre in April 1915 [76DI, 64 DI].

The corps moved into the Verdun Salient on 21st June 1916 where it manned the line between Marre and the Hayette, on the left bank, until 24th January 1917 [64DI, 65DI, 151DI]. On that date it shuffled to the left to the Argonne sector between Four de Paris and Avocourt.

The corps left the Argonne on 29th September 1917 and moved to Italy where it entered the Monte Tomba sector of the Piave front on 5th December 1917. It remained in line until 9th February 1918 [64DI, 65DI, 46DI, 47DI].

It returned to France and joined First Army in Picardy on 8th April: it remained with that army for the rest of the war. It fought to secure the line in the Santerre between Hangard and Villers-Bretonneux [29DI, 2DCP, 64DI]. When the allied advance began on 8th August, it fought at Moreuil [42DI, 66DI, 37DI, 153DI and 126DI]. From there it advanced via Nesle to Grand Seraucourt and Hinacourt by the end of August. It fought towards Neuville St Amand and Urvillers during the battle for St Quentin [56DI, 152DI, 169DI, 64DI], and then, it crossed the Oise at Mont-d'Origny on 11th October [34DI, 60DI, 56DI]. The corps took Guise on 4th November [33DI, 34DI, 166DI] and reached the line between La Capelle and Haudroy by 10th November.

XXXII CORPS D'ARMÉE

Formed as Detachment Humbert 25.09.14 retitled Corps Combiné Humbert 26.09.14 and XXXII CA 12.10.14

Commanders
25.09.14-Georges Humbert
09.03.15-Denis Duchene
03.08.15-Henri Berthelot
19.09.16-Eugene Debeney
19.12.16-Fénelon Passaga

Organic divisions
DM   -10.14
38 DI -1.15
40 DI 1.15-   62DI   6.17-
42 DI 10.14-   165DI 11.16-

Corps Troops
6.15-63 RIT   7.18-M Bn/63 RIT
6.15-145 RIT-8.18
10.14-10 R Ch-11.14
7.15- 5 RCA –2.16
2.16- 20 R Ch
10.14-two groups/46 RAC ex VI CA

12.17 third group formed
12.18 6.18 46 RAC to RGA
6.15-gr/40 RAC   7.18 merged as 132 RAL
1.16-gr/116 RAL added
Genie-15/4T 15/5 29/1 4/22 Cies
Aviation
1915-F41
1918-Sal41, Sal122, Spa258

A temporary grouping [23DI, 52DI, DM. 9DC] which defended the eastern outskirts of Reims, 21st September-25th October 1914, the corps arrived in Flanders in time to hold the line between Nieuvepoort and Diksmuide until January 1915 [38DI, 42DI, 89DT]. It moved to the Vauquois sector of Third Army and served between the Aisne and Four de Paris, 15th January-6th August 1915 [40DI, 42DI, 128DI]. During the second battle of Champagne, it fought with Fourth Army in the Aubérive/Ste Hilaire sector, 29th August 1915 until 23rd March 1916. It fought in the Marre/Cumières/Bethincourt sector of Verdun, until 10th June [40DI, 42DI, 69DI].

After a quiet period in the Chapelotte/Parroy sector of Lorraine, 16th June-24th August, the corps entered the battle of the Somme. It fought between Rancourt and Sailly Saillisel from 20th September until 17th November 1916 [40DI, 42DI, 66DI]. After a very brief spell in Champagne [3rd-28th January 1917] the corps joined Fifth Army on the Aisne front. It fought in the Berry-au-Bac/Miette sector and attacked Mont Sapigneul, from 16th April until 21st May [40DI, 69DI]. It returned to Verdun, and occupied the line between Louvemont and Damloup from 2nd July-2nd October 1917. As such, it took part in the offensive launched on 20th August.

The corps spent the rest of the war holding the line in the quieter parts of Lorraine. It held the line between Limey and Chenicourt, 5th January-22nd August 1918, [40DI, 42DI, 165DI], and then, between Port sur Seille and Bezange-la-Grande, from 22nd August onwards [40DI, 162DI, 125DI, 165DI and 1DM].

XXXIII CORPS D'ARMÉE

Formed as CAP d'Urbal 31.09.14 –retitled XXXIII CA 12.10.14

Commanders
03.10.14-Victor d'Urbal
25.10.14-Philippe Pétain
21.06.15-Emile Fayolle
22.02.16-Alphonse Nudant
06.10.16-Jacques de Riols de Fonclare
17.12.17-Gaston Leconte

Organic divisions
45 DI   9.14-2.15
76 DI   9.14-
77 DI   9.14-

Corps Troops
7.15-25 RIT   7.18-M Bn/25 RIT
4 RCA
10.14-RMCA
1.16- 4RS
7.17-19 RD
 10.14-two groups/53 RAC –transferred to
88DT 4.15 and replaced by- gp/20 RAC ex 88DT
gp/44 RAC ex 84DT
gp/14 RAC ex 92DT –8.15 to 74DI

4.1917 remaining two gps became 264 RAC
no third group formed
9.15-gr/103 RAL added   7.18 became 133 RAL Genie-9/2T 7/1T 20/22 20/17 Cies
Aviation
1915-F1
1918-Sal1, Br272

From the date of formation on 1st October 1914 until 25th February 1916, the corps served with Tenth Army in Artois. At first it fought around the eastern outskirts of Arras; then held a thin line from Carency to Roclincourt and Blagny. As other corps arrived its line was shortened to the area between La Targette and Ablain-St-Nazaire: from which it attacked Vimy Ridge in May 1915. During the third battle of Artois, it fought at Souchez and Carency. [70DI, 77DI].

Between 8th March 1916 the corps spent a month fighting on the heights above Verdun between Douaumont and Eix [70DI, 77DI], after which it was sent south to Lorraine. It served between Fey-en-Haye and St Agnant from 31st May until 29th July 1916. On 20th August it entered the battle of the Somme when it fought at Feuillières, Biaches and Barloy until 13th November [70DI, 77DI].

The corps spent a long period on the Oise front with First, Third and Sixth Armies. It served between Quennevières and Pernant, 20th November 1916-17th March 1917 and moved into the desolated area left as the Germans retreated to the Hindenburg Line. It advanced to Nampcel and then to a line between Barisis, Coucy and Quincy Basse, fro where it took part in the second battle of the Aisne until 20th May 1917 [70DI, 77DI, 52DI, 81DI]. It moved eastwards along the Chemin des Dames on 5th June and remained in line between Chevregny and Courtecon until 3rd August [5DI, 77DI, 168DI].

From 13th September 1917 until 29th January 1918, the corps manned Seventh Army's line in the Vosges from Leimbach to Fulleren. Recalled to Picardy by the German offensive, the corps joined Third Army's line between Plémont and the Oise on 28th March;it fought at Mont Renaud and advanced to Varesnes [35DI, 53DI, 1DI, 72DI]. On 7th May it was pulled out and sent back to the Vosges, where it served from the Chapelotte to Leimbach, 17th May-4th October. The corps joined the American Army on 6th October, and served briefly on the eastern fringes of Verdun, and finished its war at Custines preparing for Tenth Army's offensive towards Metz.

XXXIV CORPS D'ARMÉE

Formed as GA Vosges 28.08.14 – retitled XXXIV CA 21.10.14 and disbanded 08.12.14

Reformed as Groupe Cordonnier, 03.02.15
09.05.15-Groupe Contades
18.05.15-Groupe Demange
15.09.15-RF Belfort
20.03.16-XXXIV CA

Commanders
28.08.14-Georges Toutee
07.09.14-Henri Putz
03.02.15-Emilien Cordonnier
09.05.15-Erasme de Contades-Gizeux
18.05.15-Georges Demange
06.10.16-Alphonse Nudant

Organic divisions
41 DI 8-10.14
66 DI 8-10.14
133 DI 3-9.16
134 DI 8.16-

157 DI 3.16-
Corps Troops
284 RIT –8.17
340 RIT –8.16
7.16- 5 RIT   7.18-M Bn/5 RIT
6.16-2 RCA –7.17
6.16-5 RCA –8.16
7.17-1 R Ch
10.14-gp/26 RAC –7.16 to 66DI
4.16- gp/27 RAC7.16 to 46 DI
4.16- gp/40 RAC7.16 to 66DI
no field artillery 7.16-9.17
9.17 59 RAC reformed with two groups ex
87 and 97DT-third group formed 3.18
7.17 –gr/112 RAL added 7.18 became 134 RAL
Genie-28/2 28/51 16/25 Cies
Aviation
1915-C61
1918-Sal61, Br271

Formed at St Dié, the corps fought in the Vosges between the Col de la Schlucht and Col du Bonhomme until 5th December 1914. [41DI, 58DI].

From its reformation on 3rd February 1915 until 16th June 1917, the corps manned the defences between Thann and the Swiss frontier. On 12th July, it took over Fifth Army's lines to the north of Reims, and served between Mont Spin and the Cavaliers until 28th March 1918.

From 7th April 1918, it served with Third Army, between the Plémont and the Berlière, and fought on the Matz, between Ressons and Elincourt from 6th June, and advanced to Wacquemoulin. [62DI, 77DI, 125DI]. On 2nd August it moved to Courselles-Epayelles and fought between Plessis and Bois des Loges during the allied advance which began on 8th August 6DI, 165DI, 121DI, 129DI]. From 28th August, it advanced to the Hindenburg Line, from Lagny to the Crozat canal and then to Travency and Vendeuil by 14th September.

On 18th September, the corps moved to Flanders, where it advanced on Roulers on 14th October, and then, from 20th October, it moved forward to reach Paulatem and Gavere by 11th November [70DI, 77DI, 128DI].

XXXXV CORPS D'ARMÉE

Formed 15.12.14 in 6GDR, Sixth Army

Commanders
15.12.14-Charles Ebener
29.04.16-Charles Jacquot

Organic divisions
37 DI   12.14-8.15   61 DI 12.14-6.17
53 DI   10.15-   121 DI 8.15-

Corps Troops
6.15- 68 RIT -6.18
6.15- 69 RIT   7.18-M Bn/69 RIT
2 RMS
1.16-7 RS
7.17-7 RD

12.14-gp/37 RAC
12.14-gp/1 RACC   12.16 to 11DIC
12.14-gp/19 RAC ex 75DI 2.15 to 48DI
6.15- gp/9 RAC ex 85DT
4.1917 two groups form 203 RAC
1.18 –third group added
1.15-gr/5 RAL added   7.18 merged as 135 RAL
7.16-gr/113 RAL added
Genie- 19/14 4/24 11/19 11/24 Cies
Aviation
1915-C10
1918-Sal10, Br282

Formed from 6GDR, the corps served with Sixth Army on the Aisne, between Autreches and Bailly until 27th April 1916 [37DI, 61DI, 121DI, 53DI]. It transferred to the Somme sector and held the line between Fontaine-les-Cappy and Maucourt from 30th May until 19th September 1916 [121DI, 61DI, 51DI, 53DI]. It moved leftwards and took over positions between the Bois des Loges and Ribécourt on 25th November 1916. It followed the German retreat to the Hindenburg Line in March 1917. It advanced to Chauny, Tergnier and Vendeuil and established a new line at Essigny-le-Grand and then moved to Moy/Urvillers on 4th April [121DI, 61DI, 25DI]. There it remained until 7th August. The corps spent the winter of 1917-18 on the Chemin des Dames, where it manned the trenches from Braye to Hurtebise [19th August-20th November] and Cerny to Chevreux [21st November-26th March][121DI, 53DI].

The corps was rushed to Picardy at the end of March 1918 and joined Third Army between Montdidier, Assaincourt and Rollot on 27th March [36DI, 70DI, 169DI]. Temporarily assigned to Mangin's Group, it fought at Domflans, Courcelles-Épayeres, Mézy and Ressons during the battle of the Matz [11DI, 30DI, 1269DI]. From 13th June until 9th August it held the line Wacquemoulin, Courcelles-Épayeres, Ayencourt. Taken over by First Army, it advanced from that line to Bois des Loges, and then to the Avre and Beuvraignes, 8th-28th August [169DI, 133DI]. After a brief rest, the corps joined Tenth Army at Jouy and Presles, on 21st September. It advanced to Ostel, Athies, and Monceau-les-Wast on 10th October as Tenth Army fought the battle of St Quentin. By the time Third Army took over on 27th October, the corps moved to the Souché. From there it advanced to Montcornet, Romigny and had reached Rocroi when hostilities ended.

XXXVI CORPS D'ARMÉE

Formed from DAB 22.05.15 along with RF Dunkerque. Merged into RFD 15.08.15 and demerged as XXXVI CA 10.08.16.

Commanders
25.05.15-Alexis Hely d'Oissel
03.08.16-Jean Piarron de Mondesir
17.09.16-Maurice Balfourier
04.03.17-Charles Nollet

Organic divisions
29 DI 6.17-
133 DI 6.17-

Corps Troops
103 RIT –1.18
10.17-76 RIT -3.18
3.18- 14 RIT   7.18-M Bn/14 RIT
7.17-2 RCA No RAC
7.17-gr/119 RAL added   7.18 became 136 RAL Genie-1/3T 2/1T 15/5T Cies
Aviation
1917-C74

1918-Sal74, Sal276

The corps was formed to command those French units assigned to assist the Belgian army in the defence of the Flanders coast. It remained here until 13th November 1917. During this time, it spent a long period-until 20th June 1917, in line between Wieltje and Steenstraat. During Haig's offensive in the summer and autumn of 1917, it fought between Drie Grachten and Bikschote, until relieved by Belgian troops.

From 30th March until 14th April 1918, the corps served with First Army in Picardy to stem the German offensive there. It served at Bois Sénècat, Hangard, Moreuil and Mailly-Raineval. It returned to Belgium on 21st April and fought around Dranouter and the Monts de Cats area until 31st May [34DI, 133DI, 2DC].

From 5th June until 31st July, it was stationed in the 'quiet' sector of Lorraine between Clémery and Bezange-la-Grande, after which it returned to Picardy. It served between Lihons and the Chavette until relieved by British forces on 25th September. Thereafter, it took part in all of First Army's operations during the autumn offensives [34DI, 35DI, 133DI]. It advanced via Nesle to Savy and Grand Séraucourt, and took St Quentin on 1st October. From there it advanced to Bernouaille and Montigny-en-Arrouais and crossed the Sambre/Oise canal at Tupigny during the battle of Mont-d'Origny. Finally, it moved northwards to the Forêt du Nouvion, and was west of Chimay when the armistice came into effect.

XXXVII CORPS D'ARMÉE

Formed from 5GDR 10.06.15

Commanders
10.06.15-Celeste Deprez
05.11.15-Henri Wirbel
28.05.16-Emile Taufflieb

Organic divisions
10 DI 12.16-6.17
22 DI 5-9.16
55 DI 12.15-6.16
62 DI 6.17-
63 DI 6.15-6.16
69 DI 12.16-
81 DI 6.17-
89 DI 6.15-2.16
158 DI 9.16-6.17

Corps Troops
65 RIT –1.18
66 RIT –9.17
5.16-25 RD
7.17-10 RD
6.15-gp/32 RAC ex 85DT   1.17 to 169DI
6.15-gp/5 RAC   12.16 to 153DI
11.15-gp/32 RAC ex 5RAL   1.16 to 163DI
no field artillery after 1.17
6.15-gr/2 RAL added
1.16 gr/101 RAL added – disb 12.17
Genie- 19/3 7/15T 4/19 13/25 Cies
Aviation 1915- C30

The corps spent its entire career in the Aisne-Oise sector of the Western Front. From 10th June 1915 until 6th February 1916 it served between Condé-sur-Aisne and Pernant with Sixth and Fifth Armies [the latter from 4th August 1915]

[63DI, 89DT]. Then it served with the latter army on the eastern slopes of the Chemin des Dames, between Beau Marais and Neuvillette, 19th February 1916 to 19th January 1917 [63DI,

55DI]. It returned to Sixth Army for service between Pernant and Chavonne on 29th January 1917 and remained there until 4th April [158DI, 127DI]. Its final period of service was with Third Army. It held the line between Nanteuil-la-Fosse and Jouy, 29th January-10th August; and between Urvillers, Moy and La Fère, 14th August-11th January 1918. It was disbanded on the latter date.

XXXVIII CORPS D'ARMÉE

Formed as Secteur de Reims 25.10.14-retitled Groupe Reims 20.02.15 and .XXXVIII CA 22.06.15

Commanders
25.10.14-Charles de Pélacot
10.02.15-Olivier Mazel
25.03.16-Joseph Micheler
04.04.16-Eugene Debeney
19.09.16-Jean Piarron de Mondesir

Organic divisions
27 DI	9.16-1.17	71 DI	6.17-
30 DI	8.15-6.16	74 DI	6.17-
52 DI	6.15-6.16	97 DI	9.15-12.16
56 DI	6-10.16	123 DI	6-8.15
67 DI	4-8.16	151 DI	8.16-6.17

Corps Troops
23 RIT   7.18-M Bn/23 RIT
118 RIT –2.18
6 RCA –9.16
21 RD-11.15
7.17-10 R Ch
6.15-group/30 RAC ex 154DI
6.15-group/34 RAC ex 154DI
6.15-gp/3 RAC ex 153 DI
1.17-group/34RAC to 166DI
4.17-two remaining groups became 214RAC
and third group formed 4.18
6.18- 214 RAC to RGA
6.15-gr/104 RAL added   7.18 merged as 138 RAL
11.15- gr/115 RAL added
Genie-7/12 2/15T 8/25 2/24 2/19 Cies
Aviation
1915-C39
1918-Sal39, Sal273

The corps operated in the Reims area from 25th October 1914 until 10th May 1918. Originally assigned 51DI and 52DI, it defended the city along the line from Neuvillette to Marquises. For the second battle of the Aise, it moved to the adjacent sector between Cavaliers and Neuvillette on 16th April 1917.

Re-assigned to Sixth Army on 30th May 1918, it joined the fighting for the Marne, at Vaux, Château-Thierry, Jaulgonne and Courthiézy on 1st June. [47DI, 48DI –later 10DIC, 4DC and 5DC]. After a brief spell with Ninth Army, it fought at Mézy and Jaulgonne on 15th July, and, then, from 18th July, from Château-Thierry northwards to Charmel, Ronchères and Mont St Martin until 10th August [39DI].

On 29th August, the corps joined Fourth Army between Mesnil and Vienne-le-Château for the final advance. It moved to Beauséjours and the Main de Massiges, from which it advanced to Binarville and reached Vaux- les-Mouron by 1st October. It reached the line Termes-Olizy by 9th October, and Falaise, four days later. In the battle for Chesne, it advanced from Brieulles-sur-Bar to Boult aux Bois by 6th November. Then it retired to reserve at Vitry.

XXXIX CORPS D'ARMÉE

Formed 26.03.16

Commander
26.03.16-Henri Deligny

Organic divisions
74DI   4.16-??
129DI   4,16-??
67 DI   6-11.17
88DI   6-12.17

Corps Troops
47 RIT –4.17
HQ/1RD & HQ/7RH-7.17
6.16 gp/33 RAC ex 9DC
8.16 gp/4 RAC ex 8DC
4.16-gp/110 RAL-disb 12.17
Genie- 3/2 T 3/52T 9/19 Cies
Aviation 1917-C9

The corps was formed in Lorraine to control the line between Pont-à-Mousson and the Sanon. It extended its sector to the left on 24th October 1916 to include the west bank of the Moselle to Vargévaux. It left Lorraine on 2nd July 1917 and joined Sixth Army on the Aisne.

Between 3rd August and 1st December 1917 it operated in the Panthéon/Braye sector. During the battle of Malmaison, it advanced towards the Ailette at Filain and Chevregny. The corps was disbanded on 1st December 1917.

XXXX CORPS D'ARMÉE

Formed 17.12.16

Commander
17.12.16-Jean Paulinier

Organic divisions
None

Corps Troops
None

Purely a static line-holding corps, it held Eighth Army's sector, between the Sanon and Chapelotte, from 28th December 1916 until 27th May 1917. It took over Seventh Army's sector between Fulleren and the Swiss frontier on 20th July 1917 and remained there for the rest of the war.

I CORPS D'ARMÉE COLONIAL

Termed Corps d'Armée Colonial and based at Paris in 1914. Retitled ICAC 21.06.15

Commanders
02.08.14-Jules Lefevre
22.01.15-Henri Gouraud
29.04.15-Pierre Berdoulat
29.07.17-Emile Mazillier

Organic divisions
2 DIC   8.14-
3 DIC   8.14-
16 DIC 2.16-11.16

Corps Troops
5 BIC 8-9.14   9.14 to 3DIC
21 RIC
22 RIC

1 BIC 9.14-6.15
1 RIC
2 RIC
7.15- 88 RIT   7.18-M Bn/88 RIT
7.15-134 RIT-10.17
3 RCA [4 escadrons]
3 RACC [4 groups]   9.14 one group to 3DIC and replaced 12.14 by gp/53 RAC which went to II CAC 6.15
                                  6.15 one group to 15DIC
                                  1.16 one group to 156DI and replaced by gp/7RAC which went to 11DIC in 11.16
                                  1.17 group returned from IICAC
                                  3.18 third group reformed
6.15-gr/17 RAC added   7.18 merged as 141 RAL
1.16-gr/120 RAL added
Genie- 22/2 22/4 22/16 22/31 Cies
Aviation
1915-C51
1918-Sal51, Br260

The Colonial Corps fought with Fourth Army from August 1914 until 1st June 1915. It took part in the battles in the Ardennes at Rossignol and Valansart-et-Pin, and then retired southwards via Jaulny and Dieules, then to Faremont, Cernay and Dormois. It fought the battle of the Marne at Thieblesmont and Matignicourt, to the south-east of Vitry. Then, it advanced northwards to Ville-sur-Tourbe and Massiges where it held the line until June 1915. During the first battle of Champagne, it fought at Beauséjours [2DIC, 3DIC].

After a period of rest and retraining, the corps returned to the Champagne front on 8th August 1915: this time, under command of Group Pétain/Second Army. It held the sector between Massiges and the Aisne until 20th December 1915, and fought at Ville-sur-Tourbe and Mont Teton during the second battle of Champagne.

The corps moved to Picardy and joined Sixth Army in January 1916. From 18th February until 23rd August 1916 it held the line between Armaucourt and Fontaine-lès-Cappy. It attacked at Frise and Dompierre on 1st July, and later, at Barleux [2DIC, 3DIC, 16DIC]. After a long rest, it moved south to Third Army's sector on the Oise on 1st December 1916. There it held positions between Andechy, Bois des Loges, and Tilloloy, from which it moved eastwards into the devastated area left when the Germans retreated to the Hindenburg Line. It established a line between Beuvraignes and the Crozat canal [2DIC, 3DIC, 16DIC].

On 4th April 1917, the corps was shuffled leftwards to join Sixth Army, in preparation for its diversionary role in Nivelle's offensive [2DIC, 3DIC]. Fom Quincy Basse and Bois Mortier it attacked Laffaux until 16th June. After a short rest in the

Vosges between Leimbach and the Swiss frontier, the corps took up new positions on the Chemin des Dames on 28th July. It occupied the Casemates/Chevregny line until 28th November 1917 [2DIC, 3DIC].

From 21st January until 30th September 1918, the corps was stationed on the northern and eastern outskirts of Reims, between Betheny, Prunay and Marquises. It fought in the third battle of the Aisne, the battle for the Montagne de Reims, and the second battle of the Marne whilst in this sector. [2DIC, 3DIC, 134DI, 45DI].

During the last phase of the war, the corps advanced from Reims to reach the Suippe and Herpy areas by the end of September. From there, it moved from Herpy to Château Porcien by 6th November [2DIC, 3DIC, 136, 28DI]. The last few days of the war saw the corps in Lorrraine where it was preparing to take part in Tenth Army's assault on Metz.

II CORPS D'ARMÉE COLONIAL

Formed 21.06.15

Commanders
21.06.15-Ernest Blondlat
27.10.18-Henri Claudel
Organic divisions
10 DIC 6.15-
15 DIC 6.15-

Corps Troops
7.15-18 RIT   7.18-M Bn/18 RIT
7.15-129 RIT –8.17
2 RS
7.17-13 RD
Gp/53 RAC ex 1 CAC   3.17 to XIII CA
Gp/3 RACC [new]   1.17 to I CAC
Gp/3 RACC [new]   6.15 to 10DIC
3.16 two gps 3 RACC added as 23 RACC
1.18 third group/23 RACC formed
6.15-gr/17 RAC added   7.18 merged as 142 RAL
1.16-gr/107 RAL added
Genie-16/1T 21/25 16/22 12/17 Cies
Aviation
1915-C47
1918-Sal47, Sal277

Formed in Champagne, the corps operated with Fourth Army between Wacques and Bois Sabot until 14th October 1915 [10DIC, 15DIC]. During the second battle of Champagne it fought north of Souain.

Transferred to the Oise front, it held the line between Armancourt and the river from 12th February until 14th August 1916 [10DIC, 15DIC, DM]. It took part in the battle of the Somme, 19th September-28th December 1916 when it fought at Belloy-en-Santerre and Bernay. This included an attack on the Tranchée de Calmon on 14th October.

From 9th January until 27th April 1917, it held the line between Troyon and Hurtebise. During Nivelle's offensive it attacked towards the river Ailette until pulled out of the line for a long rest in Lorraine [10DIC, 15DIC, 38DI]. It held Eighth Army's 'quiet' sector between the Sanon and the Chapelotte from 27th May until 29th August 1917.

The corps spent the rest of the war in the Verdun region. It held positions between Mormont and Damloup, 2nd October –18th November 1917 [10DIC, 15DIC, 37DI, 60DI]; along the apex of the St Mihiel Salient from 18th November 1917 until 23rd March 1918; and between Damloup and Maizey-on the northern flank of that salient, 17th April-6th November 1918. The corps was transferred to American command on 30th August and took part in the elimination of the St Mihiel

Salient [10DIC, 15DIC, 39DI, 2DCP]. In the last few days of the war, it held postions on the Woëvre, between Etain and Damvillers.

GROUPEMENTS DE DIVISIONS DE RÉSERVES

On mobilisation in 1914, many of the reserve divisions were detached from their parent corps and allocated to a number of reserve groups. These had a relatively short existence and were either disbanded or transformed into army corps by 1915.

1 GDR
QG= Clermont Ferrand
Commander :Louis Archinard
58DR 63DR 66DR
11th August 1914-joined Armée d'Alsace-disbanded 25th August 1914
Fought in front of Mulhouse, 14th-24th August.

2 GDR
QG=Châteauroux
Commander: Léon Durand, 21.09.14– Maurice Joppé
59DR 64DR 68DR 74DR
10.8.14-Second Army   16.9.14-First Army
20th August-fought at Morhange between Nomeny and Manoncourt
25th August-battle of the Grand Couronne
13th September 1914-11th March 1915: in line between Pont-à-Mousson and Avricourt
11th March 1915-absorbed into DAL

3 GDR
QG= Chartres
Commander: Paul Durand
54DR 55DR 56DR
10th August 1914 Third Army 17th August-Army de Lorraine
Assembled between Etain and Pont-à-Mousson and fought on the Orne during the battle of the Ardennes.
Retreated to Revigny and fought with Third Army at Julvécourt, Ippecourt and Souilly during the battle of the Marne. Fought at St Mihiel, 23rd-29th September, and then held the line between Maizey and Koeur-la-Grande until disbanded on 3rd November 1914.

3 bis GDR
Formed out of 3GDR 27th August 1914
Commander: Henri Beaudenom de Lamaze
55DR 56DR 65DR
27th August 1914-Armée de Lorraine   28th August-Sixth Army Fought in the battle of the Ardennes to the northeast of Verdun Became 5 GDR on 5th September 1914

4 GDR
QG= Verdun
Comamnder: Mardochée Valabrèque
51DR 53DR 54DR 69DR
15th August 1914-Fifth Army
Advanced to the Sambre near Charleroi, and then between Moy and Urvillers during the battle of Guise. In the battle of the Marne, it advanced from Villers St Georges to Berry-au-Bac and established positions there, from 13th to 29th September 1914
30th September 1914- disbanded

5 GDR
Formed from 3 bisGDR on 5th September 1914.
Commander: Henri Beaudenom de Lamaze 21.11.14-Henri Berthelot 23.01.15-Francois Loyzeau de Grandmaison 22.02.15-Celeste Deprez
55DR 56DR 63DR 69DR 89DT
Served in Sixth Army and fought along the Ourcq during the first battle of the Marne. It advanced to the Aisne between Pernant and Soissons, and remained in line until 10th June 1915 when it was retitled XXXVII Corps d'Armée.

6 GDR
formed in Sixth Army on 27th August 1914
Commander: Charles Ebener
61DR 62DR 37DI
27th August 1914-Sixth Army 1st September-GMP   11th September-Sixth Army
Fought in the battle of theMarne at Crepy-en-Valois and Jaulzy. It advanced to Bailly, Tracy and Moulins- sous-Touvent during the battle of the Aisne. It established the line between Tracy and Quennevières until retitled XXXV Corps d'Armée on 15th December 1914.
In addition to the above GDR's, the gap between the BEF and the Channel coast was covered by a group of territorial divisions from 17th August until 22nd October 1914.

Groupement de Divisions Territorial [GDT]
Commander: Albert d'Amade 17.09.14-Brugère
81DT, 82DT, 84DT under GQG command until 8th October then part of Second Army.
Initially held the line from Dunkerque to Maubege then held in reserve in Picardy, 26th August-11th September. Fought around Albert, Bapaume and Arras until disbanded on 22nd October 1914.

CAVALRY CORPS
As there were no cavalry corps before the outbreak of the war, a number of provisional corps were formed in August 1914. Named after their commanders, they operated during the mobile phase of warfare until the end of September. Two permanent cavalry corps were formed on 26th September. A third would be formed September 1915.

Corps de Cavalerie Conneau
Initially allocated to Second Army but transferred to First Army on 19th August, the corps supported the advance on Saarebourg with 2DC, 6DC and 10DC. After the retreat to Nancy the corps was moved to the Marne region. There it joined Fifth Army and advanced from the river, via Château Thierry to Oulchy and Reims, which it reached on 18th September.

It was transformed in 1st Cavalry Corps.

Corps de Cavalerie Sordet
The corps provided the screen for Fifth Army's advance towards Namur and then fought to the west of Charleroi with 1DC, 3DC and 7DC. During the battle of the Marne, it fought between Betz and Nanteuil-le-Haudouin. On 8th September it became CC Bridoux, then CC Buisson on 21st September, when it fought at Cléry-sur- Somme and Combles.

It was transformed into 2nd Cavalry Corps.

After the formation of both cavalry corps, they were grouped together on 5th October 1914 as the Groupement de Corps de Cavalerie, under command of Conneau. Until disbandment on 16th October 1914, Conneau co-ordinated the efforts of both corps to stem the German advance in Artois and in Flanders, between Notre Dame de Lorette and Estaires.

CCP de Abbonneau
Served with Fourth Army in the advance to Neufchateau and Paliseul, 18th-25th August 1914. Had 4DC and 9DC under command.

CCP de l'Espee

Served with Ninth Army during the battle of the Marne, at Sommespuis and Mailly-le-Camp to protect link with Fourth Army. Had 6DC and 9DC under command.

A further provisional corps served in the Vosges from 3rd February 1915 until 15th August 1915.

Commanded successively by Cordonnier, Contades, and Demange, it controlled 6DC and 10DC.

I CORPS DE CAVALERIE

Commanders
30.09.14-Louis Conneau
02.03.17-Eugene Feraud

Organic divisions
1 DC 9.14-
3 DC 9.14-
5 DC 4.17-
9 DC 12.14-8.15
10 DC 9.14-11.14
1 DCP 1.18-

Corps Troops
9.18 two groups/52 RAC ex XII CA
　　　and one group/106 RAL added
Genie 1918-14/4 14/5 5/17 Cies Aviation
1916-F63
1918-Sal30, Spa63

The corps fought in Picardy and Artois from the date of formation on 26th September until 12th October, with engagements at Bapaume, Arras and Givenchy. This was followed by fighting around Laventie and Estaires. From 16th October, the corps fought in and around Ypres, and especially at Mesen. Then, it held the line between Leivin and Aix-Noulette on the northern flank of Tenth Army until 26th January 1915.

Between January and November 1915 the corps was kept in reserve behind various sectors of the front. It was held in reserve for the second battle of Artois, for the battle of the Somme, and for the second battle of the Aisne. Occasionally it supervised the rotation of its divisions into the line, in the dismounted role, in the Santerre and Oise regions 1916-1917. A major period was spent in the line, as a dismounted corps, from 20th May 1917 until 5th February 1918. During that period it was stationed in Third Army's sector between the Oise and Quincy Basse.

The corps was employed actively in the defence of the Noyon area in the spring of 1918. From 28th May until 12th June it fought between the Vesle and the Marne, between Arcis, Tardenois and Châtillon sur Marne, and then at Oeuvilly and Montvoison. Held in reserve behind Fourth Army at the start of the autumn offensive, it ended the war in reserve behind the newly-relocated Tenth Army in Lorraine.

II CORPS DE CAVALERIE

Commanders
30.09.14-Antoine de Mitry
17.12.16-Robert de Buyer
30.09.17-Felix Robillot

Organic divisions
2 DC 7.16-

4 DC 9.14-6.16 & 12.16-
5 DC 9.14-7.16
6 DC 9.14-2.15 & 8.15-
7 DC 2.15-7.17
2 DCP 1.18-

Corps Troops
9.18- two groups/264 RAC and one group
109 RAL added.
Genie 1918-11/6 27/5 6/18 Cies
Aviation
1917-F24
1918-Sal24, Br279

An active period of service began in the Lens area on 3rd October 1914. As the 'Race to the Sea' developed, the corps moved north into the Lestrem/Estaires area and arrived in the emerging Ypres Salient on 16th October. Between that date and the end of the year, it fought at the Forêt d'Houthoulst and then at Langemark and Bikschote. It garrisoned Nieuport from 12th December 1914 to 5th February 1915.

For most of 1915, the corps was held in reserve for the second battle of Artois and for the second battle of Champagne. From 21st October 1915 until 7th July 1916, it operated in the dismounted role in the Marquises/Aubérive sector of Champagne. After a period in reserve, during the battle of the Somme, it held Sixth Army's sector along the Chemin des Dames between Pernant and Chavonne, from 10th December 1916 until 29th January 1917. After a further period in reserve during the second battle of the Aisne, it took on the dismounted role between the Cavaliers and Marquises, around Reims, from 9th June 1917 to 21st January 1918.

The corps was rushed to Flanders in the spring of 1918 and fought at Mount Kemmel, 8th April-5th May. During the third battle of the Aisne, fought to the north of Neuilly St Front, and then at Dammard and Troesnes. In the fourth battle of Champagne, it fought near Vierzy and then moved to Picardy. Between 2nd and 17th August, it fought at Givillers and Bus. It returned to Flanders on 23rd September, and fought to Roeselare and Tielt. It was moving towards the Schelde when the conflict came to an end.

III CORPS DE CAVALERIE

Commander:
Robert de Buyer

Organic divisions
5 DC   8.16-12.16
6 DC   8.15-12.16
8 DC   8.15-8.16
9 DC   8.15-6.16

Corps Troops
Genie 1916- 5/17 Cie

Formed on the Champagne/Argonne boundary for use by Pétain's Group, it occupied the rearward line between Valmy and Bussy-le-Château until 8th October 1915.

Therafter, the corps's entire service took place in Lorraine. It held the line between Parroy and Bezange-la- Grande, 4th October 1915-23rd July 1916, and then, between the Sânon and the Chapelotte from 24th August until 12th December 1916. It disbanded on the latter date.

PROVISIONAL GROUPEMENTS

Groupement Bidon
Served on the Ijzer between 13-23.10.14 and 2-24.11.15
87DT, 89DT later 81DT

Groupement Hély d'Oissel
Served on the Ijzer, 5.12.14-30.12.14
87DT, 89DT, 7DC

Groupement de Nieuport
Operational 14.12.14-22.5.15 when it was absorded into XXXVI CA II CC 14.12.14-5.2.15
38DI 5.2.15-22.5.15
81DT 3.3.15-22.5.15

Groupement Baquet
Served with Fifth Army between Pernant and Soupir, 22.7.16-11.12.16
89 DI   22.7-11.12.16
127DI   22.7-11.12.16
30DI   26.8-16.9.16
7DC   2-10.12.16

Groupement Mesple
Served with First Army on the Avre, 26-30.3.18
133DI, 4DC, 163DI

Groupement Mangin
Served with Third Army on the Matz 10-13.6.18
XXXV CA plus 133DI, 152DI, 165DI and 48DI

'Affectation Organique' of Divisions and Corps d'Armee

I CA	1DI	2DI	51DI	122DI	162DI			
II	3DI	4DI						
III	5DI	6DI	130DI	158DI				
IV	7DI	8DI	124DI	163DI				
V	9DI	10DI	55DI	125DI				
VI	12DI	40DI	42DI	56DI	65DI	67DI	127DI	166DI
VII	14DI	41DI	37DI	48DI	63DI	121DI	128DI	164DI
VIII	15DI	16DI	58DI	169DI				
IX	17DI	18DI	59DI	152DI				
X	19DI	20DI	60DI	131DI				
XI	21DI	22DI	61DI	151DI				
XII	23DI	24DI						
XIII	25DI	26DI	63DI	120DI	167DI			
XIV	27DI	28DI	129DI	154DI				
XV	29DI	30DI	123DI	126DI				
XVI	31DI	32DI						
XVII	33DI	34DI						
XVIII	35DI	36DI						
XIX	37DI	38DI						
XX	11DI	39DI	153DI	168DI				
XXI	13DI	43DI	167DI	170DI				
XXX	72DI	132DI						
XXXI	64DI	65DI	76DI					
XXXII	38DI	40DI	69DI	165DI	DM			
XXXIV	41DI	42DI	66DI	133DI	134DI	157DI		
XXXV	37DI	53DI	61DI	121DI				
XXXVI	29DI	133DI						
XXXVII	55DI	62DI	63DI	71DI	74DI	97DI	158DI	
XXXVIII	30DI	52DI	67DI	71DI	74DI	97DI	123DI	
XXXIX	88DI							
XXXX	-----							
I CAC	2DIC	3DIC	16DIC					
II CAC	10DIC	15DIC						
1GDR	58DI	63DI	66DI					
2GDR	59DI	64DI	68DI	74DI				
3GDR	55DI	56DI	65DI	67DI	74DI			
4GDR	51DI	53DI	54DI	69DI				
5GDR	56DI	56DI	63DI	69DI	89DI			
6GDR	37DI	61DI	62DI					
Conneau	1DC	2DC	3DC	4DC	5DC	6DC	8DC	10DC
Sordet	1DC	3DC	5DC					
Bridoux	1DC	3DC	5DC					
L'Epee	6DC	9DC						
ICC	1DC	3DC	5DC	9DC	10DC	1DCP		
IICC	2DC	4DC	5DC	6DC	2DCP			
IIICC	5DC	6DC	8DC	9DC				
Ceo/AO	30DI	57DI	76DI	122DI	156DI	11DIC	16DIC	17DIC
Isolee	44DI	46DI	47DI	57DI	73DI	73DI	87DT	90DT

	99DT	100DT	101DT	102DT	103DT	104DT	105DT	161DI	2DM	
only										
1DI	ICA	ICA								
2DI	IICA									
3DI	IICA									
4DI	IIICA									
5DI	IICA									
6DI	IVCA									
7DI	IVCA									
8DI	VCA									
9DI	VCA									
10DI	XXCA									
11DI	VICA									
12DI	XXICA									
13DI	VIICA									
14DI	VIIICA									
15DI	VIIICA									
16DI	IXCA									
17DI	ICXCA									
18DI	XCA									
19DI	XCA									
20DI	XICA									
21DI	XICA									
22DI	XIICA									
23DI	XIICA									
24DI	XIIICA									
25DI	XIIICA									
26DI	XICVCA									
27DI	XIVCA									
28DI	XVCA									
29DI	XVCA	8.15-Isolee		6.17-XXXVICA						
30DI	XVCA	8.15-XXXVIIICA		12.16-AO						
31DI	XVICA									
32DI	XVIXA									
33DI	XVIICA									
34DI	XVIIXA									
35DI	XVIIICA									
36DI	XVIIICA									
37DI	XIXCA	10.14-6GDR		12.14-XXXVCA		1.15-				
38DI	XIXCA	10.15-XXXIICA		1.15-Isolee						
39DI	XXCA									
40DI	VICA	1.15-XXXIICA								
41DI	VIICA	8.14-		10.14-XXXIVCA		12.14-Isolee		7.16-		
42DI	VICA	10.14-XXXIVCA								
43DI	XXICA									
44DI	Isolee									
45DI	Isolee									
46DI	Isolee									
47DI	Isolee									
48DI	VIICA	5.17-Isolee								

51DI	4GDR	10.14-Isolee	11.15-ICA		
52DI	Isolee	6.15-XXXVIIICA	7.16-Isolee		
53DI	4GDR	10.14-Isolee	10.15-XXXVCA		
54DI	4GDR				
55DI	3DR	8.14-5GDR	5.15-XXXIIICA	6.15-Isolee	12.15-XXXVIIC
		6.16-Isolee	6.17-VCA		
56DI	3DR	8.14-5GDR	10.14-Isolee	9.15-VICA	
57DI	Isolee	10.15-AO			
58DI	1GDR	8.14-Isolee	6.17-VIICA		
59DI	2GDR	3.15-Isolee	6.17-IXCA		
60DI	Isolee	6.17-XCA			
61DI	Isolee	8.14-6GDR	12.14-XXXVCA	6.17-XICA	
62DI	Isolee	8.14-6GDR	10.14-Isolee	6.17-XXXVIICA	1.18-Isolee
63DI	1GDR	8.14-VIICA	2.155GDR	6.15-XXXVIICA	
		6.16-Isolee	6.17-XIIICA		
64DI	Isolee	8.14-2GDR	10.14-XXXICA		
65DI	Isolee	10.14-3DR	11.14-Isolee	12.14-VICA	1.15-Isolee
		5.16-XXXICA			
66DI	1GDR	8.14-Isolee	10.14-XXXIVCA	12.14-Isolee	
67DI	Isolee	8.14-3GDR	11.14-Isolee	1.15-VICA	9.15-Isolee
		4.16-XXXVIICA	8.16-Isolee	6.17-XXXVIICA	17.17-Isolee
68DI	2GDR	3.15-Isolee			
69DI	4GDR	10.14-5GDR	12.14-Isolee	6.17-XXXVIICA	6.17-XXXIICA
70DI	2GDR	10.14-XXXIIICA			
71DI	Isolee	6.17-XXXVIIICA			
72DI	Isolee	1.16-XXXCA			
73DI	Isolee				
74DI	Alpes	8.14-2DR	3.15-Isolee	6.17-XXXVIICA	
75DI	Alpes	8.14-3DR			
76DI	XXXICA	5.16-Isolee	12.16-AO		
77DI	XXXIIICA				
81DT	Isolee	8.14-GDT	10.14-Isolee	6.17-XXXVIICA	
82DT	Isolee	8.14-GDT	10.14-Isolee		
83DT	GMP				
84DT	Isolee	8.14-GDT	10.14-Isolee		
85DT	GMP	12.14-Isolee			
86DT	GMP	12.14-Isolee			
87DT	Isolee				
88DT	Isolee	8.14-GDT	10.14-Isolee	6.17-XXXIXCA	

89DT	GMP	10.14-GDT	4.15-5GDR	6.15-XXXVIIXA	2.16-Isolee
90DT	Isolee				
91DT	Alpes	9.14-Isolee			
92DT	Isolee				
93DT	Only 155BI-GMP				
94DT	Isolee				
95DT	Not formed				
96DT	Isolee				
97DT	Isolee	9.15-XXXVIIICA	12.16-Isolee		
98DT	Not formed				
99DT	Isolee				
100DT	Isolee				
101DT	Isolee				
102DT	Isolee				
103DT	Isolee				
104DT	Isolee				
105DT	Isolee				
120DI	XIIICA				
121DI	VIICA	8.15-XXXVCA			
122DI	ICA	10.15-AO			
123DI	XXXVIIICA	8.15-XVCA			
124DI	IVCA				
125DI	VCA				
126DI	XVCA				
127DI	VICA				
128DI	Isolee	2.17-VIICA			
129DI	Isolee	6.17-XIVCA			
130DI	IICA				
131DI	XCA				
132DI	Isolee	1.16-XXXCA			
133DI	XXXIVCA	9.16-Isolee	5.17-XXXVICA		
134DI	XXXIVCA				
151DI	XICA				
152DI	IXCA				
153DI	XXCA				
154DI	XIVCA				
155DI	None				
157DI	Isolee	3.16-XXXIVCA			
158DI	Isolee	9.16-XXXVIICA	6.17-IIICA		
161DI	Isolee				
162DI	ICA				
163DI	IVCA				
164DI	Isolee	11.16-VIICA			
165DI	XXXIICA				
166DI	Isolee	11.16-VIICA			
167DI	XIIICA	6.17-XXXICA			
168DI	XXCA				

169DI	VIIICA			
170DI	XXICA			
1DM	Isloee	9.14-XXXIICA	10.14-Isolee	
2DM	Isloee			
2DIC	ICAC			
3DIC	ICAC			
10DIC	Isloee	6.150-IICAC		
11DIC	AO			
15DIC	IICAC			
16DIC	Isloee	2.16-ICAC	10.16-AO	
17DIC	CEO			
1DC	Sordet	9.14-Bridoux	9.14-Conneau	9.14-ICC
2DC	Isolee	8.14-Conneau	8.14-Isolee	11.16-IICC
3DC	Sordet	9.14-Bridoux	9.14-Conneau	9.14-ICC
4DC	Isolee	9.14-Conneau	9.14-Isolee	9.14-IICC
5DC	Sordet	9.14-Bridoux	9.14Conneau	9.14-IICC
		8.16-IICC	12.16-Isolee	5.17-ICC
6DC	Isolee	8.14-Conneau	8.14-Isolee	8.14-l'Espee
		9.14-Isolee	9.14-IICC	11.14-Isolee
		8.15-IIICC	12.16-Isolee	7.17-IICC
7DC	Isolee			
8DC	Isolee	8.14-Conneau	9.14-Isolee	8.15-IIICC
9DC	Isolee	9.14-l'Espee	9.14-Isolee	10.14-ICC
		7.15-Isolee	8.15-IICC	
10DC	Isolee	8.14-Conneau	8.14-Isolee	8.14-Coneau
		9.14-ICC	11.14-Isolee	
1DCP	ICC			
2DCP	IICC			

Part Six

Orders of Battle, 1914-1918

Introduction & List of Battles

The following pages provide two types of order of battle.

1. General surveys, of the deployment of the French army on the western front, at specific dates. This is intended to indicate the extent and strength of French ground forces on those dates, and, to illustrate the relationship between those formations which were actually engaged with the Germans, and those in reserve, rest and recuperation, and retraining. As the war progressed, the percentage of formations out of the line grew as the French high command sought to reduce the levels of loss and stress which reached a peak in the spring of 1917.

2. Lists of formations employed at the beginning of specific battles. Lack of space precludes more detailed lists illustrating movements and developments during each battle. Such details can be found in the histories of individual armies, corps and divisions.

In the following listings, the convention adopted is to list formations from left to right across the front-line. An indication of the location of each formation is given to illustrate the scale of the front-line.

List of Battles on the Western Front 1914-1918

07.08.14	Alsace	VIICA		
19.08.14	Alsace	Armée d'Alsace		
20.08.14	Sarrebourg	1 Army		
20.08.14	Morhange	2 Army		
21.08.14	Charleroi	5 Army		
22.08.14	Ardennes	3 Army	4 Army	6 Army
24.08.14	Grand Couronne	2 Army		
26.08.14	Mortange	1 Army		
27.08.14	Meuse	3 Army	4 Army	
29.08.14	Guise	5 Army		
29.08.14	Somme/1st Picardie	6 Army		
06.09.14	1st Marne/Ourcq	6 Army		
06.09.14	1st Marne/Deux Morins	5 Army		
06.09.14	1st Marne/Marais St Gond	9 Army		
06.09.14	1st Marne/Revigny	3 Army		
06.09.14	1st Marne/Vitry	4 Army		
13.09.14	1st Aisne	6 Army	5 Army	9 Army
19.09.14	Lassigny/Roye/1st Picardie	2 Army	6 Army	
20.09.14	Woëvre	1 Army		
27.09.14	Flirey	1 Army		
06.10.14	Arras/1st Artois	2 Army		
23.10.14	Yser/1st Ypres/1st Flandres	DAB		

Date	Battle	Army 1	Army 2	Army 3	Army 4
15.12.14	1st Champagne (i)	4 Army			
15.01.15	Vauquois (i)	3 Army			
19.01.15	Hartmannwillerkopf	DAV			
16.02.15	1st Champagne (ii)	4 Army			
17.02.15	Éparges	RFV/3 Army			
28.02.15	Vauquois (ii)	3 Army			
05.04.15	1st Woëvre	1 Army			
22.04.15	2nd Ypres/Flandres	DAB/8 Army			
09.05.15	2nd Artois	10 Army			
22.07.15	Lingekopf	DAV/7 Army			
25.09.15	2nd Champagne	4 Army	2 Army		
[6.10.15]	[Navarin]	4 Army			
25.09.15	3rd Artois	10 Army			
21.02.16	Verdun	RFV/2 Army			
[09.04.16]	[Mort Homme]	2 Army			
[23.05.16]	[Mort Homme]	2 Army			
[07.06.16]	[Vaux]	2 Army			
[11.07.16]	[Souville]	2 Army			
[01.05.16]	[Thiaumont/Fleury]	2 Army			
[23.10.16]	[1st Offensive/Douaumont]	2 Army			
01.07.16	Somme	6 Army			
[24.08.16]	[Maurepas]	6 Army			
[03.09.16]	[attack]	6 Army			
[12.09.16]	[Bouchavesnes]	6 Army			
[18.10.16]	[Sailly-Saillisel]	6 Army			
[05.11.16]	[Sailly Saillisel]	6 Army			
17.03.17	Retreat to H Line	10 Army	3 Army		
17.03.17	St Quentin	3 Army			
25.03.17	Essigny/Moy	3 Army			
14.04.17	Monts/Moronvillers	4 Army			
16.04.17	2nd Aisne	6 Army	5 Army	10 Army	1 Army
[05.05.17]	[Laffaux]	10 Army			
[03.06.17]	[Californie]	10 Army			
[25.06.17]	[Caverne du Dragon]	10 Army			
[17.07.17]	[Pomerieux]	10 Army			
[19.07.17]	[Croanne]	10 Army			
31.07.17	3rd Ypres/2nd Flandres (i)	1 Army			
[04.10.17]	[3rd Ypres/2nd Flandres (ii)]	1 Army			
20.08.17	2nd Verdun Offensive	2 Army			
23.10.17	Malmaison	10 Army			
20.11.17	Cambrai	---			
21.03.18	German Offensive	6 Army	5 Army	1 Army	
22.03.18	1st Noyon/2nd Picardie	1 Army	3 Army		
25.03.18	L'Avre/2nd Picardie	1 Army	3 Army		
09.04.18	Lys	DAN			
27.05.18	3rd Flandres	DAN			
28.05.18	3rd Aisne	6 Army	5 Army	10 Army	
09.06.18	Matz	3 Army			
18.06.18	Reims	5 Army			

15.07.18	Montagne de Reims	5 Army			
15.07.18	4th Champagne	4 Army			
18.07.18	2nd Marne/Soissonais-Ourcq	10 Army	6 Army	9 Army	5 Army
30.07.18	Tardenois	10 Army	6 Army		
08.08.18	3rd Picardie-Montdidier	1 Army			
18.08.18	2nd Noyon	1 Army			
12.09.18	St Mihiel	US Army			
13.09.18	St Quentin	1 Army			
14.09.18	Vauxillon	10 Army			
26.09.18	Champagne et Argonne	4 Army	US Army		
26.09.18	Somme-Py	4 Army			
30.09.18	St Thierry	5 Army			
28.09.18	Cretes de Flandres				
30.09.18	To Hindenburg Line	1 Army	10 Army	6 Army	5 Army
08.10.18	Monfaucon	US Army			
09.10.18	Mont d'Origny	1 Army			
13.10.18	Laon/Croanne	10 Army			
15.10.18	Roulers	6 Army			
30.10.18	Serre	1 Army	10/3 Army	5 Army	
01.11.18	Chesne	3 Army	4 Army		
04.11.18	2nd Guise	1 Army			
06.11.18	Thierrache/to Meuse	1 Army			
08.11.18	2nd Belgique	6 Army			
09.11.18	Lys/Escaut	6 Army			

Orders of Battle 1914

French Army, 13th August 1914

Fifth Army [Lanrezac]

Concentration area: between Vouziers, Rethel and Aubenton
HQ=Rethel
ICA [Franchet d'Esperey] [ex Lille]
    2DI [Deligny]   Meuse between Givet and Revin
    1DI [Gallet]   Meuse between Hastiere and Ansermine
CAV CA [Sordet]
    1DC [Buisson]   Charleville-Mézières
    3DC [de Lastours]   Charleville-Mézières
    5DC [Bridoux]   Charleville-Mézières
III CA [Sauret]   [ex Rouen]
    6DI [Bloch]   Meuse between Château de Belleville and Nouvion
    5DI [Verrier]   Nouvion-sur-Meuse and Poix Terran
XICA [Eydoux]   [ex Nantes] (to 4th Army 16th August)
    21DI [Radiquet]   Sedan-Bouillon
    22DI [Pambet]   Ponts de Meuse near Remilly-sur-Meuse
X CA 20DI [Boe]   Attigny/le Chesne
    19DI [Bonnier]   Les Alleux/Vouziers
    37 DI [Comby]   ex North Africa- disembarking at Marseille
    38DI [Muteau]   ex North Africa –concentrating at Chimay
    4 DC   [Abonneau]   Sedan
    52 DR [Coquet]   Mézières
    60 DR [Joppe]   Pauvres

Fourth Army [de Langle de Cary]

Concerntration area: the Argonne – in reserve behind 3rd Army – along line Mouzon-Mangiennes
HQ=Saint Dizier
XVII CA [Poline]   [ex Toulouse]
    33DI [de Villemejane] Grand Pré
    34DI [Alby]   Apremont
COL CA [Lefevre]   [ex Paris]
    2DIC [Leblois]   Vaubecourt
    3DIC [Raffener]   Bar-le-Duc
XII CA [Roques] [ex Limoges]
    24DI [du Garceau]   Rarecourt-Malandry
    23DI [Leblond]   Valennes-Stenay
II CA [Gerard]   [ex Amiens]
    3DI [Regnault]   Marville-Stenay
    4DI [Rabier]   Mangiennes-Spincourt
9 DC [de l'Espee]   Tours
DICM [Humbert]   ex North Africa-disembarking at Bordeaux

Third Army [Ruffey]
Concerntration area: Meuse region facing Metz along line Mangiennes-Conflans-en-Jarnisy-Chambley-Pont- a-Mousson

HQ=Verdun
IV CA [Boelle]   [ex Le Mans]

```
        7DI [Trentinian]          L'Othain at Mangiennes
        8DI [Lartique]            Ormes-Damvillers
VI CA [Sarrail]    [ex Orleans]
        12DI [Souchier]           Hendicourt-Thillot-Étain
        42 DI [Hache]             Fresnes -en-Woevre Eparges
V CA [Brochin]   [ex Châlons sur Marne]
        9DI [Peslin puis Martin]  Diene-sur-Meuse
        10DI [Auger]              Genicourt-sur-Meuse
40DI [Hache]                      Thiaucourt-Flirey-Pont-a-Mousson
7 DC [Gillain]                    Fresnes-en-Woëvre
72 DR [Heymann]                   Verdun
3 GDR [Paul-Durand]
54DR [Chailley]                   Damvillers-Ornes
55DR [Leguay]                     Lionville-Buxerelles
56DR [Micheler ]                  Creue –St Remy
```

Second Army [de Castelnau]

Concentration ares: Neufchateau-Toul along line Pont-a-Mousson-Nomeny-valley of the Seille-Brin-Xures

```
HQ= Neufchateau
IX CA [Dubois]  [ex Tours]
        18DI [Lefevre]            Seille between Nomeny and Clémery
        17DI [Dumas]              Seille between Armaucourt and Brin
XX CA [Foch]    [ex Nancy]
        11DI [Balfourier]         Grand Couronne de Nancy to Armaucourt
        39DI [Dantant]            Art sur Meurthe to Moncel
        70DIR [Bizard]            NE of Nancy
XV CA [Espinasse]       [ex Marseille]
        29DI [Garbillet]          Dombasle
        30DI [Colle]              Serre between rivers Pissott and Sanon
XVI CA [Taverna]        [ex Montpellier]
        31DI [Vidal]              transit to Luneville
        32DI [Bouchez]            transit to Rehainviller
XVIII CA [de Mas] [ex Bordeaux] (diverted to Fifth Army 18th August)
        35 DI [Exelmans]          Colombey les Belles/Pont St Vincent/Domevre en Haye
        36 DI [Joannic]           Vannes le Chatel/Pont St Vincent/Menil la Tour
2 DC    [Lescot] (diverted to 5th Army-Conneau)
10 DC [Conneau]         (diverted to 5th Army-Conneau)
2 GDR [Durand]
59DR [Charlery de la Masseliere]   Laxou
68DR [Brun d'Aubignosc]            Vandoeuvre
```

First Army [Dubail]

Concentration area: Moselle valley and upper valley of the Meurthe along line- Xures-Blamont-Badonviller- Senones-Fraise-Col de Schlucht-Col de Bussang-Belfort-Swiss border

```
HQ= Épinal
VIII CA [de Castelli]     [ex Bourges]
        15DI [Bajolles]           Meurthe at Vathimenil and Fraimbois
        16DI [Maud'huy]           Meurthe at Glonville and Flin
XIII CA [Alix]   [ex Clermont-Ferrand]
        26DI [Silholl]            Cirey-Petitmont
        25DI [Deletoille]         Montigny-Ancerville
```

XXI CA [Le Grande-Girarde] [ex Epinal]
    13DI [Bourderiat]   Baccarat-Senones-Montigny
    43DI [Lanquetot]   Saales -Col du Bonhomme
XIV CA [Pouradier-Duteil/Barret] [ex Lyon]
    27DI [Barret/Blazer]   Col du Bonhomme
    28DI [Putz]   Cols d'Urbeis and le Hingerie
6 DC [Levillain]   Avricourt
71 DR [Kaufmant]   Épinal
73 DR [Chatelain]   Toul

Armee d'Alsace   [Pau]
VII CA [Bonneau]   [ex Besançon]
    41DI [Superbie]   Rougemont le Château
    14DI [Villeret]   Reppe
8 DC [Aubier/Mazel]   Belfort
57 DR [Belrnard]   Belfort

<u>1 GDR</u> [Archinard]
58DR [Besset]   Luxeuil
63DR [Loimbard]   Vesoul
66DR [Voirhaye]   Montbèliard

Armee d'Alpes [d'Amade]
44 DI   [Soyer]   Lyon
64 DR   [Hollender]   Gap -Embrun
65 DR   [Bizot]   to St Mihiel
74 DR   [Bigot]   Charmes-Bayon
75 DR   [Vimard]   Dugny

Ministry of War Reserve
61 DR [Virvaire] Paris
62 DR [Ganeval]   Paris
67 DR [Marabail]   Suippes

<u>4 GDR</u> [Valabreque]   to Fifth Army 15th August
51 DR [Boutegourd]   Vervins
53 DR [Perruchin]   Vervins
69 DR [Le Gros]   Vervins

THE BATTLES OF 1914

ALSACE, 7th August 1914

On 7th August the French moved through the Belfort Gap and took Mulhouse and Altkirch next day. Attacked by German 7th Army on the 10th and retreated to start line by 12th August

VIICA 07.08.14
14 DI
41 DI

Pau's army formed on 14th August – defeated Germans at Dornach on 19th and re-occupied Mulhouse on 20th. Forced to withdraw because of German successes further north but French retained control of Belfort Gap and the passes across the Vosges.

Armee d'Alsace 20.08.14 [pau]
    8DC   north towards Sulz.Feldkirch

116BI	Thann/Sennheim
41DI [82BI]	ne of Mulhouse
14 DI	Mulhouse
66 DR	Mulhouse/Altkirch
44 DI	Mulhouse/Altkirch
57DR	Altkirch/Dannemarie
63 DR	in reserve
4 Ch d'Afrique	to east of Altkirch

LORRAINE, 10th-28th September 1914

With 470,000 French against 400,000 Germans, under the terms of Plan XVII, the two French armies were to invade Lorraine and northern Alsace. Second Army was to advance north-east towards Metz between Chateau Salines and Saarburg and First Army on Strasbourg via Saarburg and the Col de Saales while keeping a link southwards along the Vosges to Belfort.

Second Army began its advance on 16th August, began its attack on 18th August. This ground to a halt on 23rd August.

First Army moved forward on the 14th, reached Morhange on the 17th and the German defences on 20th Both armies began to withdraw westwards on 21st August –they retreated to the line of Verdun-Nancy which they held during the first battle of the Marne.

Second Army [de Castelnau] HQ at Nancy

IX CA	transferred to 4th Army with 17 DI: 18DI remained with Second Army
2 GDR	Grand Couronne, north east of Nancy –advanced to Delme. Fought at Érbéville 5th September and then at Pont-à-Mouson, 12th September
59DR	
70DR	
68DR	
XXCA	east of Nancy between Amance and Dombasle-advanced to Morhange 14th August. Retired to St Nicholas-du-Port and fought at Crévic, Courbesaux and Léoront until 13th September.
39DI	
11DI	
XV CA	between Dombasle and Luneville –advanced to Dieuze and then back to Dombasle. Fought at Xermamésnil and Hèrimésnil during Grande Couronne
30DI	
29DI	
XVICA	on line of the Vezouve east of Luneville-advanced to Rorbach and fought at Bissing on 20th August. From 25th, engaged at Einvax, Gerbéviller and Xermamésnil
32DI	
31DI	

First Army [Dubail] [HQ at Blamont]

6 DC

VIII CA from Frombisn and Glonville, advanced to Saarburg which it took on 18th August. Fought at Réding and Gosselaing, 20th August, then retired behind the Mortagne to Hallainville and Essy-le-Cote, then advanced from Valois and Mattexey to the Meurthe.

15DI
16DI

XIII CA	Advanced from Darnieulles to Saarburg-fought at Hartzwiller, Schenecknderf and Brouderof then retired to positions north of Ramberviller from which it attacked towards the Meurthe at Xaffevillers and Bois d'Anglemont

25DI

26DI

XXI CA	Advanced from Voyer and Foret St Quirin to Col Donon and Schirmeck and towards Saarburg. Retired to Baccarat from which it fought to Col de la Chipotte and Ste Barbe.
43DI	
13DI	detached to cover Col du Donon
XIVCA	between Foret du Donon and Col de Saales. Retired to Raon-l'Etape and Baccarat.
27DI	
28DI	

ARDENNES, 21st-22nd Augusr 1914

Third Army concentrated between Verdun and Longwy and Fourth Army to the north-west on the Meuse between Verdun and Sedan. Originally Third Army was to advance eastwards towards Thionville-between Metz and Luxembourg. Fourth Army would remain in a reserve role.

The German advance through Belgium brought about a change of axis. Fourth and Third Armies would advance north into the Ardennes to meet the advancing German Third and Fourth Armies between Neufchâteau and Arlon. They began their advance on 21st August but were forced to retreat on the 22nd.

In response to this setback the Armée de Lorraine was established to hold the heights of the Meuse between Sedan and Verdun. The subsequent battle is described as the Battle of Virton by some authorities but as the Battle of the Ardennes by French official history.

Fourth Army [de Langle de Cary]

IX CA	between Mézières and Gedinon
17DI	
DM	joining
XI CA	Sedan-Maisson
21DI	
22DI	
XVIICA	Chiers-Bertrix
33DI	
34DI	
XIICA	Carignan-Neufchâteau
24 DI	
23 DI	
Colonial Corps	Neufchâteau-Izel-Montmédy
2DIC	
3DIC	
II CA	Montmédy-Virton
4DI	
3DI	

Third Army [Ruffey]

IV CA	Virton-Velosne
8DI	
7DI	
V CA	Longuyon-Longwy
9DI	
10DI	
VICA	Longwy-Arrancy
12DI	
40DI	
42DI	
4DC	

Armee de Lorraine/Sixth Army [Durand –later Manoury]
3 bis GDR
54DR
67DR
75DR
72DR
56DR
55DR

CHARLEROI, 21st August 1914

Fifth Army concentrated along the line Maubege-Givet from which it began to advance northwards in to Belgium in an endeavour to reach and hold the line of the river Sambre between Charleroi and Namur where it could stop the advance of the German Second Army. Between 21st and 23rd August, Fifth Army fought in the southern approaches to Charleroi but was forced to retreat after two days of fighting. Partly, this was because of Lanrezac's fears about the security of his flanks. The BEF fought at Mons on 23rd August, and Fourth Army was unable to stop the German advance from Liege to Namur and the line of the Meuse.

Fifth Army 21st-24th August [HQ at Chimay then to Aubenton on 25th August]

53 DR	Maubege
69 DR	Maubege/Thuin
Sordet CC	north-east of Maubege-advanced as far as Gembloux-then line of Sambre. Between Thun and Maubege
1DC	
3DC	
5DC	
11BI [ex 6DI]	
XVIII CA	Thuin on right bank of the Sambre, south-west of Charleroi
35DI	
36DI	
38DI	
III CA	south of Charleroi
6DI [less 11BI]	
5DI	
X CA	east of Charleroi
20DI	
19DI	
I CA	facing east to the Meuse at Dinant
2DI	
1DI	
51DR	line of Meuse between Dinant and Givet

Fifth Army retreated from Charleroi to the line of the Grand Morin and Petit Morin, south of the Marne between Esternay and Coulommiers. During this retreat, it fought a major rearguard action at Guise on 29th August. The fortress of Maubege was left besieged until it fell on 7th September.

1ST GUISE 29th August 1914

This battle took place between the rivers Oise and Serre on a front which extended from the Oise, west of Renansart to Vervins. Army HQ was at Laon at which city a further battle took place on:

XVIIICA	IIICA	ICA	XCA	4GDR
35DI	5DI	1DI	19DI	51DR
36DI	6DI	2DI	20DI	53DR
				69DR

also
37DI
38DI
4DC [at Vervins]

As this retreat occurred, a new Sixth Army was formed to the north-east of Paris, and a new Ninth Army was formed under Foch on the upper reaches of the Seine near Aube.

81DT took part in some of the early fighting in Picardy on 29th August.

FIRST BATTLE OF THE MARNE, 6th September 1914

As the retreat of the Allied armies halted, Joffre planned a counter-offensive to take advantage of the growing exhaustion of the Germans and the extended line of communication of the latter. The offensive which began on 6th September involved advances along a line from Paris to Verdun by the Sixth Army, BEF, Fifth Army, Ninth Army, Fourth Army and Third Army. In Lorraine, the Second army and the First Army would hold the line of the Moselle between Nancy and Toul.

Under Joffre's plan, the Sixth Army would advance eastwards along the north bank of the Marne and take the line of the river Ourcq, from which it would continue to advance eastwards towards Chateau Thierry. Its opponent was the German First Army.

Sixth Army [Manoury] Cavalry Corps

5DC	Foret de Compiègne/Nanteuil
3DC	Nanteuil
1DC	Nanteuil/Betz
6 GDR	from 7th September
61DR	Betz/Villers St Gonet
62DR	kept in rear on defence works between Plessis and Monthyon
IVCA	south of Nanteuil le Haudouin
7DI	Silly-le-Long/Bouillarcy
8DI	in reserve at Bourget [GMP] and then joined at Fublaines on 7th Septemebr
VIICA	
14DI	Bouillancy/Acy-en-Multien
63DR	Bregy/Fosse Martin/Puisieux/Vincy/Manoeuvre
5GDR	
56DR	Montgre/St Soupplets/Marcilly
55DR	Iverny/Monthyon/Barcy
Army command	
45DI	Penchard/Chambay/Bracy/Etrepilly

The BEF would advance from its positions south of the Seine, near Melun, towards the Marne between Meaux and La Ferte sous Jouarre, and continue the pressure on the German First Army.

Fifth Army would fight the German Second Army. It would advance across the Grand Morin and Petit Morin rivers- southern tributaries of the Marne, and then advance northwards via Montmirail towards Château Thierry [which it took on 9th September]. It would then advance to Reims in conjunction with Ninth Army. [The former retook Reims on 12th September].

Fifth Army [Franchet D'Esperey] Conneau Cavalry Corps

4 DC	Aizy/Ouchy-le-Chateau
8 DC	Amifontaine/Prouvais
10DC	Provins/to Chateau-Thierry
XVIIICA	
35DI	Villers St Georges/Monceaux-les-Provins
36DI	St Martin des Champs

38DI	in reserve north of Provins
III CA	
5 DI	Courgivaux
6 DI	north east of Montmirail to Champfleurey/Chataigney
37DI	Verneuil/Courgnaux-Petit Provins
I CA	
1 DI	soutb of Esternay to Maclanay-Margny -to Dormans
2 DI	south of Esternay
X CA	[to Ninth Army]
19DI	Sezanne-Boissy-les-Repos
20DI	Sezanne-le Thoult
51DR	Sezanne-north of Esternay

Army command
42 DI
In reserve- 4GDR

53DR	Villers St Georges
69DR	Villers St Georges

From its startline at Sezanne, Foch's Ninth Army would fight the battle of the Marais de St Gond , to the west of Fere-Champenoise, and then advance towards the Marne at Epernay. Its opponent was the German Third Army.

Ninth Army [Foch] [DA Foch 29th August to 7th September] IX CA

17DI	Mont Toulon/Mont Aout/Broussy-le-Grand
DM	Chateau de Mondemont
52DR	Connantre [or Connantray] XI CA
21 DI	
60 DR	Sommesous/Montrpreux
9DC	Sommesous

Army Command

42DI	Villeneuve-le-Charleville
18DI	Euvy and Fere Champenoise [ex Second Army 4th September]

Fourth Army, in Champagne, would fight the battle of Vitry-le-Francois, and then advance northwards along the line of the Marne towards Chalons and then to the open plains to the east of Reims. It would attack the German Fourth Army.

Fourth Army [de Langle de Cary] XXI CA [to Ninth Army]

13DI	Sommepuis/Camp de Mailly
43DI	Sompuis/Mairy-sur-Marne/Suippes/Souain

Army command

9DC	XVIICA
33DI	Dampierre/Grandes/Perthes
34DI	Certine/la Perrieres/Perthes
XIICA	
23DI	St Ouen/near Sommpuis/Hamauville
24DI	Courdemangy/Chatel Rouald St Laurent
CAC	
2DIC	Matiguicourt/Goncourt/St Remy
3DIC	Ecriennes/Thieblemont/Matiguicourt
IICA	
3DI	Heiltz le Hutier/Haussignement
4DI	Cheminon le Ville/Sermaize les Baines

Third Army would continue to hold the Verdun salient and the approaches to the Argonne at Ste Menehould against the onslaught of the German Fifth Army. Its contribution to victory was the battle of Revigny.

Third Army [Sarrail]
XV CA   [ex Second Army 7th September]
29DI   Revigny/Vassincourt
30 DI   in reserve south of Bar-le-Duc
V CA
9DI   Vauquois/Merchines/Sommaise/Pretz en Argonne
10DI   Nettancourt/Brabant-le-Roi/Villers-aux-Vents
VI CA
12DI   Rembercourt -aux-Pots/Sommaise
40DI   Deuxnouds-devant-Beauzee/Courcelle-sur-Aire/Neuville-en-Verdun
Verdun Fortress
72DR   Verdun
3GDR [in reserve]
65DR   Beauzee-sur-Aire/Amblaincourt/Seraucourt
67DR   Ippecourt
75DR   Souilly/Ippecourt
Army Command
7DC   Vanincourt in the Argonne-moved to Meuse at St Mihiel

The Second and First Armies did not play an active role in the First Battle of the Marne. Their deployments were:

Second Army [De Curières de Castelnau]
2DC
XVI CA   Grand Couronne/Gerbevillers
31DI
32DI
74DR
XX CA   Grand Couronne/Einville
11DI
39DI
70DR
2 GDR   Moselle
59DR   Loissy-sur-Moselle/Pont-a-Mousson
64DR   Sorneville
68DR   Erbeviller/Foret de Champenois
Toul
73DR

First Army [Dubail]
6DC
VIIICA   [to Second Army 14th September]
15DI   Mortagne to Meurthe
16DI   Mortagne to Meurthe
XIII CA   [to Sixth Army 11th September]
25DI   Mortagne-Xaffevillers
26DI   Mortagne-D'Anglemont
XIV CA
27DI   Meurthe
28DI   Meurthe
CAP   formed 5th September
DPr Vassin

DPr Barbot
GAV=	41DI
Gp Sud=	66DR
1 GDR	58DR
	44DI
Belfort=	57DR
Épinal=	71DR

The following battles took place on the eastern flank in the autumn of 1914

Woëvre	20th September	- 12DI		
Flirey	27th September	-	7DC	64DR
VIIICA	15DI 16DI			
XVICA	31DI 32DI			73DR
				76DR

First Battle of the Aisne 13th September 1914-28th September 1914

The first result of Joffe's success in the battle of the Marne was to continue the pursuit of the Germans north to the river Aisne. The Allied armies attacked on a wide front between Compiègne and Reims.

They secured the line of the Aisne, retook Soissons and Reims, but failed to achieve control of the Chemin des Dames. The heights above the north bank of the Aisne proved too much of an obstacle and this failure led to the establishment of trench warfare.

Sixth Army attacked between Ribécourt and Soissons. They crossed the Aisne at Attichy and Vic and moved on towards the valley of the Oise. At the latter point, a new army under Castelnau [Seventh Army] began to occupy the Oise up to Noyon.

Sixth Army [Manoury] [HQ at Villers Cotterêts]

XIIICA	IVCA		6GDR	VIICA	5GDR
25DI	7DI	61DR	14DI	55DR	
26DI	8DI	62DR	63DR	56DR	

The BEF advanced towards the line of the Aisne between Soissons and Vauxelles from which they mde an unsuccessful attack on the Chemin des Dames on 17th September. HQ BEF at Fére-en-Tardenois.

III Corps   II Corps   I Corps

Fifth Army occupied the riverline between Vauxelles and Berry-au-Bac and retook Reims on 12th followed up with attacks around the city and north-west towards the eastern end of the Chemind des Dames.

Fifth Army [Franchet D'Esperey] [HQ at Château Thierry]

XVIIICA	4GDR	III CA	I CA	X CA	Conneau
35DI	53DR	5DI	1DI	19DI	4DC
36DI	69DR	6DI	2DI	20DI	9DC
38DI			51DR		

Foch's Ninth Army advanced to seize positions to the east of Reims, after which it disbanded and its units were divided between Fifth Army and the Fourth Army in Champagne.

Ninth Army [Foch]   [HQ at Châlons sur Marne]

IXCA		XICA	XIIICA	
17DI		21DI	13DI	
DM		22DI	43DI	
52DR		60DR		
18DI	from 14/9		18DR	to 14/9

Although there were no further major offensives on the Aise front until Nivelle's attack in April 1917, the Chemin des Dames sector remained an important part of the French frontline until 1918. Command of this sector was shared between at least two armies. Until 12th April 1916 these were Sixth Army, on the left; and Fifth Army on the right. From that date, Tenth Army took over from Sixth Army, and, in turn was succeeded by Third Army on 30th June 1916. First Army replaced Third Army on 29th October 1916, and was succeeded by Sixth Army on 6th January 1917. After the heavy losses of April 1917, Tenth Army replaced Fifth Army. When the former army left for Italy, Sixth Army assumed sole responsibility for the Aisne sector. As such, it succumbed to the German offensive of 27th May 1918.

For most the period up to the spring of 1917, the Chemin des Dames was held by at least three corps under the varying army command. This was increased to nine corps during 1917: this was reduced to six corps by the end of 1917. As a result of demands elsewhere, Sixth Army was reduced to only three corps by the spring of 1918. A total of twenty corps served in this important theatre: several did more than one tour. They were I, II, III, V, IX, XI, XII, XIII, XIV, XVI, XVIII, XX, XXI, XXX, XXXIII, XXXV, XXXVII, XXXIX, ICAC and IICAC.

The Race to the Sea 18th Septmeber 1914-15th October 1914

Failure to take the Chemin des Dames resulted in the 'Race to the Sea' which involved French and British forces in successive operations to seize and hold territory in the Oise region, in Picardy, in Artois and in Flanders, where British and French forces joined up with the Belgian Army.

As this last phase of open warfare evolved, some major changes took place in the organisation of the French forces. Sixth Army extended its area of operations north into Picardy and conducted operations at Lassigny, Roye, Chaulnes and Péronne. The newly-formed Seventh Army was transferred to Artois but became Tenth Army on 2nd October. HQ Second Army was transferred from Lorraine to northern Picardy on 24th September. As French forces gathered in Flanders they were organised into Eighth Army on 20th October. Before then, on 5th October, Foch arrived at Doullens to take over responsibility for the Northern part of the frontline.

By mid-October, the deployment of the French army was as follows:

Northern Group [Foch]
8th Army [D'Urbal]
10th Army [Maud'Huy]
2nd Army [Castelnau]

Southern Group [Joffre] (Joffre remained CinC)
6th Army [Manoury]
5th Army [d'Esperey]
4th Army [de Langle de Cary]
3rd Army [Sarrail]
1st Army [Dubail]

Divisions involved in the 'Race to the Sea'
1DC	3DC	4DC	5DC	10DC	DC Beaudemoulin
7DI	21.9-27.12		Andechy/2A		
8DI	22/9-27.12		Avre/Andechy/2A		
11DI	??/9-21.11		Flanders		
13DI	6/10-		Loos/La Bassee		
19DI	5/10-		Arras		
20DI	2/10-		Arras		
21DI	29/9-		Somme-Beaumont Hamel/Serre		
22DI	22/9-		Somme-Albert/Orvillers/La Boiselle		
25DI	16/9-		Lassigny/Beuvraignes		
26DI	15/9-		Lassigny/Bois des Loges		
27DI	24/9-		Maucourt		
28DI	24/9-		Santerre		
39DI	25/9-3/11		Somme-Fricourt/Mametz		

43DI	5/10-1/11	Notre Dame de Lorette
45DI	5/10-	Arras
53DR	7/10-	Somme
56DR	3/10-	Somme
58DR	14/10-	La Bassée/Vermelles
62DR	4/10-	Maucourt
70DR	3/10-	Vimy
77DR	1/10-	Vimy
81DT	27/8-	south of Arras
82DT	26/9-	Somme
84DT	26/8-	south of Arras
88DT	26/9-	Lens/Arras
99DT	27/9	Maucourt
92DT	12/10-	Vermelles/La Bassée

Flanders October-November 1914
De Mitry Cavalry Corps
89 DT
87 DT
89 DT

IX CA
17DI
18DI
31DI

XXXIICA from 10/11-
38DI

later [see 8th Army notes] IICA
XVICA

Orders of Battle 1915

Western Front, 1st January 1915

GPN
81 DT   Nieuvepoort/Dunkerque

II Corps de Cavalerie [de Mitry]
4 DC   Nieuvepoort/St Georges
5 DC   Nieuvepoort/St Georges
7 DC   Reserve at Wormhoudt

Eighth Army [D'Urbal]   QG at Rousbrugge-Haringhe
XX Corps d'Armée [Balfourier]
11 DI   Steenstraate/Poelkapelle
39 DI   Poelkapelle/Ypres-Roulers Rlwy
87 DT   Canal Ijzer/Maison de Passeur
89 DT   Resting-elements with 11 & 39 DI's

IX Corps d'Armée [Dubois]
17 DI   Ypres-Roulers Rlwy/Polygon Wood
18 DI   Polygon Wood/Zwarteleen

XVI Corps d'Armée [Grossetti]
31 DI   Zwarteleen/Hollebeke/St Eloi
32 DI   St Eloi/Wijtschate

Tenth Army [de Maud'huy]   QG at St Pol
I Corps de Cavalerie [Conneau]
1 DC   Reserve at Ailly sur Noye
3 DC   Reserve at St Pol
9 DC   Aix-Noulettes sector

XXI Corps d'Armée [Maistre]
58 DR   Vermelles
13 DI   Noulette/Notre Dame de Lorette
43 DI   NDL/Ablain-St-Nazaire
92 DT   Rear-Calonne/Angres

XXXIII Corps d'Armée [Pétain]
70 DR   Ablain-St-Nazaire/Carency
77 DI   Carency/Targette
45 DI   Targette/Roclincourt
84 DT   Labour-sw of Arras

X Corps d'Armée [Wirbel]
20 DI   Maison Blanche/Blagny/Agny
19 DI   Agny/Bretancourt
88 DT   Bretancourt/Belles-aux-Bois

Second Army [de Castelnau]   QG at Cagny
XX Corps d'Armée [Balfourier]
56 DR   Belles-aux-Bois/Hébuterne

82 DT   Labour-NE of Amiens

XI Corps d'Armée [Bydoux]
21 DI   Hébuterne/Beaumont Hamel
22 DI   Beaumont Hamel/Fricourt

XIV Corps d'Armée [Alix]
53 DR   Fricourt/Bray
28 DI   Frise/Herleville
27 DI   Herleville/Maucourt

XIII Corps d'Armée [Baret]
62 DR   Maucourt/Boichoir
26 DI   Amines-Roye Road/Beuvraignes
25 DI   Beuvraignes/Lassigny

XXXII Corps d'Armée [Humbert]
38 DI   Rest-Montdidier
42 DI   Rest-Guyencourt

Army
82 DT   Labour-NE of Amiens
86 DT   Rest-Liancourt/Clemery

Sixth Army [Manoury] QG at Villers Cotterêts
Army
6DC   Reserve at Compiègne
85 DT   Labour-Crepy en Valois

XXXV Corps d'Armée [Ebener]
37 DI   Oise/Quennevières
61 DR   Quennevières/Autrechies

VII Corps d'Armée [de Villaret]
14 DI   Rest-Hartennes
63 DR   Vingré/Pernant

5 Group de Divisions de Reserve [Berthelot]
55 DR   Pernant/north of Soissons

Fifth Army [Franchet d'Esperey]   QG at Jonchery-sur-Vesle

XVIII Corps d'Armée [Marjoullet]
69 DR   Condé/Chavonne/Mouss
35 DI   Ferre Temple/Moulin Pontoy
36 DI   Moulin Pontoy/Hurtebise

III Corps d'Armée [Hache]
5 DI   Berry-au-Bac
6 DI   Godat/Loivre
Guerin Loivre/Neuvillette
Group de Reims [de Pelacot]
52 DR   Cernay/Bétheny
51 DR   Reims/Pompelle
DM   Pompelle/Marquises

Fourth Army [de Langle de Cary] QG at Châlons-sur-Marne
XII Corps d'Armée [Rocques]
24 DI   Marquises/Baconnes
23 DI   Baconnes/Wacques
60 DR   Wacques/Bois Sabot
90 DT   Aubérive/Moscou

XVII Corps d'Armée [Dumas]
34 DI   Perthes-lès-Hurlus
33 DI   Mesnil-lès-Hurlus
96 DT   Labour-Prosne

I Corps d'Armé e [Deligny]
1 DI   Beauséjours
2 DI   Rest- at Laval

Corps d'Armée   Coloniale [Lefebvre]
2 DIC   Beauséjours/Ville-sur-Toube
3 DIC   Ville-sur-Toube/Bois d'Hauzy

II Corps d'Armé e [Gérard] (to Third Army 8.1.15)
3 DI   Aisne/Vienne-Binarville Road
4 DI   Bagatelle/Four-de-Paris
10 DI   (temp ex V CA/Third Army)   Four-de-Paris/river Aire

IV Corps d'Armée [Boelle]
7 DI   Rest-Courtisols
8 DI   Rest-Courtisols

Third Army [Sarrail]   QG at Verdun
Cavalry Division
8 DC   Reserve at Revigny

V Corps d'Armée [Micheler]
9 DI   River Aire/Pont de Quatre Enfants

XV Corps d'Armee [Heymann]
29 DI   Vauquois/Avocourt
30 DI   Avocourt/Malancourt
72 DR   Brabant-sur-Meuse/Étain

Verdun [   ]

132 DI   Étain/Trésauvaux
VI   Corps d'Armée [Herr]
12 DI   Trésauvaux/Bois Loclont
67 DR   Vaux-les-Palameix/Maizey
65 DR   Maizey/Keour-la-Grande
40 DI   Rest-Souilly

First Army [Dubail]   QG at Neives-Maisons
Cavalry Division
2 DC   Rest at Blainville sur L'Eau

VIII Corps d'Armée [Piarron de Mondésir]

15 DI   Meuse/Bois d'Ailly
16 DI   Meuse/Bois d'Ailly

XXXI Corps d'Armee [Delatoille]
76 DR   St Agnant/Rambucourt
64 DR   Ribecourt/Seicherey
73 DR   Mort Mare/Bois-de-la-Prêtre

2 Group de Divisions de Reserve [Joppé]
59 DR   Pont-a-Mousson/Armaucourt
68 DR   Armaucourt/Bezange-la-Grande
74 DR   Arracourt/Avricourt

DA Vosges [Putz]   QG at Remiremont
71 DR   Avricourt/Chapelotte
41 DI   Chapelotte/Col du Bonhomme
66 DR   Col du Bonhomme/Steimbach
57 DR   Steimbach/Swiss Frontier
10 DC   Labour at Aspach-le-Bas

THE BATTLES OF 1915

VOSGES, November 1914-March 1916

Divisions involved:

66DI	15.09.14-20.07.16	Fave/Col du Bonhomme
41DI	29.09.14-11.06.16	Chapelotte/Fave
129DI	20.07.15-26.08.15	Linge
28DI	08.12.15-29.01.16	Altkirch/Burnhaupt
129DI	17/12/15-21.12.16	Linge
27DI	10.01.16-	
157DI	17.01.16-	

Battle of Hartmannswillerkopf 25/12/14
BCA- 28BCA & 30BCA
115 BI
57DI
66DI
10 DC –in reserve

Attack of 28.01.15
47DI   attacked 29.01.15 –also 41DI and 57DI

66DI   attacked 7/6/15 –also 47DI

ARGONNE 1914-1915 [Third Army]
IIICA   06.09.14-05.01.15
3DI
4DI
VCA   16.09.14-00.08.16
9DI
10DI
XV CA   16.09.14-21.03.16 –eastern sector
29DI

30DI   to 08.05.15
126DI
XXCA   1.15-8.15
40DI   [also VCA]
42DI
XXXIICA –western sector

ÉPARGES 1915
12DI
75DI
also April-June 1915
VICA
2DI
67DI

1ST BATTLE OF WOEVRE, April 1915
DA GÉRARD

Brigade Nayral -164RI, 362RI, 351RI attacked to Etain, Warcq and Buzy respectively
I CA   [Guillaumat]
2DI   to Parfondrust
1DI   to Bois de Pared
II CA   [Gérard] (covers front Morlaincourt to Marcheville)
4DI   to Maizerdy
3DI   to Marcheville

ARTOIS, 1915

Orbat of December 1914

HQ Tenth Army [Maud'Huy] HQ at Savy-Berlette
IX CA	58DI	17DI		Vermelles
XXICA	92DT	43DI	13DI	Grenay/Notre Dame de Lorette XXXIICA
	70DI	77DI	DM	Ablain-St Nazaire/Mont St Eloi
XXCA	39DI	11DI		Maroueil
XVIICA	33DI	34DI		Ecurie/Roclincourt
XCA	19DI			Arras and southwards
Reserves	2DC	53DI		

Attack of 9th May 1915
XXI CA
43DI   Aix-Noulette
13DI   Notre Dame de Lorette
70DI   Ablain-St Nazaire
XXXCA
77DI   Carency/Givenchy
DM   Berthonal/Carency
39DI   La Targette
11DI   Labyrinthe
17DI   Labyrinthe/Ecurie

Attack of 25th September 1915

Tenth Army [D'Urbal]

[10 divisions/700 field and 380 heavy guns with a further 7 divisions in reserve]
XXXICA   Lieven/Souchez
81DT
43DI
13DI
XXXIIICA   Souchez
70DI
77DI
55DI
IIICA   Neuville-Saint-Vaast
6DI
5DI
XIICA   Fourie
24DI
23DI

Oise May 1915-the attack on Quennevières by Sixth Army [Dubail] XXXV CA [Ebener]
61 DI [Nivelle]
73 BI
121BI

CHAMPAGNE, 1915

First Battles of Champagne, December 1914

Fourth Army [de Langle de Cary]
60DR   Moulin de Suain/Bois Sabot

XVII CA [J Dumas]
33DI   Perthes/Mesnil
34DI   Perthes

I CAC [Lefebvre]
2DIC   Beaséjours/Massiges

FIRST BATTLES OF CHAMPAGNE, early 1915
XXI CA   west of Souain
43DI
ICA   Hurlus/Beauséjours
1DI
2DI
II CA   Mesnil/Cote 196/Mamelles
3DI
4DI
also –48DI   Mesnil/Cote 196
XVICA
31DI   Ferme de Beauséjours
32DI   Mesnil/Cote 196/Bois Sabot
IVCA
7DI   Perthes/lès Hurlus
8DI   Perthes/lès Hurlus

Second Battle of Champagne 25th September 1915
[30 divisions, 1200 field and 850 heavy guns]

Fourth Army [de Langle de Cary] IV CA [Putz]
124DI   Mont sans Nom
7DI   Aubérive

XXXIICA [Berthelot]
42DI   Aubérive/St Hilaire
40DI   north of St Hilaire
8DI   Epine de Vedegrange   [27/9 to VII]

VII CA [Villaret]
37DI   Epine de Vedegrange
14DI   north-west of Wacques

II CAC [Blondlat]
15DIC   north west of Souain
10DIC   Ferme de Navarin
DM   Bois Sabot/Trou Bricot

VI CA [Paulinier]
12DI   west of Navarin
127DI   Navarin/Butte de Souain
56DI   Navarin/Butte de Souain

In Army Reserve
II CC   [Mitry]   4DC, 5DC, 7DC
129 DI   north of Wacques 29/9
48DI   Ferme de Navarin 29/9
64DI   north of Wacques 26/9
51DI   east of Navarin 6/10

Second Army [Petain] XIV CA [Baret]
28DI   Trou Bricot
27DI   east of Côte 193

XI CA [Baumgarten]
22DI   Butte de Tahure
21DI   north of Mesnil
31DI   west of Tahure
53DI   Butte de Tahure

XXCA [Balfourier]
11DI   Ferme Beauséjours/Côte 193
39DI   Maisons de Champagne
153DI   Maisons de Champagne

I CAC [Berdoulat]
2DIC   Main de Massiges
3DIC   east Main de Massiges/Ville sur Tourbe
151DI   Ville sur Tourbe to river Aisne
32DI   west of Massiges

In Army Reserve
16DIC   Côte 193 28/9
3DC
8DC

XVI CA [Grossetti]
15DIC west of Tahure 6/10
3DI Butte de Tahure 30/9

Orders of Battle 1916

Western Front, 1st January 1916

DAN
XXXVI Corps d'Armée [Hély d'Oissel]
37 DI	Training-Bergues
38 DI	Nieuport
45 DI	Nieuport
87 DI	Steenstraate/Boesinghe

GAN [Foch] QG at Château de Cercamp

Tenth Army [D'Urbal] QG at St Pol
IX Corps d'Armée [Curé]
17 DI	Grenay/Loos
18 DI	Grenay/Loos
152 DI	Rest-Fillievre

XXXIII Corps d'Armée [Fayolle]
77 DI	Givenchy
70 DI	Givenchy/Folie
130 DI	Givenchy/Souchez

XXI Corps d'Armée [Maistre]
13 DI	Rest-Hurieres
43 DI	Souchez/Angres
81 DI	Angres/Fosse Calonne

XII Corps d'Armée [Descoing]
24 DI	Neuville St Vaast/Ecurie
23 DI	Écurie/Roclincourt
58 DI	Rest-Avesnes

XVII Corps d'Armée [Dumas]
33 DI	Scarpe/Agny
34 DI	Agny/Ficheux

I Corps de Cavalerie [Conneau]
1DC	Berles-aux-Bois/east of Bailleuvac
3DC	Berles-aux-Bois
88 DR	Ransart/Bretoncourt

Sixth Army [Dubois] QG at Verberie
III Corps d'Armée [Nivelle]
5 DI	Frise/Foucaucourt
6 DI	Rest-Domart sur Luce
99 DT	Herleville/Maucourt
62 DI	Maucourt/Boichoir

XIII Corps d'Armée [Alby]
120 DI	Andechy/Bois des Loges
25 DI	Bois des Loges/Thiescourt
104 DT	Belval/Oise

26 DI   Rest-Crevecouer

XXXV   Corps d'Armée [Ebener]
103 DT   Tracy-sur-Oise
61 DI   Touvent
DM   Training-Couevres
121 DI   Training-Coeuvres
53 DI   Touvent/Pernant

I Corps d'Armée Coloniale [Berdoulat]
2 DIC   Training-Betz
3 DIC   Training-St Soupletts

II Corps d'Armé e Coloniale [Blondlat]
10 DIC   Training –St Ricques
15 DIC   Training-Crecy-en-Ponthois
16 DIC   Rest-Gournay-sur-Aronde

Army
102DT   Labour-Montdidier and Amiens

GAC [de Langle de Cary]   QG at Avize

Fifth Army   [Franchet d'Esperey] QG at Jonchery-sur-Vesle
XXXVII Corps d'Armée [Wirbel]
63 DI   Pernant/Venizel
89 DI   Venizel/Condé-sur-Aisne
97 DI   Labour-Reims

XVIII Corps d'Armée [Marjoulllet]
69 DI   Condé-sur-Aisne/Moussy
35 DI   Moussy/Paissy
36 DI   Paissy/Pontivy

I Corps d'Armée [Guillaumat]
2 DI   Pontivy/Berry-au-Bac
1 DI   Loivre/Neuvillet

XXXVIII Corps d'Armée [Mazel]
30 DI   Neuvillet/St Leonards
52 DI   St Leonards/Marquises

XVI Corps d'Armée [Grossetti]
31 DI   Rest-Mareuil
32 DI   Rest-Cumieres

Army
55 DI   Training-Ville-en-Tardenois

Fourth Army [Gouraud]   QG at Bouy-moves to St Memmie 2.1.16
II Corps de Cavalerie [de Mitry]
4DC   Baconnes/Moscou
5DC   North of Prosnes
7DC   Prosnes/Marquises

II Corps de Cavalerie [de Mitry]
60 DI   Moscou/Aubérive
100 DT   Rest-Billy-le-Grand

VI Corps d'Armée [Paulinier]
12 DI   Aubérive/Epine de Vedegrange
56 DI   Vedegrange/Wacques
127 DI   Wacques/Souain

XXXII Corps d' Armée [Bertholet]
40 DI   Rest-Sarry
42 DI   Rest-Chalons

Second Army [Petain]   QG at Châlons-sur-Marne
XI Corps d'Armée [Baumgarten]
151 DI   Souain/Tahure to Somme-Py road
21 DI   Somme-Py to Tahure road/Tahure
22 DI   Tahure/Mamelles

XV Corps d'Armée [de Maud'Huy]
126 DI   Mamelles/Côte 196
123 DI   Côte 196/Maisons

IV Corps d'Armée [Putz]
8 DI   Maisons/Massiges
124 DI   Massiges/Ville-sur-Toube
7 DI   Ville-sur-Toube/Vienne

Third Army [Humbert]   QG at Nettancourt
X Corps d'Armée [Anthoine]
20 DI   Binarville/Houyette
19 DI   Houyette/Fontaine de Charmes
131 DI   Fontaine des Charmes/Four-de-Paris

V Corps d'Armée [Hallouin]
125 DI   Four-de-Paris/Haute Chevauchée
9 DI   Haute Chevauchée/river Aire
10 DI   River Aire/Vauquois

Army
29 DI   Malancourt/Bethincourt
14 DI   Training-Aulnes/Perthes
48 DI   Tranist from 3Army to 2Army

RFV [Herr]   QG at Verdun

Army
72 DI   Brabant sur Meuse/Étain
51 DI   Étain/Éparges
132 DI   Rest-Verdun
15 DI   Training-Boran

II Corps d'Armée [Duchêne]
3 DI   Éparges/Vaux les Palameix
67 DI   Vaux les Palameix/Maizey4 DI   Rest-Souilly

GAE [Dubail] QG at Gondrecourt

First Army [Roques]   QG at Toul
VIII Corps d'Armée [Cordonnier]
16 DI   Apremont/Bois d'Ailly

XXXI Corps d'Armée [Deletoille]
76 DI   St Agnan/Rambucourt
64 DI   Labour near Toul & Lucey
101 DT   Labour near Flirey

Army
65 DI   Regnieville/Fey-en-Heye
73 DI   Fey-en-Haye

DAL [Gérard]   QG at St Nicholas-du-Port
III Corps de Cavalerie [de Buyer]
8 DC   Arracourt/Sânon
9 DC   Sânon/Parroy
6 DC   Sanon/Parroy

XX Corps d'Armée [Balfourier]
11 DI   Rest-Vezelise
39 DI   Rest-Vezelise
153 DI   Rest-Pont St Vincent

Army
59 DI   Pont-à-Mousson/Armaucourt
68 DI   Armaucourt/Bezange-la-Grande
74 DI   Training at Saffais
128DI   Vezouse/Avricourt Rlwy
71 DI   Avricourt/Chapelotte

Seventh Army [de Villaret]   QG at Lure
XIV Corps d'Armée [Baret]
27 DI   Training at Camp d'Arches

Army
41 DI   Chapelotte/Col du Bonhomme
47 DI   Col du Bonhomme/Metzeral
66 DI   Fave
129 DI   Ban de Sapt
154 DI   Rest-Valdoie
Belfort
28 DI   Burnhaupt/Altkirch
157 DI   Labour-Belfort
105 DT   Largue/Swiss Frontier
2DC   Entering line Burnhaupt/Leimbach
10DC   Swiss Frontier-labour & patrol
VII Corps d'arm ée –no divisions attached

Battles of 1916

Verdun, 1916

RFV 20th February 1916 [Herr]
Groupement Bazelaire [Left Bank of Meuse] [VIICA]
29DI   Avocourt/Bethincourt
67DI   Bethincourt/Meuse
Groupement Chrétien [Right Bank of Meuse] [XXXCA]
72DI   Meuse/Bois des Caures [with Driant's two bns of Chasseurs under command]
51DI   Bois des Caures/Ornes
14DI   Ornes/Fromezay
Groupement Duchêne [Woevre] [IICA]
132DI
3DI
4DI   Reserves
37DI   Souilly
48DI   Chaumont sur Aire
16DI   Pierrefitte les Paroches

Second Army 26th February 1916 [Pétain]
Groupement Bazelaire [VIICA]   between Avocourt and the Meuse
29DI
67DI
96BI
38BI
Groupement Guillaumat [ICA]   Meuse/Douaumont
39BI
63DI
Groupement Balfourier [XXCA] Douaumont/Eix
153DI
14DI
2DI
31BI
95DT
212BIT
Groupement Duchêne [IICA]   Eix/Paroches
3DI
4DI
68DI
132DI
32BI
211BIT

German attack on the Mort Homme position 9th April 1916- six German divisions resisted by-
42DI & 11DI

Battle for Fleury, 13th May 1916
5DI
71BI ex 36DI
Vaux 2nd June   6DI
Fleury 21st June   129DI, 130DI, 12DI
Souville 11th July   2BCh, 7RI/131DI, 167RI/128DI, Arty/131DI

1st Offensive at Douaumont, 24th October-3rd November 1916
38DI   133DI   74DI

Attack between Louvemont and Damloup, 23rd November 1916 [Mangin]
38DI   [Guyot de Salines]
133DI [Passaga]
74DI   [Lardemelle]

Offensive of 15th December 1916
126DI [Muteau]   Cote du Poivres
38DI   [Guyot de Salines]   Louvemont
37DI   [Garnier Duplessis]   Louvement
133DI [Passaga]   Bezonvaux/d'Haudromont
9DI   [Andlauer]   Douaumont

Divisions employed within the Verdun Salient during 1916

1DI	27.2-26.3.16	ICA	Poivre/Haudromont
2DI	17.2-8.3.16	ICA	Douaumont
4DI	10.4-27.4.16	IIICA	Thiaumont/Etang de Vaux
5DI	2.4-15.6.16	XXXIIICA	Thiaumont/Vaux/Eix
6DI	8.4-6..7.6.16	IIICA	Etang de Vaux/Damloup
6DI	15.12.16-	XICA	Bezonvaux
7DI	29.8-25.9.16	XICA	Thiaumont
7DI	22.10-14.12.16	XICA	Haudromont
8DI	3.7-5.8.16	XICA	Haudromont/Froidterre.
9DI	23.10- 14.12.16	XICA	Dicourt/Vaux devant Damloup
11DI	30.3-12.4.16	XXCA	Avocourt/Bethincourt
12DI	15.6-28.6.16	VICA	Bois Fumin/Vaux
13DI	3.3 -20.3.16	XX/XXICA	Douaumont/Etang de Vaux
14DI	25.2-3.316	XXX/XXCA	Bezonvaux/Etain
14DI	11.4-16.5.16	IIICA	Etang de Vaux/Damloup
15DI	27.7.-11.8.16	XICA	Vuax Chapitre/Fleury
16DI	11.7.-15.7.16	VICA	Bois Fumin/Damloup
17DI	18.4-8.5.16	XX/IXCA	Hayette/Bois Camard
18DI	13.4.-8.5.16	IX/XX/IXCA	Bois Camard/Bois d'Avocourt
19DI	2.6.-29.7.16	XXXII/XXXI	Cattancourt/Marre
19DI	7.8-2.9.16	XICA	Haudromont/Thiaumont
21DI	22.6.-23.6.16	XICA	Hudromont/Froidterre
21DI	20.11.-26.12.16	XICA	Douaumont/Chambrettes/Bezonvaux
22DI	30.3.-22.4.16	I/XIICA	Haudromont/Thiaumont
22DI	11.1.16-	XI/XIV/XVCA	Vaux devant Damloup/Dicourt
23DI	6.4.-24.6.16	I/XII/IXCA	Meuse/Haudromont
24DI	4.4.-26.7.16	I/XII/IXCA	Chattancourt/Marre
25DI	27.2.-8.3.16	XIII/VIICA	Forges
26DI	28.2.-28.3.16	XIIICA	Bois d'Avocourt
27DI	8.3-5.4.16	XXI/XXXIII	Thiaumont/Damloup
27DI	5.5-13.5.16	IIICA	Thiaumont/Damloup
27DI	12-28.8.16	XIVCA	Vaux devant Damloup/Damloup
28DI	2.3.-15.4.16	II/XIVCA	Haudromont/Damloup
28DI	22.4.-17.5.16	XIICA	Haudromont/Damloup
29DI	21.2.-26.3.16	XVCA	Malancourt/Avocourt
30DI	22.6.-25.8.16	XICA	Meuse/Haudromont
31DI	5.8-15.8.16	XICA	Haudromont/Thiaumont
32DI	11.8-30.8.16	XICA	Thiaumont/Vaux Chapitre

33DI	20.7.-15.8.16	XICA	Thiaumont/Vaux Chapitre
33DI	15.8.16-25.11.16	XICA	Meuse/Haudromont
34DI	29.3.-24.4.16	VIICA	Bois d'Avocourt
35DI	2.5-20.5.16	IIICA	Etang de Vaux/Thiaumont
36DI	20.5.-28.5.16	IIICA	Etang de Vaux/Thiaumont
37DI	21.2-26.2.16	XXX/XXCA	Poivre/Louvemont
37DI	29.3.-24.4.16	VIICA	Avocourt/Bois Carre
37DI	12.7.-29.7.16	XICA	Souville
37DI	30.10.16-	XICA	Douaumont/Chambrettes/Bezonvaux
38DI	22.6.-27.7.16	XVCA	Cote 304
38DI	3.8-21.8.16	XICA	Thiamont/Vaux
38DI	21.10.-12.12.16	XICA	Thiamont/Dicourt
39DI	21.2.-11.3.16	XX/ICA	Haudromont/Damloup
39DI	12.3.-21.4.16	XXCA	Cote 304
40DI	26.3-2.6.16	XXXIICA	Mort Homme
42DI	10.3-31.3.16	ICA	Haudromont/Damloup
42DI	6.4.-19.5.16	XXXIICA	Hayette/Meuse
43DI	5.3.-19.3.16	XX/XXICA	Etang de Vaux/Eix
43DI	20.3.-11.4.16	XXXIII/IIICA	Etang de Vaux/Damloup
45DI	20.4-23.5.16	IX/XVCA	Hayette/Bois d'Avocourt
48DI	25.2-8.3.16	XXCA	Douaumont
48DI	25.4.-11.5.16	IIICA	Thiaumont/Etang de Vaux
51DI	21.2.-26.2.16	XXX/XXCA	Beaumont/Bezonvaux
52DI	4-15.6.16	IIICA	Thiaumont/Vaux Chapitre
55DI	12.7.-1.9.16	XVCA	Cote 304
55DI	22.9-22.10.16	XICA	Haudromont/thiaumont
55DI	9.11.16-	XXXICA	Bois d'Avocourt/Camard
56DI	16-31.5.16	XIICA	Haudromont/Thiaumont
60DI	27.6.-13.7.16	XICA	Haudromont/Froidterre
63DI	1-18.6.16	III/VICA	Bois Fumin/Damloup
63DI	1-30.10.16	XICA	Bois Fumin/Dicourt
64DI	26.7-13.10.16	XXXICA	Chattancourt/Marre
64DI	24.10.16-	XV/XXXICA	Bois Camard/Cote 304
65DI	4.6-1.7.16	XXXII/XXXI	Chattancourt/Marre
65DI	11.10.16-	XXXICA	Hayette/Meuse
67DI	21.2-8.3.16	XXX/VIICA	Bethincourt/Meuse
67DI	2.9-22.9.16	XICA	Vaux Chapitre/Thiaumont
68DI	22.6-8.8.16	XVCA	Bois Carre/Avocourt
68DI	25.8-13.9.16	XICA	Thiaumont/Vaux Chapitre
69DI	8.4.-10.4.16	IIICA	Vuax
69DI	10.4-24.5.16	XXXIICA	Hayette/Cumieres
70DI	20.3-5.4.16	XXXIIICA	Etang de Vaux/Thiaumont
71DI	6.7.-15.7.16	VICA	Bois Fumin/Damloup
72DI	21.2.-25.2.16	XXX/XXCA	Brabant/Bezonvaux
73DI	28.8.-11.9.16	XI/XIVCA	Vaux Chapitre/Dicourt
74DI	7.9-30.10.16	XICA	Vaux Chapitre/Dicourt
76DI	16.3-16.4.16	XIIICA	Bois d'Avocourt/Bethincourt
77DI	16.3-5.4.16	XXI/XXXIIICA	Vaux devant Damloup/Dicourt
120DI	29.2-9.3.16	XXCA	Vaux devant Damnloup/Eix
123DI	19.5-30.10.16	XVCA	Bois d'Avocourt/Cote 304
123DI	25.11.16-	XICA	Meuse/Haudromont
124DI	16.5.-8.6.16	IIICA	Etang de Vaux/Damloup
126DI	21.3.-2.11.16	XVCA	Malancourt/Avocourt/Cote 304
126DI	11.12-22.12.16	XICA	Meuse/Haudromont

127DI	24.6.-6.7.16	VICA	Bois Fumin/Dicourt
128DI	13.7.-20.7.16	XICA	Froidterre/Vaux Chapitre
128DI	18.12.16-	XICA	Louvemont/Chambrettes
129DI	23.6.-3.7.18	XICA	Haudromont/Froidterre
130DI	15.6-28.6.16	VICA	Vaux Chapitre/Thiaumont
130DI	25.9.-25.10.16	XICA	Vaux Chapitre/Thiaumont
131DI	28.6.-15.7.16	VICA	Thiaumont/Vaux Chapitre
132DI	16.2-19.3.16	IICA	Eix
133DI	17.9.-20.12.16	XICA	Thiaumont/Damloup
151DI	27.5-14.6.16	XIICA	Haudromont/Froidterre
151DI	24.6.-15.8.16	XXXI/XICA	Chattancourt/Marre
152DI	5.5-12.5.16	IXCA	Hayette/Camard
153DI	25.2-24.4.16	XXCA	Esnes/Avocourt
154DI	27.7.-22.9.16	VI/XIVCA	Tavannes
154DI	20.12.16-	XICA	Chambrettes/Bezonvaux

BATTLE OF THE SOMME

Sixth Army 1st July 1916 [Fayolle]

Attacked 1st July 1916:
- XX CA
  - 11 DI — Maricourt
  - 39 DI — Maricourt
- I CAC
  - 3 DIC — Dompierre
- XXXV CA
  - 61 DI — Fontaines-les-Cappy

In line but not involved in the attack of 1st July:
- XX CA
  - 153 DI — Hamel
- I CAC
  - 2 DIC — Dompierre/Somme river
  - 16 DIC — Dompierre/Somme river
- XXXV CA
  - 51 DI — Foucaucourt/Amiens to Chaulnes railway
  - 121 DI — Marcelcave
- Army Command
  - 47 DI — Harbonnieres [ex XXXV CA]
  - 53 DI — Harbonnieres [ex XXXV CA]

In Reserve:
- II CA
  - 3 DI — south of Amiens
  - 4 DI — Poix
- X CA
  - 20 DI — Crevecour
- XX CA
  - 72 DI — labour duties south west of Amiens
- I CAC
  - DM — Amiens
- I CC

1 DC
3 DC

Somme: monthly summaries 1st August-1st November 1916

1st August	1st September	1st October	1st November
Sixth Army	Sixth Army	Sixth Army	Sixth Army
XXCA	ICA	ICA	IXCA
11DI	1DI	46DI	152DE
	45DI	2DI	17DI
VIICA		56DI	
48DI	VIICA		VCA
41DI	48DI	VCA	125DI
	41DI	10DI	
ICAC	66DI	125DI	XXXIICA
2DIC			40DI
3DIC	XXXIIICA	XXXIICA	42DI
16DIC	70DI	42DI	
	77DI	40DI	VICA
IICA			12DI
3DI	TENTH ARMY	VICA	127DI
4DI	IICA	12DI	47DI
121DI	3DI	127DI	56DI
	4DI		
XXXVCA	121DI	XXXIIICA	XXXIIICA
61DI	15DIC	70DI	70DI
51DI		77DI	77DI
132DI	IICAC	47DI	
	10DIC		TENTH ARMY
TENTH ARMY		TENTH ARMY	IICA
XCA	XXXVCA	IICA	IICAC
20DI	61DI	IICAC	XXICA
26DI	132DI	XXICA	XCA
	43DI	XCA	XXXCA
	also XXXCA	XXXCA	

Sequence of army corps in the Somme/Picardy area of operations 1.7.16-1.1.17

XXCA	21.8.16-ICA	8.10.16-IXCA	[Tenth Army 12.12.16]
	15.9.16-VCA	)14.1.16-XXCA –10.12.16	
	18.9.16-XXXIICA	)	
26.7.16-VIICA	18.9.16-VICA	22.12.16-XVIIICA	[Tenth Army 12.12.16]
ICAC	23.8.16-XXXIIICA	13.11.16-XIICA	[Tenth Army 13.11.16]
23.7.16-IICA-28.12.16			[Tenth Army 5.8.16]
	3.8.16-IICAC		[Tenth Army]
	5.8.16-XXXVCA	28.12.16-VIIICA	[Tenth Army]
	3.9.16-XXICA	-29.12.16	[Tenth Army]
12.7.16-XCA			[Tenth Army 5.8.16]
XXXVCA	-19.9.16		[Tenth Army 5.8.16]
XXXCA			[Tenth Army 28.6.16]

Divisions which served in the Battle of the Somme, 1st July-30th November 1916

01.07.16-10.12.16   11DI   XX/6

01.07.16-07.12.16	39DI	XX/6		
01.07.16-28.11.16	153DI	XX/6		
01.07.16-23.08.16	2DIC	ICAC/6		
01.07.16-04.08.16	3DIC	ICAC/6		
01.07.16-22.08.16	16DIC	ICAC/6		
01.07.16-15.07.16	DM	ICAC/6		
01.07.16-20.07.16	53DI	XXXV/6		
01.07.16-08.09.16	61DI	XXXV/6	5.8-XXXV/10	
01.07.16-28.12.16	121DI	XXXV/6	23.7-II/6	5.8-II/10
01.07.16-16.10.16	51DI	XXX/10	25.8-X/10	
	58DI	XXX/10		
01.07.16-08.12.16	62DI	XXX/10	26.10-XXI/10	
11.07.16-26.12.16	47DI	XX/6	14.9-XXXIII/6	
			3.10-VI/6	
13.07.16-17.01.17	132DI	XXXV/6	5.8-XXXV/10	
			10.9-XXI/10	
		24.9-XXXV/10		
16.07.17-27.07.16	41DI	VII/6	21.7-XXI/6	
16.07.16-18.09.16	48DI	VII/6		
16.07.16-02.01.17	20DI	X/10		
16.07.16-30.11.16	26DI	X/10		
23.07.16-23.12.16	3DI	II/6	5.8-II/10	
01.08.16-23.12.16	4DI	II/6	5.8-II/10	
03.08.16-21.11.16	10DIC	IICAC/10		
10.08.16-18.09.16	14DI	VII/6		
14.08.16-25.12.16	15DIC	II/10	5.11-IICAC/10	
14.08.16-01.12.16	72DI	XXX/10		
15.08.16-27.10.16	66DI	VII/6	10.10.-XXXII/6	
17.08.16-18.11.16	43DI	XXXV/10	10.10-XXI/10	
18.08.16-10.10.16	46DI	XX/6	21.8-I/6	
19.08.16-30.09.16	1DI	I/6		
20.08.16-29.09.16	45DI	I/6		
23.08.16-21.11.16	70DI	XXXIII/6	13.11-XII/10	
23.08.16-11.11.16	77DI	XXXIII/6		
03.09.16-05.10.16	2DI	I/6		
03.09.16-17.12.16	13DI	XXI/10		
08.09.16-26.10.16	120DI	XXXV/10	19.9-XXI/10	
14.09.16-29.10.16	10DI	V/6		
18.09.16-18.12.16	12DI	VI/6		
18.09.16-19.12.16	127DI	VI/6		
20.09.16-03.11.16	42DI	XXXII/6		
27.09.16-23.02.17	56DI	I/6	21.10-VI/6	
29.09.16-14.11.16	125DI	V/6		
30.09.16-17.11.16	40DI	XXXII/6		
09.10.16-21.10.16	18DI	I/6	10.10-IX/6	
15.10.16-13.12.16	25DI	X/10		
20.10.16-04.12.16	152DI	IX/6		
20.10.16-20.01.17	23DI	XXXIII/6	6.11-XII/10	
27.10.16-21.11.16	17DI	XXXII/6	7.11-IX/6	
17.11.16-06.01.17	24DI	XII/10		
17.11.16-28.12.16	DM	IICAC/10		

Orders of Battle 1917

Western Front, 1st January 1917

GAN [Franchet d'Esperey]   QG at Clermont
XXXVI Corps d'Armée [Balfourier]
45 DI   Nieuport

Tenth Army [Duchêne]   QG at Moreuil
IX Corps d'Armée [Niessel]
18 DI   Bouchavesnes/Bois l'Abbé
17 DI   Bois l'Abbé/Clermont

XII Corps d'Armée [Nourrison]
23 DI   Maisonette/Cléry sur Somme
24 DI   Rest-Pois
129 DI   Barleux/Belloy

XVIII Corps d'Armée [Hirschauer]
29 DI   Rest-Grandvillers
35 DI   Belloy/Berny
36 DI   Berny/Genermont
152 DI   Rest-Quevauvillers

VIII Corps d'Armée [Hély d'Oissel]
15 DI   Ablaincourt
16 DI   From front to Fresnes
124 DI   Training-Songeres
169 DI   Training-Ste Menehould

XXI Corps d'Armée [Maistre]
43 DI   Rest-Beauvais
72 DI   Ablaincourt/Pressoire

X Corps d'Armée [Anthoine]
8 DI   Pressoire
20 DI   South of Pressoire
58 DI   Maucourt
DM   Training-Crevecouer

II Corps d'Armée Coloniale [Blondlat]
10 DIC   Training-Marseille-en-Beauvais
15 DIC   Training-Marseille-en-Beauvais

Army
100 DT Rest-Poix

Third Army [Humbert]   QG at Noailles –to Maignelay 3.1.17
XXX Corps d'Armée [Chrétien]
132 DI   Maucourt/Andechy

I Corps d'Armée Coloniale [Berdoulat]
62 DI   Andechy/Armancourt
2 DIC   Montdidier/Roye road

3 DIC	Beuvraignes

Army
81 DT	Labour-Montdidier

First Army [Fayolle] QG at Verberie
Army
121 DI	Bois des Loges/Plessis

I Corps de Cavalerie [Conneau]
1DC	Tracy/Oise/Quennevières [elements]
3DC	Tracy/Oise/Quennevières [elements]

XXXV Corps d'Armée [Jacquot]
61 DI	Plessis/Ecouvillon
53 DI	Ecouvillon/Ribécourt

XXXIII Corps d'Armée [Leconte]
70 DI	Quennevières/Hautbraye
77 DI	Hautbraye/Pernant

Army
87 DT	Labour-Senlis
120 DI	Transit-Verberie
163 DI	Training-Villers Cotterêts

GAC [Pétain]   QG at Châlons-sur-Marne

Sixth Army [Mangin] QG at Oulchy-le-Château
HQ out of line-reformed 16.1.17 at Fismes

Fifth Army [Mazel] QG at Jonchery-sur-Vesle
II Corps de Cavalerie [de Buyer]
2DC	Venizel/Condé
4DC	Condé/Soupir
7DC	East of Soissons/Pernant

XXXVII Corps d'Armée [Taufflieb]
158 DI	Soupir/Troyon
10 DI	Troyon/Pontoy

V Corps d'Armée [de Boissoudy]
69 DI	Pontoy/Berry-au-Bac
125 DI	Rest-Coulognoy

XXXVIII Corps d'Armée [Piarron de Mondésir]
9 DI	Berry-au-Bac/Godat
27 DI	Godat/Loivre
151 DI	Cavaliers/Reims

VI Corps d'Armée [de Mitry]
12 DI	Rest-Coulognes
56 DI	Rest-Condé-en-Brie
127 DI	Rest-Ville-en-Tardenois

Army
89 DT	Labour-Fismes
97 DT	Labour-Fismes
2DC	Condé-sur-Aisne/Venizel
4DC	Soupir/Condé-sur-Aisne
7DC	South-west of Pernant

Fourth Army [Roques]
QG at St Memmie

XVII Corps d'Armée [Dumas]
34 DI	Marquises/Moscou
42 DI	Aubérive
19 DI	Aubérive/Vedegrange

I Corps d'Armée [de Riols de Fonclare]
162 DI	Navarin/Côte 193
60 DI	Côte 193/Tahure
51 DI	Courtive/Massiges
1 DI	Training-Courtisols
2 DI	Training-Mailly

VII Corps d'Armée [de Bazelaire]
14 DI	Massiges/Maisons
40 DI	Maisons/Aisne
165 DI	Four de Paris/river Aire
41 DI	Transit to Mailly

Army [ex VII CA]
37 DI	Transit to Wassy
38 DI	Transit to Gondrecourt

Second Army [Guillaumat]   QG at Bar-le-Duc

XVI Corps d'Armée [Grossetti]
32 DI	Aire/Haute Chevauchée
31 DI	Haute Chevauchée/Avocourt
71 DI	Training-Triaucourt

XXXI Corps d'Armée [Rozée d'Inferville]
55 DI	Avocourt/Camard
64 DI	Camard/Côte 304
65 DI	Hayette/Charny

XI Corps d'Armée [Muteau]
123 DI	Meuse/Louvement
128 DI	Louvement/Chambrettes
154 DI	Chambrettes/Bezonvaux
6 DI	Bezonvaux/Vaux devant Damloup
21 DI	Rest-Avincourt
59 DI	Training-Verdun

XV Corps d'Armée [de Maud'huy]
22 DI	Damloup/Château-sous-les Côtes
130 DI	Châtillon/Tresauvaux
5 DI	Éparges/Vaux-les-Palameix

III Corps d'Armée [Lebrun]
- 74 DI   Haute Meuse/Dompcervin
- 63 DI   Domcervin/Koeur-la-Grande
- 33 DI   Koeur/Etang de Vargevaux

XIV Corps d'Armée [Marjoullet]
- 28 DI   Training-Gondrecourt

Army
- 126 DI   Rest-Bar le Duc
- 133 DI   Rest-Bar le Duc

GAE   [de Castelnau]   QG at Gondecourt

Eight Army [Gérard]   QG at Tantonville
Formed from DAL 2.1.17

Army
- 131 DI   Vargevaux/Limey
- 5DC   Embermesnil/Sânon

XXXIX Corps d'Armée [Deligny]
- 67 DI   Fey-en-Heye/Limey
- 167 DI   Pont-à-Mousson/Nomeny
- 11 DI   Nomeny/Brin
- 48 DI   Training-Neufchâteau

Army
- 68 DI   Brin/Amaucourt./Sanon

XXXX Corps d'Armée [Paulinier]
- 73 DI   Sanon/Vezouse
- 7 DI   Vezouse/Chapelotte

II Corps d'Armée [de Cadoudal]
- 3 DI   Training-Bois l'Eveque
- 4 DI   Training- Toul

XIII Corps d'Armée [Demange]
- 25 DI   Rest-Neufchâteau
- 26 DI   Rest-St Buin

XX Corps d'Armée [Claret de la Touche]
- 39 DI   Rest-Bayon
- 153 DI   Rest-Bayon
- 168 DI   Rest-Saffais

Army
- 88 DT   Labour-Nancy

Seventh Army [Debeney]   QG at Lure
Army
- 47 DI   Chapelotte/Col Ste Marie
- 66 DI   Col Ste Marie/Metzeral
- 46 DI   Metzeral/Leimbach

13 DI   Training-Villersexel
52 DI   Training-Valdahon
161 DI   Labour-Belfort
170 DI   Training-Vesoul

XXXIV Corps d'Armée [Nudant]
164 DI   Carlspach/Ammmertsville
157 DI   Ammertsville/Canal du Rhine et Rhone
134 DI   Canal/Swiss Frontier
6DC   Swiss Frontier –patrols & training

XXXII CA- no divisions under command

THE BATTLES OF 1917

GERMAN WITHDRAWAL TO HINDENBURG LINE, 17th March 1917

THIRD ARMY	XIVCA	27DI
Reserve-154DI		62DI
DM	XCA	28DI
	ICAC	3DIC
		2DIC
FIRST ARMY	XIIICA	26DI
Reserve-53DI	XXXVCA	25DI
61DI		121DI
	XXXIIICA	81DI
		70DI
		77DI
SIXTH ARMY	XXXVIICA	127DI

* First Army formations transferred to Third Army 22nd March

ST QUENTIN, 13th April 1917

THIRD ARMY [Humbert]   2nd German Army
XIIICA   36
25DI advances to St Quentin   47
26DI advances to St Quentin   7th German Army
XXXVCA   46R
121DI Urvillers 13
61DI Alaincourt
53DI Vendeuil
XXXIIICA
70DI Foret de Coucy/Foret de St Gobain
77DI Coucy le Chateau/Foret de St Gobain

MORONVILLERS, 17th April-20th May 1917 [Third Champagne] Fourth Army [Anthoine]
VIIICA [Hély d'Oissel]
16DI Bois de la Grille
34DI Cornillet/Mont Haut
XVIICA [Dumas]
45DI Mont Haut/Le Casque
33DI?? `Le Têton
XII CA [Nourisson]
24DI east of Aubérive
128DI later-east of Aubérive

Added 26th April:
X CA [Vandenburg]
19DI   26th April-
20DI   30th April-
72DI   Mont Haut/le Casque to XVIICA
48DI   to XVIICA- Mont Cornillet
131DI   to XVIICA- Mont Haut/le Casque
8DI   to XVIICA- Le Têton

Laffaux, 5th May 1917

3DI   Mont Spin 4th May
4DI   Sapigneul 4th May
11DI   Ferme Malval
12DI   Ferme Froidmont 5th May
22DI   Chemin des Dames 5th-7th May
35DI   Casemates 5th-6th May
168DI   nort of Verneuil

Third Ypres 31st July

First Army [Anthoine] ICA
51DI
1DI XXXVICA
133DI
29DI

Verdun: French Offensive, 20th-24th August

Formation	Second Line	First Line	Location
XIIICA [Linder]			
	97DI	25DI	Avocourt
	120DI	26DI	Esnes
XVI CA [ ]			
	32DI	31DI	west of Chattancourt
	48DI	DM	east of Chattancourt
XVCA [Fonclare]			
	7DI	126DI	Côte du Poivre
	20DI	123DI	Côte du Poivre
XXXIICA [Passaga]			
	40DI	165DI	Caurières
	69DI	42DI	Caurières

Army Reserves
63DI
73DI
not involved in the offensive
X CA
                        129DI??   Vaux
                        19DI   Tavannes

Malmaison 23rd October [Chemin des Dames]

Tenth Army [Maistre]
XIV CA   Quincy Basse to Vauxillon
129DI
154DI
28 DI

27 DI
151 DI
XXI CA   Mennejean to Panthéon
43 DI
170 DI
13 DI
167 DI
AS8 & AS11 [24 tanks]
XI CA   Panthéon to Jouy
38 DI
22 DI
66 DI
AS12 [12 tanks]
27DI & AS31 [28 tanks]
28DI & AS33 [28 tanks]

CAMBRAI, 20th November [held in reserve in case of need by BEF] XXICA
129DI
170DI

NIVELLE'S OFFENSIVE/SECOND AISNE, French Forces, 16th April 1917

Nivelle employed four armies under the command of General Micheler of the Reserve Army Group to provide the principal assault on the German positions in April 1917. Secondary attacks would take place around Arras by the BEF from 9th April, by the Third Army on St Quentin on the 11th, and then east of Reims by Fourth Army from 17th April. Nivelle's strategy was to employ two armies-Sixth and Fifth-to attack the German defenses along the line of the Chemin des Dames, north of the river Aisne, between Soissons and Reims. Once the Germans had been committed he would drive Tenth Army forward on a very narrow front at the junction of Sixth and Fifth Armies. The anticipated breakthrough by Tenth Army would create a narrow corridor as far as Laon, beyond the hilly region of the Chemin des Dames. Once this had been achieved, First Army would move up from its reserve positions on the Marne, move through the corridor, and exploit northwards across the open plain from Laon to Sedan and the Belgian border.

Sixth Army [Mangin]
Holds line from Coucy le Chateau to Hurtebise along the Chemin des Dames

I CAC [Berdoulat]   Coucy-le-Chateau to Missy
3 DIC   Quincy Basse/Vauxillon-attacks Bois Mortier
2 DIC   south of Vauxillon/Aisne-attacks Laffaux
158 DI   faces Laffaux-not engaged

VI CA [de Mitry] Vailly-Soupir
56 DI   Moussy-sur-Aisne- attacks Ferme des Bovettes
127 DI   Condé-sur-Aisne/Soupir- attacks Chavonne
12 DI   2nd line west of Craonne
166 DI   at Soupir-not engaged

XX CA [Maziller] Soupir-Paissy
39 DI   Moussy-sur-Aisne/Civy- attacks Braye en Laonnais
153 DI   Troyon/Chivy- attacks up to Chemin des Dames
11 DI   at Neuilly St Front-not engaged
168 DI   at Neuilly St Front- not engaged

II CAC [Blondlat]   Paissy-Hutrebise
38 DI   attacks south of Ailles
15 DIC   Chivy-Hurtebise –attacks towards Cerny-en-Laonnaise

10 DIC Hurtebise- attacks same

XI CA [Maud'huy] in reserve behind XX CA
21 DI St Remy Blanzy
22 DI Oulchy-le-Chateau
133 DI Longeuval
5 DC

Fifth Army [Mazel]
Holds line from Hurtebise through Craonne to Aisne and city of Reims

I CA [Muteau] Hurtebise-Craonne
66 DI moving from Tenth Army-elements engaged Vauclair
162 DI Ferme et Cruette de Hurtibise-attacks Plateau de Vauclair
1 DI Craonne-attacks plateau and village
2 DI Craonne/le Ployon- attacks plateau
51 DI 2nd line at Craonne

V CA [de Boissoudy] Craonne-Berry-au-Bac
9 DI Bois des Buttes/la Miette-attacks Juvincourt
10 DI le Ployon/Bois des Buttes-attacks Ville aux Bois

XXXII CA [Passaga] Berry au Bec-Sapigneul
69 DI La Miette/Berry-au-Bac-attacks Claques Dents
42 DI Berry-au-Bac- attacks north of the Aisne
40 DI Aisne/Sapigneul- attacks Cote 108/Mont de Sapigneul

VII CA [de Bazelaire] Mont Spin-Courcy
37 DI north of Godat/La Neuville-attacks Mont Spin/Sechamps
14 DI north of Godat/Ferme de Luxemburg-attacks Bermericourt
41 DI Ferme de Luxemburg/south of Loivre-attacks Loivre
152 DI in reserve at Jonchery-sur-Vesle

XXXVIII CA [Piarron de Mondesir] Reims
151 DI Cavaliers-de-Courcey/Reims
89 DI Reims/Marquises
6 DC

Tank Force
Group Chaubès: 7, 3, 8 Sqns [48 tanks] Group Bossut: 2, 4, 5, 6, 9 Sqns [80 tanks]

Tenth Army [Duchêne]
Breakthrough force stationed south of the river Aisne
Corps listed in order of expected commitment to the Laon corridor

XVIII CA [Hirschauer] Fismes
35 DI
36 DI
154 DI

II CA [de Cadoudal] Concevreux/Beaurieux
3 DI
4 DI
46 DI

III CA [Lebrun]   Fismes
5 DI
6 DI
47 DI

IX CA [Niessel]   Ville-en-Tardenois/Lagery
17 DI
18 DI
I CC [Feraud]   ??
1 DC
2 DC
3 DC

First Army [Fayolle]
General reserve in the Marne region
4 DC
7 DC

X CA [Vandenberg]   Chalons sur Marne
19 DI
20 DI
131 DI   moving to join Fifth Army

XXI CA [Maistre]   Château-Thierry
13 DI
43 DI
167 DI

ORDERS OF BATTLE 1918

Western Front, 1st January 1918
GAN_ [Maistre] QG at Avize

CSN_ [Putz]   QG at Amiens

XXVI Corps d'Armée [Nollet]
29 DI   Nieuvepoort
133 DI   Rest-Dunkerque

Third Army [Humbert] QG at Noyon
I Corps de Cavalerie [Féraud]
1DC   Barisis-aux-Bois/Fresnes
5DC   Fresnes/Quincy Basse
3DC   Reserve at Pontoise
III Corps d'Armée [Lebrun]
5 DI   Pontruet/Selency/Dallon
6 DI   Dallon/Urvillers
XXXVII Corps d'Armée [Taufflier]
81 DI   Urvillers/Moy
62 DI   Moy/Fere
154 DI   Rest-Lassigny

Sixth Army [Duchêne]   QG at Belleu
XI Corps d'Armée [de Maud'huy]

22 DI	Quincy Basse/Mortier
151 DI	Mortier/Chavignon
21 DI	Chavignon/Vauxmaire
61 DI	Training-Ecurie
161 DI	Rest-Attichy

XXXV Corps d'Armée [Jacquot]
53 DI	Chevregny/Brunin
121 DI	Brunin/Vauclerc

V Corps d'Armée [Pellé]
125 DI	Vauclerc/Ployon
10 DI	Ployon/Miette
9 DI	Rest-Serzy-et-Prin
55 DI	Rest-Fere en Tardenois

I Corps d'Armée [Lacappelle]
1 DI	Training-Lizy sur Ourcq
2 DI	Training-Senlis
51 DI	Training-Crecy en Brie
162 DI	Training-Montmerency

Fifth Army   [Micheler]   QG at Jonchery-sur-Vesle

II Corps de Cavalerie [Robillot]
2DC	Reserve at Provins
4DC	Bétheny/Pompelle
6DC	Training at Sézanne

XXXVIII Corps d'Armée [Piarron de Mondésir]
74 DI	Miette/Sapigneul
71 DI	Sapigneul/Godat
157 DI	Godat/Courcy

XXXIV Corps d'Armée [Nudant]
134 DI	Courcy/Bétheny
58 DI	Bétheny/Reims
48 DI	Training-Damery

I Corps d'Armée Coloniale [Mazillier]
2 DIC	Training-Vertus
3 DIC	Training-Château-Thierry

II Corps de Cavalerie [Robillot]
2 DC	Bétheny-Pompelle
4 DC	Bétheny-Pompelle
6 DC	Bétheny-Pompelle

Army
67 DI	Rest-Ville-en-Tardenois

Fourth Army [Gouraud]   QG at St Memmie

IV Corps d'Armée [Pont]
7 DI	Marquises/Cornillet
124 DI	Cornillet/Mont Haut
163 DI	Mont Haut/Têton

8 DI   Labour-Cuperly/Vadenay

XXX Corps d'Armée [Chrétien]
97 DI   Téton/Aubérive
132 DI   Aubérive/Vedegrange

XVIII Corps d'Armée [d'Armade de Pouydraguin]
36 DI   Mamelles
35 DI   Côte 193

VIII Corps d'Armée [Hély d'Oissel]
15 DI   Mesnil/Maisons
72 DI   Maisons/Aisne
169 DI   Aisne/Four de Paris
16 DI   Training-Ste Menehould

XIV Corps d'Armée [Marjoullet]
27 DI   Rest-Mailly
28 DI   Rest-Mailly
129 DI   Rest-Mailly

Army
38 DI   Labour-Mourmelon
87 DI   Training-Mairy sur Marne

GAE   [de Castelnau] QG at Mirecourt

Second Army [Hirschauer]   QG at Bar-le-Duc
XIII Corps d'Armée [Linder]
60 DI   Four de Paris/Aire
120 DI   Aire/Avocourt
26 DI   Rest-Laheycourt/Revigny

II Corps d'Armée [de Cadoudal]
4 DI   Avocourt/Haucourt
3 DI   Haucourt/Bethincourt

VII Corps d'Armée [de Bazelaire]
14 DI   Bethincourt/Forges
48 DI   Forges/Meuse
63 DI   Mormont/Côte 344
34 DI   Rest-Bar-le-Duc
168 DI   Training-Verdun

XVII Corps d'Armée [Graziani]
68 DI   Beaumont/Bois Chaume
33 DI   Bois Chaume/Bezonvaux
25 DI   Bezonvaux/Damloup
11 DI   Labour-Bar-le-Duc
153 DI   Transit-Vanault les Dames

X Corps d'Armée [Vandenburg]
131 DI   Damloup/Haudiomont
20 DI   Haudiomont/Éparges
19 DI   Éparges/Calonne

II Corps d'Armée Coloniale [Blondlat]
15 DIC   Loclont/Paroches
52 DI   Paroches/Koeur le Grande
10 DIC   Koeur/Etang de Vargevaux

First Army [Debeney]
HQ moving to Lorraine-operational from 11.1.18 at Toul
DM –from 1.1.18 Vargevaux/Limey

Eighth Army [Gérard]   QG at Flavigny-sur-Moselle
XXXII Corps d'Armée [Passaga]
42 DI   Limey/Bois Prêtre
40 DI   Bois Prêtre/Clémery
165 DI   Clémery/Chenincourt
39 DI   Labour-Pont-à-Mousson

XV Corps d'Armée [Riols de Fonclare]
126 DI   Chenincourt/Brin
123 DI   Moncel/Bezange la Grande
37 DI   Training-Dormay/Nancy

IX Corps d'Armée [Mangin]
18 DI   Bezange-la-Grande/Sanon
41 DI   Bezange-la-Grande/Sanon
59 DI   Embermesnil/Domevre
152 DI   Vezouve
128 DI   Vezouve/Chapelotte
17 DI   Rest –Custines
164 DI   Training-Rosières aux Salines

Army
69 DI   Training with US Army-St Blin

Seventh Army [de Boissoudy]   QG at Lure
VI Corps d'Armée [de Mitry]
170 DI   Chapelotte/Fave
166 DI   Provenchèsnes sur Fave/Bonhomme
167 DI   Bonhomme/Metzeral
56 DI   Metzeral/Leimbach

XVI Corps d'Armée [Corvisart]
66 DI   Guebwiller
31 DI   Burnhaupt
32 DI   Training-Montreux Vieux

XXXIII Corps d'Armée [Leconte]
70 DI   Burnhaupt/Canal de Rhone et Rhine
77 DI   Canal/Fulleren

XXXX Corps d'Armée [Paulinier]
13 DI   Labour-Héricourt
12 DI   Labour-Swiss Frontier
43 DI   Labour-Swiss Frontier
127 DI   Labour-Swiss Frontier

73 DI   Fulleren/Swiss Frontier

CA's without divisions under command: XXCA, XXICA

21st March 1918: French front-line forces

GAN [Franchet d'Esperey]
7DI   Scherpenberg, Flanders

Third Army [Humbert]
9 DI   reserve at Estrées St Denis
10 DI   reserve at Crecy-en-Brie

Sixth Army [Duchene]
161DI   Barisis-Quincy Basse

XICA
61DI   Bois-Mortier-Chavignon
21DI   Chavignon-Les Vaumaires

XXXVCA
53DI   Pont de Chevregny-Brunin
121DI   Brunin-Ailette-Foret de Vauclerc

ICA
2DI   Miette-Ployon
162DI   Miette-Ployon
51DI   Maizy-Concervaux

Fifth Army [Micheler] XXXVIICA
71DI   Miette-Sapigneul
74DI   Sapigneul-north of Godat

XXXIVCA
157DI   south of Godat-Courcy
45DI   Courcy-Betheny
134DI   Béthany-Reims

ICAC
3DIC   Reims-Fort de la Pompelle
2DIC   Fort de la Pompelle-Marquises

Fourth Army [Gouraud] IVCA
8DI   Mont Cornillet-Mont Haut
124DI   Mont Haut-Teton

XXXCA
87DI   Teton-Aubérive
72DI   Aubérive-Road from Vaudessincourt to Prosnes
132DI   Aubérive-Epine de Vedegrange

IIICA
6DI   Les Mamelles-Cote 193
5DI   Cote 193-West of Navarin
58DI   Butte de Mesnil-Maisons de Champagne

VIIICA
16DI   Maisons de Champagne-river Aisne

GPE [de Castelnau]

Second Army [Hirschauer] XIIICA
63DI   Bois de Beaurain-Four de Paris
25DI   Four de Paris-Aire
60DI   Four de Paris-Aire
120DI   Aire-Avocourt

IICA
3DI   Avocourt-Haucourt
68DI   Haucourt-west of Forges

XXCA
168DI   west of Forges-east of Samogneux
39DI   Cote 344-Mormont
4DI   Mormont-Bois de Chaume

XVIICA
153DI   Bois de Chaume-Bezonvaux
20DI   Bois de Chaume-Bezonvaux
26DI   Bezonvaux-Damloup
131DI   Damloup-Haudiomont

XCA
33DI   Haudiomont-Calonne
34DI   Eparges-Calonne
52DI   Calonne-Maizey

First Army [Debeney] IICAC
15DIC   Maizey-Kouer la Grande
10DIC   Kouer-Etang de Varegvaux

VIIICA
DM   Etang de Vargevaux-Limey

XXXIICA
69DI   Etang de Vargevaux-Limey
42DI   Limey-Bois de la Pretre
40DI   Bois de la Pretre/Clemery

Eighth Army [Gerard] XVCA
126DI   Seille-Brin and Chenincourt
37DI   Seille-Brin and Chenincourt
123DI   Moncel-Bezange la Grande

VIICA
41CA   Bezange la Grande-Sanon
164DI   Sanon-Embermesnil
14DI   Embermesnil-Domevre
128DI   Vezouse-Chapelotte

Seventh Army [de Boissoudy] XXICA

170DI	Chapelotte/Fave
63DI	Provenchery-Cold de Bonhomme
167DI	Col de Bonhomme-Metzeral
13DI	Metzeral-Baillon de Guebvillers

XVICA

66DI	Guebvillers-Leimbach
32DI	Leimbach-Burnhaupt le Haut

XIVCA

27DI	Leimbach-Rhone/Rhine Canal
28DI	Rhone/Rhine Canal-Fulleren

XXXXCA

73DI	Fulleren-Swiss Frontier

Spring 1918

Forces in North pre 21st March 1918

133DI	XXXVICA	GAN
7DI	XVICA	DAN
41DI	VIICA	DAN

HQ Third Army sent north to help British Fifth Army on 24th March. Covered gap between Montdidier and Amiens with only three cavalry divisions. IICC [Robillot]
2D C3DC and 6DC

HQ First Army then moved from Lorraine to plug gap to left of Third Army. By 1st April it became the main source of resistance to the German attack in Picardy. The following divisions had been moved to Picardy:

56DI	24/03/18	VICA ex 7 Army
12DI	25/03/18	VICA ex 7 army
166DI	26/03/18	VICA ex 7 Army
17DI	27/3/18	IXCA ex 8 Army
59DI	27/03/18	IXCA ex 8 Army
127DI	27/03/18	VICAex 7 Army
163DI	27/03/18	IVCA ex 4 Army
45DI	28/03/18	XXXIVCA ex 5 Army
152DI	28/03/18	IICAC ex 5 Army
162DI	29/03/18	ICA ex 6 Army
2DCP	29/03/18	IIICA ex 8 Army
18DI	01/04/18	IXCA ex 8 Army

By 1st April, the French forces in the north were deployed in the following fashion.

DAN	FIRST ARMY	THIRD ARMY
3DC	VICA	XXXVCA
	133DI	5DC
154DI	56DI	70DI
XXXVICA	162DI	36DI
17DI	Mesole Gp	169DI [joins 1.4.18]
65DI	4DC	V CA
133DI	10DI	77DI
	163DI	9DI to 1/4

```
                29DI [XXXVI]        35DI to 1/4
                IXCA                53DI to 1/4
                127DI               IICC
                166DI               22DI
                                    62DI
                                    1DC
                                    38DI
                                    67DI
```

LYS/FOURTH YPRES, April 1918 [de Mitry]

IICC	[Robillet]		XXXVICA	[Nollet]	DAN
28DI	to 27/4	34 DI	from 19/4	17DI	to 20/4
154DI	to 29/4	133DI	from 19/4	65DI	to 20/4
3DC	to 29/4	2 DC	from 21/4	31DI	from 29/4
39DI	from 25/4				

OISE FRONT [Third Army]

NOYON 22nd March 1918 [covers retreat of British Fifth Army] VCA [Pelle]
9DI
1DI
35DI

MONT RENAUD –SW of Noyon, March 1918
35DI

THIRD BATTLE OF THE AISNE

Sixth Army, 27th May 1918 [Duchêne] XXX CA
151DI	Quincy Basse/Mortier
19 DI	Champs/Manicamp
55 DI	Manicamp/Varesnes
2DCP	Pont St Mard/Champs in reserve=
39DI	at Soissons
1DI	at Villers Cotterêts

XICA
61DI	Bois Mortier/Chavignon
21DI	Chavignon/Vaumaires
22DI	Vauclerc/Vaumaires in reserve
74DI	at Condé-sur-Aisne
157DI	at St Mard/Maizey

XXICA
22 DI	Vauclerc/Soissons
13 DI	reserve at Ville-en-Tardenois
39 DI	reserve at Soissons

Fifth Army 27th May 1918 [Micheler] ICC
| 120DI | Olizy/Chatillon |
| 13DI | joins at Fismes |

V CA

28 DI   Ardre/Bligny
154 DI   Ville-en-Tardenois/Ardre
40 DI   Fleury/Montagne de Reims

I CAC
45 DI   Loivre/Courcy
134 DI   Cavaliers/Bétheny/Reims
2 DIC   Vigny/Reims
3 DIC   Reims

THIRD AISNE - situation 1st June 1918

Tenth Army [Mangin] XXXCA
55 DI   Nampcel/Thiolet
19 DI   Thiolet/Confrecourt
162 DI   Confrecourt/Pontarcher
170 DI   Pontarcher/Mercin-et-Vaux
35 DI   Mercin-et-Vaux/north of Chaudun
51 DI   north of Chaudin/Vierzy [plus elements of 74DI] In reserve= 61DI, 2DI, DM, 151DI

XI CA
131 DI   Vierzy/Louatre
128 DI   Louatre/Troesnes in reserve= 21DI

Sixth Army [Duchêne] VII CA
26 DI   arriving at Troesnes/Passy-en-Valois

XXI CA
4 DI   Passy-en-Valois/Sommelans [and elements 73DI]
43 DI   Sommelans/Étrepilly
164 DI   Étrepilly/Ferme de Grand Ru
73 DI {-}   Ferme de Grand Ru/Monneaux

XXXVIII CA
10 DIC   Monneaux/Chierry
22 DI   Chierry/Fossoy
3 US DI   Fossoy

Group la Tour
5 DC   Fossoy/Dormans
20 DI   Dormans/Soilly

Fifth Army [Micheler] Group Simon
Elements 4DC/167DI/170DI –Dormans/south bank of the Marne

I CC
120 DI   Verneuil/Olizy [elements 13DI/1DC]
40 DI   Olizy Violaine/Ville en Tardenois

V CA
19 Br DI   Ville-en-Tardenois/Côte 183
28 DI   Côte 183 south of Aubilly/Colommes-la-Marne
154 DI   in reserve north of Chaumuzy

I CAC

45 DI	Coulommes/Reims [elements 2DIC]
134 DI	Reims
3 DIC	east of Reims

BATTLE OF THE MATZ, 9th-12th June 1918

Third Army [Humber] XXXV CA
36 DI	Ployron/Courcelles-Epayelles
169 DI	Tricot
58 DI	Rollet/Orviller-Sorel

XXXIV CA	to 10/6	
125 DI		Orvillers/Sorel-fought at Ricquebourg/Vignecourt/Antheuil- Army from 10/6
1 DCP		Thiescourt/Plessis du Roye -to XVCA 10/6
II CA		
53 DI		Plemons/Thiescourt-fought Chevincourt/Melicoq/Marchermont
72 DI		Oise/Cannectaecourt –fought at Marchermont

XV CA
126 DI	Antheuil/Villers-sur-Condon
123 DI	line Orvillers/Sorel-fought at Ricquebourt/Vignecourt/Antheuil

Army Troops
11 DI	10/6 to Gp Mangin	-Bois de Ressons/Mery/Courcelles-Epayelles
18 DI	10/6-XXXIV CA	-Ressons/Marquelin
69 DI	10/6-XXXIV CA	-Antheuil
133 DI	reserve at Noroy	

Reinforcements-
10/6-152DI	Gp Mangin	-Breteuil/Mery
10/6-165DI	Gp Mangin	-Belloy/Lataule
10/6-129DI	Army	-Courcelles-Epayelles/Mery
11/6-48DI	Gp Mangin	-Wacquemoulin/St Maur
11/6-67DI	XV CA 12/6-IICA	-Mont de Chaumont-line Chevincourt/Machermont

List of Corps d'Armée Involved in Battles of the Aisne and Marne 1918
I CA	29.05.18-Sixth Army	02.06.18-Tenth Army	
II CA	19.06.18-Sixth Army		
III CA	08.07.18-Sixth Army	17.07.18-Ninth Army	
V CA	30.05.18-Fifth Army		
VI CA	27.05.18-Sixth Army -08.06.18	31.07.18-Tenth Army	
VII CA	31.07.18-Tenth Army		
XI CA	27.05.18-Sixth Army	02.06.18-Tenth Army-09.08.18	
XIVCA	09.07.18-Ninth Army	15.07.18-Fifth Army	
XX CA	06.06.18-Tenth Army		
XXI CA	27.05.18-Sixth Army –21.06.18		
XXX CA	27.05.18-Sixth Army	02.06.18-Tenth Army	
XXXVIII CA	30.05.18-Sixth Army	17.07.18-Ninth Army	20.07.18-Sixth Army
I CAC	29.05.18-Fifth Army		
I CC	29.05.18-Fifth Army	19.07.18-Ninth Army	23.07.18-Sixth Army
II CC	29.05.18-Sixth Army	16.06.18-Tenth Army –02.08.18	

List of Divisions Engaged in Battles of the Aisne and Marne 1918
1DI	28.05.18-6/XI	02.06.18-10/XI –28.07.18

2DI	29.05.18-6/I	02.06.18-6/IICC	20.06.18-6/II-27.07.18
4DI	31.05.18-6/VII-08.06.18	16.07.18-6/III 19.07.18-9/III	30.07.18-6/III
5DI	18.07.18-6/XI	26.07.18-10/XI –29.07.18	
7DI	09.07.18-5/ICAC	15.07.18-5/V –31.07.18	
8DI	17.06.18-5/V –18.07.18		
9DI	12.07.18-9/XIV	18.07.18-5/V –30.07.18	
10DI	31.07.18-5/V		
11DI	20.06.18-10/I	13.07.18-10/XX 15.07.18-10/I	
12DI	23.07.18-10/XX		
13DI	27.05.18-6/XXI	29.05.18-5/ICC-05.06.18	
14DI	16.07.18-5/II Italian	24.07.18-5/V 01.08.18-5/XIV-04.08.18	
16DI	03.08.18-5/XIV		
17DI	02.08.18-10/XX		
18DI	16.07.18-6/III	17.07.17-9/III 25.07.18-5/III 30.07.18-6/III	
19DI	27.05.18-6/XXX	02.06.18-10/XXX 12.07.18-10/I 15.07.18-10/XXX	
20DI	29.05.18-6/XXI	01.06.18-6/XXXVIII –27.06.18 15.07.18-6/III	
		17.07.18-9/III 20.07.18-5/XIV 31.07.18-5/V	
21DI	27.05.18-6/XI –02.06.18		
22DI	27.05.18-6/XXI-03.06.18		
25DI	26.07.18-10/XXX		
26DI	01.06.18-6/IICC-20.06.18		
28DI	30.05.18-5/V –12.06.18		
33DI	20.06.18-6/II –01.08.18		
35DI	30.05.18-6/I	02.06.18-10/I-04.06.18	
39DI	28.05.18-6/XI	02.06.18-10/XI-03.06.18 22.06.18-6/XXXVIII 17.07.18-	
		9/XXXVIII 20.07.18-6/XXXVIII-30.07.18	
40DI	29.05.18-5/ICC	12.06.18-5/V- 20.07.18	
41DI	15.07.18-10/XI	25.07.18-6/XI 26.07.18-10/XI	
43DI	29.05.18-6/XXI –06.06.18		
45DI	29.05.18-5/ICAC-02.06.18	01.07.18-5/ICAC	
47DI	04.06.18-6/VII	17.07.18-6/II –18.07.18	
48DI	08.07.18-10/XI	15.07.18-10/XXX –21.07.18	
51DI	31.05.18-6/I	02.06.18-10/I –15.06.18	
01.07.18-5/V	08.07.18-6/III	17.07.18-9/III-18.07.18	
52DI	18.07.18-6/VII	27.07.18-6/II	
55DI	27.05.18-6/XXX	02.06.18-10/XXX	12.07.18-10/I-15.07.18
58DI	20.07.18-10/XX –24.07.18		
61DI	27.05.18-6/XI	02.06.18-10/XI-08.06.18	
62DI	27.07.18-6/II		
63DI	16.07.18-6/II		
68DI	26.07.18-10/XI		
69DI	16.07.18-10/XX	21.07.18-10/I	
71DI	08.07.18-9/XIV		
72DI	14.07.18-10/I		
73DI	27.05.18-6/XXI	03.06.18-6/VII-03.07.18 17.07.18-9/III-25.07.18	
74DI	27.05.18-6/XI	02.06.18-10/XI-05.06.18	
77DI	15.07.18-6/III	16.07.18-5/ICC 19.07.18-9/ICC 20.07.18-5/ICAC	
		01.08.18-5/XIV	
87DI	02.06.18-6/XI	06.06.18-10/XI 18.07.18-10/XX	
120DI	30.05.18-5/ICC	12.06.18-5/V 09.07.18-5/II Italian –27.07.18	
125DI	24.06.18-6/XXXVIII	08.07.18-6/III –17.07.18	
127DI	01.08.18-10/XXX		
128DI	01.06.18-6/XI	02.06.18-10/XI-18.07.18	

131DI	29.05.18-6/XI	02.06.18-10/XI-11.06.18 16.07.18-5/ICC 19.07.18-9/ICC 20.07.18-5/XIV 22.07.18
134DI	29.05.18-5/ICAC	
151DI	27.05.18-6/XXX	01.06.18-6/I 02.06.18-10/I-12.06.18
153DI	13.06.18-10/XX-08.07.18	15.07.18-10/I-22.07.18
154DI	28.05.18-6/IX British	29.05.18-5/ICC 30.05.18-5/V-31.05.18
157DI	27.05.18-6/XI	28.05.18-6/XXI-29.05.18
162DI	29.05.18-6/I	02.06.18-10/I –18.07.18
164DI	30.05.18-6/XXI	01.07.18-6/VII –27.07.18
167DI	03.06.18-6/XXI	21.06.18-6/III 04.07.18-I US Corps-27.07.18
168DI	19.07.18-9/III	21.07.18-5/V 23.07.18-5/ICAC
170DI	28.05.18-6/XI	30.05.18-6/I 02.06.18-10/I-05.06.18
2DIC	29.05.18-	5/ICAC –06.08.18
3 DIC	29.05.18-5/ICAC	
10DIC	30.05.18-6/XXI	01.06.18-6/XXXVIII-27.06.18 05.07.18-9/XIV 08.07.18-5/V- 28.07.18
DM	29.05.18-6/XI	30.05.18-6/I 02.06.18-10/I-20.06.18 05.07.18-10/XX-22.07.18
2DCP	31.05.18-6/I	05.06.18-10/I 06.06.18-10/XX-22.07.18
1DC	29.05.18-5/ICC-07.06.18 15.07.18-5/ICC 16.07-5/V 19.07-9/ICC 20.07.18-5/ICC-22.07.18	
2DC	29.05.18-6/IICC-06.06.18 12.07.18-6/IICC –20.07.18	
3DC	29.05.18-6/IICC-06.06.18 20.07.18-5/ICC 23.07-6/ICC-30.07.18	
4DC	27.05.18-6/ICC 29.05.18-6/XXI 01.06.18-6/XXXVIII-07.06.18 13.07.18-6/IICC 16.07-10/IICC –20.07.18	
5DC	27.05.18-6/ICC 29.05.18-6/XXI 01.06.18-6/XXXVIII-06.06.18 16.07.18-5/ICC 19.07-9/1CC 20.07-5/ICC-22.07.18	
6DC	29.05.18-6/IICC 04.06.18-6/VII –06.06.18 18.07.18-10/IICC-20.07.18	

SECOND BATTLE OF THE MARNE, 1918

Overall French Deployment 14th July 1918
GAN
Tenth Army [Mangin] Sixth Army [Degoutte] Fifth Army   [Berthelot] Fourth Army [Gouraud]
In reserve- Ninth Army [Mitry]

CHAMPAGNE 'FRIEDENSTURM', 14th-15th July 1918

Fourth Army [Gouraud]

IV CA [Pont]
1st wave-
163 DI Prunay/Cornillet
124 DI Cornillet/Mont sans Nom
132 DI Mont sans Nom/Aubérive
2nd wave-
27 DI   Moscou/Suippe
71 DI   Moscou/Cornillet
10 DI   Cornillet/Prunay

XXICA [Naulin]

170 DI   Auberive/Vedegrange
13 DI   Vedegrange/Côte 193
43 DI   Côte193/Mamelles
46 DI   Souain/Perthes
42 US DI

VIII CA [Hély d'Oissel]
161 DI   Memelles/Massiges
16 DI   Massiges/Ville-sur-Tourbe
1 DCP   Ville-sur-Tourbe/l'Aisne
63 DI   Aisne/Ravine Houyette

Army Reserves [not used]
9 DI
52 DI
131 DI
1 DC

Situation 15th July 1918

Tenth Army

XVIII CA
70 DI   Oise/Tracy-le-Mont
15 DI   Tracy-le-Mont/Moulin-sous-Touvent
55 DI   Moulin-sous-Touvent/Confrecourt

I CA
162 DI   Confrecourt/Aisne
11 DI   Aisne/Cutry

XX CA
DM   Cutry/St Pierre-Aich

XXXCA
48 DI   St Pierre-Aich/Longpont
19 DI   in reserve

XICA
128 DI   Longpont/Ancienville
36 DI   in reserve

Sixth Army
II CA
33 DI   Ancienville/Troesnes
2 DI   Troesnes/Passy-en-Valois
168 DI   in reserve
2 US DI   in reserve

VII CA
47 DI   Passy/Chezy-en-Oxois
164 DI   Chezy/Veuilly-la-Poterie
I US CA
167 DI   Veuilly/Lucy-le-Bocage200
26 US DI   Lucy/Monneaux

XXXVIII CA
39 DI   Monneaux/Chierry
3 US DI   Chierry/Crezancy
III CA
125 DI   Crezancy/Dormans
51 DI   Dormans/Bouquigny

Ninth Army [in reserve] XIV CA
XVI CA II CAC

Fifth Army
V CA
8 DI   Verneuil/Cuisles
40 DI   Cuisles/Champlot
10 DIC   in reserve
77 DI   in reserve
II ITALIAN CA
8 IT DI   Champlat/Chambery
3 IT DI   Chambrecy/Coulommes
120 DI   in reserve
I CAC
2 DIC   Coulommes/Reims
134 DI   Reims
3 DIC   south east of Reims
45 DI   towards Prunay
7 DI   in reserve

FOCH'S COUNTERATTACK, 18th July 1918

Tenth Army [Mangin]   Sixth Army [Degoutte]
18 divisions [including 2 US]   9 divisions [including 2 US]
3 groups of 123 tanks   1 AS of 10 tanks
3 groups of 90 tanks   3 battalions of 125 light tanks
3 battalions of 130 light tanks   230 batteries
470 batteries   28 squadrons of aircraft
40 squadrons of aircraft

Situation 1st August 1918

Tenth Army
I CA
162 DI   Confrecourt/Pernant
72 DI   Pernant/Mercin
11 DI   Mercin/Vaubuin
69 DI   Vaubuin/Berzy-le-Sec

XX CA
87 DI   Berzy/Villemontoire
15 Br D I   Villemontoire
12 DI   Villemontoire/Tigny

XXX CA   [127 DI in reserve]
19 DI   Tigny/Parcy
25 DI   Parcy/Plessier-Huleu
34 Br DI   Plessier/Grand Rozoy

XI CA
68 DI   Grand Rozoy/Wallee
1 DI   Wallee/Trugny

Sixth Army
II CA   [52DI & 33DI in reserve]
63 DI   Trugny/Fere-en-Tardenois
62 DI   Fere-en-Tardenois
I US CA [4 US & 28US DI in reserve]
42 US DI   Seringes/Sergy

XXXVIIICA
32 US DI   Sergy/Bois Meunnier

III CA   [73DI in reserve]
4 DI   Bois Meunnier/Ste Gemme
18 DI   Ste Gemme/Passy-Grigny

Fifth Army
V CA   [7DI & 9DI in reserve]
20DI   Passy/Grigny
10 DI   Berthenais/Ville-en-Tardenois

XIV CA [16DI in reserve]
14 DI   Ville-en-Tardenois/Bligny-a-Ville
77 DI   Bligny/Ste Euphraise
I CAC
2 DIC   Ste Euphraise/Vrigny
168 DI   Vrigny/Reims
134 DI   Reims
3 DIC   south east of Reims
45 DI   towards Prunay

25th September 1918: French Army Deployment on the eve of Final Advance Group Armee Francais [Belgium] [to become Sixth Army]
IICC
2 DC   movement to Proven/ Roosbrugge Haringe 18/9-27/9
4 DC   movement to Proven /Roosbrugge Haringe 18/9-27/9
6 DC   movement to St Omer from 18/9

VII CA
128 DI   movement from Loon Plage to Bikschote 24/9
164 DI   rest at Gravelines
41 DI   movement to Ypres

First Army
VIII CA
37 DI   2nd Noyon-Oise/east of Tergnier
58 DI   Oise/Vendeuil from 25/9
60 DI   Hinacourt/Vendeuil   [ex XVCA]
67 DI   Oise/Barisis-aux-Bois [ex XVIIICA]
123 DI   moved to VIIICA near Tergnier ex XVCA
46 DI   rest at St Just-en-Chaussee/Wavignies [ex XVCA] XV CA
126 DI   rest at Bonneuil-les-Eaux/Nesle [joined XVCA 22/9] XXXI CA

47 DI   rest at Nesle [to XV CA 27/9]
56 DI   Andechy/Avre –attacked Echelle-St-Aubain 26/9
152 DI   east of Nesle/Canal du Nord
169 DI   Essigny-le-Grand

XXXVI CA
34 DI   rest south east of Amiens from 22/9
133 DI   in action at Epine de Dallon/St Quentin
166 DI   in action at Epine de Dallon/St Quentin

Army Command
15 DI   rest at Neuilly en Thelle [ex XVIIICA]
64 DI   rest at Ham
70 DI   rest at Compiègne/Estrées St Denis [to GAF 28/9]
121 DI   west of Braine –transferring to Tenth Army 27/9

Tenth Army
VIICA
55 DI   2nd Noyon-north of Ailette/Pont St Mard

XVI CA
31 DI   Quincy Basse/Bois Mortier
32 DI   Fresnes/Barisis aux Bois
33 DI   Fresnes/Barisis aux Bois

I CA
29 DI   Vauxillon/south of Allemant [to XVIII CA 28/9]
127 DI   north of Sanaey 29/8 to river Ailette

XXX CA
36 DI   Allemant/Plateau de Pinon
59 DI   Vauxillon

XXXV CA
25 DI   Presles/west of Vailly
162 DI   Vailly/Aizy
72 DI   Aizy/Jouy

Army Command
5 DI   rest at Crépy-en-Valois [27/9 to GAF in Flanders]
11 DI   rest at Crécy-en-Brie
12 DI   rest at Crouy-en-Ourcq
17 DI   rest at Vezaponin
35 DI   rest at Antheuil
66 DI   rest at Compiègne
132 DI   rest at Ivors
1 DM   en route to Rosières aux Salines [8th Army]

Fifth Army
III CA
6 DI   rest at Fismes
52 DI   Braine/Coureullot to the Vesle
62 DI   Villers en Prayeres/Glennes

XX CA

45 DI	Glennes /Romain/Baslieux
153 DI	rest at Hatillon sur Marne

V CA
9 DI	Romain-Arbre de Romain
10 DI	north of Vendeuil/Jouchery-sur-Vesle

XIII CA
16 DI	Jouchery-sur-Vesle/Muizon
168 DI	Vesle/Muizon -west of Reims

I CAC
77 DI	Neuvillette/outskirts of Reims
2 DIC	Reims/Prunay
3 DIC	rest at Tours sur Marne

Army Command
53 DI	rest at Épernay
134 DI	rest at Fismes

Fourth Army
IV CA
7 DI	Prunay/south of Mont Cornillet
8 DI	south of Mont Cornillet/Moscou
163 DI	Moscou/Aubérive
124 DI	rest at Mourmelon-le-Grand

II CA
3 DI	Mesnil-lès-Hurlues 26/9-
4 DI	Mesnil/Perthes -ex XXICA 25/9
14 DI	west of Mesnil/Perthes from 26/9
48 DI	rest Somme-sur-Tourbe until 26/9

XXI CA
13 DI	Trou Bricot/Mesnil –2nd line at Perthes
43 DI	move to Perthes/Trou Bricot
167 DI	ex Perthes/Trou Bricot to Souain
170 DI	moving up from Châlons-sur-Marne 26/9

IX CA
2 DM	Butte de Mesnil 26/9
120 DI	rest at Gizaucourt
157 DI	rest at Valmy 28/9 to Dormois
161 DI	rest at Beauséjours

XI CA
21 DI	at Suippes –to north of Py 26/9
22 DI	Navarin/Butte de Souain
61 DI	at Suippes- to north of Py 26/9
151 DI	attack towards St Marie-à-Py 26/9

XIV CA
68 DI	Wacques/Auberge de l'Esperance
28 DI	Epine de Vedegrange/west of Souain
154 DI	to front at Epine de Vedegrange 26/9

XXXVIIICA
71 DI   Aisne/Vienne le Château
1 DCP   Aisne/Vienne le Château

Army Command
73 DI   rest at Auve
I CC
1 DC   at Suippes
3 DC   at Suippes

Second Army/United States Army
5 DC   Argonne –in support at Passavent en Argonne

XVII CA
18 DI   Samogneux/Bezonvaux
10 DIC   Bezonvaux/Damloup
15 DIC   Damloup/Fresnes
26 DI   moving to Verdun sector at Bois de Caurières

II CAC
2 DCP   St Mihiel sector at Hauts-de-Meuse/Tillot/Hattonchattel
39 DI   St Mihiel sector at Hattonchattel/Bois de Chaufour

Eighth Army
69 DI   rest at Nancy in I US CA VI CA
27 DI   Domevre/Leintrey
87 DI   Embermesnil/Sanon
129 DI   Sanon/Bezange la Grande
131 DI   Vezouve/Chapelotte

XXXII CA
40 DI   Bezange la Grande/Brin
42 DI   Brin/Han
125 DI   to Brin/Arraye sector 25/9
165 DI   Arraye/Clémery

Seventh Army
XXXIII CA
20 DI   Chapelotte/Fave
19 DI   Fave/Weiss
1 DI   Lauch/Leimbach

XXXX CA
2 DI   Leimbach/Burnhaupt le Haut
38 DI   Burnhaupt/Fulleren
51 DI   Fulleren/Swiss Frontier

Advance to Victory 1918

Amiens/Third Picardy, 8th August 1918

First Army
XXXI CA
37DI   Hailles/Bois Senecat

42DI	Bois de Moreuil
126DI	Roye
153DI	Hangest/Arvillers/Erches
47DI	9/8-Berny sur Noyon
56DI	9/8-Andechy/Avre

IX CA
3DI	Mailly-Raineval/Bois St Herbert
15DIC	to the Avre
66DI	Morisel/Moreuil 8-10/8 [Army Command?]

X CA
60DI	arrived Montdidier 8/8
152DI	Grivesnes/Cantigny 9/8 to Pierrepont
166DI	support role-Grivesnes/Beuvraignes to Roye

XXXV CA
169 DI	Assainvillers/Faverolle
46 DI	Pieneuex/Rollet

Army Command
133DI	Ployron/Courelles-Epayelle attacks 9/8-Tilloloy/Beuvraignes
1 DM	rest at Breteuil

St Mihiel, 12th September 1918

First US Army
V US CA II CAC
2DI
26DI
39DI
IV US CA I US CA

Verdun XVII CA
18DI
10DIC
15DIC

Argonne/Monfaucon, October 1918
18DI
26DI

Champagne et Argonne: Somme-Py, 26th September 1918

Fourth Army [Gouraud] Iv Ca [Pont]
7 DI	Cornillet
8 DI	south of Cornillet
124 DI	Moscou/Aubérive
163 DI	Moscou/Aubérive

XIV CA [Marjoulet]
68 DI	Esperance/Wacques
28 DI	west of Souain/Vedegrange
154DI	Vedegrange

XI CA   [Prax]
21DI   north of the Py [2nd line]
22DI   Navarin/Butte de Souain
61DI   north of the Py [2nd line]
151DI   Ste Marie-à-Py

XXI CA [Naulin]
167 DI   Trou Bricot/Butte de Souain
43 DI   Trou Bricot/Perthes
170DI   north of Somme-Py [2nd line]
13DI   Perthes/Souain [2nd line]

II CA [Philipot]
14DI   Perthes/Butte de Tahure
3DI   Galoche/Mamelles
48DI   Aure/Lorisy [2nd line]
4DI   Perthes/Beauséjours [2nd line]

IX CA [Garnier-Duplessis]
2 DM   Massiges/Beauséjours
29/9-120DI   Plateau de Soudain
6/10-125DI   Monthois/Châlons
161DI   Butte de Mesnil/Maisons de Champagne
29/9-157DI   Dormois
14/10-134DI   Vouzier

XXXVIII CA [Piarron de Mondésir]
74DI   Massiges/Ville sur Tourbe
71DI   Aisne/Vienne le Château
1 DCP   Aisne/Vienne le Château

First US Army
I US CA
77 US DI

VAUXILLON, 14th-15th September 1918

Tenth Army
I CA   NE of Soissons
29 DI
128 DI

XXXV CA Joy/Presle
1DM

ST QUENTIN, 13th September-8th October 1918

First Army
XXXVI CA   St Quentin
34DI
133DI
166DI
XXXI CA   Grand Seraucourt/Hinacourt
60DI

46DI
126DI
129DI
XVCA   Hinacourt/Vendeuil
46DI
47DI
VIII CA –joining First army at Tergnier

St Thierry, 30th September 1918

Fifth Army
VCA   Villers-en-Prayeres
9DI
10DI
III CA   Basileux-lès-Fismes
52
XX CA   Beuil-sur-Vesles
6 DI
134 DI
153 DI
XIII CA   Jonchery-sur-Vesle
15 DI
168 DI
I CAC   Reims
2 DIC
3 DIC

Mont-d'Origny, 9th October 1918 to Second Guise, 4th November 1918

First Army
XV CA   Seboncourt to Etreux –to Nouvion-en-Thièrache
46DI
66DI
XXXVI CA   Bernoville to Tupigny and east of Sambre-Oise Canal
34DI
152DI
XXXICA   Neuville St Amand to Guise
33DI
56DI
VIIICA   Bernot-Chevresis-Monceaux to Sains Richaumont-Hirson
35DI
58DI
123DI

Battle for the Serre, 30th October 1918

Third Army
XVI CA   Anizy le Château to Chalandry and Cul de Saarts
31DI
32DI
XVIII CA   Barenatn-Cel to Verneuil-sur-Serre to Aubenton
17DI
127DI
29DI

59DI
XXXV CA   Monceau-le-Wast to Montcornet-Rocroi
25DI
72DI
121DI

Fifth Army
VCA   Malmaison & Selve to Sissonne-Liart-Renwez
9DI
52DI
XIIICA   Thour/St Germaincourt to St Fergeux, Arreaux and Varidon
16DI
45DI
151DI
28DI
9DI
13DI
XXICA   Thour to Recouvrance to Nizy, Hannogne and Signy L'Abbaye
43DI
170DI
167DI
167DI
62DI
1CAC   Heroy-Château-Porcien
2DIC
3DIC
IV CA   Thugy-Tugny to Charleville
8DI
163DI
124DI

2ND BATTLE OF GUISE, 4th November 1918

First Army
XXXVI CA
34 DI
64 DI
152 DI VIII CA
37 DI XX CA
47 DI XV CA
66 DI XXXI CA
166 DI

CHESNE, 1st November 1918

Fourth Army
XIVCA   joined 5th November, and advanced to Meuse near Sedan
22DI
124DI
163DI
XI CA   West of Attigny to Mézières
21 DI
7 DI
2DCP

IX CA	Voncq to Alluex, Ardenens Canal and Quatre Champs	
134DI		
40 DI		
120 DI		
53DI		
XXXVIIICA	Olizy to Falaise, Boult au Bois, and Brieulle-sur-Bar	
71 DI		
74 DI		
1 DCP		
125DI		

BELGIUM, October–November 1918

Sixth Army
VIICA
128DI
41DI
164DI XXXIVCA
70DI
77DI
11DI XXXCA
132DI
5DI
12DI Army
2DC
4DC
6DC

WESTERN FRONT, 11th November 1918

FLANDERS

Sixth Army [Degoutte]   QG at Roulers

II CC	Robillot		
2DC	Lasson	Schelde	
4DC	Lavigne-Delville	Schelde	
6DC	Mesple	Schelde	
XXXIV CA	Nudant		
5 DI	Roig-Bourdeville	Schelde	
11 DI	Vulliemot	Tielt	
XXX CA	Penet		
12 DI	Chabord	Eine	
132 DI	Sicre	Wannegem/Lede	
VII CA	Massenet		
41 DI	Bablon	Oudenaarde	
164 DI	Gaucher	Gand	
Army Command			
70 DI	Tantôt	Deinze	
77 DI	Serrigny	Ruysslede	
128 DI	Segonne	Waregem	

Reserve Army Group [GAR] [Fayolle] QG at Nettancourt
First Army [Debeney] QG at Homblieres

XV CA	De Fonclare	
123 DI	De Saint-Just	Robechies
51 DI	Ecochard	Liessies
XXXVI CA	Nollet	
166 DI	Cabaud	Fourmies/Momignies
133 DI	Valentin	Chinay
XXXI CA	Toulorge	
-		
VIII CA	Hély d'Oissel	
58 DI	Priou	Fôret de Signy-le-Petit
37 DI	Simon	Seloigne-Baileux
XX CA	Berdoulat	
-		
Army Command		
67 DI	Bousquier	Sains Richauront
35 DI	Mareschal	La Fère
48 DI	Schuhler	La Capelle
126 DI	Mathieu	Guise
46 DI	Gratier	Trelon
66 DI	Brissaud-Desmaillots	Ham
47 DI	Dillemann	Eglancourt/Froidestrees
153 DI	Goubeau	Marle
169 DI	Serot Almera Latour	Guise
33 DI	Leconte	La Capelle
34 DI	Savatier	Guise
152 DI	Andrieu	Nouvion
64 DI	Colin	Rumigny
15 DI	Arbancre	To Paris
168 DI	Peschart D'Ambly	La Capelle

Third Army [Humbert] QG at Laon

XVI CA	Deville	
17 DI	Gassouin	Signy-le-Petit
32 DI	Daydrein	Cul de Saarts
59 DI	Vincendon	Cul de Saarts
XXXV CA	Jacquot	
25 DI	Joba	Montcornet
72 DI	Ferradini	Notre Dame de Liesse
121 DI	Targe	Rocroi
XVIII CA	De Pouydraguin	
-		
Army Command		
19 DI	Trouchaud	Crecy sur Serre
29 DI	Barthelemy	Marle/Vervins
36 DI	Mittelhauser	Crépy-en-Valois
31 DI	Martin	Transit to Paris

CENTRE ARMY GROUP [Maistre] QG at St Memmie
Fifth Army [Guillaumat] QG at Reims

XXI CA	Naulin Gamelin Michel, C	
9 DI	Girard	Château Regnault/Meuse
43 DI		Chaumont Porcien
62 DI		Monthermé
IV CA	Pont	
8 DI	Tetart	Meuse/Charleville
V CA	Pellé	
10 DI	Pichat	Aubigny-les-Pothes
52 DI	Boyer	Revin/Laifour
XIII CA	Linder	
13 DI	Tabouis	Signy l'Abbaye/Belval
151 DI	Biesse	Signy l'Abbaye
Army Command		
6 DI	Poignon	Sissonne
16 DI	Le Gallais	Ay/St Image
28 DI	Madelin	West of Épernay Condé-en-
45 DI	Michaud Cot	Brie Pont Faverger
124 DI	Mangin, J	SE of Rethel Boult sur Suippe
125 DI	Schmidt	Jouchery sur Vesle. Nouvien-
167 DI	Bernard	Porcien
170 DI	Mordrelle	
2 DIC		

Fourth Army [Gouraud] QG at St Memmie

XI CA	Prax	
61 DI	Blondin	Mézières
2 DCP	Hennocque	Mézières
XIV CA	Marjoulet	
22 DI	Pire	Mézières
163 DI	Boichut	Flize
IX CA	Garnier Duplessis	
7 DI	Bulot	Sauville-Vendresse
40 DI	Laignelot	Sedan
48 DI	Schuler	Vouziers/Tourteron
120 DI	Mordacq	Suippes
XXXVIII CA	Piarron de Mondésir	
42 DI	De Barescut	Courtisols
71 DI	Barbier	Chaussée sur Marne
74 DI	De Lardemelle	Possessee
87 DI	Dhers	Monthois/Bony
Army Command		
14 DI	Baston	Tourtern/Balon
21 DI	Giraud	Touligny

53 DI	Guillemin	Transit to Vittel
134 DI	Petit	Pont Faverger
1 DCP	Brècard	Valmy

United States Army

HQ 2nd Army [Hirschauer] QG moving from Laheycourt to Nancy

HQ XVII CA [Hellet]
HQ XXXIII CA [Leconte]

II CAC	Claudel	
10 DIC	Marchand	Étain
15 DIC	Guerin	Damvillers

Eastern Army Group   [de Castelnau] QG at Mirecourt

Tenth Army   [Mangin,C] QG at Tantonville
XXXII CA	Passaga	
69 DI	Poindron	Han/Brin
165 DI	Arraye/Clémery	
1 DM	Daugan	Brin/Bezange-la-Grande
I CAC	Maziller	
3 DIC	Poyperoux	Xeuilluy
III CA	Lebrun	

Army Command
1 DI	Grégoire	Mirecourt
2 DI	Mignot	Centrey
18 DI	Andlauer	Bayon
20 DI	Desvoyes	Arches/Thaon
26 DI	De Belenet	Liverdun
27 DI	Roux	Rosières-aux-Salines
39 DI	Pougin	Nancy
56 DI	Demetz	Mirecourt
127 DI	Rampont	Transit to Charmes

Eighth Army [Gérard] QG at Flavigny-sur-Moselle

II CA	Philipott	
41 DI	Bablon	Leintrey-Sanon
129 DI	De Corn	Sanon-Bezange-la-Grande
VI CA	Duport	
3 DI	Nayral Martin de Bourgon	Domevre-Leintrey
73 DI	Lebocq	Chapelotte-Vezouve

Army command
131 DI	Chauvet	Lunéville

Seventh Army [de Mitry] QG at Lure

X CA	Vandenburg Jacuemot Goybert	
60DI		Chapelotte/Fave
157DI		Fave/Weiss
I CA	LaCappelle	Weiss/Metzeral
162DI	Messimy	
161DI	Modelin	Metzeral/Leimbach
XXXX CA	Paulinier	Leimbach/Burnhaupt
68DI	Menville	
154DI	Breton	Burnhaupt/Fulleren
2DM	Modelon	Fulleren/Swiss Frontier
Army Command	Dufieux	Transit to Remiremont
38DI		

GOG Formations

ICC	Féraud	Moving to Nancy
1 DC	De Rascas de Château-Redon	
3 DC	De Boissieu	
5 DC	Simon	

Outside France

23DI	Italy
24DI	Italy
30DI	Macedonia
57DI	Macedonia
76DI	Macedonia
122DI	Macedonia [en route to Turkey]
156DI	Macedonia
11DIC	Macedonia
16DIC	Macedonia
17DIC	Macedonia [en route to Hungary]

OVERSEAS OPERATIONS

GALLIPOLI, 1915

After the failure of the naval assault to force the passage of the Dardanelles, the French committed an ad hoc corps to the ground forces which sought to secure the Gallipoli peninsula between April 1915 and January 1916. The Corps Expéditionnaire d'Orient commanded two divisions which fought on the right flank of the allied force as it sought to move up the peninsula towards Krithia. The divisions were:

1 Division du CEO	2 Division du CEO
1 Metropolitan Brigade	3 Metropolitan Brigade
2 Colonial Brigade	4 Colonial Brigade

MACEDONIA, 1915 – 1918

British and French troops began to arrive in Salonika in October 1915 in response to a request from the Greek government for military assistance against a possible Bulgarian invasion. As the force landed the pro- allied Greek government was overthrown and replaced by one which favoured neutrality. In spite of this the allied army remained in order to pose a threat to Bulgaria and to provide a base for the liberation of Serbia. The allied force did very little until the autumn of 1918 when it did begin an offensive which lead to the collapse of the Central Powers in the Balkans. This force was to include 6 British infantry divisions and two mounted infantry brigades, 6 Serbian infantry divisions and one cavalry division; one Italian infantry division and two Russian brigades.

The initial French commitment was 57DI, 156DI and 122DI. This became the Armée d'Orient. When an allied high command was established on 11th August 1916, the French component became the AFO-the Armée Française d'Orient with a total of eight divisions. These were 57DI, 156DI, 122DI, 16DIC, 17DIC, 11DIC, 76DI and 30DI. These were organised into three ad-hoc corps.

On 11th September 1918, French forces were distributed as follows-
Armee Francais d'Orient

2 Group	3 Group	Army Cmd
30DI	57DI	Gp de Cavalry-2 RChd'A, 1 Spahis
76DI	Regt/156DI	122DI
11DIC	Algerian bn	17DIC
156 DI[-]		

Commandement des Allies en Orient

1 Group	British Army
16DIC	RZ

When Bulgaria collapsed, an Armée du Danube was formed with 30DI and 76DI.

ITALY, 1917-1918

After the Italian defeat at Caporetto, British and French re-inforcements were sent to Italy. Most of this force returned to the Western Front in the spring of 1918, but some divisions remained for the rest of the war. Paradoxically, an Italian corps was sent to the Western Front in 1918.

The initial French force was commanded by Tenth Army [Duchêne] and comprised:

XIICA	23DI	24DI
XXXICA	64DI	65DI
Army command	46DI	47DI

After the return of Tenth Army to France, the force was reduced to XII Corps d'Armée with 23DI and 24DI. In June 1918, the corps served with the Italian Sixth Army, but, in October 1918, the corps was split up when 23DI was moved to the newly-formed Italian Twelfth Army.

Part Seven

An Alphabetical Listing of French Generals, 1914-1918

Abonneau, Pierre	4DC & Prov CC	02.08.14-13.10.14
Aime, Ernest	67DI	10.08.15-08.09.16
Alby, Henri	34DI	02.08.14-11.04.15
	XIIICA	11.04.15-06.10.16
Aldebert, Adalbert	8DI	02.01.17-24.08.18
Alix, César	XIIICA	02.08.14-01.04.15
Allenou, Louis	5DC	28.09.14-31.03.17
Amade, Albert d'	Alpes	02.08.14-00.09.14
	GDT	00.09.14-00.12.14
	CEO	24.02.15-15.05.15
Andlaeur, Joseph	63DI	02.06.16-03.07.17
	18DI	12.12.17-11.11.18
Andrieu, Francois	152DI	27.01.16-09.07.18
Anselme, Philippe d'	127DI	22.01.16-11.11.18
Anthoine, Francois	COS 2nd Army	02.08.14-07.10.14
	20DI	08.10.14-10.10.15
	X CA	10.10.15-23.03.17
	4 Army	23.03.17-15.06.17
	6 Army	15.06.17-21.12.17
	CGS	21.12.17-05.07.18
Arbanere, Louis	15DI	09.03.17-11.11.18
Archinard, Louis	1GDR	02.08.14-25.08.14
Arlabosse, Louis	24DI	05.01.15-10.01.15
	23DI	10.01.15-30.05.15
	9DI	30.05.15-08.11.16
	87DI	05.04.17-02.06.18
Armau de Pouydraguin, Louis d'	15DI	14.10.14-24.03.15
	47DI	24.03.15-22.08.17
	XVIII CA	22.08.17-02.06.18
Aubier, Louis	8DC	02.08.14-16.08.14
Auger, Michel	10DI	02.08.14-26.08.14
Aymerich, Joseph	2DIC	22.06.17-10.11.17
Bablon, Pierre	41DI	31.05.18-11.11.18
Bailloud, Maurice	156DI	16.03.15-26.08.16
	CEO	01.07.15-04.10.15
Bailly, Henri	19DI	05.09.14-16.09.16
Bajolle, Léon	15DI	02.08.14-14.10.14
	81DI	08.12.14-10.01.18
Balfourier, Maurice	11DI	02.08.14-29.08.14
	XXCA	29.08.14-17.09.16
	XXXVICA	17.09.16-04.03.17
Bapst, Etienne	23DI	22.08.14-27.08.14
	72DI	31.10.14-03.03.16
Baquet, Louis	13DI	27.08.14-13.10.14
	89DI	01.07.15-17.06.17
Baratier, Albert	8DC	04.09.14-10.08.16
	134DI	10.08.16-19.10.17
Barbier, Paul	71DI	28.10.18-11.11.18
Barbot, Ernest	77DI	08.09.14-11.05.15 KIA
Barescut, Maurice de	6DI	06.12.16-02.05.17

	42DI	26.08.18-11.11.18
Baret, Jospeh	27DI	02.08.14-24.08.14
	XIVCA	24.08.14-31.08.16
Barthelemy, Joseph	27DI	08.06.16-03.06.17
	29DI	07.04.18-11.11.18
Baston, Paul	156DI	26.08.16-01.05.18
	14DI	11.06.18-11.11.18
Bataille, Desirée	41DI	03.09.14-13.09.14
Battesti, Jules	52DI	02.09.14-27.09.14
Baucheron de Boissudy, Antoine	43DI	03.12.15-16.10.16
	V CA	16.10.16-01.05.17
	7 Army	04.05.17-15.10.18
Baumgarten, Maurice	62DI	15.11.14-10.02.15
	XICA	10.02.15-04.06.16
Bazelaire, Georges de	38DI	12.11.14-13.01.15
	27DI	13.01.15-02.11.15
	VII CA	02.11.15-04.06.18
Beaudemoulin, Antoine	103DT	14.07.15-19.05.16
	101DT	19.05.16-28.01.17
	157DI	28.10.17-04.05.18
Beaudenom de Lamaze, Henri	3bisGDR	24.08.14-21.11.14
Belenet, Jean de	26DI	28.02.18-11.11.18
Bellin, Emile	CGS	02.08.14-22.03.15
Berdoulat, Pierre	69DI	01.11.14-29.04.15
	I CAC	29.04.15-19.07.17
	XX CA	19.07.17-11.11.18
Berge, Paul	30DI	31.10.14-15.09.15
Bernard, Frederic	57DI	02.08.14-03.02.15
Bernard, Joseph	29DI	14.04.17-07.04.18
	170DI	14.04.17-11.11.18
Bernard, Louis	40DI	19.12.16-16.09.18
Berthelot, Henri	ACGS	02.08.14-21.11.14
	5GDR	21.11.14-23.01.15
	53DI	23.01.15-03.08.15
	XXXIICA	03.08.15-19.09.16
	Rumania	00.12.16-00.05.18
	5 Army	05.07.18-07.10.18
	Danube	00.11.18-00.05.19
Bertin, Simon	36DI	19.09.14-19.08.15
	152DI	14.10.15-27.01.16
Besset, Césare	58DI	02.08.14-31.08.14
Biesse.Camille	151DI	29.05.18-11.11.18
Bigot, Louis	74DI	02.08.14-29.02.16
Bizard, Charles	70DI	02.08.14-13.08.14
Bizot, Brice	65DI	02.08.14-19.09.14
	97DT	24.10.14-10.03.16
Blanc, Auguste	33DI	14.01.15-02.06.15
	158DI	23.07.15-21.03.17
Blazer, Ferdinand	26DI	20.08.14-24.08.14
	27DI	24.08.14-13.01.15
	47DI	13.01.15-24.03.15
	15DI	24.03.15-15.07.15
	157DI	23.12.15-23.05.16
Bloch, Georges	6DI	02.08.14-31.08.14
Blondin, Anatole	65DI	14.05.16-15.07.18
	61DI	15.07.18-11.11.18
Blondlat, Ernest	DM	08.08.14-21.06.15
	II CAC	21.06.15-27.10.18
Bodin de Galembert, Joseph de	157DI	04.05.18-30.05.18

Boe, Elie	20DI	02.08.14-05.09.14
Boelle, Victor	IV CA	02.08.14-17.06.15
Boichut, Edmond	163DI	16.06.17-11.11.18
Boissieu, Claude de	3DC	05.04.16-11.11.18
Bolgert, Edouard	41DI	13.09.14-22.09.14
	58DI	22.09.14-22.08.15
Bonet, Paul	35DI	06.11.16-16.06.17
Bonfait, Hemri	9DI	23.01.15-30.05.15
	23DI	30.05.15-11.11.18
Bonneau, Louis	VII CA	02.08.14-12.08.14
Bonnier, Francois	19DI	02.08.14-05.09.14
	35DI	03.10.14-07.05.15
	16DIC	23.06.16-30.07.16
Bordeaux, Joseph *	11DIC	04.10.17-15.06.18
	17DIC	01.01.18-29.05.18
Bordeaux, Joseph*	163DI	29.10.16-13.06.17
	18DI	22.08.17-12.12.17
Borius, Albert	156DI	01.05.18-11.11.18
Boucher de Morlaincourt, Francois	132DI	23.09.14-02.10.15
Bouchez, Achille	32DI	02.08.14-28.02.17
Boulangé, Albert	51DI	28.01.16-26.08.18
Bourdériat, Frederic	13DI	02.08.14-27.08.14
	89DT	12.09.14-16.11.14
Bousquier, Léon	67DI	04.05.18-11.11.18
Boutegourd, René	51DI	02.08.14-13.05.15
Bouyssou, Pierre	22DI	30.09.14-10.07.17
Boyer, Jean	52DI	13.12.15-11.11.18
Brasier de Thuy, Emile	59DI	22.12.14-08.09.15
Brécard, Charles	161DI	18.10.16-31.03.17
	5DC	31.03.17-06.01.18
	1DCP	06.01.18-11.11.18
Breton, André	154DI	04.09.16-11.11.18
Briant, Francois	127DI	10.06.15-22.01.16
Bridoux, Joseph	5DC	02.08.14-10.09.14
	I CC	08.09.14-17.09.14
Brissaud-Desmaillets, Georges	12DI	23.09.16-09.04.17
	66DI	19.04.17-11.11.18
Bro, Joseph	1DI	03.10.14-08.03.15
	15DIC	14.06.15-21.11.15
Brochin, Charles	V CA	02.08.14-23.08.14
Brugere, Henri	GCT	17.09.14-00.10.14
Brulard, Jean-Marie*	38DI	13.09.14-12.11.14
	2DI	21.09.14-16.07.15
	17DIC	06.08.15-29.02.16
	CEO	04.10.15-00.01.16
	157DI	23.05.16-28.01.17
	131DI	28.01.17-09.01.18
Brun d'Aubignosc, Emile	68DI	02.08.14-17.09.14
Buat, Edmund	121DI	18.06.16-31.12.16
	II CA	31.12.16-02.01.17
	33DI	18.02.18-30.03.18
	XVII CA	30.03.18-20.06.18
	6 Army	10.06.18-05.07.18
	CGS	05.07.18-11.11.18
Buisson, Clément	1DC & CC	02.08.14-28.09.14
Buisson d'Armandy, Eugene	75DI	25.09.14-06.11.14
	55DI	06.11.14-16.01.15
Bulot, Jospeh	7DI	22.10.17-11.11.18
Bunoust, Georges	90DT	12.08.14-16.09.14

De Buyer, Robert	4DC	13.10.14-01.07.15
	17DI	01.07.15-25.08.15
	III CC	25.08.15-17.12.16
	IICC	17.12.16-30.09.17
Cabaud, Paul	166DI	23.12.16-11.11.18
Cadoudal, Henri de	13DI	13.10.14-05.06.15
	57DI	12.08.15-15.10.15
	31DI	15.10.15-02.01.17
	II CA	02.01.17-11.06.18
Calvel, Henri	92DT	02.08.14-01.09.14
Capdepont, Francois	48DI	21.03.15-15.09.16
	22DI	10.07.17-27.03.18
Carbillet, Jean-Baptiste	29DI	02.08.14-28.01.16
Care, Ernest	3DI	19.09.14-20.10.14
	6DI	20.10.14-05.11.14
	125DI	14.05.15-06.10.15
Caron, Alphonse	165DI	19.11.16-11.11.18
Castaing, Jean	30DI	15.09.15-03.11.17
	122DI	02.11.17-01.03.18
Castelli, Jospeh de	VIII CA	02.08.14-12.10.14
Curières de Castelnau, Noel de	2 Army	02.08.14-21.06.15
	Army Group Centre	22.06.15-12.12.15
	CGS	11.12.15-00.11.16
	Army Group East	27.12.16-02.01.17
	Army Group East	01.04.17-11.11.18
Chabord, Rémy	12DI	10.06.18-11.11.18
Chailley, Jules	54DI	02.08.14-27.10.14
Challe, Georges	4DI	07.09.17-11.10.17
Chandezon, Henri	25DI	08.09.14-17.09.14
Chapel, Tell	85DT	02.08.14-09.01.15
Chateau, Louis	105DT	12.12.14-17.04.15
Chatelain, Joseph	73DI	02.08.14-29.08.14
	11DI	29.08.14-27.09.14
	84DT	30.09.14-07.07.15
Chauvet, Paul	131DI	18.04.18-11.11.18
Cherrier, Joseph	152DI	24.05.15-14.10.15
	61DI	23.12.15-11.06.16
Chomor, Nicolas	Supreme War Council	1911-1914
Chretien, Adrien	3DI	03.02.15-22.01.16
	XXXCA	19.01.16-10.06.18
Claret de la Touche, Georges	58DI	31.08.14-22.09.14
	41DI	22.09.14-17.09.16
	XX CA	17.09.16-19.02.17
Claudel, Henri	59DI	20.05.17-10.06.18
	XVIICA	10.06.18-24.10.18
	II CAC	27.10.18-11.11.18
Codet, Alexandre	DM	21.06.15-03.08.16
Colin, Paul	64DI	28.0.516-11.11.18
Collas, Francois	7DI	05.10.14-15.05.15
	15DI	15.06.15-09.03.17
Colle, Francois	30DI	02.08.14-31.10.14
Comby, Louis	37DI	02.08.14-09.01.15
	85DT	09.01.15-14.06.15
Compagnon, Jules	64DI	07.09.14-28.05.16
Conneau, Louis	10DC	02.08.14-13.09.14
	I CC	30.09.14-02.03.17
Contades-Gizeux, Erasme de	10DC	13.09.14-01.06.16
	XXXIVCA	09.05.15-18.05.15
	100DT	06.10.16-05.01.17

Coquet, Hyacinthe	52DI	02.08.14-02.09.14
Cordonnier, Emilien	3DI	02.09.14-19.09.14
	3DI	20.10.14-03.02.15
	57DI XXXIVCA	03.02.15-08.05.15
	VIIICA	03.02.15-09.05.15
	AFO/Macedonia	08.05.15-03.08.16
		11.08.16-19.10.16
Corn, Alfred de	129DI	30.06.17-11.11.18
Cornille, Alfred	35DI	07.05.15-06.11.16
Cornullier-Lucierne, Gustave	89DT	24.04.15-01.07.15
	4DC	01.07.15-12.11.17
Corvisart, Charles	123DI	14.06.15-30.04.17
	XVICA	30.04.17-26.08.18
Cot, Jean	124DI	28.10.18-11.11.18
Coutanceau, Michel	????	????
	XXX CA	12.08.15-19.01.16
Crepey, Etienne	14DI	16.01.15-31.08.16
Cugnac, Gaspard de	77DI	24.01.16-17.12.16
Cure, Louis	14DI	02.08.14-12.08.14
	88DI	12.08.14-16.11.14
	39DI	16.11.14-13.03.15
	IXCA	13.03.15-14.05.16
Dantant, Georges	39DI	02.08.14-16.11.14
	100DT	13.02.15-26.06.15
	124DI	14.06.15-08.12.16
Darteint, Théodore de	56DI	16.09.14-28.01.16
Daugan, Albert	DM	01.09.17-11.11.18
Dauvin, Sainte-Foye	21DI	25.10.14-27.08.18
Daydrein, Guillaume	32DI	28.02.17-11.11.18
Debeney, Marie-Eugene	57DI	08.05.15-18.06.15
	25DI	18.06.15-04.04.16
	XXXVIIICA	04.04.16-19.09.16
	XXXIICA	19.09.16-19.12.16
	7 Army	19.12.16-04.05.17
	CGS	02.05.17-21.12.17
	1 Army	21.12.17-11.11.18
Deffontaines, Achille	24DI	22.08.14-26.08.14
Degoutte, Marie-Joseph	DM	03.08.16-01.09.17
	XXI	01.09.17-10.06.18
	6 Army	10.06.18-11.11.18
Deshayes de Bonneval, Léon	37DI	09.01.15-22.02.16
Delarue, Gabriel	48DI	08.02.15-21.03.15
Delbousquet, Francois	20DI	10.09.15-19.01.16
Delétoille, Gaston	25DI	02.08.14-08.09.14
	XXXICA	08.09.14-02.01.17
Deligny, Henri	2DI	02.08.14-08.09.14
	ICA	04.09.15-25.02.15
	153DI	29.03.15-26.03.16
	XXXIXCA	26.03.16-11.11.18
Delmotte, Nicolas	33DI	02.06.15-17.01.16
Demange, Georges	COS/2 Army	02.08.14-??????
	25DI	17.09.14-18.05.15
	57DI	18.06.15-12.08.15
	XXXIVCA	18.05.15-
	XIIICA	06.10.16????
		06.10.16-19.03.17
Demetz, Georges	56DI	29.06.17-11.11.18
Dennery, Justin	88DT	02.08.14-12.09.14
Deprez, Césare	ACGS	02.08.14-30.08.14

	61DI	31.08.14-22.02.15
	5GDR	22.02.15-10.06.15
	XXXVIICA	10.06.15-05.11.15
	DAL	05.11.15-31.12.16
Descoings, Henri	24DI	26.08.14-05.01.15
	XIICA	05.01.15-12.05.16
Desforges, Gilbert	X CA	02.08.14-10.11.14
Dessort, Antoine	59DI	11.03.16-27.02.16
	16DIC	30.07.16-11.11.18
Desvaux, Francois	7DI	25.09.14-05.10.14
	33DI	09.12.14-14.01.15
Devoyes, Auguste	24DI	13.06.18-15.06.18
	125DI	22.06.18-24.06.18
	20DI	24.06.18-11.11.18
Deville, Louis	42DI	09.03.15-26.08.18
	XVI CA	26.08.18-11.11.18
Diebold, Jospeh	125DI	06.10.16-22.06.18
	20DI	22.06.18-24.06.18
	125DI	24.06.18-08.08.18
Dillemann, Phillipe	18DI	19.10.16-22.08.17
	47DI	22.08.17-11.11.18
Drude, Antoine	45DI	02.08.14-26.12.14
Dubail, Auguste	1 Army	02.08.14-05.01.15
	Army Group East	05.01.15-31.03.16
	Military Governor of Paris	06.04.16-14.06.18
Dubois, Pierre	IXCA	02.08.14-13.03.15
	6 Army	13.03.15-22.02.16
	RFV	26.02.16-00.00.17
Duchêne, Denis	42DI	07.11.14-09.03.15
	XXXIICA	09.03.15-03.08.15
	IICA	10.08.15-29.12.16
	10 Army	27.12.16-11.12.17
	Italy	10-12.17
	6 Army	11.12.17-10.06.18
Dufieux, Jullien	38DI	16.10.18-11.11.18
Dumas, Jean-Baptiste	17DI	02.08.14-06.09.14
	XVIICA	???
Duport, Pierre	131DI	21.08.14-20.05.17
	XIVCA	11.09.15-02.09.16
	131DI	31.08.16-02.09.16
	VICA	09.01.18-18.04.18
Durand, Leon	2GDR	02.08.14-21.09.14
Durand, Paul	3GDR	02.08.14-21.08.14
	A de L	17.08.14-21.08.14
Ebener, Charles	6GDR	27.08.14-15.12.14
	XXXV CA	15.12.14-29.04.16
Ecochard, Joseph	63DI	03.07.17-28.08.18
	51DI	28.08.18-11.11.18
Éon, Auguste	33DI	17.01.16-18.02.18
Éspee, Jean-Francois de l'	9DC & ProvCC	02.08.14-01.06.16
Espinasse, Louis	XVCA	02.08.14-31.10.14
Exelmanns, Charles	35DI	02.08.14-04.09.14
Eydoux, Joseph	XICA	02.08.14-10.02.15
Faës, Alexandre	14DI	17.11.14-16.01.15
Farret, Léon	11DIC	15.06.18-11.11.18
Fayolle, Marie-Emile	70DI	13.08.14-21.06.15
	XXXIIICA	21.06.15-26.02.16
	6 Army	26.02.16-19.12.16
	4 Army	19.12.16-31.12.16

	1 Army	31.12.16-06.05.17
	Army Group Centre	04.05.17-00.11.17
	Italy	00.11.17-00.02.18
	Army Group Reserve	23.02.18-11.11.18
Féraud, Eugene	7DC	21.04.16-02.03.17
	I CC	02.03.17-11.11.18
Ferradini, Louis	72DI	03.03.16-11.11.18
Ferron, Henri de	84DT	02.08.14-30.09.14
Ferry, Edmond	11DI	27.09.14-11.04.16
Foch, Ferdinand	XXCA	02.08.14-29.08.14
	Det Foch/9 Army	29.08.14-04.10.14
	Army Group North	04.10.14-27.12.16
	Army Group East	21.01.17-31.03.17
	CGS	00.05.17-00.10.17
	Italy	00.10.17-00.10.17
	Allied War Council	00.11.17-00.03.18
	Allied CinC	00.30.18-11.11.18
Franchet d'Esperey, Louis	ICA	02.08.14-04.09.14
	5 Army Army	04.09.14-31.03.16
	Group East Army	31.03.16-27.12.16
	Group North	27.12.16-10.06.18
	CAOA/Salonika	18.06.18-11.11.18
	Turkey	00.11.18-00.11.20
François, Maurice	62DI	10.02.15-04.08.17
Gadel, Henri	10DIC	26.09.15-22.12.15
	3DIC	19.11.15-02.07.16
	9DI	08.11.16-07.05.17
Gallet, Alexandre	1DI	02.08.14-03.10.14
	89DT	16.11.14-21.11.14
	88DT	28.02.17-20.12.17
	83DT	20.12.17-11.11.18
Gallieni, Joseph	Supreme War Council	1909-1914
	Military Governor of Paris	26.08.14-05.11.15
	War Minister	00.11.15-00.03.16 [died]
Galon, Henri	70DI	26.02.16-28.11.16
Galopin, Alfred	83DI	23.09.14-20.12.17
Gamelin, Maurice	168DI	11.12.16-19.12.16
	9 DI	07.05.17-11.11.18
Ganeval, Francois	62 DI	02.08.14-21.09.14
Ganter, Jules	71DI	07.06.17-28.10.18
Garbit, Louis	129DI	31.12.15-30.06.17
Garreau de la Mechenie, Charles de	24DI	02.08.14-22.08.14
Garnier-Duplessix, Noel	2DI	08.09.14-21.09.14
	37DI	29.10.16-06.06.18
	IX CA	06.06.18-11.11.18
Gassouin, Joseph	17DI	09.01.18-11.11.18
Gaucher, Léon	164DI	11.11.16-11.11.18
Gendron, Jean	8DC	27.08.14-04.09.14
Genin, Léon	57DI	05.03.18-11.11.18
Gérard, Augustin	IICA	02.08.14-24.07.15
	DAL	24.07.15-05.11.15
	1 Army	31.03.16-31.12.16
	8 Army	31.12.16-11.11.18
Gerome, Auguste	17DIC	29.02.16-23.03.17
	122DI	23.05.17-02.11.17
Gillain, Edmond	7DC	02.08.14-25.08.14
	155DI	29.03.15-28.04.15
	157DI	28.04.15-15.09.15
Girard, Nicolas	62DI	29.03.18-11.11.18

Giraud, Emile	21DI	27.08.18-13.11.18
Girondon, Pierre	12DI	23.05.16-23.09.16
Goubeau, Fernand	153DI	01.05.17-11.11.18
Goullet, Georges	3DIC	12.09.14-19.11.15
Gouraud, Henry	10DI	17.09.14-23.01.15
	I CAC	22.01.15-29.04.15
	CEO	15.05.15-01.07.15
	4 Army	11.12.15-19.12.16
	1 Army	01.06.17-15.06.17
	4 Army	15.06.17-11.11.18
Goureau, Felix	4DI	09.07.18-11.11.18
Goybert, Mariano	157DI	30.05.18-11.11.18
Gramat, Antoine	12DI	24.07.15-23.05.16
Gratier, Jules	46DI	04.03.16-11.05.17
	25DI	10.05.17-24.08.18
	46DI	24.08.18-11.11.18
Graziani, Jean	28DI	03.04.17-12.12.17
	XVIICA	12.12.17-29.03.18
	XIICA	29.03.18-11.11.18
Gregoire, Léon	1DI	06.10.16-11.11.18
Grossetti, Paul	COS/3 Army	02.08.14-30.08.14
	42DI XVI CA	30.08.14-07.11.14
	AFO/Macedonia	07.11.14-13.01.17
		01.02.17-30.09.17
Groth, Charles	83DT	02.08.14-23.09.14
Guerin, Etienne	15DIC	21.11.15-11.11.18
Guerrier, Arthur	66DI	06.10.14-29.01.15
Guignabaudet, Pierre	17DI	06.09.14-01.07.15
	2DI	16.07.15-17.06.17
	41DI	17.06.17-31.05.18
Guillaumat, Marie-Louis	33DI	02.08.14-09.12.14
	4DI	09.12.14-26.02.15
	I CA	26.02.15-17.12.16
	2 Army	15.12.16-11.12.17
	Salonika	22.12.17-18.06.18
	Military Governor of Paris & Supreme War Council	14.06.18-03.10.18
	5 Army	07.10.18-11.11.18
Guillemin, Amédée	121DI	14.06.15-18.06.16
	131DI	02.09.16-28.01.17
	53DI	05.04.17-11.11.18
Guillemot, Marius	77DI	17.12.16-09.01.18
Guyot d'Asnieres de Salins, Arthur	29DI	28.01.16-22.04.16
	38DI	22.04.16-16.10.18
Hache, Emile	40DI	02.08.14-25.08.14
	III CA	25.08.14-23.12.15
Hallier, Eugene	168DI	09.01.18-24.08.18
Hallouin, Louis	26DI	30.09.14-07.07.15
	V CA	07.07.15-15.10.16
Hellot, Frederic	56DI	28.01.16-29.06.17
	????	29.06.17-27.10.18
	XVII CA	27.10.18-11.11.18
Hély d'Oissel, Alexis	COS/5Army	02.08.14-28.09.14
	7DC	28.09.14-14.01.15
	38DI	14.01.15-21.05.15
	XXXVI CA	22.05.15-03.08.16
	VIII CA	03.08.16-11.11.18
Hennocque, Edmond	20DI	19.01.16-17.01.18
	2DCP	06.01.18-11.11.18

Henrys, Paul	59DI	27.07.16-20.05.17
	XVII CA	20.05.17-20.12.17
	AFO/Macedonia	31.12.17-11.11.18
Herr, Frederic	12DI	17.09.14-15.11.14
	VI CA	15.11.14-24.07.15
	II CA	24.07.14-10.08.15
	RFV	10.08.15-00.02.16
	XVI CA	13.01.17-30.04.17
Heymann, Jules	72DI	02.08.14-31.10.14
	XV CA	31.10.14-02.04.16
Hirschauer, Auguste-Edouard	63DI	30.12.15-20.06.16
	XVIII CA	20.06.16-22.08.17
	IX CA	22.08.17-17.12.17
	2 Army	11.12.17-11.11.18
Hollender, Charles	64DI	02.08.14-07.09.14
Huguenot, Eugene	132DI	28.03.17-07.09.18
Huguet, Charles	97DT	10.03.16-12.06.16
Humbert, Georges	DM	18.08.14-08.10.14
	XXXIICA	25.09.14-09.03.15
	DAL	00.03.15-00.07.15
	3 Army	22.07.15-11.11.18
	7 Army [temp]	temp 15-23.10.18
Jacquemot, Charles	57DI	16.01.17-14.12.17
	60DI	24.02.18-11.11.18
Jacquot, Charles	6DI	05.11.14-30.04.16
	XXXV CA	24.04.16-11.11.18
Joba, Joseph	48DI	15.09.16-23.07.17
	25DI	24.08.18-11.11.18
Joffre, Joseph	Commander in Chief	02.08.14-17.12.16
	War Council	00.01.17-00.03.18
Joppé, Maurice	60DI	02.08.14-25.09.14
	2GDR	21.09.14-00.03.15
	152DI	29.03.15-24.05.15
	87DT	24.05.15-05.04.17
Jouannic, Théophile	36DI	02.08.14-19.09.14
	81DT	06.10.14-08.12.14
Journée, Felix	53DI	07.09.14-18.10.14
Jullien, Georges	63DI	17.11.14-30.12.15
Kaufmant, Joseph	71DI	02.08.14-13.03.15
	68DI	13.03.15-25.04.15
Kopp, Jean	59DI	20.08.14-22.12.14
Lacapelle, Gustave	66DI	12.05.16-19.04.17
	I CA	19.04.17-11.11.18
Lacombe de la Tour, Alphonse	5DC	06.01.18-18.09.18
Lacroisade, Paul	91DT	02.08.14-08.01.15
Laffon de Ladebat, Etienne	War Council-Rear Services	02.08.14-30.11.14
Laguiche, Pierre	161DI	31.03.17-11.12.17
Laignelot, Joseph	40DI	16.09.17-11.11.18
Lallemand de Marais, Valther	5DC	10.09.14-28.09.14
Lancrenon, Paul	17DI	29.08.15-09.01.18
Langle de Cary, Fernand de	4 Army	02.08.14-11.12.15
	Army Group Centre	12.12.15-02.05.16
Lanquetot, Pierre	43DI	02.08.14-06.02.15
	151DI	01.04.15-20.05.17
Lanrezac, Charles	5 Army	02.08.14-03.09.14
	Inspector of Military Schools	00.10.14-00.00.17
	Inspector-General	00.00.17-00.04.17
Laporte d'Hulst, Henri de	55DI	16.01.15-14.08.16
Lardemelle, Charles de	122DI	14.06.15-20.12.15

	74DI	29,02,16-11.11.18
Laroque, Jean	59DI	08.09.15-11.03.16
Lartigue, Raoul de	8DI	02.08.14-06.10.14
	99DT	03.12.15-13.08.16
Lasserre, Jean-Baptiste	101DT	19.05.15-19.05.16
Lasson, Antide	2DC	08.02.18-11.11.18
Lastours, Aymard Dor de	3DC	02.08.14-05.04.16
Lavigne-Delville, Paul	4DC	12.11.17-11.11.18
Leblois, Paul	2DIC	02.08.14-23.01.15
	57DI	23.10.15-16.01.17
	AFO/Macedonia	19.10.16-01.02.17
Leblond, Charles	23DI	02.08.14-22.08.14
	3DIC	27.08.14-12.09.14
	86DT	01.10.14-27.05.15
Lebocq, Henri	73DI	09.09.14-11.11.18
Lebouc, Georges	53DI	25.03.16-15.01.17
	161DI	11.12.17-27.06.18
Lebrun, Léonce	4DI	03.08.15-21.04.16
	III CA	21.04.16-11.11.18
Leconte, Gaston	40DI	25.08.14-19.12.16
	XXXIII CA	17.12.16-11.11.18
Lefevre, Jules	I CAC	02.08.14-22.01.15
Lefevre. Justinien	18DI	02.08.14-19.10.16
Le Gallais, Alexandre	16DI	09.08.16-11.11.18
Legrand, Edmond	XXI CA	02.08.14-12.09.14
	27DI	03.11.15-08.06.16
Le Gros, Henri	69DI	02.08.14-08.09.14
	65DI	19.09.14-08.02.15
	105DT	17.04.15-12.08.15
Leguay, Louis	55DI	02.08.14-05.11.14
Lejaille, Claude	97DT	12.06.16-02.01.18
Léorat, Henri	7DC	14.01.15-21.04.16
Leré, Pierre	92DT	01.09.14-12.02.15
Leroux, Charles	58DI	26.02.16-13.06.16
Lescot, Antide	2DC	02.08.14-13.08.14
Lestoqui, Charles	36DI	19.08.15-10.08.16
Levillain, Georges	6DC	02.08.14-27.08.14
Lévi, Camille	25DI	04.04.16-11.05.17
	46DI	11.05.17-24.08.18
Linder, Henri	4DI	21.04.16-23.03.17
	XIII CA	24.03.17-11.11.18
Lobit, Paul de	34DI	11.04.15-14.12.17
Lombard, Léon	63DI	02.08.14-17.11.14
	43DI	06.02.15-03.12.15
Loyzeau de Grandmaison, Francois	53DI	18.10.14-23.01.15
	5GDR	23.01.15-22.02.15
Lyautey, Herbert	Morocco	1912-1916
	War Minister	00.12.16-00.03.17
Madelin, Jean	28DI	12.12.17-11.11.18
Magnan, Georges	153DI	26.03.16-19.12.16
	168DI	19.12.16-09.01.18
Maistre, Paul	COS/4 Army	02.08.14-12.09.14
	XXI CA	12.09.14-01.05.17
	6 Army	04.05.17-11.12.17
	10 Army	11.12.17-10.06.18
	Army Group North	10.06.18-11.11.18
Mangin, Charles	5DI	31.08.14-04.06.16
	XI CA	04.06.16-19.12.16
	6 Army	19.12.16-04.05.17

	IX CA	17.10.17-06.06.18
	10 Army	10.06.18-11.11.18
Mangin, Joseph	55DI	14.08.16-28.08.18
	125DI	28.08.18-11.11.18
Manoury, Michel	A de L	21.08.14-26.08.14
	6 Army	26.08.14-13.03.15
	Military Governor of Paris	05.11.15-06.04.16
Marabail, Henri	67DI	02.08.14-10.08.15
Marchand, Jean-Baptiste	10DIC	14.06.15-26.09.15
	10DIC	22.12.15-11.11.18
Marcot, Lucien	81DT	02.08.14-06.10.14
Mareschal, Henri	163DI	13.06.17-16.06.17
	35DI	16.06.17-11.11.18
Margot, Eugene	62DI	14.08.17-29.03.18
Marjoullet, Albert	35DI	04.09.14-03.10.14
	XVIIICA	30.09.14-20.06.16
	XIV CA	02.09.16-11.11.18
Martin, Emile	9 DI	12.08.14-23.01.15
Martin, Pierre	31DI	02.10.17-11.11.18
Martin de Bouillon, Albert	13DI	05.06.15-22.09.18
Martin de la Porte d'Hulst, Charles	73DI	29.08.14-09.09.14
Mas-Latre, Jacques de	XVIIICA	02.08.14-04.09.14
Masnou, Joseph	23DI	27.08.14-10.01.15
	17DIC	16.03.15-06.08.15
Masseliere, Julien Charley de la	59DI	02.08.14-20.08.14
Massenet, André	39DI	25.10.16-02.06.18
	VIICA	04.06.18-11.11.18
Mathieu, Paul	126DI	19.12.16-11.11.18
Matuzynski, ???	105DT	14.10.14-12.12.14
Maud'Huy, Louis de	16DI	02.08.14-08.09.14
	XVIICA	04.09.14-30.09.14
	10 Army	03.10.14-02.04.15
	7 Army	02.04.15-03.11.15
	XV CA	02.04.16-25.01.17
	XI CA	25.01.17-03.06.18
	Governor Metz	00.11.18-
Mayniel, Raymond	86DT	02.08.14-01.10.14
Mazel, Olivier	8DC	16.08.14-27.08.14
	66DI	27.08.14-06.10.14
	1DC	28.09.14-10.02.15
	XXXVIIICA	10.02.15-25.03.16
	1 Army	25.03.16-31.03.16
	5 Army	31.03.16-22.05.17
Mazillier, Emile	2DIC	23.01.15-19.02.17
	XX CA	19.02.17-19.07.17
	I CAC	19.07.17-11.11.18
Menissier, Alphonse	20DI	22.08.14-05.09.14
Menvielle, Jean-Louis	68DI	02.03.17-11.11.18
Meric, Antoine	24DI	09.01.15-17.01.16
Mesple, Hemri	53DI	18.01.17-05.04.17
	6DC	05.04.17-11.11.18
Messimy, Adolphe	162DI	09.09.17-11.11.18
Michaud, Roger	45DI	04.06.18-11.11.18
Michel, Camille	43DI	23.07.17-11.11.18
Michel, Victor	War Council	1908-1914
	Paris	02.08.16-28.08.16
Micheler, Frederic	56D	02.08.14-16.08.14
	I V CA	23.08.14-07.07.15
Micheler, Joseph	53DI	03.08.15-25.03.16

	XXXVIIICA	25.03.16-04.04.16
	10 Army	04.04.16-27.12.16
	Reserve Army Group	01.01.17-05.05.17
	1 Army	06.05.17-01.06.17
	5 Army	22.05.17-10.06.18
Mignot, Paul	41DI	17.09.16-17.06.17
	2DI	17.06.17-11.11.18
Mitry, Antoine de	6DC	27.08.14-30.09.14
	II CC	30.09.14-17.12.16
	VI CA	17.12.16-17.04.18
	DAN	17.04.18-00.06.18
	9 Army	06.07.18-00.08.18
	7 Army	23.10.18-11.11.18
Mittelhauser, Eugene	36DI	26.04.18-11.11.18
Modelon, Louis *	61DI	19.03.17-15.07.18
	65DI	15.07.18-11.11.18
	or	or
	161DI	27.06.18-11.11.18
	2DM	04.08.18-11.11.18
Moiner, Charles	Military Governor of Paris	03.10.18-11.11.18
Mollandin, René	43DI	16.10.16-23.07.17
Monroë dit Roë, Louis	69DI	28.05.16-11.11.18
Monterou, Alphonse	30DI	01.05.18-22.05.18
Mordacq, Henri	24DI	17.01.16-17.11.17
Mordacq, Lucien	120DI	11.09.16-11.11.18
Mordrelle, Joseph	68DI	27.09.14-13.03.15
	71DI	13.03.15-07.06.17
	2 DIC	10.11.17-11.11.18
Muteau, Paul	38DI	02.08.14-13.09.14
	92DT	12.02.15-16.02.15
	126DI	04.06.15-19.12.16
	XI CA	19.12.16-25.01.17
	I CA	25.01.17-19.04.17
Naulin, Stanislaus	45DI	23.09.16-10.06.18
	XXICA	10.06.18-11.11.18
Nayral Martin de Bourgon, Pierre	3DI	22.01.16-11.11.18
Neraud, Henri	69DI	08.09.14-05.11.14
Nerel, Antoine	30DI	22.05.18-11.11.18
Nicholas, Améde	86DI	27.05.15-14.06.15
	120DI	14.06.15-11.09.16
Niessel, Henri	58DI	22.08.15-26.02.16
	37DI	26.02.16-29.10.16
	IXCA	29.10.16-22.08.17
	XICA	03.06.18-19.07.18
Nivelle, Robert	61DI	22.02.15-23.12.15
	IIICA	23.12.15-21.04.16
	2 Army	01.05.16-15.12.16
	Commander in Chief	17.12.16-17.05.17
Nollet, Charles	129DI	14.06.15-31.12.15
	66DI	31.12.15-12.05.16
	XIICA	12.05.16-25.01.16
	XXXVICA	04.03.17-11.11.18
Nourisson, Pierre	39DI	13.03.15-15.12.16
	XIICA	25.10.16-29.03.18
Nudant, Alphonse	70DI	21.06.15-22.02.16
	XXXIIICA	22.02.16-06.10.16
	XXXIVCA	06.10.16-11.11.18
Odry, Dominique	24DI	15.06.18-11.11.18
Palat, Barthelemy	95DT	21.09.14-04.10.14

	96DT	04.10.14-15.07.15
	104DT	15.07.15-30.04.16
Pambet, Joseph	22DI	02.08.14-30.09.14
Paquette, Gabriel	36DI	10.08.16-22.04.18
Passaga, Fénelon	105DT	28.02.16-03.03.16
	133DI	03.03.16-19.12.16
	XXXIICA	19.12.16-11.11.18
Passard, Flavien	4DI	26.02.15-03.08.15
Patey, Henri	60DI	16.02.16-24.02.18
Pau, Paul	Alsace	10.08.14-00.08.14
Pauffin de Saint Morel, Charles	26DI	07.07.15-27.11.17
Paulinier, Jean	62DI	10.11.14-15.11.14
	12DI	15.11.14-24.07.15
	VICA	24.07.15-17.12.16
	XXXXCA	17.12.16-11.11.18
Peillard, Raoul	28DI	19.03.16-03.04.17
Pelacot, Charles de	52DI	27.09.14-25.10.14
	XXXVIIICA	25.10.14-10.02.15
Pellé, Maurice	CGS	22.03.15-20.12.15
	153DI	11.12.16-01.05.17
	V CA	01.05.17-11.11.18
Penet, Hippolyte	12DI	19.04.17-10.06.18
	XXXCA	10.06.18-11.11.18
Pentel, Horace	65DI	08.02.15-16.05.16
	IXCA	14.05.16-29.10.16
	4DI	23.03.17-07.09.17
Perruchon, Georges	53DI	02.08.14-07.09.14
Peschard d'Ambly, Antoine	77DI	09.01.18-17.04.18
	168DI	24.04.18-11.11.18
Peslin, Pierre	9DI	02.08.14-12.08.14
Pétain, Philippe	6DI	31.08.14-20.10.14
	XXXIIICA	25.10.14-21.06.15
	2 Army	21.06.15-01.05.16
	Army Group Centre	02.05.16-04.05.17
	CGS Commander	04.05.17-17.05.17
	in Chief	17.05.17-11.11.18
Petit, Henri	134DI	19.10.17-11.11.18
Philipot, Edme	14DI	31.08.16-11.06.18
	IICA	11.06.18-11.11.18
Piarron de Mondesir, Jean	16DI	08.09.14-12.10.14
	VIIICA	12.10.14-08.05.15
	52DI	21.05.15-03.12.15
	XXXVICA	03.08.16-17.09.16
	XXXVIIICA	19.09.16-11.11.18
Pichat, Camille	10DI	29.03.18-11.11.18
Pigault, Celestin	127DI	09.07.18-27.09.18
Pillot, Stephaine	26DI	26.08.14-30.09.14
	77DI	14.05.15-24.01.16
Poignon, Camille	6DI	02.05.17-11.11.18
Poline, Arthur	XVIICA	02.08.14-21.08.14
Pont, Ferdinand	6DI	30.04.16-06.12.16
	CGS	12.12.16-01.0.517
	XXICA	01.05.17-01.09.17
	IVCA	19.12.17-11.11.18
Pougin, Armand	39DI	02.06.18-11.11.18
Pouradier-Duteil, Paul	XIVCA	02.08.14-24.08.14
Prax, Léon	68DI	25.04.15-02.03.17
	7DC	02.03.17-00.07.17
	48DI	23.07.17-19.07.18

	XICA	19.07.18-11.11.18
Priou, Jules	158DI	21.03.17-00.11.17
	24DI	19.11.17-13.06.18
	58DI	13.06.18-11.11.18
Pruneau, Ernest	17DIC	29.05.18-11.11.18
Putois, Emmanuel	20DI	17.01.18-16.06.18
Putz, Henri	28DI	02.08.14-07.09.14
	XXXIVCA	07.09.14-00.12.14
	DAB	00.04.15-00.05.15
	IVCA	17.06.15-19.12.17
	CSN	00.07.18-11.11.18
Puypéroux, Richard	3DIC	02.07.16-11.11.18
Quiquandon, Fernand	45DI	02.12.14-23.09.16
Rabier, Charles	4DI	02.08.14-09.12.14
	154DI	29.03.15-04.09.16
Radiquet, René	21DI	02.08.14-25.10.14
	91DT	08.01.15-22.06.15
	100DT	22.06.15-23.12.15
Raffenel, Léon	3DIC	02.08.14-27.08.14
Ragueneau, Camille	4DI	11.10.17-12.10.17
Rampont, Camille	127DI	10.11.18-11.11.18
Rascas de Chateau Redon, Joseph de	1DC	30.09.17-11.11.18
Rauscher, Emile	162DI	23.10.16-09.09.17
Regnault, Charles	3DI	02.08.14-02.09.14
	122DI	20.12.15-23.05.17
	AFO/Macedonia	30.09.17-31.12.17
Remond, Nicolas	4DI	12.10.17-09.07.18
Renaud, Louis	89DT	02.08.14-12.09.14
	132DI	02.10.15-28.03.17
Renouard, Jean	22DI	27.03.18-28.08.18
Requichot, Henri	6DC	06.09.14-03.04.17
Réviellac, Geraud	60DI	25.09.14-16.02.16
Riberpray, Georges	128DI	10.06.15-14.09.17
Riols de Fonclare, Jacques de	1DI	08.03.15-06.10.16
	XXXIIICA	06.10.16-17.10.16
	I CA	17.10.16-25.01.17
	XVCA	25.01.17-11.11.18
Robillot, Felix	1DC	10.20.15-30.09.17
	IICC	30.09.17-11.11.18
Rogerie, Martial	20DI	05.09.14-08.10.14
Riog-Bourdeville, Henri de	5DI	04.06.16-11.11.18
Rondeau, Georges	170DI	26.12.16-06.06.18
Roques, Charles	10DI	26.08.14-17.09.14
Roques, Pierre	XIICA	02.08.14-05.01.16
	1 Army	05.01.16-25.03.16
	War Minister	00.03.16-00.12.16
	4 Army	31.12.16-23.03.17
Rouqueral, Jean-Gabriel	52DI	25.10.14-21.05.15
	38DI	21.05.15-22.04.16
	29DI	22.04.16-17.04.17
Rouqueral, Jean-Joseph	16DI	07.01.15-09.08.16
Rouvier, Claude	51DI	13.05.15-28.01.16
	102DT	28.01.16-30.04.16
	104DT	30.04.16-05.11.16
Roux, Edouard	27DI	08.06.17-11.11.18
Roy, Francois	87DT	02.08.14-24.05.15
Rozée d'Infreville, Sixte	8DI	06.10.14-02.01.17
	XXXICA	02.01.17-25.02.18
Ruault, Joseph	92DT	16.02.15-06.07.15

	131DI	06.07.15-11.09.15
Ruffey, Pierre	3 Army	02.08.14-30.08.14
Sadorge, Laumer	2DIC	19.02.17-22.06.17
Saint-Just, Victor de	123DI	30.04.17-11.11.18
Sarda, Jean	30DI	03.11.17-01.05.18
Sarreil, Maurice	VICA	02.08.14-30.08.14
	3 Army	30.08.15-22.07.15
	CinC Salonika	03.10.15-22.12.17
Sauret, Henri	IIICA	02.08.14-25.08.14
Savatier, Victor	34DI	14.12.17-11.11.18
Savy, Joseph	67DI	08.09.16-04.05.18
Schmidt, Henri	167DI	05.12.16-11.11.18
Schuhler, Louis	48DI	19.07.18-11.11.18
Segonne, Etienne	128DI	14.09.17-11.11.18
Serot Almeras Latour, Augustin	169DI	31.12.16-11.11.18
Serret, Marcel	66DI	29.01.15-31.12.15
Serrigny, Bernard de	77DI	17.04.18-11.11.18
Siben, Ernest	57DI	14.12.17-05.03.18
	76DI	08.03.18-11.11.18
Sicre, Jean	17DIC	01.01.17-02.07.17
	132DI	07.09.18-11.11.18
Silhol, Gustave	26DI	02.08.14-20.08.14
Simon, Henri	37DI	06.06.18-11.11.18
Simon.Louis	5DC	18.09.18-11.11.18
Sorbets, Emile	28DI	07.09.14-19.03.16
Sordet, Jean-Francois	I CC	02.08.14-30.09.14
Souchier, Louis	12DI	02.08.14-17.09.14
Soyer, Albert	44DI	11.08.14-22.08.14
Spire, Joseph	22DI	28.08.18-11.11.18
Stirn, Paul	77DI	11.05.15-14.05.15
Superbie, Paul	41DI	02.08.14-03.09.14
	130DI	06.07.15-19.01.16
Tabouis, Georges	13DI	22.09.18-11.11.18
Tanant, Albert	33DI	30.03.18-11.11.18
Tantot, Emile	70DI	28.11.16-11.11.18
Targe, Antoine	121DI	31.12.16-11.11.18
Tassin, Henri	157DI	15.09.15-23.12.15
	100DT	23.12.15-06.10.16
Tatin, Georges	124DI	08.02.16-28.10.18
Taufflieb, Emile	69DI	29.04.15-28.05.16
	XXXVICA	28.05.16-11.11.18
Taverna, Louis	XVICA	02.08.14-07.11.16
Têtart, Georges	17DIC	23.03.17-01.01.18
	8DI	24.08.18-11.11.18
Topart, Paul	122DI	01.03.18-11.11.18
Toulorge, Paul	130DI	19.01.16-11.11.17
	26DI	27.11.18-08.02.18
	XXXICA	25.02.18-11.11.18
Toutee, Georges	XXXIVCA	28.08.14-07.09.14
Trentinian, Louis de	7DI	02.08.14-25.09.14
	88DT	16.11.14-21.11.14
	89DT	21.11.14-25.04.15
Trouchard, Pierre	19DI	16.09.16-11.11.18
Urbal, Victor d'	7DC	25.08.14-28.09.14
	XXXIIICA	03.10.14-25.10.14
	DAB/8 Army	20.10.14-02.04.15
	10 Army	02.04.15-04.04.16
Valabreque, Mardochée	4GDR	02.08.14-00.09.14
Valdant, Henri	10DI	23.01.15-29.03.18

Valentin, Joseph	133DI	19.12.16-11.11.18
Vallieres, Pierre des	151DI	20.05.17-29.05.18
Vandenberg, Charles	16DI	12.10.14-07.01.15
	61DI	01.06.16-09.03.17
	XIIICA	19.03.17-24.03.17
	X CA	24.03.17-11.11.18
Varin, Jean	2DC	13.08.14-08.02.18
Vassart d'Andernay, Jean de	44DI	24.08.14-08.09.14
	76DI	08.09.14-08.03.18
Vautier, Frederic	VIICA	02.08.14-17.11.14
Venel, Paul	11DIC	02.07.17-04.10.17
	127DI	07.09.18-10.11.18
Verraux, Martial	42DI	02.08.14-30.08.14
	VICA	30.08.14-15.11.14
Verrier, Elie	5DI	02.08.14-31.08.14
Vidal, Jean-Jacques	31DI	02.08.14-15.10.15
Vidalon, Jean	63DI/1DIP	06.08.18-11.11.18
Vigy, Charles	82DI	02.08.14-29.06.15
	105DT	12.08.15-28.02.16
Villeret, Etienne	14DI	12.08.14-17.11.14
	VIICA	17.11.14-02.11.15
	7 Army	03.11.15-19.12.16
Villemejane, Jean-Francois de	33DI	02.08.14-31.08.14
	102DT	19.05.15-28.01.16
Vimard, Charles	75DI	02.08.14-25.09.14
Vincendon, Joseph	59DI	10.06.18-11.11.18
Virvaine, Paul	61DI	02.08.14-31.08.14
Voirhaye, Francois	66DI	02.08.14-27.08.14
Vuillemot, Eugene	11DI	11.04.16-11.11.18
Weygand, Maxime	CGS to Foch	00.04.18-11.11.18
Weywada, Charles	7DI	15.05.15-22.10.17
Wirbel, Henri	62DI	21.09.14-10.11.14
	X CA	10.11.14-10.09.15
	XXXVIICA	05.11.15-25.05

PART EIGHT

FRANCE OVERSEAS: THE GREAT WAR, 1914-18

AN ESSAY BY PETER ABBOTT

Introduction

The period after 1901 saw a massive increase in the overseas troops, not also in terms of their numbers but also in their responsibilities. The underlying reason for this a perception that the demographic tide was running against France. Her birth rate was declining, whereas that of Germany was still high. In an age of mass armies this was critical, for as long as the Germans could put more men into the field, the chances of the French being able to reclaim her lost provinces of Alsace and Lorraine were slight.

Moreover, France's very success in creating her 'third empire' in Africa, Madagascar and Indochina worked against the achievement of this national aim, for although the pacification process had been largely completed by 1901, the new territories still had to be held. This called for white troops as well as coloured ones, for the French were well aware, as were the British in India, of the need to provide a reliable core of white rank and file.

These white troops were long service regulars. Their value as far as colonial expeditions were concerned had been demonstrated during the 1890s in Madagascar, when the Marine troops lost far fewer men from fever than the 'unsalted' Métropolitaine volunteers. However, this and other campaigns demonstrated that la Marine were increasingly likely to be employed side by side with Métropolitaine and Armée d'Afrique units, and it made sense to bring them under the control of the Ministry of War, at the same time recognise their 'colonial' vocation by re-naming them 'Troupes Coloniale'. This step was taken at the start of the century.

The white units (who soon came to be known as '*Coloniale Blanche*') could only provide a nucleus, especially in the unhealthier colonies, and even more so in the light of their continued obligation to garrison the French naval ports and provide an Army Corps for the defence of France's land frontiers. To a limited extent they could be supplemented by *Métropolitaine* troops, as had already happened in China, Indochine, Crete and Morocco. However, the main resource consisted of the *Tirailleurs Coloniaux*. Like their North African counterparts, these had initially been seen as local auxiliaries, designed to combat indigenous armies while being stiffened by white cadres, but this perception was changing.

There was already a long established tradition that the *Armée d'Afrique* should come to the aid of the *Métropolitaine* Army in the event of a European war, along with the *Coloniale Blanche* Army Corps stationed in the homeland. Now the enthusiastic *Coloniale* officers who advocated the creation of a '*Force Noir*' had persuaded French opinion to accept that the *Coloniale Tirailleur*s should do so too. The result was that France was the only combatant to field large numbers of non-white troops in Europe (the British brought some Indians to France in 1914 but they soon deployed most of these elsewhere).

France's North African *Tirailleurs* had already been blooded in the France-Prussian War. They were in action right from the start of the new conflict and served throughout it. France also drew units from West Africa, Equatorial Africa, Djibouti, Madagascar and Indochina, although most of these were used as line of communication troops or pioneers rather than front line soldiers. Those who did serve in that capacity hardly ever did so in units larger than a battalion, and even these were withdrawn from the fronts for the winter. Nevertheless, a few elite battalions such as *43ᵉ Tirailleurs Sénégalais* or *12ᵉ Chasseurs Malgache* showed the potential of the African troops.

France had already taken steps to produce the numbers required by introducing conscription in both North, West and Equatorial Africa before the war actually broke out. The draft was not applied to the new protectorate of Morocco, but that territory produced more than enough volunteers. In practice the percentage of the adult male population conscripted was always far lower than in France itself, partly because of the lower standards of general health, with the result that the *Tirailleurs* retained a substantial volunteer component. Nevertheless, the process aroused much resentment, especially in West Africa.

Indigenous North African and the Colonial troops were mostly infantry. There were a few *Spahi* units, but the artillery were almost all *Métropolitaine* or *Colonial Blanche*, albeit with native drivers or porters. The *Troupes Coloniale* had no Engineers or other service units other than a limited number of white Medical and Veterinary staff. This, of course, was largely a matter of educational standards: one of the results of the increasing sophistication of the war in the trenches was that the *Tirailleur's* white cadres had to be increased to provide the required signallers, mortarmen and clerks.

One of the peculiarities of the French system was that all the North African units were described as '*Algerien*' even though some of them had come to be based in Tunisia (Morocco only became a major source of manpower after 1918). In the same way, all the West and Equatorial African troops were known as '*Sénégalais*', even though by 1914 most of them came from other territories such as Guiné, Soudan, Dahomey or the Congo. There was some justification for this practice inasmuch as Dakar had long been the capital for the region as a whole and Senegalese provided the NCOs (and a few native officers) for all its *Tirailleurs*, but the term was still ambiguous as far as the Equatorial units were concerned. In fact, 'local' titles such as *Régiment du Gabon* were used during the first decade of the century, but this practice again at the start of the Great War.

At the outset of the war in August 1914, France was faced with a German Army which was known to be superior in numbers and which quickly proved to be superior in terms of equipment and training as well. The main threat was to France's own northern-eastern borders, and the greater part of the French Army was accordingly concentrated there.

However, France also faced other threats. Morocco was anything but pacified, and there were fears that its unsubdued tribes might be stirred up by German agents. Italy had not yet subdued the pro-Turkish Senussi in Libya, who were quite capable of creating trouble in the French Sahara. Moreover, Algeria and Tunis had their own internal security needs.

Some of the colonies bordered on German territories. Togo was not a serious threat, but Kamerun (recently enlarged by the transfer of some French territory) was a different proposition. Djibouti was close to Turkish territory, and had to be garrisoned. Fortunately France had no interest in German East Africa, where the conflict was to drag on until the end of the war, although there was a proposal (quickly turned down by the British) that an expeditionary force might be sent from Madagascar. The remainder of the Empire was relatively free from attack, but many territories had their own internal security problems.

In addition, the French had interests to protect in Syria and the Lebanon, especially in the event of a possible Turkish collapse. They could not let the British act against the Turks alone (except in Mesopotamia) and were thus compelled to provide contingents for the Dardanelles and Macedonia, Palestine and Arabia.

All these factors should be kept in mind when following the often complicated story of France's overseas troops during the War.

The Armée d'Afrique, 1914-18

The *Armée d'Afrique* did not fit the *Métropolitaine* organization pattern (its infantry regiments differed in size and it had no artillery of its own). Moreover, many of its units were split between Algeria, Tunisia and Morocco. In August 1914 it was distributed as follows (readers should note that after 1912 the North African *Tirailleurs* were styled *Tirailleurs Indigènes*, so the regimental abbreviation was officially '*RTI*', though I have retained the more familiar '*RTA*' throughout):

Div d'Alger	*1ᵉ Bde Inf (1ᵉRZ, 1ᵉ, 5ᵉ & 9ᵉRTA); 1ᵉ Bde Cav (5ᵉ RCA & 1ᵉ RS); 1ᵉ GACA, bties 6ᵉ GAPA.*
Div d'Oran	*2ᵉ Bde Inf (2ᵉRZ, 2ᵉRTA), 4ᵉBde Inf (1ᵉ & 2ᵉRE, 1ᵉBILA, 6ᵉRTA); 2ᵉ Bde Cav (2ᵉ RCA & 2ᵉ RS); 2ᵉ GACA, btie/6ᵉ GAPA.*
Div de C'tine	*3ᵉ Bde Inf (3ᵉRZ, 3ᵉ & 7ᵉRTA); 3ᵉ Bde Cav (3ᵉ RCA & 3ᵉ RS); 3ᵉ GACA, btie 6ᵉ GAPA.*
Div de Tunis	*1ᵉ Bde Inf (4ᵉRZ, 5ᵉBILA), 2ᵉ Bde Inf (4ᵉBILA, 4ᵉ & 8ᵉRTA); Bde Cav de Tunis (4ᵉ RCA & 4ᵉ RS); 5ᵉ GACA & 7ᵉ GAPA.*

Western Morocco		RdM1eZ (I, II & III/1eRZ), RdM3eZ (II & IV/3eRZ), RdM4eZ (I & VI/4eRZ),2e & 3e BILAs, RdM2eRE (III & VI/2eRE), III/1eRTA, RdM3eRTA (I & IV/3eRTA), RdM4eRTA (III & IV/4eRTA), RdM5eRTA (I & III/5eRTA), RdM7eRTA (I & IV/7eRTA), RdM8eRTA (I, V & VI/8eRTA), II/9eRTA;1eRCA (five *escadrons*), RdMS (gp/1eRS, gp/3eRS, gp/4eRS); 4eGACA, 9eGACA, 10eGACA, plus seven other *batteries*.
Eastern Morocco		II & III/2eRZ, 1eBdMILA, RdM1eRE (I, II & VI/2e RE), III & IV/2e RTA, III/6e RTA,.
Southern Morocco		II/6e RTA.

In addition, there were three battalions of the Légion in Indochine.

There were ten Groupes d'Artillerie de Campagne d'Afrique (GACAs), numbered 1e to 10eGACA. 1e, 2e, 3e, 4e, 5e, 6e and 7e were based in AFN, and 8e, 9e and 10e in Morocco.

1e RCA was in Maroc, 2eRCA in Oran, 3eRCA in Constantine, 4eRCA in Tunis, 5eRCA in Alger, and 6eRCA in Oranie. 1e, 3e & 4e RS supplied a groupe to the Régiment de Marche de Spahis in Western Morocco, while 2e RS supported operations in Eastern Morocco.

Note: There had been some movements of Zouave and Tirailleur battalions between Algeria/Tunisia on the one hand and Morocco as compared with the 1st July 1914 Moroccan OB detailed below. This was due to the normal process of 'roulement' or rotation.

*   *   *

The *Armée d'Afrique* immediately provided two divisions for France by raising *Régiments de Marche* along the previously agreed lines (they were usually made up of two active and one reserve battalion each). These divisions were named the *37e Constantinois* and *38e Algérois*, though they also drew on units from Oranie and Tunisia. Their numbering fitted the pre-war Corps sequence, although the numbers themselves do not seem to have been allocated until 1914. The divisional artillery and service units were provided by the *Métropolitaine* Army, though the North African artillery had been identified as '*d'Afrique*' since 1910. The *Groupes d'Artillerie de Campagne d'Afrique* sent batteries to the French and other fronts.

Since the *Tirailleur* regiments were larger than the *Métropolitaine* ones they were able to field additional battalions. This allowed the formation of the *45e* (Oranie) *Division* (the regular pre-war divisional sequence went up to '*43e*' while the number '*44e*' had already been allocated to a *Métropolitaine* formation on mobilization). The *45e* was composed of duplicate *Oranie* and *Constantinois* units. It arrived shortly after the *37e* and *38e* and like them was badly cut up in the early battles.

A significant number of the *Armée d'Afrique*'s active battalions were serving in Morocco in 1914. This disrupted the planned mobilization pattern. However, some of them were hurriedly formed into ad hoc *Régiments de Marche* which were then assembled into a *Division Marocaine* (*1e* and *2e Brigades du Maroc*) and separate *3e* and *4e Brigades du Maroc*. The *Division Marocaine* was not allocated a number until 1918, when it was split into *1eDM* and *2eDM*. Despite their titles, the '*Maroc*' formations contained no Moroccan troops as such until 1918.

The initial infantry compositions of these formations was as follows:

37e Div:	73e Bde:	RdM2eZ (I, V, 11/2eRZ); RdM2eT (II, V, XI/2eRTA); RdM5e&6eT (II/5e RTA 1, IV/6e RTA).
	74e Bde:	RdM3eZ (I, V, XI/3e RZ); RdM3eT (II, IV, V/3e RTA, III/3e RTA).
38e Div:	75e Bde:	RdM1e Z (IV, V, XI/1e RZ); RdM1e & 9eT (I/1e, II, III/9e RTA).
	76e Bde:	RdM4eZ (III, IV, V, XI/4e RZ); RdM4eT (I, VI/4e RTA); RdM8eT (IV, V/8e RTA).
45e Div:	89e Bde:	RdM1ebisZ later 7eRdMZ (VI, XIV/1e, VI/4e RZ); 3ebisRdMZ (III, VI, 12/3e RZ).
	90e Bde	RdM2ebisZ (IV, XIV & 'E' bn/2eRZ); RdMT (II/1e, VI/2e, II/8e RTA).
Div Maroc	1e Bde	RMC (VI, VII & IX BIC); RdMZ (I/1e, II, III, IV/3e RZ).
	2e Bde	RdMTMOc (V/4e, I/5e, IV/7e RTA); RdMTMOr (1, IV/2eRTA, IV/7e RTA).
Non-divisional	3e Bde Maroc	RdMZ (II & III/1e RZ, I/4e RZ); RdMxZT (II & III/1eZ, I/7e RTA).

4e Bde Maroc	RMxdMICM (4e BIC, 8e & 12eBTS)*; RdMT (II/4e RTA, 1/8e RTA, VI/8e RTA).
For 38e Div:	RdMMxMaroc (II/4e RZ, III/4e RTA, I/9e RTA).

The North African divisions continued to be made up of *Armée d'Afrique* units, but North African regiments were also attached to *Métropolitaine* divisions for varying periods.

The changing designations of the various *Zouave* and *Tirailleur Régiments de Marche* are confusing, but certain stages in the process can be identified. Initially, they were numbered after their parent regiments (eg *Régiment de Marche de 1ᵉ Zouaves*). However, this was not possible in the case of mixed units. Moreover, some of the parent units had also raised '*bis*' or duplicate *Marche* regiments. Consequently an attempt was made to renumber the '*Marche*' regiments consecutively and without reference to their battalions' parent regiments. This process seems to have begun in September 1914 and to have continued through to December, producing a series of titles such as *2ᵉ Régiment de Marche de Zouaves*. However, it still left some anomalies, and although most of these were corrected in 1915 some units (eg *3ᵉ bisRdMZ*) retained their anomalous titles right through the war. A further complication was that some *Zouave* and *Tirailleur* battalions were combined to produce *Régiments Mixtes des Zouaves et Tirailleurs* (RMxZT), usually of one *Zouave* and two *Tirailleur* battalions (though *4ᵉRMxZT* reversed this ratio). A final change occurred late in the war when the growing shortage of French recruits forced the disbandment of some *Métropolitaine* regiments and the creation of some new *Tirailleur Régiments de Marche* to replace them. This shortage also led to the conversion of two *Mixte* regiments to *Tirailleur*-only status (they were promptly renumbered). A detailed account of these developments on a unit-by-unit basis can be found in the Unit Summaries at the end of this section.

Most of the *Zouave* and *Tirailleur regiments de marche* served on the Western Front, but some battalions were used to form the *1ᵉ* and *2ᵉ Régiments de Marche d'Afrique (RdMdA)* which fought at Gallipoli and then Salonika. The *2ᵉbisRdMZ* was also sent to Salonika. The parent regiments served as depot units (they also had subsidiary depots in France) and the *Zouaves* raised a number of supplementary battalions from various sources. A number of territorial *Zouave* battalions were also embodied to provide security in AFN.

The *Légion* benefitted from a flood of hostilities-only volunteers. This allowed each of the pre-war regiments to form *Régiments de Marche*. There were six of these in all, of which *1ᵉRdM1ᵉRE* and *1ᵉRM2ᵉRE* remained in Morocco and the others (*2ᵉ*, *3ᵉ* and *4ᵉRdM1ᵉRE* plus *2ᵉRdM2ᵉRE*) served in France (*4ᵉRdM1ᵉRE* was an 'Garibaldian' Italian unit). The experiment of combining war-only volunteers with hardened pre-war legionaries was not a success, and many of the former demanded transfers back to their own national armies. In November 1915 the two remaining regiments in France were combined into one *Régiment de Marche de Légion Etrangère* (RMLE) which served throughout the rest of the war as part of the *Division Marocaine*, ending up as one of the two most decorated regiments in the French Army (the other being the *Régiment d'Infanterie Coloniale du Maroc*). Once again, the development can be found in the accompanying Unit Summaries.

The first three *BILA* sent *Bataillons de Marche* to France while their parent units remained in garrison in AFN. To begin with these three *BdM* fought separately. In 1915 *1ᵉ* and *3ᵉ BdMILA* were combined as a *Régiment de Marche* in *45ᵉ Division*, and in 1918 they were joined there by the *2ᵉ* as the *Groupe de Bataillons d'Afrique* (GBA).

The *1ᵉ Chasseurs d'Afrique* sent squadrons to France while *2ᵉ* went as a unit. Elements of the two were combined as a *Régiment de Marche* in 1915. In 1914-15 they served as infantry before the squadrons reverted to a cavalry role, being joined by the pre-war *3ᵉ*, *4ᵉ*, *5ᵉ* and *6ᵉ RCA* and newly-formed *7ᵉ* and *8ᵉ RCA*. The *1ᵉ*, *4ᵉ* and *8ᵉ RCA* were moved to Salonika in 1916, and two squadrons went on to the *1ᵉ Régiment Mixte de Cavalerie de Levant* (*1ᵉRMxCL*) for the Palestine campaign.

Elements of all four *Spahi* regiments were sent to France in August 1914 and were used as infantry. A *Régiment de Spahis Auxiliares Algériens* filled the gap in Algeria until it was disbanded in 1917. A new *5ᵉRSA* was formed and elements of this also fought in France. As with the *Chasseurs d'Afrique*, some of the units were later redeployed, *2ᵉ RSA* going back to Morocco and other squadrons being used with the *Chasseurs d'Afrique* to form *1ᵉRMxCL*.

* * *

The indigenous infantry companies belonging to the Moroccan *Troupes Auxiliares Marocains* had been combined into five battalions (*I* and *II* Central, *III* Meknès, *IV* South, *V* Khenifra) of *Chasseurs Indigènes* before the war began. These were then formed into a *Brigade* of two *Régiments de Marche* (*1ᵉ RdMCI* had III, IV & V Bns, *2ᵉ RdMCI* I & II Bns). This formation went to France in 1914. The title '*indigènes*' had been adopted because Morocco was technically neutral. However, it was quickly dropped.

In December 1914 the Brigade became the *Régiment de Marche de Tirailleurs Marocains* (RdMTM) and remained in France until 1918. In 1918 it was split into *1e* and *2e RdMTM*.

The *Spahi* squadrons were sent to France as the *1e Régiment de Marche de Spahis Marocains*. Used as infantry at first, it was re-horsed and sent to Salonika in early 1917, where it served with the *Armée d'Orient* and subsequently the occupation forces in Hungary, then Turkey and finally the Levant.

The status of the Moroccan troops as auxiliaries handicapped them in terms of pay and pension entitlement, and there was a move in 1915 to recognize them as regulars on the same basis as the other North African troops. However, this was not approved until 1923.

*   *   *

The Moroccan *Goums Mixtes* were expanded during the war. There were sixteen when it began, numbered from *1e* to *16e*. Two more (*17e* and *18e*) were raised in 1915, three (*19e*, *20e* and *21e*) in 1917, and two (*22e* and *23e*) in 1918. They remained in Morocco.

The Troupes Coloniales 1914-18

In 1914 the *Troupes Coloniales* formed a wholly French *Corps d'Armée* in France, together with a number of mixed garrisons overseas. The Order of Battle was as follows:

France		
1e DIC	*2e Bde* (Lyon)	*5e & 6e RIC*
	5e Bde (Paris)	*21e & 23e RIC*
2e DIC	*4e Bde* (Toulon)	*4e & 8e RIC*
	6e Bde (Marseilles)	*22e & 24e RIC*
3e DIC	*1e Bde* (Brest)	*1e & 2e RIC*
	3e Bde (Rochefort)	*3e & 7e RIC*
	Bde Art Coloniale	*1e* (Lorient), *2e* (Cherbourg & Brest), *3e* (Vincennes, Toulon, Marseilles) *RAC*
Antilles		One company IC and one bty (Martinique) AC, one platoon IC (Guadeloupe), one company IC (Guyane).
Morocco		Six *Régiments de Marche d'Infanterie Coloniale* (1-6e RMxICMaroc) each consisting of one BIC and two BTS, plus one squadron Spahis Sénégalais and two mixed groupes of Artillerie Coloniale (each of three horse and four mountain batteries).
Algeria		1e & 2e BTS de Algérie.
AOF		1e RTS (Saint-Louis), 2e RTS (Kati, Soudan), 3e RTS (Cote d'Ivoire), 4e RTS (Dakar) plus separate 1e BTS (Mauritanie) 2e BTS (Tombouctou) & 3e BTS (Zinder); Depot Spahis Sénégalais; 6e RAC (Dakar). 1e & 2e RTS, the Spahis and a mountain battery formed the Groupe Mobile de Bas-Sénégal.
AEF		RTSdTchad, RTSGabon, BTS 2 du Moyen-Congo & BTS 3 de l'Oubangui-Chari.
Madagas'r		BIC -DS (Diego-Suarez), BIC-E (Tananarive) 1e RTMal, (Tananarive), 2e RTMal, (Tamatave), 3e RTMal (Diego-Suarez), BTSdMadagascar (Majunga); 7e RAC (Tananarive & Diego-Suarez).
Djibouti		Cie de Garde Somalis.
Indochine	1e Bde (Hanoi)	9e RIC, 1e & 4e RTTon plus 4e RAC
	2e Bde (Bac-Ninh)	10e RIC, 2e & 3e RTTon
	3e Bde (Saigon)	11e RIC, 1e TAn plus 5e RAC
Chine		16e RIC

Pacifique   Two companies IC (Noumea), one platoon IC (Tahiti)

Of the active units in France, *1ᵉ DIC* was broken up on mobilization, *2ᵉ* and *3ᵉ DICs* going to form the *Corps d'Armée Coloniale* with *5ᵉ Bde* and *3ᵉ RAC*. *2ᵉ Bde* served with *14ᵉ Corps d'Armée*. In 1915 new *10ᵉ, 11ᵉ, 15ᵉ, 16ᵉ & 17ᵉ DICs* were raised. Of these, the *11ᵉ, 16ᵉ & 17ᵉ DICs* went to Salonika.

The twelve active *RICs* in France were 'doubled' on mobilization, each regiment forming a second from reservists. These duplicate regiments took the number of their active parent plus '30' (lower numbers) or '20' (this yielded *31ᵉ - 38ᵉ* and *41ᵉ - 44ᵉ RIC*). Many of the reservists had previously served in the *Zouaves*. These regiments served in various *Métropolitaine* divisions. The *Régiments de Marche* in Morocco also contributed some of their battalions: these subsequently formed the basis for the famous *Régiment d'Infanterie Coloniale du Maroc* (RICM), one of the two most decorated regiments in the French Army (the other being the *Régiment de Marche de Légion Etrangère*), together with the *52ᵉ - 58ᵉ RIC*. Heavy losses meant that not all the regiments lasted for the whole of the 1914-18 war.

In theory, the *RICs* remained all-white. However, there were also some '*Régiments Mixtes*' (these included the *4ᵉ, 6ᵉ, 7ᵉ* and *8ᵉ RMxIC* formed for service in the Dardanelles in 1915), and most of the others had *Sénégalais* units attached from 1915 onwards, effectively as third or fourth battalions. In 1916-17 the *57ᵉ, 58ᵉ* and the short-lived *59ᵉ RIC* were all-*Sénégalais*.

The regiments were moved around to meet changing circumstances, but for the most part they stayed with the same brigades (*Brigades d'Infanterie Coloniale*). These were as follows:

1ᵉ BdeIC	*1ᵉ & 2ᵉ RICs*. In *3ᵉ DIC* 1914, then *15ᵉ DIC* 1915: remained in France.	
2ᵉ BdeIC	*5ᵉ & 6ᵉ RICs*. Attached to 14th Army Corps 1914, then *15ᵉ DIC* 1915: remained in France.	
3ᵉ BdeIC	*3ᵉ & 7ᵉ RICs*. In *3ᵉ DIC* 1914: remained in France.	
4ᵉ BdeIC	*4ᵉ & 8ᵉ RICs*. In *2ᵉDIC* 1914, then to *16ᵉ DIC* in Salonika 1917.	
5ᵉ BdeIC	*21ᵉ & 23ᵉ RICs*. Initially independent. In France throughout.	
6ᵉ BdeIC	*22ᵉ & 24ᵉ RICs*. In *2ᵉ DIC* 1914. In France throughout.	
7ᵉ BdeIC	*41ᵉ & 43ᵉ RICs*. Replaced *4ᵉBdeIC* in *2ᵉ DIC* 1917. In France throughout.	
19ᵉ BdeIC	*33ᵉ & 52ᵉ RICs*. Formed 1915 for *10ᵉ DIC*. In France throughout.	
20ᵉ BdeIC	*42ᵉ & 53ᵉ RICs*. Formed 1915 for *10ᵉ DIC*. In France throughout.	
21ᵉ BdeIC	*34ᵉ, 35ᵉ & 44ᵉ RICs*. In Salonika with *11ᵉDIC* from 1917.	
22ᵉ BdeIC	*42ᵉRIC, 2ᵉbis RdMZ*. In Salonika with *11ᵉDIC* from 1917.	
30ᵉ BdeIC	*41ᵉ & 43ᵉ RICs*. In *16ᵉ DIC* 1916, but units later transferred to *7ᵉBdeIC* (see above).	
31ᵉ BdeIC	*34ᵉ, 35ᵉ & 36ᵉ RICs* (latter broken up '16). In *16ᵉ DIC* 1916, but units later transferred to *21ᵉBdeIC* (see above).	
32ᵉ BdeIC	*37ᵉ & 38ᵉ RICs*. In *16ᵉ DIC 1916*. Salonika 1917.	
33ᵉ BdeIC	*54ᵉ & 56ᵉ RICs* ex Dardanelles. In Salonika with *17ᵉ DIC* 1917.	
34ᵉ BdeIC	*1ᵉ & 3ᵉ RICs*. In Salonika with *17ᵉ DIC* 1917.	

The *Brigades* were broken up in 1917 when divisions became triangular ones: the final divisional compositions were as follows:

2e DIC	22e, 24e & 43e RICs; 1e RAC.
3e DIC	7e, 21e & 23e RICs; 2e RAC.
10e DIC	33e, 52e & 53e RICs; 41e RAC.
11e DIC	34e, 35e, 42e & 44e RICs; 21e RAC.
15e DIC	2e, 5e & 6e RICs; 22e RAC.
16e DIC	4e, 8e & 37e RICs; 42e RAC
17e DIC	1e, 3e & 54e RICs; 4e RAC.

* * *

The French made considerable use of the *Tirailleurs Sénégalais* from September 1914 onwards. Something like one hundred and fifty battalions had been raised by the end of the war, and many of them were used on the Western Front (the others served in North Africa, the Middle East and Salonika or in the tropical African colonies). The majority of those serving in France were attached to *Coloniale Blanche* infantry regiments. In 1918 this practice was extended to *Métropolitaine* regiments.

After the first winter they were withdrawn to winter quarters in the south of France until spring. Practice regarding attachment varied: in most instances the *Sénégalais* were treated as a fourth battalion, but in some cases the units were merged with the white battalions on a company basis. This became official policy after the *Sénégalais* battalions had failed to perform as well as had been hoped during Nivelle offensive in 1917, but morale suffered as a result and regimental commanders' freedom to experiment was restored in 1918. The number of French cadres was also increased in that year (in part as a response to the need for more specialists).

The raising of the *Tirailleurs Sénégalais* battalions and their overall allocation to theatres is discussed below.

The Overseas Campaigns, 1914-18

The first campaign in sub-Saharan Africa was against the small German colony of Togo, which bordered upon Dahomey and the British colony of the Gold Coast. A joint Franco-British invasion overran the territory in August 1914. The French force consisted of a 100 strong *Compagnie de Réserve Européene*, a 310 strong *Brigade de Gardes de Dahomey*, a 210 strong *Brigade de Réservistes de Dahomey*, a *Brigade de Volontaires du Dahomey* and a section of 80cm guns, plus one Mossi and one Dahoméen *Goum Monté*. Both the *Gardes*, the *Réservistes* and the *Volontaires* were in practice *Tirailleurs*, while the Europeans were *Coloniale Blanche* reservists. The *Brigade de Gardes de Dahomey* was actually a *marche* unit sent from Côte d'Ivoire prior to the war to put down a tribal insurgency. There were also elements of the regular *Bataillon Indigène de Ouagoudugu*, which probably belonged to 2e*RTS*.

* * *

The second sub-Saharan African campaign was against the larger German colony of Kamerun. This was also a Franco-British operation, with a small Belgian contribution. There had been a retitling of the French units in AEF in 1913, and in August 1914 they consisted of the *Régiment du Gabon, BTS 2 du Moyen-Congo, BTS 3 de l'Oubangui-Chari* and the *Régiment de Tirailleurs du Tchad* (the latter three battalions with two companies of *méharistes*, a *spahi* squadron and a section of mountain artillery)[1]. Not all of these troops could be employed against Kamerun, as Tchad in particular remained unpacified.

In September 1914 the French sent a contingent from Sénégal to the Allied Expeditionary Corps. This invaded Kamerun from the sea at Duala and advanced north and east. The French units were a *Coloniale Blanche* company, two newly-formed Senegalese battalions known as *BTS 1* and *BTS 2*, a mountain artillery battery (80mm guns) plus Engineer and Services sections, all from West Africa (these two *BTS* should not be confused with the Central African units mentioned above). The Senegalese battalions were formed into the *Régiment de Marche de Tirailleurs Sénégalais du Cameroun (RdMTSC)* in 1915. The *Coloniale Blanche* company was withdrawn in February 1915 because of sickness. The British Official History observed that the troops from Sénégal (which is is in the savannah belt) had little experience of fighting in thick forest.

Smaller French columns also invaded Kamerun from the north, east and south. The northern column was drawn from *RTS du Tchad* (initially its *12e, 15e* and *17e cies*), the south eastern ones from the *Moyen-Congo* (its *2e, 4e, 5e and 6e cies*) and *Oubangui-Chari's BTS No.3* (its *2e, 4e* and *5e cies* - the *4e* later becoming the *7e* - plus a *Cie Garde*), and the southern one from the *Régiment du Gabon* (its *1e, 2e, 4e* and *5e cies*) as *Colunne Mitzig*. Further units were added as the campaign progressed, including *RTST"s 1e, 2e* and *3e cies*, and *RG's 8e cie*. By February 1915 *Colunne Mitzig* had the *Régiment du Gabon's 2e, 4e, 5e 7e & 8e cies*, while *Colonne Muahadi* had its *1e cie*, later *5e & 7e*, and later still *1e* & *3e cies*. In the North, the original *RTS du Tchad compagnies* had gone into the Reserve, and the *Colonne Brisset* had its *1e, 2e* and *3e cies* instead.

The combined Allied offensive was successful and the conquest was completed in March 1916.

* * *

Turkey's entry into the war meant that Djibouti had to be strengthened, and a *BTS* was accordingly sent there in 1915 to reinforce the existing *Compagnie de Garde Somalis*. The *tirailleurs* intercepted a German attempt to infiltrate Ethiopia via the territory in 1916.

---

[1] The British Official History calls the Gabon Regiment the '1st', the Moyen Congo battalion the '2/2nd', the Oubangui-Shari battalion the '3/3rd' and the Tchad Regiment the '4th' but there seems to be no support for this in the French sources.

A *Bataillon de Tirailleurs Somalis* was recruited in 1916 and sent to France. The men protested when they were assigned to labouring duties (Somalis traditionally disdain such work) and were sent to the front. The unit fought as part of the *RICM*, its companies being split up among the regiment's battalions.

* * *

In 1915 French forces were involved in the Dardanelles expedition. The first contingent (April) consisted of a division-sized *Groupement Français* which took part in the initial landings. The groupement was reinforced in May by a further division and the two became 1er and 2e *Divisions, Corps Français Expéditionnaire*. The composition of these two formations was as follows:

1e Div:	1e Bde:	*175eRI, 1e RMdAf.*
	2e Bde:	*4e & 6eRMxIC, 8eRMCd'A* plus arty (three *groupes*) etc.
2e Div	3e Bde:	*176eRI, 2eRMdAf.*
	4e Bde:	*7e & 8eRMxIC*, arty (three *groupes*) etc.

The *RIs* were newly raised *Métropolitaine* units. *1eRMdAf* had two *Zouave* battalions ('C' Bn *4eRZ* and an un-numbered bn of *3e RZ*) and one *Légion* battalion, *2e RMdAf* three *Zouave* battalions (ex *1e, 2e* and *4eRZ*). No use was made of *Tirailleurs Algériens* initially because of fears that the Moslem *Tirailleurs* might not be willing to fight enthusiastically against the Moslem Turks. The four *RMxICs* were made up of *Blanche* and *TS* battalions, the latter being ex-North African garrison units withdrawn from the Western Front, as follows:

4e RMxIC:	*1eBn* (ex *4eRIC)*, *2eBn* (ex *1eBTSd'Algerie*) *3eBn* (ex *2eBTSd'Algerie*)
6e RMxIC:	*1eBn* (ex *6eRIC)*, *2eBn* (ex *3eBTSdeMaroc*) *3eBn* (ex *4eBTSdeMaroc*)
7e RMxIC:	*1eBn* (ex *7eRIC)*, *2eBn* (ex *8eBTSdeMaroc*) *3eBn* (ex *12eBTSdeMaroc*)
8e RMxIC:	*1eBn* (ex *8eRIC)*, *2eBn* (ex *5eRIC*) *3eBn* (ex *7eBTSdeMaroc*)

In May 1915 the arrival of *Infanterie Coloniale* reinforcements allowed the *Coloniale* battalions to be given a uniform white/black composition. In August the regiments were renumbered, each adding '50' to become the *54e, 56e, 57e* and *58eRIC*.

In August the *Métropolitaine* and *Armée d'Afrique* units were regrouped to form the *156e Division* (*175e & 176eRIs, 1e & 2eRdMd'Af*), which was then withdrawn and sent to Salonika. The *Coloniale* regiments were regrouped as *17e Division d'Infanterie Coloniale*, comprising *2eBde Coloniale* (*54e* and *56eRIC*) and *4eBde Coloniale* (*57e* and *58eRMxIC*), the latter's regiments containing the *Tirailleurs Sénégalais*. During October the white *Coloniale* troops were replaced by 'Creoles' (ie, mulattos and blacks with French citizenship from Réunion, the Antilles and the old communes of West Africa). *17e DIC* was withdrawn to winter on Lemnos.

The French forces in Salonika were spearheaded by the *156e Division*, which arrived early in October 1915. It was followed between then and November by the *57e* and *122e Divisions d'Infanterie*, together with two regiments of *Chasseurs d'Afrique*. In late February 1916 they were joined by a reorganized *17e Division Coloniale*. In August 1916 these formations became the *Armée Française d'Orient*. The *11e Division Coloniale* arrived in December 1916, and the *16e Division Coloniale* in January 1917, followed shortly afterwards by the *Métropolitaine 30e* and *76e Divisions d'Infanterie*. The composition of the *Coloniale* Divisions was as follows (most French divisions became 'triangular' in late 1917 to early 1918):

11e DIC:	21e BdeIC (34e, 35e & 44eRICs) and 2e BdeIC (42eRIC & 2ebisRZ); later 34e, 35e, 42e & 44eRICs. In Apr'18 20, 26, 30 & 39 BTS were attached.
16e DIC:	4e BdeIC (4e & 8eRICs) and 32e BdeIC (37e & 38eRICs); later 4e, 8e & 37eRICs. In Apr'18 56e, 85e, 97e & 98e BTS were attached.
17e DIC:	33e BdeIC (54e & 56eRICs) and 34e BdeIC (1e & 3eRICs); later 1e, 3e & 54eRICs. In Apr'18 89e, 93e, 95e & 96e BTS were attached.

In Apr'18 49e & 99e BTS were attached to the Armée.

The contribution of *la Coloniale* to the Salonika expedition was thus three divisions out of eight. The *Armée d'Afrique* contribution was equivalent to another division.

* * *

The French provided a contingent for the war in Palestine. Initially this *Détachement Française de Palestine (DFP)* was to consist of two battalions of the *115ᵉ Régiment Territorial d'Infanterie* plus one squadron of *1ᵉ RS*, which were to act as 'flag escort' and not become involved in any fighting. However, when the *DFP* arrived in Egypt in April 1917, its composition had been altered to *V/115ᵉRTI, VII/1ᵉRTA, IX/2ᵉRTA* and *esc/1ᵉRS*.

By October 1917 it had been decided to involve the *DFP* in operations, and it had been strengthened by the addition of the *Légion d'Orient (Ld'O)*, a locally raised unit recruited from Armenian refugees and a few Syrians (this unit was formed in Cyprus in 1916 and grew to a strength of three battalions: a fourth battalion was formed in 1918 but did not become operational, while a V (Syrian) Bn later became the nucleus of a separate Syrian *Légion*). In 1917 the DFP consisted of two infantry regiments (a two-battalion *RIdMd'Af* composed of *Tirailleurs Algériens*, and the *Ld'O*), a *1ᵉ Régiment Mixte de Cavalerie du Levant* (*Chasseur d'Afrique* and *Spahi* squadrons) and two batteries of artillery.

In March 1918 the formation became the *Détachement Française de Palestine et Syrie (DFPS)* and participated in the Allied offensive which took Damascus.

*   *   *

In addition to the Palestine contingent, the French also sent a small detachment of troops to aid the Arab Revolt. In 1916 this consisted of eight MG sections, two artillery batteries (one mountain) and an engineer company. The officers and men were drawn from the Arabic-speaking *Armée d'Afrique*.

French North Africa during the War

Algeria and Tunisia remained surprisingly quiet throughout the conflict. There was some unrest due to the increase in conscription and other wartime exactions, but for the most part detachments from the home-based *Zouave* and *Chasseur d'Afrique* regiments and the *Tirailleur Sénégalais* garrison battalions were able to contain this. The only exception was when it proved necessary to bring two *Métropolitaine* regiments across to help deal with one serious revolt in the Batna region of Algeria in late 1916. These were *77ᵉ* and *91ᵉ RIs* (from *125ᵉ Division*). They arrived in December and left again in March 1917.

When the war began there had been forty *Armée d'Afrique Tirailleur* battalions in AFN, of which nineteen were in Morocco. Thirty-two of these battalions were sent to France in autumn 1914. Six remained in Morocco (they were the *III/1ᵉ, III/4ᵉ, IV/4ᵉ, III/5ᵉ, II/6ᵉ* and *III/8ᵉRTA*). Apart from drafts, only two were left in Algeria (the *III/2ᵉ* and *II/7ᵉRTA*).

The active *Zouave* battalions were sent to France and replaced by twelve of *Zouave* territorials. *1ᵉ, 2ᵉ, 3ᵉ, 10ᵉ & 11ᵉ BZs* belonged to *Div 'Alger', 4ᵉ, 5ᵉ, 6ᵉ & 12ᵉ BZs* to *Div 'Oran'*, and *7ᵉ, 8ᵉ & 9ᵉ BZs* to *Div 'Constantine'*. Proposals to send some of these to France in 1915 were opposed by the colonists on the grounds that it would have an adverse effect on agricultural production. However, *2ᵉ* and *10ᵉ BZs* later went to the Dardanelles and Salonika for varying periods.

As noted earlier, the *Zouaves* also raised a number of '*alphabétique*' battalions from reservists, convalescents and individuals from Alsace-Lorraine. The latter were legally German citizens and could not be permitted to risk capture on the Western Front. The practice of using letters to identify battalions may have been adopted in order to avoid having to allocate the number '*13*'. Battalions designated '*L*', '*M*' and '*N*' consisted of men from Alsace-Lorraine. *1ᵉ RZ* raised Bns '*F*', '*K*', '*L*' & '*M*'; *2ᵉ RZ* raised Bn '*E*' and possibly '*K*' and '*L*' as well; *3ᵉ RZ* raised Bns '*F*', '*J*', '*L*', '*M*' & '*N*'; and *4ᵉ RZ* raised Bns '*C*', '*E*', '*F*', '*J*', '*L*' & '*R*'. Most of these units served in AFN, but one ('*M*'/*2ᵉ RZ*) went to Tonkin and three ('*E*'/*2ᵉRZ*, '*C*' & '*E*'/*4ᵉRZ*) to Salonika.

The first three *Infanterie Légère d'Afrique* battalions sent *bataillons de marche* to France in 1914, while their parent units remained in AFN along with the *4ᵉ* and *5ᵉ BILA* (though these units were sometimes described as '*de marche*' as well). '*Bat d'Afrique*' reservists were formed into a varying number of *Groupes Speciaux*, which rank among the most obscure units of the whole French army during this period. They seem to have consisted of one or two infantry companies, a section of mule-mounted mountain artillery (two old 80mm guns) and either a platoon of *Spahis* or *Goumiers*, and were said to be the equivalent of a battalion in strength. A number were employed in Morocco, and others in the south of Algeria and Tunisia.

Certain *Métropolitaine Régiments Territoriaux d'Infanterie* were sent across to bolster the garrisons. They were chosen from those recruited in the south of France in the hope that the men would be able to withstand the climate better. They included the *113e, 114e, 116e, 125e, 126e, 127e, 128e, 132e & 139e RTIs*.

The *Coloniale* contingent in Morocco sent a number of units to France. The first to arrive there in mid September was the *Régiment Mixte de Marche d'Infanterie Coloniale (4e BIC, 8e & 12e BTSM)* which formed part of *4e Bde Marocaine*. This was followed later in the same month by *1e Régiment de Marche d'Infanterie Coloniale (9e BIC, 4e & 7e BTSM)* and *2e Régiment de Marche d'Infanterie Coloniale (6e BIC, 1e BTSA & 3e BTSM)*, which made up a new *Brigade Coloniale* in the depleted *Division Marocaine*. However, further heavy losses meant that these formations were only temporary ones. There was clearly some rotation of the *BICs* because *6e BIC* was back in Morocco in late 1915.

The *Tirailleurs Sénégalais* battalions withdrawn for service in France were replaced by new ones from Senegal. These were numbered *14e* to *25e BTS*. Such battalions continued to move in and out during the war.

The small *Garde Beylical de Tunis* (one battalion, an artillery battery and a cavalry platoon) remained in existence. Its infantry provided security in Tunis and its guns helped to defend the harbour. These units were probably manned by those not fit for more strenuous service, for *Garde* reservists were called up and mustered into the Tunisian *Tirailleur* regiments, and it seems likely that its active members would have been transferred in the same way.

The garrison situation in Algeria and Tunisia in December 1917 was as follows:

Two active *Zouave* battalions (from *1e* and *4e RZ*) in south Tunisia, four other *Zouave* battalions (*alphabétiques* made up of men from Alsace-Lorraine) and the *Zouave* depots; seven battalions of *Zouave* Territorials, five battalions of *Metropolitaine* Territorials (one from *116e RTI* and two each from *125e* and *126e RTIs*, all reduced and numbering some 2,450 in total) all in Tunisia, the depots of *1e* and *2e Régiments Étranger*, *4e* and *5e BdMILA* and two depots, one *BdM Speciale* and five *Groupes Speciaux*, four battalions of *Tirailleurs Algériens* (two from *4e RTA* and one each from *1e* and *8e RTAs*) and nine depots, fifteen battalions of *Tirailleurs Sénégalais* sent over to AFN for the winter, six *Compagnies Sahariens*, two *Escadrons Chasseurs d'Afrique* (earmarked for Palestine), twenty-three *Escadrons de Spahis* and nine artillery batteries.

* * *

The situation in Morocco was particularly delicate in August 1914. The Protectorate was no more than two years old, much of the country remained unsubdued, and the French had every reason to doubt the loyalty of the portions that they occupied.

Many of the French units involved in the initial occupation had been drawn from the *Armée d'Afrique*, drafted in on an ad hoc basis, but 1913 had seen a significant strengthening of the *Coloniale* presence there. These units were then consolidated into six *Régiments Mixtes d'Infanterie Coloniale de Maroc (1e* to *6e RMxICM)*, each made up of one *Blanche* and two *Tirailleur* battalions.

The organization of the *Zouaves* and the *Tirailleurs Algériens* units in Morocco was taken in hand in 1914. By June five *Régiments de Marche* had been formed, with all their battalions drawn from the same regiments. The 1st July 1914 OB (the last available prior to the start of World War I) was as follows:

Métropolitaine: *14e BCP* only.
Armée d'Afrique RdM1eZ (I, II & III/1eRZ), RdM3eZ (II & IV/3eRZ), RdM4eZ (I & II/4eRZ), 4RdM2eRE (III & VI/2eRE), 2e & 3e BILAs, III/1eRTA, RdM3eRTA (I & III/3eRTA), RdM4eRTA (I, II & III/4eRTA), RdM5eRTA (I, II & III/5eRTA), RdM7eRTA (I & IV/7eRTA), RdM8eRTA (I, V & VI/8eRTA); 1eRCA (five *escadrons*), RdMS (gp/1eRS, gp/3eRS, gp/4eRS); 4eGACA, 9eGACA, 10eGACA, plus seven other *batteries*.
Coloniale BdMIC, 5e BTS, 1eRMxICM (1eBIC, 1e & 12e BTS), 2eRMxICM (7eBIC, 9e & 10e BTS), 3eRMxICM (9eBIC, 4e & 13e BTS), 4eRMxICM (8eBIC, 8e & 11e BTS), 5eRMxICM (4eBIC, 2e & 3eBTS), 6eRMxICM (6eBIC, 6e & 7e BTS); Esc Spahis Sénégalais.

A comparison of this OB with earlier ones shows that both the *Zouaves* and the *Tirailleurs* had been consolidated into 'family' *Régiments de Marche*. There were still four isolated battalions (one *BCP*, one *BTA*, one *BIC* and one *BTS*). Despite this apparent rationalization, the battalions were still often split up. In practice, the operational unit was the *Groupe Mobile*. This was made up of three to six infantry battalions, two or three cavalry squadrons and two or three artillery batteries.

In July 1914, with war looming, Paris told Resident General Lyautey that he would be required to send the bulk of his troops to France, and instructed him to withdraw the rest to the coastal towns and the northern corridor via Fès to Algeria. Backed by his Generals, he decided to do the opposite and 'hollow out the carcass and leave the shell' as he put it. What this meant was that he placed his remaining good troops around the periphery of the newly pacified territory, and garrisoned the interior with second line troops. Surprisingly, this policy worked, and although an ill-advised sortie by the French commander in Khenitra led to the French forces there suffering a serious defeat in November 1914, the country as a whole did not rise in revolt.

In summary, the troops Lyautey sent to France consisted of the one remaining battalion of *Chasseurs Alpins*, nine battalion of *Zouaves*, one *BdMILA*, thirteen battalions of *Tirailleurs Algériens*, four battalions of *Infanterie Coloniale*, eleven battalions of *Tirailleurs Sénégalais*, seven battalions of *Tirailleurs Marocains*, eight *escadrons* of *Chasseurs d'Afrique*, four *escadrons* of *Spahis* and eleven artillery batteries.

This left him with six battalions in the Fès region, one at Bou Denib (south of the Atlas) and seven in the corridor between Taza and Oujda, with twelve more facing the dissident massif of which Khenifra was the centre. The interior of the French-occupied zone was left denuded of regular troops, but in due course Lyautey began to receive a number of French Territorial battalions, one replacement *BdMZ* recruited in Morocco, two other *BdMILAs*, some *Groupes Speciaux*, a number of locally recruited Territorial units, and some largely untrained *Sénégalais*.

Various auxiliary units were formed in Morocco to maintain security. They included the *Bataillons de la Chaouia*, the *Bataillon de Réserve de Rabat, Compagnie de Reservistes de Marrakech* and the *Compagnies Mobalisies de Mazagan, Meknes, Mogador and Safi*.

The Order of Battle for September 1915 (repeated unchanged in October and November) shows how the composition of the French forces in Morocco had altered since the start of the war in France:

Métropolitaine	113eRTI (I, II & III bns), 114eRTI (IV, V & VI bns), 121eRTI (I & II2 bns), 125eRTI (II bn only), 127eRTI (I, II & III bns), 128eRTI (I, II & III bns), 139eRTI (I & II bns).
Armée d'Afrique	BdM/4eRZ, 1eRE (I, II & VI bns), 2eRE (III & VI bns), 1e, 2e & 3e BILA, 2eBdMILA, 10e, 11e, 13e, 14e, 16e & 17e Groupes Speciaux, I/1eRTA, V/2eRTA, II/4eRTA, II/5eRTA, IV/6eRTA, III/8eRTA; 1eRCA (three escadrons), 2eRCA (three escadrons), RdMSpahis de Maroc Occidental (groupes ex 1e, 3e & 3eRS), RdM2eRS (111,VI,VII, VIII & IX esc), Gp 5eRS (two escadrons); 4eGACA (three bties), 8eGACA (five bties), 9eGACA (three bties), 11eGACA (four bties) plus Artillerie de Position.
Coloniale	2eRICM (9e BIC, 10e, 11e, 19e & 22e BTS), 3eRICM (13e & 16e BTS only), 5eRICM (6e BIC, 14e, 15e, 18e & 21eBTS), 6eRICM (17e & 18eBTS only), 25eBTS (bn d'instruction); Esc Spahis Sénégalais; 1e & 2eGps Artillerie Coloniale.
Raised locally	Bataillon Territorial de Chauia, Bataillon de Réserve de Rabat, Compagnie Territorial de Rabat, Compagnies de Réserve de Mogador et de Mazagan and Section de Safi.
Troupes Aux.	Garde Noire, 2e & 6e Bns (2e Bn ex France, 6e new); 4e Esc Cav, four sections d'Artillerie, plus eighteen Goums.

The actual structure changed slightly as the months passed. By January 1916, for instance, the single-battalion *Tirailleurs Algériens* units were being listed as 'Régiments de Marche' (RdM2eRTA, RdM4eRTA and RdM5eRTA, with no *6e RTA* or *8e RTA* battalions there at all) and there were sixteen *Groupes Speciaux*.

The country remained generally quiet, but the Germans encouraged yet another pretender to arise to the north of Taza. They also supported the southern pretender el Hiba, who required yet another expedition by the Great Caids' tribal warriors, this time supported by four regular battalions, some cavalry and some mountain guns. This force defeated el Hiba in March 1917, but the nothern operations dragged on until November 1918.

Despite his weakness, Lyauty continued with his pacification operations. May 1917 saw French columns cross the centre of the Atlas mountains near Khenifra, cutting the dissident area into two.

In December 1917 the Morocco garrison (in outline) was as follows:

One BdMZ du Maroc, two other BdMZ (described as 'Loi Mourier'), five Légion battalions, four battalions of ILA and eight Groupes Speciaux, six Tirailleurs Algériens battalions, two battalions of Infanterie Coloniale, thirteen battalions of Tirailleurs Sénégalais, seventeen French Territorial battalions, three battalions of locally recruited French Territorials, four battalions of Tirailleurs Marocains, seventeen escadrons of Spahis Algériens, five escadrons of Spahis Marocains, one escadron of Spahis Sénégalais, fourteen batteries of Metropolitaine (ie Armée d'Afrique) artillery and six of Artillerie Coloniale.

There were some changes in early 1918, when the French were desperate for manpower. I have not been able to track down full orders of battle for this period, but there was an exchange of correspondance in late 1917 in which Paris insisted on sending five *Sénégalais* battalions (the *6ᵉ, 54ᵉ, 67ᵉ, 68ᵉ* and *69ᵉ BTS*) from southern France to replace five 'white' battalions urgently needed in France (the latter were to have been *2ᵉ BdMILA, 6ᵉ & 9ᵉ BICs* and *1ᵉ & 4ᵉ BTMs*, the last two of which had been sent back to Morocco in 1916, pesumably to recover from their losses). Clearly, 'white' simply meant 'non-black' here. If these units were currently involved in operations in the interior, they were to retire to the coast to meet the ships bringing the *Sénégalais*. In fact BdM/*4ᵉRZ* replaced *4ᵉBTM* when the 'white' units were actually sent to France in February 1918.

Lyautey did his best to resist any further reductions, pointing out that although his *Tirailleurs Algériens* were good, his *Légion* battalions were made up of Germans and Austrians due for relief and liable to desert if stationed too near Spanish Morocco, the *BILAs* were mediocre (the best had already been sent to France), the *Tirailleurs Marocains* good material but only recruits, and the *Sénégalais* mediocre troops who could not be used in the colder regions. This shortage of reliable units forced him to extemporize. A *Bataillon Mixte du Maroc* was formed in March 1917 from *Légion* and *BILA* companies, presumably as a mobile reserve unit, and in August 1917 the *Compagnies Mobalisées de Mogador* and *Safi* were expanded into *1ᵉ* and *2ᵉ Bataillons de Marche du Maroc*, using 'comb-outs' (hospital staff, drivers and the like) who were of little value as combatants but who could be split up among the *Sénégalais* units as machine gunners and other specialists.

The French weaknesses necessitated a partial retreat in the Tafilalet region south the the High Atlas. This was accomplished in mid 1918. It encouraged the dissidents, who united behind another pretender. Once again the leader of the Great Caids came to the aid of the French, who succeeded in retaining a foothold. However, the south remained in dissident hands.

* * *

The Saharan tribes remained a source of concern given the weakness of the French garrison, and steps were taken to deal with them by forming a number of *Groupes Spéciaux*. As noted earlier, their infantry were *BILA* reservists, but there were not enough of those so a number of *Ligne* companies had to be brought across from France to provide additional *compagnies de marche*. There seem to have been at least twenty such *Groupes* (*2ᵉ, 3ᵉ, 4ᵉ, 5ᵉ, 8ᵉ, 9ᵉ, 14ᵉ, 15ᵉ, 18ᵉ & 20ᵉ* are known to have existed, together with a *Groupe Spécial des Oasis Sahariennes*), and the *40ᵉ, 45ᵉ, 66ᵉ, 113ᵉ, 117ᵉ, 119ᵉ, 124ᵉ* and *169ᵉ Régiments d'Infanterie* can be shown to have contributed companies to them from late 1914 onwards, even though these regiments continued to be engaged in France.

Two further *Compagnies Sahariennes* were raised, that of *Ouargla* in 1915 and that of *Touggourt* in 1916.

* * *

AFN's Eastern Saharan frontier was another source of concern[2]. Turkey's entry into the war encouraged both the Tripolitanians and the Cyrenaican Senussi to rise against the Italians in Libya, and the latter were forced back to the coastline.

This worried the French, who had nothing more than two Saharien *Groupes Spéciaux* (*4ᵉ* and *5ᵉ*), a platoon of *Spahis*, a section of mountain artillery and a company of *méharistes* available at first. In August 1915 these were reinforced by *5ᵉ BILA*, the three-battalion *126ᵉ RTI (Territorial)*, two squadrons *4ᵉ Spahis*, two squadrons of *Chasseurs d'Afrique*, two batteries and two sections of artillery, and the *9ᵉ, 20ᵉ* & 'Oasis' *Groupes Speciaux*. These became the *Détachement Sud-Tunisien*.

The Senussi then attacked Southern Tunisia in September 1915. Further French reinforcements included two battalions of *125ᵉ RTI (Territorial)*, *1ᵉ RZ's* bns *'K', 'L'* and *'M'* bns, *3ᵉ RZ's 'L'* and *'N'* bns, and *4ᵉ RZ's 'F', 'L' 'M'* and *'R'* bns, *4ᵉ BILA*,

---

[2] The following brief account is based on Jean-Louis Lagarde's magnificent *'Zouaves et Tirailleurs, Vol.2'*.

elements of *1ᵉ* and *4ᵉ RTA, 104ᵉ, 110ᵉ* and *117ᵉ BTS* (the latters' numbers indicate that these only arrived in 1917 or '18), squadrons from *3ᵉ* and *6ᵉ RCA* and *1ᵉ, 3ᵉ, 4ᵉ* and *5ᵉRS*, plus additional artillery, some armoured cars and more *Goumiers*. The Senussi raids continued until October 1918. As can be seen, the covering force amounted initially to about a brigade, but it was later expanded to a force more like a division.

The Senussi offensive encouraged the Toureg and Tebou of Tibesti, and the Central Sahara saw a good deal of unrest. This was contained by the use of local Algerian forces, mainly local *Goums* and *Saharienne* camel companies supported by *RTA* detachments.

The Other Colonies During The War

West Africa was not threatened, but the French authorities there were increasingly called upon to provide troops for the other theatres, and this led to unrest. An extension of conscription in 1915 led to disturbances in Haute Volta, and a further extension in 1916 caused a revolt in Dahomey. This resistance led to the French entrusting their 1918 appeal to a Senegalese Deputy, Blaise Diagne. It was notably successful, though few of the new units actually saw service.

As noted, most of the fourteen *BTS* serving in Algeria and Morocco in mid-1914 were sent to France, being replaced by reserve units. A three-battalion *Régiment de Marche de Tirailleurs Sénégalais de l'Afrique Occidental (RdMTSAO)* drawn from *1ᵉ* and *2ᵉ RTS* was also sent to France in September 1914. This unit was made up of raw recruits and did not perform as well as the veteran Moroccan ones: it was withdrawn to Morocco and disbanded there, the survivors being merged with the *16ᵉ, 17ᵉ* and *18ᵉ BTS*. Also as noted, new *1ᵉ* and *2ᵉ BTS* were sent to join the Kamerun expedition in October 1914.

Most of the *Tirailleur* units were battalions. The only exceptions were the short-lived *RdMTSAO* of September 1914, a new *Régiment de Marche de Tirailleurs Sénégalais du Cameroun (RdMTSC)* formed in October 1915, and the survivors of the seven *Sénégalais* battalions sent to the Dardanelles in 1915. As has been seen, these had been consolidated into the *57ᵉ* and *58ᵉ RMxIC*, which were transformed into the *57ᵉ* and *58ᵉ Régiments d'Infanterie Colonial Sénégalais (RICS)* at the end of the year (their Senegalese battalions were re-numbered, the *57ᵉRICS* having the *66ᵉ, 67ᵉ* and *70ᵉ BTS*, the latter later replaced by the *64ᵉ*, the *58ᵉRICS* the *68ᵉ, 69ᵉ* and *71ᵉ BTS*). These two regiments were transferred to France in early 1916 and fought there before being disbanded in mid 1917. A third (*59ᵉRICS*) existed briefly in 1917.

The other units were all independent battalions. They were numbered consecutively. The sequencing was relatively simple, with only a few unexplained omissions. It was as follows:

- 1914 The pre-existing units in 1914 were the *1ᵉ* and *2ᵉ BTS d'Algerie* and the *1ᵉ* to *4ᵉ* and *8ᵉ* to *13ᵉ BTS du Maroc* (the *5ᵉ* to *7ᵉ* had been disbanded earlier). The reserve battalions sent to Morocco were numbered *14ᵉ* to *25ᵉ BTS*. The three battalions of the *RdMTSAO* notionally accounted for the next three numbers (ie *26ᵉ, 27ᵉ & 28ᵉ*), which remained blank. *1ᵉ* and *2ᵉ BTS du Cameroun* were numbered in a separate sequence.

- 1915 The following *BTS* were formed: *31ᵉ* to *37ᵉ, 39ᵉ* to *43ᵉ, 45ᵉ & 46ᵉ*. Ten battalions fought on the Western Front, plus two loc battalions, and a further eight in the Dardanelles. A battalion was also sent to Djibouti, but it is not clear whether this was one of the numbered ones or not.

- 1916 The gaps in the earlier sequence were filled in during 1916. One way in the force was expanded was by 'tripling' the existing *31ᵉ, 32ᵉ & 34ᵉ BTS* which were still in AOF in January'16. The following *BTS* were formed during the year: *29ᵉ, 30ᵉ, 38ᵉ, 44ᵉ, 47ᵉ* to *56ᵉ, 61ᵉ* to *88ᵉ & 90ᵉ*. Thirty-seven battalions fought in France, together with four loc battalions. The *43ᵉ BTS* distinguished itself in the fighting at Verdun.

- 1917 This year saw the formation of the following *BTS: 89ᵉ & 92ᵉ* to *107ᵉ*. Thirty-five battalions fought in France (these were the *5ᵉ, 6ᵉ, 8ᵉ, 20ᵉ, 27ᵉ, 28ᵉ, 29ᵉ, 30ᵉ, 32ᵉ, 35ᵉ, 39ᵉ, 43ᵉ, 44ᵉ, 45ᵉ, 48ᵉ, 51ᵉ, 52ᵉ, 54ᵉ, 61ᵉ, 64ᵉ* to *71ᵉ, 74ᵉ, 77ᵉ, 80ᵉ, 84ᵉ, 86ᵉ & 88ᵉ*) with six more on loc duties (*58ᵉ, 75ᵉ, 78ᵉ, 81ᵉ, 82ᵉ, 83ᵉ*). A further fourteen (see under 'Salonika' above) served in the Middle East and there were twelve more in Algeria and Tunisia.

- 1918 This year saw a major call on West African manpower. The units formed were *108ᵉ* to *133ᵉ, 135ᵉ* to *137ᵉ, 141ᵉ & 150ᵉ BTS*. In all, some forty-two battalions plus four depot units were sent to France. There were also twenty-three plus three service battalions in Salonika, fourteen in Algeria and Tunisia and thirteen in Morocco.

The garrison regiments remained the *1ᵉ, 2ᵉ, 3ᵉ* and *4ᵉRTS*. These acted as depots for the creation of the *BdMTS*.

*   *   *

The inhabitants of the 'four communes' of Sénégal together with those of Guadeloupe, Martinique, Réunion and Pondichery returned deputies to the French Assembly, but they were not actually citizens and thus not subject to conscription. This exemption was abolished in 1915, though the decree prescribed that they should serve in *Coloniale Blanche* units. Subsequently some 10,000 recruits came from Réunion, 17,000 from the Antilles/Guyane, 500 from St Pierre et Michelon, 1,000 from Océanie, 500 from Pondichéry and 5,400 from the 'four communes' of Sénégal. Some of the Senegalese served in a special *Bataillon d'Afrique Occidental Française*: others together with the Indians and West Indians went to the *RICs* serving in the Dardanelles. A number served in or near their home territories: for example, many Réunionais served in Madagascar.

*   *   *

French Equatorial Africa was concerned with the reduction of the German garrison in Kamerun until mid 1916. Thereafter it furnished an increasing number of men for the *Tirailleurs*, especially in 1918. However, these continued to be known as '*Sénégalais*', and no distinction was drawn in terms of origin as far as the battalion titles were concerned. Between 1914 and 1918, Gabon sent 2,000 men to France, Moyen-Congo 1,500, Oubangui-Chari 3,500 and Tchad 7,000.

The garrison units in AEF remained the *RTSdTchad, RIGabon, BTS 2 du Moyen-Congo* and *BTS 3 de l'Oubangui-Chari*. Presumably these also acted as depot units for the creation of the *BdMTS* sent to Europe.

After Kamerun (now 'Cameroun') was conquered, it was decided that the garrison was to be two *Tirailleur* battalions, one from AOF and the other from AEF. The latter had two companies from Tchad and one each from Oubangui-Chari, Moyen-Congo and Gabon. In July 1916 the two battalions were combined to form a new *RTS du Cameroun*. The eastern parts of the French territories taken over when Kamerun was enlarged in 1911 were garrisoned by *Bataillons Nos.2* and *3*, while the *RIGabon* garrisoned the southern part. In late 1918 a *Compagnie de Marche de Tirailleurs* was formed for service outside the territory, but it is not clear whether there was time for this to leave before the war ended.

The Senussi offensive in the Sahara impinged on Tchad, and there were disturbances in Borku and Ennedi. These involved the *RTSdTchad's 7ᵉ* and *8ᵉ Méhariste Compagnies*, and then its *1ᵉ Bataillon*, which was based in the north of the territory. Four new *Compagnies* (*15ᵉ, 16ᵉ, 17ᵉ & 18ᵉ*) had to be raised to reinforce the north.

*   *   *

In 1914 the garrison in Madagascar consisted of two *BICs* (*Bataillon de Diego-Suarez* and *Bataillon de l'Emyrne*, the latter being the plateau region around Tanaraive), one *BTS* (at Majunga), three *RTM* and *7ᵉRAC* of six batteries. *1ᵉRTM* was stationed at Tananarive, *2ᵉRTM* at Tamatave and *3ᵉRTM* at Antsirane.

Paris asked that a *Corps Mobile* of four battalions and two batteries be prepared for use elsewhere. The local authorities said this was not possible, but proposed two Malagasay *Bataillons de Marche* instead. Paris declined the offer but asked for their white cadres. Before these could be despatched, it changed its mind and asked that three battalions (one of *IC*, one of *TS* and one of *TM*) plus two batteries be got ready with a view to possible intervention in German East Africa. The local authorities countered by offering one *BTM* and a mixed battalion (to consist of two *compagnies* of Europeans and Creoles, one of Sénégalais and one of Comoriens). Paris agreed, but in early 1915 the British said that French help would not be necessary and the proposed expeditionary force was finally stood down in July.

During the war the Madagascar garrison was modified by the withdrawal of most of the *Coloniale* regulars. The *1ᵉ, 2ᵉ* and *3ᵉRégiments de Tirailleurs Malgache* remained in existence and acted as depot units for a number of *Bataillons de Marche*. The Governor was enthusiastic and helped to recruit large numbers of Malagasays, so much so that by mid 1916 *1ᵉRTM* had expanded to 12,000 men. However, the French High Command had a low opinion of Malagasay fighting qualities, and in early 1916 recruitment was suspended. Most of the battalions sent to France or the Balkans were used as labourers.

A *Bataillon de Marche of Tirailleurs Malgache* (BdMTM) left the island in 1914, being stationed in Tunisia until it went to France in 1916. It was an all-regular unit and was used at the front in 1917. Subsequently twenty other battalions were formed (these were the 2e, 3e, 4e, 5e, 7e and 12e BdMTM in 1916 (the 6e was the *Bataillon Somali*) the 13e, 14e, 15e, 16e, 17e, 18e, 19e, 20e, 21e, 22e, 23e, 24e and 25e BdMTM in 1917, and the 26e BdMTM in 1918)[3]. However, not all of these units existed simultaneously because some were broken up in 1917 to provide men for MG, artillery or service units (many were trained as drivers). A considerable number of Malagasays were transferred to the heavy artillery, a service for which they were deemed particularly suited.

The only other battalion to serve in the front line was the *12e BdMTM*, which confounded French preconceptions by acquitting itself with such distinction on the Western Front that it was honoured by being re-titled *12e Bataillon de Chasseurs Malgache* in August 1918.

*   *   *

The Indian Ocean territory of Réunion was not affected directly by the war, and simply contributed men to *la Coloniale*.

The *Gendarmerie Indigène* which had succeeded the *Cipayes* in Pondichéry were too weak to be involved in the war, but some sections went to Indochine in 1918-19 to help deal with unrest there.

*   *   *

Indochina remained quiet, apart from some unrest in Upper Laos and North Tonkin. The garrison was weakened by the disbandment of *10e RIC* in 1914, and by the withdrawal of many of the French cadres. One of the *Zouaves' bataillons alphabétiques* (Bn 'M' of *3e RZ*, made up of men from Alsace-Lorraine) arrived in late 1916 to relieve a *Légion* battalion (IV/1eRE) and remained until 1919 (one unlucky company was even sent on to join the *Bataillon d'Infanterie Coloniale Sibérien* in 1919-20!)

A number of *Bataillons de Tirailleurs Indochinois* (BTIs) were raised for service in Europe, though not all actually served there. Apart from those noted as combat units, they were used for LOC work. They were:

1e BTI	1916-19	Salonika (combat)	14e BTI	1916-19	France
2e BTI	1916-19	Salonika (combat)	15e BTI	1916	Annam only
3e BTI	1916-19	Madagascar then France	16e BTI	1916-19	France
4e BTI	1916-19	Salonika	17e BTI	1916-17	France
5e BTI	1916	Cambodge only	18e BTI	1916	France
6e BTI	1916-19	France (4e Cie in combat)	19e BTI	1916	Cochinchine only
7e BTI	1916-19	France (combat)	20e BTI	1916-19	Salonika
8e BTI	1915-16	Dijibouti	21e BTI	1916-19	France (combat)
9e BTI	1916-19	France	22e BTI	1917-19	France
10e BTI	1916-20	Salonika	23e BTI	1917-19	France
11e BTI	1916-19	France	24e BTI	1917-19	France
12e BTI	1916-19	France	25e BTI	1918-19	France
13e BTI	1916-19	France			

*   *   *

The French garrison in China became very weak during WW1. *16e RIC* was reduced to one small battalion by 1915 and had to be reinforced by a *BdMTTon* from *3e RTTon*[4]. This was incorporated into *16e RIC* in 1916. In 1917 a number of white reinforcements arrived (unfit *Coloniale Blanche*, Alsaciens of uncertain loyalty and a hundred mutineers from *129e RI*) and were presumably also incorporated into *16e RIC*.

In 1919 *16e RIC* contributed two companies to a *BCSibérien* (the remaining three companies came from Indochine). This unit was disbanded in 1920.

---

[3] Three of these served in Macedonia, but I have not been able to establish which they were apart from *4e BTM*

[4] This was actually the first complete *Indochinois* unit to serve abroad.

There were few troops in Océanie (ie the Pacific) at the start of the First World War. There was concern when the German cruisers *'Scharnhorst'* and *'Gneisenau'* approached Tahiti, and the local police and volunteers were hastily mobilized to support the platoon which was the only regular unit stationed there However, the ships contented themselves with shelling the port and then steamed off without attempting a landing. The regulars have been described as *'Tirailleurs Canaques'*, but in fact they belonged to *la Coloniale*, the term *'Tirailleurs'* only coming into use to describe the indigenous troops raised later in the war. Like the inhabitants of Réunion and Pondichéry, the Pacific islanders returned deputies to the French Assembly, but they were not actually citizens and thus not subject to conscription. This exemption was abolished in 1915, the decree prescribing that they should serve in *Colonial Blanche* units. Subsequently some 10,000 such conscripts came from Réunion, 1,000 from Océanie and 500 from Pondichéry.

In 1916 a *Bataillon de Tirailleurs de Pacifique* was raised and sent to France. Originally comprising only two companies from Nouvelle Calédonie, it was later brought up to strength with 500 Tahitiens, renamed the *Bataillon Mixte du Pacifique* and sent to the front. It became the *Bataillon de Marche du Pacifique* in 1917.

* * *

There were no problems in the American possessions, and no changes to their garrisons.

* * *

As a minor footnote to the story of France's overseas troops during the First World War, the Germans assembled all their Muslim prisoners of war (ex British Indian as well as French North African *Tirailleurs*) at camps near Zossen in Prussia, where they were invited to volunteer to fight for the Ottoman Sultan, who was also the Caliph. Some 1,150 did so and formed a battalion which was sent to Turkey in early 1916. It served in Iraq and was then sent to the Caucasian front to fight the Russians, where it began to disintegrate. The Turks disbanded it in October 1918.

Unit Summaries, 1914-18

This period saw many raisings and re-raisings and a number of changes of title. The summaries cover units in existence in August 1914, or which were raised or re-raised between then and November 1918. They are listed under their final titles.

European Régiments d'Infanterie de l'Armée d'Afrique

1eRZ	Formed pre 1914. In Aug had I, II & III Bns in Maroc. Acted as depot throughout war.
2eRZ	Formed pre 1914. In Aug had II & III Bns in Maroc. Acted as depot throughout war.
3eRZ	Formed pre 1914. In Aug had II & IV Bns in Maroc. Acted as depot throughout war.
4eRZ	Formed pre 1914. In Aug had I & VI Bns in Maroc. Acted as depot throughout war.
1eRdMZ	Formed Aug'14 as RdMd1eRZ de 38eDI ex IV, V & XI/1eRZ. Became 1eRdMZ Dec'14. Fought throughout war in France in 38e, 25e and 48eDIs.
2eRdMZ	Formed Aug'14 as RdMd2eRZ de 37eDI ex I, V & XI/2eRZ. Became 2eRdMZ Mar'15. Fought throughout war in France in 37eDI.
2eRbisZ	Formed Aug'14 as RdMd2eRZ de 45eDI ex IV, XII & XIV/2eRZ. Became 3eRdMZ Dec'14, then 2eRbisZ Jan'15. In France with 45eDI to Oct'15, then Salonika as Army unit.
3eRdMZ	Formed Aug'14 as RdMd3eRZ de 37eDI ex I, V & XI/3eRZ. Fought throughout war in France with 37eDI.
3eRbisZ	Formed Aug'14 as RdMd3eRZ de 45eDI ex III, VI & XII /3eRZ. Became 5eRdMZ Dec'14, then 3eRbisZ Jan'15. Fought in France throughout war in 45eDI.
4eRdMZ	Formed Aug'14 as RdMd4eRZ ex III, IV, V & XI/4eRZ. Became 6eRdMZ Dec'14, then 4eRdMZ Jan'15. Fought in France throughout war in 38eDI.
7eRdMZ	Formed Aug'14 as RdMd1eRZ de 45eDI ex VI & XIV/1eRZ & VI/4eRZ. Became 7eRdMZ Dec'14, then 3eRMxZT Jul'15 by exchanging VI/4RZ for III/4RdMTA. Rec'd XII/3RbisZ May'17, but broken up Apr'18 and became 6eRdMT.
8eRdMZ	Formed Aug'14 as RdMZ de Div Marocaine ex I/1eRZ, II/2eRZ, & IV/3eRZ. Became 8eRdMZ Dec'14. Fought throughout war in France with Div Maroc.
9eRdMZ	Formed Sep'14 as RdMZ de 3eBde Maroc ex I/4eRZ, II & III/1eRZ. Became 9eRdMZ Dec'14. Fought throughout war in France, with 153eDI from Dec'14.

BILA	There were five battalions in 1914. They were drawn on to provide first two and then three Bataillons de Marche (1e, 2e and 3e BdMILd'Afrique) which formed a Groupe des Bataillons d'Afrique and which served in 45eDI.
1eRE	Formed pre 1914. Acted as depot throughout war.
2eRE	Formed pre 1914. Acted as depot throughout war.
1eRdM1eRE	Raised pre 1914 for service in Maroc. Remained there during war.
1eRdM2eRE	Raised pre 1914 for service in Maroc. Remained there during war.
2eRdM1eRE	Formed Sep'14 ex volunteers. In Div Maroc till merged to form RdMLE Nov'15.
3eRdM1eRE	Formed Nov'14 ex volunteers, disbanded Mar'15.
4eRdM1eRE	Formed Nov'14 ex volunteers, mainly Italians. Disbanded Mar'15.
2eRdM2eRE	Formed Sep'14 ex volunteers. In Div Maroc, then 10eDI till merged to form RdMLE Nov'15.
RdMLE	Formed Nov15 ex 2eRdM1eRE & 2eRdM2eRE. In France with Div Maroc throughout rest of war. One of two most decorated regiments in Army.

Mixed Régiments d'Infanterie de l'Armée d'Afrique

1eRMxZT (1)	Formed Aug'14 ex V/3eRTA, I/5eRTA & IV/7eRTA (it was meant to have a Zouave bn but this never joined). Became RdMT de Div Maroc Oct'14 and then 7eRdMT (see below).
1eRMxZT (2)	Formed Aug'14 as 2eRdMZT (no 'Mixte' in title) ex II/2eRZ & I/7eRTA only. Became 1eRMxZT Dec'14. Lost its Zouave bn mid'18 but no change of title. Fought throughout in France in 37e, 153e & 72eDIs.
2eRMxZT (1)	Formed Aug'14 ex III/2eRZ, I & IV/2eRTA, VI/6eRTA. Merged with 1eRMxZT Oct'14, then became 7eRdMT (see above).
2eRMxZT (2)	Formed Sep'14 ex II/4eRZ, III/3eRTA & I/9eRTA, possibly as '1eRMxZT'. Became 2eRMxZT Dec'14. Became 13eRdMT Jun'18 with III/5eRTA, IV & XI/9eRTA (see above). Fought throughout in France with 38e & 48eDIs.
3eRMxZT	Formed Aug'14 as RdM1eRZ de 45e Div. Became 7eRdMZ Dec'14, then 3eRMxZT Jun'15. Became 6eRdMT Apr'18 (see above).
1eRdMd'Afrique	Formed Feb'15 ex bn/3eRZ, bn/4eRZ & bn/1e&2eREs. Served in Salonika to 1919.
2eRdMd'Afrique	Formed Feb'15 ex bn/1eRZ, bn/2eRZ & bn/4eRZ. Served in Salonika, disbanded Oct'17.

European Régiments de Cavalerie de l'Armée d'Afrique

1eRCA	Formed pre 1914. In Maroc,e remained there but sent escadrons to RdMCA. This became 1eRdMCA Apr'15. Fought in France, then Salonika to '18.
2eRCA	Formed pre 1914. To France Aug'14, split between RdMCA and divisional escadrons. Latter rejoined those ex RdMCA to form 2eRdMCA Apr'15. Fought in France throughout. 1e & 2eRdMCA See 1e & 2eRCA above.
3eRCA	Formed pre 1914. To France Aug'14 as Rgt de Cav for Corps Colonial. Fought in France throughout.
4eRCA	Formed pre 1914. To France Aug'15, in 44eDI, then to Salonika Nov'15. Fought there to '18.
5eRCA	Formed pre 1914. To France Aug'14, with different divs to Sep'16 when split, half going to Div Maroc, rest to Salonika with 76eDI.
6eRCA	Formed pre 1914. To France Aug'14. Fought there throughout.
7eRCA	Formed Apr'15 as 3eRdMCA ex V/1e, V/5e & I/6eRCAs. Became 7eRCA Aug'15 but disbanded Jan'16.
8eRCA	Formed Feb'15 as RdMCA (no number) ex depots in Algeria. Sent to Egypt and fought in Dardanelles. Became 8eRCA Aug'15. To Salonika '15 but disbanded Dec'17.

Indigenous Régiments de Cavalerie de l'Armée d'Afrique

Note: These were known simply as *Régiments de Spahis* until c1915, when *'Algérien'* or *'Tunisien'* had to be added to their title because Moroccan *Spahis* had begun to be raised.

1eRSA	Formed pre 1914. In Maroc, to France Aug'14
2eRSA	Formed pre 1914. In Maroc, to France Mar'15, back to Maroc 1917.
3eRSA	Formed pre 1914. To France Aug'14, then to Salonika.
4eRST	Formed pre 1914. In Tunisie, but sent escadrons to France.

5eRSA	Formed Aug'14. Part went to Maroc, part to France.
6eRdMS	Formed as 1eRdMS 1914, became 6eRdMS 1915, disbanded 1917.
7eRdMS	Formed as 2eRdMS 1914, became 7eRdMS 1915, disbanded 1917.
1eRdMSM	Formed as Escadrons Auxiliaires de Spahis Marocains 1912. Some formed RdM de Chasseurs Indigènes à Cheval Aug'14. Became RdMS Marocains 1915. Sent to Salonika and served there for rest of war.
RSAA	Formed as Régiment de Spahis Auxiliares Algériens 1914 for Algerie garrison. Disbanded in 1917.

Indigenous Régiments d'Infanterie de l'Armée d'Afrique

Note: The Algerian and Tunisian *Tirailleur* Regiments were officially '*Régiments de Tirailleurs Indigènes*' between 1912 and 1920. However, they continued to be known as '*Tirailleurs Algériens*' etc and I have retained this usage. The term '*Indigènes*' does not appear to have applied to the *Régiments de Marche*.

1eRTA	Formed pre 1914. In Aug had I & II Bns in Alger, III Bn in Maroc. Depot throughout war.
2eRTA	Formed pre 1914. In Aug had I, II, III & V Bns in Oran, I & IV in Maroc. Depot throughout war.
3eRTA	Formed pre 1914. In Aug had II & IV Bns in C'tine, I & III in Maroc. Depot throughout war.
4eRTA	Formed pre 1914. In Aug had I, II & VI Bns in Tunisie, III, IV & V in Maroc. Depot throughout war.
5eRTA	Formed pre 1914. In Aug had II Bn in Alger, I & III in Maroc. Depot throughout war.
6eRTA	Formed pre 1914. In Aug had I & IV Bns in Oran, II & III in Maroc. Depot throughout war.
7eRTA	Formed pre 1914. In Aug had II & III Bns in C'tine, I & IV in Maroc. Depot throughout war.
8eRTA	Formed pre 1914. In Aug had II, IV & V Bns in Tunisie, I, III & VI in Maroc. Depot throughout war.
9eRTA	Formed pre 1914. In Aug had III Bn in Alger, I & II in Maroc. Depot throughout war.
1eRdMT	Formed Aug'14 as RdMT, then 2eRdMT, then 6eRdMT Nov'14, then 1eRdMT Apr'15. Initially II/1eRTA, II/8eRTA & VI/2eRTA; ended war with I, III & IV/1eRTA. Fought throughout in France with 45eDI.
2eRdMT	Formed Aug'14 ex II & V/2eRTA, II/5eRTA. Decimated in opening battle, reconstituted as 1eRdMT de 37eDI ex II & V/2eRTA, V/5eRTA & IV/6eRTA. Became 2eRdMT Apr'15. Ended war with II, III & VI/2eRTA.
3eRdMT	Formed Aug'14 ex II, IV, V/3eRTA & III/7eRTA. Decimated in opening battle, reconstituted as 2eRdMT de 37eDI. Became 3eRdMT Apr'15 and ended war with I, IV, VI/3eRTA. Fought throughout in France, changing to 51eDI in mid 1916. Note that 9eRdMT was known as 3eRdMT briefly prior to Mar'15 (see below).
4eRdMT	Formed Aug'14 as RdM4eRTA with I & VI/4eRTA. V/4eRTA added Oct. Became 7eRdMT and then 4eRdMT Dec'14. Fought throughout in France mostly with Div Maroc.
5eRdMT	Not formed till Jan'18 ex I, V & XI/5eRTA. Fought in France with various divs.
6eRdMT	A RdM6eRT was formed Aug'14 ex I & IV/6eRTA but disappeared after opening battle. A 6eRdMT formed Nov'14 was renamed 1eRdMT Apr'15 (see above). Another 6eRdMT was formed Apr'18 from disbanded 3eRdMZT (see below) with V, VII & XI/6eRTA. Fought in France with various divs.
7eRdMT	Descended from 1e & 2eRéginents Mixte Zouaves et Tirailleurs de Div Maroc formed Aug'14 (1e with V/4eRTA, I/5eRTA & IV/7eRTA but no Zouaves despite title; 2e with III/2eRZ, I & IV/2eRTA & III/6eRTA). These combined Oct'14 to form RdMT de Div Maroc with II/2eRTA, I/5eRTA, III/6eRTA & IV/7eRTA. Became 7eRdMT Dec'14. After further changes ended war with III/6eRTA, VIII & X/7eRTA. Fought throughout in France in Div Maroc.
8eRdMT	Formed Aug'14 ex IV & V/8eRTA as RdM8eRT. II/8eRTA added Aug'15 and rgt became 8eRdMT. Fought throughout in France, mostly with 38eDI. Note that the RdMT Indigènes (later 4eRMxZT) was also known as 8eRdMT unofficially.
9eRdMT	Formed Aug'14 ex I/1eRTA, II & III/9eRTA. Became 3eRdMT Dec'14, then 9eRdMT Mar'15. Fought throughout in France.
10eRdMT	Not formed till Jan'18 ex XI/2RTA, III & XI/3eRTA. Replaced a disbanded RI in 52eDI.
11eRdMT	Not formed till Jan'18 ex IV, IX & XI/7eRTA. Replaced disbanded RIs in 58eDI.
12eRdMT	Not formed till Nov'18 (bns not known) to replace a disbanded RI in 68eDI.
13eRdMT	Not formed till Jun'18 by conversion of 2eRMxZT (see below).
15eRdMT	Not formed till Nov'18 ex XV/7eRTA and two Métropolitaine inf bns.

17eRdMT	Not formed till Nov'18 ex XV/1eRTA, XVI/5eRTA & XV/9eRTA. Replaced a disbanded RI in 166eDI
21eRdMT	Not formed till Oct'18 with XII & XVII/7eRTA, XVI/9eRTA. Replaced a disbanded RI in 8eDI.
RdMT	Originated in Détachement de Palestine-Syrie formed May'17 ex VII/1eRTA & IX/2eRTA. Served in Palestine.
	1e & 2eRdMTM Formed ex Troupes Auxiliaries Marocains Aug'14 as 1e & 2e Rgs Chasseurs Indigènes à Pied. Combined as RdMTMarocains Jan'15. Doubled again Feb'18.

Régiments d'Infanterie Coloniale

1eRIC	Formed pre 1914, fought in France in 1e BdeIC; then Salonika in 31e BdeIC 1917 on.
2eRIC	Formed pre 1914, fought throughout war in France in 1e BdeIC.
3eRIC	Formed pre 1914; fought in France in 3e BdeIC; then Salonika in 31e BdeIC 1917 on.
4eRIC	Formed pre 1914, in France to '15, then Salonika in 4e BdeIC.
5eRIC	Formed pre 1914, fought throughout war in France in 2e BdeIC.
6eRIC	Formed pre 1914, fought throughout war in France in 2e BdeIC.
7eRIC	Formed pre 1914, fought throughout war in France in 3e BdeIC.
4eRIC	Formed pre 1914, in France to '15, then Salonika in 4e BdeIC.
9eRIC	Formed pre 1914, Tonkin garrison throughout war.
10eRIC	Formed pre 1914, Annam garrison throughout war.
11eRIC	Formed pre 1914, Chochinchine garrison throughout war.
16eRIC	Formed pre 1914, China garrison throughout war.
21eRIC	Formed pre 1914, fought throughout war in France in 5e BdeIC.
22eRIC	Formed pre 1914, fought throughout war in France in 6e BdeIC.
23eRIC	Formed pre 1914, fought throughout war in France in 5e BdeIC.
24eRIC	Formed pre 1914, fought throughout war in France in 6e BdeIC.
31eRIC	Formed 1914 ex 1eRIC, fought throughout war in France.
32eRIC	Formed 1914 ex 2eRIC, fought throughout war in France.
33eRIC	Formed 1914 ex 3eRIC, fought throughout war in France in 19e BdeIC.
34eRIC	Formed 1914 ex 4eRIC, in France, then Salonika 1917 in 31e then 21e BdeIC.
35eRIC	Formed 1914 ex 5eRIC, in France, then Salonika 1917 in 31e then 21e BdeIC.
36eRIC	Formed 1914 ex 6eRIC, in France in 31e BdeIC, broken up 1916.
37eRIC	Formed 1914 ex 7eRIC, in France then Salonika 1917 in 32e BdeIC.
38eRIC	Formed 1914 ex 8eRIC, in France then Salonika 1917 in 32e BdeIC.
41eRIC	Formed 1914 ex 21eRIC, fought throughout war in France in 30e then 7e BdeIC.
42eRIC	Formed 1914 ex 22eRIC, in France, then Salonika 1917 in 22e BdeIC.
43eRIC	Formed 1914 ex 23eRIC, fought throughout war in France in 30e then 7e BdeIC.
44eRIC	Formed 1914 ex 24eRIC, in France, then Salonika 1917 in 21e BdeIC.
52eRIC	Formed Apr'15 as 2eRégiment Mixte Coloniale; then 52eRIC Aug'15. Fought in France throughout in 19e BdeIC.
53eRIC	Formed Apr'15 as 3eRégiment Mixte Coloniale; then 53eRIC Aug'15. Fought in France throughout in 20e BdeIC.
54eRIC	Formed Mar'15 as 4eRégiment Mixte Coloniale (Dardanelles); then 54eRIC Aug'15; to Salonika '16.
56eRIC	Formed Mar'15 as 6eRégiment Mixte Coloniale (Dardanelles); then 56eRIC Aug'15; to Salonika '16.
57eRIC	Formed Mar'15 as 7eRégiment Mixte Coloniale (Dardanelles); 57eRIC Aug'15; to Salonkia as all-black unit, then to France '16, but broken up May'17.
58eRIC	Formed Mar'15 as 8eRégiment Mixte Coloniale (Dardanelles); 58eRIC Aug'15; to Salonkia as all-black unit, then to France '16, but broken up May'17.
59eRIC	Formed and disbanded Apr'17.
RICM	Formed 1914 as Régiment d'Infanterie Coloniale du Maroc; then Régiment Mixte d'Infanterie Coloniale du Maroc Jly'15; fought throughout war in France. One of two most decorated regiments in Army.

Régiments d'Artillerie Coloniale

1eRAC	Formed pre 1914, fought throughout war in France.
2eRAC	Formed pre 1914, fought throughout war in France.

3eRAC	Formed pre 1914, fought throughout war in France.
4eRAC	Formed pre 1914, Tonkin garrison throughout war.
5eRAC	Formed pre 1914, Cochinchine garrison throughout war.
6eRAC	Formed pre 1914, AOF garrison throughout war.
7eRAC	Formed pre 1914, Madagascar garrison (Diego-Suarez) throughout war.
13eRAC	Formed May'18 in France. Disbanded Jan'19.
21eRAC	Formed Apr'18 in France. Disbanded Apr'19.
22eRAC.	Formed Apr'18 in France. Disbanded Mar'19.
23eRAC	Formed Apr'18 in France. Disbanded Mar'19.
41eRAC	Formed May'18 in France. Disbanded Feb'19.
42eRAC	Formed May'18 in France. Disbanded Jun'19.
43eRAC	Formed Apr'18 in France. Disbanded May'19.
141eRAC	Formed Mar'18 in France (heavy artillery). Disbanded 1919.
142eRAC	Formed Mar'18 in France (heavy artillery). Disbanded 1919.
143eRAC	Formed Mar'18 in France (heavy artillery). Disbanded 1919.
182eRAC	Formed Aug'18 in France (heavy artillery). Disbanded 1919.
183eRAC	Formed Aug'18 in France (heavy artillery). Disbanded 1919.
341eRAC	Formed Mar'18 in France (heavy artillery). Disbanded 1919.
342eRAC	Formed Mar'18 in France (heavy artillery). Disbanded 1919.
343eRAC	Formed Mar'18 in France (heavy artillery). Disbanded 1919.

Régiments de Tirailleurs Coloniaux

1eRTS	Formed pre 1914, Sénégal garrison throughout war.
2eRTS	Formed pre 1914, Soudan garrison throughout war.
3eRTS	Formed pre 1914, Côte d'Ivoire, Dahomey & Togo garrison throughout war.
4eRTS	Formed pre 1914, Sénégal garrison throughout war.
RdMTSAO	Formed 1914 in AOF but broken up before end of year.
RTS Tchad	Formed pre 1914, Tchad garrison throughout war.
Rgt Gabon	Formed pre 1914, Gabon/Congo garrison throughout war.
RTSC	Formed 1915 as Régiment de Marche de Tirailleurs Sénégalais du Cameroun; then Régiment de Tirailleurs Sénégalais du Cameroun to garrison territory.
1eRTM	Formed pre 1914, Madagascar garrison throughout war.
2eRTM	Formed pre 1914, Madagascar garrison throughout war.
3eRTM	Formed pre 1914, Madagascar garrison throughout war.
RTAnnam	Formed pre 1914, Cochinchine garrison throughout war.
1eRTTon	Formed pre 1914, Tonkin garrison throughout war.
2eRTTon	Formed pre 1914, Tonkin garrison throughout war.
3eRTTon	Formed pre 1914, Tonkin garrison throughout war.
4eRTTon	Formed pre 1914, Tonkin garrison throughout war.